William Henley Jervis

The Gallican Church

A History of the Church of France. Vol. II

William Henley Jervis

The Gallican Church
A History of the Church of France. Vol. II

ISBN/EAN: 9783337004194

Printed in Europe, USA, Canada, Australia, Japan

Cover: Foto ©ninafisch / pixelio.de

More available books at **www.hansebooks.com**

J. BÉNIGNE BOSSUET,

Bishop of Meaux

Frontispiece. Vol II

THE GALLICAN CHURCH.

A

HISTORY

OF THE

CHURCH OF FRANCE,

FROM THE CONCORDAT OF BOLOGNA, A.D. 1516, TO THE REVOLUTION.

WITH AN INTRODUCTION.

By REV. W. HENLEY JERVIS, M.A.,
PREBENDARY OF HEYTESBURY;
AUTHOR OF 'THE STUDENT'S HISTORY OF FRANCE.'

"Fluctuat, nec mergitur."

IN TWO VOLUMES.—Vol. II.

WITH PORTRAITS.

LONDON:
JOHN MURRAY, ALBEMARLE STREET.
1872.

LONDON:
PRINTED BY WILLIAM CLOWES AND SONS, STAMFORD STREET,
AND CHARING CROSS.

CONTENTS OF VOLUME II.

CHAPTER I.

	PAGE
Extension of system of Seminaries	1
Vincent de Paul on ecclesiastical Seminaries	2
Collége des Bons Enfans	3
Congregation of St. Sulpice	4
Seminary of St. Nicolas du Chardonnet	5
Congregation of Eudistes	6, 7
Closing labours of Vincent de Paul	8
Foundation of Hospital of Sainte Reine	9, 10
Death of Vincent de Paul	11
Rise of Bossuet. His early studies and preferments	12, 14
The 'Perpétuité de la Foi'	15
Other works of Arnauld and Nicole against Calvinism	16
Renewal of controversy. Bishop Arnauld of Angers	17, 18
'Nouveau Testament de Mons'	19
Complaints against Antoine Arnauld. He retires to Brussels	20, 21
Renewed persecution of Port Royal	22

CHAPTER II.

The "Droit de Régale"	23
Feudal view of episcopal sees	24
Extension of the Régale by Louis XIV.	25
The exempt Cathedrals. Bishops Pavillon and De Caulet	26
They resist the Régalistes	27
Briefs of Innocent XI. to Louis XIV.	28
Death of the Bishops of Alet and Pamiers	29
Innocent XI. excommunicates the Régalistes	30
Breach between Louis and Innocent	31
Extraordinary meeting of French bishops	32
Report of Committee on the Régale	33
Policy of the Jesuits	34
The Advocate-General, Talon, on the Régale	35
Bossuet on the approaching Assembly of the Clergy	36, 37
Bossuet's Sermon on the Unity of the Church	38—42
Letter of the Assembly to Pope Innocent	44

	PAGE
The Pope's reply	45
Origin of the Four Gallican Articles	46
Bishops Bossuet and De Choiseul	47
Their dispute on the Infallibility of the Pope	48
The "Declaration of the Clergy of France"	49–51
Resentment of the Pope	52
Antoine Arnauld on the Four Articles	53
Innocent refuses institution to bishops-designate	54
Ultramontane strictures on the Declaration	55
Bossuet's "Defensio Declarationis"	56–59

CHAPTER III.

The "Avertissement Pastoral" to the Protestants	60
Efforts of the clergy towards their conversion	61, 62
The "Caisse des Conversions." Pélisson-Fontanier	63
The King urged to measures of coercion	64
Further restrictions imposed on Huguenots	65
Revocation of the Edict of Nantes	66, 67
Antoine Arnauld approves it	68
General assent of the nation	69
Organized Missions to the Protestants	70
Fénelon preaches in Poitou and Saintonge	71
Measures of concession adopted, but too late	72
The Protestant emigration	72, 73
Affair of the Franchises. Louis appeals to a General Council	74–76
Negotiations. Reconciliation with Innocent XII.	77, 78
Malebranche on Moral Causation	79
Malebranche on Grace and Mediation	80
His errors exposed by Bossuet	81, 82
Arnauld and Fénelon write against Malebranche	83, 84
Arnauld on "Péché philosophique"	85
The "Fourberie de Douai"	86
Death of Antoine Arnauld	87
Panegyrics pronounced upon him	88
Archbishop De Harlai succeeded by De Noailles, Bishop of Châlons	89
Pastoral Instruction of Archbishop De Noailles	90
Father Quesnel of the Oratory. The 'Réflexions Morales'	91
The 'Problème ecclésiastique'	92, 93
Bossuet persuaded to refute it. His 'Avertissement'	94
De Noailles becomes identified with the Jansenist party	95

CHAPTER IV.

The Controversy on Quietism	96
Rise of Mysticism	97
The Hesychasts of Mount Athos	98

CONTENTS OF VOLUME II.

CHAPTER I.

	PAGE
Extension of system of Seminaries	1
Vincent de Paul on ecclesiastical Seminaries	2
Collége des Bons Enfans	3
Congregation of St. Sulpice	4
Seminary of St. Nicolas du Chardonnet	5
Congregation of Eudistes	6, 7
Closing labours of Vincent de Paul	8
Foundation of Hospital of Sainte Reine	9, 10
Death of Vincent de Paul	11
Rise of Bossuet. His early studies and preferments	12, 14
The 'Perpétuité de la Foi'	15
Other works of Arnauld and Nicole against Calvinism	16
Renewal of controversy. Bishop Arnauld of Angers	17, 18
'Nouveau Testament de Mons'	19
Complaints against Antoine Arnauld. He retires to Brussels	20, 21
Renewed persecution of Port Royal	22

CHAPTER II.

The "Droit de Régale"	23
Feudal view of episcopal sees	24
Extension of the Régale by Louis XIV.	25
The exempt Cathedrals. Bishops Pavillon and De Caulet	26
They resist the Régalistes	27
Briefs of Innocent XI. to Louis XIV.	28
Death of the Bishops of Alet and Pamiers	29
Innocent XI. excommunicates the Régalistes	30
Breach between Louis and Innocent	31
Extraordinary meeting of French bishops	32
Report of Committee on the Régale	33
Policy of the Jesuits	34
The Advocate-General, Talon, on the Régale	35
Bossuet on the approaching Assembly of the Clergy	36, 37
Bossuet's Sermon on the Unity of the Church	38–42
Letter of the Assembly to Pope Innocent	44

	PAGE
The Pope's reply	45
Origin of the Four Gallican Articles	46
Bishops Bossuet and De Choiseul	47
Their dispute on the Infallibility of the Pope	48
The "Declaration of the Clergy of France"	49–51
Resentment of the Pope	52
Antoine Arnauld on the Four Articles	53
Innocent refuses institution to bishops-designate	54
Ultramontane strictures on the Declaration	55
Bossuet's "Defensio Declarationis"	56–59

CHAPTER III.

The "Avertissement Pastoral" to the Protestants	60
Efforts of the clergy towards their conversion	61, 62
The "Caisse des Conversions." Pélisson-Fontanier	63
The King urged to measures of coercion	64
Further restrictions imposed on Huguenots	65
Revocation of the Edict of Nantes	66, 67
Antoine Arnauld approves it	68
General assent of the nation	69
Organized Missions to the Protestants	70
Fénelon preaches in Poitou and Saintonge	71
Measures of concession adopted, but too late	72
The Protestant emigration	72, 73
Affair of the Franchises. Louis appeals to a General Council	74–76
Negotiations. Reconciliation with Innocent XII.	77, 78
Malebranche on Moral Causation	79
Malebranche on Grace and Mediation	80
His errors exposed by Bossuet	81, 82
Arnauld and Fénelon write against Malebranche	83, 84
Arnauld on "Péché philosophique"	85
The "Fourberie de Douai"	86
Death of Antoine Arnauld	87
Panegyrics pronounced upon him	88
Archbishop De Harlai succeeded by De Noailles, Bishop of Châlons	89
Pastoral Instruction of Archbishop De Noailles	90
Father Quesnel of the Oratory. The 'Réflexions Morales'	91
The 'Problème ecclésiastique'	92, 93
Bossuet persuaded to refute it. His 'Avertissement'	94
De Noailles becomes identified with the Jansenist party	95

CHAPTER IV.

The Controversy on Quietism	96
Rise of Mysticism	97
The Hesychasts of Mount Athos	98

CONTENTS OF VOLUME II.

	PAGE
Western Mystics. The School of St. Victor	99
Quietism of Michel Molinos	100
Madame de la Mothe Guyon	102
First imprisonment of Madame Guyon	103
Madame Guyon patronized by Madame de Maintenon	104
Quietism at Saint Cyr	105
Fénelon and Madame Guyon	106–108
Quietism attacked by the Bishop of Chartres	109
Madame Guyon dismissed from Saint Cyr	110
Madame Guyon's writings examined by Bossuet	111
Misgivings of Fénelon	112
The Conferences of Issy	113
Fénelon's protests of submission	114
Fénelon appointed Archbishop of Cambrai	115
The Articles of Issy	116
Submission of Madame Guyon	117
Consecration of Fénelon	118
Bossuet's 'Instruction sur les états d'oraison'	119–121
Fénelon declines to approve it. His reasons	122–124
Second imprisonment of Madame Guyon	125
Fénelon's 'Explication des Maximes des Saints'	126, 127
Resentment of Bossuet	128
Unfavourable reception of the 'Explication'	129
Displeasure of Louis XIV.	130
Breach between Bossuet and Fénelon	132
Fénelon appeals to the Pope	134
His letter explaining his opinions	135, 136
His book inconsistent with the Articles of Issy	137
Fénelon banished from Court	138
Good faith of Fénelon and Bossuet	133
Counter-appeal to Rome against Fénelon	141
Supporters of Fénelon at Rome	142
Publications on both sides of the controversy	143
Fénelon's friends displaced	144
Renewed persecution of Madame Guyon	145
Calumnious insinuations against Fénelon	146
Vindication of Fénelon	147
Louis XIV. remonstrates with Innocent XII.	148
Condemnation of Fénelon's 'Explication'	149
Reception of the Pope's Brief at Paris	150
Edifying submission of Fénelon	151, 152
Provincial Councils for reception of the Brief	153–155
D'Aguesseau's 'Réquisitoire'	156
Cessation of the Controversy	158
Results on the Gallican cause	159

CHAPTER V.

	PAGE
The Gallican Church at the opening of the eighteenth century	160
Intellectual activity. Resuscitation of Jansenism	161
Assembly of the Clergy in the year 1700	162
Doctrine of Probabilism. Its condemnation	164, 165
Question of the "Chinese ceremonies"	166–168
The "Cas de Conscience"	169
Secretly approved by Cardinal de Noailles	170
Condemned by Bossuet	171
The Doctors retract their approval	ib.
Condemned by Clement XI. Ordonnance of Cardinal de Noailles	172
Question of Church authority on "doctrinal facts"	173
Letter of the Bishop of Saint Pons	174
Death of Bossuet	175
Incompetence of Cardinal de Noailles	176
The bull "Vineam Domini"	177
Reception of the bull by Assembly of Clergy	178, 179
Different interpretations put upon it	180
Negotiations between De Polignac and Cardinal Fabroni	182
Hostility of Fabroni to Cardinal de Noailles	183
Difficult position of Cardinal de Noailles	184
Suppression of Port Royal des Champs	185
The Nuns refuse to accept the "Vineam Domini"	188
They are finally expelled from the Convent	190
Demolition of Port Royal. Violation of the cemetery	191
Remorse of Cardinal de Noailles	193
State of parties. Michel Le Tellier. Godet-Desmarais	194, 195
The Duc de Saint Simon. Le Tellier intrigues against De Noailles	197
"Declaration" to satisfy the Pope	198
Ascendency of Le Tellier and Ultramontanes	199

CHAPTER VI.

Efforts to condemn Quesnel's 'Réflexions'	200
Pastoral Instruction of the Bishops of La Rochelle and Luçon	201
Imprudent conduct of Cardinal de Noailles	202
He incurs the King's displeasure	203
Discovery of Le Tellier's intrigue against the Cardinal	205
De Noailles inhibits the Jesuits	207
Quesnel's 'Réflexions' suppressed by Council of State	208
Louis XIV. demands a bull against Quesnel	209
Letter of De Noailles to the Bishop of Agen	210
The Constitution "Unigenitus"	212–215
Measures for its acceptance in France	216
Report of the Committee of bishops	217

CONTENTS OF VOLUME II.

	PAGE
Agitation excited by the bull	218
Protest of the nine prelates	219
The bull registered in Parliament	220
And by the Sorbonne after considerable opposition	221
Overtures of accommodation to De Noailles	222
Demands for explanation. Negotiations with the Pope	223, 224
Mission of Amelot to Rome	225
Singular confession of Clement XI.	226
Project of a National Council. Last illness of Louis XIV.	227
Death of Louis XIV.	228
Death of Fénelon	229
Change of policy under the Regent Orleans	230
Cardinal de Noailles in power	231
Mortification of the Ultramontanes. Le Tellier exiled	232
Reaction against the "Unigenitus"	233
Appeal of the four Bishops to a General Council	234
Supported by the Theological Faculty of Paris	235
The Regent beset by the Ultramontanes	236
General agitation. Acceptants and Appellants	237
Pope Clement's letter to Cardinal de Noailles	238
Refusal of bulls to bishops. The appeals condemned at Rome	239
Cardinal de Noailles publishes his appeal	240
The Court changes sides, and supports the "Unigenitus"	241
Intervention of Dubois. His character	242
Ordination and Consecration of Dubois	243, 244
The "Accommodement" of 1720	245
Dubois created Cardinal. Triumph of Ultramontanes	246

CHAPTER VII.

New Conseil de Conscience. Rise of Fleury	247
Letter of the seven bishops to Innocent XIII.	248, 249
Persecution of "Anti-Constitutionnaires"	250
De Noailles and F. de Linières	251
Death of Dubois. Death of the Regent Orleans	252
Fleury in power	253
Negotiation between Benedict XIII. and De Noailles	254, 255
De Noailles draws up Explanatory Articles	256, 257
The negotiation fails. Council of St. John Lateran	258, 259
Fleury made Cardinal and Prime Minister	260
Soanen, Bishop of Senez	261
Archbishop De Tencin. The Council of Embrun	262–264
Bishop Soanen condemned and exiled	265
Remonstrance of the appellant prelates	266
Consultation of the Paris Advocates	267
Failing health of Cardinal de Noailles. He accepts the "Unigenitus"	268
His death	269

	PAGE
Recantation of eight bishops and of the Sorbonne	270
De Vintimille, Archbishop of Paris. He enforces the "Unigenitus"	271
The "Lit de justice" to enforce submission	272
Resistance of the Parliament to the Crown	273
The Advocates support the appellant clergy	274
They close their chambers. Ten of them exiled	275
The clergy condemn the "Legend" of St. Hildebrand	276
Remonstrances of Bishops Colbert and Caylus	277
Jansenism identified with Gallicanism	278

CHAPTER VIII.

Deterioration of the Gallican Clergy	280
Jansenist fanaticism. Miraculous pretensions	281
The deacon François de Pâris	282
The Miracles at the cemetery of St. Médard	283, 284
The Convulsionnaires	285
Division of opinion among the Appellants	287
The "Nouvelles Ecclésiastiques"	288
Parliament summoned to Compiègne. Pucelle and others exiled	290
The controversy assumes a political shape	291
Refusal of the Sacraments to Appellants	292, 293
Parliament suppresses bull for canonization of Vincent de Paul	294
Bossuet, Bishop of Troyes, and Archbishop Languet	295
Death of Bishops Colbert and Soanen	296, 297
Cardinal de Tencin. "Les Questions de l'écho"	298
Death of Cardinal Fleury	299
Boyer, Bishop of Mirepoix	300
Death of Massillon	301
Fitz-James, Bishop of Soissons	302, 303
Christophe de Beaumont, Archbishop of Paris	304
His difficulties on coming to the See	306

CHAPTER IX.

Attack on the revenues and immunities of the clergy	307
The "Vingtième"	308
Satirical publications. "Ne repugnate vestro bono"	309
The "Billets de confession"	310
Bouettin, Curé of St. Étienne du Mont	311
Affair of the Hôpital-Général at Paris	313
Further strife on the "Billets de confession"	314–316
Parliament suspends business. Violence of the Court	317
Reconciliation on the birth of the Duc de Berri	318
Archbishop De Beaumont exiled, with other prelates	319
Remonstrances of clergy on secular encroachments	320

CONTENTS OF VOLUME II.   ix

	PAGE
Appeal to Benedict XIV. Archbishop De Beaumont's Mandement	321
The encyclical "Ex omnibus"	322
Resignation of magistrates	323
The assassin Damiens. Negotiations for peace	324
Memorial of the Assembly on rise of Scepticism	325
Origin of the "new philosophy"	327
Protestantism weakened the dogmatic principle	328
Effect of Protestant dissensions. Bayle	329
Voltaire and his school	330
Various views of the philosophers	331
Jean Jacques Rousseau	332
The Abbé de Prades	333
The 'Encyclopédie'	334–336
Rousseau's 'Émile'	337
Apologists for Christianity. Antoine Guénée	338, 339
Decay of ancient institutions. Prediction of Buffon	340
Forecastings of revolution	341

CHAPTER X.

Fall of the Jesuits. Its significance	342
Their expulsion from Portugal	343
Causes of animosity against them in France	344, 345
Affair of Father Lavalette	346, 347
The Jesuits appeal to Parliament of Paris	348
Sentence against them	349
Jesuit publications condemned by Parliament	350
The Crown interferes in vain	351
Appeal to the bishops on the conduct of the Jesuits	352
They report in favour of the Society	353
A compromise proposed, but rejected by the Jesuits	ib.
Jesuits expelled from their Colleges	354
The final sentence against them	355
Remonstrances of Clement XIII. and of Archbishop De Beaumont	356
Jesuits expelled from France	357
Abolition of the Order demanded from Clement XIII.	358
Clement excommunicates the Duke of Parma. His death	359
Intrigues in the Conclave. Election of Clement XIV.	360, 361
Suppression of the Jesuits by Pope Clement XIV.	363
Death of Clement	ib.
Conflicting opinions as to its cause	364
Archbishop De Beaumont's letter to Clement XIV.	365
Struggle between the Crown and the Parliaments	366–368
Latter days of Louis XV. Sermon of Abbé de Beauvais	369
Death of Louis XV. First measures of Louis XVI.	370
Warnings of Assembly of Clergy against unbelief	371
Memorials drawn up by Dulau, Archbishop of Arles	372

Attempt to suppress the works of Voltaire	375
Death of Voltaire	376
Death of Archbishop De Beaumont	377
Cardinal de Rohan. Affair of the "collier"	377–379
Last General Assembly of the Clergy of France	380
Calonne and the Notables	381
Archbishop Loménie de Brienne	382
Edicts rejected. Parliament exiled	383
Edict in favour of the Protestants	384
The Clergy demand the States-General	385
Resignation of Archbishop De Brienne	386

CHAPTER XI.

Necker. The "double representation" of the Tiers-état	387
Meeting of the States-General	388
Disputes on the verification of powers	389
Henri Grégoire. The Abbé Sièyes	390
The clergy join the Tiers-état	391
The Constituent Assembly and the Church	392
Abandonment of Feudal rights	393
Abolition of tithes. Speech of Archbishop De Juigné	394, 395
Madame de Staël on the tenure of Church property	396
Speech of Talleyrand, Bishop of Autun	397
His scheme for alienating Church property	398
Adopted by the National Assembly	399
The "Constitution Civile du Clergé"	400, 401
Protest of the bishops against the new constitution	402
Schism among the clergy. Jurors and Nonjurors	404
Oath to the Constitution Civile	405
Consecration of Constitutional bishops	406
The Constitution denounced by the Pope	407
Strife between conforming and nonconforming Clergy	408
Decree of the Assembly against nonjuring Clergy	409
Law of "déportation"	410
Later efforts of the Constitutional Clergy	411
Ineffectual attempt to heal the schism	412
Napoleon Bonaparte. The second Concordat	413
Resignation of the episcopate demanded by the Pope	414
The bull "Qui Christi Domini." The "Articles Organiques"	415
The new episcopate. Restored National Establishment	416
Reaction towards Ultramontanism	417
The Church enslaved under the first Napoleon	418
Recapitulation. Church Government in ancient and feudal times	419
The Concordat, hostile to Gallicanism	420
Its injurious effects upon the Church	421
Institution of bishops by the Pope, a modern innovation	423

	PAGE
Refusal of bulls of Institution. Confusion resulting from it	424
Letter of Louis XIV. to Pope Clement XI.	425
Tendency of Concordat towards Ultramontanism	426
Anomalous character of the "Constitution civile"	427
General result on Church feeling in France	428
Conclusion	429, 430

List of the archiepiscopal and episcopal sees before the Revolution of 1789 .. 431–434

NOTE TO CHAP. VI., VOL. II. 1.—Correspondence between Archbishop Wake and Louis-Ellies Dupin .. 435–441

ERRATA.

Page 236, for "Dorsanne, *Journal*, tom. ii.," read "Dorsanne, *Journal*, tom. i. p. 324."

Page 240, line 23, add note at the word "course,"—Lafiteau, 'Hist. de la Constit. Unigen.,' tom. ii. p. 41.

THE GALLICAN CHURCH.

CHAPTER I.

In the midst of the "harsh din" of controversial strife, the Church of France exhibited, at this period, no declension from the practical zeal and fruitfulness in pious undertakings which distinguished the earlier years of the century. The results of the impulse given by the example and labours of Vincent de Paul became increasingly manifest. During the thirty-five years which had passed since he commenced his work, a new race of clergy had overspread the land, who in all the most important qualifications for their office contrasted favourably with their predecessors. This change was effected principally through the multiplication of ecclesiastical *Seminaries* under the direction of the Priests of the Mission, and the general adoption of this system of clerical training by the bishops throughout France. Experience had taught Vincent to regard the formation and management of Seminaries as the most indispensable of the duties to which he was called for the edification of the Church.

Addressing his Congregation at one of their conferences, in the year 1641, he expressed himself thus:—"At first our little company did not contemplate being serviceable to ecclesiastics; we thought only of our own spiritual advancement, and of evangelizing the poor. It pleased God that no more than this should appear at the outset; but in the fulness of time He called us to contribute to the training of good priests, to furnish parishes with efficient pastors, and to point out to them what they ought to know, and what to practise. How lofty and sublime is this employment! Who among us ever thought about the exercises of candidates for Ordination, or about

Seminaries? We never imagined any such undertaking until God signified His will thus to make use of us; He has guided the Society to this field of exertion, without any choice on our part. Hence He demands of us a serious, humble, devout, and constant application to the task, corresponding to the excellence of its object. It is a great thing, doubtless, to minister to the poor, but it is far more important to instruct ecclesiastics; since if *they* are ignorant, the flock whom they direct must of necessity be ignorant also. The question might have been asked of the Son of God, Wherefore art Thou come? Is it not to 'preach the Gospel to the poor,' according to the command of the eternal Father? Why then dost Thou appoint *priests?* Why dost Thou take such pains to instruct and discipline them? Why confer on them the power to consecrate, to bind and loose, &c.? To which the Saviour might have replied, that He was come not only to teach the truths which are essential to salvation, but also to provide for His Church good priests, superior to those of the ancient Law. God, having rejected the polluted priests of the old Covenant, promised to raise up others, who from east to west and from north to south should fill the earth with their voices and their Message. And by whom did He fulfil that promise? By His Son our Lord, who ordained priests, and through them gave power to His Church to ordain others, saying, "Sicut misit me Pater, et Ego mitto vos." Thus He designed to perpetuate throughout all ages that which He himself had done at the close of His earthly life. There is nothing greater than a good priest; ponder as we will, we shall never discover any nobler work in which to engage than that of forming a good priest; one to whom our Lord grants such power over His body natural and mystical, the power to consecrate and to absolve from sin. O my Saviour, how ought poor missionaries to devote themselves to Thee for the training up of good ecclesiastics, since it is of all works the most arduous, the most exalted, the most weighty for the salvation of souls and for the advance of Christianity!"*

Such were the sentiments with which Vincent and his priests of the Mission entered on this momentous branch of their operations. It was attempted in the first instance to model the

---

* Collet, *Vie de S. V. de Paul*, tom. ii. p. 77.

Seminaries in France according to the plan prescribed by the Council of Trent;* namely by admitting as pupils boys from twelve to fourteen years of age, who, it was hoped, by means of a long systematic course of training, would retain through life the habits of discipline, self-restraint, and devotion acquired in early youth. But this scheme, after a fair trial, proved unsuccessful. Vincent opened an institution of this kind in 1635, at the Collège des Bons Enfans, and maintained it in that form for several years, but without encouraging results. The expense thrown upon parents was in most cases beyond their means; the benefit to the Church was remote and uncertain, whereas the demand for an efficient priesthood was immediate and pressing; and, unhappily, very many of the young students, on reaching the age of deliberate personal choice, renounced their ecclesiastical prospects, and fell back into a worldly life. Similar disappointments occurred in the provinces. The Seminaries of Bordeaux, Agen, and Limoges, after some years of struggling existence, were left destitute of scholars; and the Archbishop of Rouen was forced to confess that in the course of twenty years he had not been able to secure the services of more than six approved priests out of all the young men upon whom he had expended so much care and labour. The rest had returned to the world, under the plea that they had taken the ecclesiastical habit at an age when they were incapable of intelligent reflection.† In 1642 Vincent modified the plan of his Seminary by receiving as pupils young men of the age of eighteen and upwards, who had already finished their elementary studies. These became inmates of the Collège des Bons Enfans, to which Cardinal Richelieu made a donation of a thousand crowns on the occasion; while at the same time, out of respect for the recommendations and authority of the Council of Trent, the younger class of pupils were transferred to another residence in the precincts of St. Lazare, which the founder named the Seminary of St. Charles. From this time the system of "Grands Séminaires," as they were called, began to prevail throughout the country. One of the first to follow the example was Alain de Solminiac, Bishop of Cahors, who instituted a

---

* *Conc. Trident.*, Sess. xxiii. cap. 18.
† Collet, *Vie de S. V. de Paul*, Liv. iv. p. 69.

Seminary on this type for his diocese, and confided it to the management of the Priests of the Mission, making it obligatory on candidates for the subdiaconate to reside for one year at least within its walls, while a further term of one year or more was required before their promotion to the priesthood. This excellent prelate, who was one of the ecclesiastical celebrities of his time, wrote to St. Vincent a few years before his death, to the following effect: "You would be delighted to see my clergy, and you would bless God a thousand times if you knew all the good that your Missionaries have done in my Seminary—good which has been diffused throughout the province."

It must not be forgotten, however, that in the great work of theological Seminaries the Gallican Church was indebted to other societies besides that of the "Priests of the Mission." The Congregation of St. Sulpice possessed a Seminary on a vast scale, adjoining the church of that name at Paris, erected at his own cost by M. Le Ragois de Bretonvilliers, who was one of the most zealous fellow-labourers of the Abbé Olier, and succeeded him both as Curé of St. Sulpice and Superior of the Seminary. The members of this community soon extended their operations, at the invitation of the bishops, into the provincial dioceses. At Bordeaux, at Villefranche in the diocese of Rodez, at Limoges, at Bourg St. Andéol in the Vivarais, at Nantes in Brittany, at Clermont in Auvergne, and at Aix in Provence, they established colleges which were eminently successful in training candidates for the priesthood, and increasing the efficiency of those who had already taken Holy Orders. After the death of Olier in 1657, the Seminary of St. Sulpice was governed for nearly twenty years by the Abbé de Bretonvilliers, who, being possessed of an ample fortune, liberally fostered all the works of charity with which it was connected, and at his death bequeathed to it considerable property. He was succeeded by Louis Tronson, a man of the highest attainments both intellectual and spiritual, under whose wise rule the Society acquired additional lustre, and rendered invaluable services to the Church. It was to the care of Tronson that the Marquis de Fénélon entrusted his nephew, the future Archbishop of Cambrai, who acquired his clerical education at St. Sulpice. The respect of Fénélon for Tronson was unbounded. "I congratulate myself," he wrote on one occasion to Pope

Clement XI., "on having had M. Tronson for my instructor in the Word of life, and having been formed under his personal care for the ecclesiastical career. Never was any man, unless I am mistaken, superior to him for love of discipline, for skill, prudence, piety, and sagacity in the discernment of character."*

On an appointed day in each year the Seminarists of St. Sulpice assembled at the house in Paris, and attended mass in the chapel, which was usually celebrated by the Archbishop or some distinguished prelate. After service each priest approached the altar in turn, and kneeling before the Bishop, renewed the promise of self-dedication to God and separation from the world, which he had made on his admission into the community. This was expressed in a sentence from the 16th Psalm—"Dominus pars hæreditatis meæ et calicis mei; Tu es qui restitues hæreditatem meam mihi." †

The Seminary of St. Nicolas du Chardonnet was formally recognised in 1644 by the Archbishop of Paris as his Diocesan Seminary, and confirmed as such by royal letters-patent the same year. Its founder, as recorded in a former chapter, was Adrian Bourdoise; to whom indeed is frequently assigned the honour of having been the first to take successful steps towards establishing Seminaries in France. St. Nicolas du Chardonnet acquired a very high reputation as a nursery for the ministry, and its internal organization served as a model for many similar foundations in different parts of the country. In order to supply the necessary funds, Bourdoise formed an association which he styled "La Bourse cléricale," consisting of persons willing to contribute, or to collect contributions, for the support both of students at the college and of ecclesiastics after entering on their profession. In this way considerable sums were realised; the Assembly of the Clergy voted a grant to the Seminary in 1660; and the collegiate buildings were secured to the society by the liberality of the Prince de Conti, who purchased them for 36,000 livres. During the troubles of the Fronde, when hostile armies occupied the neighbourhood of Paris, the Seminarists of St.-Nicolas distinguished themselves by their devoted ministrations among the sick and wounded.

---

* *Correspondance de Fénélon*, tom. iii. p. 104, Lettre cxxvi.
† Helyot, *Ordres Monastiques*, l'art vi. chap. xviii.

Several of them died from excess of exertion or exposure to epidemic disease; and not long afterwards the Superior was taken away in the midst of his exemplary labours, finishing his course on the 19th of July, 1655, at the age of seventy-one. Bourdoise was a man of eminent endowments; stern in outward manner, but full of ardent charity within; plain-spoken almost to a fault, courageous in defence of the truth, thoroughly disinterested; one who sought the glory of God and the welfare of the Church without the slightest admixture of selfish ends. Throughout life he preserved relations of the closest friendship with Vincent de Paul, Olier, F. Condren of the Oratory, and all the foremost ecclesiastics of the day.

Subsequent benefactors endowed St. Nicolas du Chardonnet with such an ample annual revenue that the "Bourse cléricale" discontinued its operations in 1695.

A fourth Congregation of secular priests devoted to the work of clerical education was that called Eudistes, from Jean Eudes its founder, formerly a priest of the Oratory. His conduct in separating from that society has been severely criticised, but, as it appears, without justice. Eudes was conscious of a peculiar talent, which he undoubtedly possessed, for influencing the minds and character of his younger brethren; and believed himself specially called to the supervision of seminaries. The Oratory imposes no vows upon its members; and cases had occurred repeatedly of persons ceasing to belong to it when summoned by circumstances to a different sphere of labour. Acting under the advice of experienced friends, Eudes opened an institution at Caen, on a very modest footing, in March, 1643. He placed it under the invocation of "Jesus and Mary," but it was afterwards better known as the Congregation of Eudistes. Its object was twofold,—the training of candidates for the ministry, and the conduct of missions, on the same plan as those organized with so much success by Vincent de Paul. At first Eudes had no more than five associates; but ere long they acquired such high estimation for earnest zeal and general ability, that their numbers multiplied greatly; and under the sanction of the Bishop of Bayeux, and other prelates, they planted theological colleges in all the larger towns of Normandy. The great Seminary at Caen, which became the head-quarters of the Congregation, was not completed till 1657; but previously to this the Eudistes had founded houses at Rouen, Coutances, and Lisieux; and subsequently they established themselves at Rennes, Blois, Dol, and Senlis. Their work as missionaries also became widely extended. In 1660 Eudes was summoned to preach before the Court at Paris;* on which occasion his vehement impassioned eloquence made a deep impression upon the Queen Mother Anne of Austria, and secured her special favour for the society. Some years later, Louis XIV. having expressed a wish that a mission should be given at Versailles, where immense works were then in progress at the palace, the duty was entrusted by the Archbishop of Paris to Eudes and his companions. They fulfilled it with memorable effect, and received marked encouragement from the king and the royal family, who frequently came to attend the services. Soon afterwards, Louis invited the Eudistes on a similar errand to St. Germain; and this was followed by a grant from the monarch of a domicile for the Congregation at Paris. Eudes had now taken his place in public opinion as one of the most admirable preachers of the day; in consequence his ministrations were eagerly sought for on all sides. The Bishop of Evreux, in whose diocese his labours had met with great acceptance, endeavoured to get him nominated as his coadjutor in the see; but it was felt that he was more usefully employed for the interests of the Church in carrying on the works he had already undertaken; and to these he continued to devote himself with indefatigable ardour, until at length incapacitated by the infirmities of age. Having resigned his post of Superior of the Congregation, Eudes died at Caen in August, 1680, at the age of seventy-nine. He was the elder brother of the celebrated historian Eudes de Mezeray.

The Eudistes, like other Congregations instituted for the same ends, were simply secular priests; they took no vows except those at their ordination, and their dress was not different in any way from the usual clerical costume. They accepted no engagement without the express sanction of the Bishop of the diocese; and in whatever direction they were sent to labour,

---

* His first sermons at Paris were preached on the occasion of a mission which he was invited to give at St. Sulpice, by his friend the Abbé Olier, in the year 1650. It was attended with wonderful success.—*Vie de M. Olier*, tom. ii. p. 112.

their first care was to place themselves at the disposal of the parochial clergy on the spot.

The closing labours of St. Vincent de Paul, notwithstanding a complication of maladies which afflicted him at his great age, exhibited the same wisdom and the same disinterested self-sacrifice which had characterised him through life. In 1658 he completed the code of statutes of his Congregation of the Mission, containing the last and well-weighed results of his experience. For thirty years the Missionaries had fulfilled their vocation without written rules; but Vincent felt that, in the near prospect of his own removal, it was necessary to provide them with fixed precepts for their future guidance. These regulations he based on the cardinal principle of conformity with the pattern of Jesus Christ, in the two chief branches of His ministry, as a teacher and as an evangelizer. "Our rules," he said, "are almost entirely taken from the Gospel, and they all tend to conform our life to that which our Saviour led on earth. For we are told that the Divine Saviour came and was sent by His Father to preach the Gospel to the poor; and this, likewise, is the object of our mission. Yes, brethren, the poor are our inheritance. What happiness, to do the same thing for which our Lord declared that He was come from heaven to earth, and by means of which we hope, with His grace, to pass from earth to heaven! What an inducement have we here to observe strictly the rules which conduct to such a blessed end! You have long waited for them, brethren, and we have long deferred giving them to you; partly with a view to imitate our Saviour, who began to act before He began to teach. 'Jesus began to do and to teach.' For thirty years of His life He practised virtue, and employed only the three last years in preaching and teaching it. The Company, then, has endeavoured to imitate Him, not only in the work which He came to do, but also in the manner in which He performed it. Thirty-three years have passed since we began to work, and during the whole of that time we have, by the grace of God, practised the rules which we are now about to prescribe to you. You will find in them, therefore, nothing new, nothing that you have not put in practice for many years past with great profit and edification. . . . . . Those practices which have always been observed, and are observed among us to this day, it is now thought advisable to reduce to writing, and to enact as rules. I trust that the Company will receive them as emanating from the Spirit of God, from whom all good things proceed, and without whom we are not sufficient to think or to do anything as of ourselves." Vincent concludes with an affecting peroration, in which, after the example of Moses, he invokes blessings and favours of every kind from above upon all who should faithfully obey the rule thus promulgated for the governance of his Society.

Under the general head of conformity to the life of Christ, the priests are enjoined to emulate specially (1) His poverty, (2) His purity, (3) His obedience, (4) His charity. They are likewise exhorted to cultivate, throughout the cycle of their ministrations, five characteristic qualities, the impression of which ought to be left upon every act of the Congregation;— namely, simplicity, humility, gentleness, self-mortification, and zeal for the salvation of souls.

One of the last charitable undertakings of Vincent de Paul was the foundation of a hospital at Sainte Reine, near Dijon in Burgundy, for the accommodation of the numerous pilgrims and afflicted persons annually visiting that spot, some for the purpose of devotion at the shrine of the saint, others for the benefit of the mineral springs of the locality. The project was first started by M. des Noyers, a worthy citizen of Paris, whose health had been recruited by the use of the waters. He was moved with compassion for the crowds of poor helpless patients, who, after the fatigues of travel, found no better lodging at Sainte Reine than a farm or an outhouse, and not seldom were obliged to lie without shelter in the open street. Des Noyers, with the assistance of a few friends, made an effort to remedy the evil, but soon found that it was too serious and weighty to be dealt with by the scanty means at their command. In their embarrassment they applied to Vincent de Paul, addressing him by the expressive title of "steward of the affairs of God." He received them with warm cordiality, encouraged them with judicious counsel and assurances of support, and directed them to begin the work forthwith, in full confidence of a successful issue. Within two years, in spite of the public difficulties arising from the war with Spain, and his increasing personal infirmities, which kept him a constant prisoner in the house, Vincent had collected the funds required for building the hospital, which was completed early in the year 1660. Anne of Austria, at Vincent's request, took the institution under her special protection, and obtained royal letters-patent in its favour, which were registered in the parliament of Burgundy. "Such," says Collet, "was the commencement and the progress of this famous Hospital, where, without reckoning three or four hundred sick patients who are received there every year, more than twenty thousand poor pilgrims of all ages, of both sexes, of every nation, and of every religious persuasion, find year after year all the attention and assistance, both temporal and spiritual, that it is possible to procure for them. These various functions are divided among good ecclesiastics and virtuous Sisters of Charity. God has repeatedly blessed their zeal in a manner which has been celebrated even in distant foreign countries; and many a one who, on coming to these healing waters, thought only of recovering a transient soundness of body, has gained health of another kind, infinitely more precious." He proceeds to mention that the great services of Vincent in this good work were acknowledged with deep gratitude by all who had taken part in it; and that when the Bishop of Autun (to which diocese Sainte Reine belongs) wrote to Pope Clement XI. to demand his beatification, he specified as two important services which he had rendered to his diocese, first, that he had obtained, by his influence in the Council of Conscience, the reform of a large Benedictine abbey at Autun; and secondly, that he had procured the blessing of a hospital for the pilgrims of Sainte Reine, for want of which it was well known that numbers of them had perished.*

The decline of Vincent's health was gradual; and it was not till he had passed his eightieth year that his bodily infirmities were accompanied by any visible diminution of mental vigour. Many of those who had been his most valued friends and fellow labourers through life preceded him to the grave. He lost, within two years, Antoine Portail, one of his first colleagues when he commenced his work at the Collège des Bons Enfans; Charles Du Fargis, a connection of the De Joigny family, who

---

* Collet, *Vie de St. Vincent de Paul*, tom. ii. pp. 617-624.

had long been domiciled among the Lazarist community; Mademoiselle Legras, foundress of the Sisters of Charity; and Louis Rochechoart de Chandenier, Abbot of Tournus, nephew of Cardinal de la Rochefoucauld. At length Vincent found himself incapacitated by a partial paralysis of the limbs, and other symptoms of organic decay; and he at once prepared himself for the last summons in the same spirit of calm, simple self-devotion to the Divine will which had been the leading feature of his saintly life. Pope Alexander VII. consoled him on his deathbed by an Apostolical Brief full of expressions of veneration and affection; and three Cardinals wrote to him with the same object. Being requested to bestow on the sorrowing members of his Congregation some parting word of counsel and benediction, Vincent contented himself with repeating the words of the Apostle, "Qui cœpit opus bonum, Ipse perficiet;" "He who hath begun a good work in you will also perform it." Shortly afterwards this much-honoured servant of God expired in perfect peace, on the 27th of September, 1660, in the eighty-fifth year of his age. Pope Benedict XIII. declared him among the number of the "bienheureux," upon the "humble and pious demand" of Louis XV., his Queen, the prelates of France, the Assembly of the Clergy, and the whole Congregation of the Priests of the Mission, on the 13th of August, 1729. His canonization was published by Clement XII. on the 24th of June, 1737.

It will not be inappropriate, after recording the death of one to whose faithful labours the Church of France was so largely indebted for the late wonderful restoration of religious life and energy, to introduce to the reader a name which was ere long to rival that of Vincent de Paul in ecclesiastical celebrity and public influence, and which must be placed, beyond all dispute, at the head of the illustrious roll of Gallican theologians. It is that of JACQUES BÉNIGNE BOSSUET;—"a man," to borrow the words of Massillon, "who, had he but been born in the primitive ages, would have been the luminary of Councils, and the soul of assembled Fathers of the Church; would have dictated Canons, and presided at Nicæa and Ephesus."* The seventeenth century, however, was perhaps not less competent than the

---

* Massillon, *Oraison funèbre du premier Dauphin.*

fourth or the fifth to judge of the merits and genius of Bossuet; and no Council of antiquity could have exalted him to a higher pinnacle of renown than that which was accorded to him by the unanimous verdict of his contemporaries.

Bossuet was born at Dijon on the 27th of September, 1627. His father was a magistrate of high respectability, a councillor of the parliament of Metz. Being obliged by the duties of his office to be frequently absent from home, he entrusted his son to the care of his brother, Claude Bossuet; and the boy received the first rudiments of education at the college of the Jesuits at Dijon. Here his extraordinary talents were quickly discovered, and the fathers made an attempt to attach him permanently to their Society; but this was frustrated by his uncle, under whose advice Bossuet was sent, at the age of fifteen, to pursue his studies at Paris. He was already destined for the Church, and had been named, through the influence of his father, to a canonry in the cathedral of Metz. Such abuses were still by no means uncommon in France.

Bossuet reached Paris on the same day that Cardinal Richelieu re-entered the capital on his return from the south, after the submission of Roussillon and the suppression of the conspiracy of Cinq Mars. The great minister was in a dying state, borne in a huge litter of woodwork by eighteen of his guards. This scene, and that of the Cardinal's funeral obsequies which took place a few weeks afterwards, made an impression upon the mind of the young student which was never effaced.

Bossuet joined the College of Navarre, of which a divine of distinguished reputation, Nicolas Cornet, was at that time Grand Master. He formed a just estimate of the lofty endowments of his pupil, and predicted with confidence the brilliant career which awaited him. Before the close of his academical course, the name of Bossuet had become known in some of the first circles of Parisian society; he had been introduced at the Hôtel de Rambouillet, the resort of all the literary celebrities of the day; and had there astonished and charmed a fastidious auditory by delivering an extempore sermon, without the aid of books, and with little, if any, previous meditation, which both as to matter and manner surpassed all expectations.*

---

* Bausset, *Histoire de Bossuet*, tom. i. p. 22.

Having taken the degree of Bachelor in Divinity, Bossuet repaired to Metz, and devoted himself to his duties as a member of the cathedral chapter; during this interval he was ordained subdeacon and deacon by the Bishop of Langres. Returning to Paris in 1650, he resumed his studies in theology under the personal superintendence of the Grand Master Cornet; and it was now that he was led to adopt definite principles with reference to the perplexing questions which were beginning to be controversially agitated in the Church;—principles which he consistently maintained throughout life. Upon the doctrine of grace he became an attached follower of St. Augustine and St. Thomas Aquinas; adhering, according to the Abbé Ledieu's account, even to the theory of the "premotio physica" propounded by the last-named doctor.* It is clear, from his 'Traité du libre arbitre,' and his 'Défense de la Tradition,' that he considered St. Thomas as the safest and most philosophical expositor of the profound mysteries of moral causation; but he upheld that view with true moderation and charity. He did not pretend to make it a matter *de fide*, of necessary Catholic dogma; and though decidedly averse to the opposite system of Molina, he gladly acknowledged that this also, since it had never incurred the censure of the Church, was a permissible opinion, entitling those who held it conscientiously to all the benefits of Christian liberty. Having thus laid broad and deep the foundations of his theology in the teaching of the Fathers and the unvarying tradition of the Church, Bossuet embraced the only sure preservative from the spirit of sectarianism, and never permitted himself, throughout the polemical discussions which abounded in his time, to be made the mere instrument of a party.

He completed, in 1652, the lengthened course of probation prescribed by the rules of the Sorbonne for those who aspired to the higher grades of theological distinction. He was received Doctor in the spring of that year, and about the same time was ordained priest, and appointed Archdeacon of Sarrebourg, in the diocese of Metz. It was on this occasion that he became known to St. Vincent de Paul; having made a retreat under his guidance at St. Lazare (as we have already mentioned) previously to his ordination.†

---

* Ledieu, *Mémoires sur Bossuet*, tom. i. p. 38.   † See vol. i. p. 325.

During the next few years Bossuet was constantly in residence at Metz, distributing his time between his active functions in the cathedral and laborious study in private. His first essay in the arena of controversy was made in 1665, when he entered the lists against the Calvinist minister Paul Ferri, a man of superior talent, learning, and character, who had published a 'Catechism' in defence of the Reformation. Bossuet undertook to refute this production, in which the author had advanced that, "although it was possible, before the Reformation, to obtain salvation in the Church of Rome, this was no longer possible since the Reformation." The Abbé Bossuet overthrew this sophism by a powerful chain of reasoning on the perpetuity, the visibility, and the infallibility of the Church Catholic; and such was the impression which his arguments produced upon the mind of his Protestant antagonist, that, during his last illness in 1669, he announced to his family his full intention to abjure the Calvinist creed, and seek re-admission to the Church through the ministry of Bossuet. His purpose was defeated by his co-religionists; but the fact transpired, and led to numerous conversions to Catholicism in Metz and the neighbourhood.

Bossuet was summoned to Paris in 1659 to preach a course of Lent sermons; and opportunities now quickly occurred which enabled him to exhibit the full splendour of his oratorical powers. His fame having reached the ears of the young king, he was appointed to preach before him in the chapel of the Louvre during the Advent of 1661. Louis was captivated by his eloquence, and expressed his admiration without reserve; and from that moment his success, in a worldly point of view, was a matter of certainty. Several years elapsed, however, before he was preferred to a more dignified station in the Church. He was consecrated Bishop of Condom in 1669; and in September, 1670, was named by Louis XIV. preceptor to his son the Dauphin.

The leaders of the Jansenists, upon the restoration of peace in the Church, hastened to give public proof of their zeal for the true faith by turning their arms against the Calvinists. In 1669 was published the first volume of one of their most celebrated works, the 'Perpétuité de la Foi de l'Église Catholique sur l'Eucharistie.' This was composed almost entirely by

Pierre Nicole; but such was the author's modesty, that he insisted on its appearing under the name of Antoine Arnauld, on account of his superior position and reputation in the Church. Some years previously, Nicole had drawn up a short treatise on the same subject,* which had been attacked by Jean Claude, one of the most eminent ministers of the Reformed Communion. Two of his colleagues, Aubertin and Blondel, had likewise written with ability against the doctrine of the Real Presence; and to these various strictures Arnauld and Nicole thought it necessary to put forth a general reply.

The 'Perpétuité de la Foi' made its appearance with printed testimonials of approval from twenty-seven prelates, including Cardinals d'Estrées, Forbin-Janson, and Le Camus. To these were added the suffrages of twenty doctors of the Sorbonne, of whom Bossuet was one. The latter divine extols the work not only as establishing, by proof amounting almost to demonstration, the truth of the Church's belief as to the Sacrament of the Altar, but as furnishing principles upon which to construct an entire system of controversial divinity. "What strikes me especially," he says, "is that the author appeals throughout to those irrefragable maxims which preserve the faithful in their attachment to the authority of the Church—that divine Teacher who is constantly at hand to instruct them in every age of the world." Bossuet had been requested by Arnauld and Nicole to revise their work before publication. By the express command of Louis XIV., he undertook this duty; and each of the three volumes was accordingly submitted to his censorship.† In the passage above quoted, he alludes, no doubt, to the absurd calumny, which had been so long rife against the Port-Royalists, of being in league with the Calvinists to subvert the fundamental verities of the Catholic faith. The suspension of the controversy on the Five Propositions afforded Arnauld and his friends a desirable opportunity of convincing the world that they had no sort of sympathy with those who dissented from the tradition of the Church as to the Sacraments,

---

* This went by the name of *La petite Perpétuité*, to distinguish it from the subsequent larger work.

† *Histoire de Bossuet*, par le Card. Bausset, tom. i. p. 207. The second volume of *La Perpétuité* appeared in September, 1671; the third in February, 1674. Two more volumes were afterwards added by the Abbé Renaudot.

particularly that of the Eucharist, which had been so vehemently contested from the very outset of the Reformation. They therefore spared no pains to prove that the great central truth of the Real Presence rests on the unvarying evidence of all Christian centuries; and that the Eastern Church, in spite of important differences upon other topics both of discipline and doctrine, has always upon this head been in substantial agreement with the West. This fact they established beyond dispute by official certificates* signed by the Oriental patriarchs. The argument from prescription, as Nicole terms it, was at once the most natural and the most conclusive in such an enquiry, which confessedly originated in mutual charges of doctrinal innovation. The *history* of religious belief must needs be, under these circumstances, the groundwork of the whole investigation. But it was precisely in this direction that Claude and other Calvinist writers seem to have been conscious that their cause was weak. They showed great ingenuity in avoiding it; preferring to base the discussion on the interpretation of Scripture, and the various modern systems which had been devised for the purpose of confuting the alleged errors of Rome, and introducing a more spiritual view of the great mystery in question.

The 'Perpétuité de la Foi' was warmly applauded, and had considerable effect upon the public mind. Marshal Turenne had the advantage of perusing it in manuscript, and his conversion is said to have been produced in some measure by its influence.†

Arnauld and Nicole pursued this new line of controversial activity by a succession of attacks, great and small, upon the Calvinistic theology. The Antinomian tendency of one of the prominent dogmas of the Reformation was forcibly exposed by Arnauld in his 'Renversement de la Morale par la doctrine des Calvinistes touchant la Justification,' and in another treatise styled 'L'impiété de la Morale des Calvinistes.' Nicole contributed, on the same theme, 'Préjugés légitimes contre les Calvinistes,' which, like the 'Perpétuité,' was examined and ap-

---

* Arnauld obtained them through M. Picquet, a missionary priest, afterwards Bishop of Babylon, who had formerly been Consul at Aleppo.—

B. Racine, *Hist. Eccles.*, tom. xi. pt. ii. art. xiv.

† St. Beuve, *Port Royal*, tom. iv. p. 334.

proved by Bossuet. These productions were welcomed with cordial satisfaction at Rome. Arnauld and others of the Port-Royalists were distinguished by Clement X., and during the early years of Innocent XI., with repeated and flattering marks of Pontifical favour.*

The so-called "Peace of Clement IX." proved to be only an armistice of brief duration. Which of the two parties was the aggressor in the recommencement of hostilities was, as might be expected under the circumstances, a disputed question. It cannot be denied, however, that the elaborate work entitled, 'La Morale pratique des Jésuites, extraite fidèlement de leurs livres,' proceeded from the Jansenist camp, and that in spirit, if not in actual letter, it was an infraction of the late treaty. The new Archbishop of Paris caused it to be examined by the Doctors of the Sorbonne, and it was pronounced by them to abound with scandalous calumnies, monstrous falsifications of fact, and heretical propositions. Upon this an *arrêt* of the Parliament sentenced it to be destroyed by the hangman on the Place de Grève.†

The hollowness of this superficial truce soon became more clearly apparent. It seems to have been taken for granted by the Jansenists, that the distinction between the *droit* and the *fait*, upon the strength of which the four protesting bishops had been induced to accept the Formulary, would continue to be allowable in all subsequent subscriptions. They were therefore greatly disconcerted when they found that in most cases the signature was exacted "pure and simple," without distinction or qualification of any kind. One of the party, Feydeau, doctor of the Sorbonne and théologal of Beauvais, was deprived of his preferment and sent into exile for having refused to take the test without the saving clause.‡ The Bishop of Angers

---

* Innocent XI. held Arnauld in the highest estimation, and at one time designed to have created him a cardinal. Baylo (*Dict. Hist.*, sub v. Arnauld) quotes the following passage from the preface to the *Causa Arnaldina*:— "De Arnaldo in purpuratorum procerum ordinem adlegando aliquando Sanctitatem suam cogitasse, etsi certum est et pluribus notum, nollem tamen hic commemorare, nisi eminentissimus Cardinalis, intimorum Romanæ Aulæ consiliorum testis locuples, id nuper Parisiis evulgasset, asseruissetquo per unum Arnaldum stetisse quominus in eminentissimâ illâ dignitate ornaretur."

† D'Avrigny, *Mém. Chronol.*, tom. iii. p. 98. The first two volumes of the *Morale pratique* (those here referred to) were written by M. de Pontchâteau, the rest by Antoine Arnauld.

‡ See Arnauld's *Lettres* (Nancy, 1727), tom. iii. Lett. clvi.

(Henri Arnauld) attempted to establish in that diocese a greater latitude of interpretation; and apparently forgot, in his anxiety to secure favourable terms for his own friends, that he was bound to respect the liberty of those who differed from him. He issued a mandement which was complained of as making the reservation of the "fact of Jansenius" not only a permissible, but an indispensable, condition of subscription. He contended that the distinction between the doctrine of the propositions and the fact that they were taught by Jansenius, was the basis upon which the late pacification rested; and that the signatures of the four bishops, notoriously obtained upon that understanding, had been declared satisfactory by the Pope himself. Hence he insisted that the same distinction was essentially requisite in all cases. The University of Angers protested against this view, and appealed from the bishop to the Crown. The result was an arrêt of the Council of State, dated the 30th of May, 1676, from the camp at Ninove (Louis XIV. being engaged at this time in his invasion of Holland), which is said to have been suggested, if not actually drawn up, by De Harlai, Archbishop of Paris.* It condemned the mandement of Bishop Arnauld, as falsely interpreting the terms upon which peace had been concluded, and as an abuse of the condescension of the Holy See in permitting, in favour of some few individuals, a special explanation of the sense of their subscription. "Such a proceeding was virtually a revocation of the bull which prescribed the signature upon oath of the said Formulary, without making mention of any exceptional interpretation. It was also manifestly unjust to those who had subscribed it simply as it stood; since, if the distinction of the fact were necessary, their conduct was blameable instead of praiseworthy." Upon receiving this royal ordonnance, the Theological Faculty of Angers announced that no one would henceforth be admitted to exercises or degrees without signing the Formulary in the mode prescribed by the Faculty of Paris; and that all persons who had graduated since 1668 must sign it within the space of a month. The bishop now put forth a second mandement, which was virtually a retractation of the first. He declared that his meaning had been misunderstood, and that he had never

---

* *Hist. de Port Royal,* Pt. i. Liv. xi. § xxii.

intended to prohibit the acceptance of the Formulary "pur et simple," by those who felt able to take this step with a safe conscience. The University enforced its injunctions; the great majority of the students signed without hesitation; a few recusants were expelled; and the affair terminated.

But the profound animosity which had taken root in the Church during more than thirty years of contention was not to be stifled by any temporary efforts of repression. Fresh trouble was stirred up by an ecclesiastic named Mallet, who attacked the 'Nouveau Testament de Mons,' a work which had been published by the Port-Royalists in 1667, and printed at Mons in Flanders, because the necessary official sanction could not be obtained in France.* This translation had been denounced by the late Archbishop Péréfixe soon after its appearance, upon various grounds. It differed from the Vulgate; it followed the version of Geneva in many passages which are known to have been wrested so as to favour the heresy of Calvin; it was pervaded by a general tendency towards Jansenism; it distorted the sense of Scripture in such a way as to weaken belief in it, and to invalidate the evidence for some of the most important truths of religion. Other prelates proscribed it in like manner; and Pope Clement IX. suppressed it by a brief issued in April, 1668. Mallet accused the authors of systematically falsifying Scripture for the sake of obtaining countenance for their heterodox opinions. Arnauld composed a reply, but thought it prudent, before he again embarked in forbidden controversy, to forward a memorial to the king requesting his permission.† The Prince of Condé undertook to ascertain his Majesty's pleasure in the matter. Louis, prompted doubtless by the Jesuit influences which surrounded him, gave notice that any one who might venture to present the "requête" of M. Arnauld would be provided forthwith with a lodging in the Bastile. This was grossly unfair to the Jansenists. Breaches of the

---

* Ellies-Dupin, *Hist. Ecclésiastique du XVIIᵐᵉ Siècle*, Liv. iv. chap. i.; *Histoire de Port Royal*, tom. vi. p. 25. Isaac de Saci was the author of this translation. It was carefully revised by Arnauld, Nicole, the Count de Tréville, and others, who met for the purpose under the roof of the Duchess of Longueville. The official "privilege" was refused by the Government on the pretext that a sufficiently good translation was already in existence, namely, that of Father Amelotte, which had been approved by the Assembly of the Clergy.

† His "Requête au Roi" is printed among his *Lettres*, tom. iii. p. 140.

peace were committed with impunity on the one side, while on the other every movement in self-defence was sternly prohibited.

Other indications occurred of a fresh ebullition of persecuting spite against Port Royal and its friends. In 1677 the Bishops of Arras and St. Pons determined to address Pope Innocent XI. on the subject of certain corrupt maxims of morality alleged to be taught by the casuists. They applied to Nicole for assistance; and the letter which he indited on this occasion, in concert with Arnauld, was animadverted upon as a further violation of the peace of the Church.* Louis ordered the Marquis de Pomponne, Secretary of State, Arnauld's nephew, to inform his uncle that the king had hitherto been satisfied with his conduct and that of his friends as to the observance of the terms of pacification; but that lately complaints had been made against him in various quarters, and that he was accused of seeking to provoke a renewal of strife. Shortly afterwards it was notified to him that his mode of life at Paris had excited suspicion; that his house in the Faubourg St. Jacques had become the resort of the intriguing and disaffected; that he assembled his friends too often, and in numbers which had an air of faction and cabal. His Majesty desired that he would change his residence for a time.

Arnauld, finding that his enemies had succeeded in poisoning the king's mind against him, and knowing that no mere temporary change of domicile was likely to dislodge the determined prejudice which clung to his name, now took the resolution of withdrawing into voluntary exile from France. His letter to Archbishop de Harlai, explaining his reasons for this step, is written in a tone of remarkable moderation, though at the same time he does not shrink from setting forth the facts in their true light.† His enemies, he says, being no longer in a position to impugn his orthodoxy, had shifted their ground, and now maligned him as one whose character and habits were prejudicial to the State. Such an accusation, in his case, was of all others the most palpably devoid of credibility. Was it conceivable that a mere theologian, with no fortune and no powerful

---

* Arnauld to M. de Pomponne, *Lettres*, tom. iii. p. 102.
† Arnauld, *Lettres*, tom. iii. p. 188, Lettre clxxxii. See also his letters on the same occasion to M. de Pomponne and the Chancellor le Tellier, Letters clxxvii. and clxxxiii.

connexions, who had spent four-and-twenty years in complete retirement from the world and the concerns of active life, could inspire with alarm a monarch who had withstood all Europe leagued together to arrest the progress of his arms, and whose conquests had been terminated only by a glorious peace, of which he himself had dictated the conditions? If any such apprehensions really existed, they would at all events disappear as soon as he had withdrawn once more into seclusion, and renounced all visible share in the ordinary occupations of society. His Majesty would then perceive how incapable he was of lending himself to the disloyal machinations which were imputed to him; and would, he trusted, follow the impulse of his natural equity and justice in his treatment of a community which now seemed destined to a fresh persecution. For himself, he would reckon it a privilege to have contributed to such a change of policy, by sacrificing to the repose of the Church even the sweetest consolation which this world has to offer, namely that of living among our friends, and dying in their arms.

Arnauld took refuge at first with a friend at Fontenay-aux-Roses near Paris; but upon being apprised by the Duke of Montausier that the king was constantly beset by those whose counsels threatened his personal safety, he no longer delayed to seek a retreat abroad. For a moment he had thoughts of proceeding to Rome, where the Pope would doubtless have received him with all honour; but eventually he turned his steps towards Flanders, and arrived at Mons on the 20th of June, 1679. Afterwards he established himself at Brussels.

Allusion is made, in the letters above quoted, to a renewal of vexatious measures against the convent of Port Royal. The king had been induced, either by the jealous insinuations of the Jesuits, or by his hatred of whatever might by possibility become a centre of political agitation, to give orders which seriously troubled the repose of that much-tried community. He found in De Harlai, who was rather a time-serving politician than a faithful pastor of the Church, a ready instrument of his purpose. The archbishop had formerly seemed disposed to protect the Port Royalists; but his good-will vanished on the first intimation of royal displeasure; whatever might be his own feelings, the will of the sovereign must be carried into effect with passive and unreasoning submission. Louis, on returning victorious from his campaign in the Netherlands, had been provoked to find that the theological atmosphere was again overcast, and that fresh strife loomed in the distance. It so happened that in the troublesome affair of the *régale*, which belongs to this period, the two impracticable prelates, Pavillon and Caulet, were known partisans of the Jansenists, and had been among the most vehement opponents of the Formulary. Louis was heard to exclaim, in a tone of irritation, that the Jansenists were always in his way: "Ces Messieurs de Port Royal; toujours ces Messieurs!" but that he was determined to root out the sect from France, and would prove himself in that respect "more of a Jesuit than the Jesuits themselves." *

Madame de Longueville, whose friendship had thrown a powerful shield of protection round Port Royal for ten years past, died in April, 1679; and within a month afterwards the Archbishop of Paris conveyed to the abbess the king's order that the numbers of the inmates of the convent should be considerably reduced; the establishment was henceforth to consist of no more than fifty professed sisters and twelve "converses." †
With this view, the postulants, novices, and "pensionnaires" were to be dismissed immediately; and the male occupants of the cloister were informed at the same time that the king required them to disperse. The object of this policy was to break off the connexion which Port Royal had maintained with numerous families of noble birth and great influence throughout the country, and thus to destroy its importance as a focus of party spirit, religious and political. The mandate was executed without delay. Thirty-four pensionnaires—all of them belonging to the higher orders—quitted the convent, and were followed by many ecclesiastics who had resided there ever since the restoration of peace; among these were De Sacy, Tillemont, Pontchâteau, Sainte Marthe, De Luzancy, and Bourgeois. This act of wholesale dismemberment was too clearly "the beginning of the end." Port Royal after this declined rapidly in prestige and resources; it continued to exist for a period of nearly thirty years; but it is evident that its final extinction was a step resolved upon by the Government, whenever a plausible conjunction of circumstances might occur.

---

* St.-Beuve, *Port Royal*, tom. v. p. 7.   † *Hist. de Port Royal*, Pt. i. Liv. xi. § xxii.

CHAPTER II.

The conduct of Louis XIV., both in the case of Arnauld and in this latter stage of the persecution of Port Royal, is to be attributed in great measure to the pressure of the struggle in which he was engaged at the time with the Court of Rome; a struggle which, in its results, gave rise to some of the most critical occurrences in the history of the Church of France.

The origin of the prerogative called the "droit de régale" is obscure from its extreme antiquity.* Some authors have represented this question as in itself of small importance; but the truth is that it was closely connected with a principle which had for ages been fruitful in collisions between Church and State. The *régale* implied, not merely that the king was the legitimate guardian of the temporalities of vacant sees, but also that he had a right to the patronage belonging to them; in virtue of which he conferred Cathedral dignities, and benefices of all kinds, without any form of ecclesiastical institution. A difficulty was thus raised identical in substance with that which had engendered the great War of Investitures. That this privilege had been exercised by royalty in France from a very early date is an indisputable fact; but different explanations have been given of the mode in which it was acquired. According to one theory, a grant of this nature must have proceeded from the Church herself; the institution to benefices, even if restricted to those without cure of souls,† being clearly an exercise of spiritual authority, and beyond the province of the civil power. It has been attempted, therefore, to show that such concessions were made by Gallican Councils to Clovis and other Merovingian princes, and, again, by Pope Adrian I. to Charlemagne, in return for munificent donations of land and

---

* Some general observations on the *régale* will be found in the Introduction, vol. i. p. 77.

† Such was the rule, but in practice it was transgressed as often as it was observed.

other temporal advantages with which these monarchs had endowed the Church.* Much stress has also been laid upon a canon of the Council of Lyons in 1274, which sanctioned the continuance of the *régale* in churches where it was already established, prohibiting at the same time its introduction where it was hitherto unknown. Others have argued, on the contrary, that this right is inseparably inherent in the office of the sovereign; who, in his quality of supreme protector of the Church, is bound to undertake the external administration of a diocese when deprived of its ecclesiastical head. But it seems probable that the *régale* arose out of the provisions of that singular mediæval organization which we call the Feudal System. Episcopal sees were, in the language of those days, fiefs; ecclesiastical fiefs, but still fiefs, and subject, as such, to uniform laws and conditions of tenure.† The feudal tenant had no more than a life-interest in the estate; upon his decease it reverted to the seigneur, who retained it in his own hands, together with the revenues accruing from it, until a successor had been appointed, and had taken the oath of homage; whereupon he obtained what was called the "mainlevée de la régale"—in other words, was put into possession of his temporalities. Thus episcopal fiefs, on the death of the incumbents, were resumed, like others, by the king; not precisely in right of his crown, but in right of his feudal suzerainty. The same practice was followed by the dukes and counts, and other feudal potentates; and when their territorial jurisdiction was in course of time extinguished, their ecclesiastical patronage was transferred in like manner to the monarchy.

There were, however, in various parts of the country, churches which had been immemorially exempt from the *régale;* and when the Crown attempted to enforce the prerogative as universal, it encountered a resistance which proved to a great

---

* *Mémoires du Clergé*, tom. xi. pp. 179, 529 *et seqq.*

† "Baroniæ episcoporum de eleemosyna regis esse dicuntur, ideòque ab iis alienari non posse. Cùm igitur omnia ferè ecclesiarum prædia, episcopatuum nempe, et monasteriorum à regibus dotatorum, regalia sint, *i.e.* à regibus olim iis concessa, eodem jure reguntur quo beneficia militaria seu feuda, iisdemque sunt, quibus ea, servitiis obnoxia. Extinctis quippe personis ecclesiasticis, ad regem ipso jure redeunt, donec alia iisdem investiatur. Unde in chartâ Caroli IV. ann. 1354, pro episcopo Tullensi, dicitur is investiri de regalibus et feudis."—Ducange, *Glossar.*, sub v. Regalia.

extent successful. Henry IV., in 1606, published a Declaration stating that he did not purpose to establish the *régale* in any dioceses but those in which it had been enjoyed by his predecessors. But two years later the Parliament of Paris, on the requisition of the Avocat-Général Servin, pronounced an opposite decision in the case of the Deanery of the Cathedral of Belley; affirming that the *régale* was in force in that church "as throughout his Majesty's dominions."* This was complained of by the clergy; an official investigation was instituted in consequence; and the affair remained in the same position till the year 1637, when the prelates who claimed to be exempt from the *régale* were ordered to exhibit to the Council of State the documentary proofs upon which they founded such prescription. From this step no decisive result followed. The clerical Assembly of 1655 entered upon a detailed examination of the subject; and Archbishop de Marca, at the request of his brethren, embodied their views in a memorial of great learning and ability, which was presented to the king by Cardinal Mazarin. That minister professed himself convinced of the force and justice of the representations of the clergy; satisfaction was promised, and it would even seem that an edict was issued in accordance with the Declaration of 1606; but, if issued, it was certainly not executed.†

At length, on the 10th of February, 1673, appeared the famous Declaration of Louis XIV., alleging that the "droit de régale" belonged to him in all the archbishoprics and bishoprics throughout his kingdom, with the exception of those which were exempt "à titre onéreux;" *i. e.*, in virtue of distinct cessions or exchanges formerly effected at their cost and to the advantage of the Crown. The bishops of dioceses hitherto exempt were now summoned to register their oath of allegiance in the Cour des Comptes, in order to obtain restitution of their temporalities, which they were considered to have enjoyed up to this date without title.

The exempt Cathedrals were situated, for the most part, in the south; in Provence (where the *régale* had never been in force at all), Dauphiné, Languedoc, and Guienne. There were

---

* *Mémoires du Clergé*, tom. xi. p. 419; tom. x. p. 353.
† *Procès-verbaux des Assemb. Gén. du Cl. de France*, tom. iv. pp. 311 *et seqq.*

a few, likewise, in the northern provinces,—Nevers, Auxerre, Besançon, Bourges, and Arras.

Most of the bishops—in consideration, probably, of the general good-will evinced by the king towards the Church, of the uselessness of resistance, and of various other principles of prudence and discretion,*—submitted to the royal will, and connived at an encroachment which had never been tolerated by their predecessors. But there were two whom no arguments, no entreaties, no menaces, could reduce to compliance; these were Nicolas Pavillon, Bishop of Alet, and François de Caulet, Bishop of Pamiers; prelates revered throughout France for their fervent piety, pastoral devotedness, and disinterested character.

The two bishops were bosom friends. De Caulet, who was the younger, had been converted to Jansenist sentiments by his brother of Alet, and had ever since been accustomed to defer implicitly to his counsels and guidance. Their dioceses were contiguous; and they had acted in concert, as we have seen, in the affair of the Formulary, and throughout the negociations which led to the "Peace of Clement IX." They had thus become in an equal degree obnoxious to the Jesuits; but it appears that, in addition to more general grounds of conflict, they had come into collision with that Society on matters of diocesan discipline. The Bishop of Pamiers, in 1668, had found it necessary to inhibit the Jesuits of that city from hearing confessions. They set the mandate at defiance, and published libellous attacks upon the bishop; the latter made repeated, but ineffectual, attempts to bring them to submission, and at length launched against them a sentence of excommunication.

The part enacted by the Jesuits in the affair of the *régale* has been attributed to their determination to be revenged on the two Jansenist prelates for the stigma thus inflicted on the Company. Father Lachaise, who became Confessor to Louis XIV. in 1675, is said to have been the instigator of the extreme measures by which the king enforced the execution of his arbitrary edicts. And thus the memorable rupture which ensued between France and Rome, resulting, as it did, in the defiant affirmation of the four Gallican Articles, and in a movement of

---

* De Bausset, *Histoire de Bossuet*, tom. ii. p. 112.

national irritation which had all the appearance of incipient schism, may be traced in great measure to the intrigues of a Society whose *raison d'être*, so to speak, consists in devotion to the person, interests, and absolute authority of the Pope.

In 1676 the king, finding that the two bishops, after repeated admonitions, still neglected to register their oath of homage, proceeded to make nominations in virtue of the *régale* in their dioceses, as if the sees had been vacant. The Bishop of Alet pronounced a decree of suspension on the "Régalistes," and on all who might take part in their installation. His mandements were suppressed by the Council of State; his acts of suspension were annulled by the metropolitan, the Archbishop of Narbonne; upon which Pavillon, after remonstrating by letter both with the king and the archbishop, appealed to the judgment of the Sovereign Pontiff. The Bishop of Pamiers followed in the track of his colleague. The king appointed an ecclesiastic named Poncet to a canonry and archdeaconry in that Cathedral. Caulet, taking his stand upon the often-quoted canon of the Council of Lyons, forbade the chapter, under pain of suspension, to receive the royal nominee, and the latter to attempt taking possession, under pain of excommunication. Poncet sought redress from the Archbishop of Toulouse. The archbishop supported him, and cancelled the ordonnance of his suffragan; and the bishop then executed a formal appeal to the Holy See.

Innocent XI., who at this time occupied the Papal chair, possessed many admirable qualities. His intellectual gifts were small; but he was virtuous, upright, scrupulous in points of conscience, single-minded, devout, self-denying. His failings were those of a mind so penetrated with the supreme importance of certain master-principles, that in defence of them it allows zeal to outstrip discretion, and confounds firmness with obstinacy. He was keenly sensitive to those usurpations of modern royalty, which had so seriously impaired the authority and abridged the liberties of the Church; and was prepared to resent such enterprises with all the uncompromising energy of his predecessors in the middle ages. Added to this the Pope had imbibed a strong prejudice, amounting to personal dislike, against Louis XIV.; while, on the other hand, he warmly esteemed the Jansenists, whose severe morals and strictness of life were congenial to his own character. M. de Pontchâteau, one of the Port Royalist recluses, proceeded to Rome in the quality of their confidential agent, and was treated with the utmost consideration by Cardinal Cibo, minister of state, and by Favoriti, the Pope's secretary.

Innocent espoused with vigour the cause of the two appellant bishops. His first brief to Louis on the subject of the *régale* is dated March 12th, 1678. He points out that the recent attempt to extend his prerogative is an invasion of the most sacred rights of the Church; he attributes it to the sinister counsels of men who thought only of paying court to his Majesty for the sake of their own private ends; and who, while seeking at all hazards to augment his earthly power, cared little for the misery which he might have to endure hereafter from remorse of conscience, in the prospect of appearing before the tribunal of God. Those who advised him in this matter were men who, however they might pretend to be absolutely devoted to him, were, in fact, the bitterest enemies of his greatness and glory.

The Pope's conduct in this affair was dictated, beyond a doubt, by high principle and deep conviction; at the same time it must be confessed that the whole dispute was somewhat out of date. When we recollect that by the Concordat of 1516 the Curia had deliberately surrendered to the Crown the right of nomination to all the bishoprics in France, it was too late in the day to demur to the assertion of a privilege which was at once far more ancient and far less important. Such an anachronism was self-condemned to failure.

The good Bishop of Alet departed this life in December, 1677; and the whole weight of the contest with the Crown thus devolved upon the Bishop of Pamiers. He sustained it with unflinching resolution. At length he was threatened with the seizure of his temporalities unless he took the oath of allegiance within two months, and received the clergy who had been intruded into his diocese by royal patronage. He replied that he was ready to submit to the spoiling of his personal goods for the truth's sake, but entreated the king to spare his two diocesan seminaries, his cathedral (which he was rebuilding), and the various charities which he had instituted for the poor. Orders were given to proceed to the last extremity, and the bishop's property was accordingly confiscated. He suffered little, however, in a temporal sense from this act of cruelty, for his losses were more than covered by the eager liberality of private friends; his clergy taxed themselves to provide him with a regular income; and he was heard to complain that he had not been counted worthy to endure poverty for the love of Jesus Christ. A second, and again a third, brief from Innocent to Louis, couched in the same tone of urgent and solemn remonstrance, warned the monarch to desist from a course which could not but issue in disastrous consequences. On the latter occasion (December 27, 1679) the Pope announced that he should not employ any further entreaties by letter, but proceed to apply the remedies placed in his hands by his spiritual authority—remedies which he could no longer neglect without being unfaithful to his apostolical commission. "No perils, no commotions, no privations, can shake our resolution; we know that we are called to suffer such privations; and we do not esteem life itself more dear than your salvation and our own." *

Innocent wrote at the same time to the Bishop of Pamiers, warmly commending his patience under persecution, and exhorting him to constancy and perseverance. But the bishop's trials and confessorship approached their close. His death occurred in August, 1680.

This event was followed by strange scenes of agitation and confusion. The chapter of Pamiers elected grand-vicars to administer the diocese *sede vacante*, without admitting the intrusive "Régalistes" to vote on the occasion. This was resisted on the part of the Government; the Régalistes forced their way into the cathedral, and attempted to annul the election; whereupon they were violently denounced from the pulpit by one of their opponents, and threatened with excommunication. Such was the tumult, that it was necessary to send an armed force from Toulouse to restore order. The Archbishop of Toulouse now interfered, displaced Aubaréde, one of the nominees of the chapter, and installed another ecclesiastic in his place. The chapter, on their part, instantly appointed F. Cerle, an intimate friend of the late bishop. Cerle was unable to act publicly, as the adverse party reigned at Pamiers, with the support of the civil authority; but from

---

* *Histoire de Bossuet*, tom. ii. p. 115.

his hiding-place he poured forth pastoral letters, ordonnances, appeals to the Pope, and anathemas against his adversaries, with a rapidity and virulence which provoked angry reprisals. The parliament of Toulouse caused him to be prosecuted for sedition and treason; and, as he refused to appear, he was condemned to death for contumacy, and executed in effigy both at Toulouse and Pamiers. Innocent XI., transported beyond all bounds of moderation, exhaled his wrath in a brief declaring the appointment of vicars-general by the metropolitan null and void, cancelling their proceedings as devoid of jurisdiction, and excommunicating *ipso facto* all who might encourage them in disobeying his commands, not excepting the metropolitan himself. He also proclaimed that confessions made to priests under the sanction of this pretended authority were of no effect, that marriages celebrated by them were invalid, and that persons so married would live in concubinage, their offspring being illegitimate.*

Other incidents added to the exasperation on both sides. A Carmelite friar at Paris had maintained, in a public thesis, not only that the claims of the Crown in the matter of the *régale* were well founded, but a variety of other sentiments derogatory to the authority of the Pope, which in the ordinary course of things would probably have been passed over without notice. At this moment of excitement, however, Innocent inflicted an interdict on the offender, deprived him of the privileges granted to regulars by the Holy See, and threatened the superiors of the Order with excommunication and deposition if they should oppose this decree. The monks showed a disposition to obey the mandate; whereupon the Parliament interfered, cited the prior and two of his brethren to its bar, and admonished them to forbear all further proceedings in the case, under pain of exemplary punishment.† Another grievance to the Pope arose out of the conduct of Louis in the affair of the Augustinian sisterhood of Charonne. That Society had been in the habit of electing its own Superior at intervals of three years. Upon the death of the abbess in 1679 the king took upon himself to nominate a successor; and Marie Angélique De Grandchamp

---

* See the Brief in the *Collection des Procès-verbaux*, &c., tom. v. "Pièces justificatives," No. 4.
† D'Avrigny, *Mém. Chronol.*, tom. iii. p. 201.

was accordingly installed in the office, by virtue of a commission from the Archbishop of Paris. Some of the nuns protested against this as a violation of their privileges; upon which the Archbishop removed them summarily from the convent. They now complained to the Pope. Innocent, in reply, commanded them to elect a superior in conformity with their statutes, and they complied immediately. The law officers of the Crown appealed against this measure, *comme d'abus* to the Parliament; and the Court ordered that the government of the convent should be maintained in the hands of the king's nominee. Fresh briefs on one side and *arrêts* on the other embittered the dispute. A Papal bull condemned the decrees of the Parliament to be burnt; and this document was at once suppressed by the magistrates at Paris.[*]

The state of affairs had now become such that Louis and his advisers judged it necessary to take steps of a decisive nature for securing the independence of the royal authority, which they considered to be no less seriously endangered in the present case than it had been by the Papal enterprises of the thirteenth and fourteenth centuries. The Pope, on his part, viewed the question in an equally important light; for in his judgment it involved the principle of ecclesiastical liberty,—a principle for which he was bound, by the most sacred obligations of his office, to contend, if necessary, even to the shedding of his blood. In particular, he considered himself to be defending the legislative jurisdiction of the Church; for it was to the decree of the Œcumenical Council of Lyons that he unceasingly appealed, as expressing the verdict of antiquity upon the point in dispute.

There can be no doubt that the Gallican episcopate at this time was pervaded by a spirit of profound subserviency to the will and pleasure of the sovereign. Louis XIV. had reached the culminating point of his prosperity; he was feared and courted abroad, extolled to the skies at home; the arbiter, in fact, of the destinies of Europe. The bishops, although many of them were men of high character and attainments, were not exempt from the weaknesses of humanity; and it is by no means surprising, under the circumstances, that they were

---

[*] D'Avrigny, *Mém. Chronol.*, tom. iii. p. 182.

found ready to swell the general chorus of courtly adulation. De Harlai, Archbishop of Paris, Le Tellier of Reims (son of the minister of that name), Montpezat of Sens, De Bonzi of Narbonne, with others of less note, were prelates whose views of ecclesiastical duty never failed to lie in the same direction with the genial sunshine of royal favour. If it had rested with them to guide the public action of the Gallican clergy at this crisis, the result might have been deplorable; but, happily for the Church, there were some among their brethren who possessed more elevated aims, deeper knowledge, and sounder judgment; and their counsels ultimately prevailed.

On the application of the Agens-Généraux, the king permitted the bishops to hold an extraordinary meeting in March, 1681, to discuss the measures necessary to be taken with reference to the obnoxious briefs of the Pope, especially the last of the three, which was pronounced to be wholly irreconcilable with the maxims and liberties of the Church of France. Forty-one prelates assembled accordingly, under the presidency of the Archbishop of Paris; and a committee was appointed (the Archbishops of Reims, Embrun, and Alby, the Bishops of La Rochelle, Autun, and Troyes) to draw up a general report upon the matters in hand. The following were the chief points submitted to them:—

Whether the universality of the "droit de Régale" was clearly and absolutely determined by the second Council of Lyons?

Whether, considering the different sentiments held by theologians, the Church ought not to declare positively what is the true meaning of that Council?

Supposing the Pope to be correct in his interpretation of the Council, to whom does it belong to judge concerning the Régale? Who have taken cognizance of it from the time of Innocent III. to the present day?

Supposing the Pope to be the proper judge, ought he to adjudicate in person at Rome, or by commissioners acting on the spot?

Whether, inasmuch as the case is doubtful—the King asserting that the jurisdiction belongs to himself or to his Parliament, while the Pope maintains that he is the sole judge of a question which turns upon the interpretation and execution of a General Council—the prelates ought not to interfere for the purpose of checking further proceedings on the part of the Pope, especially if they should feel that such pretensions are more likely to engender scandals than to put an end to the dispute?

The report of the Committee, presented on the 1st of May, is a lengthy and plausibly-argued document, virtually answering all the above-mentioned inquiries in favour of the Crown. It begins by endeavouring to prove from historical records that the *droit de régale* was authorised by the Church herself; for instance, that it was sanctioned by Popes Alexander III., Innocent III., Clement IV., Gregory X., Gregory XI., and by the Gallican Council of Bourges. The right of collation to benefices is one that can only be conferred by the act of the Church, or with her express consent. Upon this principle, those churches which were subject to the *régale* in 1274 (the date of the Council of Lyons) had no reason to complain; while, again, those which up to that time had preserved their canonical liberty were clearly right in defending it until the appearance of the royal declaration in 1673. But no sooner does the report proceed to treat of the *régale* as a branch of the royal prerogative, than the force of these considerations is altogether ignored. "Ever since the time of Philip the Fair this has been accounted a *jus regium*—so inalienably and imprescriptibly annexed to the crown, that in that respect the king is not subject to the laws and discipline of the Church. Since there is no human power to control him, the extension of the prerogative to churches where it had not hitherto been exercised is a matter which lies exclusively in his own hands. Moreover, it appears that the canon of the Council of Lyons, upon which so much reliance is placed, was never executed; that it was caused by complaints made against the royal officers, who were accustomed to plunder and destroy the property of the Church—an abuse which no longer exists, since the present practice is to preserve the entire revenue for the benefit of the newly-appointed bishop. Nor is it by any means certain that the canon in question has any reference whatever to the modern institution known by the name of the *régale*." Upon the whole, the Committee were of opinion that, for the sake of peace, and in order to avoid greater evils which there was much reason to apprehend, the Church would do well to tolerate the application of the *régale* according to the terms of the royal Declarations of 1673 and 1675; and that this conclusion, together with the grounds on which it had been arrived at, should be respectfully notified to the Pope.

The report animadverted with severity upon the Pope's briefs to the Chapter of Pamiers. Their tendency, it states, was to sow discord between the secular and ecclesiastical powers, to nullify the Canons received in France, and to destroy the Concordat; for they assumed that the Pope could adjudicate although no appeal had been made to him, "omisso medio;" that he could confirm, "ex motu proprio," illegal uncanonical elections; that he could deprive bishops of their authority, and reverse the established order of ecclesiastical jurisdiction. As to the clause declaring sacraments administered by the nominees of the Archbishop of Toulouse to be invalid and sacrilegious, its effect was to set up altar against altar in the same diocese, and to foment the spirit of schism.

The report was unanimously adopted; and in conformity with its advice, the prelates signed a petition to his Majesty, requesting him to convoke a National Council, according to various ancient precedents, or at least a General Assembly of the clergy of France; in order that the final decisions in a matter of such moment might be taken with all the imposing solemnity, and all the air of collective authority, which the occasion required;—a course which could hardly fail to secure for the Gallican Church a fair consideration of its claims at the hands of the Sovereign Pontiff.

The Jesuits, as has been already observed, were on this occasion in a false position, inconsistent with their past history and with the fundamental rules of their Order. On the appearance of the Pope's outrageous briefs in the affair of Pamiers, they were sorely embarrassed; for on the one hand they could not openly oppose the mandates of the Holy See, while on the other they dared not offend the king, particularly as they themselves had instigated his proceedings in the extended application of the *droit de régale*. In this dilemma they affected to disbelieve the authenticity of the briefs, and ignored them on that pretext. But Innocent, hearing of this manœuvre, ordered their general at Rome to communicate those documents officially to the Provincials at Paris and Toulouse, with an express injunction to all members of the Society to make them public throughout France, and to attest their genuineness. They now, with characteristic dexterity, informed the legal authorities of the orders forwarded from Rome; and in consequence, the Superiors residing at Paris were summoned by the Parliament to undergo an examination on the affair. They obeyed, and, on attending the court on the 20th of June, 1681, were complimented by the President Novion on the prudence and fidelity with which they had acted under such difficult circumstances. It was fortunate, he remarked, that the despatch from Rome had fallen into the hands of persons so well known for their incorruptible probity and honour. Father Verthamont, Rector of the "maison professe," then briefly stated the facts of the case; after which the Advocate-General, Talon, made an elaborate harangue upon the whole question at issue. He said that this mode of attempting to publish, and in some degree to execute, Papal briefs in France was new, contrary to law, and of dangerous consequence. If connived at, the Pope might in time to come introduce, by means of the religious Orders, documents seriously detrimental to the laws and welfare of the realm; it was necessary, therefore, to check such innovations, though at the same time the utmost endeavours should be used to preserve a good understanding between the king and the Pope, between the Apostolic See and the Gallican Church. "Whatever may happen, we will never on our part cause a breach in the sacred union between the Priesthood and the Crown, so essential to the glory of both, and to the preservation of religion. On the other hand, we will not tolerate a yoke unknown to our forefathers, nor the abolition of liberties of which they were so justly jealous. As we desire to observe the Concordat, so we expect the Pope to fulfil it also in things favourable to France, which we do not regard as privileges granted by the See of Rome, but as points of common law, and the groundwork of our immunities. Those persons who are the authors of the brief of the 1st January, and of many others similar, are misleading the Pope into conflicts far more likely to curtail his authority than to augment it. The *régale* being one of the most important rights of the Crown, how can it be imagined that the king will tolerate during his reign any diminution or suspension of that prerogative? His Majesty can no more renounce it than he can annul the Salic law, or abandon any of the provinces which compose the realm of France. It is useless to threaten him with spiritual censures; the execution of such menaces can never be permitted in this kingdom. We have a sovereign remedy at hand under such circumstances, namely, the 'appel comme d'abus.' This is an infallible expedient for repelling the usurpations of the Court of Rome, for maintaining the liberties of the Church, and for securing the subject against ecclesiastical denunciations which our ancestors invariably disregarded whenever there was no legal ground for them."

The court, upon the requisition of the Advocate-General, issued a prohibition to the superiors of the Jesuits to publish the said briefs, or to further their execution directly or indirectly, upon any pretence whatever, under pain of forfeiting all the privileges enjoyed by the Society in France. Verthamont and his colleagues were then dismissed with an intimation that the Parliament was satisfied with their obedience.*

The incident is eminently grotesque. The fathers of the Order of Jesus, it is well known, take a special vow of implicit obedience to the Sovereign Pontiff; yet here we find them ranged in direct opposition to him; invoking the interference of the civil authority—of an imperious temporal potentate—to protect them against the mandates of the Holy See, which by their constitution they are bound to receive as laws of paramount obligation. Nor is it less comic to hear them eulogized by the Parliament for their inviolable loyalty to the king and the State, while it is but too clear that the real motive of their conduct was enmity against a rival theological party, which for forty years past they had been moving heaven and earth to destroy.

The General Assembly of the clergy, which was convoked for the 1st of October, 1681, was looked forward to with considerable anxiety by those who were best able to judge of the real complexion of affairs at this crisis. This is especially apparent in the correspondence of Bossuet. He had recently been appointed Bishop of Meaux, and elected to the Assembly

---

* *Procès-verbaux des Assembl. Gén.*, tom. v. "Pièces justif.," No. 9.

as one of the representatives of the province of Paris. In September, 1681, we find him writing thus to his friend De Rancé, Abbot of La Trappe: "I fear I shall be deprived for this year of the consolation which I hoped for, (that of visiting him at La Trappe). The Assembly of the clergy is about to be held; and it is desired, not only that I should be a member of it, but that I should preach the opening sermon. I may perhaps be able to steal ten days or a fortnight, if this sermon should be deferred, as is rumoured, till the month of November. Be this as it may, if I cannot go to pray with you, pray at all events for me; the affair is one of importance, and well worthy to engage your thoughts. You know what the Assemblies of the clergy are, and the sort of temper which usually prevails in them. I perceive certain dispositions which lead me to augur well of the present one; but I dare not trust these hopes, and, to say the truth, they are mingled with much apprehension."* He expresses the same feelings in writing to M. Neercassel, Bishop of Castoria, Vicar Apostolic in Holland, and to Dirois, theologian to Cardinal D'Estrées, the French minister at Rome.† The danger which he foreboded was this; that the bishops of the Court party on the one hand, out of complaisance to the sovereign and his ministers, and prelates of extreme Gallican views on the other, in their eagerness to reprobate the late uncanonical proceedings of the Pope, might be misled into a line of action tending to a positive breach of union with the Holy See. Colbert, the leading statesman of the time, was quite capable of encouraging, if not of suggesting, a movement in that direction; and Bossuet well knew that in French clerical assemblies there was no lack of men too ready to follow blindly a sudden impulse from high quarters, without perceiving or pausing to examine how far it was likely to carry them. The special favour which he enjoyed with the king, and the general confidence and esteem in which he was held by the clergy of all ranks and parties, enabled him to interfere with success at this moment as an advocate of moderation and discretion. He was too devoted a Catholic to listen to any

---

* *Correspondance de Bossuet*, "Lettres Diverses," No. lxxxv.
† *Lettres Diverses*, lxxxii., lxxxiv. To the former he writes:—" Deus nos pacem sectari donet, atque Ecclesiæ vulnera curare, non multiplicare. Id futurum spero; nec sine timore spes."

proposals of which the drift was to place the National Church in open antagonism to the Cathedra Petri, the centre of unity. He was too profound a theologian, too familiarly acquainted with the whole stream of ecclesiastical tradition from its original sources, to abandon any of those principles which are essential to the liberty of the Church, according to its just and genuine interpretation.

The Assembly met at Paris on the 9th of November, 1681, under the presidency of Archbishop de Harlai; on which occasion Bossuet delivered, in the church of the Grands-Augustins, his magnificent sermon on the "Unity of the Church." This has always been considered one of the most masterly efforts of his genius. Taking his text from the prophetic "parable" of Balaam, "How goodly are thy tents, O Jacob, and thy tabernacles, O Israel,"* the preacher enlarges, first, on the beauty and glory of the Church Catholic, as exhibited in its inviolable union with its head, the successor of St. Peter. This union is founded on the promises of Christ to that great apostle, whose prerogatives were not to cease with his life, but to survive in his successors to the end of time, so that the primacy of the Universal Church was to reside for ever in the apostolic See of Rome, and the chair of St. Peter was to be indefectible in maintaining the true faith. "Everything concurs to establish the primacy of Peter; everything, even his faults, which admonish his successors to exercise this vast authority with humility and condescension. They should learn from the example of Peter to listen to the voice of their subordinates, when, though far inferior to St. Paul both in position and in wisdom, they address them with the same object, namely, that of restoring peace to the Church. Humility is the most indispensable ornament of exalted rank; there is something more worthy of respect in modesty than in all other gifts; the world is better disposed to submit when he who demands submission is the first to yield to sound reason; and Peter, in amending his error, is greater, if that be possible, than Paul, who reprehends it."

Bossuet proceeds to point out that the pastoral authority first conferred on St. Peter was afterwards extended to the college

---

* Numbers, xxiv. 5.

of the Apostles, and therefore to the collective episcopate in all ages. "It was manifestly the design of Jesus Christ to place primarily in a single individual what was subsequently to be placed in many. All receive the same power, and all from the same source; but not all in the same degree, or to the same extent; for Christ communicates Himself in what measure He pleases, and always in that mode which most conduces to the preservation of the unity of His Church. He begins with the first, and in the first He forms the whole. By virtue of this constitution the Church is strong throughout; because every part is divine, and all the parts are united in the whole. Hence our predecessors, who declared so often in their Councils that they acted in their churches as Vicars of Christ and successors of the Apostles who were sent immediately by Him, have said also in other Councils that they acted as "Vicars of Peter," "by the authority given to all bishops in the person of St. Peter." Because everything was vested first of all in St. Peter; and such is the correspondence which reigns through the whole body of the Church, that whatever is done by each single bishop, according to the rule and spirit of Catholic unity, is done together with him by the whole Church, by the whole episcopate, and by the head of the episcopate." From this fact he takes occasion to exhort his brethren to cast aside personal feelings and private ends, and to act in the spirit of cordial harmony and sympathy with the Church universal. "Let no one of us do, or say, or think anything which the Church universal would hesitate to acknowledge. May our resolutions be such as are worthy of our fathers, and worthy to be adopted by our descendants; worthy to be numbered among the authentic acts of the Church, and to be registered with honour in that celestial chancery, which contains decrees relating not to this present life only, but also to that which is future and everlasting."

Bossuet discusses, in the second place, the most difficult part of his subject, namely the distinctive position of the Gallican Church, and the true nature of its so-called "liberties." The turn which late events had taken made it unavoidably necessary that he should touch upon this tender point; and the considerations which governed him in doing so are set forth in an interesting letter which he addressed to Cardinal D'Estrées soon after the sermon was preached.* His leading principle, he says, was to uphold the ancient Gallican tradition without derogating in any way from the true greatness and just authority of the See of Rome; and in order to this, he took care to expound the "liberties" "in the sense put upon them by the bishops, and not as they are understood by the magistrates of the courts of Parliament." "There are three particulars in which I have specially sought to avoid wounding the sensitive ears of the Romans;—the temporal independence of kings, the jurisdiction of the episcopate as derived immediately from Jesus Christ, and the authority of Councils. These are matters upon which your Eminence knows that we do not equivocate in France; and I have studied to speak of them in such a way as to keep clear of any offence to the majesty of Rome, without sacrificing the real doctrine of the Gallican Church. More than this cannot be expected of a French bishop, who is compelled by circumstances to handle these topics. In one word, I have spoken plainly, for we are bound to do so at all times, and especially in the pulpit; but I have spoken with due respect, and God is my witness that I have acted with the best intentions." After tracing, from the time of St. Irenæus downward, the intimate union which had always subsisted between the Gallican Church and the See of Rome, and showing that French monarchs have ever been the foremost defenders of the dignity and authority of the Sovereign Pontiff, he refers to the legislation of St. Louis in the Pragmatic Sanction which bears his name, and cites that edict as containing the pith and marrow of the Gallican liberties. The declared object of St. Louis was to maintain in his dominions "the common law and the canonical jurisdiction of ordinaries, according to the decrees of œcumenical Councils, and the institutions of the holy Fathers."

"Behold," exclaims Bossuet, "the liberties of the Gallican Church! they are all comprised in these precious words of the ordonnance of St. Louis; we know, and desire to know, no other liberties but these. We place our liberty in being subject to the canons; and would to God that this principle were equally effective in practice as it is comprehensive in theory!" To the neglect of it he attributes the existing abuses of the

---

* *Lettres Diverses*, No. xci.

Church; lamenting a state of things "in which privileges overwhelm the law; in which exemptions (*grâces*) are so multiplied that they almost take the place of the common law; in which the ancient regulations seem only to exist in the formalities which are required to obtain a dispensation from them." "How necessary, then, to preserve at least that portion of the primitive discipline which still remains to us! If the bishops solicit from the Pope the inviolable observance of the canons, and of the power of ecclesiastical ordinaries in all its grades, let it be remembered that they are but following the footsteps of St. Louis and of Charlemagne, and imitating the saints whose sees they occupy. This is not to disjoin ourselves from the Holy See, God forbid; on the contrary, it is to sustain, down to its minutest ligaments, the organic coherence between the head and the members. This is not to lessen the plenitude of the Pontifical authority; the ocean itself has its appointed bounds; and were it to break through those limits, its plenitude would become a cataclysm which would engulf the universe."

Bossuet next reminds his hearers of that memorable application of the Gallican maxims to the pressing exigencies of the Church, which was so signally successful in the time of the great Schism. France pointed out the way to cure that monster evil; and was followed, in the Councils of Pisa and Constance, by the whole Church. "The same maxims will be held in deposit for ever by the Church Catholic. Factious spirits may seek to make them the means to breed disturbance; but the true children of the Church will employ them according to rule, and for the sake of substantial advantages. It were easy to specify the cases in which that course should be adopted; but we prefer to hope that the deplorable necessity of dealing with such cases will never occur, and that we shall not be so unhappy in our days as to be forced to resort to such remedies." An allusion follows to the Councils of Basle and Bourges, and the second Pragmatic Sanction; and the policy of France under the perplexing circumstances of those times is extolled as a model of wisdom and moderation. None knew better than the preacher that he was here treading on extremely delicate ground, and that the Roman Curia, together with the entire school of Ultramontane divines, must needs view this part of his argument with unqualified dissent. Indeed it admits of a question whether he was justified, strictly speaking, in appealing to the enactments of the Pragmatic Sanction of Bourges; inasmuch as it had been annulled by the Concordat of 1517, which formed part of the statute law of the land, and was recognized as obligatory by the Gallican canonists.

On the subject of the relations between the ecclesiastical and the temporal power, Bossuet expresses himself with admirable judgment. "Woe to the Church when the two jurisdictions began to regard each other with jealous eyes! Why should division spring up between the ministers of the Church and the ministers of Sovereigns, when both are alike ministers of the King of Kings, though constituted in a different manner? How can they forget that their functions are in fact identical; that to serve God is to serve the State, and that to serve the State is to serve God? But authority is blind; authority is ever seeking self-aggrandizement; authority thinks itself degraded when any attempt is made to fix its limits." He then appeals to the legislation of past times, especially that of Charlemagne, in proof of the care which was then taken to avoid encroachment by one power into the province of the other. At this point he introduces a glowing *éloge* of the religious zeal of Louis XIV.; of his efforts to suppress the Calvinist heresy, and of the great advantages enjoyed by the Church under his auspices. "Why should a Pope of such known saintliness delay to unite himself to the most religious of monarchs? Such a Pontificate, so holy, so disinterested, ought to be memorable above all things for peace, and for the fruits of peace; and these, I venture to predict, will be the humiliation of unbelievers, the conversion of heretics, and the re-establishment of discipline. Such are the objects of our desires; and if it were even necessary to make some sacrifice in order to realise such blessings, ought we to be afraid of being blamed for submitting to it?"

The prelate concludes his discourse by insisting on the vital importance, in all circumstances of difficulty between Church and State, of assembling the Episcopate in Council; citing various historical examples of the success of that expedient. Nothing can be more apposite than a quotation which he makes from an epistle of St. Bernard to Louis VII., exhorting that prince to convene a meeting of bishops on the occasion of some difference which had arisen with the Pope of the day. "If Rome," he says, "in its Apostolic authority, has acted with any excess of rigour, so as to give your Majesty just cause of offence, your faithful subjects will use their best efforts to obtain a revocation, or at least a modification, of what has been done, to that extent which is necessary to maintain your honour." *

This noble sermon undoubtedly gave the tone to the deliberations of the Assembly. The bishop had submitted it beforehand to the Archbishops of Paris and Reims and the Bishop of Tournay, and also to the king, who expressed his entire approval of it. The Assembly received it with distinguished favour, and ordered it to be printed—an unprecedented honour.

The first business submitted to the Assembly was the affair of the *régale*. The committee on this question, of which Bossuet was the most influential member, had made proposals with a view to its settlement by way of compromise. Negociations were accordingly opened with the court; and it was at length arranged that the clergy should recognize the general extension of the *régale* as declared by the royal edict of 1675, while the king, on his part, consented to make an important concession to the spiritual jurisdiction, by enacting that, in all cases of benefices having cure of souls, his nominees should apply to the bishop of the diocese or his representatives for canonical institution, before taking possession. This removed, in point of fact, the most objectionable of the pretensions of the Crown; it guaranteed the principle of Church authority, and the substance of Church discipline; and, under all the circumstances, it was perhaps the wisest and most politic method of putting an end to the dispute. The Assembly felt, of course, that they were making a sacrifice thereby for the sake of peace; but it was the sacrifice of a right which they did not regard as essential or indispensable, and which, moreover, was already lost beyond all chance of recovery; while, on the

---

* "Si quid ex Apostolicæ auctoritatis rigore processit, unde se merito esse turbatam Celsitudinis vestræ serenitas arbitretur, qualiter hoc ipsum revocetur aut temperetur, prout oportet ad honorem vestrum, fideles vestri qui aderant totis viribus enitentur."—St. Bern., *Epist.*, 255 (Migne, *Patrol.*, tom. 182).

other hand, the terms of the new settlement were such as to give the Church a great and manifest advantage.

The royal edict regulating the future exercise of the *régale* appeared in January, 1682, and an act of the Assembly in accordance with it was signed immediately afterwards.* It had been expected that the Pope would signify his acquiescence without difficulty.† The Assembly addressed a letter to his Holiness, setting forth the reasons which had governed them, and entreating him to take a favourable view of their proceedings. They reminded him that there had been occasions in history when the bishops, not apprehending any danger to the essence of faith or morals, had thought proper to yield to circumstances of pressing necessity—necessity of such a kind as might even justify an alteration of the law itself; and they quoted, with considerable force, the words of Ivo of Chartres,— "even if the canons, taken in their strict application, were opposed to the concession which we have made, we should not have hesitated to make it, because the repose of the Church imperatively required it; for, inasmuch as charity is the fulfilment of the law, it is clear that we obey the law when we do what charity demands."‡ They were persuaded, they said, that the present was a case for the employment of a wise condescension; and therefore they had cheerfully resigned a right which might be held justly to belong to them, in favour of a sovereign from whom they were constantly receiving so many benefits.§

Innocent did not answer this letter till more than two months afterwards, April 11th, 1682. In his brief of that date he severely rebukes the Assembly for their pusillanimity in

---

* See the act of the clergy in Isambert, *Anc. Lois Françaises*, tom. xix. p. 374.

† Bossuet writes to M. Dirois, Feb. 6, 1682:—"Pour ce qui est de la Régale, il n'est plus question d'en discourir. Vous verrez, par la lettre que nous écrivons au Pape, que la matière a été bien examinée, et si je ne me trompe, bien entendue. Nous n'avons pas cru pouvoir aller jusqu'à trouver bon le droit du roi, surtout comme on l'explique à présent; il nous suffit que le nôtre, quelque clair que nous le croyions, est contesté et perdu; et ainsi que ce seroit être trop ennemi de la paix, que de le regarder tellement comme incontestable, qu'on ne veuille pas même entrer dans de justes tempéraments, surtout dans ceux où l'Église a un si visible avantage. Nous serions ici bien surpris qu'ayant trouvé dans le roi tant de facilité à les obtenir, la difficulté nous vînt du côté de Rome, d'où nous devons attendre toutes sortes de soutiens." — *Lettres Diverses*, No. xciv.

‡ Ivo Carnot. *Epist.*, 190.

§ *Collect. des Procès-verbaux*, tom. v. p. 227.

surrendering to the temporal power a point which he deemed of vital and paramount importance to the interests of the Church. "The bishops and clergy of France, once the joy and crown of the Apostolic See, are now conducting themselves in a way which makes us sorrowfully repeat the complaint of the Prophet, "The sons of my mother have fought against me;" though it is rather against yourselves that you are fighting, since the cause in hand involves nothing less than the safety and the liberty of the Gallican Church. Your letter appears to be dictated by fear; a motive which never yet prompted bishops to be magnanimous in defence of religion and ecclesiastical discipline, courageous in attack, and constant in endurance. You have yielded to fear where you ought to have felt no fear. You ought only to have feared incurring the just reproofs of God and man for having betrayed your honour and your duty. You ought to have called to mind the ancient Fathers, and those great bishops in all ages who have left you examples of episcopal boldness and heroism. It was for you to combine your efforts with the authority of the Apostolic See, and to plead the cause of your churches before the king with true pastoral energy and humility, even at the risk of exciting his irritation against you; that so you might be entitled to address God in the words of David, "I have spoken of Thy testimonies even before kings, and have not been ashamed." Forgetting your responsibility, you seem to have kept silence in a matter of such moment. We do not see what right you have to say that you have been vanquished in discussion—that you have lost your cause. How can he have fallen who never stood upright? How can he have been defeated who never took the field? Which of you has vindicated in the king's presence a cause so weighty, so just, so sacred? Who has emulated the ancient freedom of speech in defence of the house of Israel? According to your account the king's ministers clamoured in behalf of their master, and that in a bad cause; but you, whose cause is unexceptionable, you have never opened your lips to contend for the honour of Christ." The Pope goes on to say that he had read with dismay their statement that they had abandoned their rights and transferred them to the king; "as if they were the masters, instead of the guardians, of the churches committed to their custody; as if spiritual franchises could be given away to the secular power by bishops, who ought to submit to bonds and imprisonment themselves rather than permit the Church to be enslaved." Urged by such considerations, Innocent concludes by annulling all that had been done by the Assembly in the matter of the *régale*, as well as everything that had been done in consequence of their resolution, and whatever might be attempted to the same effect for the time to come. This vigorous, but ill-judged and intemperate effusion was of course utterly impotent to arrest the march of events in France. The consent of the Pope to the Concordat arrived at between the Sovereign and the National Church had been asked as a matter of respect; but it was one of those cases in which his refusal was of no practical consequence, except so far as it might add to the bitterness of the existing discord.

There is reason to believe, however, that the tone of Innocent's letter to the bishops on the affair of the *régale* was considerably affected by another, and a far more serious, proceeding on the part of the Assembly of 1682;—a proceeding which was all the more mortifying, inasmuch as it was scarcely possible for him to take notice of it in the way of direct reprimand or condemnation. During the long interval which elapsed between the letter of the bishops and the arrival of the reply from Rome, the Assembly adopted the four celebrated "Articles" on the independence of the temporal power and the constitutional limits of the authority of the Pope, which have been quoted from that day to the present as forming the authorised *résumé* of the Gallican tradition on those subjects.

This step was resolved upon in opposition to the wishes and advice of Bossuet. That prelate was satisfied with what had been already done to check the exaggerated pretensions of the Papacy in the matter of the *régale*, and was averse to any further measures which might tend only to aggravate and prolong the quarrel. The minister Colbert was the real instigator of the four Gallican articles. He represented to the king that the existing dispute with Rome was precisely the opportunity for reviving the ancient national doctrine as to the power of the Popes in relation both to the State and to the Church; since, in times of peace and concord, the desire to preserve a good understanding, and reluctance to be the first to stir up strife, would naturally tell against any such movement.* To these views he won over his colleague Le Tellier, the Archbishop of Reims, and finally the king himself; and the cringing parasite De Harlai submissively followed in their wake. In vain Bossuet pointed out that to proclaim solemnly, and, as it were, synodically, propositions notoriously odious to the Holy See would be the way to drive the Pontiff to extremities, and to render reconciliation impossible. "The Pope has provoked us," exclaimed De Harlai; "he shall repent of it!"†

It was intimated to the Assembly, by the king's orders, that they were expected to put forth a formal statement of the doctrine of the Church of France as to the relations between the spiritual and the temporal authorities; and a committee was named in consequence, of which Gilbert de Choiseul, Bishop of Tournay,‡ was chairman. In due course that prelate presented to the house an admirable report upon the subject, tracing the tradition of the Church as to the independence of the civil power from the earliest age to that of Gregory VII., who was the first to assert for the Apostolic See an absolute supremacy over temporal sovereigns. Then follows a masterly sketch of the Ultramontane doctrine from that date, both as to this first question and as to the assumed autocracy of the Pope in the government of the Church. The whole document is a model of learned and conclusive argument, and was received with unanimous approbation by the Assembly.§

The duty of drawing up the official Declaration which was to be founded upon it, and which was to embody the doctrinal articles expressing the sentiments of the Gallican Church, was entrusted to the Bishops of Tournay and Meaux; and there ensued between these two theologians, who were close personal friends, a remarkable dispute upon the vexed question of infallibility; where it resides, and what are its true conditions

---

* Bausset, *Hist. de Bossuet*, tom. ii. p. 161. We learn this fact from the Journal of the Abbé Ledieu, Bossuet's confidential secretary, who became acquainted with the circumstances in a conversation with the bishop in January, 1700. See *Mémoires et Journal de l'Abbé Ledieu*, edited by Dr. Guettée, tom/ ii. p. 8.

† *Nouveaux Opuscules de l'Abbé Fleury*, par l'Abbé Emery.

‡ Formerly Bishop of Comminges; the same who was so active in promoting the negociations between the Jesuit Ferrier and the leaders of the Jansenists in 1663. He was translated to the See of Tournay in 1670, and died in 1689.

§ It is given at length in the *Collection des Procès-verbaux*, tom. v. p. 489 *et seqq.*

and extent. Of this we have an interesting account from the pen of Fénélon, in his treatise 'De Summi Pontificis auctoritate,'* who declares that he had heard the particulars repeatedly from Bossuet himself. The Bishop of Tournay, in his draft of the Declaration, had stated that the Apostolic See, as well as the individual Pope, is liable to fall into heresy. Bossuet denied this, and maintained, both from the promises of Scripture and from the universal tradition of the Church, that the "faith of Peter" can never fail from the seat of his Divinely-ordained authority. "But such a privilege," rejoined De Choiseul, "is tantamount to infallibility; and you must therefore acknowledge that all decrees emanating from Rome are absolutely unalterable (*prorsus irreformabilia*), since they rest upon infallible authority. This objection Bossuet met by distinguishing between infallibility and indefectibility. The See of Peter is indefectible in holding the true faith; but the particular decisions of each reigning Pope are not incapable of error. "How can that be?" asked his colleague. "If it be possible that an individual Pope, speaking ex cathedrâ, may promulgate heresy instead of Catholic truth, does it not follow that the See of Peter may, *pro tanto*, depart from the faith, and, consequently, is not indefectible? And if this be not possible, is it not clear that every Pope must be virtually infallible?" The Bishop of Meaux, however, adhered to his position. "The Apostolic See," said he, "is by Divine promise the perpetual foundation and centre of the Church; and therefore it can never so fall away from the faith as to remain permanently in heresy or schism, after the example of those churches of the East, which, having been originally Catholic, are now committed to formal misbelief. Such a calamity can never happen to the See of Rome. If that See should ever err concerning the faith, it will not persist in error; as soon as it perceives its error, it will repudiate it; it will be promptly brought back to the right path by the fellow members of its communion. Thus, although a Pope may chance to be carried away by some transient blast of vain doctrine, the faith of Peter will remain, nevertheless, irreproachable; the See will be always Catholic in intention and affection, and can therefore never be heretical.

---

* Fénélon, "De Summ. Pontif. Auctor.," cap. 7 (*Œuvres*, tom. i. p. 659. Paris, 1838).

I assert, accordingly, that the Roman See is indefectible; but, at the same time, I utterly reject the fictitious infallibility of the Ultramontanes."

These reasonings, based as they are upon distinctions and refinements which are by no means beyond the reach of criticism, failed to carry conviction to the mind of the Bishop of Tournay; and the result of the discussion was that he begged to be relieved from the task which the Assembly had imposed upon him. It devolved, in consequence, upon Bossuet; and the authorship of the Declaration, with its four dogmatic Articles, must be regarded as belonging undividedly to him.

It appears that he took for his model in framing it the six articles put forth by the Sorbonne on the same subject in 1663; introducing such alterations of form and style as he considered suitable to an assembly of bishops pronouncing judgment in the name of a great National Church upon matters of such grave and critical import. After much consultation, the following document was ultimately sanctioned and subscribed on the 19th of March, 1682.

Declaration of the Clergy of France concerning the Ecclesiastical Power.

"There are many who labour to subvert the Gallican decrees and liberties which our ancestors defended with so much zeal, and their foundations which rest upon the sacred canons and the tradition of the Fathers. Nor are there wanting those who, under the pretext of these liberties, seek to derogate from the primacy of St. Peter and of the Roman Pontiffs his successors; from the obedience which all Christians owe to them, and from the majesty of the Apostolic See, in which the faith is taught and the unity of the Church is preserved. The heretics, on the other hand, omit nothing in order to represent that power by which the peace of the Church is maintained, as intolerable both to kings and to their subjects; and by such artifices estrange the souls of the simple from the communion of the Church, and therefore from Christ. With a view to remedy such evils, we, the archbishops and bishops assembled at Paris by the king's orders, representing, together with the other deputies, the Gallican Church, have judged it advisable, after mature deliberation, to determine and declare as follows:—

1. "St. Peter and his successors, vicars of Christ, and likewise the Church itself, have received from God power in things spiritual and pertaining to salvation, but not in things temporal and civil; inasmuch as the Lord says, My kingdom is not of this world; and again, Render unto Cæsar the things which be Cæsar's, and unto God the things which be God's. The Apostolic precept also holds, Let every soul be subject unto the higher powers, for there is no power but of God; the powers that be are ordained of God; whosoever therefore resisteth the power resisteth the ordinance of God. Consequently kings and princes are not by the law of God subject to any ecclesiastical power, nor to the keys of the Church, with respect to their temporal government. Their subjects cannot be released from the duty of obeying them, nor absolved from the oath of allegiance; and this maxim, necessary to public tranquillity, and not less advantageous to the Church than to the State, is to be strictly maintained, as conformable to the word of God, the tradition of the Fathers, and the example of the Saints.

2. "The plenitude of power in things spiritual, which resides in the Apostolic See and the successors of St. Peter, is such that at the same time the decrees of the Œcumenical Council of Constance, in its fourth and fifth sessions, approved as they are by the Holy See and the practice of the whole Church, remain in full force and perpetual obligation; and the Gallican Church does not approve the opinion of those who would depreciate the said decrees as being of doubtful authority, insufficiently approved, or restricted in their application to a time of schism.

3. "Hence the exercise of the Apostolic authority must be regulated by the canons enacted by the Spirit of God and consecrated by the reverence of the whole world. The ancient rules, customs, and institutions received by the realm and Church of France remain likewise inviolable; and it is for the honour and glory of the Apostolic See that such enactments, confirmed by the consent of the said See and of the churches, should be observed without deviation.

4. "The Pope has the principal place in deciding questions of faith, and his decrees extend to every church and all churches; but nevertheless his judgment is not irreversible until confirmed by the consent of the Church."

"These articles, expressing truths which we have received from our fathers, we have determined to transmit to all the churches of France, and to the bishops appointed by the Holy Ghost to preside over them, in order that we may all speak the same thing, and concur in the same doctrine."

The Declaration was signed by the sixty-eight members who composed the Assembly,—thirty-four bishops and the same number of the second order—and was afterwards presented to the king at St. Germain; who thereupon ordered it to be registered by the Parliament, and published an edict enjoining that the four Articles should be taught in all colleges of every University, and subscribed by all Professors of Theology before entering on their functions. The archbishops and bishops were likewise exhorted and admonished to employ all their authority to enforce the reception of the Articles throughout their dioceses.*

The studied moderation, and withal the strict theological precision, which characterise this Gallican manifesto, deserve the highest praise. The language was so carefully chosen, and the doctrine so undeniably identical with that which the Church, by the mouth of her most illustrious teachers, had sanctioned in all ages, that no one occupying the Chair of St. Peter could venture openly to repudiate or condemn it. The French clergy, it must be observed, made no assumption of a degree of authority beyond that which rightfully belonged to them. They enunciated their own opinions, but they did not pretend to impose them upon Christendom as necessary articles of faith; they did not intrude upon the functions of a General Council; they simply made a Declaration, without passing any synodical judgment upon those who might differ from them. Bossuet, as has been already mentioned, was personally disinclined even to such a qualified expression of sentiments which he felt to be uncalled for and inopportune; but the pressure from official quarters was not to be resisted; and if any such protest

---

* *Collection des Procès-verbaux*, tom. v. p. 255.

were to be made at all, it was assuredly made, through the discreet and skilful management of that great prelate, in the most inoffensive way possible under the circumstances. Nevertheless, the dissatisfaction excited at Rome was intense. The Pope appointed a congregation of Cardinals and divines to frame a censure of the propositions; and for some time it was feared that his wrath would impel him to indefensible severities. "The affairs of the Church," writes Bossuet to the Abbé de Rancé (October 30, 1682), "are going on very badly. The Pope threatens us with constitutions of an outrageous kind, and even, it is said, with new formularies of faith. Goodness of intention, combined with small enlightenment, is a great evil in such an exalted position. Let us pray, let us weep."* And again, in a letter to Dirois, "Your picture of the present state of things at Rome makes me tremble. What? Is Bellarmine to be all in all, and monopolise in his own person the whole of Catholic tradition? Where are we if such is the case, and if the Pope is about to condemn whatever that author condemns? Hitherto this has never been attempted; they have not dared to impugn the Council of Constance, nor the Popes who approved it. What answer are we to make to the heretics, when they throw this Council in our teeth and appeal to its decrees, reaffirmed as they were at Basle with the express approbation of Eugenius IV.? If Eugenius did right in solemnly approving those decrees, how can they be attacked? and if he did wrong, what becomes, they will ask, of this pretended infallibility? Are we to get rid of the authority of all these decrees, and of so many other like decrees ancient and modern, by means of scholastic distinctions, and the sophistries of Bellarmine? Is the Church, which up to this time has stopped the mouths of heretics with irrefutable arguments, now to be reduced to defend herself by such pitiful equivocations? God forbid. Do not cease, Sir, to set before them the true position to which they are about to commit themselves, and to which we shall all be committed. I doubt not that his Eminence (Cardinal d'Estrées) will speak on this occasion with all possible vigour, as well as with all possible ability. He holds the well-being of the Church in his hands."†

---

* Bossuet, *Lettres Diverses*, No. xcix.   † Ibid., No. xcviii.

It must be mentioned to the honour of Antoine Arnauld, who was at this time a refugee at Brussels, that he cordially sympathised with the French clergy in the doctrine of their four Articles, and exerted himself, through his friend M. de Vaucel, to dissuade Innocent XI. from publishing any formal disavowal of them. In the case of the *régale* he had sided with the Pope, in common with the rest of the Jansenist party; but upon the question of infallibility he was thoroughly Gallican, and was too conscientious to conceal his convictions; although it would have been easy for him, by acting otherwise, to make himself almost all-powerful at Rome, and to inflict no small humiliation upon many who had shown themselves his enemies.* "It would be giving his Holiness bad advice," writes Arnauld, "to induce him to condemn as erroneous the four Articles of the clergy: for the clergy would be at no loss for writers to defend them; whereas advocates are not easily to be found with reference to other points on which their views are mistaken. This would only call forth a quantity of publications on one side and the other, the effect of which would be to throw immense advantage into the hands of heretics, to make the Roman Church odious, to raise up obstacles to the conversion of Protestants, and to provoke a still more cruel persecution of the poor Catholics in England." He then adverts to an extravagant Ultramontane treatise which had just appeared under the title of 'Antigraphum ad Cleri Gallicani de ecclesiasticâ potestate declarationem,' by the Marquis Ceroli de Carreto. This author argued that, since Jesus Christ is the supreme sovereign of the

---

* It appears that Innocent was constantly urged by his confidential advisers, particularly by Favoriti and Casoni, to proceed to extremities against Louis by a Bull of Excommunication. They appealed to the Jansenists to support them in this project, and entreated Arnauld to take the lead in an attack upon the doctrine of the Four Articles. But he firmly declined to enter into their views. The following explanation of his motives is given in a contemporary narrative (Addit. MSS., Brit. Mus. No. 20,401) :—" Les mêmes raisons qui avoient engagé ces Messieurs plusieurs années auparavant à se déclarer pour le Richerisme, et contre l'infaillibilité du Pape fit rejeter par M. Arnauld la proposition qui lui avoit été faite d'écrire contre la doctrine du clergé. Il n'avoit garde de recounoître pour infaillibles tant de Papes qui ont condamné Jansenius ; souvenir qu'ils peuvent se méprendre lors même qu'ils prononcent sur le dogme. . . . . Ni M. Arnauld ni les Louvainistes ne pouvaient être soupçonnés d'agir en cela par complaisance pour les intérêts de S. Majesté, contre lesquels ils travaillirent depuis tant de temps. Eux-mêmes disoient à qui le vouloit entendre qu'ils combattaient l'infaillibilité du Pape pour ne pas abandonner leur propre cause, ce qu'ils eussent fait en déclarant infaillibles les Papes qui ont condamné Jansenius."

whole earth, and the Pope is His vicar, the latter must possess in like manner an universal monarchical authority, comprehending, by the force of the terms, princes as well as their subjects. "I pity the Holy See," continues Arnauld, "for having such defenders; it is a terrible judgment of God upon the Church, if Rome should condescend to such methods of self-vindication against the bishops of France." He concludes by quoting a passage from the well-known work of Duval "on the supreme authority of the Roman Pontiff," to the effect that it is not an erroneous, nor even a rash opinion, that the Sovereign Pontiff may be mistaken in his decisions.*

Innocent, after a time, viewed the affair more calmly, and abandoned the project of passing a judicial censure on the obnoxious Articles. But, in order to testify his displeasure, he refused the bulls of institution to all ecclesiastics named by the king to bishoprics, who had been members of the Assembly of 1682; and so pertinaciously was this policy adhered to, that at length no less than thirty-five dioceses—nearly a third of the whole number in the kingdom—were destitute of pastors canonically instituted.† Such a state of things stirred up a ferment of rebellious feeling against the See of Rome, and vague rumours were set afloat that the form of Papal institution was to be dispensed with for the future, and that French bishops were to be consecrated, according to the ancient rule, by the metropolitans, without any application for license to a foreign power. Louis XIV., however, contented himself with directing that, since the Pope declined to grant institution to some of his nominees, he should not be solicited to bestow it in the case of others, against whom he had no such ground of objection. The consequence was that this provision of the Concordat of Bologna fell into disuse, and remained so until the reconciliation between the French court and Innocent XII. in 1693. Meanwhile, the bishops nominated by the Crown enjoyed their revenues and temporal prerogatives, but were incapable, ac-

---

* Duval, *De suprem. auct. Roman. Pontif*, tom. ii. c. 1; Arnauld, *Lettres*, No. ccclxxxviii. (*Œuvres*, tom. ii. p. 170).

† The bishops-designate were empowered to administer their dioceses by virtue of Commissions from the Cathedral Chapters appointing them vicars-general or grand-vicars, according to the usual practice in the case of vacant sees.

cording to the terms of the Concordat, of executing any part of the spiritual functions of the episcopate.

There cannot be a clearer or more forcible proof of the false position in which the Gallican Church had been placed by that unfortunate compact. The Concordat proceeded on the principle that there can be no ecclesiastical mission except through the direct ministry of the Roman patriarch;—a doctrine unknown to antiquity, and at variance with the organic constitution of the Church. The jurisdiction of the Metropolitans, to whom it belonged originally to confirm and consecrate their suffragans, was thus annihilated; and in addition to this, it was put into the power of the Roman Pontiff to suspend, and *pro tanto* to suppress, the action of that Apostolic form of diocesan government which in all ages had been esteemed essential to the perfection of the Church. Such machinery might work smoothly in ordinary times; but it was liable to derangements and dislocations, which, as in the present instance, might throw the relations between Church and State into confusion, and might even prove subversive of the framework of Catholic unity.

Louis, having attained his object by the acceptance of the *régale* and the proclamation of the Four Articles, showed considerable self-control and moderation in repressing ulterior measures, which could only have served to prolong the existing state of embroilment with the court of Rome. The Assembly had adopted a circular letter to the prelates of France, which was intended as an indirect reply to the late reproachful brief from the Pope. The king intimated his pleasure that this should not be forwarded; and on the 23rd of June a royal message somewhat abruptly put an end to the session of the Assembly. It was prorogued, *pro formâ*, to the 1st of November following, but did not in reality meet again till the spring of 1685.*

The Gallican Declaration was not allowed to pass without vehement adverse criticism from the Ultramontanes. Various writers attacked it with more or less ability; Nicolas Dubois,† a professor at Louvain, and an anonymous divine of the same

---

* *Collection des Procès-verbaux*, tom. v. p. 554.
† He published *Ad illustrissimos et reverendissimos Galliæ Episcopos disquisitio Theologico-juridica super Declarationem Cleri Gallicani.*

university; the Archbishop of Gran or Strigonia, Primate of Hungary; Charlas,* a priest who had been banished from France on account of his zeal in defence of the Bishop of Pamiers; Father Gonzalez, General of the Jesuits; the learned Cardinal d'Aguirre;† Sfondrati, Abbot of St. Gall, afterwards cardinal;‡ and lastly, Roccaberti,§ Archbishop of Valencia in Spain, whom Bossuet describes as the most bitter of all his opponents. Bossuet felt it to be his duty, as the prelate upon whom the chief responsibility had rested in this memorable transaction, to undertake its public vindication; and with this view he now commenced the noblest and most renowned of all his works, the 'Defensio Declarationis Cleri Gallicani.' He was engaged three years upon this treatise, and completed it, in its original shape, in 1685. But there were strong reasons for not giving it to the world at that moment. Louis was negociating for a settlement of his differences with the Pope; the affair was complicated and difficult, and it would have been the height of imprudence to take any step which might be construed as an additional grievance. Years elapsed before an arrangement was effected; and Bossuet's work seemed to be doomed by circumstances to an indefinite suppression. But in the beginning of the year 1696, after the commotion caused by the violent attack of Roccaberti, and the prohibition of his volumes by the parliament, the bishop revised his manuscript, and made an important change in its original plan. It was now, probably, that he obtained the king's permission to prepare the work for the press; but other concerns of urgent importance intervened, and it was postponed from year to year, though never abandoned. It never saw the light during the great

---

* Author of the *Tractatus de Libertatibus Ecclesiæ Gallicanæ*.

† His work, of great size, was entitled, *Auctoritas infallibilis et summa Cathedræ S. Petri, extra et supra Concilia quælibet, atque in totam Ecclesiam, denuò stabilita*.

‡ He wrote, in 1684, under an assumed name, *Regale sacerdotium Romano Pontifici assertum;* and in 1688, *Gallia vindicata*.

§ Roccaberti published, in 1695, three folio volumes, *De Pontificiâ Potestate*, headed by two briefs full of commendation from Pope Innocent XII. Bossuet upon this presented a memorial to Louis XIV., representing that such an extravagant tirade against the Church and Crown of France, from one in the eminent position of a Spanish archbishop, could not be left wholly unnoticed. An *arrêt* of the Parliament prohibited its circulation in France, December 20, 1695; the Avocat-Général Lamoignon remarking that the volumes were so badly digested, and the propositions there advanced, without proof, so absurd in themselves, that they did not deserve any serious refutation.

prelate's lifetime. At his death in 1704 he bequeathed it to his nephew, afterwards Bishop of Troyes, expressly charging him to let it fall into no hands but those of his Majesty himself, who had hitherto, for grave reasons of state, objected to its publication, and who might very probably, in his (Bossuet's) opinion, continue to be opposed to it. The MS. was accordingly presented to the king by the Abbé Bossuet, and it appears that in the year 1708 a proposal was made to publish it; but the design was combated by the abbé himself, who feared that opprobrious reflections might be provoked at Rome against his uncle's memory, and that the edification to be derived from his works might thus be in great measure lost to the Church.*
The king yielded to these arguments, and the matter dropped. In the year 1730, however, an edition of the 'Defensio' was printed at Luxemburg, from an incorrect and imperfect copy which had belonged to Cardinal de Noailles. This contained none of the additions and emendations made by the author in his latter years; the preliminary dissertation (Dissertatio prævia) did not appear in it at all. The Bishop of Troyes, to whose custody the precious manuscript appears to have been restored after the death of Louis and of the Regent Orleans, at length took the resolution of placing it in a complete form before the public; and it issued from the press in 1745, in the shape in which we now possess it. In consequence of the alterations which are known to have been made in the original text, and the singular history of the work during the forty years which intervened between its composition and its publication, doubts have been expressed in some quarters as to its authenticity. These, however, are without foundation. The testimony of the Abbé Ledieu proves beyond question that Bossuet was occupied, in 1699 and three following years, in revising his work from beginning to end; that he made extensive changes in it, not with regard to its general scope and character, but by introducing fresh matter and correcting mistakes; and that, in particular, he suppressed the first three books of the original draft, and substituted for them a preliminary Dissertation, to which he gave the title of 'Gallia orthodoxa, sive Vindiciæ Scholæ Parisiensis.' Moreover, the

---

* *Mémoires et Journal de l'Abbé Ledieu*, tom. iii. p. 202.

identical manuscript which Bossuet entrusted to his nephew, and which the latter, by his uncle's instructions, placed in the hands of Louis XIV., was discovered in 1812, in the Royal Library at Paris. Cardinal Bausset, author of the 'Histoire de Bossuet,' had an opportunity of examining it, and remained fully satisfied of the accuracy of the printed work as now circulated.*

The 'Defensio Cleri Gallicani' possesses an importance, both in regard to theological doctrine and to the true principles of political government, which can hardly be over-estimated. All the contested questions affecting the limits and exercise of spiritual authority, all the critical passages in the manifold feuds between Popes, emperors, and kings—the continuous tradition of Œcumenical Councils ancient and modern, and the controversies which have arisen from their acts—the testimonies of the Fathers of the East and West, of the Schoolmen, and of other illustrious doctors whose names the Church can never cease to venerate—all are passed in review with consummate analytical talent, in a tone of never-failing moderation, and with exhaustive fulness and minuteness of detail. The impression which the work produced, in quarters where it was least likely to be regarded with partiality, may be gathered from two remarkable attestations which have been put on record by Cardinal Bausset, the biographer of Bossuet. The first is that of Cardinal Orsi, in the preface to his treatise on the Infallibility of the Pope. "I have heard," he says, "both at Rome and elsewhere, many persons distinguished for their virtues, learning, and experience, declare that, after having perused this work of Bossuet's with the utmost attention, they were convinced that Roman theologians ought no longer to persist in maintaining the cause which he impugns, but that it must be abandoned as desperate, since it was impossible to find arguments wherewith to combat truths so transparently clear."

The second is extracted from a letter of Pope Benedict XIV. to the Archbishop of Santiago, dated July 21st, 1748. "You are doubtless aware that a few years ago a work was published, the object of which was to support the propositions adopted by the clergy of France in the Assembly of 1682. Although

---

* Bausset, *Hist. de Bossuet*, tom. ii., "Pièces justif." du Liv. 6ième.

the name of the author is not given, all the world knows that it was composed by Bossuet, Bishop of Meaux. In the time of our immediate predecessor, Clement XII., it was seriously debated whether this work ought to be proscribed; but it was finally determined that no censure should be passed upon it. This decision was arrived at, not only out of regard for the author's memory, who in other respects so worthily served the cause of religion, but also out of just apprehension of provoking fresh dissertations, and renewing the dispute." *

The same salutary dread of resuscitating a hopeless controversy — hopeless because it exhibits Ultramontanism in a position of irreconcilable conflict with the stubborn facts of history—has never ceased to operate from that day to the present. Whatever other measures may have been taken to overthrow the authority of the Articles of 1682, the 'Defensio' of Bossuet remains uncensured, and without an answer. It is a monument, not of mere evanescent agitation or insubordinate self-assertion, but of a system which has lived through all the storms and revolutions of all Christian centuries, and is imperishable.

* Bausset, *Hist. de Bossuet*, tom. ii. pp. 427, 428. Versailles, 1814.

CHAPTER III.

In addition to the series of measures connected with the memorable Declaration, the Assembly of 1682 distinguished itself by putting forth an "Avertissement Pastoral" to the Protestant sectaries, exhorting them to reconcile themselves to the Church. This was couched in terms of much tenderness and charity; but it contained an intimation, nevertheless, that if they turned a deaf ear to these timely admonitions, they must prepare for a more rigorous line of treatment for the future than they had ever yet experienced. This was a significant warning of the severities which were already resolved upon, and which, to the disgrace of the government and the irreparable injury of France, followed shortly afterwards. For many years past, indeed, there had been a marked departure from those wise principles of toleration which Richelieu had observed towards the separatists, even while he destroyed for ever their importance as a party in the State. Successive ordonnances had suppressed their National Synods, deprived them of the protection guaranteed by the "Chambers of the Edict," imposed on them vexatious restrictions as to commerce and industry, excluded them from various lucrative public offices, interdicted their ministers from preaching beyond their place of residence, and prohibited them from quitting the kingdom under any pretence.* These acts of oppression goaded the Protestants in certain districts† into an attitude of resistance; seditious outbreaks took place here and there, which were promptly repressed; a few of the ringleaders were capitally punished; and the government took advantage of the occasion to demolish many of the conventicles, and to quarter bodies of troops on the inhabitants of the disturbed localities. The numbers of the Reformed had much diminished since the last open revolt under Louis XIII.,

---

* See De Rulhière (Claude Carloman), *Éclaircissements sur les causes de la revocation de l'Édit de Nantes.*
† Chiefly in the Vivarais and Dauphiné.

and were still on the decrease. According to a contemporary journal, the 'Mercure de Vizé,'* they amounted, in 1682, to something over 564,000;† the pastors numbered about twelve hundred, and the "temples" eight hundred and forty-four.

It was long before Louis XIV. resolved to attempt the restoration of religious unity by measures of violence. He directed that no exertion should be spared to reclaim his misguided subjects by gentler methods—by personal influence, by argument, persuasion, and intelligent conviction.‡ In his circular to the provincial officers, which accompanied the pastoral letter of the Assembly, he desires them to deal with the religionists in the spirit of wisdom and discretion, to employ no force but that of reason, and by no means to infringe the terms of the edicts of toleration.§ The "Avertissement" of the Assembly was communicated to the Protestant consistories, and the clergy were ordered to support it by suitable addresses; but fairness and considerateness seem to have prevailed, and public discussions were held in all freedom between the divines of the two communions.

The Gallican bishops and their clergy now bestirred themselves in the work of conversion with laudable activity. Conferences, missions, controversial tracts, special devotional services, abounded on all sides. Bossuet took the lead, in this as in all the great ecclesiastical movements of his time. He established missions in his diocese, where there were then but few Protestants, although it was at Meaux that the leaders of the Reformation had first found protection and encouragement in France. He published his 'Conference with the minister Claude,' and his 'Traité de la Communion sous les deux'

---

* Vizé was the name of the editor. He commenced publishing the *Mercure galant* in 1672, and continued it in monthly volumes for many years. Thomas Corneille, brother of the great poet, was one of his collaborateurs.

† This calculation is greatly below the mark. They numbered at this time at least one million.

‡ Such was the policy recommended by D'Aguesseau, Intendant of Languedoc, one of the most enlightened and conscientious public men of the time. He looked upon Protestantism as "a fortress which the Government ought never to attempt to carry by assault, but which should rather be attacked by sapping and undermining its foundations, by gaining ground upon it inch by inch, until it is reduced insensibly to such small proportions that in the end it falls of itself." (See the Chancellor D'Aguesseau's Memoir of his father, *Œuvres*, tom. xiii. p. 38.) D'Aguesseau resigned office as soon as he saw that the King was fully resolved upon measures of active persecution.

§ Isambert, *Anc. Lois Françaises*, tom. xix. p. 393. D'Avrigny, *Mém. Chronol.*, tom. iii. p. 244.

Espèces.' His 'Exposition de la Doctrine catholique' was circulated far and wide.* By his advice also the king ordered 50,000 copies of the French translation of the New Testament by Father Amelotte to be printed for distribution, together with an equal number of selected prayers from the Catholic Liturgy; the object of both publications being to combat the mistaken notion so common among heretics, that the Church, by using a Latin version of the Scriptures, and celebrating her offices in the same tongue, designed to keep the common people in ignorance both of one and the other. The efforts of Bossuet were seconded by several of his colleagues; by Le Camus, Bishop of Grenoble; De Breteuil, of Boulogne; De La Broue, of Mirepoix; De Laval, of La Rochelle; De Sève, of Arras; De la Hoguette, of Poitiers. The Jesuits, Capuchins, and other religious orders, sent forth armies of preachers and controversialists; and a perfect ferment of missionary ardour prevailed among Catholics of all classes, laity as well as clergy. Of the results of this great propagandist enterprise it is impossible to speak without some hesitation. That there were many sincere conversions is unquestionable. Alexandre de Bardonnèche, a magistrate of Grenoble; Arbaud de Blansac, a wealthy seigneur of Languedoc; the ministers Desmahis, Gilli, and Vignes; Ulric Obrecht, a learned pastor of Strasburg; Isaac Papin and Joseph Saurin; were men who stood too high in reputation and character to be suspected of any unworthy motive in changing their religious profession. But when we are told that in certain parts of the country,—Poitou, Languedoc, Saintonge, Béarn, Dauphiné—the abjurations of Calvinism were counted by thousands; that sixty thousand persons recanted in a single town in three days;† that the Bishop of Montpellier, on a visitation tour, was besieged by the whole population of parish after parish, demanding to be reconciled to the Church; we are tempted to assign such startling phenomena to causes of a less elevated kind. The king and his ministers seem to have acted in this matter under a singular illusion. The numerous cases which occurred of *bonâ fide* conversion among the intelligent

---

* This treatise is printed at length in the *Mémoires du Clergé de France*, tom. i. pp. 141-191.

† This is recorded by the Intendant D'Aguesseau to have happened at Nismes. — *Œuvres d'Aguesseau*, tom. xiii. p. 55.

classes led them to imagine that Protestantism was on the point of disappearing altogether—that it had lost its influence and was effete; and that if a determined effort were made at this moment, the blessing of unanimity in doctrinal belief might be secured to the nation without much difficulty. With this view they set in motion two engines which few are capable of resisting, namely, money and military oppression; the "Caisse des conversions" and the "Dragonnades."

The chief agent of the Court in its scheme of bribing the Nonconformists into orthodoxy was Paul Pélisson-Fontanier; himself a convert from Calvinism, a man of talent and intellectual culture, an author of repute, a member of the Academy, and a councillor of state. The Assemblies of the clergy had for some years past been accustomed to vote large sums towards the maintenance of Protestant ministers who might be induced to return to the Church, and who, but for this succour, would have been left destitute of the means of subsistence. The king established a fund of the same character on a far more extensive scale, by allotting to it the yearly revenues of two great abbeys, and a third of the income of all vacant benefices, which belonged to the Crown in virtue of the "droit de régale." The management and application of this treasure—the "administration des économats," as it was called—was entrusted to Pélisson; whose plan of operations was simple, and proved widely successful. He communicated with the bishops, and placed in their hands sums of money, with instructions to employ them in indemnifying persons who might abjure heresy for any loss they sustained, or imagined they sustained, by taking that step. They were to report to the minister at stated times, furnishing him with a list of the conversions effected, a copy of each abjuration, an account of their disbursements, and a receipt for the number of livres expended in each instance. Nothing could be more perfectly organised, nothing more business-like, than this system of wholesale traffic with the conscience. Forty, fifty, even a hundred livres, were in many cases given in testimony of the king's good-will towards the newly converted; but in the rural districts the ordinary tariff was six livres. "M. Pélisson works wonders," wrote Madame de Maintenon in 1683; "he may not be so learned as Monseigneur Bossuet, but he is more persuasive. One could never have ventured to hope that all these conversions would have been obtained so easily."* "I can well believe," are her words in another letter, "that all these conversions are not equally sincere; but God has numberless ways of recalling heretics to Himself. At all events their children will be Catholics. If the parents are hypocrites, their outward submission at least brings them so much nearer to the truth; they bear the signs of it in common with the faithful. Pray God to enlighten them all; the king has nothing nearer to his heart."†

But if the "caisse des conversions" was a discreditable mode of making proselytes, what is to be thought of the "dragonnades?" Happily it is needless, in a work like the present, to enter into any description of these frightful atrocities, which have left so indelible a stigma of disgrace upon the "age of Louis XIV." But the reader must, nevertheless, be reminded that, although the scandalous expedient itself was suggested by civil functionaries, such as Louvois and Châteauneuf, the principle from which it sprang was explicitly sanctioned by men who spoke in the name of religion; by the king's confessor La Chaise, by his Jesuit brethren, and by two, at least, of the leading prelates of the Gallican Church, Le Tellier and De Harlai. They urged upon Louis that it was his duty to enforce external conformity to the established Church, however rigorous the measures that might be required for the purpose. Internal assent, they assured him, would follow in due time. At the worst, those whose conversion was only nominal would but be consigned to perdition as hypocrites, instead of suffering the same punishment as heretics. As to the lawfulness of penal enactments against heresy, they defended it on the authority of St. Augustine, in his epistles to Vincentius the Donatist bishop, and to the Tribune Boniface.‡ "The fear of suffering," says that great Father, "tends to dislodge obstinacy; it makes men open their eyes to the truth; it helps them to rid themselves of error and prejudice, and causes them to desire that which formerly they were most averse to." And, again, "This authority of which they (the Donatists) complain

---

* Madame de Maintenon to Madame de St. Géran, November 13, 1683.
† Madame de Maintenon to Madame de St. Géran, October 25, 1685 (La Beaumelle, *Lettres et Mémoires de Madame de Maintenon*, tom. viii. p. 90).
‡ Aug., *Epp.*, 93, 185.

is wholesome and useful to them, inasmuch as it has reclaimed and is reclaiming every day, numbers of men who praise God for having cured them of such a dangerous infatuation, and who, prompted by the same charity that we have shewn to them, now join us in demanding that others shall be treated in like manner who still persist in error, and with whom they themselves were once involved in all the peril of perdition." The Scriptural precept, "Compel them to come in," was likewise appealed to in justification of this policy.* Nor were such sentiments peculiar to any one school of theology; they were those of the clergy in general; even Bossuet did not scruple to defend them openly.† More than this, they were not confined to the Church of Rome, but were common to all Christian denominations. It is scarcely necessary to remind the reader that Protestant governments, as well as Catholic, have sanctioned coercive legislation against those whom they deemed dangerously heterodox. The penal laws of the English Statute Book at that period, and those of other European states, were more sanguinary than those of France; and it may be proved, without any extraordinary amount of historical research, that on occasions they were put in execution with a no less barbarous cruelty.

The Assembly of 1685 presented to the throne a series of resolutions embracing the further measures of disability which they considered necessary against the Huguenots. They desired that their worship might be interdicted in Cathedral cities, and in places where the seigneurial fiefs were held by ecclesiastics; that their ministers should be incapable of receiving legacies and endowments; that members of the so-called Reformed religion should be excluded from the profession of the law, and from employment as secretaries, notaries, lawyer's clerks, booksellers, printers, and officers of municipal corporations; and that wherever there was no public exercise of their religion their children should be baptized by the Catholic clergy, tho

---

* The Protestant Bayle combated, with remarkable force, the exaggerated conclusions drawn from this maxim, in his *Commentaire philosophique sur le Compelle intrare*, published in 1687. His latitudinarian tone, however, gave offence to his co-religionists, who were scarcely less intolerant in principle than Louis and his ministers. A bitter contest ensued upon this subject between Bayle and his brother-professor Jurieu.

† See his letter "A un réfugié," *Lettres Diverses*, No. cxxvii.; also *Hist. des Variations*, Liv. x. c. 56.

parents being compelled to give them due notice for this purpose. Most of these demands had been anticipated by various royal edicts; and the king promised to grant the rest without delay. The Assembly, moreover, complained of libellous attacks upon the doctrine of the Church which were continually issuing from the Protestant press; and a memorial to the king was drawn up, setting forth, side by side, the genuine tenets of Catholicism as opposed to the misrepresentations, falsehoods, and perversions, disseminated in the works of the pretended Reformers.* Thereupon an ordonnance appeared forbidding Huguenots to preach or publish anything injurious to the Catholic religion, to impute to Catholics doctrines which they disavowed, or even to discuss their belief directly or indirectly. The Archbishop of Paris published an "Index expurgatorius" of the books thus stigmatized; and they were immediately suppressed by an *arrêt* of the Parliament.†

The ultimate conclusion towards which all these preliminary steps had long been converging was reached on the 18th of October, 1685, on which day Louis XIV. signed what is called the "Revocation of the Edict of Nantes." By a single stroke of his despotic pen he annulled all that had ever been enacted in favour of the Huguenots; decreed the immediate demolition of their remaining places of worship, forbade them to hold any meetings whatever for the exercise of their religion, and ordered their pastors to quit the kingdom within fifteen days, unless they were willing to embrace Catholicism. To those who might make abjuration considerable advantages were promised; they were exempted from the "tailles" and the obligation of lodging troops; and were to receive, moreover, pensions exceeding by one-third the salaries which had been paid to them as ministers. Their flocks were prohibited, under severe penalties, from leaving France; all children hereafter born to them were to be baptized and educated as Catholics. As to those who had already emigrated, they were exhorted to return within four months, in which case they were to be re-admitted to their privileges as French citizens, and to the enjoyment of their confiscated property.

---

* 'Requête présentée au Roi contre les calomnies de ceux de la Religion prétendue Reformée,' *Collect. des Procès-verbaux*, tom. v.; "Pièces justificat.," No. 2.
† D'Avrigny, *Mém. Chronol.*, tom. iii. p. 262.

The Chancellor Le Tellier, on affixing the great seal to this celebrated edict, testified aloud his joy and satisfaction in the words of the aged Simeon, "Lord, now lettest thou thy servant depart in peace, for mine eyes have seen Thy salvation." He looked upon it as the most fortunate act of his long official career, which was brought to a close by death within a month afterwards. Bossuet, in his Funeral Oration for the deceased minister, did not hesitate to refer to the edict of Revocation in terms of unequivocal and impassioned admiration. " Our fathers had not witnessed, as we have, the fall of an inveterate heresy; the deluded flocks returning to the fold in troops; our churches too narrow to receive them; perfect calmness maintained in the midst of such a mighty movement; the world contemplating with astonishment so decisive and at the same time so felicitous an exercise of sovereign authority, and a proof that the merits of the sovereign are more highly estimated than even his authority itself. Impressed by such marvels, let us raise our acclamations to the skies! Let us say to this second Constantine, this second Theodosius, this second Marcian, this second Charlemagne, what the six hundred and thirty fathers said of old at the Council of Chalcedon:—You have confirmed the Faith, you have exterminated the heretics; it is a work worthy of your reign. Through your exertions heresy exists no longer. God alone could have wrought this miracle. O King of Heaven, preserve our earthly monarch; this is the prayer of the Church; this is the prayer of the bishops!"*

It is curious to find that Antoine Arnauld, who certainly had no inducement to regard either the person or the policy of Louis XIV. with undue partiality, approved no less decidedly of the repeal of the laws of toleration, and the compulsory suppression of Protestantism. In one of his letters to De Vaucel he quotes the sentiment of Grotius, who had warned the Nonconformists not to imagine that the Edict of Nantes, and others of like tenor, were treaties of alliance; whereas they were simply royal ordonnances passed for the good of the public, and liable to be revoked whenever it might appear that the public interest would be served by such a step. "The laws against the Donatists," Arnauld continues, "are sufficient to authorize

---

* Bossuet, *Oraison funèbre de Michel Le Tellier*, janvier 25, 1686.

what has been done in France against the Huguenots as to any temporal injury inflicted on them by the quartering of troops and the banishment of their ministers. The laws of the Empire were not only directed against the criminal excesses of the Circumcellions, but had in view the complete extirpation of the heretical sect; private persons who refused to submit to the Church were mulcted with heavy fines; and the bishops, priests, and other ecclesiastics who would not renounce the schism, were condemned to exile." He thought it as well, indeed, that no rejoicings had been made at Rome on the occasion of the Revocation, since the measures taken had undoubtedly been somewhat violent; but he adds that "he could not allow that they were unjust."*

The biographer of Bossuet has taken great pains to prove to the satisfaction of his readers that that illustrious prelate was not consulted by the government as to the final decree which suppressed the Reformed religion in France. It appears, he says, from a memoir on the subject drawn up by the Duke of Burgundy, that two theologians were summoned to assist at the " Conseil de Conscience " in which the question was discussed; but their names were not mentioned, and he had failed to ascertain them.† The point, however, is of small importance. Most probably Bossuet was not personally consulted; but from what we know of his opinions it is clear that he would have given his assent to the measure had it been required; and it may be added that Louis and his ministers must have been perfectly well assured of the general views and wishes of the Gallican clergy before such an important change of ecclesiastical policy was resolved upon. We may well believe, indeed, that not only Bossuet, but the great majority of his colleagues in the episcopate, revolted with heartfelt indignation from the barbarities which were afterwards perpetrated on their fellow-countrymen in execution of the Edict; and it is even doubtful whether Louis himself was cognizant of the extent of persecution of which his officers were guilty in carrying out his orders.‡ But one thing is certain, that bishops and clergy,

---

* Arnauld, *Lettres*, Nos. 537, 538, 541; (*Œuvres* tom. iii.). Cf. Sainte Beuve, *Port Royal*, tom. v. p. 165.

† H. Martin (*Hist. de France*, tom. xiv. p. 45) conjectures that they were La Chaise and De Harlai.

‡ Those injunctions, nevertheless, were stringent enough to cover any

sovereign and ministers, parliaments and universities,—in a word the whole French nation,—concurred in stamping with their sympathy and approval an act which destroyed the legal status of schism and heresy, and re-established, so far as outward profession went, the one religion of their forefathers.* They must be judged in this matter, not by the standard of the nineteenth century, but by that of their own age. Their mistakes were those of the state of society in which they had been born and educated; of a system which may be defended without difficulty on the score of logical consistency, although it has long since been abandoned as impossible in practice. Their error consisted, not in 'desiring that all professed Christians should agree in doctrinal belief, but in imagining that it was possible to compass that end by means of external constraint and violence. The mischievous effects of this great moral solecism were not at once apparent; but there can be no question that it contributed indirectly to a result precisely opposite to that designed and desired by its authors. It tended to discredit the principle of religious dogma, and to prepare the way for indifferentism and scepticism. The attempt to impose by physical force an iron stereotyped uniformity produced a formidable recoil, and that at no distant date, against the whole theory of authoritative teaching. The Revocation of the Edict of Nantes furnished a magazine of specious argument for the school of Bayle and the "philosophes," the "libertins," the freethinkers, which rose into notice almost immediately afterwards;— a school which was destined eventually, not only to subvert the National Church of France, but to imperil the very existence of Christianity, and to sap the foundations of the social fabric. Nothing in all history is more solemnly instructive than the progress of that momentous reaction.

The bishops now received orders to repair to their several dioceses for the purpose of furthering the work of the recon-

---

enormities. Louvois instructed his subordinates as follows:—"Sa Majesté veut qu'on fasse sentir les dernières rigueurs à ceux qui ne voudront pas se faire de sa religion; et ceux qui auront la sotto gloire de vouloir rester les derniers, doivent étro poussés jusqu'à la dernière extrémité." Elsewhere ho says, "Qu'on laisse vivre les soldats fort licencieusement."—*Hist. de l'Édit de Nantes*, tom. v. p. 869.

* "Si Louis XIV s'est trompé, il s'est trompé avec tous ses ministres, avec tous les grands hommes de son siècle, avec tous les corps de son royaume. Cette erreur fut l'erreur commune de toute la France."—Bausset, *Hist. de Bossuet*, tom. iv. p. 69.

ciliation of the Protestants with the Church; and for many years in succession their labours in that field were incessant. Bossuet published at this time his 'Lettre pastorale aux nouveaux Catholiques sur la Communion Pascale;' his 'Avertissement aux Protestants;' and that truly original work, the interest of which is scarcely less vivid in our own day than when it was first written, the 'Histoire des Variations des Églises Protestantes.' The Bishops of Mirepoix, Montauban, Tournay, Auxerre, and Boulogne, exerted themselves in the cause with distinguished zeal. The operations of the missionary clergy, regular and secular, were carefully organized under the direction of Archbishop de Harlai, and the Assembly voted ample funds for their support. The Jesuit Bourdaloue was sent to exhibit his marvellous eloquence at Montpellier, and the accomplished De la Rue preached in other parts of Languedoc. Upwards of a hundred priests of the Oratory devoted themselves to the work. The Lazaristes, the Congregation of St.-Sulpice, the Pères de la Doctrine chrétienne, the Théatins, all contributed their full quota of labourers. The opportunity, too, gave scope for the exercise of his talents to a young ecclesiastic whose name was to become one of the household words of the French Church—the Abbé de Fénélon. François de Salignac de Lamothe Fénélon, son of a nobleman of ancient family in Périgord, was at this time thirty-four years of age. He was attached to the Congregation of St. Sulpice, and was Superior of the "Nouvelles Catholiques," an institution founded at Paris for the training of converted Protestant females. He already stood high in the esteem of Bossuet, and was recommended by him to the king as leader of the missions in Poitou, Saintonge, and the Pays d'Aunis. He commenced the undertaking with the assistance of nine trusty fellow-labourers, among whom were the Abbé de Langeron, his confidential friend through life; Claude Fleury, afterwards the celebrated author of the 'Histoire Ecclésiastique;' and the Abbés Bertier and Milon, who became bishops of Blois and Condom. We are told by his biographer that the only condition made by Fénélon with the king was that before he entered on his ministry all troops should be removed from the district, and that no demonstration of military force should be made during his stay. His treatment of the "dévoyés" was marked by invariable gentleness, forbearance, and charity; so much so, that the Secretary of State De Seignelay felt it necessary to intimate to him that he was complained of as lax and over-indulgent in his duty. The only pretext for this charge was that Fénélon was less rigid than some other missionaries in enforcing both the extreme doctrines and the system of devotional observances which, though recommended by certain sections of the Church of Rome, have never been declared indispensable by the authorities of the Church herself. Fénélon made it his object to soften the bitterness of Protestant prejudice against Catholicism, by tracing a clear line of distinction between what is necessary and what is permissible; by separating articles of faith from matters of opinion; precepts of obligation from counsels of perfection. The same method had been pursued with eminent success by Bossuet in his 'Exposition de la Doctrine catholique.'

The labours of the missionaries were not unrewarded; but the obstacles they had to encounter were gigantic, and their progress was slow and partial. On the whole, Fénélon seems to have been disappointed with the results of his mission.* Juriu, Claude, and others of the proscribed ministers, commenced a course of fanatical agitation, which ere long bore fruit in the disastrous insurrection of the Cévennes;† and the work of religious re-union was thus interrupted and indefinitely adjourned. In process of time Louis discovered that conversions made by violence are of little or no value; that the remedy is worse than the disease. A more moderate tone was adopted in dealing with the "nouveaux convertis." Orders were given to desist from the practice of compelling them to receive the Eucharist according to the Catholic rite, and to wink at their neglect of Extreme Unction and other ceremonies. The magistrates were enjoined to leave it to the ecclesiastical authorities and confessors to judge of the fitness or unfitness of the converts, as of all others, to partake with profit of the Sacraments. The royal instructions to the Intendants, and the circular letter addressed at the same time to the bishops, breathe an eminently wise, discreet, and tolerant spirit.‡ The subject, however, was

---

* See his letter to Bossuet, 8 mars, 1686. *Correspondance de Fénélon*, No. 10.
† See Voltaire, *Siècle de Louis XIV.*, chap. xxxvi.
‡ Bausset, *Hist. de Bossuet*, tom. iv. p. 98 *et seqq.*

one which gave rise to considerable differences of opinion. Bossuet discussed it with his usual vigour in a correspondence with Lamoignon de Basville, Intendant of Languedoc, and certain of the bishops of that province, which may be read at length in his collected works.*

But these measures of concession on the part of the government came too late. The edict of Revocation was practically a failure. The outward semblance of unity which it produced was hollow and fallacious; the "mauvais convertis" infinitely outnumbered those who embraced Catholicism from conviction; and the result was a mask of equivocal conformity, which served no cause save that of irreligion and unbelief.† The tide of emigration, too, in spite of numberless precautions and inhuman penalties, proved irresistible. Among the many conflicting calculations it is impossible to ascertain the real number of those who became refugees in foreign lands; but the conjecture of the Duc de Noailles may be taken as a probable one, that it did not much exceed one hundred thousand.‡ Benoît, author of the 'History of the Edict of Nantes,' raises it to two hundred thousand.§ On the other hand, the Duke of Burgundy, in the memoir already referred to, reduces the number to sixty-eight thousand in twenty years. The majority of these were intelligent manufacturers and skilled artisans, who carried away with them experience, ingenuity, and energy which France could ill afford to lose; and there were also among the exiles names of high distinction in the world of science, philosophy, and general literature. "True Catholics," says Saint-Simon, "wept bitterly over the lasting and irremediable odium cast upon their religion by these melancholy events; while, on the other hand, our neighbours exulted at seeing us thus weaken and ruin ourselves by our own acts; and, profiting by our folly, gathered materials for plots against us out of the hatred which we had drawn upon ourselves from all Protestant powers."‖

Such was the deep-rooted antipathy borne by Innocent XI.

---

* *Œuvres de Bossuet*, tom. xvii. pp. 392-459 (ed. Besançon, 1841).
† This is forcibly described by d'Aguesseau in his biographical memoir of his father, the Intendant of Languedoc.—*Œuvres*, tom. xiii. p. 53.
‡ De Noailles, *Hist. de Madame de Maintenon*, tom. ii. p. 525.
§ Tom. iii. Pt. v. p. 1014.
‖ *Mémoires de* St. Simon, tom. viii. chap. xi. p. 145 (edit. Paris, 1857).

to Louis XIV., that he even expressed disapprobation of the act by which that monarch had extirpated heresy from his dominions. "It is true," said the Pope, "that he has driven away the Huguenots from France; but he did so merely from political motives, and not at all out of zeal for religion. We gave Cardinal d'Estrées to understand as much when he presented to us his Sovereign's edict of Revocation. We altogether disapprove of these forced conversions, which, generally speaking, are not sincere. It is a misfortune for the king that all his measures are successful. He has already received his reward."* But whatever may have been his private sentiments, it is certain that the Pope subsequently wrote to congratulate his Majesty on the zeal and piety he had displayed in the great work of uprooting Protestant error. He moreover made a speech to the Consistory expressing his satisfaction at this glorious enterprise, and ordered it to be celebrated by a Te Deum and public rejoicings.†

The mutual enmity which reigned between the French court and the Vatican was aggravated by the affair of the Franchises, as it is called, which occurred in 1687. Foreign ambassadors at Rome enjoyed by custom the privilege of independent jurisdiction not only within their own mansions, but also in the surrounding district of the city; these localities swarmed in consequence with thieves and criminals of all kinds, who found there a secure asylum from the terrors of the law. The abuse had been denounced by several preceding Popes, and Innocent resolved to put an end to it. He notified to Louis that other European sovereigns had acquiesced in his regulations for this purpose, and begged that his most Christian Majesty would follow their example. Louis returned a disdainful answer, and his newly-appointed ambassador, the Marquis de Lavardin, insisted on the privilege to its full extent, and with more than usual arrogance. This brought him within the terms of a bull of excommunication which the Pope had published before his arrival;‡ and the Ambassador having presumed to attend mass notwithstanding, the French Church of St.-Louis, in which the act took place, was laid under an interdict. The Ambassador

---

* See a Report addressed to Cardinal Gualterio, afterwards Nuncio at Paris.—Brit. Mus. Add. MSS., No. 20,401.

† De Noailles, *Histoire de Madame de Maintenon*, tom. ii. chap. iv.

‡ May 12, 1687.

protested, and the Procureur-Général at Paris entered an appeal "comme d'abus" against the Papal proceedings to the next General Council lawfully assembled. Talon, the Avocat-Général, made an energetic speech on this occasion, and roundly censured the Pope for employing spiritual weapons in an affair of a purely temporal nature.* He next touched upon the sore point of the refusal of the bulls of institution to the Gallican bishops-designate. "Who would believe," he exclaimed, "that so saintly a Pontiff would leave thirty-five Catholic churches without pastors, merely because we are not disposed to acknowledge his infallibility?" The evil, however, he proceeded to point out, was not without a remedy. In times anterior to the Concordat, bishops-elect were consecrated by the Metropolitan, and received from him canonical institution without reference to Rome; nor was there anything to hinder a recurrence to that discipline. Since the Pope refused to perform the part assigned to him by the Concordat, it was to be presumed that his age and infirmities made him wish to be relieved in some degree from the burden of the pastoral care; and under these circumstances the heads of the Gallican Church were perfectly justified in proceeding to consecrate those who had been nominated by the Sovereign to vacant sees. Moreover, if the Pope thought proper to neglect the execution of the Concordat, there could be no necessity to continue sending money to Rome for the provisions of benefices and dispensations, which might easily be supplied within the realm.† Talon likewise reproached his Holiness for his alleged indulgence towards the Jansenists and the new-fangled vagaries of the Quietists. He concluded by demanding that Provincial Councils, or a National Council, should be summoned to take measures for filling up the vacancies in the episcopate; that his Majesty should be requested to maintain the franchises of his ambassadors with the whole weight of his authority; and that French subjects should be forbidden to hold intercourse with Rome, or to make any payments to the Papal coffers. The Parliament assented

---

* See *Coll. des Procès-verbaux*, &c., tom. v. p. 308 *et seqq.*, "Pièces justificatives."

† The Avocat-Général seems to have forgotten, however, that the Pope was entitled by the terms of the Concordat to refuse the bulls of institution if he saw cause to do so. The only condition was that he should specify his reasons.

to these requisitions by an *arrêt* of the 23rd of January, 1688.*
In the month of September following a formal act of appeal
from the Pope to a future General Council was deposited on
behalf of the king at the "officialité" of Paris; his Majesty at
the same time declaring that it was his full intention to remain
inviolably attached to the Holy See as the centre of unity,
to maintain its rights and authority with the same zeal which
he had shown on so many important occasions, and to treat the
head of the Church with all due respect and deference. This
document was communicated to the bishops, who in reply
respectfully congratulated the king on the wisdom of his conduct. Innocent remained inexorable, and refused to receive
a letter which Louis wrote to him on this occasion with his own
hand; and thereupon the monarch, according to the usual precedent in such circumstances, ordered his troops to take possession of Avignon and the County of Venaissin.† These events
spread serious alarm among good Catholics in France. But
their apprehensions of an imminent religious disruption were
in reality groundless; Louis XIV., however peremptory in
asserting what he deemed the just prerogatives of his Crown,
had not the slightest intention of proceeding to extremities
which would have isolated France from the rest of Catholic
Christendom.

In this state of perturbation affairs remained until the death
of Innocent XI., which occurred in August, 1689. Soon after
the election of his successor, Alexander VIII., the French court
opened negotiations with a view to accommodate its differences
with the Holy See; and for this purpose Louis restored
Avignon, and offered considerable concessions in the matter of
the franchises. The Abbé de Polignac was sent as a special
envoy to treat with Alexander, but his mission proved unsuccessful. The Pope required, as a *sine quâ non*, a distinct
retractation of the Declaration of 1682, and of the act of consent
by the clergy to the extension of the *droit de régale*.‡ The
king appointed a Commission of French prelates to discuss the
terms specified by his Holiness, and it was unanimously determined to reject them. Louis now gave the Pope to understand
that if the bulls of institution for the vacant dioceses were not

---

* D'Avrigny, *Mém. Chronol.*, tom. iii. p. 316.   † October 7, 1688.
‡ *Œuvres d'Aguesseau*, tom. xiii. p. 418.

granted before the ensuing feast of Easter, he should be compelled to re-establish the Pragmatic Sanction, or at least that part of it which provided for the consecration of bishops irrespectively of the court of Rome. Alexander, upon this, relaxed in his demands to some extent; but continued to stipulate that the execution of the king's edict enforcing the acceptance of the Declaration should be suspended, and that the bishops-nominate should address a letter to his Holiness, so expressed that it might be regarded as an act of apology; assuring him that, in the part they had taken in the proceedings of the Assembly, they had not intended to define or ordain anything that could give offence to the Apostolic See. Louis accepted these conditions, and the negotiation proceeded; but it was found impossible to arrange the terms of the proposed letter to the Pope. The king refused to sanction anything that could be construed as a retractation of the principles enunciated by the Parisian divines; and although less than this would doubtless have satisfied Alexander had it been offered promptly, he lost patience at length, and assumed an openly hostile attitude. By a constitution bearing date August 4th, 1690, he annulled all the deliberations and resolutions of the Assembly of 1682, as well as all the acts of the authorities, ecclesiastical and civil, founded upon them. From prudential considerations, however, he kept this document secret for several months. In January, 1691, he became aware that his end was approaching; and on the 30th of that month he communicated the bull to the Cardinals, and ordered it to be published with the usual formalities. It reached France at the same moment with the tidings that the Holy See was vacant; and under these circumstances Louis signified to the Parliament that it was unnecessary to take any official notice of it. It might be hoped, he added, that the next Pope would refrain from confirming this injudicious act of his predecessor.*

This anticipation was happily realized. Cardinal Pignatelli, who succeeded to the Chair under the name of Innocent XII., lost no time in assuring the King of France of his friendly dispositions. The negotiation was resumed; the bull of the deceased Pontiff, without being revoked, was quietly sup-

---

* D'Aguesseau, *Mém. sur les affaires de l'Égl. de France.*

pressed; and, after some further delay, both parties agreed upon the draft of a letter to the Pope to be signed individually by the bishops nominated to French sees; which his Holiness consented to accept as a sufficient reparation for the part they had acted in the Assembly of 1682.

It is obvious beforehand, that any document which, after a contest of such magnitude, was to prove satisfactory at once to the court of Rome and to the King of France must be to some extent of an equivocal character. "This letter," says D'Aguesseau, "was so worded that it might be considered as merely expressing the sorrow which the bishops experienced on finding that the Pope was ill-disposed towards them on account of what had passed in the Assembly of the clergy in 1682." But it is certain, likewise, that it might be interpreted as a disavowal of theological tenets promulgated by that Assembly, which were well known to be in the highest degree distasteful to the Roman See. It runs as follows:—"Prostrate at the feet of your Holiness, we confess and declare that we are profoundly and beyond all words distressed by those acts of the aforesaid Assembly which have given such serious offence to your Holiness and your predecessors. Accordingly, whatever may have been deemed to be decreed in that Assembly concerning the power of the Church and the Pontifical authority, we hold as not decreed, and declare that it ought to be so held. Moreover we regard as not synodically determined that which may have been taken so to be determined by that Assembly to the prejudice of the rights of Churches." * This language sounded so like a renunciation of the unpalatable *doctrines* contained in the four Gallican Articles, that the Pope was fairly justified in understanding it in that sense, and agreeing to a reconciliation on these terms.

But it was very far from the design of the authors of the famous Declaration to stultify themselves by an unconditional

---

* "Ad pedes Beatitudinis vestræ provoluti profitemur et declaramus nos vehementer quidem, et suprà omne id quod dici potest, ex corde dolere de rebus gestis in Comitiis prædictis, quæ Sanctitati vestræ et ejusdem prædecessoribus summoperè displicuerunt; ac proinde quicquid in iisdem Comitiis circa Ecclesiasticam Potestatem et Pontificiam Auctoritatem decretum censeri potuit, pro non decreto habemus et habendum esse declaramus. Præterea pro non deliberato habemus illud quod in præjudicium jurium Ecclesiarum deliberatum censeri potuit."

surrender. They were willing to admit that the Four Articles did not amount to an episcopal judgment, a synodical definition of doctrine; they did not pretend to enforce them as universally binding on the conscience; but they adhered to them nevertheless, as expressing the long-descended tradition which they had received from their forefathers, and they maintained that they never had been—never could be—condemned with justice as opposed to the Catholic faith. They forbore to insist on the particular document which had excited such grave displeasure at Rome; but the truths and principles propounded in it were too ancient, too venerable, and too precious, to be abandoned. "As for the Declaration," says Bossuet, "it may go wherever it pleases; but the time-honoured doctrine of the Parisian Faculty remains unshaken, and altogether free from censure."*

It must be observed, further, that the letter to the Pope above quoted was only the act of individuals, and not that of the General Assembly of the clergy which adopted the Four Articles; far less did it carry with it the authority of the whole National Church of France. Even supposing, therefore, that it involved a retractation of doctrine, the responsibility of the proceeding cannot be laid upon the Gallican Church in its corporate capacity.

Conjointly with the letter of the bishops-designate, Louis himself wrote to the Pope to inform him that he had given orders that the edict issued in pursuance of the Declaration should not be put in execution; and the obligation to inculcate the doctrine of the Four Articles in all the great seats of National Education was thus withdrawn. "By this act," says D'Aguesseau, "his Majesty established complete liberty upon these questions, in common with many other problematical opinions which do not affect the Faith, and which are left to the speculations of the schools." These important documents had the effect of restoring the relations between France and

---

* "Abeat ergò Declaratio, quo libuerit; non enim eam, quod sæpe profiteri juvat, tutandam hic suscipimus. Manet inconcussa, et censuræ omnis expers, prisca illa sententia Parisiensium; et quanquam Hispani, Belgæ, alii, qui in Gallos calamum distrinxerant, extrema omnia intentabant, Sedis tamen Apostolicæ gravitas non his se fluctibus abripi sinit, et antiquam, probatissimam, sanè quod nunc sufficit, probabilem insontemque doctrinam, ut ab initio fuerat, intactam relinquit."—Bossuet, Def. Declarat. Præv. Dissert., cap. x.

the Holy See to their ordinary footing. They are dated September 14th, 1693.*

The restless spirit of controversy on the mysteries of Grace, which had already agitated Christendom for near a century, had reappeared of late in a somewhat different shape, engendering fresh complications and new dangers to the Church. The discussion was resumed by a disputant of no ordinary powers, Nicolas Malebranche, a priest of the Oratory; who published, in 1674, his 'Recherche de la Vérité,' and in 1680 his 'Traité de la Nature et de la Grâce.' Malebranche had derived his first lessons in the science of ideas from Descartes; but, being a man of original genius, and at the same time of sincere piety, he was not content to pursue the path of abstract investigation traced by his master, but diverged from it into the sphere of revealed theological doctrine. He applied himself to the task of harmonizing Christianity with philosophy, and vindicating the perfect consistency of the Divine attributes.

Malebranche made many disciples, and became widely celebrated as one of the most profound metaphysicians, as well as one of the most attractive writers, of his day. Nevertheless the tendency of his system was in many respects dangerous. His theory of causation is open to grave objection in reference at once to natural religion, to Scripture, and to the cardinal truth of man's moral freedom. God, according to Malebranche, is the sole absolute Reality, the sole effective essential Substance. He contains in Himself all that has substantive existence. All ideas reside in Him, and are communicated to us from Him. We can neither see nor know, neither purpose nor perform, anything, except in and through God.† Our mental perceptions, and the movements of our will, are but impressions wrought upon our souls by His Supreme Intelligence. Creatures have no strength in themselves; it is God who does everything,

---

* D'Avrigny, *Mém. Chronol.*, tom. iii. p. 404 *et seqq.*; d'Aguesseau, *Mém. sur les affaires de l'Égl. de France*; Bausset, *Hist. de Bossuet*, tom. iii. p. 212; Guettée, *Hist. de l'Égl. de France*, tom. xi. p. 110 *et seqq.*

† See *Recherche de la Vérité*, Liv. iii. chap. vi. In support of this leading principle of his system, "Que nous voyons toutes choses en Dieu," Malebranche cites the authority of St. Augustine:—" Insinuavit nobis Christus, animam humanam et mentem rationalem non vegetari, non beatificari, non illuminari, nisi ab ipsâ substantiâ Dei."
—Aug., in *S. Joann. Tract.* 25..

in the region of the intellect as well as in that of outward physical action. By His power the character of the mind is moulded; from His wisdom its ideas emanate; by the impulse of His love all its motions are determined.

Such statements, though they undoubtedly exhibit one side of a sublime truth, are exaggerated and hyperbolical. It were easy to show that they lead almost inevitably to inferences which are fatal to any true belief in man's free will and personal responsibility.

But difficulties still more serious arise from the views propounded by Malebranche as to the economy of Grace. God, he argues, produces His most perfect works by the most simple methods. He governs for the most part by fixed general laws, not by constantly repeated acts of volition. As the primary, paramount Cause, He does not interfere in the details of secondary action, but leaves them to the control of secondary agents—of "occasional causes."* God desires, in a general sense, the salvation of all men; but He acts, in the order of grace, through a mediate, ministerial, or "occasional" cause, namely through His Son, the Word Incarnate. The Incarnation of Christ was part of God's original design in the creation of the world; it was absolutely necessary to the perfection of His work, and would have been so even if Adam had never fallen.† Christ is the instrument through whom all Divine gifts and graces are dispensed to mankind. Those individuals in behalf of whom He intercedes with His Father are called into the way of Life, obey the call, and are finally saved; but Christ, in respect of His human nature, is a being of limited capacities and faculties. He is continually making choice of living stones to be built up in the spiritual Temple which He is rearing to His Father's honour; but, being finite, He cannot think of all, cannot attend to all; and hence it happens that

---

* Malebranche attributes, e.g., the miracles of the Old Testament to "occasional causes," namely, to the ministry of angels.

† "Quoique l'homme n'eût point péché, une Personne Divine n'auroit pas laissé de s'unir à l'univers, pour le sanctifier pour le tirer de son état profane," &c. Malebranche, *Entretiens sur la Métaphysique*, ix. 5. See Emile

Saisset, *Essai de Philosophie Religieuse*, p. 55. This theory of the moral necessity of the Incarnation has been reproduced in our own days by Professor Forschammer of Munich, and other writers of the Naturalistic school. It conducts, unhappily, to a negation of some of the primary truths of revealed religion.

many are omitted from His intercession, receive no grace, are never added to the mystical Temple, and perish eternally. Consequently Christ, considered in His humanity, is chargeable with all the deficiencies and inequalities which occur in the operation of Divine grace.* Such is the strange expedient by which Malebranche proposes to reconcile the justice and omnipotence of the Deity with His attributes of perfect benevolence and love. What is this but to solve one difficulty by substituting another? In what sense is the Divine goodness vindicated by the interposition of a Mediator who is incapable, after all, of fully effecting the object of His mission? The practical result remains the same, that the majority of mankind are left to perish. How then is God justified by attributing this to the imperfection of the Mediator in His human character, when, by the hypothesis, He was thus constituted by the Sovereign Creator? †

These rash speculations, and the credit and popularity acquired by their author, alarmed the orthodox clergy. Bossuet, with his usual penetration, discerned at a glance the pernicious principle which lay at their root, and the sinister results, both in theology and morals, towards which they pointed. "Pulchra, nova, falsa," was his terse annotation on the 'Traité de la Nature et de la Grâce,' which Malebranche had submitted to him in manuscript. In one of his letters he explains at some length the grounds of his apprehensions as to the general drift of the new philosophy. "I will not conceal from you that I foresee not only in this question of nature and grace, but also in reference to many other points of deep religious importance, the approach of a grand attack upon the Church, under the name of the Cartesian philosophy. From its principles, wrongly understood, more than one heresy may take its rise; and I prophesy that the consequences which are drawn from it in opposition to the doctrinal belief of our fathers will render it odious, and deprive the Church of all the beneficial results

---

* "Dieu n'agit point dans l'ordre de grâce, si l'âme de Jésus-Christ, comme cause occasionelle, ne le détermine à agir. D'où il est évident qu'il faut rejeter sur Jésus-Christ, comme homme, toutes les difficultés qui se trouvent dans la distribution de la grâce."

† The theory broached by Malebranche is likewise clearly incompatible with Catholic teaching as to the Hypostatic union of the two Natures in Christ, and, as depending on this, with the "communicatio idiomatum."

which might have been hoped from it." He proceeds to expose the dangers which might follow from a misinterpretation or abuse of the Cartesian axiom, that nothing is to be admitted as true but what the reason clearly comprehends. "Within certain bounds," he says, "this is quite true; but upon this pretext people take the liberty to approve or reject whatever they please, according as they fancy that they understand it or the contrary; without considering that, besides those ideas which we apprehend with perfect distinctness, there may be some of a mixed and obscure nature, which nevertheless contain truths so essential, that in denying them you would deny everything. Such is the freedom of judgment thus engendered, that men recklessly advance whatever happens to occur to them, without regard to traditional teaching; and this license has never been carried to greater lengths, in my opinion, than by the new system (that of Malebranche), which seems to me to embrace the aberrations of all the sects, and in particular of Pelagianism. I grant that you demolish Molina in some respects no less than the Thomists; but since you have nothing positive to propose in their place, you only amuse the world with fine speeches. What you have adopted from Molina you push to an extreme which he himself would never have ventured on; and his disciples will disown you as well as the rest, when once they perceive, on examining your doctrine to the bottom, that you have only been flattering their vanity. . . . So long as Father Malebranche listens only to persons who, for want of deep acquaintance with theology, do nothing but admire and worship him for the beauty of his language, there can be no remedy for the evil which I anticipate, and I cannot feel at ease with regard to the heresy which I feel will originate from your system. I speak as in the presence of God, and as a bishop who is bound to watch over the integrity of the Faith. The evil is spreading. Either I very greatly deceive myself, or I perceive a grand conspiracy forming against the Church; and in due time it will break forth, unless an early opportunity is taken of coming to an understanding, before matters proceed to extremities."*

With what singular accuracy the presentiments of this far-

---

* Bossuet, *Lettres Diverses*, No. cxxxix., "A un disciple du Père Malebranche."

reaching intellect were verified by the event, will appear in the sequel. Bossuet, however, was too sagacious to attribute the rise of Rationalism, which he thus scented from afar, exclusively to the abuse or perversion of Cartesianism. He well knew that the seeds of that monster heresy had been sown at a much earlier date; and that Descartes and Malebranche were but incidental factors, however powerful and damaging, in the work of its development.

It appears that Bossuet had some intention of personally entering the lists against the accomplished Oratorian; but the Prince of Condé, by repeated and earnest entreaty, succeeded in inducing him to renounce the idea. Antoine Arnauld, however, at the bishop's request, consented to undertake the task of refuting him.* In reply to the 'Recherche de la Vérité' he published, at the age of seventy-four, his treatise 'Des vraies et des fausses idées;' † to the dissertation 'De la Nature et de la Grâce' he opposed his 'Reflexions philosophiques et théologiques sur le système de la Nature et de la Grâce.' ‡ Both must be placed among his happiest productions.

Bossuet likewise persuaded Fénélon, whose position in the world of letters was not yet completely established, to employ his pen in the same cause, and promised to revise his manuscript. The 'Refutation du système du Père Malebranche' was the earliest of Fénélon's efforts in the polemical arena.§

---

* See *Epist. CVI.*, 'Castoriensis Meldonsi,' Bossuet, *Lettres Diverses.*
† A. Arnauld, *Œuvres*, tom. xxxviii.
‡ A. Arnauld,' *Œuvres*, tom. xxxix. To this work are prefixed eight letters from Arnauld to Malebranche. They had been on terms of private friendship for many years. On the controversy between Malebranche and Arnauld, see Darimon, *Hist. de la philosophie en France*, tom. ii. p. 364, 365. See also *Epist. CV.*, 'Meldensis Castoriensi' (M. de Noercassel):—"Accepi à vestris, ut credo, regionibus, cum aliis multos viri omni eruditione præstantis libros, tum etiam eum cui est titulus, De veris ac falsis Ideis; quo libro gaudeo vehementissimè confutatum auctorem eum, qui Tractatum de Naturâ et Gratiâ Gallico idiomate, me quidem maximè reclamante, publicare non cessat. Hujus ego auctoris detectos paralogismos de ideis aliisque rebus huic argumento conjunctis, eo magis lætor, quod ea viam parent ad evertendum omni falsitate repletum libellum de Naturâ et Gratiâ. Atque equidem opto quamprimùm edi, ac pervenire ad nos hujus tractatûs promissam confutationem; neque tantum ejus partis quâ de gratiâ Christi tam falsa, tam insana, tam nova, tam exitiosa dicuntur; sed vel maximè ejus quâ de ipsâ Christi personâ, sanctæque ejus animæ, Ecclesiæ suæ structuræ incumbentis, scientiâ, tam indigna proferuntur; quæ mihi legenti horrori fuisse isti etiam auctori candidè, ut oportebat, declaratum à me est; atque omnino fateor enisum esse me omni ope, ne tam infanda ederentur. Quæ tamen .... validè confutari è re Ecclesiæ est, ipsâquo argumentandi arte, quâ pollere is auctor putatur."—Bossuet, *Lettres Diverses.*

§ This treatise, for some unexplained

It evinces an extensive knowledge of the nature of the difficult problems in dispute, and considerable argumentative power; but in parts it is inconclusively reasoned, and lacks perspicuity. On the whole it gave satisfaction to the Bishop of Meaux, who corrected it throughout. That Fénélon should have commenced his theological career by attacking Malebranche is a circumstance worth noting in the history of both. The future Archbishop of Cambrai had not as yet betrayed any tendency towards the hallucinations of Mysticism; but before many years had passed he had embraced, with a warmth of sympathy almost amounting to enthusiasm, the sentiments held by Malebranche as to the union of the soul with God, together with other singularities of the school in question. These kindred spirits were little aware that their mental proclivities lay so strongly in the same direction; nor does it appear that at any time of their lives relations of confidence were established between them. Fénélon's theology during his earlier years was free from the slightest taint of heterodoxy. So long as he wrote under the vigilant superintendence of Bossuet, he was not likely to wander from the paths of truth and soberness; and had he but faithfully adhered to the guidance of that consummate master of Catholic tradition, he would have been preserved, in all probability, from those sophistical snares which afterwards proved so injurious to his fame. But there was that in the nature of Fénélon which could not rest satisfied with the trite paths of scientific and historical religion. Louis XIV., no mean judge of character, early divined his passion for the ideal, the imaginative, the transcendental. "He is a genius," said his Majesty, after a long conversation with the gifted abbé; "but he has the most chimerical mind in the kingdom." The works of Malebranche were denounced in due course to the Congregation of the Holy Office, and were successively placed on the 'Index.' The treatise on Nature and Grace was proscribed in May, 1690; the 'Recherche de la Vérité' in March, 1709; the 'Entretiens sur la Métaphysique' in January, 1714.

The controversy with Malebranche was one of the last under-

---

reason, was never given to the world during the author's life. It appeared for the first time in the collected edition of his works published at Paris in 1820.

takings of the great Arnauld. His whole life had been a conflict; and even in extreme old age he found it impossible to lay down his arms. In 1690 he denounced to the Pope the erroneous doctrine known by the name of "Péché philosophique," which had lately been inculcated by certain Jesuit professors. Like others of their favourite maxims, it was full of plausibility, but capable withal of being so perverted as to excuse an indefinite laxity of morals. One of the Company, F. Meunier, had taught at Dijon that "a sin against the law of nature or the light of reason, if committed by one who has no knowledge of God, or who at the moment has no thought of God, is *philosophical* sin, as contradistinguished from theological; and as such, does not offend God or deserve everlasting punishment." With the help of this ingenious device, how many gross crimes might be transformed into venial infirmities, and proved to be harmless to the soul! Father d'Avrigny, however, assures us that no such proposition was seriously maintained by any Jesuit teacher; and that if F. Meunier ever broached it at Dijon, it was in a "hypothetical" sense, and not as a matter of positive fact; as an opinion commonly received in the schools, but which the Society by no means wished to adopt or recommend.* Be this as it may, the "Péché philosophique" was condemned by a decree of the Holy Office in August, 1690. Arnauld's five 'Denunciations' of the error are printed among his works.†

By way of retaliation, the Jesuits procured from the Pope (Alexander VIII.) a condemnation of a long list of propositions in moral theology derived chiefly from the writings of the disciples of Jansenius. Some of them were quoted almost verbatim from Arnauld's famous treatise 'Sur la fréquente Communion,' which, as the reader will remember, had been examined at Rome no less than forty years previously, and was then pronounced irreprehensible.‡ Such, for instance, was the statement that "the order of Penance is subverted by the practice of giving absolution immediately after confession, and that the modern custom of administering that Sacrament is a grave abuse." And again, "that it is sacrilege to presume to receive the Communion before one has made satisfaction by deeds of

---

* D'Avrigny. *Mém. Chronol.*, tom. iii. p. 338 *et seqq.*
† Arnauld, *Œuvres*, tom. xxxi.   ‡ See vol. i. p. 398.

penance proportioned to the greatness of one's sins;" that "it is necessary to repel from the Holy Table persons who have not attained to the love of God in a very elevated and transcendent degree." These sentiments are indisputably those of the book on Frequent Communion; but on what principle the court of Rome consented to condemn them on the present occasion, after having formerly declared that the work was undeserving of censure, it is somewhat difficult to understand. Such a proceeding was scarcely consistent with the theory of Papal infallibility.

The malice of the Jesuits pursued Arnauld even to the confines of the grave. In 1691 they contrived to subject him to fresh annoyance by means of a disgraceful machination which is known in history as the "Fourberie de Douai." Some professors of that University, practising on the vanity and ignorance of one of their junior colleagues, addressed forged letters to him under the name of Arnauld, one of which contained an exaggerated version of the doctrines commonly imputed to the Jansenists, purporting to be the substance of a thesis lately maintained in public at Malines. The young divine was requested to express his approbation of this document, in testimony of his zeal for the truths which had been defended with so much constancy by the "disciples of St. Augustine" against the persecution of a tyrannical majority. Flattered beyond measure by such a mark of consideration and confidence from one of the most celebrated personages of the day, De Ligny fell into the snare, and signed the fictitious thesis, together with several friends who, like himself, sympathised with Arnauld. The authors of the fraud had thus in their hands evidence sufficient to convict their opponents of heresy, and to procure their removal from their posts at the University, which was their principal object. But not content with this, they proceded to play off a further hoax on their unlucky dupe De Ligny. The false Arnauld invited him to leave Douai for Paris, where he promised to meet him secretly, and engaged, moreover, to obtain for him, through his influence with one of the French bishops who favoured the party, an honourable and lucrative appointment in a remote southern diocese. Such was the almost incredible simplicity of De Ligny, that this second part of the plot was equally successful with the first. He forwarded his books and papers to the address of his correspondent (thus placing himself, without knowing it, completely in the power of his enemies), and repaired to Paris, where, it is needless to say, he found no trace of Antoine Arnauld. Still unaccountably blind to the delusion, he traversed the whole of France to Carcassonne, the residence of the prelate to whom he believed himself to be so powerfully recommended. His arrival was, of course, altogether unexpected; and, to cut the story short, he at last discovered the whole tissue of deceit by which he had been victimised. He at once retraced his steps to Douai, and lost no time in apprising the real Arnauld of the cheat which had been perpetrated in his name. Arnauld indignantly demanded justice of the Bishop of Arras, to whose diocese Douai belonged. The bishop cited the parties before him; but the Jesuits had taken the precaution to deposit all the original documents in the hands of the Rector of their college, and that official, when called upon to produce them, was not forthcoming. Eventually the papers were forwarded to Father La Chaise, and by him were laid before the king, who, as D'Avrigny assures us, was already aware of the circumstances, and considered the trick as nothing more than "a stratagem of war." The doctors of the Sorbonne, being consulted, pronounced the doctrine of the Douai professor to be identical with that of the first three propositions of Jansenius, and directly opposed to the Papal constitutions. Thereupon De Ligny and his friends were deprived of their offices, and banished to distant parts of the kingdom. Meanwhile a report was spread, and widely credited, that the letters addressed to De Ligny were, after all, indited *bonâ fide* by Arnauld himself; that he had been robbed by a faithless servant, who had betrayed his secrets to the adverse party. The tale passed current, in spite of its palpable absurdity; and the cause represented by Arnauld suffered in proportion. The real projectors of this vile imposture escaped without punishment.*

Antoine Arnauld departed to his rest, after a short illness and with little suffering, on the 8th of August, 1694, in the 83rd year of his age. He died at Brussels, in an obscure and humble dwelling in the faubourg, and was buried in the church of St. Catherine, under the steps of the altar. The place of his sepulture was kept mysteriously secret for many years, through appre-

---

* See *Œuvres d'Arnauld*, tom. xxxi.; *Histoire de Port Royal*, tom. vi. p. 114 *et seqq.*; D'Avrigny, *Mém. Chronol.*, tom. iii. p. 352 *et seqq.*

hension, it is said, of the unrelenting vengeance of those who had been his foes through life. His heart, embalmed and encased in silver, was sent to the abbey of Port Royal, and presented to the community, in a few touching words, by M. Ruth d'Ans, Canon of St. Gudule at Brussels.

Two of the most distinguished members of the sacred College, Cardinals D'Aguirre and Casanate, harangued the Consistory in eloquent praise of the illustrious deceased. The former said of him, that although M. Arnauld had never attained any more elevated title or dignity in the Church than that of priest, he did not hesitate to rank him higher than any living prelate, and to place him on a level with the most celebrated and most saintly ecclesiastics of antiquity; that he had done no less honour to Paris and to France than Clement, Alexander, and Origen had done to Egypt, St. Jerome to Dalmatia, Claudian Mamertus to Dauphiné, Tertullian, before his perversion, to Carthage; that he deserved, more truly than St. Claudian, the eulogy passed upon the latter by Sidonius Apollinaris, that he was the most accomplished of all philosophers, and the most learned of all the learned. D'Aguirre also observed that the place which he occupied in the College of Cardinals had been at first designed by Pope Innocent for M. Arnauld;—a place which he would have filled with far greater merit and success than himself.

On the other hand we need not be surprised, considering the position which Arnauld had filled as an energetic party leader during a long period of unexampled excitement, to find that his removal from the world was looked upon in some quarters as a subject of thankfulness and satisfaction. His friends were much pained by a passage in a letter written on the occasion by De Rancé, Abbot of La Trappe, to M. Nicaise, a canon of Dijon. "So M. Arnauld," he said, "is dead at last. His career having been prolonged to the furthest extreme, its termination was inevitable. Let people say what they will, many questions must now be brought to a conclusion; his learning and authority were of infinite importance to the Party. Blessed are they who know no party save that of Jesus Christ!" De Rancé, on being upbraided for these disparaging expressions, willingly gave testimony to Arnauld's extraordinary gifts and virtues, but avoided, nevertheless, anything which could be taken in the sense of a retractation. It is on record, also, that Bossuet, whose admiration of Arnauld was unbounded, frequently lamented that he should have applied his vast talents to such an unworthy task as that of persuading the world that the doctrine of Jansenius had not, after all, been condemned.*

Archbishop De Harlai died in August, 1695, at the age of seventy. This prelate, though far from irreproachable as to his private conduct, had at least the merit of preventing, by his tact and skilful management, any fresh ebullition of the contending passions which had been tranquillized by the "Peace of Clement IX." It was very generally expected that Bossuet would be appointed to succeed him; but Louis XIV. was fastidious upon the point of aristocratic birth, and the lineage of the Bishop of Meaux was not sufficiently distinguished to entitle him to such an exalted dignity. The royal choice fell upon Louis Antoine de Noailles, Bishop of Châlons, brother of the Duc de Noailles; a man who in most respects was a perfect contrast to his predecessor. His moral character was stainless, his piety unquestionable, his pastoral zeal universally acknowledged; but he was of an irresolute temper, and deficient in intellectual depth and solidity of judgment. He laboured, consequently, under great disadvantages as an administrator. He was already an object of suspicion to the Jesuits, and this prejudice was augmented by the fact that he had been selected for the See of Paris without their recommendation or concurrence. He showed at first a disposition to conciliate their confidence, and studied to preserve neutrality in all matters of party controversy. It was not long, however, before he was driven from this position.

Father Gerberon, a noted Jansenist, published, in 1695, a posthumous treatise by the Abbé de Barcos, nephew of the celebrated St. Cyran, entitled 'L'Exposition de la Foi Catholique touchant la Grâce et la Prédestination,' which was reported to renew the condemned necessitarian errors. A loud clamour arose instantly; the work was denounced to the Chancellor, and all the copies at Paris were seized; the Archbishop was appealed to, and found himself compelled to notice the affair judicially. On the 20th of August, 1696, he issued a "Pastoral Instruction" in condemnation of Gerberon's publication.† This document

---

* *Lettres et Journal de l'Abbé Ledieu*, février 1703, tom. i. p. 388.
† See Bossuet, *Œuvres*, tom. viii. p. 630 (ed. Besançon, 1840).

consisted of two parts. In the first the prelate reviewed the notorious facts of the history of Jansenism; lamented that a system which had been branded as heretical by so many Papal constitutions, and by the whole episcopate of France, should again be attempting to raise its head; and pointed out that the lately published brochure was all the more dangerous, inasmuch as, being written in the vulgar tongue, it was addressed to the ignorant as well as the learned. He proceeded to declare that the 'Exposition de la Foi' comprised all the poison of the Five Propositions; that the doctrine therein propounded was "false, rash, scandalous, derogatory to the goodness of God, and heretical;" and that "the author was specially to be censured, in that not only he had taught as matter of faith what is not of faith, but also tenets contrary to the Faith, and abhorred by the whole Catholic Church." The second part of the Instruction sets forth the genuine doctrine of the Church Catholic as to grace and election; which, based on the authority of the great Augustine, is shown to be as far removed from Molinism as from the exaggerations and misrepresentations of Jansenius. In conclusion, the Archbishop announced that, "while he would firmly oppose those who might either speak or write, directly or indirectly, in contravention of the decisions of the Popes, at the same time he would not suffer persons as devoid of authority as they were of charity to set themselves up as judges of the belief of their brethren, and to injure their reputation by groundless suspicions."

The Abbé Ledieu, in his Journal,[*] mentions a fact of much significance and interest, namely that the dogmatic portion of this manifesto was penned by Bossuet, at the request of his Metropolitan, with whom he was on terms of cordial confidence. This is a sufficient guarantee that it faithfully represents the mind and teaching of the "Doctor of Grace." No divine, probably, was ever better qualified than Bossuet to speak with authority upon that question.

The step taken by the Archbishop was prompted by the best motives; but the result was, as it commonly happens in like circumstances, that the attempt to mete out praise and blame in equal measure to two hostile parties satisfied neither, and

---

[*] *Mémoires et Journal de l'Abbé Ledieu*, tom. ii. p. 303.

drew upon him no small amount of ill-will from both. The Jansenists were offended by the sweeping terms which he had used in speaking of the condemnation of the doctrine of Jansenius, which most of them maintained to be untouched by the Pontifical censures;* while the Jesuits resented still more deeply the concluding paragraph of the Instruction, which they felt to be aimed against themselves. The Archbishop, they said, could not help deciding in their favour as a matter of official form, inasmuch as they were manifestly supported by the verdict of the Apostolic See; but it was clear that in his heart he shared the convictions of the Jansenists, even at the very moment when he verbally condemned them.†

The impression which prevailed that the new Archbishop sympathised to a considerable extent with the theology of Port Royal was not without foundation. A few years previously, while Bishop of Châlons, he had been induced to give his sanction to the 'Reflexions morales sur le Nouveau Testament' by Father Quesnel of the Oratory;—a work which was destined to engender a no less violent tempest in the Church than even the redoubtable 'Augustinus' itself. Pasquier Quesnel was an ecclesiastic of superior talent, learning, and piety, but withal a vehement propagandist of the Jansenistic system of divinity. He had quitted the Oratory in 1684, in consequence of his repugnance to subscribe a formulary against Jansenism and other errors, which that Society had imposed as a test upon its members. Soon afterwards he retired to Holland, where he joined Antoine Arnauld; he lived for many years in intimate companionship with that illustrious exile, and ministered to him in his last moments. After his death, Quesnel was recognised by common consent as the leader of the party;— "the Elisha," as Cretineau-Joly expresses it, "of the Jansenist Elijah;‡" and if indefatigable energy and industry are suffi-

---

* Some of the party, however, took a more reasonable view of the Archbishop's Ordonnance. The Oratorian Duguet declared that the harsh language of the first part might well be forgiven in consideration of the sound doctrine enunciated in the second, which could not but be infinitely serviceable to the cause of truth. Father Gerberon observed that in the second part he recognised the accents of a pastor who spoke with the tender affection of a father for his children, while he saw in the first nothing but the prejudices and perverseness of a stranger, whose voice he knew not, and whom he could not follow without losing his way.

† D'Aguesseau, "Mémoires sur les affaires de l'Égl. de F." (*Œuvres*, tom. xiii. p. 166).

‡ *Hist. de la Comp. de J.*, tom. iv. p. 433.

cient qualifications for such a post, no party was ever more worthily governed. The work in question was, in its original shape, a modest duodecimo volume, consisting of short practical notes on the Gospels, and designed chiefly for the use of the younger brethren of the Oratory. It appeared in 1671, with the approbation of the excellent Felix Vialart, Bishop of Châlons, who recommended it to the clergy and laity of his diocese. Being well received, it was gradually enlarged by the author, and when reprinted in 1693, it filled four octavo volumes. It was this latter edition that bore the endorsement of De Noailles, who had succeeded Vialart in the see of Châlons. The bishop described it in highly laudatory terms, as containing the substance of the best Patristic commentaries on the New Testament, as giving a clear explanation of many difficulties, as treating the most sublime truths of religion with a power and sweetness which could not fail to touch the hardest heart, and in short, as abounding with wholesome nourishment and edification for the flock of Christ. Soon after De Noailles was translated to Paris, application was made to him to repeat his approval of the work for his new diocese; but it would seem that in the interval unfavourable comments had been passed upon it in various quarters, and that it was already stigmatized as being more or less deeply imbued with Jansenistic heterodoxy. Under these circumstances, the Archbishop declined to authorize it afresh until it should have undergone a searching revision; and he submitted it to Bossuet and other theologians for this purpose. A new edition was in contemplation; and it was hoped that with the help of certain corrections and omissions it might be brought into full accordance with the standard of Catholic teaching. But the Archbishop's compliance in the first instance had placed him in a false position. The Ordonnance of 1696, taken in connexion with his antecedents, offered a tempting opportunity of twitting a great dignitary with inconsistency and tergiversation; and it was not neglected.

While the work of Quesnel was under examination, an anonymous pamphlet made its appearance with the title of 'Problème ecclésiastique, proposé à M. l'Abbé Boileau de l'archevêché; à qui l'on doit croire, de M. Louis Antoine de Noailles, Évêque de Châlons en 1695, ou de M. L. A. de

Noailles, Archevêque de Paris en 1696.' It was an argumentum ad hominem; and it must be confessed that the difficulty which it propounded was in no small degree embarrassing. The doctrine of the 'Reflexions morales,' the writer urged, was identical with that of the 'Exposition de la Foi.' How then could the same prelate approve the former and condemn the latter without falling into palpable self-contradiction? He illustrated this by comparing together various passages from the works in question, and showed that, although differing in form, the sentiments they conveyed were in substance precisely the same. He offered no opinion as to their soundness or unsoundness, but affected entire impartiality; simply requesting to be informed which of the two episcopal utterances was to be received and obeyed; that of Châlons, which sanctioned the views thus advocated, or that of Paris, which proscribed them?

We learn from D'Aguesseau that the Jesuits were at first credited with the authorship of this production; but, as it was afterwards discovered, erroneously. It was written in reality by an "outrageous Jansenist,"* Dom Thierri de Viaixne, a Benedictine of the Congregation of St. Vanne, who was subsequently imprisoned in the Bastille by the king's orders. The archbishop felt it necessary to vindicate his honour; and, after consulting the king, he brought the affair before the Parliament of Paris. D'Aguesseau, at that time Avocat-Général, eloquently denounced the 'Problème' as a defamatory libel, the very title of which was an insult. It was not known, he said, who were the authors of this mystery of iniquity; but it was certain that a prelate of such exemplary and unblemished life could have no other enemies than those of

---

* "Janseniste des plus outrés." D'Aguesseau, "Mém. sur les affaires de l'Égl. de F." (*Œuvres*, tom. xiii. p. 196). The Archbishop himself, as St. Simon tells us (*Mémoires*, tom. i. chap. 43), firmly believed that the attack proceeded from the Jesuits, and would not be persuaded to the contrary. "Ils eurent beau protester d'injure en public et en particulier, et aller lui témoigner leur désaveu et leur peine qu'il prit cette opinion d'eux; ils furent froidement écoutés, et comme des gens qui ne persuadoient pas, mais qu'on voulait bien faire semblant de croire. Le livre fut condamné et exécuté au feu par ordre du Parlement, et les Jésuites, contre qui tout se souleva, en eurent toute la honte, et ne le pardonnèrent jamais à M. de Paris." St. Simon adds that a M. Boileau was the author of the 'Problème;' but this is not likely. Boileau was a thorough-paced Jansenist, but he was at the same time an intimate personal friend of the Archbishop, and was domiciled at the palace when the satire appeared.

the Church herself. Upon his demand, the court sentenced the pamphlet to be publicly torn and burned by the "exécuteur de haute justice" in the parvise of Notre Dame; which was done accordingly on the 29th of January, 1699. It was afterwards suppressed by a decree of the Holy Office at Rome.*

The Archbishop, however, was anxious that his opponent should be repulsed by force of argument as well as by the iron hand of judicial authority. He appealed to Bossuet to write in refutation of the Problème. That prelate consented, and drew up an 'Avertissement sur le livre des Reflexions morales,' which was designed as a sort of preface to the forthcoming edition of Quesnel's work. This 'Avertissement' is an ingenious attempt to excuse and justify the Reflexions, by showing that even the author's strongest statements did not amount to any of the heretical dogmas of Jansenius, and that his views on the subject of Grace harmonized with those of the Thomist school, which had ever been held admissible in the Church. Bossuet placed the result of his labours at the archbishop's disposal, only stipulating that, if it were published, his name should not appear. But, for some reason which has never been clearly explained, De Noailles thought proper to abstain from making use of the 'Avertissement' for the purpose contemplated by the author. Instead of printing it entire, he contented himself with causing certain parts of it to be embodied in a series of letters which were published anonymously by way of reply to the Problème.† Bossuet complained of this proceeding, declaring that the most important and conclusive portion of his argument had been suppressed. Cardinal Bausset asserts ‡ that Bossuet made it a condition of his assistance that numerous passages of the work should be expunged, and others materially altered; that the friends of Quesnel refused to acquiesce in this demand, and that thereupon the negotiation fell to the ground. De Noailles, whose apprehensions were excited by the objections urged by Bossuet,

---

* D'Avrigny, *Mém. Chronol.*, tom. iv. p. 106; d'Aguesseau, *Œuvres*, tom. xiii. p. 197.

† *Journal de l'Abbé Ledieu*, tom. ii. p. 445. 'Lettres d'un Théologien à un de ses amis, à l'occasion du Problème ecclésiastique adressé à M. l'Abbé Boileau.' A Anvers, chez Henri van Rhyn, 1700.

‡ Bausset, *Histoire de Bossuet*, tom. iv. pp. 44-47 (Versailles, 1814); cf. d'Avrigny, *Mém. Chronol.*, tom. iv. p. 296.

declined to grant any fresh approval of the 'Reflexions,' and accordingly the edition of 1699 appeared without the sanction of his name as Archbishop of Paris, although that which he had formerly given as Bishop of Châlons was carefully reprinted. Bossuet's 'Avertissement' was laid aside among his papers, and was afterwards published surreptitiously in Holland. It now finds a place in the collection of his works.*

It is not improbable that the archbishop's conduct in this matter was determined by an intimation from the king, that he would do well to withhold any further direct token of favour from an individual in the suspicious predicament of Father Quesnel. The rooted antipathy borne by Louis to the Jansenists was notorious; the recent renewal of agitation had doubtless embittered his mind; and such feelings of alarm and resentment would be encouraged by his Jesuit confessor. Some expression of them was possibly conveyed to De Noailles.† He could not avoid acting in accordance with it, and indeed probably welcomed it with satisfaction, as furnishing him with the means of escaping from a somewhat perplexing difficulty. But it was of no advantage to him whatever as regards the character for impartiality which he desired to enjoy with the two great antagonist parties in Church and State. From that time forward De Noailles was unalterably identified in the eyes of the nation with the Jansenistic faction. It was to no purpose that he and his friends on all occasions deprecated and repelled the insinuation. It clung to him for the rest of his days; and the conviction was deepened by the unfortunate mixture of obstinacy and weak concession which he displayed in the stormy scenes of his subsequent career.

* *Œuvres de Bossuet*, tom. ii. p. 473 *et seqq.* (ed. Besançon, 1840).
† Guettée, *Hist. de l'Égl. de France*, tom. xi. p. 144.

CHAPTER IV.

In the midst of the excitement caused by these attempts to resuscitate the half-extinguished embers of the strife on the Five Propositions of Jansenius, another theological conflict was proceeding simultaneously, which involved circumstances of a specially painful character, though in its results it was not lastingly injurious to the Church. This was the memorable dispute on Mysticism, or Quietism.

The peculiar form of devotional religion known under these names was not, as most readers are aware, the offspring of the seventeenth century. It rests, in fact, on a substratum of truth which is coeval with man's being, and expresses one of the elementary principles of our moral constitution. Although, in the course of ages, that truth was overlaid and obscured by successive accretions of error, it survived by its intrinsic vitality; and its manifold modifications served at once to attest its Divine origin, and to exhibit the industry of man in applying it, sometimes rightly, sometimes wrongly, to the details of his interior life and experience. The system of the Mystics arose from the instinctive yearning of man's soul for communion with the Infinite and the Eternal. Holy Scripture abounds with such aspirations—the Old Testament as well as the New; but that which under the Law was "a shadow of good things to come," has been transformed by Christianity into a living and abiding reality. The Gospel responds to these longings for intercommunion between earth and heaven by that fundamental article of our faith, the perpetual presence and operation of God the Holy Ghost in the Church, the collective "body of Christ," and in the individual souls of the regenerate. But a sublime mystery like this is not incapable of misinterpretation; and history teaches us that no Christian century has been exempt from one or another of the endless fallacies and extravagances for which it has been made the pretext. The Church has ever found it a difficult matter to distinguish and adjudicate between what may be called legitimate or orthodox Mysticism and those corrupt, degrading, or grotesque versions of it which have exposed religion to reproach and contempt. Some Mystics have been canonized as saints; others, no less deservedly, have been consigned to obloquy as pestilential heretics.

It was in the East—proverbially the fatherland of idealism and romance—that the earliest phase of error in this department of theology was more or less strongly developed. We find that in the fourth century the Church was troubled by a sect called Massalians or Euchites, who placed the whole of religion in the habit of mental prayer; alleging as their authority the Scriptural precept "That men ought always to pray, and not to faint." They were for the most part monks of Mesopotamia and Syria; there were many of them at Antioch when St. Epiphanius wrote his Treatise against heresies, A.D. 376. They held that every man is from his birth possessed by an evil spirit or familiar demon, who can only be cast out by the practice of continual prayer. They disparaged the Sacraments, regarding them as things indifferent; they rejected manual labour; and, although professing to be perpetually engaged in prayer, they slept, we are told, the greater part of the day, and pretended that in that state they received revelations from above; on the strength of which they uttered predictions, which were proved to be false by the event. They believed, moreover, that it is possible for man to attain in this life to a condition in which he is not only like God, but equal to Him; and that those who reach this summit of perfection are altogether incapable of sin, even of thought, or of ignorance. The Massalians did not openly separate from the Church; they were condemned, however, by two Councils—one at Antioch in 391, the other at Constantinople in 426.*

Delusions of the same kind were reproduced from time to time in the Oriental Church; and, as is commonly the case, the originators of error were followed by a race of disciples who advanced considerably beyond them. The Hesychasts, or Quietists of Mount Athos in the fourteenth century, seem to have been fanatics of an extreme type. They imagined that, by a process of profound contemplation, they could discern internally the light of the Divine Presence—the "glory of God"—the

---

* Fleury, H. E., Liv. xix. 25, 26; Liv. xxiv. 44.

very same which was disclosed to the Apostles on the Mount of Transfiguration. Hence they were also called Thaborites.* The soul to which this privilege was vouchsafed had no need to practise any of the external acts or rites of religion, but remained in imperturbable and ineffable repose in perfect union with God. Such, they maintained, is the Beatific Vision enjoyed by saints and angels. They admitted, however, that this supernatural Light was not of the actual essence of the Godhead, though it was uncreated and incorruptible; and that in all instances in which the Almighty has revealed himself to mankind, they have not beheld His essence, but only this mysterious Effulgence distinct from it. They called it His energy, or operation. The strange and self-contradictory notions of these Greek ascetics were vehemently combated by Barlaam, a Calabrian monk of great learning, and were as strenuously defended by Gregory Palamas, Archbishop of Thessalonica. Councils were held repeatedly to discuss the intricate questions thus raised concerning the Divine Essence. The principal opponents of the Thaborites belonged to the Latin communion; and hence the affair assumed the aspect of an international quarrel between the two great sections of Christendom. The decision was in favour of the visionaries of Mount Athos, whose doctrine was declared to be part of the authoritative teaching of the Greek Church; and Barlaam was finally condemned at Constantinople in 1351.†

The theory of abstract contemplation, with the extraordinary fruits supposed to be derived from it, travelled in due course into the West, and there gave birth to the far-famed school of the Mystics, of which there were various ramifications. The earliest exponent of the system in France was John Scotus Erigena, the contemporary and friend of Charles the Bald; who, by his translation of the treatises ascribed to Dionysius the Areopagite,‡ and by his original works, greatly promoted the

---

* Their argument is thus summarized by one of themselves:—" Posse fieri ut oculis corporeis quispiam Divinum et increatum lumen contempletur, perspicuè demonstrare licere; evangelistam enim scribere Dominum ante mortem suam principes discipulos assumpsisse, et cùm ascendisset in Montem Thabor, transfigurntum esse ante eos, resplendissoque faciem Ejus sicut solem; cujus fulgorem discipulos non sustinentes intueri in terram cecidisse. Si igitur illi et homines et adhuc imperfecti circumfulgens ipsos Divinum et increatum lumen videre potuerunt, quid mirum si et nunc sanctos supernè à Deo collustratos dicamus lumen cernere?"—Raynald. Annal. ad ann. 1341. No. lxxi.

† Fleury, H. E., Liv. lxxxvi. §§ 1, 2.

‡ The late Archbishop of Paris, Mon-

growth of that transcendental idea of personal religion which was afterwards so widely accepted in the Latin Church. Erigena sought to engraft the Neo-Platonism of Alexandria upon the dogmatic theology of Rome; an attempt which succeeded to a certain point, but which involved throughout a dangerous tendency. In insisting on the perfectibility of human nature through assimilation and union with the Deity, he lost sight of the essential distinction between matter and spirit, and lapsed insensibly into the snares of Pantheism. Erigena incurred the censures of the Holy See; but the results of his teaching were permanent. A current of thought and feeling set in from his time, which, while in some minds it inspired much genuine devotion and exalted saintliness, betrayed itself elsewhere in outbursts of extravagant enthusiasm and deadly self-deception.

The Mystics, or Theosophists as some style them, attained a position of high renown and influence at Paris towards the close of the twelfth century. Here two of the ablest expositors of the learning of the middle age, Hugh and Richard of St. Victor, initiated crowds of ardent disciples into the mysteries of the "via interna," and of "pure love"—that marvellous quality by which the soul, sublimated and etherealized, ascends into the very presence-chamber of the King of kings; which is the bond of ecstatic and indissoluble union between the creature and the Creator.* The school of St. Victor opposed itself vigorously to the dry disputatious spirit of the dialectic philosophy, and became a real and lasting power in the Gallican Church. The path thus traced was trodden by many who were to take rank eventually as the most perfect masters of spiritual science; among them are the venerated names of Thomas à Kempis, St.-Bonaventura, John Tauler of Strasburg, Gerson, and St.

---

seigneur Darboy, published in 1846 (when Professor of Theology at the Seminary of Langres) a French translation of these celebrated writings, preceded by an Introduction, in which he argues, with much plausibility, in defence of their authenticity. He considers that the works of "S. Denis the Areopagite" formed the basis of the whole structure of mediæval Mysticism.

* A single sentence from the treatise of Hugh of S. Victor *De Sacramentis* will serve to show how faithfully his characteristic dogma was perpetuated by the modern Mystics:—"If thou shouldest hold eternal life itself to be other than the Supreme Good, which is God, and shouldest serve Him solely with a view to attain that object, it would be no perfect service, no disinterested love." "Etiam si vitam æternam aliud aliquid esse cogitaveris, et diversum ab ipso bono quod Deus est, et pro ipso adipiscendo tantùm servieris, non est pura servitus, neque dilectio gratuita."—H. de S. Victor, *De Sacram.*, Lib. ii. par. xiii. cap. 8 (Migne, *Patrolog.*, tom. clxxvi.).

Vincent Ferrier. It was the same burning consciousness of supernatural intuition—of immediate intercourse with the Unseen through the power of Divine love—that produced in later days a St. Theresa, a St. Jean de la Croix, an Ignatius Loyola, an Alfonso Rodriguez, a St. François de Sales, a St. Jeanne Françoise de Chantal.

But, on the other hand, it is not less true that emotional religion has been found to degenerate, in modern as well as in ancient times, into manifold forms of moral aberration. The fallacy originally engendered by Manichean Dualism has proved more or less seductive in every age. To exalt above measure the dignity and privileges of the spiritual element in man carries with it the danger of disparaging the material part of our nature; and this results in the preposterous notion that, provided the soul be absorbed in the contemplation of things Divine, the actions of the body are unimportant and indifferent. How often the Church has combated and denounced this most insidious heresy is well known to all who have a moderate acquaintance with its history. Under the various appellations of Beghards, Fratricelli, Cathari, Spirituals, Albigenses, Illuminati, Guerinets, and Quietists, the self-same delusion has been sedulously propagated in different parts of Christendom, and with the same ultimate consequences. A revival of the last-named sect, the Quietists, took place in Spain about the year 1675, when Michel de Molinos, a priest of the diocese of Saragossa, published his treatise called 'The Spiritual Guide,' or, in the Latin translation, 'Manuductio spiritualis.' His leading principle, like that of his multifarious predecessors, was that of habitual abstraction of the mind from sensible objects, with a view to gain, by passive contemplation, not only a profound realisation of God's presence, but so perfect a communion with Him as to end in absorption into His essence.* This

---

* Ruysbroek, the great German Mystic of the fourteenth century, teaches in like manner that the contemplative soul sees God with a brightness which is in fact the Divine Essence itself; and, more than this, that the soul *is* that same Divine radiance; that it ceases to be what it was previously in its own natural character, and is changed, transformed, absorbed, into the essence of the Uncreate; that it is so lost in the infinite abyss of its new existence, that thenceforward it is not cognizable by any created intelligence. See his work *De Ornatu Nuptiarum Spiritualium* quoted by Bossuet in the *Instruction sur les États d'oraison.* "Without entering into this question," adds that prelate considerately, " it is sufficient to observe that this author, and others of the same class, abound with like expressions, to which

spiritual perfection supersedes all conscious exercise of the reason, and all definite acts of penitence, faith, and devotion; it implies an utter abandonment of the active faculties to God, so that the soul rests in silent immoveable tranquillity on Him, absolutely indifferent to everything except His inward voice and operation. But while the inner man was thus concentrated upon the Invisible—while self was thus immolated and annihilated, to the extent of suppressing every movement of the natural intellect and the natural will—it was apparently forgotten that the grand principles of distinct personality and direct moral responsibility were in the same ratio obscured and disowned. The door was opened, in fact, for a renewal of the wildest disorders of ancient Gnosticism.

The danger, however, was quickly discovered, and the remedy applied with promptitude and vigour. Cardinal Caraccioli, Archbishop of Naples, in a letter to the Pope in January, 1682, laid before his Holiness the peculiar tenets and practices of the rising sect, and the scandals which he apprehended from them in his diocese; and in February, 1687, Cardinal Cibo, Prefect of the Congregation of the Holy Office, addressed a circular upon the subject to the bishops, directing them to institute the necessary enquiries with a view to judicial proceedings which had been already determined on. These measures of the Roman authorities are said to have been instigated by Louis XIV., who ordered his ambassador, Cardinal d'Estrées,* to urge upon the Pope the imperative duty of crushing the new upgrowth of resuscitated heresy. Persons of the highest distinction—Cardinals, Inquisitors, nay, even Pope Innocent himself—were suspected of sharing these dangerous opinions. Molinos was arrested and imprisoned, and in due time the Inquisition condemned sixty-eight propositions from his works; a sentence which was confirmed by a Papal bull in August, 1687. Having undergone public penance, he was admitted to absolution; after which, in *merciful* consideration of his submission and repentance, he was consigned for the rest of his days to the dungeons of the Holy Office. Here he died in November, 1692.

---

no sound meaning can be attached except by merciful interpretations, or, to speak plainly, by forced constructions."

* This prelate was himself an ardent partisan of Quietism, and had published an Italian version of one of the works of Father Malaval.

Many of the sentiments maintained by Molinos are highly reprehensible, both in themselves and in the conclusions towards which they tend by legitimate inference; but it seems doubtful whether his own mind was corrupted by them. Many writers describe him as personally a man of blameless life and sincere piety. It is asserted that his followers were betrayed into immoral excesses, and very probably some such cases occurred; though even this is strenuously denied by his apologists.

The principles of Quietism had struck root so deeply, that they were not to be soon dislodged either by the terrors of the Inquisition or by the well-merited denunciations of the Vatican. The system was irresistibly fascinating to minds of a certain order. Among those who were dazzled by it was the celebrated Jeanne Marie De la Mothe Guyon—a lady of good family, of superior talents carefully cultivated, attractive in person and manners, impulsive, energetic, ambitious of social power. Married, when scarcely more than a child, to a man of mature age and uncongenial temper, Madame Guyon's early life had been one of disappointment and isolation. She was left a widow while still young; and was no sooner free from the matrimonial yoke, than, disdaining the prosaic sphere to which she had hitherto been confined, she soared into the regions of supernatural illumination and ideal perfection. Nor was she content to pursue this exalted track in selfish solitude. She believed that she had an extraordinary vocation; she felt herself destined to be the instrument of converting others; to become the foundress of a school or an Order, after the example of Madame de Chantal; to originate great works of charity; to be the guide, the counsellor, the oracle, of enquiring souls. Her first step in this career was taken under the auspices of the Bishop of Geneva, Mgr. d'Arenthon, who invited her to join an establishment which he was forming at Gex for the conversion of Protestant females in that district. Here Madame Guyon made the acquaintance of the Superior, a Barnabite monk named Lacombe. His zeal for Mysticism was as fervent as her own; but he was a man of feeble judgment, and altogether of inferior mental calibre. A close friendship sprung up between them; Lacombe, from having been the director, became ere long the devoted disciple of Madame Guyon; and her connexion with this brainsick fanatic was the circumstance which first exposed her to the blasts of obloquy and persecution. The Bishop of Geneva became dissatisfied with Lacombe, and removed him from the institution at Gex; upon which Madame Guyon followed him to Thonon in the Chablais, and there exerted herself in various ways as a religious instructor, giving lectures, holding discussions, visiting the sick, and encouraging people of all classes to come to her for private advice. She travelled for like purposes in the north of Italy and the south of France; sojourning for some time at Grenoble, where her treatise called 'Moyen court et très facile pour l'oraison' was printed in 1685. At length, in 1686, she arrived in Paris, accompanied by Father Lacombe.

It was precisely at this moment that the scandal connected with the case of Molinos had reached its height. The French bishops were busily employed in hunting down his adherents (who were believed to be still numerous) and uprooting the remains of the proscribed heresy. Lacombe soon made himself notorious by his eccentricities; he was denounced to the Archbishop of Paris (De Harlai), and that prelate, apprehensive of an attempt to revive the worst features of Quietism, procured an order for his arrest.* Through the malicious intrigues of a relation, Madame Guyon became implicated in the charges against her confessor; she was arrested in January, 1688, by virtue of a *lettre de cachet*, and conducted to the Convent of the Visitandines de Ste. Marie.

Strictly speaking, it was unjust to prosecute her as a pupil of Molinos; for it appears that she had no acquaintance whatever either with that individual or his writings. Their ideas, however, were essentially the same, having been drawn from the same source, namely, the works of the Spanish Mystics, particularly those of St. Theresa and St. Jean de la Croix. The resemblance between the 'Moyen court' and the 'Guide Spirituelle' was too manifest to be mistaken. Another of Madame Guyon's works, the 'Cantique des Cantiques, interprété selon les sens Mystiques,' was a further development of the same theory; and in the 'Torrents Spirituels,' which at this time existed only in manuscript, she laid bare the most esoteric depths of the system. But the prejudice against her seems to have arisen in the

---

* Lacombe was transferred from one prison to another; at length, his mind having given way, it was found necessary to place him in the lunatic asylum at Charenton, where he died insane.

first instance not so much from any critical examination of her writings as from a general imputation of religious extravagance, including some suspicion as to incorrectness of morals.

Madame Guyon's first imprisonment lasted eight months. She regained her freedom through the influence of Madame de Maintenon, who had conceived an interest in her from the accounts given by the inmates of the convent of her edifying conduct and many engaging qualities. A reaction now ensued in her favour. Recommended by the patronage of one who, in all but the name, was Queen of France, she found herself admitted on a footing of confidential friendship into some of the highest circles of the capital. She became a frequent guest at the hotel of the Duke de Beauvilliers, governor of the Duke of Burgundy, a councillor of state, and one of the most distinguished ornaments of the Court. Here she speedily made herself the centre of attraction, and captivated all around her. The three sister Duchesses of Beauvilliers, Chevreuse, and Mortemart, (daughters of the minister Colbert), yielded to her ascendency, hung upon her words, and almost worshipped her as a messenger direct from heaven. Even the sober-minded Madame de Maintenon, who was in habits of constant intercourse with this great family, was smitten with the prevailing fascination. Here, too, Madame Guyon enjoyed the society of one who was to be the most illustrious of her adherents, the Abbé de Fénélon, at that time recently appointed preceptor to the "children of France."

Such was the impression made by Madame Guyon upon the mind of Madame de Maintenon, that after a time the latter introduced her to the "dames de St. Louis," who presided over a semi-conventual establishment which she had founded at St. Cyr, near Versailles. These ladies received her with the utmost distinction, listened in breathless excitement to her "conferences," and encouraged her to take a leading part in the religious instruction of the place. This injudicious proceeding led to complications which must for ever be regretted. It so happened that a cousin of Madame Guyon's, Madame de la Maisonfort, was at the head of the educational staff at St. Cyr, and a special favourite with Madame de Maintenon. She embraced the views of her kinswoman with enthusiasm, and propagated them both among teachers and pupils. Ere long the whole house was permeated by the atmosphere of Quietism. The books and manuscripts of Madame Guyon were passed eagerly from hand to hand. The language of the Mystics became vernacular among the nuns; they were perpetually discussing the state of contemplation, passive prayer, holy indifference, self-annihilation, the trials of the saints, and disinterested love. The contagion spread to the *sœurs converses*, who neglected their household work in their anxiety to scan these mysteries, which were all the more attractive in proportion as they were abstruse and unintelligible.*

At St. Cyr Madame Guyon frequently met with Fénélon, who was confessor to Madame de la Maisonfort, and was in fact, though not ostensibly, the ecclesiastical director of the institution. That two spirits of such an order should have been instinctively drawn towards each other is surely nothing marvellous. To some writers it seems unaccountable that one in the position and with the intellectual superiority of Fénélon should have been accessible to the spells of a woman who, however talented and accomplished, had shown herself strangely deficient in judgment, and was looked upon in many quarters as a deluded visionary. They have remarked, with a view to explain it, that Fénélon, with all his erudition, all his eloquence, all his refinement, all his spirituality, was not thoroughly trained in theological science; that he lacked precision of thought; that he was rather an orator than a philosopher; rather an idealist than a logician; rather persuasive than profound.† Without denying that there is justice in this criticism, it is important that we should

---

* De Noailles, *Histoire de Madame de Maintenon*, tom. iii. p. 236; *Mémoires de Saint Cyr*, chap. xxix.; St. Simon, *Mémoires*, tom. i. chap. xviii.

† "Un naturel si heureux fut perverti, comme celui du premier homme, par la voix d'une femme, et ses talens, sa fortune, sa réputation même, furent sacrifiés, non à l'illusion des sens, mais à celle de l'esprit. On vit ce génie si sublime se borner à dévenir le prophète des Mystiques et l'oracle du Quiétisme; ébloui le premier par l'éclat de ses lumières, et éblouissant ensuite les autres; suppléant au défaut de science par la beauté de son esprit, fertile en images spécieuses et séduisantes plutôt qu'en idées claires et précises; voulant toujours paroître philosophe ou théologien, et n'étant jamais qu'orateur; caractère qu'il a conservé dans tous les ouvrages qui sont sortis de sa plume jusqu'à la fin de sa vie."— D'Aguesseau, "Mémoires sur les affaires de l'Égl. de Fr." (*Œuvres*, tom. xiii. p. 169). See also Guettée, *Hist. de l'Égl. de Fr.*, tom. xi. pp. 149, 150. It must be borne in mind, however, that Fénélon was no friend to the Jansenists; and that on certain important occasions he openly sided with their adversaries. Unhappily this wretched ecclesiastical feud had an under-current of practical influence which it is necessary to take into account throughout this period of French history.

not exaggerate the amount of influence obtained by Madame Guyon over Fénélon. Their relations have been misrepresented; as if hers had been the governing mind, while he was little more than an apt scholar; she the heaven-sent guide, and he the submissive disseminator of her teaching. This is a false colouring of the case. No one who approached Madame Guyon could be insensible to the peculiar charm of her personal character; and Fénélon appreciated it equally with others. Moreover, the natural bias of his mind, and the direction of his studies from his youth up, predisposed him to sympathize with her views of experimental religion; but these very circumstances qualified him, in an eminent degree, to judge of their soundness and truth. Though not, perhaps, a consummate master of theology in its widest range, Fénélon was deeply versed in one important branch of it, namely, the theology of the Mystics; and he was therefore better able than most others to decide how far Madame Guyon was in accord with those whom the Church had authorized to speak on such matters in her name, and how far she was the dupe of her own overwrought feelings and exuberant imagination. That his admiration of her genius, and his predilection for the characteristic features of Mysticism, did not prevent him from discriminating between the true and the false, the laudable and the questionable, both in her writings and her conduct, is a fact of which we have abundant evidence. In his 'Réponse à la Relation sur le Quiétisme,' and in his correspondence with Madame de Maintenon and M. Tronson, he gives a transparently candid account of the rise and progress of his acquaintance with Madame Guyon, and explains his mature view of her case in all its bearings. At first, he says, he was prejudiced against her, from what he had heard reported about her travels. These impressions were dispelled by the perusal of a letter from the Bishop of Geneva; that prelate declared that he esteemed and honoured Madame Guyon infinitely; that he could not in conscience speak otherwise than in the highest terms of her piety and morals; and that he had but one fault to find with her, namely, that she sought to introduce her own system into all the religious houses of the diocese, irrespectively of the rules and statutes of their foundation. This, observes Fénélon, was merely the indiscreet zeal of a woman who was too anxious to communicate to others things which she deemed salutary and edifying.*

"I never had any natural inclination," he writes again, "either towards her person or her writings. I never remarked anything extraordinary about her, which might tend to prepossess me in her favour. While in the perfect enjoyment of her liberty, she explained to me her religious experience, and all her sentiments. There is no need to discuss her peculiar language, which I do not defend, and which is of no great consequence in a woman, provided the meaning be Catholic. She is naturally prone to exaggeration, and incautious in her mode of speaking. She is even apt to place too much confidence in those who question her. I count for nothing her pretended prophecies and revelations; and I should have but a poor opinion of her if I thought that she esteemed them very highly. A person who is devoted to God may mention incidentally something which has passed through her mind, without forming any positive judgment upon it, or wishing that others should consider it seriously. It may be an impression from God, for His gifts are inexhaustible; but it may also be a baseless imagination. The principle of loving God exclusively for His own sake, absolutely renouncing all self-interest, is a principle of pure faith, which has no sort of connection with miracles and visions. No man can be more circumspect or dispassionate than I am on that point."†

In another letter he says, "I saw Madame Guyon often, as all the world knows; I esteemed her, and I allowed her to enjoy the esteem of persons of high eminence, whose reputation is dear to the Church, and who had confidence in me. It was impossible that I should be ignorant of her writings. Although I did not examine them all completely, I became acquainted with them sufficiently to feel in doubt about her, and to question her with the greatest strictness. I repeatedly made her explain to me what she thought upon the topics in agitation. I demanded of her the precise value of each of the terms of that mystical phraseology which she employed in her writings. I ascertained distinctly, on each occasion, that she understood

* "Réponse à la Relation," chap. i. § 1 (*Œuvres de Fénelon*, tom. ii.).
† To Madame de Maintenon, 7 mars 1696, *Corresp.*, No. 53.

them in a sense perfectly innocent and perfectly Catholic. . . .
Let others, who know nothing of Madame Guyon but her
writings, interpret them, if they please, with rigour; I do not
interfere; I do not defend or excuse either her person or her
writings. But, for my own part, I am bound in equity to judge
of the meaning of her writings by her sentiments, with which I
am intimately acquainted, rather than to pronounce upon her
opinions from the literal sense of her expressions—a sense which
she never meant them to convey."*

These testimonies prove that Fénélon's approbation of
Madame Guyon was, from the first, reserved and qualified. He
regarded her as one who had made great advances in the
spiritual life, and as a dutiful daughter of the Church in intention and principle; but he was fully alive to her failings in the
way of unmeasured language, though he thought her entitled
to considerable indulgence even on that score; first by reason
of her sterling integrity, and secondly by reason of her sex.
It must be remembered, also, that Fénélon had seen only the
printed works of Madame Guyon, and knew nothing whatever
of her manuscript productions—the 'Torrents,' the 'Autobiography,' the 'Exposition of the Apocalypse,' and others;—the
latter of which were far more objectionable than the former,
both in point of rhapsodical style, and as to heterodox speculation in doctrine. In a word, the relations of Fénélon to
Madame Guyon were those of one self-reliant and independent
mind to another. He was drawn towards her by congeniality of
natural taste, and by a sympathetic interest in the deepest and
most inscrutable mysteries of personal religion; but it were a
mistake to suppose that he blindly surrendered his judgment to
hers, or that he ever exchanged the dignity of his office as a
priest for the character of a proselyte or a disciple.

Nevertheless it was natural, and perhaps inevitable, that as
soon as the name of Madame Guyon became notorious in society,
and she was known to have been the cause of serious discord
and commotion at St. Cyr, a certain amount of suspicion should
fall upon Fénélon, who was supposed, and with reason, to be her
most influential supporter in that institution. Symptoms of the
coming storm appeared in 1693. The Bishop of Chartres,

---

* To Madame de Maintenon, September, 1696, *Corresp. de Fénelon*, No. 57.

Godet-Desmarais, in whose diocese St. Cyr was at that time situated,* viewed with alarm the morbid tone of sentiment which had invaded the sisterhood, and felt it his duty, both as bishop of the diocese and as the spiritual adviser of Madame de Maintenon, to warn her against what he deemed an evil of no common magnitude. There is no need to take it for granted, with some writers, that he was actuated in this step by jealousy of Fénélon. The question of Mysticism (particularly the development of it then prevalent) was one upon which conscientious Churchmen might take opposite sides without any infusion of unworthy feeling, simply from the incentive of zeal for truth, or cogent sense of duty. Bishop Godet held Fénélon in sincere regard. For his sake he long delayed to impart his misgivings to Madame de Maintenon; and, when he did so, he scrupulously avoided saying anything which could implicate his friend in the errors which he denounced.† Madame de Maintenon was slow to be convinced. She was familiar with the 'Moyen court' of Madame Guyon (which had been recommended to her by Fénélon), and had even read some part of it to the king; but Louis, who was "not sufficiently advanced in piety to relish such a method of perfection," had dismissed it as dreamy and fantastical.‡ The monitions of her confessor opened her eyes to the danger; yet, from her great esteem for Fénélon, she refrained from moving in the affair until she had taken the opinions of other divines of the highest standing. She consulted Bossuet, de Noailles,§ Bourdaloue, Brisacier, Joly the superior of St. Lazare, and Tronson, under whom Fénélon had studied at the Seminary of St. Sulpice. Their verdict was

---

* The present See of Versailles was not erected till the Concordat of 1802.

† Bausset, *Histoire de Fénélon*, tom. i. chap. vi.

‡ Madame de Maintenon to the Ctesse. de St.-Géran, 12 mai 1694 (*Lettres et Mémoires de Madame de Maintenon*, tom. ii. p. 109. La Beaumelle).

§ The opinion of this prelate (then Bishop of Châlons) is preserved in the correspondence of Madame de Maintenon. "Les livres de Madame Guyon," he says, "renferment, sous une apparence de piété, des propositions dangereuses, et qui tendent à renouveler les erreurs du Quiétisme. On y trouve des maximes, condamnées il y a près de quatre cents ans, dans un concile général tenu à Vienne, en France, et qui étoient soutenues par des gens qui vouloient établir une nouvelle spiritualité dont les principes étoient fort conformes à ceux que Madame Guyon enseigne dans ses ouvrages. Les idées de perfection qu'elle y donne ont été non-seulement inconnues aux Apôtres à qui toute vérité a été révélée, mais sont formellement opposées aux régles qu'ils nous ont laissées, à celles des saints Pères qui les ont suivis, et à la pratique de tous les saints."—Théoph. Lavallée, *Correspondance générale de Madame de Maintenon*, tom. iii. p. 406.

unanimous against Madame Guyon and her system; and Madame de Maintenon hesitated no longer. She notified to Madame Guyon that her visits would not be acceptable for the future at St. Cyr. The sisters were forbidden to read her books; her manuscripts, together with certain papers written by Fénélon, were withdrawn from circulation; and it was hoped that by these vigorous measures order and tranquillity would soon be re-established. The Bishop of Chartres seemed satisfied with this submission to his pastoral authority; and there was no disposition to proceed further against Madame Guyon, could she have been content to take her dismissal quietly, and to remain in silence. But, unfortunately, she now appealed to the arbitration of Bossuet; who, with his masculine straightforwardness and logical rigidity of mind, was of all men the least likely to judge her leniently. She was determined to this step by the advice of Fénélon, who induced her to submit to the Bishop of Meaux not only her published works, but also her manuscript effusions, which she had never communicated even to himself.* Bossuet spent several months in perusing them, and was shocked to find that they abounded with preposterous absurdities, betokening a mind in a state of chronic disorder. Some of her pretensions were precisely those of the Spiritualists of our own times. She claimed to be "clairvoyante;" she saw into the innermost depths of souls; and not only so, but she possessed "a miraculous authority both over the bodies and the minds of those whom the Lord had given to her, so that their internal condition seemed to be wholly in her hands." She was a reservoir of superabundant grace, the overflowings of which she dispensed, by a somewhat materialistic process, to those who were placed in personal contact with her. It was in this way

---

* Fénélon, MS. note to the *Relation*, p. 5. Among the Egerton MSS. in the British Museum (No. 1664) is a copy, in small 4to, of the original edition of Bossuet's *Relation sur le Quiétisme*, profusely annotated in the margin with critical remarks in the handwriting of Fénélon himself. It is needless to point out the interest attaching to this commentary, representing, as doubtless it does, the first vivid impressions wrought on Fénélon's mind by the redoubtable manifesto of his adversary. It appears that he forwarded another copy of the *Relation*, with a similar running refutation of its contents, to the Abbé de Chanterac, his agent at Rome. It has never, to the best of my knowledge, appeared in print; the *Réponse à la Relation* being a totally distinct composition. The reader is requested to remember that the passages quoted in foot-notes, for the purpose of substantiating statements advanced in the text, are literal extracts from this manuscript.

that she obtained relief when half-suffocated by the redundance of her spiritual gifts. She spoke of herself as the appointed instrument of God's most marvellous operations; as invested with a prophetical, or rather an Apostolical, mission; as the minister of a new dispensation. "That which I bind shall be bound, and that which I loose shall be loosed; I am that stone fixed by the holy Cross, rejected by the master-builders."* In her 'Commentary on the Apocalypse' she indulged in flights of fancy of an equally exorbitant kind.

However startled and scandalized, Bossuet seems to have treated Madame Guyon on this occasion with much forbearance. He wrote letters to her replete with weighty reasoning and fatherly counsel. He held a lengthened interview with her, in which he earnestly laboured to dispel her illusions, combating more especially her strange notion that to implore anything of God (for instance, the pardon of our sins) is an act of self-interest, incompatible with "pure love" and entire conformity with the Divine will. He was unable to disabuse her of this error; but she made repeated promises of submission to his instructions, and engaged to remain for a time in retirement, according to his advice.

Bossuet next visited Fénélon, with whom he was still on terms of intimacy, and strove to open his eyes to Madame Guyon's hallucinations, by laying before him extracts from those parts of her writings which he had never before seen.† He expected that his friend's opinion of these extracts would

---

* Bossuet, *Relation sur le Quiétisme*, Sect. ii. 9, 13, 14, 15. See Madame Guyon's *Autobiography*, Pt. ii. chap. xvii. With reference to the *Autobiography*, she writes to Bossuet in an apologetic tone (February, 1694, Lettre x.):—"Ce fut par excès de confiance que je vous donnai la Vie, que j'étois prête à brûler comme le reste, si Votre Grandeur me l'avoit ordonné. Vous voyez bien que cette Vie ne se peut montrer que par excès de confiance. Je l'ai écrite, ainsi que mon Dieu est témoin, avec une telle abstraction d'esprit, qu'il ne m'a jamais été permis de faire un retour sur moi en l'écrivant. Quoique cela soit de la sorte, peu de personnes sont capables de comprendre jusqu'où vont les secrètes et amoureuses communications de Dieu et de l'âme. La confiance que notre Seigneur m'a donnée en Votre Grandeur m'a fait croire que vous les sentiriez si elles étaient incompréhensibles, et que le cœur soit frappé des mêmes choses qui répugnoient à l'esprit." After such a naïve confession, it would be harsh indeed to interpret the *Autobiography* "au pied de la lettre."

† MSS. notes of Fénélon to the *Relation*, pp. 12-15; *ibid.*, p. 27. Fénélon declares that he condemned these extracts without hesitation:—"On peut donc me croire quand je dis que je n'ai point lu des manuscrits que j'ai fait lire à M. de Meaux; et que je condamne sans hésiter sur l'exposé qu'on m'en fait."

have agreed altogether with his own; but instead of this he was met with extenuations, qualifications, and evasions; and in the end he went his way without success, mourning over the eclipse of such a noble mind.

The march of events, however, had already convinced Fénélon of the necessity of caution. After 1693 his communications with Madame Guyon were extremely rare.* He resigned the office of confessor to Madame de la Maisonfort. He requested that the letters of spiritual counsel which he had written for the benefit of certain inmates of St. Cyr might be suppressed; and he explained his principles at length to Madame de Maintenon, guarding himself against unwarrantable inferences, defending himself from the charge of innovation, and professing all reverent submission to the tradition of the Church.† He was evidently conscious that he had become an object of mistrust; and it was soon apparent that his favour and position at court were seriously in jeopardy.

Still, if Madame Guyon could have acquiesced in the advice which she had voluntarily solicited, and remained in patient seclusion, these unfavourable impressions would probably have died away without leaving injurious results. But in 1694 her restlessness returned; and she petitioned the king, through Madame de Maintenon, for a commission, half clerical and half lay, to report, not only on the soundness of her writings, but on the truth of rumours which she alleged to be current against her moral character.‡ As to the lay commissioners this request was refused, since the vague calumnies referred to were credited by none; but three ecclesiastics were named to undertake the theological enquiry—Bossuet, De Noailles, and Tronson; and they proceeded to hold a series of conferences, extending over many months, at a country-house at Issy, belonging to Tronson as Superior of the congregation of St. Sulpice. These confer-

---

* He writes thus to Archbishop de Noailles in June, 1697:—"Je n'ai vu ni pu voir bien souvent Madame Guyon. Mon principal commerce avec elle à été par lettres, où je la questionnais sur toutes les matières de l'oraison. Je n'ai jamais rien vu que de bon dans ses réponses; et j'ai été édifié d'elle, à cause qu'il ne m'y a paru que droiture et piété. Dès qu'on a parlé contre elle, j'ai cessé de la voir, de lui écrire, et de recevoir de ses lettres, pour ôter tout sujet de peine aux personnes alarmées."—*Corresp. de Fénélon*, No. 67.

† *Correspondance de Fénélon*, Nos. 30, 31.

‡ Madame Guyon to Madame de Maintenon, June, 1694 (*Corresp. de Fénélon*, tom. vii. No. 30).

ences were conducted in strict secresy. Even the Archbishop of Paris, to whose jurisdiction as diocesan the affair properly belonged, was not consulted. He took offence in consequence, and showed his feelings by forestalling, in a pastoral ordonnance of October 16, 1694, the judgment of the commissioners on the matter in hand. He condemned a treatise on Mental Prayer by Father Lacombe, and the two principal works of Madame Guyon, as containing false and pernicious doctrine, long since censured by the Councils of Vienne and Trent; and pointed out that they were essentially opposed to Christianity, by encouraging contempt for external duties and observances, by disparaging mortification and rules of asceticism, by prescribing indifference to those means which are the best calculated to promote holiness and salvation, and by fostering the mistaken persuasion that God may be possessed even in this life as He is in Himself, without any intermediate instruments.* Bossuet and his colleagues took little notice of this manifesto of their metropolitan. They pursued their task, observing that it was not their intention to act in the way of episcopal jurisdiction, but simply to lay down doctrinal conclusions for the guidance and satisfaction of those who had shown confidence in them by naming them to compose the commission.†

But what was the part reserved for Fénélon in an investigation which concerned him so nearly, and which, in respect of deep knowledge of the questions in debate, he was more competent to direct than any one of the triumvirate at Issy? His name was excluded from the Commission; partly because there was too much reason to regard him as a partisan of Madame Guyon, and partly because his friends (among whom Bossuet must still be reckoned) wished to prevent his having the opportunity of compromising himself further at this critical moment. The authority of Bossuet was paramount in the Commission; and indeed the spirit of ecclesiastical dictatorship, which by this time had become habitual to him, was but too manifest throughout the proceedings. Conscious, however, that he had but a slight acquaintance with mystical theology, he applied to Fénélon to furnish him with extracts from ancient and modern sources to

---

* D'Avrigny, *Mém. Chronol.*, tom. iii. p. 433.
† Bossuet, "Lettres sur l'affaire du Quiétisme" (*Œuvres*, tom. xviii. p. 434). Bausset, *Hist. de Fénélon*, tom. i. chap. vi.

assist the Commissioners in forming their conclusions, especially with regard to the cardinal point at issue, that of the disinterested love of God. Fénélon accordingly collected a catena of authorities on this subject from Mystics of the highest repute, from St. Clement of Alexandria down to St. François de Sales, which he forwarded to Bossuet, together with copious comments of his own, for the purpose of proving that writers of this peculiar stamp are not always to be understood literally; that exaggeration of style is one of their characteristic features, and that after making all due allowance on that score, the result would be more than amply sufficient to establish the doctrine of pure love, and to satisfy all those who, while zealous for true Mysticism, were equally alive to the dangers of illusion.* This humble office Fénélon fulfilled with all his native sincerity and simplicity; expressing himself at the same time in terms of almost abject deference to the judgment of Bossuet, and declaring that, whatever might be the ultimate decision, his own suffrage could not fail to conform to it. "Be under no anxiety about me," he writes; "I am in your hands like a little child. You are kind enough to say you desire that we should be of one mind; for my part I am ready to go further, and to say that we are already agreed beforehand, in whatever sense you may decide. Even if what I have read should seem to me more clear than that two and two make four, I should consider it less clear than my obligation to distrust my own understanding, and to prefer to it that of a prelate like yourself. Do not take this for a mere compliment; it is a serious and literal truth." † Bossuet having apparently hinted some doubts as to the orthodoxy of his views, Fénélon protests that he only desires to be instructed; that he is ready to retract and abandon the slightest error, and that even if the judgment of his superior should be mistaken, he should obey with the utmost docility and confidence, from the principle of supreme devotedness to the guidance of the Church.‡ These assurances from a friend to whom he was still attached,

---

* Je fis des recueils ... pour montrer que les anciens n'avoient pas moins exagéré que les Mystiques des derniers siècles; qu'il ne falloit prendre en rigueur ni les uns ni les autres; qu'on en rabattît tout ce qu'on voudroit, et qu'il en resteroit encore plus qu'il n'en falloit pour contenter les vrais Mystiques ennemis de l'illusion."—Fénélon, *Réponse à la Relation*, chap. ii. § xx.
† Fénélon to Bossuet, July 28, 1694, *Corresp. de Fénélon*, No. 36.
‡ Fénélon to Bossuet, December 16, 1694, *Corresp. de Fénélon*, No. 37.

though he believed him to be treading on dangerous ground, had doubtless much weight with Bossuet; nor could he refuse to admit, on the strength of the evidence adduced by Fénélon, that the consensus in favour of certain maxims to which he was personally disinclined was more emphatic than he had hitherto imagined. Hence he was led to hope that existing differences might in time disappear, and that he might be the means, on the one hand, of saving the reputation of his friend, and on the other of establishing disputed truths on a firmer foundation, to the edification of the Church.

Under these circumstances, the reports which were beginning to prevail to the discredit of Fénélon were for a time checked and silenced; and, on the recommendation of Madame de Maintenon, he was nominated to the archiepiscopal see of Cambrai in the spring of 1695.

No sooner was he designated to the highest order of the ministry, than it became plain that he could no longer be confined to the subordinate place which he had hitherto occupied with regard to the deliberations at Issy. He was admitted, therefore, ostensibly to the conferences on a footing of equality with the other commissioners; but in point of fact their labours were already terminated; and almost immediately afterwards the famous 'Articles of Issy' were presented to Fénélon for signature, though he had no share in drawing them up. This unceremonious treatment did not prevent him from expressing his readiness to accept the Articles, provided certain alterations and additions were adopted, which he specified. His suggestions were agreed to, and the 12th, 13th, 33rd, and 34th articles were inserted in order to meet his views.* Upon this he declared that he was "willing to sign them with his blood." † No doubt he spoke sincerely; he regarded the Articles as a correct exposition of the authorised doctrine, so far as they went, on the truths in question, and as a test whereby true Mysticism might be discriminated from the false, the sound from the corrupt and dangerous. One of them, the 33rd, contains a statement which, we may be perfectly sure, owed its admission to the personal solicitation of Fénélon. It runs thus :—" It is also allowable to

---

* The *Articles sur les états d'oraison* are to be found in the xivth volume of Bossuet's works (Besançon edit.) annexed to his Ordonnance of April 16, 1695.
† *Réponse à la Relation*, chap. iii. § 45.

encourage, in truly pious and humble souls, a submission and consent to the will of God, even if, by an entirely false supposition, it should please Him to keep them in eternal torments instead of that eternal blessedness which He has promised to the righteous; without depriving them, notwithstanding, of His grace and His love. This is an act of perfect abandonment; and of pure love practised by the saints; and by souls truly perfect it may be usefully practised with the special grace of God; without detracting at the same time from the obligation of other acts of piety which we have already defined as essential to Christianity." The Bishop of Mirepoix wrote to Bossuet to express his surprise that he should have assented to this article, which appeared to sanction one of the most unwarrantable speculations of the Mystics.* Bossuet replied that he had well reflected on it, and that he found the sentiment in the works of so many approved authors (among whom he instances St. Chrysostom, Theodoret, St. Isidore of Damietta, St. Theresa, and St. François de Sales), that he thought it was not possible to call it in question.† After all, he says, it was only affirming, in other words, that the love of God is in itself far more desirable than all imaginable torments are revolting to our nature.

It would appear, then, that the Articles of Issy were conceived in a spirit of forbearance and mutual concession; and as such, might well be regarded as a treaty of pacification. They were signed by the commissioners and by Fénélon on the 10th of March, 1695; and there is reason to believe that this act was understood on all hands as the seal of a cordial reconciliation.

The fate of Madame Guyon remained to be determined. She had voluntarily placed herself, with Bossuet's consent, in a convent at Meaux, during the examination of her writings, in order to be completely under his eye and control. Here her conduct was in every respect commendable; the Superior and sisterhood attested that they had been edified by her perfect regularity, sincerity, humility, gentleness, and patience, and by

---

* It must be noted, however, that the article speaks only of a hypothetical case; that supposing, *per impossibile*, God could consign a righteous soul to the pains of hell, it ought to remain unchangeably devoted to His will.

† Bossuet, *Lettres sur l'affaire du Quiétisme*, Nos. xxxiv. xxxv. xxxvi.

her deep devotion towards the mysteries of the Catholic Faith.* During this time she underwent more than one examination before the commissioners, at which Bossuet is said to have treated her with some severity. When the Conferences terminated, that prelate dictated to her an act of submission, by which she accepted the thirty-four Articles, and condemned with heart and mouth everything contrary to them, together with all other errors, whether in her own works or elsewhere. She repudiated all writings attributed to her, with the exception of the 'Moyen court' and the 'Cantique des Cantiques,' renouncing these likewise except in so far as they agreed with the Catholic and Apostolic Faith, "from which she had never intentionally swerved for a single instant." She assented to the condemnation of her books pronounced by the Bishops of Meaux and Châlons in their pastoral ordonnances. Lastly, she engaged to obey the injunctions of the Bishop of Meaux, which forbade her for the future to write books, to teach dogmatically in the Church, or to undertake in any shape the guidance of souls; professing her desire to live henceforth in entire separation from the world, and in the practice of " a hidden life with Jesus Christ." In a further statement, appended to Bossuet's pastoral letter, Madame Guyon protested a second time "that she had never intended to advance anything at variance with the doctrine and spirit of the Catholic and Roman Church, to which she had ever been obedient and submissive, and would so continue, with God's help, to the last hour of her life."

Upon the faith of these declarations, which, as we have said, were prescribed by Bossuet himself, that prelate delivered to Madame Guyon, on her quitting his diocese, a certificate, expressed as follows:—" We, Bishop of Meaux, certify to all whom it may concern, that, in consequence of declarations of submission signed by Madame Guyon, and of the prohibition which she has accepted to write, teach, or dogmatize in the Church, or to circulate her works in print or manuscript, or to engage in any way in the guidance of souls; having regard also to the testimonies which have been made to us in her favour during the six months which she has passed in the convent of St. Mary in our diocese, we continue to be satisfied with her conduct, and

---

* See their certificate in the *Lettres sur l'affaire du Quiétisme*, Lettre xlii.

have confirmed her in that use of the Holy Sacraments in which we found her. We declare, moreover, that she has always expressed herself in our presence as detesting the abominations of Molinos, and others elsewhere condemned, in which it does not appear to us that she was ever implicated; and we did not intend to include her in the mention made of those errors in our ordonnance of April 16, 1695. Given at Meaux on the 1st of July, 1695."

It cannot be denied that this document has in great measure the air of a justification of Madame Guyon, with reference both to her principles and her conduct. It proceeds upon the fact that she had candidly acknowledged and renounced her errors; it attests the purity of her morals and her many Christian virtues, and it acquits her of all complicity in the excesses of Molinos and other apostles of Quietism. Fénélon, therefore, had good reason to testify his amazement, on a subsequent occasion, that such a voucher should have been given to her, if Bossuet conscientiously believed her to be guilty of the grave delinquencies which he afterwards laid to her charge. If the Bishop of Meaux, who had scrutinized the whole of her writings, and had subjected her to searching examinations vivâ voce, could excuse her on the ground that her intentions were harmless and that she had always been orthodox at heart, why might not a similar line of vindication be open to the Archbishop of Cambrai, who knew only those of her publications which were admitted to be the least worthy of censure?*

For the time, however, all differences seemed at an end. Bossuet expressed a strong desire to officiate at the consecration of Fénélon; and persisted in seeking an arrangement to that effect, in spite of certain impediments which at first seemed likely to prevent it. The ceremony was to take place at St. Cyr, in the diocese of the Bishop of Chartres, and the question arose whether that prelate could yield precedence to another, on an occasion when by his office he would be naturally entitled to preside. High authorities pronounced in the negative; but Bossuet cited ancient Councils to prove that a diocesan

---

* Fénélon, *Réponse à la Relation*, chap. i. §§ viii. xv. xvi. Bossuet's reply was, that the certificate was granted only in consideration of her having renounced her errors, professed herself penitent, and solemnly promised obedience to his directions for the future.

bishop may, even within his own jurisdiction, give way to his senior in the episcopate, when both belong to the same province; and although there were other points on which difficulties were suggested, these were overruled, and the matter was finally settled according to his wishes. Fénélon was consecrated Archbishop of Cambrai in the chapel of St. Cyr on the 10th of June, 1695. Bossuet was the consecrating prelate; the Bishop of Châlons (De Noailles) acted as first assistant; and the third place was filled by the Bishop of Amiens, who was substituted for the Bishop of Chartres.*

But notwithstanding this demonstration of restored harmony, there still lurked in the mind of Bossuet a residuum of doubt as to the soundness of Fénélon with regard to those great principles of Christian ethics which he believed to be imperilled by the Quietism of the day. He had not been perfectly satisfied with his conduct at the time of the signing of the Articles. Fénélon had promised absolute submission; yet when the Articles were tendered to him he had hesitated and demurred, proposed alterations, stipulated for additions. His subscription was looked upon as a recantation in disguise, and with some justice; but Bossuet was not contented with this qualified success. He was seriously alarmed at the progress of the fanatical notions which were identified with Madame Guyon, and which seemed to spread more and more widely in proportion to the efforts made to repress them. He knew that Fénélon was supposed, though perhaps unjustly, to favour these errors, and he felt that the Church was likely to derive damage rather than profit from his elevation to one of its highest dignities, unless the propagators of false doctrine were precluded, once for all, from sheltering themselves under the sanction of his name. He resolved, there-

---

* Upon this subject, which became of importance when the orthodoxy of Fénélon was afterwards impeached by Bossuet, the statements of the two prelates are irreconcilable. Bossuet asserts (*Relation sur la Quiétisme*, § iii. 14) that Fénélon begged him to preside at the consecration, and adds that, two days before the ceremony, he protested on his knees that he would never hold any doctrine but his. Fénélon declares, on the contrary (*Réponse*, chap. iii. § 52), that he never asked him to undertake the office. Bossuet came into his room, he says, after his nomination, and, embracing him, exclaimed, "These are the hands that will consecrate you." "I knew not," he continues, "what reply to make to him, because I wished to ascertain the intentions of a person (Cardinal de Bouillon) to whom I owed that mark of respect. In the end, I did no more than acquiesce in the reiterated offers of the Bishop of Meaux." Cardinal Bausset decides, without hesitation, in favour of Fénélon.

fore, to give him a fresh opportunity of renouncing, distinctly and positively, the "evil communications" which had exposed him to so much sinister criticism; and for this purpose he begged him to signify his approval of a new work in which he was engaged in refutation of the false Mystics. This was his famous 'Instruction sur les états d'oraison.'

In his pastoral letter of April 1695, Bossuet had promised to put forth a more ample exposition both of the truths to be embraced and of the errors to be shunned, with regard to the obscure points of theology then so vehemently debated. To this work he applied himself with his characteristic energy, and was employed upon it during the latter half of 1695 and part of the following year. It contains a minute philosophical analysis of the state of the soul in the exercise of devotion, and especially in the so-called "passive prayer." The author shows, from the writings of approved mystics, that, while they recognize a condition in which the soul is so absorbed in the contemplation of God that conscious ratiocination and other mental acts are for the time excluded,* yet this does not imply a total or permanent, but only a temporary, suspension of the ordinary faculties. The suppression of "discursive acts" is limited to the duration of the passive prayer; instead of which, the modern mystics maintained that this "passivity" was a fixed condition, upon which they entered by an "acte perpétuel," or "universel," which had no need to be repeated; thus doing away with the duty of practising devotion by any conscious and deliberate movement of the will.† Again, he combats the mischievous notion that explicit acts of faith are unnecessary for those who pursue this novel road to perfection; that the mysteries of the Trinity and the Incarnation, the Divine attributes, the articles of the Creed, the petitions of the Lord's

---

* Molinos went so far as to exclude even religious meditation or reflection from the contemplative state. "A reflection of the soul on its own actions," he says, "hinders it from receiving the true light, and from taking a step towards perfection." *Guide Spirituel*, chap. v. p. 31, quoted by Bossuet in his *Instruction*.

† This was expressly condemned by the xixth of the Articles of Issy. "Perpetual prayer does not consist in a perpetual and single act, which is supposed to continue uninterruptedly, and therefore need not be reiterated, but in a perpetual disposition and readiness to do nothing that may displease God, and to do everything in order to please Him. The contrary proposition, which would exclude in every state—even in that of perfection —all plurality and succession of acts, is erroneous, and contrary to the tradition of all the saints."

Prayer, are no longer proper objects of direct contemplation to the soul which is already in union with the very essence of the Godhead.* It was pretended that our Lord's humanity need not, and cannot, be kept distinctly in view in such a state, because it is merged in his Divine Personality. "He who thinks of God," says Molinos, "thinks of Jesus Christ;" and he adds that "no one continues to make use of the means when once he has obtained the end." Another point attacked in this treatise with conclusive force is the abuse of the doctrine of self-abandonment and self-annihilation. The "holy indifference" vaunted by Quietists was such that the soul experienced no impulsion either on the side of enjoyment or of privation; although its love of God was immeasurable, it nevertheless had no desire of Paradise, either for itself or others; no solicitude for the success of anything done either for its own salvation or that of its neighbour. It cannot be distressed either by its own perdition or by that of any other creature. The soul must will nothing except what God himself has willed from all eternity.† Lastly, Bossuet demolishes the false position that the state of "passive contemplation" is essential in all cases to Christian perfection.‡ He points out that, according to the great masters of theology, this state does not belong to justifying grace, —"gratia gratum faciens,"—but, like the gifts of prophecy, tongues, or miracles, to extraordinary grace,—"gratia gratis data;" otherwise it would follow that some of the most admirable saints were but imperfect and inexperienced in the ways of God; for to St. Basil, St. Gregory Nazianzen, St. Ambrose, St. Augustine, St. Chrysostom, St. Bernard,—whom the Church honours as the brightest examples of spirituality,— this perpetual state of contemplation, with its "mystical incapacities," was utterly unknown. St. Theresa, speaking of these peculiar conditions of prayer—the prayer of "quietude," of "union," and the like,—says that superiority of merit does not depend upon the possession of these gifts, inasmuch as there are many saintly persons who have never received them, and that many have received them who have never become

---

* Censured in the xxivth Article of Issy.
† *Instruction*, Liv. iii. These errors are formally condemned in the vth, ixth, xivth, and xxxiiind Articles of Issy.
‡ See the xxiind and xxiiird Articles of Issy.

saintly; to which she adds that such gifts may be highly profitable towards advancement in virtue, but that he who acquires them by his labour is far more meritorious. The same doctrine is inculcated by St. François de Sales, who, though he had no personal experience of the special grace in question, attained incontestably to the loftiest degrees of the pure love of God.*

Having completed this elaborate justification of the Articles of Issy, Bossuet sent it in manuscript to the Archbishop of Cambrai, taking it for granted, apparently, that he would not hesitate to sanction it with his approval, in common with the Bishop of Châlons (now advanced to the See of Paris) and the Bishop of Chartres. He felt that he had a right to expect this; first, because Fénélon had subscribed the Articles, upon which the 'Instruction' was only an extended and methodical commentary; and next, because he had solemnly, repeatedly, and with every demonstration of sincerity, declared his resolution to abide by the judgment of Bossuet and his colleagues upon the matters in debate.† To his great surprise, however, the Archbishop declined to approve the work, and returned it after a very hasty examination,‡ through the Duc de Chevreuse, whom he commissioned to explain his reasons. The ground of refusal was that the 'Instruction' was a tissue of personal attacks upon Madame Guyon. With regard to fundamental doctrine, he declared that he could not perceive a shadow of discrepancy between himself and Bossuet; but he could not in conscience assent to such a rigorous condemnation of a person

---

* *Instruction*, Livres vii. ix. x.

† See especially his letter to Bossuet of December 12, 1694 (*Corresp. de Fénélon*, tom. vii. p. 129), in which he says:—"Si vous croyez que je doive quelque chose à la vérité et à l'Église dans laquelle je suis prêtre, un mot sans raisonnement me suffira. Je ne tiens qu'à une seule chose, qui est l'obéissance simple. Ma conscience est donc dans la vôtre. Si je manque, c'est vous qui me faites manquer faute de m'avertir. C'est à vous à répondre de moi, si je suis un moment dans l'erreur. Je suis prêt à me taire, à me rétracter, à m'accuser, et même à me retirer, si j'ai manqué à ce que je dois à l'Église." After such language Bossuet might fairly demand every mode and measure of submission; but he did not sufficiently take into account the great change in Fénélon's ecclesiastical position which had occurred subsequently. In the mouth of the Abbé de Fénélon these protestations might be quite becoming; but it was another thing to require that they should be carried out to the very letter by the Archbishop of Cambrai.

‡ "Je ne le gardai que vingt-quatre heures, et je n'en lus pas deux pages de suite; je parcourus seulement les marges. Je vis partout des passages de Madame Guyon, cités avec des réfutations atroces, où vous lui imputiez des erreurs dignes du feu, que vous assuriez qui étoient évidemment l'unique but de tout son système."—Fénélon to Bossuet, 9 févr. 1697, *Corresp. de Fénélon*, No. 61.

for whom he had entertained high esteem, and whom he believed (as, indeed, her accuser himself had formerly acknowledged) to be innocent of any evil intent.

The whole force of this objection evidently turns upon the meaning of the phrase "personal attacks." It was impossible for Bossuet, in laying bare the nature of a system which he deemed to be fraught with peril to religion and to society, to avoid alluding to the circumstances which had led to the inquiry; and among these he could not but refer to the works which had been published to the world by Madame Guyon, as well as to those of Molinos, Malaval, and other extreme mystics, which had latterly excited so much attention. These works constituted the overt facts which had occasioned the conferences of Issy; and it was in refutation of the errors therein propounded that the Commissioners had drawn up their XXXIV. Articles, to which Fénélon, in concert with them, had affixed his signature. If Fénélon was not prepared to condemn Madame Guyon, he ought never to have signed those articles; and the truth is, that he placed himself in a false position by so doing. Having signed them, he became identified with the opponents of a system of which Madame Guyon had been one of the most enthusiastic advocates; and it is clear that he could not abruptly dissociate himself from their subsequent proceedings without laying himself open to the charge of inconsistency. Was there anything in Bossuet's treatment of the controversy in his 'Instruction' that exonerated the Archbishop from adhering to the course to which his previous acts had pledged him? It would be difficult to maintain the affirmative. Bossuet had made frequent quotations, indeed, from the 'Moyen court' and the 'Cantique des Cantiques,' for the purpose of exposing what he considered to deserve censure in their principles and tendencies; but he cannot be said to have indulged in offensive imputations against the author. Nothing is spared in the way of acute and telling criticism of the mistaken theory upon which these books are based; but there is no attempt to fasten upon Madame Guyon the charge either of culpable motives or of discreditable conduct. To affirm, then, that he had represented her as a prodigy of wickedness, as the author of a "monstrous system which, under the pretence of spirituality, subverted the Divine law, established fanaticism and impurity, confounded the distinctions between virtue and vice, destroyed all social subordination, and sanctioned every species of hypocrisy and falsehood" *—such assertions savoured strongly (to say the least) of misapprehension and exaggeration.

Moreover, it must not be concealed that the Archbishop's personal estimate of Madame Guyon † was in no small degree self-contradictory. At one moment he spoke of her as a poor ignorant woman, whose books he would not attempt to defend directly or indirectly, since he considered them censurable in their true and literal sense; at another, when asked to join his episcopal brethren in denouncing the doctrine of those books, he replied that to do so would be to violate his conscience, and to "insult without cause a person whom he has revered as a saint," and from whose character and example he has derived "infinite edification." ‡ "I am not obliged," he cries, " to censure all the bad books which appear, particularly those which are absolutely unknown in my own diocese. Such a censure could not be demanded of me except for the purpose of removing suspicions which may have arisen as to my opinions; but I have other and more natural means of dispelling such suspicions, without going out of my way to torment a poor woman against whom so many others have already fulminated, and with whom I have been on terms of friendship. Nor is it expedient that I should make any distinct declaration against her writings; for the public would not fail to conclude that it was a kind of abjuration which had been extorted from me. Such a personal censure would not be required of me even by the Inquisition; and I will never consent to it unless out of obedience to the Church, whenever she may think fit to draw up a Formulary on the subject, as was done in the case of the Jansenists." §

But it is not difficult to read " between the lines " of Fénélon's correspondence, especially of his letters to Bossuet, that there were secret reasons which prompted his conduct at this moment

---

* Fénélon to Madame de Maintenon (*Corresp. de Fénélon*, No. 57).

† Thus in the *Réponse à la Relation*, he says, "I excused her books, *without meaning to approve of them*, on account of her good intentions. Although I had read them rather negligently, they appeared to me to be very far from correct." Yet it was one of these books, the *Moyen court*, that he had recommended to Madame de Maintenon as containing the quintessence of spiritual religion.

‡ Fénélon to M. Tronson, février 26, 1696 (*Corresp. de Fénélon*, tom. vii. No. 99.)

§ Fénélon to M. Tronson, *ubi supra*.

of embarrassment, besides those which he openly assigned. He had been wounded to the quick by fresh measures of inexcusable rigour which had been taken against Madame Guyon. That unfortunate person had been arrested for the second time, and was committed prisoner to Vincennes in December 1695. Orders were given to treat her well, but at the same time not to permit her to hold communication with any human being, either personally or by letter. It was soon known that this act of cruelty had been instigated by Bossuet. "It was a thunderstroke," says St. Simon, "for M. de Cambrai and his friends, and for the little flock." Not the slightest intimation had been vouchsafed to any one of them beforehand; and the Archbishop must have felt from that moment that his place in Madame de Maintenon's favour, and his general prospects of worldly prosperity, were dangerously compromised.

Madame Guyon, after her departure from the convent at Meaux, had failed to fulfil the engagements into which she had entered with Bossuet. Instead of proceeding, according to her promise, to a watering-place in the country, she returned clandestinely to Paris, and concealed herself in a lodging in the Rue St. Antoine, deceiving Bossuet as to her place of abode by giving him a false address. She continued to see her friends, to disseminate her doctrines, and to attract fresh proselytes. She was even indiscreet enough to exhibit the certificate of the Bishop of Meaux, as a proof that her orthodoxy was guaranteed by that all-powerful prelate. This provoked Bossuet; and he persuaded Madame de Maintenon, and through her the king, that it was not safe to allow such an accomplished propagandist to remain at liberty. Such was his ascendency at this period, that although Madame de Maintenon, Archbishop de Noailles, and even Louis himself, would have preferred a gentler treatment, his advice prevailed, that she should be immured in a State prison.

Madame Guyon was by no means so tractable on this occasion as before. She was examined repeatedly; but, far from betraying fear or promising submission, she defended herself with remarkable spirit and pertinacity. With a view to induce her to recant, Fénélon was appealed to with increased urgency to condemn her doctrine publicly; but this course, as we have seen, he resolutely rejected. At length, in the hope of being released from confinement, she consented to sign a form of general submission to her diocesan, the Archbishop of Paris. This document was drawn up by Fénélon, and approved by M. Tronson; and the prisoner, after signing it, was transferred from Vincennes to a house at Vaugirard, where she enjoyed comparative comfort. She was, however, strictly watched and guarded.*

The effect of these events was to place Fénélon more and more prominently before the eyes of the world as the patron of an odious sect, and especially as the indulgent apologist of Madame Guyon. The public could not appreciate his over-refined distinctions between condemning her doctrines and attacking her person; between the positive inculcation of error and mere venial slips of hyperbolical language. He had allowed himself to be drawn into an equivocal position; and in spite of all the resources of rhetoric and special pleading, it was inevitable that a certain amount of opprobrium should henceforth attach to his name.

On the other hand, he gained admiration from his contemporaries, and posterity has amply confirmed their verdict, for his generous adherence to a friend whom he believed to be the victim of injustice, even at the risk of personal reputation and worldly success. From this time must be dated his estrangement from Bossuet;—an estrangement which was too soon to be converted into active antagonism.

Fénélon was not content with rejecting the imperious demands of the Bishop of Meaux in a case in which he considered (though perhaps over-scrupulously) that his own honour was at stake. He felt it necessary to put forth, in self-justification, a statement of his views as to the true meaning of the Articles of Issy. Such was his object in undertaking the memorable treatise entitled 'Explication des maximes des saints sur la vie intérieure.' His plan was to arrange, in separate paragraphs, first those canons of mystical theology which had been

---

* "Madame Guyon a souscrit à la condamnation de ses ouvrages, comme contenant une mauvaise doctrine contraire aux articles qu'elle a signés; moyennant cela et la renonciation à son directeur, avec quelques autres choses conformes à sa déclaration faite entre mes mains, on l'a reçue aux sacrements. Il y a un peu de discours dans sa soumission. Elle n'a pas voulu souscrire, que M. Tronson ne l'ait assurée par écrit qu'elle le pouvoit, et qu'elle y étoit obligée. On ne vit jamais tant de présomption et tant d'égarement que cette personne en a fait paroître. Ce qu'il y a de meilleur, c'est qu'elle demeurera enfermée."— Bossuet to M. de la Brouc, Sept. 4, 1696, *Lettres sur l'affaire du Quiétisme*, No. lxx.

accredited as orthodox, and secondly the false deductions, misinterpretations, and abuses which had served to bring Mysticism into suspicion and contempt in modern times.* Nothing could have been better devised, had the subject been one upon which no previous action had been taken by those in authority; but under existing circumstances it only served to provoke dissension in the episcopate, and to make confusion worse confounded. Fénélon's first care was to submit his composition, with unreserved frankness, to the judgment of the Archbishop of Paris (De Noailles) and M. Tronson, as two of the commissioners who had framed the Articles of Issy. The Archbishop scrutinized it throughout, with the assistance of his confidential theologian M. Beaufort; he suggested certain alterations, which were immediately adopted by the author in his presence; and in the end he pronounced the book "correct and useful," adding that Fénélon's only fault in his eyes was that of being "too docile." He recommended, however, that the opinion of some other professed theologian should be taken; and Fénélon accordingly consulted the Abbé Pirot, one of the most eminent doctors of the Sorbonne, and well-known to be a personal friend of Bossuet. That experienced critic, after an attentive perusal, declared that the 'Explication' was "a golden book." †

But the intended publication was kept a profound secret from Bossuet; and this was a fatal mistake. Bossuet had been President of the Commission at Issy. With what propriety could a detailed commentary on the acts of that Commission be published by one who had taken part in them, without previous communication with him? Fénélon pleaded that it was impossible for him to ask Bossuet to sanction his forthcoming work, when he had just refused to approve that prelate's 'Instruction.'

---

* The *Explication des maximes*, having been condemned by the Holy See, is not printed with the rest of Fénélon's works, and has become extremely rare. I have made use of the copy in the British Museum, a small duodecimo, Paris, 1697. The plan is thus described in the *Avertissement*:—"Chaque article aura deux parties. La première sera la vraie que j'approuverai, et qui renfermera tout ce qui est autorisé par l'expérience des saints, et reduit à la doctrine suine du pur amour. La seconde partie sera la fausse, où j'expliquerai l'endroit précis dans lequel le danger de l'illusion commence. En rapportant ainsi dans chaque article ce qui est excessif, je le qualifierai et je le condamnerai dans toute la rigueur théologique." I have in my possession a translation of the *Explication* into villainously bad English, published by "E. and C. Dilly, in the Poultry," MDCCLXXV.

† "Qu'il étoit tout d'or." Fénélon, *Réponse à la Relation*, § lxix.

But the misfortune was, that he should ever have allowed himself to be placed in this invidious position. One false step entails another. Was it wise to separate himself, in a transaction so important, from such distinguished colleagues in the episcopate, to whose judgment he professed the highest possible deference? His excuse was, that the 'Instruction' was a libellous attack on Madame Guyon. But if so, why did he not press the objection to the work at the time he was asked to approve it? We have the assurance of Bossuet himself that, had he done so, anything in the way of reasonable alteration or suppression would have been agreed to in order to give him satisfaction. Was this, again, the sole motive of his refusal? Was there not, besides, an unwillingness, when it came to the point, to join in a positive condemnation of Madame Guyon's *opinions;* although, in private conversation and correspondence, he had often declared that he by no means agreed with them? Had he taken a more consistent course, the way would have been opened, in all probability, for explanations and concessions on the part of those who differed from him, which would have spared the Church the scandal of the melancholy scenes which followed.

As it was, the "eagle of Meaux" naturally resented the attempt to ignore him by re-opening, without his knowledge or consent, a controversy which he regarded as already terminated. Although Fénélon had not informed him of his purpose, he was perfectly well aware of it. "I hear," he writes to the Abbé de Maulevrier,* "that M. de Cambrai is writing on spirituality. I feel sure that this proceeding will cause great scandal; first, because after what he obliged me to say of his refusal to approve my book, he will never be willing to condemn Madame Guyon's writings, and this would be to introduce a new distinction between the 'droit' and the 'fait,' implying that M. de Paris and I condemned that lady without understanding her real meaning. I could not in conscience tolerate this; and shall feel compelled to point out that the books which he seeks to support contain a doctrine subversive of true piety. Secondly, I perceive, from M. de Cambrai's letters and speeches, that he will strive to establish the possibility of perpetual passivity;— an idea leading to illusions which are past endurance. I am

---

* *Lettres sur l'affaire du Quiétisme,* No. lxxxv. (janvier, 1697).

assured that he will leave in doubt and obscurity articles upon which it is indispensably necessary, at the present conjuncture, that he should explain himself. And if this be so, how can I be excused from making known to the whole Church the great danger of such dissimulation? It is clear that, since there has been no mutual concert among us as to what ought to be said, the object is to show that M. de Paris and I were wrong in condemning Madame Guyon; which I would acknowledge without hesitation if it were true. I am reduced to this dilemma; either it is intended to set forth the same doctrine which I have taught, or it is not. If it be the same, the unity of the Church requires that we should come to a previous understanding; if it be different, I am compelled either to write against it, or to abandon the truth."*

The Archbishop of Paris requested Fénélon to abstain from publishing his 'Explication' until the work of Bossuet on the same subject, which had been so long in preparation, should have issued from the press. Fénélon assented; but the Duc de Chevreuse and other friends, in their eagerness to secure for him the advantage of being heard before the attack of his opponent, hurried forward the printing of the book, and it appeared, without Fénélon's knowledge, in January 1697, about a month before Bossuet's 'Instruction.'

It was received with a general clamour of disapprobation. "Scarcely any one except theologians," says St. Simon, "could understand it; and they only after reading it three or four times. It had the misfortune to be praised by no one; and the connoisseurs pronounced it to contain, under a barbarous phraseology, pure Quietism, divested indeed of everything gross and offensive, but obvious at first sight; together with various subtleties quite novel, and extremely difficult both to comprehend and to practise. I am not giving my own judgment upon what is so far beyond me, but relating the universal sentiment expressed at the time; and nothing else was then talked of, even among the ladies; *à propos* to which people repeated Madame de Sevigné's

---

* "M'étoit-il défendu d'expliquer les articles sans la permission de M. de Meaux? Ne suffisoit-il pas que je les expliquasse bien? Si mon explication paroissoit mauvaise, il falloit s'en plaindre au Pape, à qui je me soumettois, et après avoir fait les objections en secret, il n'y avoit qu'à attendre la réponse du supérieur. Mais, indépendamment de cette réponse, on vouloit décider et prévaloir."—Fénélon, MS. note to the *Relation*, p. 7.

witticism in the heat of the disputes upon grace,—'I wish religion could be made a little thicker; for it seems in the way to evaporate altogether by dint of being subtilized.'* The book offended everybody; the ignorant, because they understood nothing about it; the rest, from the difficulty of comprehending and following the line of argument, especially in a barbarous and unknown dialect; the prelates opposed to the author, on account of the magisterial air assumed in distinguishing the true from the false maxims, and by reason of the errors which they detected in those which were pronounced to be sound."†

Bossuet, in his 'Relation sur le Quiétisme,' paints in vivid colours the scene of excitement that prevailed. "The city, the Court, the Sorbonne, the religious communities, the learned, the ignorant, men, women, all classes without exception, were indignant, not at the affair itself, which few were acquainted with, and which none understood thoroughly, but at the audacity of such an ambitious decision, at the over-refinements of expression, at the unheard-of novelties, at the entire uselessness and ambiguity of the doctrine. Then it was that the public outcry reached the sacred ears of the king, and he learned what we had so sedulously concealed from him;‡ he learned, from a hundred mouths, that Madame Guyon had found a defender at his Court, in his palace, and near the persons of the princes his children; with how much displeasure, may be estimated from the piety and wisdom of that great monarch. We spoke the last; every one knows that we were met with just reproaches from so good a master, for not having sooner disclosed to him what we knew."§

Great, indeed, must have been the amazement and indignation of Louis, when a prelate like Bossuet, in whom he placed unbounded confidence as the veteran and invincible champion

---

* This is one of the many bons mots which are almost untranslatable: "Épaississez-moi un peu la religion; qui s'évaporo toute à force d'être subtilisée."

† *Mémoires de St. Simon*, tom. i. chap. xxvii. (ed. Paris, 1856).

‡ The Chancellor Pontchartrain, it appears, was the first to inform Louis of the scandal occasioned by Fénélon's book (Bausset, *Hist. de Bossuet*, tom. iii. p. 286).

§ Bossuet, *Relation*, § vi. p. 4. Bossuet's account of the agitation on this occasion has been taxed with exaggeration. It is fully corroborated, however, by a letter addressed to Fénélon by the Abbé de Brisacier, one of his warmest friends, who could have no possible object in representing things more unfavourably than truth required. See *Correspondance de Fénélon*, No. 173, tom. vii. p. 379.

of orthodoxy in France, threw himself at his feet, and implored pardon for having hitherto concealed from his sovereign the "fanaticism" of his unhappy brother. Hating, as he did, sects, controversies, intrigues, and religious novelties of all kinds, the idea that he had unwittingly entrusted the education of his grandchildren and the government of a vast diocese to one who might prove to be a second Molinos, was unspeakably abhorrent to his mind. He had always disliked Fénélon,[*] the loftier qualities of whose character he was incompetent to appreciate, though he had sufficient sagacity to discern its weaknesses; and this announcement doubtless convinced him that such a man could no longer safely discharge the office of Preceptor to the princes.

Fénélon complains, in the 'Réponse à la Relation,' that Bossuet made no attempt, at this crisis of his fortunes, to soften and dispel the royal apprehensions. A word from him, he says, would have sufficed for this purpose; but he refused to utter it. Had he stated that the 'Explication des maximes' was about to be revised a second time, by enlightened prelates and divines, and that they fully hoped to come to an understanding with the author, and persuade him to retract the ill-advised language and objectionable sentiments which had justly alarmed the Church, the king would have been pacified, the mouths of scandal-mongers stopped, and concord in the end restored. Bossuet, certainly, made no such representations to the throne. Under the keen feelings of irritation which Fénélon's conduct had provoked, it was not natural that he should do so; and we may presume, moreover, that he did not deem it consistent with his duty.

It was at once resolved to make every possible exertion to induce the Archbishop of Cambrai to retract his errors. But the means chosen for this purpose were such as had little chance of success. Bossuet proposed, at first, to communicate to Fénélon privately, in writing, his remarks upon his book, and that they should afterwards examine them together, in company with the Archbishop of Paris, M. Tronson, and M. Pirot, with a view to mutual explanation and satisfaction. But Fénélon

---

[*] D'Aguesseau, "Mém. sur les aff. de l'Égl. de France" (*Œuvres*, tom. xiii. p. 171).

declined to meet Bossuet for this purpose. He was reduced, he said, to the painful necessity of no longer treating with him personally, in consequence of his unfriendly behaviour for several years past.* This widened the breach between them; and Bossuet, abandoning the hope of arriving at a pacific solution, felt himself forced into an attitude of open hostility. The result was that Fénélon, instead of excluding his opponent, was himself excluded from the proceedings instituted for the consideration and correction of his work. Bossuet withheld his promised "remarks" from month to month; and, meanwhile, arrangements were made for a series of conferences at the archiepiscopal palace in Paris, between the Archbishop, the Bishop of Meaux, the Bishop of Chartres, M. de Beaufort, and the Abbé Pirot; and here the 'Explication des maximes' was dissected with unsparing rigour, all leanings towards a more indulgent treatment being overruled by the commanding authority of Bossuet.†

The general impressions under which Bossuet entered upon this investigation may be gathered from the following extract from a letter to his nephew, the Abbé Bossuet, dated March 24, 1697:—"The book is indefensible and abandoned. The Jesuits, who at first supported it, now only talk of the best means of correcting it; and those which have been proposed hitherto are but feeble. Father La Chaise has told the king that one of their fathers, said to be a great theologian, has discovered in it forty-three propositions requiring emendation. There are in this book several statements directly contrary to the Thirty-four Articles which the author has signed; among others, to the 8th and the 11th. The doctrine which pervades the book as to indifference to salvation, and the involuntary distress of the inferior nature in Jesus Christ,‡ is erroneous and full of ignorance. The absolute sacrifice of salvation, and positive

---

* Fénélon to the Archbishop of Paris, June 8, 1697 (*Corresp. de Fénélon*, tom. vii. p. 442).

† "M. de Paris craint M. de Cambrai, et me craint également. Je le contrains; car sans moi tout iroit à l'abandon, et M. de Cambrai l'emporteroit . . . M. de Paris et de Chartres sont foibles, et n'agiront qu'autant qu'ils seront poussés."—Bossuet to his nephew, June 10, 1697 (*Œuvres*, tom.

xviii. p. 562).

‡ This refers to a passage in the book which Fénélon always declared to have been interpolated by the editors, and which he never acknowledged as authentic. It is the thirteenth in the list of propositions afterwards condemned by the Pope:—"La partie inférieure de Jésus-Christ sur la croix ne communiquoit pas à la supérieure son trouble involontaire."

acquiescence in perdition and damnation, is manifestly impious, and censured by the 31st Article subscribed by the author. A species of love which in one place is termed impious and sacrilegious, is described in another as a preparation towards justification. You will find, about page 97, the pure essence of Quietism; that is to say, the notion of waiting indolently for grace, under the pretext that it must not be anticipated.* Many passages cited as from St. François de Sales are either not to be found in the writings of that saint, or are wrested from their meaning, or even manifestly garbled. The primary definitions upon which the system turns are false and erroneous. The Advertisement, and the whole style of the work, seem unspeakably arrogant; and such is the over-refinement from beginning to end, that most persons cannot understand it at all. After reading it, nothing remains except the pain of finding religion reduced to mere phrases, subtleties, and abstractions. I write all this with grief, on account of the scandal which falls on the Church, and the dire disgrace which threatens one in whom I had hoped to find the most valued of my friends, and whom I still love sincerely. I am not at liberty to keep silence after what he says in his Advertisement—that his object is to expound the doctrine which M. de Paris and I established in the Thirty-four Articles.† We should be prevaricators were we to hold our peace, and the doctrine of the new book would be imputed to us. For the rest, he has assured the king and all the world that he means to be as docile as a child, and that he is ready to retract forthwith, if it can be shown that he has fallen into error. We shall put him to the proof; for it is with himself that we intend to commence. I will only add that the work of this prelate abounds with contradictions, and that the true and the false are mingled together throughout."‡

---

* At p. 97 of the *Explication* we read as follows:—"L'âme, pour être pleinement fidèle à Dieu, ne peut rien faire de solide ni de méritoire que de suivre sans cesse la grâce, sans avoir besoin de la prévenir. Vouloir la prévenir, c'est vouloir se donner ce qu'elle ne donne pas encore; c'est attendre quelque chose de soi-même et de son industrie, ou de son propre effort."

† "C'est pour dénicher le vrai d'avec le faux dans une matière si délicate et si importante, que deux grands prélats ont donné au public trente-quatre propositions qui contiennent en substance toute la doctrine des voies intérieures; et je ne prétends dans cet ouvrage qu'en expliquer les principes avec plus d'étendue."—'Avertissement' to the *Explication*.

‡ "Lettres sur l'affaire du Quiétisme." No. ci. (*Œuvres de Bossuet*, tom. xviii.).

In subsequent letters he thus relates the progress of the examination :—" We have continued our conferences—M. de Paris, M. de Chartres, and myself—and have fixed upon the propositions which we consider to deserve censure, and which are somewhat numerous; intending to send them at the earliest moment to M. de Cambrai, together with the precise grounds on which we object to them. We shall afterwards do whatever may be requisite, in the spirit of charity, for the defence of the truth. The good intentions of M. de Cambrai being well known to us, we cannot doubt that he will explain himself to the satisfaction of the Church ; and it would be deeply painful to us to be compelled to forward information to Rome in denouncement of errors which tend to the subversion of religion."* Shortly afterwards he writes, "As to the affair of M. de Cambrai, there is no further need to make a mystery of it. He has thought fit to write to the Pope on the subject; and he has done rightly, if he has written with all due submission and sincerity. But, since we have reason to fear that he may equivocate, and are convinced that we ought not to allow his book to circulate, we feel ourselves obliged to inform the Pope of the importance of the case, and of the motives which induce us to communicate our views to his Holiness. We see that M. de Cambrai persists in defending Madame Guyon, whom we believe to be a Molinosist, and whose books we cannot permit to remain unsuppressed without endangering the whole of religion. We have exercised all possible patience, and have made every effort to terminate the affair by methods of charity ; but, since we are driven to Rome, it will be necessary to speak out in spite of ourselves, and to show that we are by no means disposed to spare a colleague who has put religion and truth in jeopardy."†

Fénélon had, indeed, taken the bold step of appealing to Rome for a judgment on his book, which, as he thought, had no chance of being fairly dealt with in France. He was not disposed to accept the extra-judicial arbitration of three prelates, however eminent, to whom he owed no canonical obedience, and whose verdict, moreover, he looked upon as a foregone conclusion. For, although the Archbishop of Paris and the Bishop

---

* Bossuet to his nephew, April 29, 1697. No. cxiii.
† Bossuet to his nephew, May 6, 1697, Lettre cxiv.

of Chartres showed an inclination from time to time to relent in his favour, such symptoms were always peremptorily repressed by Bossuet, who was now stern and almost rancorous in his determination to coerce him into submission. He resolved, therefore, to anticipate their sentence by demanding the interposition of the Apostolic See. His letter to the Pope for this purpose is dated April 27, 1697.*

He explains to the Holy Father the reasons which had led him to write on the inward life and contemplation. There were those, he says, who had abused the approved maxims of the saints by attempting to introduce pernicious errors, which the ignorant and worldly turned into derision. The doctrines of Quietism had been favoured, unconsciously, by many mystical writers of sincere piety and the best intentions, from want of caution in their terminology, and from pardonable ignorance of theological science. It was this which had impelled two illustrious prelates to promulgate the Articles of Issy, as also to condemn certain little books,† some passages of which, taken in their obvious sense, deserved censure. But, as men are for ever falling from one extreme into another, this proceeding had been made a pretext for decrying, as chimerical and extravagant, the pure love of the contemplative life. Hence he felt called upon to do what in him lay towards fixing the boundaries between the true and the false, between the ancient and safe and the novel and dangerous. He then sketches in outline the contents of his book. "I have condemned," he says, "the 'permanent act' of the Quietists, showing that it engenders spiritual indolence and lethargy. I have asserted the indispensable necessity of the distinct exercise of every virtue. I reject that doctrine of passive prayer which excludes the co-operation of free-will in meritorious actions. I disallow all 'quietude' except that inward peace through which the acts of the soul are performed 'in such a way as to appear to simple persons not distinct acts, but an abiding condition of union with God.' I maintain that, in all grades of perfection, the Christian grace of hope must be cultivated as essential to salvation; that we must hope for, desire, and seek, salvation, and that as a personal boon and

---

* *Corresp. de Fénélon*, No. 192, tom. vii. p. 407. It is also given at length in the *Mémoires du Clergé*, tom. i. p. 389.
† *I. e.* those of Madame Guyon, the *Moyen court*, &c.

blessing, inasmuch as God wills it, and commands that we should will it as tending to His glory.* Lastly, I have taught that this state of pure and perfect love is very rarely attained; and that, though habitual, it is subject to interruption and fluctuation. It is not inconsistent with daily sins of infirmity, nor with acts which, although good, are in a lower degree pure and disinterested."

Such, according to the testimony of the author himself, are the salient points of this celebrated brochure. In a memorial to the Nuncio at Paris, Fénélon protested that his object throughout had been to conform to the Articles of Issy; that he believed *ex animo* the doctrine there enunciated; and that he was ready to prove before the Holy Father that he had never in any instance contradicted them. "As I hope," he says in the same document, "to obtain the king's permission to make a journey to Rome, which is necessary for my peace of conscience and for the honour of my ministry, I promise to submit with entire docility and without reserve to the decision of his Holiness, after he has condescended to hear me. God is witness that I have no prepossession in favour of any suspected book or suspected person. God, who searches the heart, knows that I have never held any belief beyond what is expressed in my book. I condemn and detest any interpretations of an impious or deceptive tendency which may have been assigned, without just reason, to this work. I am ready to condemn whatever doctrine and whatever writing his Holiness may think fit to condemn. If he should judge it necessary to condemn my book, I shall be the first to assent to its condemnation, to prohibit it in the diocese of Cambrai, and to publish a mandement embodying his censure."†

It is, nevertheless, incontestable that there are discrepancies which cannot easily be reconciled between the 'Explication des maximes' and the Articles of Issy. Not to mention other instances, the 'Explication' teaches that under certain circumstances the soul may carry self-sacrifice to such an extreme as

---

* Acts of hope are, in Fénélon's system, accompanied by, and as it were absorbed in, charity. It is charity that animates and inspires them; so that the perfect Christian exercises hope and all other virtues with that very disinterestedness which is the specific characteristic of charity itself. See his letter "A un ami," Aug. 3, 1697 (*Œuvres de Fénélon*, tom. v. p. 368).

† "Fénélon au Nonce du Pape," July, 1697 (*Corresp.* tom. vii. p. 520).

to abandon the desire of salvation,* and to acquiesce in its own eternal perdition, if such should be the Divine will. Whereas the Articles declare, on the contrary, that all Christians, in whatever condition, are bound to desire and seek eternal life as a direct object; that indifference to salvation, under whatever circumstances, is inadmissible; that souls under corrective suffering are not permitted to acquiesce in feelings of despair and the prospect of perdition.† Fénélon, it is true, acknowledges that the happiness of heaven is the object of desire to the perfect Christian; but he draws a distinction between the formal *object* and the actuating *motive*. Salvation, he says, is to be desired, not as a personal boon, not as our own deliverance from eternal misery, not as the reward of our merits, not as the greatest of all our interests, but because it conduces to the glory of God—because He wills it, and requires us to will it for His sake. The key to his system lies in the definition of the term self-interest. He seems to have meant by it the natural principle of self-love, or selfishness, which, without being positively vicious, is mercenary, and belongs to the "old Adam."

But it was argued on the opposite side, that this theory of disinterestedness destroys the exercise of Christian hope;—a grace which can hardly be conceived to exist independently of the motive of eternal beatitude. The Apostle says, "We are saved by hope;" now hope implies of necessity some admixture of self-interest; so that, if the pursuit of heaven is to be separated from any such consideration, it would follow that one of the three great "theological virtues" must be eliminated from the character and condition of the perfect Christian. This was, in fact, the capital error charged against Fénélon's teaching both by Bossuet ‡ and by the Bishop of Chartres. The "Pastoral Letter" of the latter prelate exposes the fallacies into which he had fallen on this subject perhaps more forcibly than anything that appeared in the course of the controversy.§

* "Dans ce trouble invincible, dans cette impression involontaire de désespoir, elle fait le sacrifice absolu de son intérêt propre pour l'éternité."—*Explication*, Article x. p. 90.
† See Articles v. ix. xxxi.
‡ See his "Réponse à quatre lettres de M. de Cambrai" (*Œuvres*, tom. xiv. p. 699).
§ This document is printed in the seventh vol. of Fénélon's works, p. 113 (edit. Versailles, 1821). See also the same bishop's letter to Fénélon (*Corresp.*, tom. vii. p. 419), in which he says:—"Ne prétendez plus justifier un livre qui, depuis le commencement jusqu'à la fin, exclut tout motif d'espérance du troisième état des justes, sans parler des autres erreurs qu'on y voit."

It was soon significantly intimated to the author of the 'Explication des maximes,' that, whatever might be the issue of his appeal to the Pope, he was already condemned by Louis XIV. He had written to the king to request that he might be permitted to proceed to Rome to defend himself in person; promising to see no one but the Pope and those whom he might appoint to conduct the examination, to live in perfect privacy, and to return immediately after the conclusion of the affair. His Majesty, in his reply, dated August 1, 1697, rejected his petition; and moreover, ordered him to quit Versailles immediately, to repair to his diocese, and not to leave it without permission. Fénélon obeyed the mandate; but was so distressed by its suddenness and severity that he fell ill before reaching Cambrai. Resolved, however, that his cause should not suffer at Rome for want of a well-qualified advocate, he lost no time in sending thither the Abbé de Chanterac, Archdeacon of Cambrai, his relation and intimate friend; one whose wisdom, learning, and virtue fully entitled him to such a mark of confidence. Bossuet, on his part, was already provided with a representative at the Papal Court, in his nephew the Abbé Bossuet;—a person whose savage animosity against Fénélon, and neglect of the ordinary rules of self-restraint, added tenfold bitterness to this deplorable strife. He was seconded by the Abbé Phélipeaux, canon and grand-vicar of Meaux; who drew up a complete account of the controversy, leaving an injunction in his will that it should not be published till twenty years after his decease.*

There is no apparent ground to doubt (though the contrary has been maintained) that the two principals in this theological duel were governed by motives equally conscientious, equally worthy of their position and profession. Both were alike convinced that they were defending truths of the profoundest moment, and forwarding the best interests of Christianity. "This is no question of personal honour," says Fénélon,† "nor of the opinion of the world, nor of the pain which must naturally follow from the humiliation of defeat. I believe that I am acting with sincerity; I am as much afraid of being presump-

---

* Phélipeaux's book, entitled *Relation de l'origine, du progrès, et de la condamnation du Quiétisme répandu en France, avec plusieurs Anecdotes curieuses*, was published, without the name of author or place, in 1732.

† L'Archevêque de Cambrai à un ami (the Duc de Beauvilliers), 3 août, 1697 (*Œuvres de Bossuet*, tom. xviii. p. 583).

tuous, as I am of being feeble, time-serving, and timid in the defence of truth. If the Pope condemns me, I shall be undeceived, and by that means the vanquished will reap all the real advantages of victory. If, on the other hand, my doctrine is not condemned, I shall endeavour, by respectful silence, to appease those of my colleagues whose zeal has been roused against me, and who have imputed to me a doctrine which I hold in no less horror than themselves. Perhaps they will be induced to do me justice, when they witness my good faith. . . . Let us not regard the purposes of men, nor their proceedings; let us see nothing in all this but God alone. Let us be children of peace, and peace will abide with us; it may be bitter, but it will be all the more pure. Let us not mar the uprightness of our intentions by perverseness, by passion, by worldly machinations, by natural eagerness to justify ourselves. Let us simply establish our good faith; let us allow ourselves to be corrected, if it be necessary; and let us endure correction, even if we deserve it not." * .

Nor would it be less unjust to attribute to the high-souled Bossuet the petty vice of jealousy towards a rival star which was supposed to threaten his own supremacy in the ecclesiastical hemisphere. He was incapable of such weakness. Standing, as he did, on the highest pinnacle of professional fame—crowned with the well-earned laurels of a life of conflict—secure of the confidence of his sovereign—the undisputed dictator of religious policy in France—he had nothing left to desire in the way of external honour and pre-eminence. His appreciation of Fénélon's powers was always frank and generous; he acknowledged without hesitation that he possessed genius superior to his own. "As for those," he says, "who cannot believe that zeal in the defence of truth may be pure and without thought of temporal interest, or that it is sufficiently attractive to be the sole motive

---

* Madame de Maintenon writes thus to Archbishop de Noailles as to Fénélon's views in this affair:—"Quant au retour de M. de Cambrai, il n'y a que Dieu qui puisse le faire. Et je suis persuadée que vous ne le croyez pas aussi imbu de ces maximes-là qu'il l'est en effet. Son cœur en est rempli; et il croit soutenir la religion en esprit et en vérité. S'il n'étoit pas trompé, il pourroit revenir par des raisons d'intérêt. Je le crois prévenu de bonne foi. Il n'y a donc plus d'espérance. J'ai tant de connaissance de cette affaire, et depuis si longtemps, que j'en parle plus hardiment que je ne ferois de toute autre."—July 13, 1697. *Lettres et Mémoires de Madame de Maintenon*, tom. x. p. 86.

of exertion, let us not be angry with them. Let us not suppose that they judge us with predetermined malice; and after all, as St. Augustine says, let us cease to be surprised if they impute to human beings the imperfections of humanity."* Again;— "I have no quarrel with M. de Cambrai, except that which exists between him and all the bishops, and the whole Church, on account of his mistaken doctrine. I beg therefore that you will call the attention of the Cardinal † to the injustice which he would do me by representing this affair as if it were at all personal to myself. You may tell him that I have not, and never have had, any private dissension with the Archbishop of Cambrai, to whom I have at all times shown every sort of kindness—a fact of which all the world, and the king himself, are witnesses." "M. de Cambrai," he writes to the same correspondent, "continues to publish everywhere that it is I, and I alone, who am stirring up the cabal against him. The only cabal that I have engaged in consists in having striven to detach him from the obstinacy of Madame Guyon—in which I only seconded the efforts of Madame de Maintenon, to whose patronage he owes everything;—and in having concealed his errors from the king, in the hope that he might be induced to retract them. The king reproved me, and with too much reason, for having caused, through my reticence on this painful topic, his promotion to the Archbishopric of Cambrai. This is the whole extent of my offences against him; this is all my cabal."‡

Bossuet expressed from the first his confidence that Fénélon's book would be condemned. He believed in the justice of his cause, and in the force of truth; but, in addition to this, he was secretly acquainted with the purpose of his royal master, and knew that he was prepared to exercise any amount of pressure upon the oracle of the Vatican, in order to extort the response which he desired. Louis had already written an autograph letter to the Pope,§ in which he described the 'Explication' as having incurred grave censure from Gallican prelates and divines, and intimated, in terms not to be mistaken, that he should not be satisfied unless their judgment were confirmed by

---

* "Préface sur l'Instruction pastorale de M. de Cambrai" (Œuvres, tom. xiv. p. 671).

† Cardinal de Bouillon, French ambassador at Rome.

‡ Bossuet to his nephew, September 16, 1697 (Œuvres, tom. xviii. p. 602).

§ This is printed in Bossuet's "Correspondence" (Œuvres, tom. xviii. p 575).

that of the Holy See. The "Declaration" of the three prelates * was, by his order, made public at the same moment, and delivered to the Nuncio for transmission to Rome. This was a clear and powerful statement of the whole case as viewed by the adversaries of Fénélon; summing up his errors in the two comprehensive charges of disparaging the virtue of Christian hope, and of pressing the duty of self-abnegation to the extreme of indifference to salvation. It was a counter-appeal to the arbitration of the Apostolic See; which was thus spontaneously invoked by both parties, and that in a cause which, according to strict Gallican principles, ought to have been decided within the jurisdiction of the home episcopate. The inconsistency was pointed out to Bossuet; who replied that, since Fénélon had been the first to seek the decision of the Pope, a corresponding step on his part was inevitable; and that it would have been far more imprudent to hazard the discussion of such a theme in a provincial Synod, or an Assembly of the clergy, which, from the multiplicity of private interests and passions, might have proved unmanageable. At all events the worst course that could be taken would be that of abandoning the defence of the truth on account of the uncertainty of success. What could be said for the zeal and courage of bishops, if it should fail them in such an emergency? Moreover, there was every reason to believe that the sentence on the book would be one of condemnation.†

Unforeseen difficulties, however, for a time obstructed and retarded this result. Fénélon found friends among the Jesuits. He had never been connected with them previously; so far from it that in his earlier years he was suspected of sympathizing with the Jansenists, and was twice excluded from promotion on that account. The 'Explication des maximes,' however, was zealously supported by some of the most eminent Jesuits, including Fathers La Chaise ‡ and de Valois; and (so far as they dared) the Order intrigued at Rome to procure the acquittal of the author. His cause was also energetically advo-

---

* *Œuvres de Bossuet*, tom. xiv. p. 411. It is dated August 6, 1697.

† Bausset, *Hist. de Bossuet*, tom. iii. p. 307.

‡ Madame de Maintenon to Archbishop de Noailles, April 3, 1697

(*Lettres et Mémoires de Madame de Maintenon*, tom. x. p. 75). La Chaise, however, changed his opinion afterwards, and followed the stream in condemnation of Fénélon.

cated by Cardinal de Bouillon, who had just succeeded Cardinal Forbin Janson as French Chargé d'Affaires at the Pontifical court. De Bouillon was a vain, pretentious, arrogant man, who had made himself ridiculous by affecting the style and privileges of a sovereign prince, and was in consequence no favourite with Louis XIV. The Dukes of Beauvilliers and Chevreuse had obtained for him the appointment at Rome; and in acknowledgment of the obligation, he engaged to employ all the influence of his office in furthering the interests of their friend the Archbishop of Cambrai. His private feelings impelled him in the same direction. Between the houses of De Noailles and De Bouillon there was an ancient grudge, which the Cardinal would very gladly have indulged by disconcerting and discomfiting the Archbishop of Paris. Bossuet was obnoxious to him by the dazzling lustre of his genius, and the oppressive ascendency which he exercised in Church and State. He was jealous, again, of the growing credit of the Bishop of Chartres, and his confidential relations with Madame de Maintenon. And finally, he was a devoted partisan of the Jesuits. All these considerations concurred to strengthen his resolution to support Fénélon, though he had little or no real acquaintance with the merits of the question in dispute.

On the whole, then, there appeared some prospect that the book might, after all, escape condemnation. Despite the pressing instances of Louis, the examination was conducted with all the deliberate tediousness prescribed by Roman usage. Sixty-four sessions, of several hours each, were held between October, 1697, and September, 1698; but little progress was made towards a decision. The examiners were the "Consultors" of the Holy Office, ten in number; and five of these uniformly declared in Fénélon's favour.* The Pope, perplexed by this division of sentiment, and unwilling to condemn a prelate whose virtues and talents were the theme of universal admiration, referred the case to the Congregation of Cardinals of the Inquisition; and fresh debates commenced, which were continued with the utmost assiduity during many months.

---

* Two of them, Rodolovic, Archbishop of Chieti, and Gabrieli, Superior-General of the Bernardines, were shortly afterwards created cardinals.

These delays irritated the king and the whole party opposed to Fénélon. Bossuet, during this tantalizing interval, betrayed his impatience by pouring forth, with feverish impetuosity, a multitude of controversial treatises, which were all marked by his accustomed power of thought and language, but which, to his infinite mortification, were invariably met with equal acuteness, and sometimes with superior felicity of argument, by his accomplished antagonist. The warfare not only arrested the attention of the learned, but excited intense interest among all classes of society in France, and even abroad. On Bossuet's side the chief publications were his 'Summary of the Doctrine of the Explication,' which appeared in Latin and French, and was laid before the examiners at Rome; his 'Préface sur l'Instruction pastorale de M. de Cambrai;' three tracts in Latin, entitled 'Mystici in tuto,' 'Schola in tuto,' and 'Quietismus Redivivus;' and lastly, the famous 'Relation sur le Quiétisme,' perhaps the ablest of his productions in this conflict, but withal characterized by an amount of personal acrimony and invective which cannot be defended. Fénélon replied to these attacks with astonishing rapidity. Every shaft from the enemy's lines called forth a swift and incisive missile in*return; 'Letters in Answer to the Bishop of Meaux,' 'Letters to Archbishop de Noailles,' criticisms on the Pastoral of the Bishop of Chartres, and, above all, the 'Réponse à la Relation sur le Quiétisme,' with the 'Réponse aux Remarques de l'Évêque de Meaux;'— a series of productions which carried the fame of Fénélon as a master of polemical science to the highest point.

These last-mentioned efforts belong to the final stage of the contest, when, through the lengthened procrastinations of the court of Rome, a grievously embittered state of feeling had set in on both sides. Bossuet's party were provoked by the difficulties which impeded, and threatened to frustrate, their design. They felt that it was necessary to strike a crushing blow, in order to convince the Pope and the Cardinals that, although Fénélon might still possess some few enthusiastic partisans, his disgrace in a political sense at Versailles was irrevocable. For this purpose it was at one time in contemplation to remove the excellent Duc de Beauvilliers from his place at court and at the Council-board; but, before taking such a serious step, the king fortunately consulted Archbishop de

Noailles; and that prelate, highly to his honour, represented matters in such a light as to induce him to abandon the idea.* The duke's services, therefore, were retained; but several functionaries of a lower rank were abruptly dismissed from office, solely because they were relatives or friends of Fénélon, and supposed to sympathize in his opinions. These were the Abbé de Beaumont, Fénélon's nephew, sub-preceptor to the princes; the Abbé de Langeron, reader; and Dupuis and L'Échelle, gentlemen of the chamber to the Duke of Burgundy. This malignant spite was even carried so far as to strip Fénélon's brother of the petty appointment of an exempt of the "garde du corps." †

The action of Bossuet was of a severer kind. He extracted twelve propositions from Fénélon's work, and caused them to be presented in an irregular way, by personal solicitation, to the doctors of the Sorbonne, accompanied by a form of censure which they were requested to subscribe. Sixty signatures were thus obtained from compliant members of the Faculty; and the document was immediately despatched to Rome, as a proof that theological opinion in France was decidedly adverse to the doctrine in question. It was not an official corporate act of the Sorbonne, but simply of the three-score individual doctors who were induced to sign it; such as it was, however, it made the designed impression upon the minds of many in authority at the Papal court. The censure was drawn up by M. Pirot, the same divine who, on a former occasion, had described the 'Explication' as worthy of the warmest consideration.‡

These angry impulses, again, prompted Bossuet to publish two letters addressed to him, under the seal of confidential friendship, by De Rancé Abbot of La Trappe, in which the work of the Archbishop of Cambrai, and the sect with which he was supposed to be in alliance, were denounced in terms of unmeasured indignation. "If the dreams of these fanatics are to be received," said De Rancé, "it will be necessary to close

---

* D'Aguesseau, "Mém. sur les aff. de l'Égl. de France" (Œuvres, tom. xiii. p. 174). Had Beauvilliers been displaced, it was the king's intention to give the reversion of his honours to the Marshal Duc de Noailles, brother of the archbishop.

† St. Simon, Mémoires, chap. xxxv.

tom. i. p. 350.

‡ It is entitled "Animadversio plurium Doctorum è Facultate theologiæ Parisiensis in diversas propositiones excerptas à libro cui titulus Explication des maximes des saints," &c. See Œuvres de Bossuet, tom. xix. p. 195.

the volume of Holy Scripture; to set aside the Gospel, with all its sacred and essential precepts, as if they were practically useless; and even to count for nothing the life and example of Jesus Christ, all adorable as it is. This is a consummate piece of impiety, veiled under a strange and affected phraseology, devised for no other purpose than the deception and seduction of souls."* Bossuet showed this, with other letters, to Madame de Maintenon, who agreed with him that it would be desirable to make them public. This was done accordingly, without previous reference to De Rancé for his consent; and copies were circulated far and wide, much to the injury of Fénélon in the minds of those who, while incapable of forming a judgment personally, knew how to appreciate that of so celebrated an authority as the Abbot of La Trappe. The abbot himself was infinitely annoyed by this unwarrantable breach of propriety.†

Meanwhile the persecution of Madame Guyon was revived; for it was hoped that, by raking up fresh suspicion against her character and proceedings, some portion of the scandal might recoil indirectly upon Fénélon. Every vestige of her former influence had been eradicated from St. Cyr. A rigorous search was made for her letters and other manuscripts, every fragment of which was removed from the convent. To make assurance doubly sure, the king expelled three of the sisters who showed a disposition to resist these measures of arbitrary repression, and ordered that they should never, under any circumstances, be permitted to return.‡ Among them was Madame de la Maisonfort, who, on quitting St. Cyr, placed herself under the direction of Bossuet at Meaux; retaining, nevertheless, her warm admiration and veneration of Fénélon, the loss of whose instructions she never ceased to lament.

Immediately afterwards (September, 1698) Madame Guyon was transferred from Vaugirard to the Bastille; and it was given out that revelations had been made by Father Lacombe, then a prisoner at Vincennes, the effect of which was to cast a dark shade upon the nature of their past relations. Lacombe, whose intellect had never been robust, was at this time in a

---

* M. de Rancé à Bossuet, 14 avril, 1697 (*Œuvres de Bossuet*, tom. xviii. p. 546).
† *Mémoires de St. Simon*, chap. xxxv.
tom. i. p. 354.
‡ August 7, 1698. De Noailles, *Hist. de Madame de Maintenon*, tom. iii. p. 244.

state of pitiable fatuity; and it was preposterous in the extreme to attach any serious import to allegations obtained under such circumstances. Nevertheless it is unhappily certain that an attempt was made by the Abbé Bossuet and others at Rome, under colour of these extorted confessions, to insinuate that the connection between Fénélon and Madame Guyon had not been altogether innocent.* Fénélon's first impulse was to treat the calumny with silent contempt; but, on the appearance of Bossuet's 'Relation sur le Quiétisme,' which contained mysterious allusions pointing in the same direction, his friends, especially Cardinal de Bouillon and the Abbé de Chanterac, represented to him that an equally public refutation of the falsehood was indispensable;† and it was now that he wrote his celebrated Apology, the 'Réponse à la Relation.' If Bossuet's attack had raised a ferment in the popular mind, the archbishop's defence produced a still more extraordinary sensation. The reaction of feeling was electrical. The public voice proclaimed that his justification on the score of morals was complete and triumphant; and, moreover, a strong presumption arose in favour of the orthodoxy of his opinions; since it was argued that his enemies would never have resorted to the disgraceful expedient of personal slander, had they not felt that the charge of heretical doctrine was likely to prove untenable. "We have already given away more than forty copies of the 'Réponse,'" writes the Abbé de Chanterac, "and numbers of people are still demanding it with incredible eagerness. The uproar is terrible; all Rome resounds with it. What comforts me the most is to witness the joy both of private friends and of the public at the entire recognition of your innocence. One of the most learned bishops here said to me, and has said pretty strongly to others, that nothing more could be desired for your justification, and that you have crushed M. de Meaux to powder."‡ "Never

---

* "Je lui fis remarquer que ce n'étoit point en vain que nos partis remplissoient le monde de ces déclarations du Père Lacombe, et de l'aveu qu'il faisoit de ses crimes et de ceux de Madame Guyon, ensuite de votre société particulière avec elle; qu'ils vouloient insinuer par là que votre livre défendoit ingeniosissimis verbis, comme dit M. de Meaux, les maximes de cette femme, et que, de ses maximes, ils passoient à ses mœurs. Il convint que c'étoit leur pensée." (The Abbé de Chanterac to Fénélon, July 19, 1698.) The third person of whom he speaks was Cardinal Casanate.

† *Corresp. de Fénélon.* tom. ix. pp. 124, 198, 240, 245, 251, 267.

‡ Abbé de Chanterac to Fénélon, Aug. 30, 1698 (*Corresp.*, tom. ix. p. 393).

did an apology meet with such general approbation. It is not only its simple unaffected elegance that is admired, but, still more, its force, its gentleness, its persuasive air of truthfulness, which convinces, and which effaces altogether the disagreeable impressions produced by the 'Relation' of M. de Meaux. The Archbishop's innocence seems to fill the public with universal joy. The Abbé Bossuet is so amazed by it, that he urgently solicited an audience of the Pope, and besought him with extreme earnestness to defer giving judgment in the affair until his uncle should be able to answer the 'Reply' of M. de Cambrai. His party no longer speak with the same pride and confidence which they displayed after the 'Relation.' Their present cue is to say that the history of the facts has nothing to do with the points of doctrine; yet it is clear enough that their great object was to confound the two together, while, on the contrary, it is M. de Cambrai's interest to keep them separate."*
"A prelate of this court, famous for his learning, and high in the esteem and confidence of several cardinals, to whom I presented a copy of your 'Réponse,' told me that it has wrought a great change in the minds of many; that the last time he saw me, he feared that the affair would end unfavourably, because he had heard certain cardinals express their apprehension that your book would be treated as an apology for Madame Guyon; but that, at present, all is going in the right direction."†

Fénélon and his friends were inspirited by this apparent change of fortune; and upon the strength of it an effort was made to settle the case by a compromise. A series of twelve dogmatic statements, or canons, was drawn up, and submitted to the Pope by Cardinal Ferrari; they were shaped affirmatively, and set forth the orthodox tradition on the points at issue, without denouncing any anathemas, or censuring any theological work by name. If the judgment could have taken such a form, the 'Explication des maximes' would have remained in reality uncensured, while at the same time the doctrine of the Church would have been clearly established in opposition to Quietism. Innocent, who was sincerely anxious to save the reputation of Fénélon, approved the project; and at one moment

---

* Abbé de Chanterac to Abbé de Langeron, Sept. 2, 1698 (*Corresp. de Fénélon*, tom. ix. p. 398).

† Abbé de Chanterac to Fénélon, Sept. 6, 1698 (*Corresp. de Fénélon*, tom. ix. p. 408).

its success seemed probable.* But the Abbé Bossuet was vigilant, well informed, and resolute. No sooner did he hear of the scheme, than he despatched an extraordinary courier to Paris, and signified to the king that, unless he was prepared to see the Archbishop of Cambrai triumphantly acquitted, he must instantly make an exhibition of authority and determination such as the Vatican could neither misunderstand nor evade. Louis had already remonstrated with the Pope on the vexatious impediments which delayed his judgment; he now exchanged complaints for menaces. "His Majesty learns with surprise and grief that after all his solicitations, and after the repeated promises of his Holiness to cut up by the root the mischief which the Archbishop of Cambrai's book has wrought throughout the kingdom, when all seemed terminated, and the book was declared by the congregation of Cardinals and by the Pope himself to abound with errors, its friends have proposed a new expedient, the tendency of which is to render all the previous deliberations fruitless, and to renew the whole dispute. . . . . . His Majesty cannot believe that, under a Pontificate like the present, such a lamentably weak policy can be entertained; and it is clear that it would not be possible for his Majesty to receive or sanction in his dominions anything except that which he has demanded, and which has been promised him, namely, a direct and precise judgment upon a book which has thrown his kingdom into flames, and a doctrine which causes division. Any other form of decision would be useless for the settlement of an affair of such importance, which has kept all Christendom so long in a state of suspense. The promoters of this new plan have manifestly no great concern for the honour of the Holy See, whose authority might by their rashness be plunged in an abyss of difficulties merely for the sake of protecting a book already pronounced to be deserving of censure. It would be too distressing to his Majesty to witness the birth of another schism among his subjects, at the very moment when he is making every available effort to extinguish that of Calvin. And if he should perceive that an affair which seemed almost at an end is being protracted through motives of indulgence which he

---

* L'Abbé Bossuet à son oncle, 10 mars, 1699 (*Œuvres de Bossuet*, tom. xix. p. 382).

is at a loss to comprehend, he will know what course he ought to adopt, and will take measures accordingly; cherishing at the same time the hope that his Holiness will be unwilling to reduce him to such painful extremities."*

As it happened, however, this indecent attempt to intimidate the aged Pontiff was unnecessary. He had taken his determination before the royal missive reached his hands; and that determination was in accordance with the dictates of Louis, and adverse to Fénélon. The project of the canons was discussed in the congregation of cardinals, but, with the exception of Cardinal de Bouillon, no one raised a voice in its support. Even Cardinal Ferrari, with whom the idea originated, and Cardinal Albani, who had warmly supported it, ultimately abandoned it as hopeless. The only remaining alternative was to pronounce a direct sentence of condemnation on Fénélon's work, according to the draft-decree which had been already agreed upon.†

On the 12th of March, 1699, Innocent XII. at length gave judgment in this memorable cause. It was expressed in the form, not of a bull, but of a brief, condemning the 'Explication des maximes des saints' in general, and, in particular, twenty-three propositions extracted from it; these were characterised as "rash, scandalous, ill-sounding, offensive to pious ears, pernicious in practice, and respectively erroneous." The faithful were forbidden, under pain of excommunication, to print, read, possess, or make use of the said book, "inasmuch as they might thereby be misled insensibly into errors already condemned by the Catholic Church." The principal passages condemned are those to which we have so often referred as comprising the leading features of Fénélon's system ; namely, the disinterested love of God exclusively for His own sake, and the notion of the absolute sacrifice of salvation by a righteous soul under circumstances of extreme spiritual trial. It was remarked, however, that some of the statements which had been most severely criticised in France were altogether untouched by the Papal censure.‡

The enemies of Fénélon felt, indeed, even in this moment of

---

* "Mémoire envoyé à Rome par le Roi, contre le projet des canons qu'on vouloit substituer à la condamnation du livre de M. de Cambrai.' (*Œuvres de Bossuet*, tom. xix. p. 404.)

† L'Abbé Bossuet à son oncle, mars 13, 1699 (*Œuvres de Bossuet*, tom. xix. p. 395).

‡ Such, for instance, as Article xli. on 'Spiritual Marriage.'

exultation, that something was wanting to the completeness of their triumph. The twenty-three propositions were pronounced erroneous, but they were not branded as heretical, nor even as "approaching to heresy." Strenuous exertions had been made to secure the insertion of those epithets, but in vain; a majority of the Cardinals decided on the more lenient course. The censure, again, was promulgated in a brief or letter, instead of the more imposing form of a bull; and certain clauses were omitted, which the Popes usually employed for the purpose of adding weight to their official utterances. On the other hand, phrases had been added which were notoriously opposed to the principles of Gallicanism; for it was presumed that Louis and his advisers, in their joy at the attainment of their main object, would not be overscrupulous as to points of minor interest, which, under other circumstances, they might have been inclined to dispute.*

The courier despatched by Cardinal de Bouillon with the announcement of the Papal judgment reached Versailles on the 22nd of March. Bossuet received the news on the same day; and when he next appeared at Court, the king arranged with him, in a private interview, the measures which it would be necessary to take with a view to the official reception of this important act by the Gallican Church. "It was then, doubtless," says the Abbé Ledieu, "that he suggested the idea, not only of the letters patent, but of the provincial assemblies, in order to render the acceptance more solemn, and to augment the lustre of the king's triumph. After this, he said to us in private, 'All will go well; what is requisite will be done; letters patent will be given; the Parliament will make no difficulty.' The common talk in Paris, however, was of a different tone. 'It is only a brief; that is nothing. The king will never grant letters patent. The Parliament cannot possibly accept the expression "motu proprio."' When I mentioned these rumours to the bishop, he merely repeated that all would turn out well . . . . The condemnation of a book against which he had been so continually writing for a long time past was universally regarded as the fruit of his exertions. The more he sought to divest himself of this

---

* St. Simon, *Mémoires*, tom. ii. chap. i.

distinction, the more eagerly was it assigned to him by the public. A perfect concourse of people of all conditions came to congratulate him. The royal family were the first to give the example, both in person and by letter; he received visits from all the bishops who were at Paris; and letters arrived from those who were absent, and from persons of consideration throughout the kingdom, during the space of two months, to wish him joy on the occasion. It was the theme of common conversation, not only in the towns but among country people, that "M. de Meaux had gained his cause at Rome against M. de Cambrai."

The conduct of the defeated party, meanwhile, was such as to entitle it to a meed of praise at least equal in degree, however widely differing in character. Few facts in the Church's annals are more familiar to the general reader than the exemplary submission of Fénélon to the supreme authority of Rome, notwithstanding the crushing humiliation now inflicted on him. The duty of such submission was one of the primary axioms of his religious creed. "Roma locuta est; causa finita est." Considering the high personal esteem in which he was held by the reigning Pontiff—considering the powerful support which he enjoyed among the Jesuits, the Cardinals, the official staff of the Inquisition—considering, again, the extremely intricate and bewildering nature of the questions which formed the subject of dispute—there is no doubt that the Archbishop, had he been so minded, might have eluded the censure, and prolonged the struggle indefinitely. He had a position as strong, to say the least, as that of the Jansenists, who, by means of their fine-drawn distinction between doctrine and fact, had set Pope after Pope at defiance, and were still, after half a century of controversy, uncondemned in their own estimation, though they were heretics in the eyes of all the rest of the Catholic world. But Fénélon disdained such sophistical artifices. It is well known how, on receiving notice of the Papal brief, he ascended the pulpit of his cathedral, where, instead of preaching, as he had intended, on the subject of the day—the Annunciation—he proceeded to enforce the duty of obedience to ecclesiastical authority; and how he drew up forthwith a mandement to his flock announcing his sincere acceptance of the sentence, at whatever cost of personal mortification.

"We adhere to this brief, most dear brethren (such are his words), both with respect to the text of the book and with respect to the twenty-three propositions, simply, absolutely, and without a shadow of reserve. Accordingly, we condemn both the book and the propositions, precisely in the same form and with the same expressions, simply, absolutely, and without restriction. Moreover, we forbid the faithful of this diocese, under the same penalty, to read or retain this book. We shall find comfort, dearest brethren, under our present humiliation, provided that the ministry of the word, which we have received of the Lord for your sanctification, be not weakened thereby, and that, notwithstanding the abasement of the pastor, the flock may grow in grace before God. With our whole heart, then, we exhort you to sincere submission and unreserved docility, lest by any means the simple duty of obedience to the Holy See should be insensibly impaired; of which obedience we desire, with the assistance of God's grace, to set you an example to the last moment of our life. God forbid that our name should ever be mentioned, except it be to call to mind that a pastor felt it incumbent on him to be more submissive than the least sheep of his flock, and that he set no bounds to his compliance."* The Archbishop wrote to the Pope to signify, in similar terms of profound humility, his submission to the censure; and received a reply from his Holiness, expressing in gratifying language his satisfaction with his conduct. In the original draft of this letter Innocent had spoken still more decidedly in praise of Fénélon, whose character he had long admired; but the Abbé Bossuet, who had displayed throughout the affair a spirit of hateful malignity, succeeded, by dint of clamour and intrigue, in procuring the suppression of these eulogistic clauses. Even the victor of Meaux could not refrain from indulging in unfair and captious criticisms on the mandement of his fallen adversary.†

Although, in consequence of the readiness shown by Fénélon to bow to the decision of the Holy See, all doubt was removed as to the practical reception of the brief in France, it was deemed necessary, before it was published officially, to observe

---

* *Mémoires du Clergé*, tom. i. p. 459.
† See his letter to his nephew, April 19, 1699 (*Œuvres de Bossuet*, tom. xix. p. 456).

certain formalities illustrating the great principles of "Gallican liberty" which had been re-affirmed with so much emphasis in 1682. According to these maxims, a judicial sentence of the Pope in a matter of faith cannot be published in France until it has been solemnly accepted in due canonical form by the archbishops and bishops of the realm. Every member of the episcopate is, by virtue of his office, a judge of theological doctrine co-ordinately with the Pope; and the judgments of the Holy Father are not irreversible or infallible unless confirmed by the collective assent of the Church.* It was arranged, therefore, that the king should address a circular letter to the metropolitans, desiring them to summon a meeting of their conprovincial bishops to deliberate on the acceptance of the brief. By this expedient it was held that the bishops would individually exercise their functions as colleagues and assessors of the Pope; and their acquiescence in the judgment would be no mere act of enforced registration, but the expression of their own independent conviction.

"The Provincial Assemblies," says D'Aguesseau, "were held successively in each province with perfect unanimity, both as to the condemnation of the Archbishop of Cambrai's book, and as to the preservation of the right of bishops to judge of doctrine, and other features of the liberties of the Gallican Church. A laudable emulation was excited among the different provinces; each aspired to the honour of having maintained most vigorously the power inherent in the episcopal character, of judging either before the Pope, or with the Pope, or after the Pope, and the right of bishops to receive the Papal constitutions only after examination, and in judicial form. The most remarkable circumstance in this solemn attestation of its doctrine by the Gallican Church was that it occurred at a time when we had no difference whatever with the Court of Rome, and when the king was living in perfect intelligence with the Pope, from whom he feared nothing and had nothing to fear. So that it was truth alone, and not the necessity arising from any external conjuncture, which gave occasion to a declaration of the sentiments of the clergy thus authoritative and unanimous.†

---

* "Nec tamen irreformabile esse judicium, nisi Ecclesiæ consensus accesserit." See the fourth Article of 1682.

† D'Aguesseau, "Mém. sur les aff. de l'Egl. de France" (*Œuvres*, tom. xiii. p. 182).

The Assembly of the province of Paris, which was designed to serve in some measure as a model for the rest, was held in the chapel of the Archbishop's palace on the 13th of May, 1699. There were present Archbishop de Noailles, the Bishops of Chartres, Meaux, and Blois, and the vicar-general of Orleans, representing Cardinal de Coislin, bishop of that see. Bossuet had feared that some opposition or dissension might arise in the course of the proceedings; but on the contrary, perfect harmony prevailed, and the *procès-verbal* was adopted without amendment or division. In this document it was carefully laid down that the acceptance of Apostolic constitutions is to be made by the authorities of the Church after deliberation; the bishops uniting themselves in spirit with his Holiness in the condemnation of error. Such acceptance, again, must include an express declaration that it is not to prejudice the right of bishops to judge in the first instance in causes of doctrine, when they may think it necessary for the good of the Church. The Assembly adverted to the defects of form in the Pope's brief, to the omission of the customary clauses "Nulli ergo" and "Si quis autem," and to the insertion of the anti-Gallican phrase "motu proprio";—all which irregularities they excused upon various specious considerations.* But they added another article, which was a most unjust and unbecoming aggravation of Fénélon's punishment. Under the plea of deterring his partisans from imitating his example, "like the followers of Gilbert de la Porrée, of whom St. Bernard says that they preferred having that prelate for their master in his error than in his retractation," they resolved that the king should be requested to revoke the permission granted for printing the condemned book, and to suppress all publications that had been made in defence of it. This was grossly inconsistent; for whereas they professed to be acting in strict accordance with the judgment of the Pope, they well knew that the archbishop's apologies for his work had been repeatedly declared at Rome to

---

* It was observed, with reference to the "motu proprio," that a decision which had been originally demanded by the author of the censured volume, which was desired by the bishops, and urgently insisted on by the secular authority, could not be in reality an arbitrary decree of the Pope, though it might be so described in the brief; and that therefore the clause might be allowed to pass without objection, in consideration of the advantages gained by the settlement of the question.

be exempt from censure, and that no mention was to be found of them in the brief which was the occasion of their meeting. The resolution passed, however, unanimously; and the maxim "væ victis" was applied without remorse. The majority of the provinces copied almost verbatim the proceedings of that of Paris; but six out of the seventeen (Toulouse, Narbonne, Sens, Vienne, Auch, and Arles) forbore to insist on the suppression of the apologetic writings.

The most trying scene in the whole drama was that enacted in the province of Cambrai; where it fell to the lot of Fénélon to preside, as metropolitan, over an assembly called together for the purpose of finally sealing the condemnation of his own work. One of his suffragans, Valbelle, Bishop of St. Omer,* had the effrontery to attack the touching mandement of his superior, and to insinuate that his professed humility was but that of outward respect, and not of the heart and conscience. It lacked, he said, some expression of penitence; and, were it not for the known integrity of the Archbishop, the door might thus be left open for a relapse into the very error which had been verbally abjured. Fénélon bore the implied insult without a sign of resentment. He calmly pointed out that the terms of his mandement expressed a far deeper acquiescence than one of mere external respect; that he had promised his flock to set them an example of docility and obedience of equal duration with his life; and that he could hardly be suspected of making use of such language with an intent to deceive and trifle with the Church. He was incapable of taking any steps, directly or indirectly, for the sake of eluding the sentence contained in the Pope's brief. He could not indeed acknowledge, against his conscience, that he had ever really held the erroneous tenets imputed to him; he had hoped that his work had been so carefully shaped, and balanced by such correctives, as to give no countenance to error; but he gladly renounced his own judgment to conform implicitly to that of the Holy Father. The bishops congratulated him on these edifying sentiments; but nevertheless they made him drink the cup of humiliation to the very dregs. He was compelled to decide, as president, in favour of the suppression of all

---

* "Homine d'esprit," says d'Aguesseau, "mais chaud comme un Provençal qu'il étoit, et chicaneur comme un Normand." (*Mém. sur les Aff. de l'Égl. de France*).

his writings in support of the 'Explication des maximes,' which was demanded by the plurality of voices; recording at the same time, in the *procès-verbal*, his own dissent from that measure.*

When the Pope's constitution had thus been accepted by the Provincial Assemblies, the king sent letters-patent to the Parliament, requiring the magistrates to register and publish it, that it might be executed according to due form and tenor. This final step took place on the 14th of August, 1699, after an eloquent "requisitoire" from the Avocat-Général D'Aguesseau, which is styled by the President Hainaut "an immortal monument of the solidity of the maxims of the Church of France, for ever honourable to the memory of that great magistrate." Bossuet, in like manner, commended it as "a work worthy of the zeal of a bishop or a theologian, rather than of a magistrate; the officers of the Parliament not being accustomed to manifest so much favour to the Church." D'Aguesseau showed indeed considerable skill on this occasion in distinguishing, while at the same time he reconciled and harmonized, the rights of the Church and of the Crown, of the Pope and of the Episcopate. "This glorious work," he says, "the success of which interested in an equal degree religion and the State, the Priesthood and the Empire, is the precious fruit of their perfect intelligence. Never did the two supreme Powers which God has established for the government of mankind concur so zealously, and I may say so felicitously, to the attainment of their common end, namely, the glory of Him who delivers His oracles by the mouth of the Church, and who causes them to be executed by the authority of sovereigns." In a few pregnant sentences he depicts the source and nature of the controversy. "Dark shades, all the more dangerous in that they borrowed the appearance and lustre of the most brilliant light, had begun to cover the face of the Church. Minds the most elevated, souls the most heavenly, deceived by the false glitter of a dazzling spirituality, were the most ardent in pursuing the shadow of an imaginary perfection; and if God had not abridged the days of illusion and aberration, even the elect (if it were possible, and if I may be permitted to adopt the language of Scripture), would have been in danger of being

---

* *Mémoires du Clergé,* tom. i. p. 466.

seduced. The truth made itself heard through the voice of the Pope and of the Bishops; they invoked the light, and light arose out of the depths of darkness. Only a word was necessary to dissipate the clouds of error; and the remedy was so prompt and so effectual, that it has effaced even the remembrance of the malady which threatened us." He then pays a just tribute of admiration to the magnanimous behaviour of Fénélon;—that pastor from whom the Church might have expected opposition, " if his heart had been the accomplice of his intellect," but who had "hastened to pronounce against himself a painful yet salutary censure, and had reassured the Church, scared as it was by the novelty of his doctrine, by solemnly announcing submission without reserve, obedience without limits, acquiescence without restriction." He next recounts the constitutional measures which had been taken for the acceptance of the brief: insisting specially on the judicial power of bishops in doctrinal causes, whether separately or in conjunction with the Pope. "Nothing," he says, "can shake this incontestable maxim, which was born with the Church; and will last as long as the Church;—that each See, being the depository of the faith and tradition of its fathers, has the right to give its testimony to the same, whether separately or in the corporate assembly of bishops; and these individual rays make up that vast body of light which, henceforth till the consummation of all things, will evermore cause error to tremble and truth to triumph. Let us, by a wise moderation, identify the interests of the Pope with those of the bishops; let us receive his judgment with profound veneration, yet without detracting aught from the authority of the other pastors. Let the Pope be always the most exalted, yet not the sole, judge of our faith; let the bishops always have their seats after him, but nevertheless *with* him, for the exercise of that power which Christ conferred on them in common, to teach all nations, and to be everywhere and in all ages the light of the world. For these reasons," he concludes, "we demand that this brief be registered, with one simple but useful protest, which we find in the subscriptions of an ancient Spanish Council:—Salvâ priscorum canonum auctoritate." *

---

* This speech is printed in the works of Bossuet, tom. xix. p. 524.

Nothing is more remarkable in the history of this affair than the fact that it was terminated by a single decision of that august tribunal, to which Catholics in all ages have been accustomed to appeal for justice in the last resort. D'Aguesseau observes that, in a case of such magnitude, the circumstance is probably without a parallel. After the events which we have just related, the vexed question of Quietism sank rapidly into oblivion. The Archbishop of Cambrai amply redeemed the pledges he had given both before and since his condemnation. He avoided all allusion to the controversy; he never complained of the sentence; he never regretted that he had bound himself to absolute and life-long submission. His friends, for the most part, pursued a similar course; and the consequence was that, although the traditional theory of Mysticism survived in individual minds, and exercised an influence which no external opposition could overthrow, it led to no display of sectarianism, and never again became openly menacing to the peace of the Church.

There are other considerations, however, which suggest a doubt whether the judgment which was thus passively accepted may not have been prejudicial, rather than favourable, to the true principles of Catholicism. Fénélon leaned towards Ultramontane opinions. Hence his sympathy with the Jesuits; hence his friendship with Cardinal de Bouillon; hence the extreme reluctance of the Pope to pronounce his condemnation. Such tendencies predisposed him, when his orthodoxy was attacked, to recur immediately to Rome; a step highly gratifying to that Court, and one from which it failed not to extract solid advantage. That a Gallican prelate of such eminence should voluntarily seek the decision of a foreign tribunal, ignoring the constitutional rights of his colleagues in the episcopate, and contradicting the maxims which his predecessors had upheld with so much ardour in all ages, was a matter of no small congratulation to the Curia and its supporters. It was, *pro tanto*, a relinquishment of the doctrine that the bishops, assembled in Provincial or National Synod, are the primary judges of ecclesiastical causes arising within their jurisdiction; it was a direct encouragement to the absolutist pretensions of the Roman Pontiffs, from which the Church had already suffered so severely. This error on Fénélon's part compromised, as we have seen, Bossuet and those who acted with him, since his appeal to Rome seemed to necessitate a similar movement on their side; and the frequent applications of Louis to Innocent placed the Crown in the same incongruous predicament. When all was over—when the oracle had spoken, and the Pope had arrogated to himself personally, "motu proprio," the supreme arbitration of the affair—then the Gallican Church bethought itself of the authority of its own episcopal assemblies; but it is obvious that it was then too late; the proper moment for the exercise of that authority was past. The forms of deliberation, references to historical precedent, protests against usurpation, saving clauses, scrupulous reservations—all were important in their measure, and it was right to employ them; but it cannot be denied that they were illusory with regard to the adjudication of the case in hand; the bishops had allowed the real functions of their office to be forestalled and sacrificed. Every successive instance of such weakness damaged the cause of Gallicanism; and hence we must not be surprised to find that the aggressions upon it became bolder and more offensive, and that, although there was not wanting a firm front of resistance, that resistance was made with diminished resources, and with less and less prospect of ultimate victory.

CHAPTER V.

THE opening of the eighteenth century found the Church of France in a condition which may be described, from many points of view, as its acme of prosperity and glory. At no former period had it stood so high in the confidence and esteem of the nation; never had its privileges been more generally respected; never had it possessed, in the various orders of the ministry, so many shining examples of learning, intelligence, pastoral devotedness, and saintliness of life. The highest rank of the hierarchy numbered at least six members whose reputation was European, and of whom any age of the Church may well have been proud;—Cardinal de Camus Bishop of Grenoble; Bossuet; Fénélon; Huet Bishop of Avranches; Fléchier Bishop of Nismes; and Mascaron Bishop of Agen. Other prelates, though less widely celebrated, were scarcely less estimable; such as Archbishop de Noailles; Des Marais Bishop of Chartres; De la Broue Bishop of Mirepoix (the intimate friend of Bossuet); Nesmond Bishop of Bayeux; and Berthier Bishop of Blois. The priesthood abounded with illustrious names. It could boast of consummate masters of pulpit oratory, such as Bourdaloue and Massillon; of enlightened commentators on Holy Scripture, such as Duguet, Bernard Lami, Richard Simon, and Lauemant; of scientific theologians, such as Tournely and Thomassin; of erudite historians, such as Claude Fleury, Noël Alexandre, Denis de Ste. Marthe, Ellies-Dupin, and Le Nain de Tillemont. The religious Orders rivalled each other as models of discipline, and had produced men who in their several lines of study became prodigies of intellectual attainment. Pre-eminent among them was the Benedictine Congregation of St. Maur, of which some account has been given in a former part of this work. Jean Mabillon, its brightest luminary, had now passed the zenith of his course; yet his declining years scarce witnessed any relaxation of those indefatigable researches which had made him beyond question the greatest ecclesiastical scholar of the age. He was surrounded by a phalanx of not unworthy lieutenants—Ruinart, Durand, Martenne, Massuet, Montfaucon, Bouquet, Constant, Blampin—who faithfully trod in his footsteps, and with almost equally glorious results. The Jesuits, again, the Fathers of the Oratory, the Seminary of St. Sulpice, the Lazarist Priests of the Mission, the Seminary of Missions Étrangères, the Frères de la Doctrine Chrétienne, though their proceedings were not always free from the bitterness of jealousy and party spirit, were energetic in their different spheres of action, and contributed to prolong that dominant influence of religion over the social system which had been founded in great measure by their earlier labours. Added to this, the great success of the Diocesan Seminaries had by this time wrought a wonderful change of tone and character among the ranks of the parochial clergy.

It must be remembered, however, that these auspicious circumstances represent only one side of the picture. Underneath this brilliant exterior the old sores and chronic maladies of the Church still lay unhealed. The Jansenist feud, though suspended for a time by the brief armistice called the "Peace of Clement IX.," was one of implacable, undying animosity. The self-styled Augustinians, not content with repudiating, in the secret recesses of their hearts, the repeated condemnations of their doctrine by the Holy See, assumed a similar tone in public whenever opportunity offered; insisting that the tenets censured by the Vatican were not, and never had been, held by them, and that in fact it was a mistake to suppose that they had ever been maintained at all. The "heresy of Jansenism," they asserted, was a phantom, a fable, a chimera; the errors proscribed under that name were defended by none; and the real views of the accused party were none other than those of the great Augustine, whose orthodoxy was guaranteed by the verdict of the Catholic Church of all ages.

Nothing could be more impolitic on the part of the Jansenists than to provoke a renewal of discussion on this worn-out controversy. For thirty years past they had been left in unmolested enjoyment of their opinions; if not favoured by those in authority, they were at least tolerated and protected; all that was required of them was an honest conformity to the text of the Pontifical Constitutions, which they were presumed to have accepted and subscribed with a good conscience. During the life of Archbishop De Harlai they remained, on the whole, quiescent; but the character and prepossessions of his successor were such as almost to invite them to make a movement in advance; and the result of their first attempt (in the case of the 'Exposition de la Foi' edited by Gerberon), though not decisive in their favour, left ground for hoping that the new archbishop might, by a bold face and skilful management, be won over to their side.

A publication entitled 'Augustiniana Ecclesiæ Romanæ doctrina,' dedicated to the Assembly of the clergy of France, which was about to hold its ordinary session, appeared early in the year 1700. It re-opened all the questions which the Church had striven to set at rest by a series of infallible decisions; affirmed the necessity of the captious distinction between the *droit* and the *fait*, and demanded a fresh judgment from Rome, as if her former utterances were inadequate and obsolete.* It was impossible to avoid noticing this production; and accordingly Bossuet, in a memorial presented to the king just before the meeting of the Assembly, pointed out to his Majesty the peril which threatened religion from the intrigues of two opposite parties, one of which laboured to sap the authority of the Church by evading its dogmatical decisions, while the other attacked its very vitals by propagating a fatal system of lax and corrupt morality. He proposed that these evils should be dealt with by the Assembly simultaneously; wisely remarking that a one-sided judgment would be worse than useless. If action were taken at all, it should be unbiassed and impartial; Jesuits and Jansenists alike should be made to feel that they were amenable to the bar of ecclesiastical opinion, and especially to the authority of the assembled Episcopate. Louis, who in matters of this nature was accustomed to yield passively to the counsels of Bossuet, signified his approval of the scheme; he authorised the Assembly to proceed to the condemnation of the errors, doctrinal and moral, fostered by the rival factions; only stipulating that neither individual authors, nor any religious community, should be stigmatised by name.

The Assembly met at St.-Germain on the 2nd of June, 1700.

---

* Father Quesnel, in his *Lettre à un députe du second ordre*, had argued very plausibly to the same effect.

Bossuet, who sat as one of the representatives of the province of Paris, was its governing spirit, though not officially its president. That post was assigned to Le Tellier Archbishop of Reims, a prelate eminently unfitted for it, both on account of his haughty unconciliating manners, and because he was notoriously a violent opponent of the Jesuits, with whom he had lately had a severe contest in his own diocese. He had the good sense, however, to perceive that he was not likely to bring the deliberations to a successful issue without the help of a colleague. It fortunately happened that just at this moment Archbishop de Noailles was promoted to the rank of cardinal; and it was felt that this accession of dignity pointed him out as the proper person to act as moderator on such an occasion, although he had no seat in the Assembly by election. With the co-operation of Bossuet, the arrangement was accordingly effected; and Cardinal de Noailles presided on the 20th of August, when the report of the Committee on faith and morals (prepared by Bossuet, who was chairman) was presented to the house.* This committee had not been appointed without opposition. The Archbishop of Auch, the Bishop of Apt, and other prelates in the Jesuit interest, resisted it on the ground that the Assembly had met for the transaction of temporal business only; and that the time allotted by the Crown for their session was too short to admit of their entering on so vast a field of discussion as that indicated by the Bishop of Meaux. Bossuet firmly but temperately combated these objections, and carried with him the great majority of the house. The committee was appointed, and in due time produced a report, specifying as worthy of the censure of the clergy one hundred and sixty propositions on various subjects, among which those relating to false casuistry largely preponderated. They were afterwards reduced to one hundred and twenty-seven. Four were impugned as savouring of Jansenism; two as tainted with Semi-Pelagianism; nine were concerned with miscellaneous points of positive theology; ten referred to the question of attrition and contrition, and the degree of charity required for acceptable penitence; while all the rest belonged to the cate-

---

* Abbé Ledieu, *Journal*, &c., tom. i. p. 90.

gory of lax morality, and in particular, to the fallacious theory of probabilism.*

The reader is aware that the dangers of this system had already been the theme of many a cutting sarcasm and many a grave remonstrance. Two successive Pontiffs, Alexander VII. and Innocent XI., had solemnly condemned its excesses. It had been satirized by Pascal in some of the most caustic of his 'Provincial Letters'; and Arnauld and Nicole, in the 'Morale pratique des Jésuites,' had done their utmost to fasten on their adversaries, not only the authorship of these slippery maxims, but likewise all the most odious consequences which might fairly or unfairly be developed from them. Bossuet had made arrangements for obtaining an expression of opinion on the subject from the famous Assembly of 1682; but was prevented by the abruptness with which its session was cut short immediately after the settlement of the affair of the Four Articles. The Church of France, in his opinion, owed it to herself to repudiate, by a definitive sentence, these monstrous perversions of the code of evangelical truth; and this was now effected after a brief show of vexatious opposition.

It may be well to repeat in this place that the doctrine of Probabilism, as well as other characteristic features of modern casuistry, though they are popularly identified with the Jesuits, did not, strictly speaking, originate with that body. The Jesuits adopted a system which they found ready to their hands; and it is difficult to explain the fact that that system should have been accepted and practised for so long a period by the clergy both regular and secular, without awakening suspicion, or provoking any expression of disapprobation from the heads of the Church. There is a true, as there is a false, doctrine of probability; the former had been taught by theologians from the commencement of the Scholastic era; the latter was first broached towards the close of the sixteenth century by a Spanish divine named Bartolomeo Medina; who, be it observed, was not a member of the Order of Jesus, but a Dominican. That of two probable opinions we ought to prefer that which appears the safer and the more strongly recom-

---

* See "Censura et Declaratio Conventûs Generalis cleri Gallicani in materiâ Fidei et morum," in the *Procès-verbaux des Assemblées Gén. du Clergé*, tom. vi. "Pièces justificatives," No. 4.

mended, is a principle which approves itself at once to reason and the moral sense; but, according to the theory started by Medina, we may with a safe conscience take a course which is *less* probable, renouncing that which has a superior weight of testimony in its favour; and not long afterwards this sentiment was endorsed by Salonias, an Augustinian, as being that of "a large number of distinguished theologians, chiefly of the school of St. Thomas."* The first Jesuit who inculcated this doctrine was the famous Gabriel Vasquez; and some of the names which the Society holds in the highest honour are to be found subsequently in the lists of its defenders; among others those of Cardinals Bellarmine and Pallavicini. The theory at length reached its extreme development; it was proclaimed that an opinion was probable, and might therefore be safely followed in practice, which had the sanction of any single theologian of established reputation. All barriers were broken through, as Cardinal De Bausset justly observes,† when once this wild persuasion had invaded the mind. Advantage was taken of it, to an extent which could not have been conceived beforehand, to involve the most elementary rules of morals in a haze of doubt and paradox which excused any amount of practical obliquity. Those who had been foremost in approving the new principle hastened to read their recantation when they witnessed these revolting consequences. Bellarmine retracted in form; Pallavicini wrote vigorously against his former opinion; Cardinal d'Aguirre tearfully lamented and abjured his error. A General of the Jesuits, Thyrsus Gonzalez, published in 1694 a volume setting forth in elaborate detail all the snares and perils to be apprehended from the growing prevalence of probabilism.‡

Bossuet made considerable use of this last-mentioned work in his report to the Assembly of the year 1700. He urged that in morals, as well as in doctrinal belief, the true rule for Catholics is that of Vincent de Lerins, "Quod semper, quod ubique, quod ab omnibus." Tried by this crucial test, probabilism cannot escape condemnation; since its direct tendency

---

* D'Avrigny, *Mém. Chronol.*, tom. ii. p. 316.
† De Bausset, *Hist. de Bossuet*, tom. iv. p. 29.
‡ Gonzalez, *Fundamentum Theologiæ Moralis, id est, Tractatus Theologicus de recto usu opinionum probabilium.*

is to accustom the conscience to repose upon the dicta of this or that fallible individual, instead of seeking to ascertain what is intrinsically good or evil, true or false, and what has been authorised by the general acceptance and practice of the Church. The reasoning was so powerful and so persuasive, that opposition was manifestly hopeless; and on the 4th of September the report was adopted without a dissentient voice. The formal censure of the propositions was a necessary consequence, and was duly inserted in the *procès-verbal* of the Assembly.* This was a deadly blow to the influence of Jesuit morality and Jesuit confessors in France; and another item was thus added to the increasing catalogue of grievances between the Order and Cardinal De Noailles; grievances which they were not likely to forget whenever the course of events might bring with it an opportunity of retaliation.

The Assembly also appointed a committee on the subject of Quietism, of which both the Bishop of Meaux and his nephew the Abbé Bossuet were named members. That prelate, it is scarcely necessary to state, directed its proceedings; and its report, of which he was the author, though it cannot be charged with falsification of facts, nor with positive unfairness, undoubtedly represented the whole case from his own point of view, and contained some expressions depreciatory of Fénélon's conduct. It bore testimony incidentally to the moral integrity of Madame Guyon, and her freedom from all complicity with the errors of Molinos.†

The question of the "Chinese ceremonies," as it was termed, was so warmly debated at this time, and wore so serious an aspect, that it had been proposed to submit it to the consideration of the Assembly during the present session. But since the cause had already been referred for arbitration to the Court of Rome, it was judged more respectful to abstain from any step which might seem to anticipate the sentence of that supreme tribunal. This was one of the manifold disputes which arose out of the crooked policy of the Jesuits. Their conduct as missionaries in China had been such as to give colour to the grave imputation which is now proverbially attached to their name, that of employing questionable means to effect a meri-

---

* *Procès-verbaux des Assembl.*, tom. vi. p. 496.
† Ibid., tom. vi. "Pièces justif.," No. iii.

torious end; of "doing evil that good may come." They had permitted their converts to continue practising many of the superstitious rites prescribed by Confucius, in combination with the ordinances of Christian worship. There were not wanting specious trains of argument to support this anomalous discipline; but it was opposed by the emissaries of two rival Orders, the Franciscans and Dominicans, and subsequently by the priests of the "Missions Etrangères," headed by their superior, Maigrot, titular Bishop of Conon. Upon the appearance of a mandement of this prelate, in 1693, prohibiting the latitudinarian indulgences which had been tolerated by the Jesuits, the latter raised the standard of resistance, refused to obey the monition, and carried their cause by appeal to Rome. Here it encountered the usual embarrassments and delays arising from the intrigues and passions of contending parties.

Meanwhile the superiors of the Foreign Missions at Paris, MM. Brisacier and Tiberge, took a step which brought the Jesuits once more in the position of defendants to the bar of the Gallican Church. In June, 1700, they denounced to the Faculty of Theology a list of propositions extracted from certain writings of Fathers Lecomte and Gobien, entitled 'Nouveaux mémoires sur l'état présent de la Chine,' 'Histoire de l'édit de l'Empereur de la Chine,' and 'Lettre sur les cérémonies de la Chine.' It was understood that this proceeding had the direct sanction of Cardinal de Noailles, of the Archbishop of Reims, and of Bossuet.

The tenor of the impugned statements was sufficiently startling. They affirmed that the people of China had preserved for near two thousand years the knowledge of the true God, and had honoured Him in a manner which might serve for a pattern and an instructive lesson to Christians. That the moral character of their religion was no less pure than its dogmas; pure morality having prevailed in China at a period when Europe, and almost the whole world, was plunged in error and corruption. That the Chinese emperor ought not to regard Christianity as a new or strange religion, inasmuch as it was precisely identical in its principles and fundamental articles with that which had been professed for ages by Chinese philosophers and sovereigns; they worshipped the same God whom Christians worship, and acknowledged Him no less devoutly as the Lord of heaven and earth.* This was carrying the maxim of "making themselves all things to all men" to an extreme for which it were vain and fallacious indeed to plead the authority of the Apostle Paul. There is a dangerous affinity between such a style of teaching and the "Jehovah, Jove, or Lord," of the poet; the tendency of both being to foster a spirit of religious indifference closely allied to infidelity. Every available engine was set in motion by the Society and their friends to avert a censure; notwithstanding which the aforesaid propositions were condemned on the 18th of October, by a vast majority of doctors, as "false, rash, scandalous, contrary to the word of God, and subversive of the Christian faith and religion." The decision was vehemently attacked by various writers of the Ultramontane school, and was defended with no less energy by Ellies-Dupin and Noël Alexandre, two of the most erudite doctors of the Sorbonne. In the end, Pope Clement XI., though as a rule he was predisposed to favour the Jesuits, found it necessary to pronounce unequivocally against them in the matter of the Chinese ceremonies. He despatched Cardinal De Tournon to China as his legate, and steadily upheld him against the refractory missionaries, who defied his authority, and subjected him to a savage persecution. The Cardinal was at length imprisoned in the Society's house at Macao, where, after enduring much privation and cruel suffering, he died in the odour of sanctity, and with courage worthy of a martyr.

That the result of these repeated defeats was to exasperate the Jesuits, and incite them towards schemes of vengeance, is beyond question; nevertheless it would appear that the next polemical movement was a contrivance of their adversaries the Jansenists, who, as we have seen, were emboldened at this moment by the hope of retrieving their fortunes through the friendly agency of Cardinal de Noailles. It was with this object that they devised the ingenious expedient known as the "Cas de conscience." The document so called was drawn up privately in 1701, but was not published to the world till more than a year afterwards, at the close of 1702 or beginning of 1703. It described a case of difficulty, real or fictitious, propounded by a

---

* *Histoire de Bossuet*, tom. iv. p. 266; D'Avrigny, *Mém. Chronol.*, tom. iv. p. 167; Picot, *Mém. pour servir à l'Hist. ecclés.*, tom. i. Introduction.

confessor in the country to the doctors of the Sorbonne. An ecclesiastic who had long been under his guidance had lately expressed sentiments on certain points which made it doubtful whether he could safely be admitted to sacramental Absolution. It appeared, on questioning him, that he condemned ex animo the five Jansenistic propositions, according to the terms of the Papal Constitutions; but that he did not believe the Pope to be infallible in matters of fact, and considered that, as to the authorship of the condemned tenets, it was sufficient to submit in "respectful silence;" that no man ought to be molested on account of his belief unless it could be proved that he had distinctly maintained some one of the heretical Propositions. Upon several other controverted topics—such as predestination, efficacious grace, attrition, the worship of the Virgin and the Saints, the Immaculate Conception—his language was of a liberal tone, and flatly contravened the favourite notions of the Jesuits. He confessed, moreover, that he was in the habit of reading Arnauld's book on Frequent Communion, the Spiritual Letters of St. Cyran, and even the New Testament in the translation of Mons, which he held to be permitted in all dioceses except those in which the bishops had formally proscribed it.*

"A large number of the doctors to whom this case was presented," says the Chancellor D'Aguesseau, "did not perceive either the snare that was laid for them, or the consequence of their decision. One of them, more clear-sighted than the rest, felt misgivings, and replied that if they would only send this ecclesiastic to him, he would soon find means to remove his scruples and restore his peace of mind. The others signed it without much consideration; and it soon became public, either from the imprudence of the Jansenists, the indiscreet zeal of the Sulpicians, or the address and activity of the Jesuits."† It bore the signatures of forty doctors, who recorded their opinion that the views of the individual in question were not reprehensible; that he was in a safe state of conscience, and could not be denied absolution.

The publication of the "cas de conscience" caused no small excitement and alarm. Jansenism had been thought virtually extinct; but here was a clear proof of its resuscitation. If the

---

* Picot, Mém. pour servir à l'Hist. ecclés., tom. i. p. 21.
† D'Aguesseau, Mém. sur les Aff. de l'Égl. de France, tom. xiii. p. 201.

authority of the Holy See in deciding the "fact of Jansenius" was again to be called in question, the peace of the Church was compromised afresh; the labours and conflicts of fifty years were little better than fruitless, and nothing remained but the prospect of multiplied perplexities and endless disorder. A paper signed by forty doctors of the Sorbonne was not a document to be despised; and, to add to the difficulty, a report was soon spread, which seemed to have some foundation, that the Archbishop of Paris himself was acquainted with the project, and had given it his approbation, though on condition that the fact should be kept a profound secret.* Such a proceeding was, unfortunately, of a piece with the Cardinal's habitual weakness and short-sightedness.

The heads of the Church were much embarrassed as to the course to be pursued. Bossuet, though he was now suffering under the combined weight of age and disease, "took fire," says his secretary Ledieu,† and, foreseeing the complications which might supervene, began to review systematically the facts and documents relating to the history of Jansenism, in order to guide both himself and others in dealing with existing circumstances. The result of this enquiry was to confirm him in the belief which he had held for forty years, that the Five Propositions were unquestionably contained in the work of Jansenius, and that their spirit was diffused throughout it. He was willing to allow, however, that the Jansenists could not in theological strictness be called heretics, since they professed to renounce the errors condemned by the Church; but they were justly chargeable with acting so as to foment heresy and schism, by giving countenance to proscribed error; an indictment which he had already preferred against them in his Report to the Assembly of 1700.‡ The great prelate also expressed his astonishment that the Four Bishops, Antoine Arnauld, and the nuns of Port-Royal, could have stooped to such a gross subterfuge as that by the help of which they signed the Formulary; since the terms of that test were so distinct and precise, both as to the point of doctrine and of fact, that they admitted of no reserve or mystification whatsoever; consequently any

---

* D'Aguesseau, *Mém., ubi supr.*; Bausset, *Hist. de Fénélon*, tom. ii. chap. iv.

† *Journal de l'Abbé Ledieu*, tom. i. p. 357; janvier 1703.
‡ Ledieu, *Journal*, tom. i. p. 389.

proceeding of that kind appeared to him a downright falsehood.*

Led by such feelings, Bossuet necessarily came to the conclusion that the "cas de conscience" must be condemned, and he used all his influence with Cardinal de Noailles to bring him round to the same opinion. The Cardinal, helpless, as usual, through the effects of his own want of judgment, hesitated to declare himself in public against an act which he had substantially sanctioned in private; and he gladly accepted Bossuet's suggestion that the doctors might possibly be persuaded to retract their decision, particularly when they found that it was likely to create a serious disturbance, and to be censured by the highest Church authority. Great exertions were accordingly made to procure this solution, and with marked success. Many of the doctors had signed under the impression that in doing so they were consulting the wishes of the Cardinal-archbishop; they now readily entered into explanations which amounted to a reversal of their former judgment. Noël Alexandre, the distinguished ecclesiastical historian, set the example; in a letter to the Archbishop he stated that, by a submission of "respectful silence," he meant one of cordial inward assent—a bonâ fide acquiescence, both of the understanding and the heart, in the decision of the Church. He declared, also, that the Church is infallibly guided in the discernment and verification of "doctrinal facts;" and that therefore no one could refuse to subscribe the Formulary without committing mortal sin. This act of quasi-recantation was numerously followed. Eleven doctors adopted it nearly verbatim; twenty-four others wrote to the Cardinal to signify their adhesion to whatever judgment he might pronounce upon the "cas de conscience." The remaining five, however, were stubbornly refractory; Petitpied, who was said to be the original author of the scheme, Bourret, Delan, De Blampignon, and the well-known Ellies-Dupin. Their obstinacy cost them dear. They were exiled in various directions by *lettres de cachet*; Petitpied and Delan were expelled from the Sorbonne; Ellies-Dupin forfeited his professorship of philosophy at the Collége de France.†

---

* Ledieu, *Mém. et Journal*, tom. i. p. 362; January 5, 1703.

† "Dupin," observes D'Aguesseau, "was as little of a Jansenist as those who drove him into exile; but he had made himself obnoxious at Rome by defending the Gallican maxims against the doctrines of the Ultramontanes."

While De Noailles was congratulating himself on the success of his manœuvre, Pope Clement XI. published a brief, dated February 12, 1703, by which he severely condemned the "cas de conscience" and its supporters. This added to the Cardinal's perplexities, and produced further complications in the general strife of parties. The Pope complained bitterly of persons "who seemed born to disturb without ceasing the peace both of the Church and of the State; who audaciously strove to render nugatory all the exertions which had been made to extirpate an infinitely malignant and dangerous heresy; turbulent, insolent, rebellious spirits, who must be silenced, repressed, overthrown." Cardinal De Noailles, on receiving intelligence that this brief was in preparation at Rome, thought that he could not do better than anticipate it by issuing an ordonnance of similar tenor; "but he anticipated," says D'Aguesseau, "not the brief itself, but only its arrival in France, since the brief was dated on the 12th, and the Cardinal's ordonnance appeared only on the 22nd. There were indeed," continues the Chancellor, "some too accurate chronologists, who affirmed that there was a slight mistake in the date of this ordonnance; and that the news of the forthcoming brief caused it to retrograde some few days, in order that it might seem to be the offspring of free and independent zeal, rather than of constrained and servile complaisance. Be this as it may, the Pope's brief and the mandement of the Cardinal made their appearance nearly at the same moment; and the latter had the fate of almost all the other proceedings of its author—that is to say, it alienated the Jansenists without attracting their opponents to his side." *

As for the Papal brief, it became, through the mismanagement of the Court and the over-scrupulous officiousness of the legal functionaries, the means of aggravating the evil which it was designed to cure. The king communicated it to the bishops, with a letter in which he expressed his determination to support the measures of his Holiness in defence of the integrity of the Faith. Some prelates, in their anxiety to gratify the government, proceeded to publish the brief in mandements to their dioceses, forgetting that such a step was premature, since it had not been received and registered in Parliament. Thereupon the

---

* D'Aguesseau, Mém. sur les Aff. de l'Égl. de France, tom. xiii. p. 203.

mandements of the Bishops of Clermont, Poitiers, Apt, and Sarlat, were attacked as "abusive" by the provincial Parliaments to whose jurisdiction they belonged, and cancelled.* The Bishop of Chartres and other friends of the Jesuits now endeavoured to persuade Louis to issue letters-patent for the registration of the brief; but they were successfully opposed by the Chancellor Pontchartrain and the Procureur-Général D'Aguesseau, who insisted that the Pontifical missive contained statements and pretensions which made its reception impossible in France. It would seem that they were needlessly punctilious in this matter; being actuated, perhaps, by a certain amount of prepossession in favour of the Jansenists. The result, at all events, was unfortunate; for the party hostile to the "cas de conscience," finding that their success in its condemnation was, after all, but partial and equivocal, urged the king to apply to the Holy See for a categorical decision upon the question of the authority of the Church in judging of doctrinal facts; which experience had shown to be in reality the turning-point of the whole Jansenist controversy.

Considerable difference of opinion prevailed among the Gallican prelates and divines upon this deeply interesting but most difficult subject. Many believed, with Cardinal De Noailles, that in the determination of non-revealed facts the Church possesses no more than a moral or natural infallibility, as distinguished from the supernatural illumination of the Divine Spirit. Others held the middle course traced by Bossuet, that a cordial internal submission is due to the decisions of the Church as to such facts, without maintaining that her authority in that respect is absolutely infallible. A third theory, of which Fénélon was the ablest advocate, was that of the Jesuits and other Ultramontanes; according to which the Church is always, equally, and absolutely infallible, whether in definitions of faith properly so called, or in questions of dogmatic fact inseparably allied to the essential truths of revelation.

Those who thus differed in theological principle necessarily differed likewise in their view of the animus of the Church in requiring subscription to the Formulary against Jansenism. Was the acceptance of the Papal constitutions in the affair of

---

* D'Avrigny, *Mém. Chronolog.*, tom. iv. p. 212; Larrey, *Hist. de France sous Louis XIV.* tom. iii. p. 263.

Jansenius imposed as a point of ecclesiastical discipline, or as an article of religious faith pertaining to salvation? If the former, it might be sufficient to submit in "respectful silence;" if the latter, nothing could satisfy such a demand short of an assent identical with that challenged by the voice of Inspiration itself.

Beneath these difficulties, again, lay the dubious problem involved in the conduct of the four recusant bishops in 1668, and the circumstances under which peace had been restored by Clement IX. Did those prelates deal honestly with the Pope, or dishonestly? Was it with his cognisance that they mentally excluded the "fact of Jansenius" from their acceptance of the Formulary, and declared as much in the written statements preserved in their diocesan archives? If Clement deliberately sanctioned their subscription on such terms, with what consistency could any real belief in the heterodoxy of Jansenius be afterwards exacted from the faithful? Why might not the anti-Jansenist test be equally ambiguous and illusory in every other instance? In the confessed uncertainty which shrouded that transaction, everyone had naturally interpreted it so as to suit his own wishes and predilections; and hence it was by no means wonderful to find that Jansenism still survived in France. What hope remained of arresting its future progress, except some fresh and (if possible) more unequivocal enunciation of the truth from the Chair of St. Peter?

The venerable Bishop of St. Pons, who was now the sole survivor of the nineteen prelates who had pleaded with Clement IX. in behalf of their four brethren, declared, in a letter to the Archbishop of Cambrai, that the Pope was fully acquainted with all the particulars of the conduct of those bishops, and that consequently the distinction between the *fait* and the *droit* had his implied, if not explicit, sanction. "The Four Bishops," he said, "were altogether guiltless of bad faith in their submission; nothing whatever was concealed from the Pope as to the contents of their *procès-verbaux*; there was nothing equivocal, nothing forced, nothing contrary to the respect due to the Holy See and to the majesty of the crown, in the letters of the bishops; during the whole of those discussions the doctrine of the Church of France as to non-revealed facts was all but uniform, and reduced itself, with some slight variety of expression, to that of respectful silence; so that, if this sentiment were now pronounced to be heretical, all the bishops who were accounted orthodox at the time of the controversy, though maintaining the sufficiency of respectful silence, would become heretics by professing the very same conviction." The Bishop of St. Pons felt called upon to make this statement by way of reply to a Pastoral Instruction by Fénélon, in February, 1704, in which he accused the four bishops of having deceived the Pope by subscribing the Formulary with a secret reservation, and hinted that, if they were innocent, there was no escaping the conclusion that the Pope himself must have acted with conscious prevarication.*

Such was the conflict of opinion on this subject, when Louis XIV., at the instance of Father La Chaise, the Bishop of Chartres, and other Jesuitical counsellors, resolved to recur once more to the Apostolic See for a final resolution of all doubts as to the meaning and force of the judgments previously delivered in the case of Jansenius. The preliminary negotiations between the two courts for this purpose occupied the whole of the year 1704.

Meanwhile the Gallican Church suffered an irreparable loss in the death of Bossuet. That illustrious prelate expired at Paris on the 12th of April, 1704, in the seventy-seventh year of his age. He had been occupied, even during his last painful illness, in preparing a treatise "on the authority of ecclesiastical judgments, and the submission due to the Church as to matters of fact," with immediate reference to the dispute upon the "cas de conscience." The fatal progress of the malady interrupted his labours, and the work was never completed. A sketch of it, from the original MS. of the author, is preserved by Cardinal Bausset at the end of the fourth volume of his 'Life of Bossuet.'

The removal of one who had played such a conspicuous part in public life, and who had attained such eminence in general estimation not only in France but throughout Europe, must have been seriously felt at any time; but, happening when it did, it was nothing short of a national calamity. Bossuet was

---

* See "Instruction pastorale sur le Cas de conscience" (*Œuvres de Fénélon*, tom. x. p. 153, 154.)

probably the only man in the kingdom who could have restrained the rival factions from plunging afresh into all the hazards and tumult of open war. He was respected and feared by Jesuit and Jansenist alike. Agitators on both sides knew well that he was not to be moved by party considerations; that he was the sworn enemy of evasion and equivocation, of mental reservation, of trickery and intrigue. Though profoundly conversant with the theology of St. Augustine, and an avowed disciple of that Father, no slur of Jansenism had ever been cast upon his name. On the other hand, he never allowed himself to be made a tool of the Jesuits; his learning, his rectitude, his firmness, the native majesty of his genius, overawed them and controlled their excesses. So long as he lived, the impress of that master-spirit was clearly discernible in the conduct of all affairs of moment connected with the Church. His influence over Cardinal de Noailles was a point of immense importance. Although it was impossible to prevent that well-intentioned but feeble-minded prelate from falling into occasional mistakes and inconsistencies which were mischievous both to himself and to the Church, Bossuet generally succeeded in warding off the consequences of his errors, and deterring him from any fatally imprudent course. But when the Cardinal was deprived of his guidance, he experienced the usual fate of those who, in troublesome times, occupy a position of dignity and responsibility for which they are incompetent. If he attempted to stand neutral, he found himself ignored and useless; if he was indulgent, he was ridiculed and imposed upon; if he acted with severity, he stirred up furious opposition. He was forced to become the instrument of measures which in his conscience he reprobated and abhorred. A sincere lover of peace, his life was embittered by perpetual strife; a patriot in the highest sense of the word, he laid the foundation of some of the heaviest disasters of his country. There is reason to believe that, if Bossuet had been spared, he would have dissuaded Louis XIV. from seeking to solve existing difficulties by repeated applications to Rome. But the royal ear was now monopolized by the Jesuits; and they had no other line of action to propose but that of crushing out all opinions differing from their own by successive denunciations from the Vatican; although experience had proved that their opponents were at least equally ingenious in evading the force of such utterances, and rendering them practically abortive.

Scrupulous precautions were taken with a view to make the forthcoming constitution acceptable both to the ecclesiastical and civil authorities in France. The Pope went so far as to communicate with Louis beforehand both as to its matter and its form; and the king submitted the draft to his law officers, in order to make sure that it contained nothing that could offend the most jealous asserters of Gallican independence. These preliminaries having been adjusted, the bull "Vineam Domini Sabaoth" was promulgated at Rome on the 17th of July, 1705; was transmitted by the Nuncio Gualterio to Versailles, and was presented by the king's orders to the Assembly of the Clergy then in session at Paris.

The Holy Father commenced by reciting the decisions of his predecessors Innocent X. and Alexander VII. in condemnation of the Five Propositions of Jansenius, and the measures which had been taken to ensure the acceptance of their sentence in France. He proceeded to complain of "turbulent men who would not acquiesce in the truth, and who contradicted the voice of authority by various distinctions, or rather subterfuges, calculated to involve the Church in endless debates and dissensions." "What is still worse," he continued, "these men avail themselves of the decrees of the Apostolic See directed against their errors, interpreting them falsely to their own exculpation." Thus they abused the letter of Clement IX. to the four protesting bishops in 1669, and the two briefs of Innocent XII. to the bishops of Belgium in 1694; "as if the former Pontiff, after requiring from the said prelates a sincere and absolute submission to the Formulary, had permitted in reality some exception or restriction, contrary to his express declaration; and as if the latter, when he pronounced that the Propositions were condemned in their obvious sense, referred not to the sense in which they were indited by Jansenius, but to some other widely different acceptation." Further, he censured the lately-revived pretext of "respectful silence;"—"a fallacious and absurd expedient, by which men concealed their error, instead of renouncing it; by which the evil was disguised, but not healed; by which the Church was cheated, but not obeyed. With the help of such equivocations men maintained that the Formulary might be lawfully signed by those who did not believe in their hearts that the work of Jansenius contained any heretical doctrine." In conclusion, the Pontiff declared that the Church expected from her children not merely tacit submission ("for even the wicked are silent in darkness"), but a cordial assent and inward conformity; that "respectful silence" by no means suffices for repudiation of the heresies of Jansenius, but that they must be rejected and condemned *ex animo;* and that the Formulary cannot be lawfully subscribed with any other sentiments or upon any other principle. Those who may hold or teach the contrary are pronounced to be violators of the Apostolic Constitutions, and liable to all the pains and penalties therein specified.

Cardinal de Noailles, in announcing the Pope's Constitution to the Assembly, made a curious exhibition of his characteristic want of tact and discretion. He inveighed against the pastoral instructions of several bishops in the matter of the "cas de conscience," which contained, he said, exaggerated statements as to the authority of the Church in determining questions of fact.* Among these he singled out for special animadversion that of Fénélon, who, as the reader will remember, held that the Pope is infallible in such decisions no less than in dogmatic definitions *de fide.* The Cardinal attacked this opinion, and pointed out that the Pope had made no such assumption of infallibility in the bull which they were now called upon to accept. These remarks were singularly unfortunate, both in point of taste and of judgment. Considering the prominent part which the Cardinal had taken in procuring Fénélon's condemnation a few years previously, common delicacy might have prompted him to avoid anything like personal reflection on his conduct on the present occasion; while the criticism on the terms of the Papal bull was equally injudicious, inasmuch as all reference to the claim of infallibility had been studiously omitted (though the existence of the claim was of course notorious) for the express purpose of securing the unanimous adherence of the clergy of France to this new edict of the Roman Curia. It was thus that De Noailles, while professing and desiring to act impartially, made himself virtually an

---

* De Larrey, *Hist. de France sous Louis XIV.* tom. iii. p. 264.

abettor of disaffection and division; his imprudence aroused suspicion in all quarters, and destroyed his usefulness. His address to the Assembly, contrary to almost invariable precedent, was not entered on the official register of the proceedings.

The Assembly received the Constitution "Vineam Domini" with all respect and submission, in accordance with the report of a committee; but adopted previously, by an unanimous vote, the three following maxims:—I. That the bishops possess, by Divine right, the power of judging concerning doctrine together with the Pope. II. That the decisions of the Holy See are obligatory upon the whole Church when they have been accepted by the pastoral body. III. That this acceptance is always made by the episcopate in the form of judgment. Why this declaration was thought necessary does not clearly appear. However true in itself, it was certainly ill-timed at a moment when it was so important that the court of Rome and the Gallican Church should be seen to act in harmonious concert. It was but too probable that the Pope would object to such statements, as suggesting that the bishops were at liberty to sit in judgment on the Vicar of Christ, and to reverse his decisions, if it seemed good to their superior wisdom. Indeed, we learn from the narrative of D'Aguesseau, that the measures taken for the acceptance of the bull excited no small disapprobation in the bosom of the Assembly itself. "The most zealous Anti-Jansenists," he says, "thought they discerned in these proceedings a covert attempt to favour the innovators, and furnish them with specious expedients for eluding the thunders of the Church. They insinuated that, from the principle that Papal constitutions are binding on the Church *when* they have been accepted by the pastoral body, it followed inferentially that *until* the Church, assembled in its corporate form, had accepted such constitutions, they do not possess the force of law; and that nothing more was needed to revive, and that with impunity, all the errors of Jansenius. For the partisans of that heresy would assert, on one side, that the body of Pastors never had solemnly accepted the decisions of the Popes concerning Jansenism, and on the other that those decisions were not obligatory until they had been so received; whence they would assuredly draw the conclusion that nothing at all had been decided against them in a binding form. By such an ambiguous proceeding the laborious efforts of fifty years would be rendered nugatory; the hopes of a party which seemed on the point of being extinguished would be reanimated; and the position and prospects of the Church would be more calamitous than when the disputes began."*

As to the contents of the bull itself, the same author remarks that it was unsatisfactory to both parties; the one being of opinion that it went too far, the other, that it did not go far enough. It went too far for the Jansenists, because it distinctly condemned their favourite resource of "respectful silence," and exacted a positive *bonâ fide* assent and consent to all the dicta of the supreme ecclesiastical tribunal. For the Ultramontanes it did not go far enough, because it abstained from declaring such dicta to be absolutely infallible, and did not require, with regard to matters of fact, a *Divine* faith, like that due to the truths of revelation. Hence disputes arose as to the interpretation of the bull. Some maintained that the Pope claimed for the "fact of Jansenius" the highest and most unqualified species of belief; others held that it was sufficient to accept it with *human* faith, as a matter of discipline and submission to authority; and a third party argued that no judgment as to the fact had been given either one way or the other, inasmuch as no distinction was drawn in precise terms between the fact and the doctrine. Respectful silence, they admitted, is no adequate acceptance of the Church's decisions as to dogma; but they pretended that, for aught that the holy Father had said to the contrary, it was still an open question whether that kind of obedience might not suffice as to external and unrevealed facts. Thus little or no ground was gained towards the termination of the controversy or the real reconciliation of the belligerents.

Clement XI., meanwhile, was seriously offended by the sentiments promulgated by the Assembly of the Clergy in their acceptation of his recent bull. He complained that he had not been treated with good faith. The bull had been almost extorted from him by importunate solicitations from France, upon the express understanding that it was to be

---

* D'Aguesseau, *op. cit.* p. 252.

accepted as it stood, without any reservation derogatory to the Holy See; but no sooner had it reached Paris than the Assembly ignored the conditions upon which it had been granted. The Constitution was subjected to a long examination by a committee of bishops in order to decide whether it should be received or not; and in the end the acceptance of it had been clogged by certain articles which restricted the power of the Pope within such narrow limits that, under a great outward show of respect, they in reality annihilated his authority. To pretend that, after the Sovereign Pontiff has pronounced judgment, it is competent to the bishops to inquire whether that judgment accords with the tradition of the Church, was manifestly to question his supremacy; to debate whether he ought to be obeyed was in itself an act of disobedience. The acceptance of a bull by the episcopate is a matter of submission, not of jurisdiction; its object is to make public the decrees of the Holy See, not to render them irrevocably binding.

The Pope gave expression to these angry feelings in two briefs directed to Cardinal de Noailles and to the king. The former excused himself from receiving the missive, on the ground that, as the Assembly was dissolved, he was no longer its president, and consequently could not act under that character. The Nuncio, upon this, refrained from presenting the second brief officially; but its purport was conveyed privately to Louis, who immediately instructed his Minister at Rome to offer explanations with a view to satisfy his Holiness. The Abbé de Polignac * was accordingly charged to negotiate with Cardinal Fabroni, a prelate who stood high in Clement's favour; and, although the latter was by no means well disposed towards his colleague De Noailles, it seemed likely that an accommodation would be speedily effected. De Noailles forwarded to the Pope a memorial, in which, while he maintained substantially the Gallican theory of episcopal jurisdiction, he softened, as far as possible, whatever might sound harsh to Roman ears, and suggested a construction of the maxims

---

* Melchior de Polignac, Auditor of the Rota, afterwards Archbishop of Auch, and Cardinal. He was highly distinguished as a diplomatist and a man of letters, and succeeded Bossuet in his chair at the Academy. He had been concerned in the reconciliation between Innocent XII. and the French Church in 1693. De Polignac was one of the principal negotiators of the Peace of Utrecht.

asserted by the Assembly which showed that they were vitally important with a view to curb the insubordination of the Jansenists. This document was not altogether relished at the Vatican. Fabroni compared it to a mine which contained large stores of gold, but likewise a quantity of clay; when he came to anything which favoured the Pontifical supremacy, he cried out "This is gold;" but when he encountered statements which wore a contrary aspect, he exclaimed "Here is the clay;" and he concluded by recommending that De Noailles should heat his crucible a second time, and repeat the process of sublimation, so as to purge out all base admixture, and leave only pure metal, worthy of a place in the Apostolic treasury. The French Cardinal agreed to undertake this; but, before the task was finished, an obscure monk, either from officiousness or of malice prepense, called the attention of the Roman Inquisition to Father Quesnel's 'Exposition of the New Testament,' which had already given rise to so much suspicion against the author. It was notorious that this work had been approved by Cardinal de Noailles; and the Abbé de Polignac, on hearing that it had been denounced to the authorities, hastened to point out that any censure of it would be unwise at that moment, since it would offend the Cardinal, and might perhaps frustrate the pending negotiations between the Holy See and the Church of France. Fabroni promised that all possible delicacy should be observed in the affair, and that, if the book were condemned at all, it should be done in such a way as to cast no reflection upon the prelates under whose sanction it originally appeared. When the expurgated letter of De Noailles at length reached Rome, it was found that, in spite of all his precautions, there was still an *argillaceous* residuum, and that it was more than doubtful whether it would give his Holiness entire satisfaction. Its fate was sealed by an unlucky *contretemps* which occurred with reference to Cardinal Fabroni. De Noailles had commenced by an allusion (sufficiently common in documents of that nature) to the parable of the Wheat and the Tares. He was deeply grieved, he said, to find that "the enemy," who was incessantly occupied in sowing tares among the fair corn-fields of the Church, had used his accustomed arts to mislead the Sovereign Pontiff as to the meaning of certain sentiments lately expressed by the clergy of France. Fabroni, on reading this, imagined, or pretended to imagine, that he himself was the enemy referred to, and resented it fiercely as a personal insult. In vain the Abbé de Polignac strove to soothe his irritation by representing that the phrase was one of no special significance, but merely a matter of conventional form on the part of the Cardinal, who could not possibly have designed to offend him in an affair in which his good offices were so indispensable. He obstinately persisted in his absurd persuasion; repeated continually, "I am the evil one," "I am the enemy!" and let fall threats, in the vehemence of his wrath, that, since such was the case, he would take care that Father Quesnel should be condemned with all possible rigour, and that the name of his patron at Paris should not be forgotten on the occasion. De Polignac attempted to renew his pacific efforts, but the Cardinal quitted him abruptly, muttering to himself, with ominous malignity, "The enemy! the enemy!"

Upon this strange scene D'Aguesseau reflects with just severity. "If the Church could perish," he observes, "it would have been destroyed long ago by these and such like causes. But God sustains it against the passions of His own ministers; and, despite Cardinal Fabroni and many others resembling him, the good seed is still preserved in the midst of the tares which "the enemy" has scattered through the world, and which he will always continue to scatter to the end of time."

Fabroni was as good as his word. So industriously did he employ his influence with the Pope, who was already personally prejudiced against De Noailles,* that in July, 1708, a decree was promulgated at Rome condemning the New Testament of Quesnel in terms of extraordinary harshness, prohibiting its circulation, and sentencing it to the flames. "The work," said his Holiness, "contains notes and reflections which have indeed the outward semblance of piety, but withal are artfully calculated to extinguish it; setting forth in divers places doctrines and propositions which are seditious, rash, pernicious, already condemned, and manifestly imbued with the Jansenistic heresy.†

---

* De Noailles was one of the five prelates who, in 1697, had denounced to Innocent XII. a work by Cardinal Sfondrati, entitled *Nodus Prædestinationis dissolutus*. This book was edited, some years after the death of the author, by Cardinal Albani, subsequently Pope Clement XI. See Ledieu, *Journal*, tom. i. p. 25.

† Cardinal de Noailles was so much

But this brief, being in certain respects at variance with the Gallican liberties and the maxims of the Parliament, was not received in France. The cabal against the Cardinal was disconcerted for the moment; but his enemies soon returned to the charge with redoubled energy.

His situation became daily more embarrassing. Madame de Maintenon, who was sincerely attached to him,* entreated him to take some steps to vindicate himself, once for all, from the imputation of patronizing a party whose heterodoxy and factious turbulence had ruined its credit both in Church and State. "I would give my blood," she wrote, " if I could only hear it said, the Cardinal has declared categorically against the Jansenists. I wish you could open your eyes to the universal prevalence of suspicion against you, from prelates down to the humblest religious. The Cardinal is not a Jansenist, but he shows them favour; the Cardinal is no Jansenist, but he is beset by them; the Cardinal is no Jansenist at heart, but he countenances their manœuvres; the Cardinal is not a Jansenist, but they boast of him, though in reality they are much dissatisfied with him. Such, Monseigneur, are the tales that reach me every day, and that grieve me to the soul. My only comfort is, that I have not yet met with any one who accuses you of Jansenism, nor with any one who does not blame you for not taking your stand vigorously against it." †

But neither these remonstrances, nor the importunities of the Bishop of Chartres, who in like manner besought him to act with becoming decision under the existing stress of circumstances, made the desired impression on the Cardinal. Whether from fear of being taunted with inconsistency, or from that obstinacy which is so nearly akin to weakness, or from conscientious approval of Quesnel's work and real sympathy with his opinions, he could not be persuaded to reconsider his position,

---

distressed by this censure of Quesnel's work, in which he believed himself to be personally involved, that he had thoughts of resigning the Archbishopric of Paris. "On dit," says the Abbé Ledieu, "que M. le Cardinal en est fort affligé, le regardant comme une flétrissure de son nom et de sa personne, qui lui est suscitée par les Jésuites; il lui en est venue la pensée, étant en retraite, de quitter sa place, et de céder au temps; mais il n'en fera rien, mieux conseillé.—*Journal de l'Abbé Ledieu*, tom. iii. p. 192.

* De Noailles was connected with Madame de Maintenon's family by the marriage of his nephew, the Comte d'Ayen, with her niece, Françoise d'Aubigné.

† *Lettres et Mémoires de Madame de Maintenon*, tom. x. Lettre ccxix., Oct. 24, 1708.

with a view to such explanations and concessions as his friends deemed necessary. On the contrary, he strove to justify himself by appealing to the authority of Bossuet, who, as the reader will recollect, had examined the 'Reflexions morales' at his request, and had drawn up an 'Avertissement' by way of preface to the edition of 1699.* This had hitherto been suppressed, since those who had undertaken to carry Quesnel's book through the press had not thought proper to adopt the recommendations which were urged by the writer. Bossuet's 'Avertissement' remained, however, among his manuscripts, and was published surreptitiously, after his death, by a zealous partisan of Quesnel's. De Noailles obtained a copy, and circulated it in Paris, as a proof that the book which he was now urged to disavow had been approved in substance by an illustrious doctor of the Church, whose orthodoxy was above all shadow of suspicion. But the sentiments of Bossuet on the general merits of the controversy were well and widely known; and the expedient proved almost wholly useless towards exonerating the Cardinal in the public mind.†

Among the results which followed from the Constitution "Vineam Domini," the most important and the most distressing was the suppression of the doomed monastery of Port-Royal des Champs. The part taken by Cardinal Noailles in this iniquitous deed was contradictory to his known feelings and his habitual policy; it was not, in fact, that of a free agent, but was forced upon him by external pressure. Hitherto he had always protected that ill-starred community; and through his forbearance the prohibition to take novices and pensioners, imposed by De Harlai in 1679, had not been carried out. The idea of lighting afresh the torch of persecution by a second anti-Jansenist test was of all others the least likely to occur to him; especially as no new subscription was prescribed in the bull itself, nor had anything of the kind been proposed by the Assembly of the

---

* See *supra*, p. 94.
† See the *Journal de l'Abbé Ledieu*, tom. iii. p. 333 *et seqq.* I have already mentioned the circumstances which cast some suspicion upon the Cardinal's conduct with respect to this work of Bossuet's, undertaken as it was at his earnest entreaty. Why was not the *Avertissement* published entire at the time when it was first written? Why were large portions of it suppressed? The natural inference is that the work, as indited by the author, was not altogether palatable to the "Quesnellistes;" and that accordingly they made use of that part which suited their purpose, and carefully withheld the rest.

Clergy. On receiving orders from the king, however, to tender the Constitution for signature to the nuns of Port-Royal, he dared not remonstrate against the injustice of the measure, for fear of giving fresh countenance to the current belief of his Jansenistic tendencies. St. Simon attributes the manœuvre to Le Tellier,* but in all probability incorrectly, for that Jesuit had not yet succeeded to the post of confessor at Versailles. There were others of his Order near the monarch's person, not to mention many courtiers of high rank devoted to their views, who doubtless made full use of the opportunity.

The Cardinal-archbishop, as if to show his impartiality, commenced by demanding subscription to the Papal bull from the sisterhood of Gif, a neighbouring convent which had always maintained a cordial friendship with Port-Royal. Here the test was accepted without difficulty; and it seems that other houses were equally compliant. Port-Royal signed in its turn; but appended to the certificate the following restrictive clause,—"without prejudice to what was done in our favour at the Peace of the Church under Clement IX." The Cardinal objected to this proviso; but the abbess reminded him that his predecessor Archbishop Péréfixe had declared himself perfectly satisfied with their signature of the Formulary in 1669, made in exact conformity with that of the four bishops, which had the sanction of the Pope himself. It was upon the strength of that arrangement that they had been reinstated in their convent; and it was clearly impossible for them now to ignore its terms, or to refrain from claiming its advantages. This reasoning was logically unanswerable. The subscription demanded to the "Vineam Domini" was either consonant with the terms of the Peace of Clement IX., or repugnant to them; in the former case, the clause proposed by Port-Royal was manifestly legitimate; in the latter, they could not obey without violating the formal engagement with their diocesan forty years before. But the nuns forgot, or did not perceive, that the Peace of Clement IX., upon which they rested their defence, was a mere compromise; and that the time for compromises was past. In 1669 the Curia, alarmed by the imminence of schism, had wisely consented to meet the Jansenists half-way in

---

* *Mémoires de St. Simon*, tom. v. chap. vi.

order to effect an accommodation; but since that time the posture of affairs had changed materially. Port-Royal had lost its ablest champions, while the chief positions of influence and command were occupied by its mortal foes. The party was no longer formidable either in respect of numbers, ability, social rank, or political importance; the only person in high station who had shown a disposition in its favour, Cardinal de Noailles, found himself compelled to retract, and was playing the game of those who had vowed its destruction. To prolong the struggle was evidently hopeless. The Cardinal himself acknowledged to Marignier the confessor of Port Royal, that even if the sisters had yielded unconditionally in the present instance, they would have been none the better off in a worldly point of view, since the extinction of their house had been long ago resolved upon in the royal counsels.*

The signature with the addition of the qualifying clause being pronounced inadmissible, Port-Royal was consigned to summary vengeance, and every principle of law and equity was outraged in order to ensure its downfall. In 1706 the abbess was prohibited by royal mandate from receiving novices for the future. In the following year the convent of Port-Royal at Paris appealed to the crown against the division of corporate property which had been made between the two houses at the time of their separation nearly forty years previously.† The decision was in their favour; the king revoked the settlement by letters patent, and decreed that the whole revenue of both houses should be appropriated to that of Paris. By this act of sudden disendowment the persecuted community was reduced to utter penury. They defended themselves, nevertheless, with admirable energy, and sustained a tedious process in the "officialité" of the Cardinal; but it was clear that no arguments would be allowed to turn the balance in their favour. The eloquence of their advocate attracted eager crowds of the

---

* *Histoire de Port-Royal*, tom. iii. p. 150.

† In May, 1668. One-third of the revenue was adjudged to Port-Royal at Paris, two-thirds to Port Royal des Champs. This arrangement was confirmed by a Bull of Pope Clement IX. in September, 1671. The details are given in the *Gualterio Papers* (Brit. Mus. Add. MSS., 20,401):—" Mémoire sur ce qu'il conviendroit faire pour réunir le monastère de Port-Royal des Champs à celuy de Paris."

Parisians to hear the pleadings, and their memorials, which abounded with intelligence and talent, were applauded on all sides. But all was unavailing to change the predetermined sentence. The Cardinal by an ordinance of November 18, 1707, pronounced them "contumacious and disobedient to the Apostolical constitutions;" he rejected their saving clause as "illusory, evasive of the law, and injurious to the Holy See;" and, having no further hope that they would submit to the wisdom of the Church, he interdicted them from the use of the Sacraments, deprived them of all voice, active and passive, in the management of the concerns of their convent, and forbade them to assemble to elect an abbess. Against this decree they appealed, but uselessly, to the primatial see of Lyons.

In March, 1708, Clement XI. published a bull, which was followed three months later by a second, definitively suppressing the Abbey of Port-Royal des Champs, and annexing its property to the establishment at Paris. But by a renewed series of petitions, protests, and other acts of resistance, the final catastrophe was adjourned till late in the year ensuing. In a last appeal to De Noailles, which contains passages of remarkable power and pathos, the nuns consoled themselves by the consideration that, if they were to be driven from their beloved home, it was not for any laxity of morals or neglect of monastic discipline, not for having incurred extravagant expense, not for having indulged in worldly habits and worldly society, not for having maintained any error contrary to the Faith, not for having failed in due submission to their superiors (unless it was deemed a want of such submission to hold sentiments approved by the Holy See, by Archbishop Péréfixe, and by his Majesty), but solely because the Port-Royalists of Paris were envious of the blessing with which God had distinguished Port-Royal des Champs; and sought to repair the ruins of their own house by destroying that of their sisters. "Alas! Monseigneur," they exclaimed, "what a wretched inheritance for them is this fatness of the earth, when they are destitute of the dew of heaven, which can never descend in benediction on such a deed of spoliation! As for ourselves, since most of us are by reason of our years and infirmities drawing near to the gates of eternity, it is of small importance to us in what condition we may finish our course, provided God will grant us grace to continue faithful to Him even to the end.*

The Cardinal, by way of ultimatum, published the letter which had been written by the late Bishop of Meaux at the desire of Archbishop Péréfixe, for the purpose of persuading the recusant sisters to sign the Formulary on the principle of "human faith." It is doubtful, as I have observed elsewhere, whether this letter was ever sent to Port-Royal; the nuns declared that no mention of it was to be found in the records of the convent, nor any evidence that it had been answered by the community. But however this may have been, the publication of the document was not likely to have any practical effect in the present state of the case. In the first place, the signature of the Formulary of Alexander VII. had been imposed upon the whole Gallican Church by the authority of the Pope and the Assembly of the Clergy; whereas subscription to the "Vineam Domini" was not exacted either by Pope or clergy, nor by any one except the king and Cardinal de Noailles. And moreover, it appeared from the very terms of the recent constitution, that the system formerly advocated by Bossuet was now considered inadmissible. Bossuet had urged compliance as a matter of external respect to authority; the bull demanded an interior conformity; an assent of the heart and of the will.

The hour at length arrived when the curtain was to fall on the last scene of this melancholy drama. In August, 1709, the abbess of the Paris convent proceeded in person to Port-Royal des Champs, armed with an *arrêt* of the Parliament, and summoned the prioress and sisters to acknowledge her as their superior, in virtue of the decree by which the two communities had been amalgamated into one. They calmly declined to obey, and executed a protest to that effect in presence of the notaries. The abbess was then put into possession, with the customary formalities, of the Church, the conventual buildings, and the dependencies of the house; after which she took her departure to St. Cyr, to report to Madame de Maintenon the success of her expedition.

Michel Le Tellier, a man of stern, inflexible, ruthless character, with whom the supremacy of his Order seems to have been the

---

* *Histoire de Port-Royal*, tom. iii. p. 179.

one paramount end of existence, now governed the conscience of Louis XIV., in succession to the easy-tempered Father La Chaise. To him, unless gross injustice has been done him by the testimony of history from that day to the present, belongs the unenviable distinction of having instigated the severities which resulted, first in the desolation, and ultimately in the demolition, of Port-Royal des Champs. He represented to the king that the new abbess could not discharge the duties of her office, by reason of the perverseness and insubordination of the community over which she had been called to preside; and insisted that the only remedy was to break up the existing sisterhood, and place the nuns separately in approved convents in different parts of the country, where they could hold no communication with each other, and would consequently be incapable of doing further mischief. Louis blindly assented, and an ordonnance authorizing this cruel project was issued by the Council of State. Its execution was entrusted to the Marquis D'Argenson, lieutenant of police; who, on the 29th of October, 1709, made his appearance at the convent gates, furnished with an ample supply of *lettres de cachet*, and attended by commissaries, exempts, and a body of three hundred soldiers. Proceeding to the chapter-house, D'Argenson seated himself in the abbess's stall, and demanded in the king's name the title-deeds and other legal documents belonging to the house. They were delivered up immediately, and he placed his seal upon the coffers. After applauding them for their compliance, he proceeded to announce that he was the bearer of commands far more painful and severe, to which, nevertheless, it was necessary to submit. The king, for various well-considered reasons, and for the good of the State, thought fit that the nuns of Port-Royal should be separated from each other, and distributed in religious houses beyond the limits of the diocese of Paris. The Prioress ventured to express her surprise that Cardinal De Noailles, being their lawful superior, should exile them to convents out of his own jurisdiction; to which the reply was that he had his reasons for so doing. Without delay, a train of coaches was drawn up in the court-yard; and the sisters, having made a few hasty preparations for departure, were consigned to the charge of the exempts, to be conducted, some singly, some in pairs, to the convents named in the *lettres de cachet.* The prioress, Louise Dumesnil De Courtiaux, was exiled to Blois; the rest to Chartres, Mantes, Meaux, Compiègne, Rouen, Amiens, Autun, and Nevers. Rigorous instructions were given as to the treatment of the prisoners in their new abodes; they were to be strictly debarred from commerce with the outer world, and not admitted to the Sacraments except in case of repentance.

The vengeance of the Jesuits against Port-Royal was not satiated even by this forcible dispersion of its inmates. The language of the bull of suppression authorized the total demolition of that "nest of heresy"; and the Pope, for that purpose, revoked "all that might have been ordained to the contrary by authority of whatever kind, even were it that of a General Council." A royal ordonnance in conformity with this sentence was published in January, 1710. His Majesty enjoined that the abbey buildings should be forthwith levelled with the ground; assigning as his motive, that the expense of maintaining and repairing them would fall heavily upon Port-Royal of Paris, and that the sale of the materials would be highly advantageous to the creditors of that community.* The services of D'Argenson were again put in requisition; and with such zeal did he superintend the work of destruction, that in a brief space not one stone was left standing on another of this celebrated cloister, which for seventy years had held so conspicuous a place in the religious history of France. The abbey church shared the same fate shortly afterwards; and, by an act of revolting barbarity, the dead were at the same time disinterred from their graves in the surrounding cemetery, and transferred, under circumstances scandalously indecent, to other resting-places in the neighbourhood. These profanations were wreaked upon the remains of some of the most illustrious denizens of Port-Royal—the Tillemonts, the Nicoles, the De Sacys, even the Arnaulds. Many tombstones removed from the violated sepulchres are to be seen to this day in the parish

---

* "La maison de P.-R. de Paris est tombée dans une extrême pauvreté; on est à la veille d'en voir tous les biens vendus par les créanciers, et les religieuses dans la nécessité de chercher des retraites dans leurs familles. Il n'y a d'autre moyen d'empêcher ce désordre que de rendre à leur maison les biens de P.-R. des Champs, qui luy ont autrefois appartenu."—*Gualterio Papers.*

churches and churchyards of St. Lambert, Palaiseau, and Magny.*

That such vile deeds should have been perpetrated in the name of Religion, of the Church of Christ, of zeal for the integrity and purity of the Catholic faith, is a fact profoundly humiliating, which may be pondered on with profit in every age of controversial irritation. The destruction of Port-Royal was a spectacle well calculated not only to disabuse mankind of the baseless fiction of Pontifical infallibility, but to suggest doubts as to the mission and authority of the Church herself. If the sisters had impugned the fundamental verities of Christianity—if they had been blasphemers, infidels, apostates, or idolators—if they had been notoriously remiss in discipline or depraved in morals—the punishment with which they were visited might not have been disproportioned to their demerits. But what was, in reality, "the head and front of their offending"? In subscribing the constitution "Vineam Domini," they had ventured to stipulate that no prejudice should be done thereby to a former decision made in their favour, at a critical moment of their history, by the selfsame Pontifical authority. In obeying Clement XI., they declined to ignore or abandon Clement IX. It is easy to say that they misinterpreted the terms of the pacification under Clement IX. This, as we have seen, is an obscure and debateable question; but, supposing that their view of those terms was mistaken, was it just that for this reason they should be subjected to an act of vengeance so sweeping and so irremediable? Might not such an error, even if aggravated (as doubtless it was) by obstinacy and insubordination, have been atoned for by a less crushing penalty than that of wholesale extirpation?

The fate of Port-Royal becomes still more mournful when we reflect that Cardinal de Noailles must have been, in these last transactions, an unwilling agent, and must have felt in his conscience that he was doing a cruel wrong. Once more that unfortunate prelate had been forced by his enemies into a false position. Practising on his nervous anxiety to clear himself of

---

* The Marquis de Pomponne interred several of his relatives (the Arnaulds) in the church of Palaiseau, placing over them the singularly appropriate epitaph, "Tandem requiescant."

complicity with Jansenism, they inveigled him step by step into a series of measures wholly foreign to his principles, which ruined his peace of mind for ever. He was not naturally prone to persecution, still less was he disposed to persecute Port-Royal; yet such was the course of events, that its overthrow was ultimately his work, and it was impossible for him to escape the responsibility and odium resulting from it. He was the victim of an inexorable fatality. "He discovered the enormity of his fault," says St. Simon, "when it was no longer possible for him to parry a blow which was beyond his foresight, and which, indeed, none could have anticipated. He gained nothing by it in the estimation of the Molinists, and lost credit grievously as regards the Jansenists, which was precisely the result contemplated by the Jesuits. From the date of that deplorable event he declined in health, and was driven headlong without intermission from one extremity to another until his life was brought to a close." *

Few scenes in history are more affecting than that drawn by the annalists of Port-Royal of the Cardinal's pilgrimage to the ruins of the desecrated sanctuary. Scourged by ceaseless remorse, he resolved to seek relief by an act of solemn penance performed on the spot. He proceeded thither, attended only by his secretary Thomassin, a faithful monitor who had earnestly laboured to dissuade him from the policy which now weighed so intolerably on his conscience. On reaching the site of the abbey, he became completely unnerved by emotion; his lamentations were piteous; he was convulsed by tears and sobs. Wringing his hands in an agony of grief, he cast himself upon the ground, and cried aloud to heaven for mercy. "O," said he, "all these dismantled stones will rise up against me at the day of judgment! O how shall I ever endure this vast, this heavy load!" It was with difficulty that the secretary succeeded in replacing him in his carriage, and bringing him back to Paris.† Nor does it appear that the poignancy of his compunction was much assuaged by the lapse of time. He was heart-broken; sinking at times into a settled gloom not far removed from despair.

---

* *Mém. de St. Simon*, tom. v. p. 76.
† Pontain, *Histoire abrégée de Port-Royal*, tom. i. p. 306, 307 (Paris, 1786).
See also the "Ruines de Port-Royal," by the Abbé Grégoire. *Annales de la Religion*, tom. xiii. p. 57.

Before proceeding with the history of a series of events which issued in fresh calamities both to Church and State in France, it may be advisable to take a brief review of the situation of parties as they existed at the beginning of the year 1710.

The reader must recollect, then, that Louis XIV. was now far advanced in age and broken in health; that fortune had latterly been adverse to him in the prosecution of the arduous "War of the Succession;" that he was often sorely disquieted by the remembrance of the scandals and disorders of his early life; and that all these causes concurred to subject him more and more absolutely to the dominion and dictation of his Jesuit confessor. Father La Chaise had died, full of years and generally regretted, in January, 1709. On his deathbed he mentioned, by the king's desire, several members of his Order out of whom his Majesty might choose a successor in the guidance of his conscience. At the head of this list was Michel Le Tellier, Provincial of the Jesuits in France; and Louis, merely because the name was the first that met his eye, appointed him to the vacant post. Writers of Jansenistic proclivities (in particular St. Simon) paint the character of Le Tellier in the most forbidding colours. According to them, he was a man profoundly false and treacherous, who owned no other God but his Society, and studied nothing except its tortuous intrigues; one who masked his designs under a thousand hypocritical disguises; one who hesitated at nothing when he had the opportunity of making himself feared; one who laughed at the most positive engagements when it no longer suited him to acknowledge their obligation, and pursued with relentless malice those with whom he had contracted them.* Some deduction should perhaps be made from this estimate in consideration of the bitterness of party spirit; but the portrait, as to its leading features, does not appear to be overdrawn. Le Tellier had a personal pique against Cardinal de Noailles; he detested the Jansenists with a deep, ferocious hatred; and it was his first object of ambition to make his Order paramount in authority, not only in France, but throughout the world. Nurtured from his youth in the theology of Molina, he not only maintained it

---

* *Mém. de St. Simon*, tom. iv. p. 289; Duclos, *Mém. Secrets*, Liv. i. (Petitot, *Collection des Mémoires*, tom. lxxvi.).

zealously, but was violently intolerant of every other school and system. All who thought differently he regarded as his natural enemies, to be resisted, humbled, discomfited, at all hazards, in order that the doctrine espoused by his Society might be in the end universally and exclusively triumphant. His predecessor La Chaise was a man of refinement and cultivation—courteous, candid, honourable, humane; Le Tellier was a parvenu, a bigot, a firebrand; one whose only idea of government was that of reckless, iron-hearted despotism. Possessing, by virtue of his office, the "feuille des bénéfices," his influence among the aspirants to ecclesiastical distinction was of course immense; and he is said to have used it, not for purposes actually corrupt, but as a means of raising to the episcopate ignorant men of narrow capacity and elastic conscience, upon whom he could depend for unscrupulous devotion to his will.*

The Bishop of Chartres, Godet-Desmarais, who since the disgrace of Fénélon had enjoyed the undivided confidence of Madame de Maintenon, together with a considerable share in the administration of the Church, expired in the autumn of the same year 1709; leaving behind him the reputation of an able theologian, an exemplary pastor, and a man of self-denying saintly life. His mantle fell, unfortunately, upon two persons of inferior calibre, with whom he had been closely associated in his later years: these were Thiard De Bissy, Bishop of Meaux, and La Chétardie, Curé of St. Sulpice. The recommendation of one who had served her so long and faithfully was all-powerful with Madame de Maintenon; she forthwith made La Chétardie her confessor, while De Bissy succeeded, through her patronage, to the influence which the late prelate had exercised upon the general direction of ecclesiastical affairs. Both the one and the other were pledged to Ultramontanism, and pliant instruments in the hands of Le Tellier.

The exiled Archbishop of Cambrai, in like manner, was a staunch adherent of the cause represented by the Jesuits, and maintained confidential relations with Le Tellier. His conduct

---

* Le Tellier had been one of the chief actors in the disgraceful affair called the "fourberie de Douai." He defended his Order with vigour and ability in the controversy on the "Chinese ceremonies." His *Défense des nou-* *veaux Chrétiens et des Missionaires de la Chine, du Japon, et des Indes, contre deux livres intitulés* ' *La Morale pratique des Jésuites*' *et* ' *L'esprit de M. Arnauld,*' was placed on the Roman Index, "donec corrigatur," Dec. 22, 1700.

at this period was prompted by a variety of motives. He was earnestly opposed by principle and conviction to the Jansenist opinions; he could not but remember with gratitude the friendly offices of the Jesuits at a moment when both his doctrinal integrity and his personal reputation hung trembling in the balance at Rome; he seems to have cherished some hope of retrieving his fortunes and reappearing on the scene of public life; and lastly (since even Fénélon had his share in the inevitable frailties of humanity), it is possible that he viewed with latent satisfaction the gathering storm which was about to burst on Cardinal de Noailles. For similar reasons, the Dukes of Beauvilliers and Chevreuse, still devotedly attached to Fénélon, and still possessed of important influence at court, readily countenanced the schemes of Le Tellier and his Order.

The party commanded powerful support, as we have seen, in the Roman Curia. "The enemy," in the shape of Fabroni, was intently on the watch for any opportunity of avenging the imaginary stigma inflicted on him by his brother De Noailles. The Pope consulted him in everything, and his ascendency at the Vatican was complete. Cardinal de la Tremoille was a man of no personal weight or merit, but he was French Chargé d'Affaires at Rome, and a brother of the celebrated Princess Orsini, on both which grounds his adhesion to the project was a point of the utmost consequence. A third auxiliary was Father Daubenton, a man of ability, learning, and experience, who held the post of French assistant to the General of the Jesuits. He had long been on intimate terms with Fabroni, and corresponded confidentially with Fénélon.

Cardinal de Noailles, on the other hand, had but few on whom he could rely for steadfast and intelligent co-operation in the approaching conflict. His chief allies in the episcopate were Hébert Bishop of Agen, De la Broue Bishop of Mirepoix (the trusted friend of Bossuet), Clermont Tonnerre Bishop of Langres, and Colbert Bishop of Montpellier.* Among the ministers of state there was a small, but distinguished, minority who sympathised with him in disputing the supremacy of the Jesuits, and who viewed with jealous eyes the encroachments of

---

* Charles Joachim Colbert, second son of Charles Colbert, Marquis de Croissy, nephew of the famous minister of Louis XIV., and brother of the Secretary of State De Torcy.

Rome on Gallican independence, ecclesiastical and political. This consisted of the Chancellor Pontchartrain; of Henri François D'Aguesseau, then Procureur-Général, subsequently Chancellor; and of the Marquis de Torcy, Secretary of State, who was a nephew of the great Colbert, and married to a lady of the Arnauld family.* The Duke de Saint Simon, again, must be quoted among those who entertained sentiments decidedly opposed to Ultramontanism, both as regards the Jansenistic controversy and the Gallican liberties.† But this nobleman possessed at that moment little or no political importance. He studiously abstained from identifying himself with any particular section of the Church, and cultivated amicable relations with all parties. He venerated Port-Royal, yet withal was on the best terms with Fathers La Chaise and Le Tellier, and other Jesuits; he enjoyed the confidence of the Duke of Burgundy, the pupil of Fénélon and Beauvilliers; and he not only contrived to persuade the court and the government that he was himself pure from all taint of Jansenism, but succeeded in clearing no less a personage than the Chancellor Pontchartrain from that most dangerous impeachment.‡ Accordingly, it was no part of St. Simon's policy to declare himself openly in defence and vindication of the Cardinal, although no man more thoroughly appreciated his virtues, or more strongly reprobated the malicious intrigues of which he was the victim.§

The first proof given by Le Tellier of his determination to mortify and depress Cardinal de Noailles was to extort from him certain explanations of the doctrines laid down by the Assembly of the Clergy on the occasion of their accepting the bull "Vineam Domini." The *procès-verbal* of the Assembly of 1705 was about to be printed; and the new confessor persuaded the king that it ought not to be made public without inserting expressions calculated to satisfy the Pope, who still resented the bold pretensions advanced by the Gallican episcopate. D'Aguesseau recounts the various efforts which

---

* Catherine Felicité, daughter of Simon Arnauld, Marquis de Pomponne, and grand-niece of Antoine Arnauld.

† St. Simon's profession of faith upon these subjects will be found in his *Mé-*

moires, tom. vi. p. 127 (edit. Paris, 1857). His *précis* of Gallicanism, from a layman's point of view, is forcibly expressed, and worthy of all praise.

‡ *Mém. de St. Simon*, tom. vi. p. 123.
§ *Ibid.*, p. 209.

were made to induce the Cardinal to explain away his own deliberate act, and the characteristic fluctuations of his mind while the affair was in agitation.* At length he consented to sign, in concert with eleven other prelates, a "Declaration" addressed to the Pope, in which the maxims which had offended his Holiness were considerably modified, if not virtually disavowed. This document stated (1) that the Assembly, in asserting that the decisions of the Pope are obligatory when they had been revised by the Episcopate, did not mean that such Constitutions are not, without such formal acceptance, to be regarded by the faithful as the rule of belief and conduct; but only designed thereby to drive the Jansenists into their last entrenchments, by employing against them a principle avowedly maintained by themselves. (2). The Assembly disclaimed all pretensions to examine the dogmatic judgments of the Pope, in the sense of submitting them to a superior tribunal of revision; it only ventured to compare its own sentiments with those enunciated by his Holiness, and rejoiced to find that its belief upon the points in question had always been in exact conformity with that expressed in the Constitution. (3). The Assembly was fully convinced that in the Papal bulls against Jansenius nothing was wanting to make them universally binding on the Church; that no appeal from them was permissible, and that it was not to be expected that they could be in any wise altered. In conclusion, the prelates earnestly protested, in their own names and in that of the Gallican Church collectively, that nothing was nearer to their hearts than to manifest their profound respect for the See of Rome and their submissiveness to its decrees, after the example of their predecessors in all ages. The letter was dated June 29, 1711, and was presented to the Pope by Cardinal de la Tremoille on the 24th of July following.

It may be easily conceived that it was no slight annoyance to Cardinal de Noailles to be made a party to this Declaration, containing as it did admissions irreconcileable with the principles of Gallicanism, and with his own previously-expressed opinions. "In this affair," says D'Aguesseau, "the Cardinal was duped by his yielding temper and defective foresight. He did what the

---

* D'Aguesseau, "Mém. sur les Aff. de l'Égl. de France" (*Œuvres*, tom. xiii. p. 290).

king required, yet without gratifying the king; he laboured for peace, yet found it not, since he was subsequently compelled to take the same measures in order to satisfy the Pope as if he had never signed the Declaration; and of those concessions the Pope failed not to make an advantageous use, as I had predicted."

De Noailles, relying on his conscious rectitude, soon fell more and more hopelessly into the toils spread for him by the Jesuitical cabal. The king regarded him with suspicion; Madame de Maintenon, once his warmest friend, became estranged, if not actively hostile; his clergy began to stand aloof from him; those who were preferred to the highest stations in the Church, such as Cardinal de Rohan and De Mailly, Archbishop of Reims, were uniformly opposed to him. And now commenced the train of events which led to the promulgation of the ill-omened Constitution "Unigenitus,"— a subject upon which volumes have been written, all illustrating with more or less power the multiplied calamities which it heaped upon France, whether considered as a Monarchy, as a Church, or as a nation. Without fear of misinterpreting the momentous lessons of history, we may reckon the ecclesiastical agitation which now arose among the indirect, yet efficient and unquestionable, causes of the Great Revolution.

CHAPTER VI.

The censure passed at Rome, in 1708, on the New Testament of Father Quesnel proved ineffectual, as we have mentioned, by reason of certain expressions which were pronounced at variance with the maxims of Gallican jurisprudence. The work continued to enjoy wide-spread estimation in France. Many bishops publicly recommended it to their clergy and their flocks; among others De Bissy, Bishop of Meaux. Father La Chaise kept it constantly upon his table, frankly declaring that he loved what was good and valuable from whatever quarter it might come, and that he never opened the book without lighting upon something by which he was instructed and edified. The opposition to it, however, was by no means abandoned. To compass its definitive condemnation was an object which the Ultramontanes kept pertinaciously in view, both from general jealousy of its celebrity as the production of an adverse theological school, and from special enmity against Cardinal de Noailles, its avowed and steadfast patron. It was resolved to make a second attempt to discredit and suppress it; and for this purpose two bishops hitherto unknown to fame, De Lescure of Luçon and Champflour of La Rochelle, issued, in July, 1710, a joint pastoral Instruction, in which they denounced the work in question as fraught with deadly heresy. This was a carefully concerted movement. According to St. Simon's account, it was projected by Le Tellier, not without the countenance and assistance of Fénélon.* A priest named Chalmette, well-instructed in the details of the scheme, communicated confidentially with the two prelates, and arranged with them, if he did not actually dictate, the terms of the afore-

---

* Fénélon himself, however, positively denied that he had any concern in it. (See his letter to the Maréchale de Noailles, *Corresp.*, tom. iv. p. 8.) The testimony of St. Simon throughout this affair must be received with reserve.

said manifesto;* which was a treatise of considerable length, designed to prove that all the errors of Jansenius on the mysteries of grace were reproduced, though covertly and stealthily, in the 'Reflexions' of Quesnel. Malissoles, Bishop of Gap, supported his colleagues by a mandement to the same effect.

The "Instruction" of the Bishops of La Rochelle and Luçon was no sooner in print, than the publisher forwarded copies of it to his correspondent at Paris; and the latter caused it to be announced by placards or handbills throughout the capital. Some of these notices were affixed to the gates of the archiepiscopal palace; a proceeding which is stated by some writers to have been customary in such cases, but which was far more probably a piece of deliberate insolence. Cardinal de Noailles was profoundly offended by it, and unhappily gave vent to his feelings in a style which ill accorded with the dignity of his position. The two bishops had each a nephew studying at the Seminary of St. Sulpice; the Cardinal, too hastily adopting the suggestions of those around him, credited these young men with the authorship of the act which had roused his indignation, and insisted upon their being immediately dismissed from the Seminary. No proof was producible against them; on the contrary, their character was excellent, and the Superior assured the Cardinal that it was impossible they could have been guilty of such gross impropriety.† They were expelled notwithstanding; whereupon the two bishops addressed a letter to the king (which is said to have been inspired by Le Tellier), bitterly remonstrating against the indignity. They protested that they did not demand justice for the injury done to themselves or their relatives, but that the cause which they pleaded was that of the Church, of the episcopate, of sound doctrine, and of legitimate liberty; ‡ after which they indulged in some severe

---

* Several letters from the Abbé de Langeron, the intimate friend of Fénélon, to Chalmette, who was a canon of La Rochelle, will be found in the *Correspondance de Fénélon*, tom. iii. (Paris, 1827). Chalmette was afterwards sent to Rome by the two bishops as their accredited agent in the dispute with Cardinal de Noailles.

† See the "Mémoire historique" on these occurrences in the *Corresp. de Fénélon*, tom. iv. p. 227. De Larroy, however, ascribes the offence, without hesitation, to the two students (*Hist. de France sous Louis XIV.*, tom. iii. p. 492).

‡ They complain, too, that Jansenistic error was greatly on the in-

reflections on De Noailles, as an abettor of innovation and heresy, and an enemy to the peace of society; comparing him to those proud prelates of imperial cities under the Lower Empire, who, abusing the authority of their station, tyrannized over their colleagues, and governed their flocks not by charity, but by cruelty and terror. The picture was ludicrously unlike the gentle-tempered, peace-loving Cardinal; nevertheless it was not without its effect, since it altered to some extent the position of parties, and represented De Noailles as the aggressor, whereas in reality he was the person sinned against.

Public opinion declared itself strongly on the side of the Archbishop. The Chapter of Notre Dame, the clergy of the diocese, the religious communities, the doctors of the Sorbonne, sent deputations to the palace to express their indignation at the affront offered to their metropolitan, and to request that the "Instruction" of the two prelates, together with their libellous letter to the king,* might be forthwith suppressed by authority. The king, though he could not approve the conduct of the Cardinal in the summary expulsion of the two seminarists, promised him satisfaction for the wrong he had sustained; and the latter would have consulted at once his dignity and his interest by awaiting the result with patience. Instead of this, he was unwise enough to publish an ordonnance, dated April 28th, 1711, condemning the Pastoral Instruction of the Bishops of La Rochelle and Luçon, and the mandement of the Bishop of Gap. He accused the Instruction of favouring one of the Five Propositions of Jansenius, though professedly designed to overthrow them; and of reproducing some of the proscribed errors of Baius. The mandement he censured as disrespectful to St.

---

crense. "L'erreur fait chaque jour d'immenses progrès par le moyen de plusieurs livres, les uns dédiés à M. le Cardinal, d'autres approuvés par lui, ou par gens à lui, tous venant d'auteurs qui lui sont chers. L'étrange situation, que celle où les évêques vont se trouver! Regarderont-ils tranquillement, chacun dans leur diocèse, la portion du troupeau que le Seigneur leur a confiée, s'empoisonner dans ces livres pernicieux? Parleront-ils, au péril, no disons point de so voir maltraités dans leurs personnes ou dans les membres de leurs familles, car ils doivent compter cela pour rien; mais au péril de voir éclater des ressentiments scandaleux qui déshonorent l'épiscopat, au péril de voir ces mauvais livres soutenus et autorisés par ceux qui devroient être les premiers à les proscrire?"—*Corresp. de Fénélon*, tom. iii. p. 327.

* It is not known by what means the letter to the king became a matter of publicity. The two bishops always denied that this was caused by any act of theirs.

Augustine, and tending to depreciate the authority of his writings in the eyes of the faithful. If such productions were allowed to circulate, encouragement would thereby be given, he said, to the renewal of the worst of those corruptions, both doctrinal and moral, which had been so often condemned by the Popes, and especially by the Gallican Assembly of 1700. This preamble was followed by a decree suppressing the documents in question, which the Cardinal affected to consider as falsely attributed to the prelates whose names they bore.

This was precisely the sort of proceeding calculated to exasperate Louis XIV. An appointment had been made with the Cardinal for an audience, at which the steps to be taken in his vindication were to be arranged; but on the very day that his Ordonnance appeared, the king sent him a message by the Chancellor, that "since he had already done justice to himself, he need not take the trouble of coming to Marly."*

Upon this his sorely-tried patience seems to have failed him. "My misfortune is complete," he wrote to Madame de Maintenon; "I am calumniated, outraged, disgraced. The Jesuits had tormented me in a thousand ways; their malice seemed to be exhausted, though my patience was not. Now they suborn two prelates to slander me in the ears of the king; they post up mandements against me on the walls of my cathedral and on the gates of my palace; and withal they require me to hold my peace, and to acquiesce, by cowardly silence, in my own dishonour. The three bishops have disseminated false doctrine in my diocese; it is my duty to repair the mischief. Is it just that, while the meanest of all the bishops are allowed to publish mandements, the right to do the same should be denied to an Archbishop of Paris? I beseech you, Madame, to read mine with attention, and to acknowledge that, after having shown so much moderation, I had no reason to expect such a letter as

---

* La Beaumelle, *Mém. de Madame de Maintenon*, tom. v. p. 102; "Le P. Lallemant à Fénélon," 17 mai, 1711 (*Corresp. de Fénélon*, tom. iii. p. 349). Madame de Maintenon writes as follows to the Duke de Noailles, May 5, 1711:— "Je ne vous parlerai plus de M. le Cardinal. J'ai fait ce que j'ai pu pour adoucir tout de part et d'autre. Je déplais aux deux partis, parceque je ne suis d'aucun; on voudroit m'y entraîner, mais les matières en question me passent. J'ai résolu de n'en plus parler; je vous dirai seulement que la lettre des évêques est publique et insoutenable; que le Roi indigné en vouloit faire raison à M. le Cardinal; et que, sans attendre le jour de l'audience, il se l'est faite lui-même."

the king has caused to be sent to me by M. de Pontchartrain."*

The king, alarmed by the spectacle of division and confusion in the episcopate, entrusted to the Duke of Burgundy, who had recently become Dauphin by the death of his father, the difficult task of interposing as mediator between the contending parties. That prince called to his assistance the Archbishop of Bordeaux, the Bishop of Meaux, the Chancellor Pontchartrain, the Duke de Beauvilliers, and the Secretary of State Voisin. They proposed, as a plan of accommodation, that the two bishops should draw up a second mandement, explaining those passages in the first which had given offence to the Cardinal and his clergy; that the Cardinal, accepting this as a reparation, should submit to mutual friends the draft of a fresh ordonnance, revoking the prohibition of the "Pastoral Instruction" of his colleagues, and disclaiming all pretension to sit in judgment on their doctrine, or to infringe the independence of their episcopal authority; and that, as soon as these documents had been exchanged, the two prelates should join in a letter to his Eminence, expressing their respect and esteem for his personal character, and their sincere satisfaction at the removal of the causes which for a time had interrupted their harmony. But this promising project was not destined to succeed. On the one hand, Cardinal de Noailles printed and circulated a somewhat indiscreet letter written by the Bishop of Agen, containing charges and insinuations which gave renewed umbrage to the Bishops of La Rochelle and Luçon, and made them hesitate to subscribe the terms of reconciliation as arranged by the Dauphin.† On the other, a singular incident occurred at this moment, which, had the Cardinal possessed sufficient tact to turn it to account, might have opened for him a triumphant issue from his difficulties. An intercepted letter fell into his hands, which revealed a dark plot concocted by Le Tellier, for inducing the bishops to denounce De Noailles in a body to the king, and forcing him to take decisive action against the obnoxious volumes of Quesnel. The letter was written by a certain Abbé

---

* La Beaumelle, *Lettres de Madame de Maintenon*, tom. iv. p. 252.
† See their letter to the Bishop of Meaux, Oct. 11, 1711 (*Corresp. de Fénélon*, tom. iii. p. 439).

Bochart de Saron to his aged uncle the Bishop of Clermont;[*] it enclosed the draft of a letter to the king, which he was requested to sign, and to return in an unsealed envelope to Le Tellier at Fontainebleau; mention was also made in it of a forthcoming mandement by the bishop, which was to be revised and approved by the same secret authority before publication. The abbé declared that Le Tellier had shown him more than thirty letters from the most influential among the prelates and clergy, urging his Majesty to take proceedings against Cardinal de Noailles; and that he expected within a week to receive as many more from other quarters. This information, which reached the Cardinal in a manner so extraordinary that he considered it a supernatural interposition, he instantly communicated to Madame de Maintenon, to the Dauphin, and to the king. He moreover caused the documents to be printed, and copies to be distributed, to the number of seven hundred, among the clergy of Paris, and other ecclesiastics throughout the kingdom.[†]

Great was the consternation of Le Tellier. The court, the clergy, the society of Paris, exclaimed against him with one voice; and for some days his disgrace was considered certain. The Abbé Bochart hastened to throw himself into the breach, and published a letter directly contradicting his former statement, declaring that Le Tellier had no share whatever in the intrigue, and taking the whole responsibility upon himself. He had used the confessor's name, he said, without his knowledge or authority, for the sake of prevailing the better with his uncle to adopt the measures prescribed to him. But few or none were deceived by this barefaced falsehood. Cardinal de Noailles felt it his duty to advise the king to dismiss an ecclesiastic who had proved himself so unworthy to direct his conscience. "What hope is there," he wrote to Madame de Maintenon, "of his Majesty's salvation, so long as he entrusts himself to a confessor who, far from recommending virtue by his example, is false to

---

[*] See the *Journal de l'Abbé Dorsanne*, tom. i. p. 11. Antoine Dorsanne was a canon of Notre Dame, and grand-vicar and official of the archdiocese of Paris. He enjoyed the entire confidence of Cardinal de Noailles, and was more than once employed by him as his special agent at Rome. The Abbé Bochart's letter is also printed by Crétineau Joly in his *Histoire des Jésuites*, tom. iv. p. 453.

[†] *Journal de l'Abbé Ledieu*, 6 août, 1711, tom. iii. p. 342; *Journal de l'Abbé Dorsanne*, tom. i. pp. 12 13.

the first principles of truth and sincerity,—having offered to declare upon oath that he had no concern in what has passed, although he was the principal author of it, as is proved by the papers which have been brought to light by such a remarkable act of Divine Providence? How much damage may be inflicted on the Church by a confessor of this stamp, who scruples not to expose it to schism for the sake of satisfying his private malice; one who corrupts the bishops by the prospect of worldly advancement; who, instead of submitting to their decisions, compels them to receive his, and to publish them in their own names; and that not only in their dioceses but in mine, and throughout France! You well know, Madame, how he is spoken of by religious persons whom you esteem. I assure you that such sentiments are widely entertained; and that were it only for the general discredit into which Father Le Tellier has fallen, there is quite sufficient reason for removing him from his post; for it is not fitting that the confidence of the king should remain in the hands of a man of such evil repute. The matter is not mended by the second letter of the Abbé Bochart; for he only covers himself with additional confusion, without exculpating Father Le Tellier."*

These representations were outweighed, however, by the influence of Le Tellier, and of others who had lately risen to conspicuous places in court favour, especially De Bissy, Bishop of Meaux. That prelate aspired to the Roman purple, which he hoped to secure through the recommendation of the Jesuits. He undertook to plead the cause of Le Tellier with Madame de Maintenon and the king; and his Majesty, whose infirmities made him shrink from the idea of changing his confessor, too easily allowed himself to be convinced that, after all, he had been unjustly accused. He accordingly retained his office, and became more powerful than ever.

De Noailles now resorted to a step which wore the appearance of deliberate retaliation and revenge, though in truth it proceeded from a conscientious conviction of his duty as a chief ruler of the Church. He deprived almost all the Jesuits at Paris of their licences to preach and hear confessions in his diocese; assigning as his reason, that "they inculcated false

---

* La Beaumelle, *Lettres de Madame de Maintenon*, tom. iv. p. 261.

doctrines, and instigated the flock to rebel against its pastor." More than forty members of the Order were thus interdicted. In the *maison professe* of Saint Louis only eleven remained who could exercise their functions.* The confessors of the royal family were alone excepted from the decree, and this solely out of the Cardinal's respect for the king. "His Majesty," he wrote, "will no doubt be displeased; but in order to gratify my sovereign I have no right to offend God. I am afraid, indeed, that I am doing this already, to prove my respect and devotion towards him: I am granting fresh powers to Father Le Tellier, though of all others he the most richly deserves to lose them. I make this sacrifice to the king, and charge it upon his conscience, praying continually that the good Lord will make known to him the peril he incurs by entrusting the care of his soul to a man of such character."†

It was not to be expected, after these occurrences, that the negotiation conducted by the Duke of Burgundy would lead to any successful result. The Cardinal was required, as a preliminary concession, to explain himself distinctly upon the subject of Jansenism, and to revoke his approbation of Quesnel's New Testament. To this sacrifice he could not in conscience submit; and the two bishops declined, in consequence, to write the proposed letter of satisfaction which was to seal the treaty of peace. These measures having proved finally abortive, there remained the expedient, which was soon seriously contemplated by all parties, of referring the whole question to the judgment of the Apostolic See. According to St. Simon, this was from the outset the real aim of Le Tellier and his coadjutors. "What he desired was, to make it an affair of so much embroilment and dissension, that it should be of necessity carried to Rome, contrary to all the laws and usages of the Church, which provide that such questions shall be decided judicially on the spot where they originate, saving the right of appeal to the Pope, who, by his legates, either corrects the former judgment or confirms it in equally judicial form. Now this latter form can only be that of a Council, where the author

---

* *Journal de l'Abbé Ledieu*, tom. iii. p. 346. Even Le Tellier was prohibited by name from giving absolution in the "cas reservés," and from hearing the confessions of nuns.

† Cardinal de Noailles to Madame de Maintenon, August 20, 1711 (La Beaumelle, tom. iv. p. 264).

of a book which has caused dispute may be heard in person in his own defence,—a privilege which Father Quesnel demanded without ceasing as long as lived. But this was not the game of Father Le Tellier. He well knew what would be the result of treating such an affair after that fashion. His object was to stifle the dispute by a stroke of authority, and to make this an instrument of persecution for future years, so as to establish their doctrine as a matter of faith, whereas hitherto it had been barely tolerated in the Church."*

It soon transpired that steps had been taken by the government in furtherance of this deep-laid scheme. The king, by a significant proof, showed that he was resolved to pursue this unhappy quarrel to the last extremity. In November, 1711, appeared an *arrêt* of the Council of State, prohibiting, "for certain important considerations," the further sale and circulation of the New Testament of Father Quesnel. "Cardinal de Noailles having been solicited by the king," says Ledieu, "to withdraw his approbation from the work, and having refused on the plea that his conscience would not permit him, the king rejoined that *his* conscience urged him to suppress the book; and an ordonnance to that effect was passed in the Council, though this was contrary to the advice of M. de Pontchartrain and M. D'Aguesseau, who stated that it was against the interest of the king and of his crown thus to sanction tacitly the condemnation passed upon it at Rome by a brief inconsistent with the liberties of the Gallican Church;" to which the king is said to have replied that his conscience was dearer to him than his crown. No one doubts that all this machinery is set in motion by Father Le Tellier, who boasts that he will obtain from Rome a bull in full form against the New Testament of Father Quesnel; and that with a view to this, he will avail himself of the *arrêt* aforesaid, which indicates the king's willingness to receive such a bull, and to cause it to be accepted by the bishops and published throughout the kingdom. But it is not believed that he will obtain it, the Pope being dissatisfied with the manner in which the bishops received his last bull against Jansenism;

---

* *Mém. de St. Simon*, tom. vi. p. 412.

on which occasion they declared themselves to be judges, in conjunction with the Pope, of the doctrine condemned."*

A month afterwards, in December, 1711, Louis demanded of the Pope, through Cardinal de la Tremoille, his Chargé d'Affaires at Rome, a bull distinctly specifying and condemning the errors contained in the Nouveau Testament of Quesnel, which the decree of 1708 had censured only in general terms. His Majesty also requested that the holy Father would not publish his decision without previously communicating with Cardinal de la Tremoille, so as to avoid anything which might raise a difficulty as to its legal reception in France. Clement accordingly appointed, in February, 1712, a special congregation of five Cardinals and eleven theologians to conduct the examination of the book. The Cardinals were Fabroni, Ferrari, Spada, Casini, and Tolomei. The theologians were chosen from all Orders and all schools of opinion: two were Augustinians, two were Thomists, two were Scotists; four were of no specially marked shade of sentiment; one only belonged to the Society of Jesus. "Never, perhaps," writes Father Daubenton to Fénélon, "has a book been subjected to a more lengthened or a more scrupulous examination. After seventeen conferences of the theologians, held in the presence of Cardinals Ferrari and Fabroni, the propositions were examined in the presence of the Pope and nine Cardinals of the Holy Office in twenty-four congregations, where, besides the theologians already named, were assembled all the Consultors of the Holy Office, and several prelates. There is not a single proposition which has not cost the Pope three or four hours of private study."† The Abbé Dorsanne informs us, however, that the members of the congregation, with one exception, did not understand French, and that their knowledge of Quesnel's book was derived from a Latin translation. Le Drou, the only one who was well versed in the original language, was adroitly removed from Rome by Fabroni and Daubenton, under the pretext of a mission to Liège.

---

* *Journal de l'Abbé Ledeieu*, tom. iii. p. 358.
† P. Daubenton to Fénélon, 16 septembre, 1713 (*Corresp. de Fénélon*, tom. iv. p. 325).

While the examination was in progress, Cardinal de Noailles published a remarkable letter to the Bishop of Agen, which was in effect a formal apology for his sentiments and conduct with reference to the Jansenistic controversy. He observed that he had been trained for the ecclesiastical profession by Father Amelotte, who was well known to be altogether opposed to the doctrine of Jansenius.* From him he had learned to reverence the authority of St. Augustine and St. Thomas Aquinas; and never would he blush to own himself a disciple of those two great saints. Although he had no sympathy with the views of Molina, he well knew that largeness of heart and mind is eminently characteristic of the true pastor, and was therefore prepared to tolerate frankly whatever the Church tolerates. He quarrelled with no man for being a Molinist. He had given employment to many persons so designated—he believed with justice,—making this sole proviso, that they were not lax or inefficient in the practical guidance of souls. "I consider myself bound," he proceeds, "to defend the liberty of theologians; I cannot allow them to be oppressed by a yoke which even General Councils have never pretended to impose; and I will never depart from that wise maxim of antiquity, "In necessariis unitas, in dubiis libertas, in omnibus caritas." In a word, if to be a Jansenist, or an abettor of Jansenism, signifies to follow literally and exactly the doctrine of St. Augustine and St. Thomas, I declare that, whatever may happen to me, I shall be in that sense a Jansenist, or an abettor of Jansenism, just as they please to call it, to the last breath of my life;† and I maintain the hope that at the judgment seat of Christ I shall find, with regard to that particular, as well as upon the other articles enjoined by religion,

---

* Denis Amelotte was a priest of the Oratory, and author of a French version of the New Testament, an *Abrégé de Théologie*, the 'Life of Father Condren,' and other works. He died in 1678. His 'Life of Condren,' which contained reflections on the Abbé de S. Cyran, involved him in a sharp conflict with Nicole and other Port-Royalists.

† The Cardinal must have been aware, however, that this vague profession of devotion to St. Augustine and St. Thomas was common in the mouths of the most notorious Jansenists. Arnauld, Pascal, Quesnel, even Jansenius himself, were in the constant habit of repeating the same phrase. It would have been more to the purpose if his Eminence had clearly pointed out the distinction between the Jansenism which he repudiated and the Augustinian and Thomist system to which he declared himself so unalterably attached.

the reward which is promised to true faith. The sheep, as St. Augustine says, must not abandon their skin because the wolves usurp it as a disguise." The Cardinal then appeals to the Ordonnance which he published soon after his translation to the see of Paris in 1696, and which had been stigmatized by his enemies as "the Jansenistic profession of faith." He recounts the numerous testimonies of approbation which he received on that occasion both from Rome and in France, particularly the letters of Cardinal D'Estrées, of Fénélon, of the late Bishop of Chartres, of the present Bishop of Meaux, of the pious Tronson, and of the Duke de Beauvilliers, whose known abhorrence of the slightest taint of Jansenism rendered his suffrage specially worthy of attention. As to its being called the creed of the Jansenists, "there are many people," says the Cardinal, "whose creed is only that of the day—*fides temporum*, instead of the belief of the Church, which never changes, and is independent of place and time." In conclusion, he recalls the circumstances under which he had given his official sanction to the 'Livre des Reflexions' of Quesnel. He had found it in use throughout the diocese of Châlons, under the direct patronage of his saintly predecessor Vialart. It had been licensed and eulogized by Archbishop de Harlai. Other prelates, some of whom died in the odour of sanctity, had recommended the work in the strongest terms, especially M. D'Urfé Bishop of Limoges, whose theology was well known to be that of the Seminary of St. Sulpice. Above all, it had been defended by the immortal Bossuet. "At any rate we cannot be mistaken as to the theological principles which that great doctor of the Church of France has established with such solidity in his Justification of this work, lately published; since they are those which the Popes distinguished by their preference upon the questions of predestination and grace, when they were agitated in the Congregations De Auxiliis. This step was taken by Bossuet on the occasion of the libellous 'Problème ecclésiastique' in 1699, which denounced the 'Livre des Reflexions' as fraught with all the venom of Jansenism. That libel was condemned to the flames at Paris, and was soon afterwards censured at Rome by Innocent XII.; a sentence which was looked upon as an indirect and tacit approval of the work which the Problème had attacked."

"I have not hesitated to say to all who chose to hear me, that I will never be the man either to cause or to permit division in the Church for the sake of a book which religion can very well afford to dispense with. If our holy Father the Pope should think proper to censure this book in solemn form, I will accept his Constitution and his sentence with all possible respect, and will be the first to give an example of perfect submission of mind and heart. I have always detested, and still detest, all innovations in matters of religion; I never pardon any attempt of that kind; and the zeal which I desire to maintain throughout life against the errors of Jansenism will not extinguish that which I am bound to exhibit against every other form of false doctrine."

We learn from the Abbé Ledieu that this letter, which was widely circulated, excited no small indignation against the Jesuits, who now attacked the party opposed to them with greater audacity and violence than ever. Unpopular as they were with the public, their credit was paramount at court; and they now began to make use of it for purposes of direct persecution. Individuals who incurred their ill-will were suddenly dismissed from their employments, or incarcerated in the Bastille. Among these victims was the famous Charles Rollin, author of the 'Histoire ancienne,' at that time coadjutor to the Principal of the Collége de Beauvais at Paris. It is even said that severe measures were contemplated against Cardinal de Noailles himself, but were prevented by the interference of Pontchartrain, who represented to the king the gross scandal which must arise from any attempt against a prelate of his rank, reputation, and unquestioned integrity.*

The Cardinal seems gradually to have recovered much of the esteem and confidence with which Louis had formerly regarded him, and his general position had become more promising, when Clement XI. pronounced his long-expected judgment in the case of Quesnel. The memorable Constitution "Unigenitus Dei Filius" was promulgated on the 8th of September, 1713. The labours of the examiners had extended over a period of eighteen months; the result was that one hundred and one

---

* *Journal de l'Abbé Ledieu*, tom. iii. p. 374.

propositions from Quesnel's Commentary were marked out for censure on various grounds and in various degrees; the main indictment being their conformity, either obvious or covert, with the heretical dogmas of Jansenius. They are faithfully extracted, almost without exception, from the original, though in some few instances the author's meaning seems to have been warped, either through the separation of a passage from its context, or from the incorrectness of the Latin translation. They were condemned with the usual qualifications; as "false, captious, ill-sounding, offensive to pious ears, scandalous, pernicious, injurious both to the Church and to the temporal powers, seditious, blasphemous, suspected of heresy, already condemned, and finally, as renewing divers heresies, principally those contained in the Five Propositions of Jansenius, taken in the sense in which they were condemned." The following are offered to the reader as fair samples of the teaching which provoked such a formidable series of anathemas from the Chair of St. Peter.

Proposition V. "When God does not soften the heart by the inward action of His grace, external exhortations and favours serve only to harden it still more."—Quesnel on Romans ix. 18.

Proposition VI. "How great is the difference, O my God, between the Jewish and the Christian covenant! Both require the abandonment of sin and the fulfilment of Thy law; but in the one case Thou exactest it of the sinner while leaving him in his inability (to obey); in the other, Thou bestowest that which Thou commandest, by purifying him by Thy grace."—Rom. xi. 27.

Proposition XX. "The true idea of grace is this; that God wills that we should obey Him, and He is obeyed; He commands, and everything is done; He speaks as the master, and all is submission."—St. Mark, iv. 39.

Proposition XXX. "All those whom God wills to save by Jesus Christ are saved infallibly."—St. John, vi. 40.

Proposition XXXVIII. "A sinner is not free, except to do evil, without the grace of the Deliverer."—St. Luke, viii. 29.

Proposition XLIV. "There are but two loves, from which spring all our volitions and all our actions; the love of God, which does everything for His sake, and which He rewards; and the love of ourselves and of the world, which does not refer to God that which ought to be referred to Him, and which for that very reason becomes evil."—St. John, v. 29.

Proposition XLVI. "Cupidity or charity renders the use of our senses good or bad."—St. Matt. v. 28.

Proposition LIV. "It is charity alone that speaks to God; it is to charity alone that God listens."—1 Cor. xiii. 1.

Proposition LIX. "The prayer of the wicked is an additional sin, and whatever God grants them is a fresh judgment upon them."—St. John, x. 25.

Proposition LXIV. "Under the curse of the law man never acts rightly, because he sins either by doing evil, or by abstaining from it through fear."—Galat. v. 18.

Proposition LXVIII. "How great is God's goodness, in thus abridging the way of salvation, so as to comprehend everything in faith and prayer."—Acts, vii. 21.

Proposition LXXI. "Man may dispense, in order to his preservation, with a law which God made by reason of its utility."—St. Mark, ii. 28.

Proposition LXXIX. "It is useful and necessary at all times, in all places, and for all classes of persons, to study Holy Scripture, and to become familiar with its spirit and its mysteries."—1 Cor. xiv. 5.

Proposition XCI. "The fear of an unjust excommunication ought never to hinder us from doing our duty. We are not severed from the Church, even when we appear to be cast out of it by the wickedness of men, so long as we are united to God, to Christ, and likewise to the Church, by means of charity."—St. John, ix. 22.

Proposition XCIII. "Jesus sometimes heals wounds which the precipitancy of chief pastors has inflicted without His command. He restores what they cut off through inconsiderate zeal."—St. John, xviii. 11.

Proposition XCIV. "Nothing gives a worse opinion of the Church to its enemies, than to see tyranny exercised therein over the faith of the faithful, and division encouraged for the sake of things which injure neither faith nor morals."—Rom. xiv. 16.

Proposition XCVI. "God permits that all authorities (*toutes les puissances*) should be opposed to the preachers of the truth, in order that its victory may not be ascribed to anything except His grace."—Acts, xvii. 8.

Proposition XCVIII. "To be persecuted as a heretic, as wicked, as profane, is commonly the last trial and the most meritorious, inasmuch as it makes us the most conformable to Jesus Christ."—St. Luke, xxii. 37.

Proposition CI. "Nothing is more opposed to the Spirit of God and the doctrine of Jesus Christ than to make oaths common in the Church; since it multiplies the occasions of perjury, spreads snares for the weak and ignorant, and sometimes makes the name and the truth of God subserve the designs of the wicked."—St. Matt. v. 37.

That such passages savour of partisanship and sectarianism—that they betray a state of feeling soured by injustice and oppression—that many of them are based upon that fundamental error of Jansenism, the irresistibility of grace—that some of them are reproductions of statements already condemned in the works of Jansenius and Baius—that their tendency is to foster a spirit of disrespect to constituted authority, both ecclesiastical and civil—all this will scarcely be denied by any candid mind. But it may be justly questioned whether it was wise or right to visit them with such a tremendous denunciation of Apostolic displeasure. In the interests of truth, of peace, and of the general edification of the Church, a more lenient sentence might surely have met the exigencies of the case;—for instance, that of placing the work upon the Index until it should be corrected. But it is easy to discern the mistakes of a false policy when a flood of light has been poured upon them by the retrospective experience of more than a hundred and fifty years. There is good reason for believing that the bull was extorted from Clement XI. in opposition to his better judgment. He asked the opinion of Cardinal Carpegna, who strongly remonstrated against the proposed measure; and his advice caused the Pope to hesitate long before giving his consent. But the empire exercised over him by Fabroni was too absolute to be resisted. The bull was published without previous consultation with the Cardinals as a body;—an omission which caused serious irritation among the majority of the Sacred College.

As soon as the Constitution reached France, the King consulted Cardinal de Noailles, through the Secretary Voisin, as to the means to be employed for its reception by the Church. The Cardinal recommended that the Provincial Councils should be convoked for this purpose, as in the case of the Archbishop of Cambrai; and this was likewise the advice of the law-officers of the Crown, who reported, moreover, that the bull contained nothing inconsistent with the usages of the kingdom or the Gallican liberties. The King, nevertheless, preferred a different method of proceeding, which had already been adopted on several important occasions,—namely, that of an extraordinary assembly of those bishops who happened to be in or near Paris. This, to use the words of Voisin to De Noailles, was "the surest and shortest way;" but it is certain, at the same time, that it was not the way prescribed by the canons; nor could any measures which these prelates might think proper to take possess binding authority over their absent colleagues, or over the National Church at large.

In compliance with the King's commands, twenty-nine prelates assembled at the Archbishop's Palace at Paris on the 16th of October, 1713, under the presidency of De Noailles. At subsequent meetings the number increased to forty-nine. A committee was appointed to report upon the Constitution, consisting of Cardinal de Rohan Bishop of Strasburg; the Archbishops of Bordeaux and Auch; the Bishops of Meaux, Soissons, and Blois.

Cardinal de Noailles had already published a mandement, on the 28th of September, revoking the approbation which he had given, as Bishop of Châlons, to Quesnel's New Testament; "both in order to redeem the promise which he had made to condemn the book as soon as his Holiness should condemn it, and to testify his submission and respect for the head of the Church." It was anticipated that, after this important concession, the Cardinal would not press any serious objection to the acceptance of the Constitution. But no sooner had the Committee presented its report, than it became apparent that there were two, if not three, parties in the Assembly. Some few extreme Ultramontanes, such as De Bissy and De Mailly, were for accepting the Pope's decree as the dictum of an absolutely infallible authority, without submitting it to any semblance of examination by the Gallican Episcopate. These joined the great majority of the prelates, who, under the leadership of Cardinal de Rohan, subscribed to the bull upon the general principle of obedience to the King, and from the desire of preserving a good understanding between the Holy See, the Sovereign, and their own order. Lastly, there were those who found themselves unable to assent to the Papal decision, at all events without requiring explanations as to the meaning and application of some of its articles. This small section was headed by Cardinal de Noailles, and owed its influence to his rank and character.

The following recommendations were made by the Committee on the 13th of January, 1714. That the Assembly should accept with submission, respect, and joy, the Constitution "Unigenitus," as expressing the faith and doctrine of the Church. That they should condemn Quesnel's book and the propositions extracted from it, in the same terms and with the same qualifications as those used in the bull. That they should write a letter of thanks to the Pope, and another to the King. And that they should draw up and publish an uniform "Instruction pastorale," containing explanations of certain parts of the bull, which had already given rise to objections and false interpretations. Forty bishops voted in favour of the Report; but Cardinal de Noailles, the Archbishop of Tours, and seven other prelates, declined to adopt it until they had an opportunity of examining the text of the proposed pastoral Instruction. That document was read in the Assembly on the 1st of February, when the same prelates expressed themselves dissatisfied with it, and regretted that in consequence they felt precluded from taking any further part in the deliberations of their brethren.* The King commanded them not to withdraw from the sittings, and they therefore continued to attend *pro formâ*, but did not join in the proceedings; considering that it was more respectful to the Pope to seek explanations directly from himself, rather than to put forth comments of their own, which might not prove acceptable either to his Holiness or to the absent bishops of France.

The Constitution Unigenitus soon became the theme of severe and passionate criticism. Fénélon thus describes the prevalent feeling in a letter to Father Daubenton. "People

---

* *Procès-verbaux des Assemb. du Clergé*, tom. vi. p. 1259 *et seqq.*

exclaim on all sides that the Pope has condemned St. Augustine, St. Paul, and even Jesus Christ. They declare that the Constitution is Pelagian, and that it serves only to demonstrate the fallibility of Rome. It is asserted that it denies the necessity of grace, and especially of that effectual grace which ensures predestination; that it wrests out of the hands of the faithful the Word of God and the Gospel of Jesus Christ; that it rejects the salutary course of probation to which penitents ought to be subjected before reconciliation; that it suggests that men ought to be deterred from doing their duty by the fear of an unjust excommunication, with the view of inspiring kings themselves with terror, and making them afraid to exercise their authority whenever it may please the Pope to threaten them with the tyrannical thunders of the Vatican. Many very scandalous writings have appeared against the Constitution; but in spite of all the artifices of an extremely bold and powerful party, the authority of the king and the zeal of true Catholics will carry the day."*

Impressions of a like character are recorded in a joint letter addressed to the King by the nine protesting bishops, February 5, 1714.† "The charity of Jesus Christ constrains us, Sire, and forbids us to conceal from your Majesty the present disposition of the souls entrusted to our care, of which we must render an account to God at the day of judgment. Since the Constitution condemns one hundred and one propositions in an indeterminate manner, each individual takes licence to interpret them in accordance with his private sentiments. Certain divines are already making use of this censure, contrary to the intentions of his Holiness, for the purpose of erecting their own opinions into dogmas of faith, and contradicting principles authorized by the Church. Others are circulating every day writings designed to show that many of the condemned propositions contain none other than the doctrine of Holy Scripture and the Fathers. The recent converts (from Calvinism) who are very numerous, and whose salvation is so dear to your Majesty, and many Catholics of long standing likewise, are alarmed by the condemnation of the extracts relating to Holy

---

* Fénélon au Père Daubenton, Nov. 20, 1713 (*Corresp. de Fénélon*, tom. iv. p. 363).
† They also drew up a letter to the Pope, but the king would not permit it to be forwarded.

Scripture. Pastors and confessors are constantly propounding to us fresh doubts as to the articles which concern the administration of the Sacrament of Penance. Magistrates apply to us for explanations of those which treat of excommunication. And we know that your Majesty is cognisant of the extravagant reproaches and scurrilities in which the enemies of the Church have indulged on the occasion of this Constitution. These facts, Sire, have induced nearly all the prelates of the Assembly to demand that the bull shall not be published without at the same time explaining to the people the truths which they are bound to believe and the errors which they are bound to reject. But while on one hand the prelates declare that they accept the Constitution only in the sense of their exposition of it contained in the Pastoral Instruction, on the other they are drawing up an Act which will make it appear to the Pope that they accept it purely and simply. We confess to your Majesty that we cannot adopt in an assembly of bishops language different from that which we purpose to address to the common Father of the faithful. Hence we cannot approve their deliberations, nor subscribe their resolutions. Nevertheless, since it is important to apply a remedy to existing troubles, we hasten to unite ourselves to the head of the Church by proscribing the 'Livre des Reflexions;' and for the rest, we entreat him to expound to us his intentions —following herein the example of the eighty-five bishops our predecessors, at whose demand Innocent X. condemned the Five Propositions of Jansenius. God is witness that we would fain extinguish with our blood, were it possible, the flames of division, and that we have nothing else in view save the welfare of the Church, the honour of the Holy See, the glory and the tranquillity of your Majesty." This letter is signed by Cardinal de Noailles, the Archbishop of Tours, the Bishops of Verdun, Laon, Châlons, Senez, Boulogne, St. Malo, and Bayonne.*

Such representations had little or no effect upon the mind of Louis. He complimented the Assembly on the completion of their labours, and expressed himself well satisfied with the conduct of the majority, whose acts he promised to support to

---

* *Gualterio Papers* (Brit. Mus. Add. MSS. 20,319).

the full extent of his authority. To the minority it was very plainly intimated that they had incurred the royal displeasure. Cardinal de Noailles was forbidden to appear at Court, and his eight colleagues were ordered to repair to their dioceses within three days.*

The bull was registered in Parliament after a brief but vigorous opposition from the Abbé Pucelle, one of the clerical councillors of the Grand' Chambre, who attacked the word "enjoignons" as applied to the bishops in the letters-patent. This, he contended, was an infraction of the rights of the episcopate, who could not recognise the interference of secular authority in a matter of which they were by their office the exclusive judges. His protest, however, was disregarded, and the letters-patent were passively accepted.† A like arbitrary pressure was exercised upon the Sorbonne, where vehement agitation was excited by the motion to accept the Constitution. Cardinal de Noailles, hearing of the proposed attempt upon the liberty of the doctors, hastened to publish beforehand a Pastoral Letter and mandement upon the subject of the bull, copies of which were distributed to the members as they entered the hall of assembly. The step was important in a twofold point of view; for, besides being Archbishop of Paris, the Cardinal was Provisor of the Sorbonne. His Eminence stated that the course of action on which he had resolved was, in his judgment, the most respectful towards the Holy See, the most conducive to the preservation of the truth, and the most likely to restore peace to his diocese—an object which he had long and anxiously desired, and which he was willing to purchase at the expense of life. He exhorted his flock not to be dismayed by the existing spectacle of division, or rather diversity of sentiment, in the episcopate, since these differences did not relate to the substance of the Faith, and did not rend the sacred bonds of charity. Not one of the bishops in the Assembly had joined the side of error—not one had declared himself in opposition to the truth. He considered that the wisest plan, under the circumstances, was to apply to the Pope, to make known to him their troubles and difficulties, and to entreat him to supply the means of

---

* Père Lallemant à Fénélon, 11 février, 1714 (*Corresp. de Fénélon*, tom. iv. p. 425).
† Dorsanne, *Journal*, tom. i. p. 103.

tranquillizing disquieted consciences, of maintaining the freedom of the Catholic schools, and of preserving peace among the faithful. He then commended himself to the prayers of all pious persons, and, after repeating the condemnation which he had previously passed upon the New Testament of Father Quesnel, he concluded by forbidding all ecclesiastics to exercise any function or act of jurisdiction with regard to the bull Unigenitus, or to receive it without his express permission, under pain of suspension *ipso facto*.

Many members of the Faculty availed themselves of this bold manifesto of their superior, to decline giving their votes in favour of the Constitution. Opinions were much divided. The king, hearing of the obstinate resistance to his orders, "was about to make an example forthwith," says D'Avrigny, "had not Cardinal de Rohan represented that the opposition arose from fear of the censures menaced by the Archbishop. His Majesty, therefore, contented himself with transmitting fresh orders to the Sorbonne on the 3rd of March; but the same contrariety of feeling was apparent, one party declaring for acceptance pure and simple, the other refusing to register the bull except with certain modifications. It is easy to conceive that those of the doctors who had signed the famous 'cas de conscience'—that Habert, whose theology had been denounced by several bishops as savouring of Jansenism—in a word, that the supporters of Quesnel as a body—found it difficult to subscribe the condemnation of a doctrine which, but for the fear of punishment, they would openly have endorsed by their suffrages. Such was the influence of that fear, that there were those among them who changed their minds three or four times, and ended by voting for the registration, which took place on the 5th, in spite of the clamour of the recusants, who were too few in number to arrest the conclusion." It seems, however, that at a subsequent meeting certain members had the presumption to attempt to reopen the question; whereupon four of them were exiled by *lettres de cachet*, and several others were prohibited from taking their seats in the Assembly. Thus all opposition was forcibly suppressed for the time.*

The Court of Rome was highly indignant at the turn which

---

* D'Avrigny, *Mém. Chron.*, tom. iv. p. 346.

events were taking in France. A violent despatch was forwarded to the Nuncio, ordering him to demand of the King the banishment of Cardinal de Noailles, and the appointment of grand vicars, who were to suspend from their functions all confessors who refused to sign the Constitution. The Cardinal was to be cited to Rome to answer for his conduct, and the Pope was to issue a commission to one of his suffragans to administer the diocese and province. But it is doubtful, says Dorsanne, whether such proposals were actually made to his Majesty; the audience of the Nuncio was a secret one, and the result was never divulged.*

The state of affairs now became so threatening, that it was judged advisable to make overtures of accommodation to De Noailles and his adherents, who, though a mere fraction of the episcopate,† were supported by a large proportion of the parochial clergy, by many of the religious Orders, by several Universities, and by the more intelligent part of the nation. Cardinals D'Estrées and De Polignac, both celebrated for their talents and success in diplomacy, undertook the office of mediators. Cardinal De Rohan and De Bissy professed themselves intensely anxious to promote a pacific arrangement, but secretly employed their influence to frustrate the measures proposed. It was suggested that, inasmuch as all parties agreed that the bull required some explanation, Cardinal de Noailles should compose a Mandement, or Instruction pastorale, containing the comments which he considered necessary, and that in the same document he should declare his respectful acceptance of the Constitution, without stating in terms that such acceptance was restricted by the foregoing observations. It was hoped that the majority of the bishops might be induced to accept this form of submission in preference to that which had been drawn up by the Assembly at Paris; and the expedient might have proved successful but for the mischievous intrigues of Le Tellier and his party, who instantly despatched an agent to Rome, charged to agitate for its rejection.‡ The Pope hesitated; and the course of the nego-

---

* Dorsanne, *Journal*, tom. i. p. 111.
† The protesting prelates were never more in number than sixteen, including De Noailles. The acceptants counted upwards of a hundred.
‡ This was Père Timothée de la Flèche, a Capuchin, surnamed the "courrier de la bulle." He is believed to have been the "obscure monk" spoken of by D'Aguesseau, who first denounced the "Réflexions Morales" to the Roman authorities. See *suprà*, p. 92.

tiation from this point becomes extremely tortuous and obscure. Sometimes Clement seemed disposed to make concessions, and explain the contested passages of his bull; at other times he breathed nothing but threats and vengeance, insisted on implicit obedience, and declared himself resolved to proceed against the refractory bishops to the last extremity. He was indeed involved in an embarrassing dilemma. The proposal of De Noailles and his friends, to accept the Constitution in accordance with their own interpretation of its meaning, was one which practically went far to annul its authority, and subjected the acts of the supreme Pontiff to the arbitrary revision of his subordinates. If such a system were to prevail, it would be easy to find excuses for any amount of false and dangerous doctrine, under the specious pretext of explaining the sentence by which it was condemned. On the other hand, it was clear that this proposal was the Cardinal's ultimatum. Fickle and inconsistent as he had hitherto shown himself through life, he was now inflexible; neither entreaties nor menaces moved him. "It is impossible," writes a correspondent to Cardinal Gualterio (October 15, 1714), "to persuade him to proceed further. It is to be hoped that the Pope will show forbearance, and admit the form of acceptance projected by Cardinal de Noailles. Otherwise, if his Holiness should not think fit to sanction this expedient, he may prefer to take into consideration the scheme of holding a National Council, to which the king would consent, if he desired it. It is therefore at the Pope's pleasure to bring the affair to a conclusion by one method or the other."

"All the world knows, and all the bishops agree, that some amount of explanation is positively necessary. So urgent was this necessity in the opinion of the bishops of the Assembly, that they would not sign the act of acceptance until the explanations were completed; and they placed their acceptance and their explanations (contained in the Instruction pastorale) under one and the same signature, in order to prove to the public that both are comprehended in a single act. If, notwithstanding, the Pope should persist in demanding an acceptance pure and simple, and absolute obedience to the Constitution, the only means of effecting this is the voice of a National Council. But I find that the wisest and most experienced persons here feel sure that the Pope will not adopt this latter course, which could not but produce vexatious results either for his Holiness or for the Church of France. For such a Council must either be perfectly free, or not be free. If it is free, there can be no doubt that the bishops of France, finding themselves assembled as a corporate body, will proceed to assert their maxims and their rights, and to repair the breaches that may have been made in them; and in so doing will express themselves in a style which cannot possibly be acceptable to Rome. On the other hand, if the Council is not free, and authority is employed to coerce it, it may be confidently expected that protests will be made against its proceedings, and that there will be appeals to a General Council. Perhaps it may be proposed to proceed judicially against the dissentients, and to compel submission by force. But this would be simply to put the finishing stroke to discord and division in the Church of France, and to expose it to confusion and calamities which cannot be contemplated without affright." The writer then refers to a memorial prepared by Cardinal de Polignac for the Pope, in which he pointed out how important it was not to outrage the feelings of Cardinal de Noailles—not to drive him to extremities—especially as he had shown himself compliant on several points connected with the doctrinal questions in hand. "Moreover," he continues, "the Cardinal de Noailles is a prelate whose morals and conduct are irreproachable; the public is altogether prepossessed in his favour; he is respected and beloved throughout Paris; and this city includes among its inhabitants a larger proportion than any other in the world of nobility, of magistrates, of communities regular and secular, of men of learning, and of persons entitled on all grounds to high consideration. To attack their Archbishop, whom they regard as a saint and as a righteous man suffering persecution, would be to disgust all these classes, and to provoke, so to speak, a general insurrection." *

The acute remarks of the author of this letter as to the probable action of a National Synod expressed, no doubt, the sentiments of the more clear-sighted portion of the Gallican episcopate. They saw that such an assembly, whether permitted to deliberate freely or not, was not likely, under existing circumstances, to promote the pacification of the Church. The

---

* *Gualterio Papers* (Brit. Mus. Add. MSS. 20, 319).

project, nevertheless, had numerous and influential supporters, though it does not appear to what party they belonged; and in December, 1714, the governmen tdespatched a Councillor of State named Amelot on a special mission to Rome, to make arrangements with the Pope for the convocation of the Council. It was already understood that the intervention of Cardinals D'Estrées and Polignac had failed, and that the explanatory comments of De Noailles were rejected at the Vatican as inadmissible. The Abbé Chalmette announces this clearly in a letter to the Bishop of La Rochelle, dated from Rome, October 1, 1714. "Upon that point," he says, "this Court will never yield. You may judge of it from the words spoken to myself by one of the most respected of the Cardinals. 'As to these explanations, he said, they no more deserve to be admitted than if, by way of acknowledging the dogma of the Trinity, it were proposed to confess belief in two Persons and a half.' In a word, what is demanded from M. le Cardinal de Noailles is an acceptance of the Constitution pure and simple; after that, he may publish as many mandements as he pleases." *

Amelot, having been received in audience by the Pope, was referred by him to Cardinal Fabroni, as the minister with whom he was to treat. The envoy interpreted this as a certain presage of the ill-success of his mission; and it soon appeared that the Curia entertained strong objections to the notion of a National Council. He pursued the negotiation, however; and in a subsequent interview with his Holiness he seems to have succeeded to some extent in overcoming his repugnance to the scheme. If such a measure was really desired in France, said Clement, after a mature consideration of the many difficulties and risks which it might involve, he would not withhold his consent; but he exacted, as an essential preliminary condition, that Cardinal de Noailles should be deposed from his rank as a member of the Sacred College. Amelot observed that this step would be useless, since it was not in the character of Cardinal, but in that of Archbishop of Paris, that De Noailles was required to accept the Constitution.

It was at one of the audiences granted to the French envoy

---

* L'Abbé Chalmette à l'évêque de La Rochelle (*Corresp de Fénélon*, tom. iv. p. 510).

that the singular conversation took place which is related by St. Simon in his 'Memoirs' upon the authority of Amelot himself. The Pope enlarged on the regret which he felt that he had allowed himself to publish the Constitution; confessing that it had been extorted from him by the letters of the king and of Le Tellier, which persuaded him that the king was so absolutely master of the bishops, the rest of the clergy, and the Parliaments, that the bull would be accepted unanimously, and registered and published everywhere without the slightest difficulty; and that, had he foreseen the hundredth part of the opposition which it had met with, he would never have sanctioned it. Upon this Amelot ventured to inquire why, when about to issue the bull, he had not contented himself with censuring some few propositions from Quesnel's book, instead of making a catalogue of one hundred and one extracts? The Pope now burst forth into exclamations and tears. "O, Monsieur Amelot, Monsieur Amelot," he cried, seizing the envoy by the arm, "what would you have had me do? I struggled to the utmost to curtail the list, but Father Le Tellier had declared to the king that the book contained more than a hundred propositions deserving censure; he did not wish to pass for having spoken falsely, and they forced me at the point of the bayonet to condemn more than a hundred in order to prove that he was right. *I have quoted only one more.* You see, Monsieur Amelot, how impossible it was that I should act otherwise!"*

The vacillation, inconsistency, and procrastination exhibited by Clement convinced Amelot that he was not disposed to consent to the Council, and that his only object was to gain time, to suggest a multitude of captious difficulties, and to consume weeks and months in discussing frivolous matters of form. Meanwhile fresh attempts were made to arrive at an understanding with Cardinal de Noailles (one of them under the auspices of the celebrated Massillon, afterwards Bishop of Clermont), but each in its turn proved nugatory. At length the Pope, though he could not summon sufficient resolution to sanction the project of a National Council, felt it imperative to act decidedly against the Cardinal; and a brief was addressed

---

* St. Simon, *Mémoires*, tom. viii. p. 246.

to him through the Nuncio, in April, 1715, commanding him to notify his acceptance of the Constitution "pure et simple" within fifteen days, under pain of being degraded from the Roman purple, and proceeded against according to the canons. Little or no attention, however, seems to have been paid to this missive, and it is doubtful whether it was ever communicated to the Cardinal. A despatch arrived immediately afterwards from Amelot, to the effect that the Pope's consent to the Council was no longer to be expected; whereupon the king determined to convoke it upon his own authority, and to exclude from it, by virtue of his sole prerogative, those prelates who declined to accept the Constitution. Louis persevered to the end in the system of high-handed despotism which had characterised his reign. De Bissy, who had distinguished himself by his zeal in the execution of the royal will, received his reward at this juncture in the shape of a Cardinal's hat; while, on the other hand, the "anti-constitutionnaires" became the victims of undisguised persecution. Several eminent divines were banished by *lettres de cachet*, and others consigned to the Bastille, simply on the ground of their conscientious objections to the bull against Quesnel.

Things were in this unsettled and complicated state, when Louis, whose health had long been visibly failing, was attacked by a malady which at his time of life could hardly terminate otherwise than fatally. Le Tellier and his confidants were in dismay. They felt that power was slipping from their hands; and with indecent importunity they urged the dying monarch to complete the necessary measures for securing a compulsory manifesto of the National Church in favour of the bull. A declaration was hastily drawn up, summoning the dissentients to make unconditional submission within a given time; this was to be registered by the Parliament in the king's presence; and the Synod, awed by this *coup d'état* into absolute unanimity, was thereupon to pronounce the acceptance of the Constitution in the name of the Gallican Church, and stifle the voice of opposition by all the terrors both of ecclesiastical and secular law. But it was too late. The king's strength declined rapidly, and when the preliminary arrangements were concluded, he was no longer able to undertake the fatigue of holding the *lit de justice*. Conscious that his days were numbered, he unburdened his mind to Cardinals de Rohan and De Bissy, in the presence of Madame de Maintenon and Le Tellier, in terms which must have raised a bitterly reproachful echo in the consciences of some of his hearers. "I die," said Louis, "in the faith and obedience of the Church. I have not sufficient learning to understand the questions which disturb her; I have simply followed your advice; I have done what you required; if I have done wrong, you are answerable for it before God, and for this I call Him to witness." The two Cardinals replied by lavish encomiums upon his conduct. The king proceeded to express a wish to be reconciled to Cardinal de Noailles, for whom he had always cherished esteem and regard; but this generous impulse was thwarted by Le Tellier, who observed that such a step might prove injurious to the triumph of "the good cause." He so far relented, however, as to say that there would be no objection to the Cardinal's presence provided he would pledge himself beforehand to accept the Constitution. De Noailles was sorely afflicted by this last stroke of malicious enmity. He answered respectfully, but demurred to the prescribed stipulation, and was not permitted to see the king.*

The Jesuits had governed Louis through life, and even on his death-bed their empire over him was exercised with undiminished vigour. It is related by Dorsanne, that he had already pronounced the three ordinary vows of initiation into the Order; and that in his last moments the fourth was administered to him by Le Tellier. Thus fortified, according to the best judgment of his confessor, against the approach of the king of terrors, he calmly expired on the morning of the 1st of September, 1715.

Several months previously, on the 7th of January, 1715, the Archbishop of Cambrai closed a career which, however chequered by temporal trials and reverses, was bright with evangelical piety, and ennobled by self-denying devotedness to the work of the ministry. He died beloved and unfeignedly lamented, not only in his own diocese, but throughout the north of France and in the Low Countries; his saintly character and unbounded charities having endeared him during the later campaigns of the war even to foreign invaders and hostile armies. It is impossible not to regret that this admirable pre-

---

* Duclos, *Mém. Secrets*, tom. i. p. 154; St. Simon, *Mémoires*, tom. viii. p. 68.

late should have attached himself with such extraordinary ardour to the policy of the Jesuits;—a line of action which exposed him to the probably unmerited charge of aspiring, through their interest, to a return to court favour and worldly power. If Fénélon ever nourished such hopes, they must have been rudely extinguished by the death, first of the Dauphin, next of his royal pupil the Duke of Burgundy,* and finally by the still more cruel blows which severed him from his devoted friends the Dukes of Chevreuse and Beauvilliers; the former of whom departed this life in 1712, the latter in October, 1714, only four months before Fénélon himself. Saint Simon declares that under the Regency of the Duke of Orleans the Archbishop would undoubtedly have been elevated to a position of the highest public authority;† but the truth is that he was in no condition, either physically or mentally, to undertake such arduous functions, even had the prospect been open to him. These fatal losses had destroyed his relish for the concerns of this world, and seem to have impressed him with the presentiment that his own end was near at hand. "We must enter into God's designs," he writes to the Duchess de Beauvilliers, "and do what we can to promote our own consolation. Very soon we shall rejoin those whom we have not lost; every day we are approaching them with rapid strides. Yet a little while, and there will be no more cause to weep. It is we who are dying; he whom we love lives, and will never more die." ‡ Three days after the date of this letter he was attacked by the illness which within a brief space brought him to the grave.

Fénélon, as we have seen, was conscientiously opposed to Jansenism as a system of doctrine; but at the same time (be it recorded to his honour) his treatment of individual Jansenists, who abounded in his diocese, was marked by invariable moderation and forbearance. The victims of persecution flocked to Cambrai as to a secure asylum, a haven of rest; here they enjoyed perfect toleration; and under such circumstances, they were content to devolve upon others the task of controversial self-defence, and never raised a dissentient voice against the

---

* The Duke of Burgundy died on the 18th of February, 1712, in the 30th year of his age.
† St. Simon, *Mémoires*, tom. vii. p. 277.
‡ Fénélon à la Duchesse de Beauvilliers, Cambrai. 28 décembre, 1714 (*Œuvres de Fénélon*, tom. v. p. 768).

universal admiration and affection in which the Archbishop was held. Such was his habitual temper of considerate kindness towards persons from whose principles and views he differed *toto cœlo*, that on one occasion he invited the arch-Jansenist Quesnel to visit him at Cambrai, that they might discuss the contested questions at leisure in the spirit of cordial goodwill and charity. "Thankful shall I be," said the prelate, "with the great Augustine, to him who will correct me in matters wherein he knows himself to be right; thankful for the friendly offices of one whose doctrine, nevertheless, I am compelled to oppose."

Louis XIV. was no sooner laid in the tomb than a startling reaction supervened in Church and State under the auspices of the Regent, Philip Duke of Orleans. Saint Simon ascribes the revolution to his own personal agency; the facts, at all events, are incontestable. Cardinal de Noailles, instead of being deposed from office, anathematized as a heretic, and driven into obscurity for the rest of his life, was placed at the head of the "Conseil de Conscience" or department of ecclesiastical affairs, and became at one stroke the most powerful churchman in the kingdom. "That *good cause* upon which, under the late king, the Catholic faith and the whole of religion appeared to depend—the cause of the Constitution—changed places instantaneously with the faction of misbelievers, of rebels, of schismatics, of proscribed heretics, the highest members of which were plunged in the depths of disgrace and degradation, openly persecuted, dispersed in exile, thrown into dungeons, without being permitted to appeal to any legitimate tribunal for the redress of their wrongs. Nothing more was needed than this great blow of the restoration of Cardinal de Noailles and his friends to power on the death of the king, to confound their enemies, to brand their foreheads with the ignominy of their ambition, their intrigues, their violence, to stigmatize their Constitution as the opprobrium of religion, the adversary of sound doctrine, of Holy Scripture, of the Fathers; to stamp their cause as the most odious and the most dangerous both for religion and for the State. Twenty-four hours sufficed to effect the change; a fortnight brought it to maturity. Grass was growing in the courts of the Archbishop's palace; none save a few secret partisans were to be seen there, trembling, Nicodemus-like, under the denunciations of the synagogue. Suddenly people began to return; a minute later all the world was on the way thither. Those of the bishops who had been the most abject slaves to the court, clergy of the second order who had intrigued the deepest to make their fortune, men of the world who had taken the most pains to please and flatter the ecclesiastical dictators, were not ashamed to throng the saloons of Cardinal de Noailles; and there were some who were impudent enough to try to persuade him that they had always beloved and respected him, and that their conduct throughout had been innocent. He felt shame on their behalf; he received them all like a true father, showing no coolness except in a few cases where deception would have been too transparent, and in these without bitterness or reproaches. He was little moved, indeed, by this sudden turn of fortune, well knowing that it might soon be followed by another in the opposite direction, if the Court happened to withdraw the favour which he now enjoyed."*

The colleagues of De Noailles on the ecclesiastical commission were Besons Archbishop of Bordeaux, a man of preeminent capacity for business, of conciliating disposition, and respected by the parochial clergy; the Abbé Pucelle, who had distinguished himself by courageously opposing the registration of the Constitution in Parliament; the Procureur-Général D'Aguesseau, soon afterwards Chancellor of France;† and Joly de Fleury, Avocat-Général, a magistrate equally well known for his attachment to Gallican principles. The Abbé Dorsanne, official of the consistory court of Paris, and author of the

---

* St. Simon, *Mémoires*, tom. viii. p. 217. It must be remembered that there were political agencies at work, which powerfully affected the course of ecclesiastical events at this crisis. The Duke of Orleans had reason to suspect that certain personages at Court were scheming to supplant him by placing the government, after the death of Louis, in the hands of the Duke du Maine, one of the king's sons by Madame de Montespan. Under this apprehension he lost no time in forming an alliance with the leaders of the opposite party, representing the national Gallicanism and the popular hatred of the Jesuits. Measures were thus concerted with Cardinal de Noailles, the Duke de Noailles his nephew, D'Aguesseau, Joly de Fleury, and other influential magistrates, which gave them a preponderance in the Parliament, and enabled them to secure the appointment of the Duke of Orleans as Regent, with the supreme administration of the kingdom during the minority of Louis XV. The Duke naturally rewarded his supporters by entrusting them with the principal offices of State.

† D'Aguesseau became Chancellor on the death of Voisin, in February, 1717.

'Journal,' was appointed secretary. The "feuille des bénéfices" was bestowed on Cardinal de Noailles.

The wrath and mortification of the "constitutionnaires" knew no bounds. To the Jesuits the new appointments were especially provoking, implying, as they did, that the tactics of the present régime were to be diametrically opposite to those of the reign which had just closed, and that at least during the minority of Louis XV., a child of five years old, the door to Royal favour and administrative power would be rigorously shut against the Order. In the bitterness of their discontent they began to hatch plots of a dangerous kind against the Regent and his government; insomuch that his Royal Highness felt it necessary to admonish them by a few wholesome examples. Father Le Tellier was ordered to retire to Amiens, although by the king's will he had been named confessor to the youthful Louis XV. That injunction was disregarded, and in the following year the place destined for Le Tellier was filled by one of strikingly opposite character,—the excellent Claude Fleury, author of the 'Histoire ecclésiastique.'*

The disgraced Jesuit, persisting in his seditious schemes, was subsequently exiled to La Flèche, where he died, despised and hated even by his own fraternity, in 1719. Louis Doucin, another prominent member of the Society, was banished in like manner to Orleans. Further intrigues having come to light, the Jesuits were interdicted in the dioceses of Metz and Verdun; and De Noailles revoked the licenses of several fathers to whom he had indulgently restored them.

One of the first measures of the Regent was to revise the *lettres de cachet* by means of which, under the tyranny of Le Tellier, those who were obnoxious to him had been imprisoned in the Bastille, and otherwise persecuted. The greater part of these arrests had been made, according to St. Simon, on the ground of Jansenism and the Constitution. He implies that their number was considerable; and Voltaire and other historians state

---

* The Regent, in announcing this appointment to Fleury, said, "Sir, I prefer you to anyone else, because you are neither a Jansenist, nor a Molinist, nor an Ultramontane." Fleury had been sub-preceptor to the Dukes of Burgundy, Anjou, and Berry. At the time of Fénélon's dismissal Bossuet interceded in his favour, and he was permitted to retain his place.

that the prisons were crowded with such victims of ecclesiastical cruelty.* But these accounts appear to be exaggerated; the truth is, so far as concerns Le Tellier, that the whole list of sufferers during the six years of his dominion did not exceed seventeen.† The prisoners were liberated, the exiles were recalled; among the latter were the four doctors of the Sorbonne who had opposed the registration of the bull Unigenitus.

It may easily be conceived that under the new administration the affair of the Constitution was contested with greater vehemence and animosity than ever. The first move of the dominant party was to obtain from the Sorbonne a retractation of its act of acceptance, upon the ground that it was extorted by fear and force. The Syndic Ravechet, a staunch supporter of De Noailles, argued energetically to that effect, and carried with him an immense majority of the doctors. Their conclusion was combated with remarkable eloquence and vigour by Honoré Tournely, one of the most accomplished theologians of the time, but to no purpose. Twenty-two doctors appealed to the Parliament, *comme d'abus*, against the proceedings of their brethren; whereupon a vote was passed excluding them from the meetings until they should give satisfaction to the Faculty and to the Syndic. In the end the decree of acceptance in 1714 was pronounced false, cancelled, and expunged from the registers of the Sorbonne. Several provincial theological Faculties adopted a similar decision.‡

The Regent, in concert with De Noailles, took an early opportunity to re-open negotiations with the Pope, with a view of persuading him to explain or modify the Constitution. Upon this point, however, Clement was immoveable. He maintained that its terms were transparently clear, and required no comment; adding that the same captious disposition which led to the demand for explanation would too surely lead the petitioners to reject or ignore it, if afforded. The mission of the Abbé Chevalier, in 1716, consequently proved altogether fruitless. The Pope consulted the Congregation of Cardinals, and the

---

* Voltaire, *Siècle de Louis XIV.* chap. xxxvii.; Lacretelle, *Hist. de France pendant le XVIIIme Siècle*, tom. i. p. 132; Duclos, *Mém. Secrets*, tom. i. p. 207.

† Crétineau-Joly, *Hist. de la Comp. de Jésus*, tom. iv. p. 478. See the authorities there cited.

‡ Those of Nantes, Reims, and Caen.

result was that four briefs were despatched to France towards the end of that year, the tenor of which was by no means favourable to the interests of peace. The first was addressed to Cardinal de Noailles, and exhorted him to accept the bull cordially and frankly, without insisting upon comments which neutralised its real meaning. The second was from the Pope to the Regent, informing him of the measures determined on by his Holiness against Cardinal de Noailles and the Sorbonne. The third was to the Sorbonne, suspending all its privileges held of the See of Rome, in punishment of its late presumptuous repudiation of the bull. The fourth was directed to the bishops who had accepted the bull; it asserted that the errors of Quesnel's book were so manifest that no man could be deceived by them, and that to demand explanations of the Constitution was to "hanker after the fruit of the forbidden tree." The Regent refused to receive these documents; the clergy were ordered to abstain from taking notice of them; the Parliaments suppressed them as contrary to law, and illegally introduced into France.

The decided ascendancy of De Noailles and the opponents of the Constitution during the earlier years of the Regency had the effect of fanning the flame of agitation which now overspread the kingdom. The accepting bishops became more and more incensed against the minority who were thus countenanced in their insubordination; while the latter gained wider influence among all classes of society, and were supported with unwearied energy by the Parliaments, who lost no opportunity of testifying their unconquerable aversion to this unfortunate specimen of Papal infallibility. The spirit of resistance showed itself in a formidable shape in March, 1717, when four bishops, De la Broue of Mirepoix, Soanen of Senez, Colbert of Montpellier, and Delangle of Boulogne, executed a solemn act of appeal to a future General Council against the bull Unigenitus. After describing the lamentable state of division and confusion which prevailed, affecting all orders of the nation—magistrates, ecclesiastics, Faculties of theology, the faithful laity, the newly converted Protestants, even heretics and enemies of the Church— these prelates declared that for three years past they had made every available effort to obtain from the Pope some measure of redress, but in vain. Scandal and dissension were increasing day by day; the peace of the Church was wrecked, and Christian truth enfeebled. They were compelled, by a deep sense of their duty to that portion of Christ's flock over which the Holy Ghost had made them overseers, to have recourse to a remedy which, under the pressure of existing circumstances, they deemed to be not less necessary than it was in itself certain and effectual. They referred the whole affair to the judgment of the Church Universal, " the supreme tribunal of the Spiritual Power, the immoveable pillar of the truth, the inviolable sanctuary of peace and charity." They included in the terms of their appeal, not only the Constitution itself, but all measures which the Pope might be induced to take against them in consequence of the present proceeding; at the same time affirming that they had no design to speak, or even to think, in contradiction to the Catholic, Apostolic, Roman Church, or to the authority of the Holy See.

On the 5th of March, the Theological Faculty of Paris declared, by an overwhelming majority, its concurrence in the appeal of the four bishops, and proclaimed with enthusiasm its readiness to join them in prosecuting it before the Œcumenical Council, whensoever duly convoked and freely assembled. The impulse thus given greatly intensified the ferment of opposition. Had Cardinal de Noailles promptly thrown his influence into the scale, and placed himself at the head of the appellants, it is not improbable that the court of Rome might have recoiled from the violence of the storm it had evoked, and sought a timely retreat by reasonable concession; the conflict might have been stayed, and a lengthened train of calamities averted from the Church and realm of France. But the Cardinal was hampered by the incurable indecision of his nature; he hesitated and temporised. He drew up and signed a form of appeal, like his bolder brethren; but for the present he could not be persuaded to make it public, and it remained locked up in his secretary's office. Meanwhile the Regent was besieged by the Ultramontanes, who denounced the appeal as an act of open rebellion, fraught with dangerous consequence, and leading straight to schism. To Philip of Orleans personally, all schools of doctrine, all forms of religion, all decrees of Popes and canons of Councils, were alike matters of indifference; he was a freethinker in sentiment and a confirmed libertine in morals.

But he was shrewd enough to perceive that the "Quesnellistes," if allowed to preponderate, were likely to prove dangerous in a political sense, and that it was the interest of the government to hold the balance even, as far as possible, between the contending parties. Hence he hearkened on the present occasion to the counsels of Cardinals de Rohan and Bissy, and De Mailly Archbishop of Reims; and under their dictation the four appellant bishops received orders to quit Paris within twenty-four hours, and retire to their dioceses. The Sorbonne was forbidden to deliberate on the subject of the Constitution; the Syndic Ravechet was banished to Lyons; the notary in whose presence the appeal had been signed was arrested and sent to the Bastille.*

The war was now waged with increased determination and activity on both sides. Archbishop de Mailly published an ordonnance excommunicating *ipso facto* all persons who might revoke their acceptance of the Constitution and subscribe to the appeal. The Appellants, whose numbers and importance augmented every day, sought redress from the Parliament; and that tribunal quickly pronounced a decision which in effect annulled the sentence of the prelate. In proportion as the excitement spread throughout the country, the whole nation was marshalled into two antagonist camps, the Acceptants and the Appellants; and it became clear that a struggle was at hand between Ultramontanism, as embodied in the Constitution Unigenitus and backed by the authority of the Crown, and the cause of national independence, represented by a not very numerous phalanx of Gallican prelates and clergy, but defended with dauntless zeal by those ancient corporations which were the traditional guardians of popular liberty—the Parliaments of Paris and the provinces. The latter party were driven by degrees into extravagant proceedings, which inflicted irremediable injuries on France. But what language is strong enough to reprobate the conduct of those who provoked such excesses by systematically abusing their authority, by turning a deaf ear to protests against patent and monstrous grievances, by sacrificing truth, honour, and duty at the sordid shrine of worldly ambition? It was owing to their gross mismanagement that the cause of a factious sect became the cause of that vast

---

* Dorsanne, *Journal*, tom. ii.

multitude of Frenchmen who loved justice, scorned oppression, and venerated the institutions which had made France great and glorious. The active sympathy shown by the Parliaments to the Jansenists of the eighteenth century materially altered the character of the memorable warfare which had so long distracted the fairest part of Christendom. The religious feud was converted into a chronic litigation between jarring orders in the secular economy. What was originally a controversy on mysterious problems of abstract theology developed into a social and political schism. The later generation of Jansenists became dangerous to the State, not because they disbelieved the "fact of Jansenius" and maintained that grace is irresistible, but because they were leagued with a powerful and ambitious public body which was constantly coming into collision with the executive Government. The course of that struggle, as it proceeded, was more and more manifestly revolutionary. In the disjointed condition towards which the nation was tending, every movement for the purpose of restraining royal absolutism within reasonable bounds served only to precipitate it further on the road to anarchy and dissolution.

The boldness and number of the appeals created alarm at Rome; and the Pope was induced to address a brief to Cardinal de Noailles in a tone of conciliation, expressing the extreme anxiety he felt to witness the re-establishment of peace in the Church. "Knowing, as we do," he said, "to how great a degree the influence, the authority, and the example of your Eminence are capable of contributing to the object which we so inpatiently desire, and unwilling to neglect any available resource of Apostolic gentleness in order to attain it, after having offered up our prayers to God, we now address them to yourself. We have constantly before our eyes the evils which have already occurred and are occurring day by day, as well as future calamities graver still, which threaten us through the abuse made of your name and support by the enemies of the Church. We therefore conjure you with all possible urgency, by the holy mysteries instituted by Jesus Christ as on this day,* that is, by the institution of the Priest-

---

* The brief is dated on Thursday in Holy Week, 1717.

hood and the Eucharistic Sacrifice, in which He has given us the symbols of unity and peace; and, again, by His passion and death, which He underwent in order that He might gather together in one the children of God who are scattered abroad,—to listen to our voice, or rather to Jesus Christ himself, who speaks to you by the mouth of one who, however unworthy, is His Vicar; and, reminding you of the divine admonition, lean not to thine own understanding, we exhort you paternally to distrust your own wisdom in an affair of such weighty moment; to make a generous sacrifice of your own feelings, preferring the tranquillity of the Church to every personal consideration; and, by your example in submitting to our Constitution, to open a way of deliverance for the kingdom from the grievous troubles which it now endures; thereby covering with shame the evil-minded and the heretic, for whom those troubles are a source of triumph. May your Eminence receive our observations as a sincere proof of the distinguished affection with which we regard you; and may you believe that this letter is dictated by the desire and hope that we may not see you charged at the judgment-seat of Christ with the loss of so many souls; as also we trust that we ourselves may be held guiltless of that crime at the same dread tribunal."

The Cardinal responded to this exhortation in a spirit of filial respect; but intimated withal that the best mode of terminating the strife would be to publish, on the part of his Holiness, such explanation of the bull as would suffice to convince and confound those who calumniously taxed it as heterodox and anti-Christian. This advice, so often and hitherto so ineffectually tendered to the Roman Court, now seemed for the first time not unlikely to prevail. Cardinals Tolomei and De Tremoille, in concert with the Jesuit Lafiteau, an unofficial agent of the Duke of Orleans, projected a new scheme of pacification. They proposed, as its basis, that a doctrinal statement, or "corps de doctrine," should be drawn up for the purpose of elucidating the obnoxious portions of the bull. This was to be subscribed by the French clergy, both acceptant and appellant; and the Pope was thereupon to declare himself satisfied with their submission to his Constitution. The Regent published a Declaration in October, 1717, enjoining absolute silence upon the matters in dispute, pending the negotiations thus opened with

Rome; and several months were occupied in laboriously discussing the details of the arrangement. But after manifold fluctuations, it appeared that the Pope had no real intention of conforming to such conditions of peace; and the Regent, irritated by his caprice, assumed a remonstrant attitude, complaining especially of the refusal of canonical institution to several prelates nominated to French sees. There were no less than twelve in this predicament; among them the Abbé Bossuet, nephew of the great Bishop of Meaux, who was designated to the see of Troyes; the Abbé de Beaumont, a nephew of Fénélon, named to Saintes; and Massillon, named to Clermont. Boldly confronting the difficulty, the Council of Regency appointed a commission of laymen, with the Duc de Saint Simon at its head, to inquire into the means of supplying these vacancies in the episcopate without the intervention of the Roman Pontiff. It was an enterprise which had already more than once terrified the Vatican; and in the present instance its result was eminently successful. The tidings no sooner reached Rome, than the bulls for the twelve bishoprics were despatched with such precipitate haste, that the courier who brought them expired from the effects of fatigue on reaching Paris.*

The settlement of the main subject of dispute, however, seemed as remote as ever. In February, 1718, a decree of the Inquisition condemned the appeals of the four bishops and of the Theological Faculties. The Parliament of Paris met this by denouncing the sentence of a tribunal which France has in all ages refused to recognise. The Pope expressed himself dissatisfied with the "corps de doctrine," inasmuch as it amounted, in his view, to no more than a conditional and relative acceptance of the Constitution, which he had so constantly repudiated. He intimated that his patience was exhausted, and that nothing remained but to take the measures which had become inevitable for vindicating the authority of the Apostolic See. On the 28th of August, 1718, he promulgated the bull "Pastoralis officii," by which, after recounting the efforts he had made to convince and convert the gainsayers, he declared that those who refused submission to the Constitution were "no longer

---

* Lemontey, " Histoire de la Régence " (*Œuvres*, tom. vi. p. 165); Picot, *Mém. pour servir à l'hist. du XVIIIme Siècle*, tom. i. p. 150.

to be regarded as children of the Church, but as disobedient, contumacious, and refractory." "Since they have departed from us and from the Roman Church," said Clement, "if not by express words, at least in fact, by manifold proofs of hardened obstinacy, they must be held as separated from our charity and that of the Church, and communion can no longer subsist between them and ourselves." The gravity of this proceeding at length impelled Cardinal de Noailles to declare himself distinctly. He published his appeal to the General Council, which had hitherto been kept secret; and this was closely followed by a further act of appeal against the "Pastoralis officii," in which he laid down the maxim that, pending the judgment of the supreme legislature of the Church, the Pope had no right to pronounce judicially upon the questions at issue. His sentiments were enthusiastically re-echoed in all directions. The University of Paris, the Chapter of Notre Dame, the curés of the city churches, the secular and religious communities of the capital, vied with each other in the fervour of their protests against the ill-advised policy of Rome. The four bishops who had originated the movement renewed their appeal, and were supported by twelve of their brethren; many Cathedral Chapters, and a multitude of the country clergy, adhered to the same course. But at this moment De Noailles abruptly resigned his seat in the Council of Conscience; foreseeing, probably, that the party opposed to him, headed by De Rohan and Bissy, were likely to regain the ascendant, and desiring to secure for himself full liberty of action. It was a needless and inglorious surrender of what in more resolute hands might have been a position of immense advantage. A prelate like Bossuet, or even De Noailles himself had Bossuet been at hand to support him, would have held it fast and rendered it impregnable. But it was the Cardinal's fate always to give way precisely when firmness was most essential to his own credit and the success of his cause. His place at the ecclesiastical board was filled by the Archbishop of Bordeaux; but it met only once after his resignation, and was immediately afterwards dissolved.*

---

* St. Simon, *Mémoires*, tom. xi. p. 29.

The Court now inclined to the side of the "constitutionnaires;" and upon the strength of this change of policy, the accepting bishops fulminated mandement after mandement, insisting upon absolute submission to the "Unigenitus" as "a dogmatic judgment of the Universal Church, all appeal against which was null and void, illusory, rash, scandalous, schismatic, injurious to the authority of the Church, to the Holy See, and to the episcopal body." The Parliaments bravely maintained their ground; they declared the mandements "abusive," and as such condemned and suppressed them. They rejected likewise the Apostolic letter "Pastoralis officii," pronouncing it inadmissible both as to form and matter.

The strife was fierce and complicated beyond example. Cardinal de Noailles, on publishing his appeal, had addressed an Instruction to his clergy, explaining at considerable length the motives of his conduct, and the dissentient view which he felt compelled to take of the late Papal utterances. Rome replied to this document, which was drawn up with much ability, by a decree of the Inquisition, stating that the holy Father, having heard with extreme sorrow that such a publication had appeared, to the scandal of all good Catholics and the grievous injury of souls, had caused consultations to be held in his presence by eminent theologians, together with the ordinary members of the Roman Inquisition, when it was determined that the said Instruction should be condemned and prohibited by reason of various false doctrines and assertions contained in it, injurious in many ways to all Catholic bishops, but especially to the prelates of France and to the Apostolic See. It was denounced in due form accordingly; the faithful being forbidden to print, read, or possess it, under pain of excommunication *ipso facto*. But when the decree reached France, the Parliament of Paris forthwith suppressed it, warning all his Majesty's subjects of the legal penalties they would incur by any act tending to further its circulation.

Seldom had the Church of France been in a more critical position; it seemed to be drifting rapidly towards schism, and even towards organic disruption. These calamities were averted, and some approach was effected towards a restoration of Christian unity and concord, through the intervention of a personage whose character and antecedents rendered him pre-eminently an unlikely instrument of such beneficent results. This was the Abbé (afterwards Cardinal) Dubois.

That it should have been possible for such a man as Dubois to act the principal part in even the temporary adjustment of a difficulty so deeply affecting the welfare of the Christian Commonwealth, is a fact which speaks volumes as to the demoralized state of opinion in France during the minority of Louis XV. Dubois was one of the most impudently vicious of mankind. He it was who, in his capacity of preceptor to the Duc de Chartres (the future Regent), had deliberately sown in his young heart those seeds of infidelity and licentiousness which afterwards bore such melancholy fruits. His own life had been a tissue of scandals. "All the vices contended within him," says St. Simon, "which of them should remain his master. Avarice, debauchery, and ambition, were his gods; perfidy, flattery, servility, his means of action; utter irreligion, his normal condition; and the opinion that uprightness and honour are mere artificial pretences which have no real existence in any one, his fixed principle; from which it followed that all means were in his estimation equally good. He excelled in low intrigues; he lived upon them, he could not do without them; but there was always some object towards which all his movements were directed, with an extent of perseverance which was bounded only by success, or by the absolute demonstration that success in that track was impossible. In the latter case, he continued to toil on in the depths of darkness until he saw daylight better at some other outlet. Thus he passed his life in sapping and mining. He would utter the grossest falsehoods quite naturally, with an air of simplicity, candour, and sincerity."* By means of these and other questionable accomplishments Dubois had rendered important services to the Regent in many a political emergency.

But it is admitted that he possessed, as a set-off against his vices, intellectual ability above the average, great knowledge of the world, firmness, persuasiveness, and indefatigable industry. More than one department of the government was already under his control. In order to reach the highest pinnacle of power, Dubois had determined to push his fortunes in the

---

* St. Simon, *Mémoires*, tom. vii. p. 315.

Church; he aimed at ruling France in the imposing character of a Cardinal, after the memorable precedents of Richelieu and Mazarin. Hitherto he had taken only the minor orders; notwithstanding which, upon the death of Cardinal de la Tremoille, Archbishop of Cambrai, in 1720, he had the effrontery to ask the Regent to nominate him to the vacant see. The duke, to do him justice, seems to have been shocked by the proposal; but Dubois pressed his application, and procured, in order to back it, a letter from George I., the Protestant King of England, requesting the Regent, as a personal favour, to bestow the coveted preferment upon one whose merits he esteemed so highly.* The duke knew not how to resist, and the promise was accordingly given. The abbé, however, could not become an archbishop without having first been ordained priest. He applied for this purpose to Cardinal de Noailles: expecting that, under the many difficulties which surrounded him, that prelate would gladly seize the opportunity of conferring an important obligation upon one who was evidently destined to play a leading part in the affairs of state. But he found himself mistaken. De Noailles not only refused to ordain him in his own diocese, but declined even to facilitate his ordination by granting him letters dimissory to one of the suffragans of the province.† The Archbishop of Rouen, Bezons, recently translated from Bordeaux, was less scrupulous. From him letters dimissory were obtained; and in February, 1720, Dubois repaired to Pontoise, at that time within the boundaries of the province of Rouen, where he received priest's orders‡ from the hands of Tressan Bishop of Nantes, premier aumonier to the Regent.§ The Pope having despatched, though with some hesitation, the "Indult" for the Archbishopric of Cambrai, he was consecrated in the Church of the Val de Grâce,

---

* Duclos, *Mém. Secrets*, tom. i. p. 400. Lemontey, *Hist. de la Régence*, chap. xiii.

† Dorsanne, *Journal*, tom. i. p. 508.

‡ The common account (originating with St. Simon, and copied by Duclos, Lacretelle, and others) is that he was ordained sub-deacon, deacon, and priest, on one and the same day; but this is not strictly correct. The precise dates are given by Dorsanne. Dubois was ordained sub-deacon on Saturday February 24, 1720; deacon on the next day, Sunday the 25th; and priest on the Sunday following, March 4. (Dorsanne, *Journal*, tom. i. p. 509).

§ Lavergne de Tressan was a prelate of disreputable character, and a shameless pluralist. His services on this occasion procured for him afterwards the archbishopric of Rouen.

with extraordinary pomp and splendour, on the 9th of June in the same year, Cardinal de Rohan officiating as the presiding prelate, with Tressan of Nantes and Massillon of Clermont for his assistants. The latter, strangely inconsistent as the fact appears with his own integrity and piety, consented to sign the certificate of the new Archbishop's correctness of life and morals.*

Impelled by the double motive of resentment against Cardinal de Noailles and anxiety to secure favour at Rome with a view to the ulterior prize of the cardinal's hat, Dubois now exerted all his influence and energy to bring about a complete acceptance of the Constitution "Unigenitus" both by the civil government and by the Gallican Church. At his instigation the Council of Regency adopted, on the 4th of August, 1720, a Declaration drawn up by the Chancellor D'Aguesseau, approving of the "corps de doctrine," and enforcing the Constitution as a law of the State, according to the explanations therein contained. This was transmitted to the Parliament, which was then in exile at Pontoise, by reason of its opposition to the Regent in a matter arising out of the disaster of the financier Law. The magistrates refused to register; relying, it is said, upon a private assurance from Cardinal de Noailles that he would never accept the Declaration until it had been sanctioned by their concurrence. Their contumacy irritated the Regent and Dubois, and they received fresh *lettres de cachet* on the 11th of November, ordering them to retire to Blois, still further from the capital. Meanwhile the Declaration was registered by the Grand Conseil, a body well known to be abjectly obsequious to the government of the day.† The Regent and his minister seemed determined to proceed to extremities against the Parliament; D'Aguesseau, alarmed at the prospect of a dangerous collision, tendered his resignation, which, however, was not accepted; and the situation of affairs became more and

---

* Duclos suggests excuses for Massillon's weakness. "L'étude et la retraite avoient pu l'empêcher d'être parfaitement instruit de toute la dépravation du nouveau prélat; ajoutez à ces raisons une sorte de timidité que la vertu bourgeoise conserve au milieu de la cour. Il obéit enfin à la necessité. Les rigoristes le blâmèrent, et les gens raisonnables le plaignirent, et l'excusèrent." —*Mém. Secrets*, tom. i. p. 404. Massillon received as his reward a seat in the Council de Conscience (*Mém. du Maréchal de Richelieu*, tom. iii. p. 208)

† Dorsanne, *Journal*, tom. ii. p. 31.

more threatening. But at this moment Cardinal de Noailles, apprehensive of the gravest consequences if the contest were further prolonged, and feeling that, under the circumstances, his engagement with the Parliament would be more honoured in the breach than the observance, signified to the Regent his readiness to endorse the Declaration; and on the 17th of November he published his Mandement to that effect, which was virtually an act of adhesion to the bull Unigenitus, though modified by the explanatory comments already adopted as the basis of an understanding.* The Parliament, after this, had no excuse for non-compliance; on the 4th of December they registered the Declaration without condition or demur;† whereupon the Regent at once expressed himself satisfied; the magistrates, to their great joy, were recalled to Paris; and within a fortnight the business of the different courts of justice resumed its usual course.

But this singular transaction (known as the "accommodement" of 1720) was scarcely more than an evasion of the questions in dispute, and could not, therefore, be permanently conclusive. The Jansenist agitators clamoured against the Cardinal for having "betrayed the truth;" the Pope kept silence, but was at heart indignant; the appeals to a future Council recommenced, and were widely multiplied. Amid the general discontent, one, at all events, of the parties principally concerned beheld his intrigues crowned with success, namely, Dubois. He took care that the merit which he had acquired by

---

* Lafiteau, *Histoire de la Constitution Unigenitus*, tom. ii. p. 116. The "Explications," or "Corps de doctrine," may be seen in the *Collection des Procès-verbaux des Assemb. du Clergé*, tom. vi., "Pièces justificatives," No. 4. They were signed by one hundred prelates. A variety of motives concurred to dispose the Cardinal to compliance. He was staggered by the attitude of the bishops in other parts of Christendom, who, though of course aware of the events which were passing in France—the difficulties urged against the reception of the Constitution, the appeals against it to the future Council, &c.—unanimously stood aloof, and abstained from showing the slightest sympathy with the dissentients. Again, the persons in whose judgment he reposed the greatest confidence—F. de la Tour General of the Oratory; Dreuillet Bishop of Bayonne; the Chancellor D'Aguesseau; Father Polinier, and the Abbé Couet—all combined to entreat him to close without delay with the proposed terms of accommodation. (Dorsanne, *Journal*, tom. ii. p. 8).

† "Mercredi 4, le Parlement a enregistré la déclaration pour la Constitution; mais comme il l'a enregistrée en 1714, de manière que c'est n'avoir rien fait. C'est un jeu que cela, et les constitutionnaires ne doivent point être contents." (*Journal historique du règne de Louis XV.*, par E. J. F. Barbier, tom. i. p. 64).

winning the authorities in France into submission to the long-contested edict of the Pope should be proclaimed at the Vatican in its fullest extent;* the victory, though by no means decisive or complete, was undeniable as to outward appearance; and it was impossible to resist his claim to reward. Clement XI. is understood to have been on the point of raising him to the Conclave when he was attacked by the illness which caused his death, on the 19th of March, 1721. Cardinal Conti, who succeeded as Innocent XIII., bound himself by a written promise, previously to his election, to carry out this purpose; and from him Dubois at length received the Cardinal's hat, which filled up the measure of his ambition.† During the brief remainder of his life he enjoyed unbounded power in France in affairs ecclesiastical and civil. The Ultramontanes were for the time triumphant, and the unhappy Jansenists were visited unsparingly with the iron scourge of persecution.

---

* His chief agent for this purpose was the shrewd and insinuating Lafiteau, who had just been elevated, through his patronage, to the bishopric of Sisteron. Dubois also reckoned among his supporters at Rome the exiled heir of the Stuarts (there recognised as King of England), Cardinal Gualterio, Cardinal de Rohan, and the too-famous Abbé (afterwards Cardinal) de Tencin.

† "On ne sçauroit dire combien on fut indigné à la cour et à la ville de la promotion de l'Abbé Dubois, et le mauvais effet qu'elle fit pour le Pape. On disoit hautement que ce nouveau Cardinal avoit répandu *deux millions* dans la famille du Pape."—Dorsanne, *Journal*, tom. ii. p. 78.

CHAPTER VII.

The new "Conseil de Conscience," or Ecclesiastical Commission, consisted of Cardinals Dubois, De Rohan, and De Mailly, together with Fleury, formerly Bishop of Fréjus, now preceptor to the young king;—men not likely to show mercy to the "anti-constitutionnaires." The last-named prelate, who was soon to rise to the highest post in the administration of affairs, had a special and personal ground of animosity against the "Quesnellists." In 1716, on the occasion of his taking leave of the diocese of Fréjus, he had published a Pastoral Letter containing severe reflections on the perverseness and obstinacy of the Jansenists. Quesnel, who at eighty years of age had lost none of his polemical energy, attacked this production in a tone of bitter sarcasm, and covered it with ridicule; and the future minister, though he took no public notice of it, never forgot or forgave the offence. Fleury's zeal against Jansenism had a suspicious air, since in his early days he had studiously kept aloof from controversy; and so far was he from being a partisan of the Jesuits, that his professional advancement was due to the warm recommendation of Cardinal de Noailles. But, although by nature modest, tolerant, and disinterested, he was not devoid of ambition; and his private resentment concurred with his political aspirations to dispose him to deal severely with those who might attempt to resist or elude the terms of the recent settlement. Fleury, nevertheless, was a man of honourable character, and even of sincere religious feeling; far superior in moral worth to his colleagues in the government. He regarded Dubois with aversion and contempt, and did his utmost to inspire Louis XV. with similar sentiments.

The "accommodement" was but a pseudo-pacification, a mere compromise; and as in the analogous case of the "Peace of Clement IX." in 1669, the factions on both sides strained and abused it to the furtherance of their own purposes. Although a certain number of the appellant bishops and clergy had imitated

Cardinal de Noailles in his submission, quite as many persisted in their defiant attitude, and invoked afresh the judgment of an Œcumenical Council—the only tribunal, they maintained, which was competent to decide in the last resort questions of such difficulty and magnitude.* The Government could not avoid noticing these proceedings, since they were in the teeth of the royal Declaration just registered in Parliament, which prohibited and suppressed such appeals; and various penalties of greater or less severity were inflicted in consequence.

The commencement of a new Pontificate was looked upon as a favourable opportunity of extorting something from Rome in the way of concession; and with this object seven Gallican bishops addressed a letter to Innocent XIII. in June, 1721, full of acrimonious complaints against the bull Unigenitus. Among these prelates were three of the original appellants— the Bishops of Senez, Boulogne, and Montpellier: the fourth, De la Broue of Mirepoix, had died in the year preceding. The other signataries were the Bishops of Tournay, Auxerre, Pamiers, and Macon. Their letter was a violent attack upon the bull, both as to its matter and its form. They represented it as accrediting an entirely novel system, both of theology and of morals; a system founded on the fallacious principles of Molina, which had been condemned by the congregation "De Auxiliis," and which the Popes had repeatedly promised to proscribe in solemn form. These errors had been reproduced of late with fresh activity in a notorious work by Cardinal Sfondrati, and by the Jesuits Francolini† and Fontaine; yet the Holy See had allowed the scandal to pass without notice, the special partiality of the late Pope for Cardinal Sfondrati being a fact but too well known. Instead of censuring these pernicious doctrines, Rome had thought fit to denounce the 'Reflec-

---

* "Si les choses s'adoucissent à Rome sur l'accommodement, elles s'aigrissent en France; nos zélés indiscrets ont engagé à certaines procédures qui ont échauffé les esprits au delà de ce qu'ils étoient, en sorte qu'ils ont renouvelé leurs appels publiquement; ainsi je crains fort que l'affaire ne devienne plus difficile, et que le Pape, voulant trop soutenir son autorité, n'augmente le trouble dans l'Église."—Cardinal de Noailles to Cardinal Gualterio; Conflans, 17 de mars 1721 (*Gualterio Papers*, MSS. 20,394).

† Balthasar Francolini, born at Fermo, in 1650, was an author of some repute, and published several treatises on dogmatic and moral theology. Those here referred to are probably his work *De disciplinâ Pœnitentiæ* and his *Tirocinium theologicum*. Francolini died at the Jesuit College at Rome in 1709.

tions on the New Testament,' which enjoyed the patronage of one of the chief Gallican prelates, universally respected for his piety and orthodoxy. The bishops then expatiate on the results of the Constitution Unigenitus; what consternation it had excited throughout Christendom, what affliction it had caused to the Episcopate, what agitation and distress among the faithful, and, more painful still, what triumph to the Protestants. They conclude by imploring the Holy Father to undertake the defence of the cause of truth under such alarming circumstances. "Attempts have been made to separate us from the communion of the Holy See; but they have only had the effect of attaching us still more closely to the centre of ecclesiastical unity. We have been persecuted by the civil power, but we have never ceased to inculcate upon our flocks the respect which is due, according to the sacred canons, to the Roman Pontiff. We have never imagined that a cause of such magnitude could be determined by our own authority, or that a few individual bishops could apply an effectual remedy to such a pressing evil. But, after endeavouring without success to dispel the clouds of prejudice from the mind of Clement XI., we have finally taken the path which is indicated to us by Jesus Christ in the Gospel; and we demand that the arbiter of our controversy shall be none other than the Church herself."

"Your Holiness will judge without difficulty which course is the more honourable to the Roman See, that of permitting a decree to continue in force which is manifestly opposed to the dogmas of the Faith and the dictates of morality, insomuch that its errors pierce through the veil by which it is vainly attempted to conceal them, or that of pronouncing, in conformity with the rules laid down by Innocent III., one of the most celebrated of your predecessors, and with the constant practice of the Church, that this decree is surreptitious, and altogether inconsistent with the laws of the Roman Church. The sacred records of the tradition of the Church teach us that the Holy See has judged it necessary, on certain occasions, to annul the decrees of Popes, and even to stigmatise their memory, when they have been so unhappy as to persevere till death in engagements unworthy of their character." The Pope, resenting this strong language, referred the document to the Inquisition, who, in March, 1722, condemned it as insulting to the Catholic episcopate, particularly that of France, to the memory of Clement XI., to the reigning Pope, and to the Apostolic See; and, moreover, as full of the spirit of schism and heresy. Innocent also addressed briefs to Louis XV. and to the Regent, in which he declared that the bull Unigenitus condemned nothing but manifest errors, and that it was not opposed either to the teaching of the Fathers or to the liberty of the Catholic schools. He complained bitterly of the conduct of the remonstrant bishops, and demanded rigorous measures against them, since such pastors were more likely to destroy the sheep than to guide them safely.* The Regent, in consequence, denounced the offensive letter by an *arrêt* of the Council of State, and declared that the authors would be proceeded against according to the canon law; but this threat was not carried into execution. The bishops wrote to the Regent in self-justification, and defended the principle of appeal to a General Council by a learned series of proofs and testimonies from ecclesiastical antiquity.

Cardinal Dubois became prime minister in August, 1722, and signalised his elevation by penal inflictions of odious severity on the contumacious clergy. The bishops were encouraged to denounce them to the government; whereupon, by the extra-judicial machinery of *lettres de cachet*, they were deprived of their benefices, driven from their homes, fined, banished from the country, immured in a dungeon, and in one way or another consigned to poverty and misery.

In the midst of this reign of terror, the Assembly of the clergy which met in 1723 was servile and pusillanimous enough to name Dubois to preside over its deliberations. The only person in high station who seems to have had the courage to cross him was Cardinal de Noailles. That prelate was not to be induced by any deference to the wishes of the minister to waive his conscientious objection to license the Jesuits in his diocese. On the retirement of Claude Fleury from the post of royal confessor,† Dubois proposed for the appointment a Jesuit named De Linières, who was already confessor to the Duchess of

---

* "Pastoribus hujusmodi oves Christi perdendas potius quàm pascendas ulterius permitti non posse." — See Dorsanne, *Journal*, tom. ii. p. 128.

† Fleury resigned office, on account of his great age, in March, 1722, and died in July, 1723.

Orleans, mother of the Regent. De Noailles, however, refused to grant to him or any other member of the Order the necessary powers to direct the conscience of the young king. He wrote to the Duke of Orleans, frankly explaining his views, and pointing out that, since the Jesuits were well known to be adverse to the recent "accommodement," it was certain that they would employ all their efforts to stir up a renewal of strife, and to insist on an absolute acceptance of the Constitution.

But Dubois was resolute, and carried his point. On the 31st of March F. de Linières was presented to Louis XV. as the person selected by the Duke of Orleans for the post of his spiritual guide; no notice having been previously given to De Noailles.* The motive of Dubois in this proceeding, as Duclos remarks,† was doubtless that of spite against the Cardinal for refusing to ordain him, for he was under no personal obligation to the Jesuits, who had had no share in his promotion. In the teeth of the Archbishop's inhibition, he persisted in the nomination; and as De Noailles was equally unyielding, the Pope was appealed to for a special faculty in favour of the Jesuit, setting aside the jurisdiction of the diocesan. This was obtained without difficulty; and in order to avoid any open breach of discipline, it was arranged that when his Majesty purposed to confess, he should proceed from Versailles to St. Cyr, within the diocese of Chartres, where the Jesuits enjoyed the requisite powers.

De Noailles took no pains to conceal from the Regent the feelings with which he viewed the partial and persecuting spirit now displayed in the conduct of Church affairs. He bluntly enquired of his Royal Highness "When he intended to set up the Inquisition in France?" and as the prince replied in a tone of irritation, he proceeded to point out that his present policy was not more opposed to the Inquisition than to the principles upon which he had acted at the commencement of his Regency. "All that you are now doing," he said, "encourages the Jesuits to believe that they will soon witness the establishment of the Inquisition, and that they themselves will be appointed grand Inquisitors."

Events, meanwhile, were impending, which once more mate-

---

* Dorsanne, *Journal*, tom. ii. p. 118.   † Duclos, *Mém. Secrets*, Liv. v. p. 473.

rially changed the situation of parties, and promised some measure of relief to the suffering Church of France. Dubois was cut short in the enjoyment of his full-blown honours; he expired, from the effects of a desperate surgical operation, on the 10th of August, 1723. His death-bed was a frightful scene. He raved and blasphemed in his last moments, and rejected with scorn the most ordinary decencies of religion.* The Duke of Orleans, prematurely worn out by his excesses, was suddenly struck with apoplexy, and followed his unworthy favourite to the grave on the 2nd of December in the same year. His loss was not regretted by any important or respectable party in Church or State. "In the Church," says St. Simon, "both pretenders to religion and the really devout were glad to be rid of the scandal of his life, and of the open support afforded to the libertines by his example; and both Jansenists and Constitutionists, either from ambition or stupidity, agreed in taking comfort from it. The former, after having been charmed by the fair promise of his earlier measures, had found themselves worse treated in the sequel than they had been under Louis XIV.; the latter, full of rage because he had not allowed them to go all lengths to annihilate the Gallican maxims and liberties, to establish the unlimited dominion of the bishops, and to make the authority of the Church formidable to all men, not excepting even sovereigns, exulted in their deliverance from a superior genius, who, although he sacrificed individuals to their malice, firmly checked them as to the main object for which they were constantly scheming. They hoped everything from a successor who would be unable to detect their intrigues, whom they might easily hoodwink, and under whom they would be free to proceed with more audacity." †

---

* See *Mém. du Maréchal Duc de Richelieu*, tom. iii. p. 324.

† St. Simon, *Mémoires*, tom. xiii. p. 92. At this point we are deprived of the invaluable stores of contemporary information supplied by this celebrated writer. The death of the Regent Orleans and the elevation of the Duke of Bourbon are the last political events recorded by St. Simon. From a passage at the close of his work it would appear that he proposed to continue it down to the death of Cardinal de Fleury; but if this design was ever executed, the world has not been permitted to profit by it. The Duke of St. Simon was a perfect type of the aristocrat of the ancient *régime;* brimfull of prejudices, partialities, crotchets, antipathies, which he makes no attempt to disguise; yet this cannot be said to detract from the general trustworthiness and accuracy of his narrative. The picture is highly coloured; the lights and shadows are

The Duke of Bourbon-Condé, an ignorant man of small capacity, succeeded nominally to the office of prime minister; but the substance of power passed into the hands of André Hercules de Fleury, ci-devant bishop of Fréjus. Ostensibly, however, Fleury contented himself with the administration of the "feuille des bénéfices," or department of ecclesiastical affairs. In the disposal of the splendid preferments and immense revenues of the Church he must be allowed the praise of disinterestedness, since he appropriated nothing to himself,* and recognised piety, learning, and pastoral efficiency as essential qualifications for advancement. At the same time it cannot be denied that as a rule he sought the objects of his patronage among the known partisans of the bull Unigenitus. Upon this point he habitually belied his general character for moderation and firmness. Private pique, doubtless, was partly his motive in this policy; but there is reason to believe that he acted likewise from a conviction, however mistaken, of the necessity of enforcing the Papal Constitution, as the only remaining chance of eradicating from the Church the festering sore of Jansenism.

Upon the death of Innocent XIII. in March, 1724, Cardinal Orsini, Archbishop of Benevento, was elected to succeed him, and took the name of Benedict XIII. The new Pope belonged to the order of the Dominicans, and was believed to be strongly attached to the Thomist theology. This encouraged the opponents of the Constitution to hope that he might be disposed to promote some conciliatory arrangement in their favour; since the Jansenists, as we have before had occasion to remark, professed to concur in the main with the teaching of St. Thomas, and with that of St. Augustine as interpreted by him. Cardinal de Noailles lost no time in attempting to profit by a circumstance of such promising augury. Since the "accommodation" of 1720 he had remained quiescent; but upon the accession of Benedict he wrote to congratulate his Holiness, and appealed to him, at the close of his letter, to apply some effectual

---

sharply contrasted, and may occasionally be charged with exaggeration; but the effect of the whole is life-like, graphic, and truthful.

* Fleury could not be prevailed upon to accept the archbishopric of Reims, one of the highest and richest dignities of the church, which the Regent offered him on the death of Cardinal de Mailly. The duke forced upon him afterwards the Abbey of St. Étienne at Caen.— Barbier, *Journal*, tom. i. p. 111.

remedy to the alarming disorders of the Church.* The Pope responded by a brief full of affectionate condescension, applauding the Cardinal's zeal for unity, and expressing his own earnest solicitude for the restoration of peace. "We are persuaded," he said, "that since you offer us your felicitations with so much fervour as being charged with the mission of re-establishing and maintaining peace, you are fully prepared and desirous to second us by doing all that lies in your own power towards the accomplishment of your wishes. In this conviction we exhort and urgently beseech you to exert all the influence that you possess for this purpose; act in accordance with what is demanded of you by your talents, your birth, your dignity; and strive by your filial and exemplary obedience to recover others into the path of unity. By such conduct you will assuage our paternal grief, since it is impossible that we, on our part, should excuse ourselves from our plain duty, or deviate from the vigilance, the resolutions, or the acts, of our predecessors."

De Noailles could hardly be surprised at the intimation conveyed in this latter sentence, that the Pope considered himself bound to adhere to the Constitutions "Unigenitus" and "Pastoralis Officii;" but he cherished, nevertheless, from his private knowledge of the views held by his Holiness, a sanguine hope that his enterprise might prove successful. One of Benedict's earliest Pontifical acts had been to address a brief to the Dominicans, in which he vindicated with considerable emphasis their known tenets on the doctrines of grace, and declared them exempt from any share in the anathemas of the bull Unigenitus. "It is not surprising," he said, "that you should take amiss the malicious assertion which has been made, that Clement XI., in condemning the errors specified in his bull Unigenitus, designed in any sense whatever to attack the doctrine of St. Augustine and St. Thomas, or sought to diminish your reputation by subjecting the principal articles of your belief to the censures denounced in the said Constitution. I applaud your sensitiveness in this matter, and recognise you thereby as the true children of St. Thomas. In the whole of this affair your cause has never been separated from that of the Holy See; far from

* Dorsanne, *Journal*, tom. ii. p. 221.

pitying you, I consider it highly to your honour to be identified with the Angelic Doctor, and to witness in your own persons that the agreement of his doctrine with the Divine oracles and the Apostolic decrees has not sufficed to restrain the unbridled license of these calumniators. It is strange that such insinuations should have been made, since the errors in question are distinctly condemned by the teaching of St. Thomas; and it has so happened, by a remarkable Providence, that his writings have been the means of overthrowing numberless forms of heresy which have arisen in the Church. I exhort you then to despise the slanders which it is attempted to propagate against your dogmas of grace efficacious by itself and of gratuitous predestination to glory without any prevision of merits, derived as they are from the works of St. Augustine and St. Thomas, from the word of God, from the decrees of Councils, and from the authority of the Fathers. We forbid, under canonical penalties, all persons whatsoever to give currency to such calumnies or spread such rumours. Continue to regulate yourselves by the teaching of our celebrated Doctor, which is more luminous than the day, and contains no alloy of error. Maintain and defend it with all vigour, inasmuch as it is the rule of Christian doctrine, and contains nothing but the pure verities of our holy religion. I announce this to you in order to dispel your fears, and to prove to you our deep interest in your welfare. This indeed is the least that we can do, having embraced your statutes, and made our profession of religion in your illustrious Order, from which Providence has now raised us to undertake the government of the Church."

Such sentiments, officially enunciated from the Roman Chair, naturally led De Noailles to anticipate that the "Unigenitus," though it could not be absolutely revoked, might even yet be supplemented by such explanations as would enable the appellant party to submit without violating the dictates of their conscience. And it is almost certain that if a confidential negotiation to this end could have been conducted exclusively between the Pontiff and the Cardinal, the desired result would have been realized. De Noailles, in a second letter to his Holiness, entered at great length into the details of the case, showing how the Jesuits had systematically abused the bull for their own malicious purposes, and exposing the intrigues by which they had deterred

Clement XI. from publishing the explanations which, as he believed, that Pontiff was personally disposed to grant. He pointed out the grievous scandal entailed upon the Church by the fact that some of her most essential doctrines had not only become matters of violent dispute, but that they were practically overthrown and destroyed. He implored the holy Father to pronounce distinctly what sentiments are to be held as to the necessity of faith in Jesus Christ, the omnipotence of the will of God, the free gift of His grace, the equilibrium between good and evil which some pretended to exist in the mind and will of man, the difference between the obedience required under the Law of Moses and the precepts peculiar to the Gospel, the proper use of Holy Scripture, and the rules for due administration of the Sacrament of penance. He concluded by protesting that he accepted the Constitution precisely in that sense, with those views, and in that disposition, with which his Holiness desired that it should be received, and in which he himself received it."

The Pope expressed himself deeply thankful for these overtures; and it appears that, after some further correspondence, it was arranged that De Noailles should draw up a statement of his own sentiments with regard to the principal points which had been so fiercely controverted in connexion with the bull Unigenitus; the Pope was thereupon to declare his approval by a brief; and the Cardinal felt assured that this act would be welcomed as amply satisfactory by all who had hitherto been conscientiously opposed to the Constitution, and that their objections would be at once withdrawn.

He accordingly reduced to twelve articles his views upon the questions in dispute; of which the following is an epitome.

"1. No man, since the fall of Adam, can attain eternal salvation without faith in the Redeemer, more or less distinct and developed, according to the difference of times and the circumstances of individuals.

"2. No man resists the absolute will of God.

"3. It is not necessary, in order to sin or merit on the part of man, that there should be an equal capacity for good and evil, or an equal tendency in both directions, or equal powers in the will.

"4. It may be safely maintained that the blinded and hardened are sometimes deprived judicially of all interior grace; but no man will be rash enough to assert that those who in that state commit mortal sin are not guilty in the sight of God.

"8. He who commits great sin offends God, although he may be ignorant of God, or may not at the moment think of God, or may not consider the gravity of his sin.

"9. We do not follow the safe path unless we require, in the Sacrament of penance, the same love of God which the Second Council of Orange and the Council of Trent exact from adults for justification in baptism.

"10. It is in accordance with the precepts of the Gospel and the rules of the Church to postpone the benefit of absolution in the case of penitents burdened with great crimes, or those who are in the habit or the proximate occasion of mortal sin; or those who give but doubtful or equivocal evidence of conversion; and generally in the case of all whom a wise confessor considers to be not sufficiently prepared and rightly disposed.

"11. The reading of Holy Scripture is doubtless useful in itself; but it is not positively necessary to the salvation of all men without exception; neither is it allowable that every private individual should interpret it according to his own fancy and his own understanding, or read it without sincere submission to the Church, to whom it belongs to judge of the true sense and interpretation of Scripture.

"12. If any sentence of excommunication should clearly forbid the exercise of a real virtue, or contravene a legitimate precept, it is to be regarded as unjust and void; and that conformably with the decrees of the Church."

These propositions were placed in the hands of the Pope by F. Gravezon, a Dominican, on behalf of Cardinal de Noailles; and we are told that Benedict signified his unqualified approbation of them.* Several of them, it is obvious, contradict some of the favourite dogmas of the Jesuitical school; they condemn, for instance, the efficacy of attrition, the Molinist theory of the equilibrium of the human mind between good and evil, the pernicious figment of "philosophical sin," and the practice of dispensing absolution without sufficient proof of penitence. But it must be acknowledged, on the other hand, that the general tone

---

* Dorsanne, *Journal*, tom. ii. p. 250.

of the document is moderate, judicious, and orthodox; and that if there had existed on the side of the Ultramontanes any honest wish for reconciliation, a fairer opportunity of effecting it could hardly have been offered. Such a policy, however, did not suit their purposes; they knew their power at Rome, and were resolved that, whatever might be the personal dispositions of the reigning Pontiff, the Constitution should be enforced upon the Church down to its smallest iota, without regard to reason, discretion, or possible consequences to the cause of religion. Accordingly the leading prelates of their party addressed vehement remonstrances to the Roman Conclave against accepting the proposed explanations; and even went so far as to assail the Pope with insults and menaces in case he should declare his concurrence with them in an official form, as he had promised Cardinal de Noailles. Their passion transported them beyond all bounds of propriety. They denounced the recent negotiation as a mystery of iniquity, a deed of darkness, a plot to betray the Church; they affirmed that the Pope had thereby excited grave suspicions as to the purity of his own faith, and that such a transaction had inflicted a lasting stigma of disgrace upon the author and the defenders of the Constitution—nay, upon the Holy See and the Universal Church. In fine, they gave Benedict to understand that the clergy of France would not hesitate to separate from his communion and head a national schism, if he should persist in countenancing this sacrilegious project.*

The result of this demonstration was such as might be expected. The Pope was intimidated, and bent before the storm; and such was the despotic pressure brought to bear upon him, that at a Council held in St. John Lateran, in April, 1725, he found it necessary to accept a decree endorsing the Unigenitus in its fullest extent and obligation, and enjoining its execution more rigorously than ever. "We command all bishops and pastors of souls to require with all possible strictness that the Constitution given by Clement XI. of saintly memory, commencing with the word Unigenitus, be observed and executed by all the faithful of whatsoever grade or condition, with the complete obedience which is due to it. If then they should learn that any one, whether within or beyond their diocese or province,

---

* Dorsanne, *Journal,* tom. ii. p. 264.

thinks ill or speaks ill of the said Constitution, let them not neglect to proceed against him by virtue of their pastoral authority, and to punish him. And should they consider that a more efficacious remedy is necessary, let them denounce to the Apostolic See these perverse rebels against the Church. Let them be equally zealous in searching for any books attacking this Constitution, or maintaining the false doctrines which it condemns, and let them cause them to be transmitted without delay for examination to the Holy See." The acts of this Council were subscribed by the Pope, thirty-two Cardinals, and forty-three prelates, besides abbots and other functionaries. At the most, however, it was no more than a Provincial Synod; and although the re-affirmation of the Unigenitus was demanded with such extraordinary urgency by the Ultramontanes on this occasion, it does not appear how, upon their principles, it could thus have obtained any additional force or authority. The bull, being the utterance of a Sovereign Pontiff speaking *ex cathedrâ*, upon matters of dogmas and morals, was already invested, according to their hypothesis, with all the attributes which made it universally binding on the faithful as part of the infallible rule of faith.

The constitutionnaires, highly elated by the submission of the Vatican and the defeat of the project of pacification, forthwith organized further measures of aggression against their protesting brethren;—a course in which they were unhappily supported by the minister Fleury, who dictated the policy of France. The General Assembly of the clergy had met in July, 1725, in a state of great irritation against the Government, excited by the new tax called the "cinquantième," which it was proposed to assess upon their order in common with the rest of the nation. After complaining to the throne, in indignant terms, against this invasion of their ancient immunities, the house proceeded to debate upon matters of theological controversy; deplored the prevailing insubordination and disorder which threatened France with schism; denounced the protection afforded to refractory ecclesiastics by several Courts of Parliament, and demanded permission to hold provincial Councils, in order to apply the remedy provided for such evils by the primitive institutions of the Church. As the discussions grew tumultuous, and an intractable spirit was displayed, the Duke of Bourbon despatched on the

27th of October an order which suddenly put an end to the session. The members, however, before separating, drew up a letter to the King, animadverting boldly upon this interference with the free action of the Assembly at a moment when the Faith was in imminent peril. This provoked the Duke to mark his displeasure still more severely. On the next day, a Secretary of State forcibly took possession of the register, carried away the original of the offensive letter, and erased the entire record of the proceedings of the 27th. The letter was afterwards suppressed by the Parliament on the requisition of the Advocate-General.

Fleury, it would appear, had no share in this unceremonious treatment of the clergy. On the disgrace of the Duke of Bourbon in the summer of 1726, he succeeded to the direction of affairs; but disclaimed, nevertheless, the title of Prime Minister, and exhorted Louis to retain the reins of government, after the example of his predecessor, in his own hands. He was immediately advanced to the rank of Cardinal * at the King's special request, in anticipation of the "nomination of the Crowns," which was to take place in the following year. Reasons of state made it important that he should acquire this dignity, since it carried with it the right of presiding in the Council of ministers; and it is believed that Fleury, in order to obtain it, pledged himself to support to the utmost of his power the Papal policy in the matter of the Constitution Unigenitus.†

One of his first acts (October 8, 1726) was to publish a Declaration acknowledging the immunity of the clergy from ordinary taxation, and explaining that the "cinquantième" had been assessed upon their property by mistake. "The rights of Churches," it was stated, "dedicated as they are to God, and beyond the range of human commerce, are irrevocable, and cannot be subjected to taxation, either by way of confirmation or of any other kind." ‡ The Assembly, at an extraordinary meeting held the same year, testified its gratitude for this distinct recognition of the privileges of the Church by voting a subsidy of five millions of livres. This was followed up by a

---

* September 11, 1726.
† Lacretelle, *Hist. de France pendant le XVIIIme Siècle*, tom. i. p. 73; De Tocqueville, *Hist. philosophique du règne de Louis XV.*, tom. i. p. 347.
‡ Isambert, *Anciennes Lois Françaises*, tom. xxi. p. 301; *Collection des Procès-verbaux*, &c., tom. vii. p. 616.

renewed appeal to the throne for license to hold a series of provincial Councils,—"a remedy," said the bishops, "which may perhaps procure for us the consolation of reclaiming some of our colleagues to concord and unanimity, of convincing them how culpable they are in their resistance to the bull, and persuading them to correct by their own act the errors into which they have been betrayed." Such language, under existing circumstances, was ominously significant; and there can be no doubt that a compact had already been entered into between Fleury and the constitutionnaires, in virtue of which a determined onslaught was to be made upon the most conspicuous of the appellant party.* Two excellent prelates, Colbert of Montpellier and Armagnac de Lorraine of Bayeux, were to have been the first objects of the attack; but a pastoral letter which was published at this juncture by Jean Soanen, Bishop of Senez, was so belligerent in its tone as fairly to entitle him to bear the brunt of the meditated crusade.

Soanen was a venerable prelate eighty years of age, who led an apostolic life among his simple-minded flock, in a remote and thinly-peopled district in the mountains of Provence. He had been a member of the Oratory, and a pupil of Quesnel; had gained celebrity as a preacher, and possessed virtues which made him universally respected and beloved. He had never attempted to conceal his deep repugnance to the Constitution Unigenitus. His name appears among the nine dissentient prelates on its first promulgation; he was one of the four original Appellants, and had twice subsequently renewed his appeal. His "Instruction Pastorale" in August, 1726, was a reiteration of the same persistent antagonism; and coming at this particular moment, it had the air of a deliberate defiance to the chief authorities of the Church. The bishop, conscious that he must shortly put off his earthly tabernacle and appear before God, reviews in this document the whole course of his conduct with regard to the Jansenistic controversy. He stigmatizes the Formulary as an act of odious tyranny, and laments that he had ever been induced to sign it. He retracts his adhesion to the bull Vineam Domini;

---

* The necessity of this course was incessantly urged upon the minister by his confessor the Abbé Polet, a man of restless talent for intrigue, wholly devoted to the Ultramontane interest.

he blames himself for having rashly prohibited the 'Livre des Reflexions,' which he confesses that he had always inwardly approved and had found conducive to edification; and he declares that he can never be a party to any arrangement on the subject of the bull Unigenitus which involved as a condition the acceptance of that unhappy measure. He warmly defends the twelve Articles lately set forth by Cardinal de Noailles, and concludes by charging the people of his diocese to continue faithful to the truth, which cannot but triumph in the end, in spite of all the storms of persecution.

Such was the production of which it was proposed to take cognizance according to the most imposing forms of ecclesiastical judicature. It was determined that the primitive action of the Provincial Council should be resuscitated for the occasion. The principal instigator of this proceeding was Pierre Guerin de Tencin, at that time Archbishop of Embrun, of which province Senez was one of the suffragan sees. The elevation of such a personage to one of the highest stations in the Church was an abuse almost as scandalous as that of Dubois himself. Tencin had been the confidant of the adventurer Law, and was deeply concerned in the mysterious iniquities of the Rue Quincampoix, by means of which he had realised immense profits.* He had been publicly charged with perjury and simony, and had never cleared himself from the imputation.† He was known to be of loose morals, and was suspected even of monstrous crime—a reproach which perhaps he owed to the profligacy of his sister, the " chanoinesse " Alexandrine de Tencin. Such was the man with whom the virtuous Fleury now condescended to ally himself, for the purpose of crushing one of the most exemplary and saintly prelates that ever adorned the episcopate of France. Tencin, who aspired to the Roman purple, caught at the opportunity afforded him of propitiating the Vatican by an exhibition of zeal for the Constitution. He applied to the Government

---

* The Abbé Tencin was the instrument of Law's somewhat equivocal conversion to Catholicism; on which occasion, however, he omitted to reclaim his proselyte from his immoral course of life. " Madame Law, qui exigeoit les respects de toutes les dames de la cour et de la ville, n'étoit qu'une concubine, enlevée autrefois à un négociant Anglois; alors on dit dans tout Paris, qu'avant d'en faire un Catholique romain, Tencin eût dû en faire un honnête homme, et réprimer son concubinage, au lieu de le tolérer." *Mémoires du Maréchal Duc de Richelieu*, tom. iii. p. 36.

† *Ibid.*, p. 276.

for permission to summon the Council of his province to sit in judgment on the fearless Soanen; and the assent of the Cardinal-minister was given but too readily. "People remarked," says Dorsanne, "that Tencin would doubtless succeed in making a heretic of M. de Senez, in the same way as he had formerly made a Catholic of M. Law."

A royal edict convoked the Council of Embrun for the 15th of June, 1727; and the Bishop of Senez was enjoined by a *lettre de cachet* to repair thither, and not to take his departure until the close of the Council without the Metropolitan's consent.* The Archbishop, in summoning his Comprovincials, spoke in general terms of the objects of the meeting, and made no mention of the measures projected against Soanen; but the latter, who had received private information of the machinations of his enemies, took the precaution to protest beforehand against the competency of the Council to adjudicate on his act of appeal, his Pastoral Instruction, or any controverted questions arising out of the bull Unigenitus. "The public voice," he said, "and the letter of convocation of the Archbishop himself, indicate clearly that this provincial Synod results from the resolution of the Assembly of clergy in 1725, when the royal permission was asked to hold Councils in certain provinces of the realm, particularly in that of Narbonne, where it was designed to proceed against the Bishop of Montpellier on account of his publications against the bull Unigenitus and in defence of the Peace of Clement IX.; works which we ourselves approved in opposing the deliberations of that Assembly. The notoriousness of these facts forbids us to doubt that a design is now formed against our person, and against the works which we have published to attest anew our devotion to those sacred truths which we are bound to defend to the last breath of our life." Soanen adopted this course upon the strength of an opinion by some of the most eminent jurisconsults of Paris, who maintained that his appeal to the future Council was lawful, inasmuch as the royal Declaration of 1720, which prohibited such appeals, had been registered with an express reservation of the Gallican liberties.†

The Council was opened at Embrun on the 16th of August.

---

* Dorsanne, *Journal*, tom. ii. p. 399.
† *Journal de E. J. F. Barbier*, tom. i. p. 262.

There were present Archbishop de Tencin as president, the Bishops of Senez, Vence, Glandève, and Grasse, with the deputy of the Bishop of Digne, and thirty-four ecclesiastics of the second order. In the next session the Abbé Gaspard d'Hugues, who acted as promoter and was the Archbishop's official, denounced the Pastoral Instruction of the Bishop of Senez as in the highest degree disrespectful and injurious to the Holy See, and to the laws and ordinances both of Church and State. The principal counts of the indictment were the language used by the prelate with reference to the Formulary of Alexander VII., his unmeasured condemnation of the Constitution Unigenitus, and his presumption in eulogising and recommending to his flock the proscribed 'Livre des Reflexions' of Quesnel. In the course of his speech the abbé took occasion to allude in terms of fulsome adulation to the Metropolitan, whom he extolled for his talents, his singular virtues, his Christian piety, and his episcopal fidelity. These encomiums must have severely taxed the gravity of the audience.

Soanen, being required either to acknowledge or to disown the authorship of the Pastoral, frankly admitted its authenticity, and signed a copy of it. He then repeated his protest against the competence of the Council; after which he retired while that act was taken into consideration. It was pronounced invalid and void, as were also the gravamina urged by the accused prelate against each of the judges individually. In the fourth session, August 20, the report on the Pastoral Instruction was publicly read, condemning it on all the charges which had been set forth by the promoter.

The Council next opened communications with the bishops of the neighbouring provinces of Vienne, Aix, Lyons, and Besançon, requesting them, according to ancient precedent, to repair to Embrun and give them the benefit of their advice and cooperation. A reinforcement of ten prelates arrived accordingly; most of whom were strongly-pronounced Ultramontanes, such as Lafiteau of Sisteron and Belzunce of Marseilles. On the 9th of September Soanen was cited before his judges for the last time; on which occasion he once more entered his solemn protest against their proceedings collectively and individually, and appealed, *comme d'abus*, to the Parliament of Paris against whatever might be attempted to his prejudice. This latter step embarrassed Tencin and his colleagues for the moment; the Parliament readily admitted the appeal, but Fleury hastened to the rescue, and evoked the cause to the Council of State; in other words, suppressed it by a stroke of irresponsible authority. Relieved from this difficulty, the Council of Embrun concluded its labours on the 22nd of September; when the "Instruction" of the Bishop of Senez was condemned as "rash, scandalous, seditious, injurious to the bishops and to the royal authority, schismatical, full of the spirit of heresy, abounding with errors, and instigating to heresy."

The penalty inflicted on Soanen was that of suspension from all episcopal power and jurisdiction, and from all exercise of ecclesiastical functions whether episcopal or sacerdotal, until he should revoke his Pastoral Instruction and all other acts in contravention of the bull. A Vicar-General was appointed to administer the diocese of Senez; and the aged bishop was exiled by *lettre de cachet* to the Abbey of La Chaise Dieu in Auvergne. He submitted at once to the iniquitous sentence; and exhibited under this last humiliation, as he had done throughout his troubles, a patience, gentleness, fortitude, and magnanimity, worthy of the days of primitive Confessorship.

These proceedings stirred up a considerable ferment of opposition and remonstrance. The advocates of Paris, to the number of fifty, including some of the most distinguished of their body, published a second Consultation,* in which they vehemently attacked the judgment of the Council of Embrun, and proclaimed it invalid on various grounds, dwelling chiefly on its incompetence to decide a cause which was already transferred by appeal to the cognizance of the supreme tribunal of the Church. They likewise passed severe criticisms on the entire line of policy whereby it had been attempted to suppress Jansenism; reprobating in round terms the Formulary, the Papal Constitutions, the mandements of the bishops, the rigorous treatment of the appellants, and the abuse of power in impeding the action of the ordinary courts of law. Barbier remarks that this publication, though an able defence of the laws of the land and the Gallican liberties, was not so much a consultation properly so called, as a libel spontaneously concocted among the

---

* October 30, 1727.

members of the bar under the excitement of party spirit. They conceived, he says, that none were so well qualified as themselves, by their independent position, to proclaim the truth upon great ecclesiastical questions, undeterred by respect for the authority of the crown, the Pope, or the bishops. "Of the fifty advocates who have signed the Consultation, there are six or seven who understand matters of this kind, and the rest know nothing about them. Happily neither my father nor I (both were pleaders in the Parliament of Paris) have allowed our names to appear as taking part in this business. I hold that we ought to discharge our duties honourably without mixing ourselves up in affairs of State, in regard to which we have neither authority nor mission."*

The movement, however, was so daring in its pretensions, and caused such general sensation, that the government could not allow it to pass in silence; and the Comte de Maurepas, Secretary of State, in a letter to Cardinal de Rohan in April, 1728, directed him to assemble the bishops to examine the document, and forward a report to the king on its contents. Almost at the same moment the prelates of the appellant party, twelve in number, with De Noailles at their head, addressed the throne in an elaborate protest against the proceedings at Embrun, setting forth the gross injustice which had been practised towards Soanen before his condemnation, declaring him irreproachable on the score of orthodoxy, and maintaining that, although he had been branded with general imputations of monstrous errors, no heretical doctrines had ever been distinctly specified, and he had been expelled from his diocese by dint of mere groundless clamour and vague reproaches. They concluded by stating that they could not recognize the sentence thus unjustly and illegally passed upon one of the most virtuous of their brethren.†
This letter was ungraciously sent back to its authors by Fleury, with an intimation that the king considered it an act of sedition, and was astonished that they should pay more attention to the complaints of an individual bishop than to the deliberate

---

* E. J. F. Barbier, *Journal*, tom. i. p. 271.

† This manifesto was the work of Laurent François Boursier, doctor of the Sorbonne, a man of superior learning and ability, who at this period was one of the chief pillars of Jansenism. He composed the letter of the seven bishops to Innocent XIII. in 1721, and many other celebrated brochures of the party.

judgment of fourteen or fifteen of his colleagues, and that without examining the authentic acts of the Council, which had not yet been made public. The prelates ventured to remonstrate, and met with a second unceremonious rebuff.

Cardinal de Rohan and the bishops who met under his presidency reported, after lengthened deliberations, that the Consultation of the advocates impugned some of the most fundamental articles both of the doctrine and discipline of the Church. It reduced to a nullity the authority of the Ecclesia docens, and the force of its judicial decisions; it represented a General Council as indispensable, and denounced the policy of the Popes in neglecting to convoke it; it was full of mistakes and false statements as to the Formulary, the Peace of Clement IX., the bull Vineam Domini, the Constitution Unigenitus, and the legality of appeal to a future Council, in the teeth of the express edict of the sovereign. In pursuance of this conclusion, the Consultation was suppressed by an *arrêt* of the Council of State on the 3rd of July, 1728.

Archbishop de Tencin obtained without difficulty from Benedict XIII. a brief confirming the acts and judgment of his Provincial Council; on which occasion the Pope expressed his admiration of the remarkable prudence and zeal with which the proceedings had been conducted.* Cardinal de Noailles, with eight of his supporters, formally opposed the registration of this brief in Parliament, together with all other decrees and edicts tending directly or indirectly to confirm the Council of Embrun. But within a fortnight the Cardinal was induced to sign a retractation of this act of opposition.† The truth is that his faculties, mental and bodily, were failing under the accumulated burden of years, conflicts, anxieties, and disappointments. He had long been a sufferer from the remorseful memories of past acts of weakness, inconsistency, and indiscretion; and his conscience became more painfully restless as he approached the close of his career. In this state of morbid depression he was

---

* Dorsanne, *Journal*, tom. ii. p. 409.

† "Voilà bien des fois que ce bonhomme-là varie, parcequ'il n'a guère été capable de prendre un parti de lui-même. Quoi qu'il en soit, l'alarme est dans le camp Jansénicn; il y en a qui n'ont pas diné le jour de la nouvelle. Cet Archevêque de Paris, honnête homme et aimé, à la tête du parti, étoit ce qui l'embarrassoit le plus."—Barbier, *Journal*, tom. i. p. 276.

besieged by officious relatives, particularly by his nephew the Duc de Noailles and his niece the Maréchale de Gramont, as well as by confidential friends such as the Chancellor d'Aguesseau and Father de la Tour of the Oratory, who implored him to desist from the hopeless struggle, and consult his own peace and that of the Church by cordially submitting to the Holy See. Their exertions were at length successful; the prelate, who was fast sinking into imbecility, allowed a mandement to appear in his name in October, 1728, by which he accepted the Unigenitus "purement et simplement,"—revoked his Pastoral Instruction of 1719, and everything else that he had published in opposition to the bull,—and assented to the judgment of the Council of Embrun.* This important act was not communicated to the clergy of the diocese in the usual manner, but copies of it were affixed by the police to the principal doors of the churches, and exempts were stationed to prevent their being defaced or destroyed. Notwithstanding these precautions, which betrayed the apprehensions of the Government, the notices were torn down in every quarter of the city, or so bespattered with mud and filth that they became illegible. The archers, it seems, had orders to make no arrests, for fear of exciting a popular tumult; and although the clergy refused to publish the Archbishop's recantation at the *prônes* in the parish churches, the authorities dared not interfere.†

The Cardinal's conversion was exultingly hailed at Rome, and Pope Benedict announced it to the Consistory as an event which called for fervent expressions of gratitude to Heaven. But the Ultramontanes were not to enjoy their triumph without challenge. It appears that the Abbé Dorsanne and other watchful Jansenists, foreseeing the advantage that might be taken of their patron in a moment of weakness, obtained from him in advance a paper disavowing and cancelling any act bearing his name which contravened the principles and sentiments by which he had so long been known to be governed; asserting his unalterable attachment to the great cause which

---

* The Cardinal's sudden defection was a fatal blow to the Abbé Dorsanne, who had hitherto fought the battle of the appellants with unwavering constancy and courage. Feeling that the cause was lost, he abandoned himself to despair, and died on the 13th of November, 1728.

† Barbier, *Journal*, tom. i. p. 282, 283; Dorsanne, *Journal*, tom. ii. p. 441.

he had defended through life in union with his illustrious colleagues in the episcopate; and authorizing those to whom he entrusted this declaration to make it public if circumstances should arise which in their judgment made it expedient.*
Upon the appearance of the Archbishop's mandement, the Jansenists instantly produced and circulated the document which they had provided in anticipation of this very emergency; they entitled it 'Le contre-poison de l'acceptation.' This added to existing complications. One party insinuated that the declaration was apocryphal, or the result of undue influence; on the other hand the acceptance of the bull was so palpably contrary to the whole course of the Cardinal's policy for upwards of thirty years past, that there was strong ground for questioning its authenticity, unless, indeed, it had been wrung from him at a time when he was scarcely responsible for his acts. The probability is that there was no positive fraud on either side; but that the rival parties practised alternately, as occasion offered, upon the sick man's scruples and fears, and that under the pressure of disease, and of the moral bewilderment resulting from two conflicting views of duty, each succeeded in carrying off the victory in turn. From these pitiable scenes De Noailles was at length happily released by death; he breathed his last at Paris on the 4th of May, 1729, at the age of seventy-eight.†
There is no need to enlarge either upon his virtues or his failings, which are alike familiar to the reader. A stern Jansenist, hearing of the controversial intrigues which incessantly tormented him even in his dying chamber, remarked that it was not to be expected that the destroyer of Port-Royal should depart this life in peace, like a consistent defender of the truth.‡

---

* It was deposited in the hands of the bishop of Senez. Dorsanne, tom. ii. p. 448.

† He had restored the Jesuits to their ecclesiastical functions in his diocese by an ordinance of March 6, 1729. No doubt he found this one of the most difficult and irksome of all his acts of repentance.

‡ Barbier, tom. i. p. 283. Cardinal de Noailles was interred in Notre Dame, in front of the altar of the Virgin. The following inscription (now no longer in existence) was placed upon his tomb:—

"Ad pedes Deiparæ
Quam semper religiosè coluerat
Hic jacet
Ut testamento jussit
Ludovicus Antonius de Noailles
S. R. E. Cardinalis, Archiepiscopus
Parisiensis,
Dux S. Clodoaldi, par Franciæ,
Regii ordinis S. Spiritus Commendator,
Provisor Sorbonæ, ac regiæ Navarræ
superior.

Viewed from the ecclesiastical standpoint, the position now gained by the Constitutionnaires was one of such superiority as to guarantee the speedy triumph of the entire system which they represented. The opposition was disorganized and broken on all sides. Its leader was dead; one of its most distinguished captains was a prisoner; while of the rank and file of the army numbers had sought safety by a hasty flight to Holland, and numbers more had made their peace with the conquerors by unconditional recantation and submission. No fewer than eight bishops—those of Blois, Agen, St. Malo, Condom, Angoulême, Dax, Agde, and Rodez — signified their acceptance of the Constitution before the end of the year 1729. A like example of sudden resipiscence was displayed by the Sorbonne, which for many years past had been a stronghold of the recusant party. It was determined to relieve the Faculty, by a summary process, of the presence of those false brethren who marred its unanimity; and forty-eight doctors, guilty of having renewed their appeal since the " accommodement " of 1720, were excluded from its councils by *lettres de cachet*. Thus purified from heretical and schismatical alloy, the Sorbonne held a session on the 8th of November, and soon arrived at the conclusion that the original acceptance of the Constitution by their body in 1714 was a free, legitimate, and authoritative act; that whatever had been done subsequently with a view to annul it ought to be buried in profound oblivion; that during that period of trouble and confusion the ancient doctrine of the Faculty had been impaired; new dogmas had been introduced which were subversive of the authority of the Church, of its head, and its chief pastors; which invested the second order of the clergy with the right of judging in matters of faith, authorized the most irregular proceedings, and

---

Commissi sibi' gregis
Sollicitudine pastor, charitate pater,
  Moribus forma,
Domui suæ bene propositus,
Domûs Domini zelo accensus,
In oratione assiduus, in labore indefessus,
  In cultu modestus, in victu simplex ;
Sibi parcus, in cæteros sanctè prodigus,
A teneris ad senium æqualis idemque,
  Semper prudens, mitis, pacificus,

Vitam transegit benefaciendo.
  Ecclesiam Parisiensem
    Annos xxxiv.
Rexit, direxit, excoluit, ornavit.
Ejus beneficentiam homines si taceant
  Hujus basilicæ lapides clamabunt.
Obiit plenus dierum, omnibus flebilis,
Die Maii 4. Ann. Domini 1729, ætatis 78.
  Viro misericordi
    Divinam misericordiam apprecare."

represented the Church as involved in darkness and almost extinct. Thereupon the doctors resolved to ratify the decrees of 1714, to renew their respectful acceptance of the Constitution as a dogmatic judgment of the Universal Church, to revoke their appeal and all acts contrary to the present decision, and in future to admit none into their body but those who should distinctly testify their submission to the bull. This vote passed with wonderful harmony, and was subscribed by upwards of seven hundred doctors of the Sorbonne in Paris and the provinces, among whom were thirty-four bishops.*

The government, elated by these instances of opportune tergiversation in quarters so influential, concluded too quickly that the time had arrived when all remaining elements of opposition might be suppressed without difficulty if the voice of authority made itself heard with sufficient emphasis and force. The new Archbishop of Paris, Gaspard de Vintimille, formerly Archbishop of Aix, was a decided partisan of the Ultramontanes; and he commenced his reign by strenuous efforts to enforce the complete acceptance of the Constitution throughout his diocese. Meeting with resistance, he appealed to the king for support; and his Majesty, under the dictation of Fleury, launched an edict † to which it was determined to extort obedience by straining to the utmost all the resources of the absolute monarchy. It commenced by bitterly complaining of the bad faith and perverse obstinacy of the refractory clergy; after which it proceeded to enact (what had already been enacted on so many previous occasions) that all ecclesiastics should forthwith subscribe the Formulary *purement et simplement*, in default of which their benefices should be vacated *ipso facto;* that the Constitution Unigenitus, which had become the law of the Church by virtue of the general consent of the Episcopate, should henceforth be regarded and respected as a law of the State; that silence should be observed upon all questions

---

* Picot, *Mém. pour servir à l'hist. ecclésiastique du XVIIIme Siècle*, tom. ii. p. 58. The forty-eight deprived doctors, with eight others who voluntarily joined them, entered a formal protest against all the proceedings of the Faculty on this occasion. The late violent interference of the government, they contended, was fatal to freedom of deliberation; and any pretended action of the corporate body under such circumstances was null and void. Barbier, *Journal*, tom. i. p. 299.

† March 24, 1730. Isambert, *Anc. Lois Françaises*, tom. xxi. p. 330.

relating to the bull, without restraining the bishops, however, from instructing their flocks as to its obligation. Lastly, it ordained that appeals *comme d'abus* upon these matters should have no suspensive, but only a devolutive effect;* and injunctions were added which tended to circumscribe the powers of the lay magistrates in taking cognizance of such appeals.

It was well known to the court that this measure, if presented for free consideration to the Parliament of Paris, would be sharply contested, and probably rejected. To obviate this, Louis held a bed of justice on the 3rd of April, 1730, and insisted on the immediate registration of the edict in his presence without discussion. And now abundant proof appeared that the spirit of resistance to the assumed dictatorship of Rome, though checked for a moment, had suffered no collapse. The Chancellor D'Aguesseau proceeded to collect the votes. The majority of the councillors were bold enough to dissent, and several stated their objections audibly, in spite of the king's prohibition. One of them took special exception to the condemnation of Quesnel's famous maxim, that "the fear of an unjust excommunication ought not to deter us from discharging our duty;" which condemnation tended, as he declared, to snatch the sceptre out of the king's hands, and to endorse the most exaggerated and dangerous pretensions of the Roman see.† In spite of the opposition, the assent of Parliament to the Royal declaration was assumed and proclaimed; after which the king retired. The councillors kept their places, and asserted their independence, at the instigation of the Abbé Pucelle, by protesting that two-thirds of their number were opposed to the edict. Next day, upon the motion of the same courageous magistrate, they adopted a set of vigorous resolutions on the independence and supremacy of the temporal power; con-

---

* See Introduction, tom. i. p. 76.

† It must be confessed, however, that this much-contested proposition (the 91st censured by the bull Unigenitus) is somewhat captiously and equivocally expressed. Fénélon's remarks on it in his 1st "Mandement sur la Constitution" (*Œuvres*, tom. xiv. p. 460) are well worth consideration. "If the injustice of the excommunication be manifest—if the duty be a real and positive duty,—the proposition contains a truth to which it is impossible not to assent. But if the excommunication is unjust only in the opinion of the individual against whom it is directed; if the duty is but an imaginary duty; if only some uncertainty should exist as to the injustice of the sentence and the reality of the duty; then the proposition becomes false, and is all the more dangerous, inasmuch as it presents itself under a specious appearance of truth."

tending that it does not belong to ecclesiastics to define the limits between civil and spiritual authority; that the laws of the Church do not become laws of the State until they are sanctioned and promulgated by the sovereign; and that the ministers of the Church are accountable to the king and the Parliament for any offence against the statute law of the realm.* So recklessly determined was the government at this moment to enforce the Constitution and to repel the first symptoms of contumacy among the magistrates, that this *arrêt* of the Parliament was immediately cancelled by an order of the Council of State. From this date commenced a dangerous agitation, which placed the Parliaments in persistent antagonism to the Crown and the hierarchy; while at the same time the animosities among the clergy waxed fiercer than ever, by reason of the systematic support afforded to the weaker party by those who held in their hands the interpretation and administration of the law.

A few months after the scene above described a collision occurred between the Parliament of Paris and the ecclesiastical authorities, which added greatly to the prevailing excitement. Three parish priests of the diocese of Orleans declined to sign the Formulary and revoke their appeal against the Constitution at the command of their bishop. The latter felt bound to enforce the penalties denounced by the recent Declaration; he declared them rebellious to the Church, and deprived them of their cures. They appealed, *comme d'abus*, to the Parliament; the magistrates admitted the appeal, and forbade, pending the adjudication of the case, the execution of the bishop's ordonnance. The curés continued, in consequence, to fulfil their accustomed functions; whereupon they were cited to answer for their disobedience before the consistory court of the diocese. They appealed a second time to the Parliament; the Parliament threw its shield over them, and inhibited the procedure in the spiritual court. The Bishop of Orleans now invoked the intervention of the Crown, and urged the necessity of upholding the Declaration against the arrogant attempts of the Parliament to ignore and nullify it. At this moment the affair was complicated by the appearance of a consultation signed by forty

---

* *Mém. du Maréchal Duc de Richelieu*, tom. iii. p. 203.

advocates of Paris, who eagerly undertook the defence of the three ecclesiastics. They expressed, in language of hitherto unexampled freedom, their views, not only with regard to the exercise of ecclesiastical authority, but also as to the jurisdiction and prerogatives of royalty. The Parliaments, they maintained, held their judicial and administrative powers by the will of the French people; they were the constitutional assessors of the throne; if the king was the head of the nation, the Parliament was its senate, and without the consent of the latter body no enactment could acquire the force of law. They enunciated other ideas by no means consistent with the traditions of an absolute monarchy; and ended by declaring that it was the right of the lay courts to protect the lower orders of the clergy against the oppressive acts of their superiors, and that their decrees suspended the execution of ecclesiastical sentences until the affair had been finally decided. The novel tone of these sentiments astonished and even alarmed the government. Fleury acted, however, promptly and resolutely. The cause of the three priests was evoked to the Grand Conseil; they were ordered to submit themselves to the judgment of their diocesan, and remained suspended from their office; and the Parliament was interdicted from taking any further notice of the case. The consultation of the avocats was suppressed as injurious to the king's authority, seditious, and dangerous to the public tranquillity; those who signed it were ordered either to disavow or retract it within the space of a month, in default of which they were to be debarred from all exercise of their profession. Upon this they drew up an explanatory memorial, which was pronounced satisfactory with reference to the rights and supremacy of the Crown, but retracted nothing as to the relations of the civil tribunals to the discipline and jurisdiction of the Church. They were admitted to an audience by Cardinal Fleury, who assured them that his Majesty had received their apology graciously, and regarded them as faithful defenders of the rights of his Crown.*

But the heads of the Church were by no means contented with this partial submission. Early in the following year the

---

* Barbier, *Journal*, tom. i. pp. 330-335.

Archbishops of Paris and Embrun and the Bishop of Laon [*] fulminated violent ordonnances against the obnoxious consultation; stigmatizing its authors as heretics and schismatics, and accusing them of a deliberate design to overthrow all constituted authority in Church and State. Archbishop de Vintimille asserted, in lofty language, the independence of the hierarchy in their judicial character; their right to legislate in matters of faith and morals, and to enforce their enactments by spiritual censures; together with other cognate dogmas which, though familiar in the mouths of mediæval theologians, were now regarded as questionable and obsolete. The Parliament was instantly in arms; the mandements of the Archbishop of Embrun (Tencin) and the Bishop of Laon were suppressed as seditious and "abusive," and the Procureur-Général appealed *comme d'abus* against the ordonnance of the Archbishop of Paris, in consequence of which that prelate was summoned to appear personally before the Court. The government met this by a proclamation (March 10, 1731) imposing absolute silence as to the articles complained of in the mandement, until measures should be taken for bringing the disputes to a termination. A circular was likewise addressed to the bishops, exhorting them to refrain from characterising the Unigenitus as a "rule of faith," and to be content with enjoining submission to it as a "dogmatic judgment of the Universal Church." But these palliatives were of no avail. The indignant Archbishop memorialised the King at Fontainebleau, when he obtained an order of Council evoking the affair of his mandement to the royal person, and granting him full authority to publish it, the appeal *comme d'abus* and the *arrêt* of the Parliament notwithstanding. This step was vehemently resented. Three hundred avocats met in a state of wild excitement, demanded the suppression of the order of Council, and resolved to close their chambers and suspend all business until satisfaction was obtained.[†] Their threat was immediately put into execution; and the sudden disappearance of the members of the bar caused a vexatious interruption in the course of public justice. The

---

[*] "M. de la Faro, qui serait un mauvais sujet étant mousquetaire, et qui néanmoins est évêque de Laon." Barbier, *Journal*, tom. i. p. 339.

[†] *Ibid.*, p. 358.

Court retaliated by exiling ten of their number by *lettres de cachet* to remote places in the country; but the rest stood firm, and were warmly supported by the rising spirit of popular independence, which gathered strength from these occurrences. In the course of a few weeks Fleury found it necessary to negotiate with the malcontents; and they were prevailed upon to resume their duties at the Palais de Justice on condition that the Government should make a formal acknowledgment of their innocence as to the imputations cast upon them by the Archbishop. This was announced accordingly by an *arrêt* of the Council of State; the exiled barristers were recalled, and on the 26th of November the pleadings recommenced in the courts as usual. These events afforded too clear an indication of the change which was already in progress in the relations of the Crown and the privileged orders to the great middle class of the nation;—a class which was now beginning to understand its importance and its strength.

At the meeting of the Assembly of the Clergy, held in the summer of 1730, fresh matter of dissension arose in consequence of an attempt of Benedict XIII., two years before, to impose upon the Church the observance of the Feast of St. Hildebrand, otherwise Pope Gregory VII. This ill-timed measure was naturally objected to in France as a new Ultramontane aggression. The Parliament of Paris, at this moment more sensitive than ever to the slightest encroachment on the Gallican liberties, reprobated the proposed office as an illegal addition to the Breviary, and suppressed it accordingly. The example was followed by the provincial Parliaments of Reims, Metz, Toulouse, and Bordeaux. It was an opportunity not likely to be neglected by that small minority of the bishops who still remained attached to the ancient principles of the Church of France. Several of them, in particular Caylus Bishop of Auxerre, Colbert of Montpellier, and Bossuet of Troyes, published mandements prohibiting the use of the office in their dioceses; and not content with condemning the "legend" of St. Hildebrand, entered into lengthened denunciations of the entire system by which Rome had laboured for so many ages to establish her autocracy, both in things temporal and spiritual. Pope Benedict annulled, by one brief, the *arrêt* of the Parliament, and by another severely censured the mandements of the bishops. Both these briefs were suppressed in their turn by order of the Parliament in February, 1730.

The Bishop of Montpellier pursued the affair with all his accustomed energy, and addressed a long letter to the King, pointing out the close connexion between the late act of significant innovation and the false policy which had given birth to the Constitution Unigenitus. He entreated Louis XV. to recur to those original laws of ecclesiastical and civil government which had been published, under the authority of his predecessor, by the famous Assembly of 1682; to declare his cordial adherence to the Four Gallican Articles; to cause the work written in defence of them by the great Bishop of Meaux (the 'Defensio Declarationis Cleri Gallicani') to be at length given to the world; and to extend his royal patronage to the 'Ecclesiastical History' of Claude Fleury, which had been slanderously defamed by the Ultramontanes. The King sent this letter to the Assembly for examination. They drew up an address to his Majesty in reply, in which, after briefly expressing their disapproval of the legend of St. Hildebrand,* they attacked the bishop vigorously on the score of his resistance to the bull Unigenitus; they claimed the support of the Crown against the scandal of a prelate thus openly rebellious to the decisions of the Church and the statutes of the realm; and begged that to this end the Archbishop of Narbonne might have leave to convoke the Council of his province, and summon his suffragan of Montpellier to the bar of that tribunal. But Fleury, apparently, thought it unadvisable to repeat the sinister precedent of the Council of Embrun; and the request of the Assembly was not acceded to.

The Bishop of Auxerre made complaints in like manner both to the King and the Assembly of the dangerous results of the system latterly pursued by the Roman Curia. In noticing this document, the Assembly stated that such conduct was specially unbecoming, inasmuch as the prelate had taken upon himself to address exhortations to an Assembly which had no need of them, and with whose sentiments he could not but be acquainted,

---

* "Légende qui n'a été adoptée dans votre royaume par aucun évêque, et dont l'usage n'a été et ne sera permis dans aucun de nos diocèses." *Collection des Procès-verbaux*, tom. vii. p. 1073.

while he himself was openly disobedient to the authority of the Church and neglectful of the orders of the King, who, as protector of the Church, was employing his power in causing her laws to be executed. The Assembly, before separating, addressed a circular letter to the bishops, in which they solemnly affirmed that the doctrine of the Four Articles of 1682 had always been, and still was, that of the clergy of France.

Thus the remonstrances of these faithful prelates were not without effect in recalling to the minds of the clergy the principles which their predecessors had so nobly and successfully asserted in many a former conflict; but such spasmodic attempts were powerless to arrest the reactionary tide towards Roman absolutism which now threatened to engulf and overwhelm the Church. Unfortunately, almost the sole defenders of the true discipline and legislation of Catholic antiquity were now to be found among the votaries of Jansenistic error; so that in combating the latter, discouragement and discredit was necessarily inflicted in like proportion upon those who were labouring to uphold the former. This circumstance materially damaged the cause of Gallicanism. There was, of course, no essential connexion between the primitive theory of Church polity and the peculiar theological sentiments condemned in the bull Unigenitus. It was quite possible to protest against the misgovernment of the Roman Curia without cherishing any extreme convictions as to "gratuitous predestination" or the orthodoxy of the "sense of Jansenius." Yet the march of events had been such as to create an intimate bond of sympathy between these two apparently distinct currents of opinion; and by degrees they were confounded together under the common denomination of mutinous resistance to the Apostolic See. Hence all the extravagances engendered by Jansenism in its later and more questionable developments recoiled, however unjustly, upon the system of ecclesiastical policy vindicated by Gerson, De Marca, and Bossuet. Jansenism became manifestly dangerous to public order and the security of the State; Gallicanism, in the view of a despotic government, seemed involved in the same odious category; and it was deemed necessary, in consequence, to visit both with an impartial exhibition of the same persecuting rigour.

The session of the Assembly was brought to a close on the

20th of September, 1730, when La Parisière, Bishop of Nismes, addressed the King in an animated harangue, certain passages of which gave rise to animadversion on the part of the ever-vigilant Parliamentary magistrates.* Their objections were disposed of by the customary expedient of referring them to the cognizance of the royal Council. The civil courts never lost an opportunity at this period of showing that they considered all public acts of the ecclesiastical authorities as within the sphere of their official criticism and control; a claim which in process of time they pushed to such an anomalous extreme, that the result was a general derangement and confusion of the jurisdiction rightfully belonging to Church and State.

---

* *Procès-verb. des Assembl. du Clergé*, tom. vii. p. 1220. One sentiment which they specially disapproved was to the effect that "the reign of his Majesty was founded upon Catholicism, and ought always to be defended by the same principles." It was alleged that this doctrine favoured the pretensions under which the rights of sovereign princes had been attacked in former ages.

CHAPTER VIII.

IT must be obvious to the reader, that those who at this epoch exercised the chief influence upon ecclesiastical affairs in France were for the most part men of a very different stamp from that of the Arnaulds and Nicoles, the Fénélons and Bossuets, of the preceding generation. An exhausting controversy had so long been preying on the vital powers of the Church, that the race of her children had degenerated; their intellectual and spiritual growth was stunted; they were altogether of a lower organisation. Those noble religious enterprises which had won the sympathies and admiration of all classes of society in the seventeenth century, though they had borne immediate fruit of the highest value, failed of success as instruments of a permanent reformation. Unhappily they were closely followed by the Regency; and the spectacle exhibited by that reign of unbridled licentiousness of manners, of cynical pyrrhonism as to revealed truth, and of political turpitude and dishonour, was sufficient in itself to counteract the salutary work of former days, and to explain any amount of national demoralisation. The preferment of men like Dubois, Rohan, Tressan, and Tencin, to the highest posts of dignity and authority in the Church, gave a shock to public opinion, and to the prestige of the ecclesiastical order, which could not be repaired by the isolated virtues of a Massillon, a Polignac, a Soanen, or a Colbert. Even under the comparatively decorous rule of Fleury the honours of the episcopate were lavished upon candidates who possessed little or no merit beyond that of blind unreasoning zeal for the Pope and the Constitution. Persecution, again, had produced its natural results. It had made the dominant party beyond measure bigoted, overbearing, merciless; it impelled the suffering minority to seize with avidity any means that offered of disconcerting and embarrassing their oppressors. In some quarters it inspired hypocrisy; in others it stimulated the busy spirit of intrigue; in others it provoked the extravagances of a reckless fanaticism. The humiliations to which the Jansenists had of late been subjected seemed to presage the approaching extinction of their power as a religious party. The doctrinal principles for which they had so long and so resolutely contended seemed to be losing their hold upon the mind of the Church; the episcopate, with but three or four exceptions, was unanimous in repudiating and proscribing them; the light which had been kindled in France by St. Cyran and the apostles of Port-Royal was on the point of succumbing before the blasts of rampant error. Enthusiasm was thus driven, so to speak, to its last entrenchments; and the desperate circumstances of the hour suggested resources and remedies of the same desperate character.

To the operation of some such causes we must assign the series of (so-called) preternatural manifestations which the Appellants claimed as proofs of Divine interposition in their favour, at various times between the years 1725 and 1732. The first case was that of a woman named Lafosse, who was reported to have been miraculously restored to health at the procession of the Holy Sacrament in the parish of Ste. Marguerite at Paris. The clergy of that church being appellants, the fact was proclaimed as establishing beyond dispute that Heaven was enlisted on their side. Cardinal de Noailles ordered an enquiry into the circumstances, which was conducted by his official the Abbé Dorsanne; and the result, as might be expected, was a solemn affirmative of the reality of the miracle. Among the names which appear in the documents connected with this occurrence is one which the reader will scarcely be prepared to meet with on such an occasion; it is that of Arouet de Voltaire. He was one of the witnesses who, by their testimony to the truth of the event, contributed to the conclusion thus promulgated by the authorities of the Church.* Other instances supervened of the sudden cure (or reputed cure) of inveterate maladies. But far the most widely celebrated are those which were ascribed to the intercession of a deceased ecclesiastic named François de Pâris.

---

* See his letter to Madame de Bernières, 20 août 1725. "Correspondance Générale" (Œuvres, tom. xxxi. p. 76), also Barbier, *Journal*, tom. i. p. 220.

"There died about a year ago,"* says Barbier, under date March, 1729, "a certain Monsieur Paris, brother of one of the councillors of the Grand' Chambre, who was a Jansenist of the most approved type. He had an income of 10,000 livres, the whole of which he gave to the poor; he ate nothing but vegetables, slept without sheets, and constantly lived a holy life. He was buried in the churchyard of St. Médard in the faubourg St. Marcel, and is regarded as a saint. All the common people of Paris, and many indeed of the upper classes, have resorted to his tomb, where, according to their account, miracles are wrought." Subsequently he writes (July, 1731):—
"This M. Pâris, of whom I spoke, has remained quiet for some time, that is, without performing any miracles; but during the last two months he has exhibited fresh vigour, and every day there is a wonderful concourse of people at his tomb. Though St. Médard is a long way off, numbers of carriages repair thither, conveying men as well as women, and persons of distinction. Several miracles have taken place, very opportunely, in cases of paralysis. The people sing of their own accord, and intone the Te Deum. This gives great pleasure to the Jansenists. A begging friar, the other day, having thought proper to pass jests upon the assembled crowd, the people drove him away, and in consequence no one in the neighbourhood will bestow any alms upon him for the future. The portrait of the *bienheureux* Pâris has been engraved, and is cried about the streets. The people will make a saint of him without the help of the Court of Rome, if this goes on."†

François de Pâris was but a deacon in the Church, having declined, from motives of humility, to proceed to priest's orders. He was an Appellant, and had repeated his appeal; and so strongly addicted was he to the exaggerations of the Jansenist school, that at one time he passed two whole years without approaching the mysteries of the Altar. His piety, if not enlightened, was genuine and sincere. He spent his whole time in prayer, study, penitential exercises, and manual labour. His habitual austerities destroyed his health, and he was no more than thirty-seven when he died. One of the earliest of

---

* Barbier is not strictly accurate; Pâris died on the 1st of May, 1727.
† Barbier, *Journal*, tom. i. p. 287, 353.

the supernatural phenomena attributed to his agency was the cure of a young female named Anne Lefranc, who seems to have been in the last stage of consumption. No sooner was she laid upon the wonder-working tomb, than the most distressing symptoms disappeared instantaneously, and within a few days her recovery was pronounced complete. As the event became a subject of loud and boastful exultation among the enemies of the Constitution, Archbishop de Vintimille instituted an enquiry into the facts. One hundred and twenty witnesses came forward to verify the prodigy; forty were examined,—among them the mother, the brother, and the sister of the patient, and the surgeons who had attended her,—and their evidence proved by no means satisfactory upon several points of essential importance. The Archbishop decided that, in the face of so many inconsistencies and contradictions, the tale was unworthy of credit. On the 24th of July, 1731, he published a mandement to that effect; he condemned a dissertation which had been circulated in defence of the miracles; and prohibited all marks of special veneration at the tomb of M. Pâris for the future. "Notwithstanding this," says Barbier, "such a crowd collected on the morrow, St. James's Day, that by four o'clock in the morning it was not possible to get into the church of St. Médard, or into the little cemetery which contains the tomb." Mademoiselle Lefranc appealed to the Parliament against the Archbishop's decision; and by way of challenging further investigation, twenty-three curés of the capital laid before their diocesan reports of fresh marvels of the same kind, which now multiplied so rapidly that their very number became an argument of no small weight against them. It appears that those who resorted to the tomb were mostly females, suffering under various forms of nervous disease, partially paralyzed, or subject to hysterical affections. These poor creatures were seized with spasms or convulsions, which led to a state of delirious frenzy; and not unfrequently, whether from abnormal tension of the imagination or from the action of some occult physiological cause, such paroxysms were followed by an abatement of the morbid symptoms. The nervous system was relieved; the crippled limb resumed its functions; a healthy reaction set in, and infirmity for the time took flight. Such phenomena are, and always will be, popularly classed as supernatural; but it is evident that they are so designated in a relative sense—relatively, that is, to our own feeble ideas and apprehensions of the organic economy of Nature. The terms natural and supernatural serve, in fact, only to express the limitations and imperfections of human knowledge. Nothing is miraculous to the Omniscient and the Omnipotent. Events which men call such may result as truly from regular laws of the Divine Government as those which occur in what we style the ordinary course of Nature;—the only difference being that in the latter case the law of causation, its principles and its effects, fall within the range of our own knowledge and uniform experience, while in the former both the cause and its mode of action are hidden from us—hidden in the infinite depths of the Divine mind.

The noted case of the Abbé Bécheran, though it was so confidently appealed to by the Jansenist agitators, will not stand the test of sober and rational criticism. He had been lame from his youth, and had one leg considerably shorter than the other. He came to Paris by the advice of the Bishop of Montpellier (who, as a good Jansenist, was strongly prepossessed in favour of the miraculous pretensions) and performed three "neuvaines" at the cemetery of St. Médard. The Penitential Psalms were chanted over him with fervent devotion as he lay extended on the tomb; from time to time he experienced convulsions of such violence that the pulse collapsed; his face became ghastly, he foamed at the mouth, and his whole body was forcibly lifted up, in spite of the attendants who held him firmly by the arms. He was visited and examined by the most eminent surgeons. Some declared that he had derived great benefit; that the sinews had recovered much of their natural elasticity, and that he was far less lame. Others, on the contrary, affirmed that he limped as much as ever; that the convulsions arose from the vehement exertions which he made, in the hope of obtaining a cure, to stretch and lengthen his leg; and that the writhings of his frame were occasioned, not by any supernatural visitation, but simply by the excess of pain. It was the example of Bécheran, we are told, that "made the convulsions fashionable;"* he was popularly surnamed "the master of the *convulsionnaires*."

---

* Barbier, tom. i. p. 387.

Throughout the year 1731 the ferment continued to increase. One case produced an extraordinary sensation; that of a woman who, being in sound health, pretended to be paralytic, and proceeded to St. Médard in a spirit of mocking incredulity. Her folly was promptly punished; she was struck with real paralysis of the whole of the right side, and was carried away on a litter to the Hotel Dieu, in the midst of an excited crowd, who proclaimed this novel portent through the streets. The procès-verbal recording the event was signed by twenty-six persons of established credit in various sections of society, including magistrates of the Parliament and canons of Notre Dame.*

Individuals of high rank were to be seen from time to time among the throng of devout suppliants at the shrine of the Jansenist saint;—the Princess-Dowager of Conti, the Marquis de Legale, the Vicomte de Nesmond, the Chevalier Folard (a literary writer of considerable reputation), the historian Rollin, and a Councillor of the Parliament named Carré de Montgéron.† The last-named personage received, according to his own account, a most memorable recompense for his assiduous pilgrimages to St. Médard. He was converted, by an inscrutable and irresistible impulse, from the extreme of scepticism to a profound acceptance of the whole cycle of Catholic belief. Montgéron recorded his own experience, together with his convictions of the truth of the miracles, and the grounds on which he formed them, in a quarto volume entitled 'La vérité des miracles operés par l'intercession de M. de Pâris.' He was imprudent enough to present this work to Louis XV., whereupon a *lettre de cachet* consigned him to the Bastille; and after being transferred from one place of confinement to another, he ended his days a prisoner in the citadel of Valence.‡

The Government, which had shown exemplary forbearance in dealing with this strange outburst of fanatical delusion, at length resolved on the decisive step of closing the cemetery of St. Médard to the public. This was effected by the Lieutenant-General of Police, without any demonstration of resistance, on

---

* Barbier, *Journal*, tom. i. p. 355.
† See *Souvenirs de la Marquise de Créquy*, tom. iii. p. 25, 36. (Paris, 1842.)
‡ Barbier, *Journal*, tom. ii. p. 157.

the 29th of January, 1732; and a royal ordonnance appeared at the same moment, in which the miracles were declared to be based on superstition, and the whole affair was denounced as an imposture.* But the leaders of the movement were not to be thus silenced; they began to assemble their followers secretly in private houses, where similar scenes were enacted, and were carried to even further lengths of extravagance. The convulsions became more frequent and more violent than ever; the patients, in their agonies, screamed for help (*secours*) and consolation; and this was administered in an anomalous shape by the bystanders, who thumped them with bludgeons, iron bars, and hammers, to an extent which under other circumstances would have been wholly insupportable.† Moreover, the convulsionnaires, after the example of religious enthusiasts in all ages, uttered discourses in their ecstacies, which took sometimes the character of prophecies, sometimes of outrageous philippics against the authorities in Church and State, sometimes of moral exhortations. They had visions of the future fortunes of the Church, which they depicted under images drawn from the prophetic Scriptures; and the expositions of some of these "figuristes" seem to have displayed no common amount of intelligence and skill. Another section of them became known as "Élisiens" or "Vaillantistes," from a priest named Vaillant, who was supposed to be the Elijah foretold by Malachi as the precursor of the final judgment. Vaillant's Jansenist zeal had already cost him an imprisonment of three years in the Bastille; on being liberated, he plunged with redoubled energy into fresh propagandist enterprises, and was in consequence arrested a second time; he languished for no less than twenty-two years in the Bastille, and died in 1761 at Vincennes.

The Convulsionist movement thus ran its course through various stages, until it reached an ultimate development of undisguised indecency, immorality, and impiety. At this point it was obviously impossible that it could be any longer defended or countenanced by men of respectable character; and the

---

* Isambert, *Anc. Lois Françaises*, tom. xxi. p. 369. This gave occasion to the famous Jansenist witticism—

"De par le Roi, defense à Dieu
De faire miracles en ce lieu."

† Madame de Créquy gives a description, the details of which are beyond measure grotesque and revolting, of the crucifixion of a certain Sister Françoise Bergerat. *Souvenirs*, tom. iii. p. 55.

leading Jansenists were accordingly compelled to repudiate all connection with it, both for themselves and for their cause.

Bishops Colbert,* Caylus, and Soanen had declared in favour of the earlier manifestations; but with regard to the absurdities and excesses which followed they used the language of unqualified condemnation. The most influential of the appellant clergy took the same line; the famous Duguet, Jerôme Besoigne, author of the 'Histoire de Port-Royal,' Boursier, Delan, D'Asfeld, Petitpied, and others, earnestly reprobated the prevailing mania, and deprecated the obloquy which it brought upon their party. Petitpied, a veteran controversialist of well-known ability, drew up in 1735 a consultation which was signed by thirty doctors of the Sorbonne, to serve as a public manifesto of their sentiments at this crisis. These divines solemnly denied that the convulsions were the work of God, and declared them to be more probably a device of Satan. It was madness, they said, fanaticism, scandal, blasphemy, to attribute to God what could not possibly proceed from Him. A reply was immediately put forth on behalf of the convulsionists, who taunted the doctors with deserting their colours and betraying their convictions. "Though standing on the same footing with them in point of principle, they now sought to deprive them of the most cogent proofs and arguments whereby those principles were established; after having furnished them with arms, they had cut away from them the vantage ground on which they hoped to confound their enemies and win the battle." The Appellants were thus divided against themselves; the learned, the right-minded, the moderate, found it necessary to stand aloof from the thorough-paced enthusiasts, drawing a broad distinction between different epochs of the same movement. Some miracles they accepted as authentic, others they branded as delusions of the devil. The public did not fail to animadvert on the inconsistency; and the general result was to cast discredit and ridicule upon the system which had given birth to the thaumaturgic claims.

---

* Colbert published two Instructions Pastorales in defence of the miracles; the first was condemned as rash, scandalous, absurd and blasphemous, by a brief of Pope Clement XII. in 1733; the second was suppressed in the following year by an order of the Council of State.

Meanwhile, the determination of the Parliament to arrogate to itself jurisdiction as to the questions controverted in the Church stirred up fresh and grave dissension between the Crown, the clergy, and the civil magistracy. In May, 1732, Archbishop Vintimille published a mandement censuring the 'Nouvelles Ecclésiastiques,' a weekly journal recently set on foot by the Jansenists, which supplied a record of passing events interesting to the party, together with a running comment of suggestive reflexions.* The principal contributor was a priest named Fontaine de la Roche, whom Picot describes as a writer of unbounded impudence and shameless mendacity. "Sophistry, abuse, artifice, calumny—everything was good in his eyes, provided it was serviceable to his party. Does he speak of the Theological Faculty of Paris? It is always "la Faculté carcassienne." He styles Archbishop Vintimille the *avocat du diable*. He is highly elated because, by a quaint arrangement of the letters in Joannes Josephus Languet, he has discovered that they make, *Oh Pelagius Senonas venit!* † In his opinion, M. de Fénélon was an author of no importance, who had the privilege of writing whatever he pleased, since no one thought it worth while to take the trouble of answering him. All his commendation he reserves for the emissaries of the party, for hawkers of libels, for the convulsionnaires, for priests who abandon themselves to intrigue, for monks who renounce their rule, for obstinate nuns who quit their cloister out of piety—in short,

---

* The first numbers of the *Nouvelles Ecclésiastiques* appeared in 1715, soon after the Bull Unigenitus arrived in France. The Journal began to be published regularly in 1729; and was continued from that date, with very brief intervals, down to the year 1803. It was printed with extraordinary secrecy, and the parties concerned in it succeeded in eluding the most energetic researches of the police. Jacques Fontaine, the original editor, died in 1761; and the Journal then passed into the hands of Marc Claude Guénin, commonly called the Abbé de St. Marc. From the year 1794 it was managed at Utrecht by a Jansenist priest named Monton, at whose death in 1803 the publication finally ceased. The whole collection forms 25 volumes quarto.

† Jean Joseph Languet, Bishop of Soissons, afterwards Archbishop of Sens, was a prelate of considerable talent, who distinguished himself by his violent hostility to the Jansenists and his ardent zeal for the bull Unigenitus. His *Instruction pastorale au sujet des prétendus miracles du diacre de St. Médard* provoked a reply from Carré de Montgéron in the work already mentioned, *La vérité des miracles*, &c. An *appel comme d'abus* was also presented to the Parliament against it by twenty-three curés of Paris, but without success. Archbishop Languet drew upon himself great ridicule by publishing the Life of a visionary called Sœur Marguerite du Saint Sacrement, otherwise the Mère Marie Alacoque.

for everyone who devotes himself to the interests of a turbulent and factious sect. The most moderate, even of the appellants, blame him loudly. The Abbé Duguet was disgusted with his audacity in recklessly satirizing and censuring all that was most entitled to respect. He said that the author of the Nouvelles, being unknown, ought to content himself with the lowest place; and that since he forgets that nobody knows who he is, nor what right he has to assume a tone of personal authority, all the world is justified in reminding him of the fact." * Archbishop de Vintimille's mandement stigmatized the Nouvelles as seditious and defamatory libels;—"a description," says Barbier, "which is perfectly correct, though they are the productions of a talented pen."† The Archbishop ordered the clergy to publish this sentence at the *prônes* in their churches. Twenty-two of them declined doing so; they agreed with him in condemning the libellous organ of the Jansenists, but they could not consent to read his mandement in Divine service, since it contained statements contrary to their convictions. Their real objection to it was, that it spoke of the Constitution as "an apostolical decree received by the whole Church." The prelate proceeded against the recreants in his court, and a monition was served on them to publish the mandement on the following Sunday. They at once appealed to the Parliament. It appears that in more than one instance where the mandate was obeyed, the congregation rose *en masse* when the priest began to read, and quitted the Church.‡

The Parliament was about to take into consideration the appeal of the curés, when a royal ordonnance forbade them to deliberate, and evoked to the Council of State all matters connected with the pretended miracles of St. Médard, and other ecclesiastical disputes. The king ordered the principal magistrates to attend him at Compiègne, where he repeated his commands in person, strictly prohibiting all interference on the part of the civil courts with the concerns of the Church. In

---

* Picot, *Mém. pour servir à l'hist. ecclésiastique du XVIIIme siècle*, tom. ii. p. 106. Picot's estimate, it must be remembered, is that of a strongly prejudiced opponent. His work is ably executed, and abounds with valuable information; but it leaves the general impression that the author "held a brief," and had a purpose to serve.
† Barbier, *Journal*, tom. i. p. 409.
‡ *Ibid.* tom. i. p. 412.

the teeth of this injunction, the Parliament held a tumultuous sitting on the 12th of May, when the Abbé Pucelle harangued his brethren with passionate indignation, railed against the government of Cardinals, and urged a policy of determined resistance. A second time they were summoned to Compiègne. The king sternly required them to execute his will, and that without offering reply or remonstrance in any shape whatever. The first President, being about to speak, was ordered to be silent. Pucelle stepped forward to present a memorial agreed upon beforehand, expressing the resolution of the magistrates to resign their offices if justice were denied them; upon which Louis turned to the Comte de Maurepas, exclaiming, "Tear it," and the minister did so immediately. The Parliament retired, crest-fallen and dismayed, yet unshaken in purpose. The next day Pucelle was exiled by a *lettre de cachet* to his abbey of Cormigny in Burgundy; and Titon, another councillor well known for his Jansenist sympathies, was conducted to Vincennes. The Parliament, on its return to Paris, accepted the appeal *comme d'abus* against the Archbishop's mandement, and sent a copy of the *arrêt* to that prelate. The court replied to this act of defiance by arresting four of the most influential magistrates, and confining them in distant fortresses. A third interview with Louis at Compiègne failed to effect an understanding; and on the 13th of June the Presidents and councillors of the Parliament, to the number of upwards of one hundred and fifty, sent in their resignation, and abandoned the Palais de Justice. A royal Declaration of the 18th of August following,[*] which tended to abridge the powers of the Parliament in taking cognizance of appeals *comme d'abus*, provoked a dogged opposition, and the courts declared it impossible to register it. They had reassembled, it appears, *pro formâ*, but refused to enter upon their ordinary duties. The minister, upon this, resorted to a sweeping stroke of authority, and banished a hundred and forty councillors from Paris within twenty-four hours, to different country towns in the ressort of the Parliament.[†]

Upon reflection, however, Fleury felt that it would be

---

[*] Isambert, *Anc. Lois Françaises*, tom xxi. p. 574.
[†] Barbier, tom. i. pp. 416-469.

unwise to persist in these severities towards a body so powerful from the importance of its functions and its popularity with the great mass of the nation. He was now far advanced in years, and hesitated to risk a serious collision with public opinion, especially for the sake of supporting a Papal Constitution which was every day becoming more and more odious throughout France. In November he revoked the *lettres de cachet* against the offending magistrates; and on the 1st of December the courts of justice were re-opened for the transaction of business. The king suspended, and virtually withdrew, his Declaration of the 18th of August, and the crisis passed without any renewal of conflict. But it became manifest to the whole French people that the Parliament had won a decided victory in its struggle with the executive government; and considering the situation of parties, this fact was by no means reassuring with reference to the safety of existing institutions and the future tranquillity of the realm.

"Sensible and disinterested people," says Barbier, "regard this as merely a patched-up reconciliation; for the main substance of the quarrel remains precisely the same as ever, namely Jansenism."

During the remainder of Cardinal Fleury's ministry, no further disturbance of a violent character occurred in the relations between Church and State. Nevertheless the course of events was such as to intensify by degrees the disunion and distrust which reigned among the different public bodies. The disputes arising out of the bull Unigenitus receded more and more from theological ground, and took the shape of a revolutionary agitation in the domain of politics. The rivalry between two opposite religious schools became merged in great measure in the grave constitutional problem, whether the Parliament, whose proper functions were judicial, was to become a deliberative assembly, and to succeed in establishing a permanent right to control the acts of the Crown and its ministers, the jurisdiction of the hierarchy, and the whole internal administration of the kingdom. The result of the late struggle had encouraged these pretensions; and the increasing weakness of the government seemed to invite a renewal of similar enterprises. Louis XV. with the connivance, it is said, of his ancient preceptor,* commenced about the year 1735 a career of licentious indulgence which soon inspired him with utter disrelish for the duties of his station; while the Cardinal-minister sank gradually into the habits of apathetic indolence natural to the decrepitude of extreme old age. The Parliamentary magistrates perceived that under such circumstances a grand opportunity was opened to them to stand forth as the champions of popular liberty and independence, more especially against the tyranny of the priesthood and the Jesuits. It happened unfortunately at this juncture that some of the bishops introduced a novel method of showing their detestation of Jansenistic error, by withholding the last Sacraments and the rites of Christian sepulture from persons who declined to accept with absolute faith the Constitution Unigenitus. They contended that a stubborn refusal to obey the acknowledged laws of Church and State exposed the offender to the penalties of excommunication; and the appeal to a future Council against the Unigenitus was placed without hesitation in that category.† The Parliament protested against this doctrine, and resented its application. Church discipline, thus unjustly and vexatiously administered, exasperated the lay mind, and the result was a strongly organised coalition to defeat it.

In 1733, a sick parishioner of St. Médard having demanded the last Sacraments, the curé, M. Coiffrel, questioned her upon the article of the Constitution, requiring that she should declare her acceptance of it as a "rule of faith." As her replies were unsatisfactory, he refused to administer the sacraments. Appeal was instantly made to the Parliament, and the magistrates proceeded to deal with the affair as within their legal competence. The Avocat-Général proposed an address to the king, requesting him to employ his authority for the prevention of abuses which harassed the consciences of the faithful by depriving them of the last consolations of religion. This was

---

* H. Martin, *Hist. de France*, tom. xv. p. 208. (4me Ed).

† The law of the Church did not sanction the refusal of Christian burial except in the case of pagans, infidels, heretics, and schismatics, those who commit suicide, persons killed in duels, and persons publicly denounced as excommunicate. Héricourt, *Lois ecclésiastiques de France*. G. xii. § 17, 19. It is hardly necessary to say that it required a violent and extreme stretch of interpretation to bring the Appellants as private individuals within either of these classes.

negatived, and it was ordered that counsel should be heard in support of the appeal against Coiffrel; but the government now interfered, cancelled the *arrêt* of the Parliament, and evoked the case to the Royal Council.

An intimation had been already given to the civil courts that matters of this kind were beyond their province; the Chancellor D'Aguesseau had admonished the Parliament of Bordeaux that it ought to have rejected an application made for the purpose of compelling an ecclesiastic to administer the Sacraments to a sick person; the court ought to have been aware that it was incompetent to entertain such questions. They should be referred to the bishop, who alone possessed the requisite authority.

In 1737 a case involving the same difficulties occurred at Douai. The Chapter of St. Amé, in that town, had been excommunicated by the bishop of the diocese for its opposition to the Unigenitus. Upon this the majority of the canons made their submission; but two or three persisted in their appeal, and even renewed it; and one of these, being on his death-bed, applied to the dean for extreme unction and the Viaticum. That dignitary peremptorily refused to grant them to an excommunicated heretic, and the canon died without them. His corpse was excluded in consequence from consecrated ground, and was at length interred in his garden. Barbier relates, though it seems scarcely credible, that because the body of the deceased was laid with the face towards the church, as usual in the case of Catholics, the authorities ordered a disinterment, and would not be satisfied till they were convinced that the head had been turned the opposite way. The relations of the deceased, indignant at this insult, complained of it publicly, and carried the case before the Parliament. A tumultuous debate followed, in spite of the efforts of the first president to stifle deliberation; but, as usual, the affair was abruptly withdrawn from their cognizance, and transferred to the Council of State.

Shortly afterwards the Parliament exhibited its irritation against the government by suppressing the bull issued by Pope Clement XII. for the canonisation of Vincent de Paul.* This

---

* Barbier, *Journal*, janvier 1738, tom. ii. p. 186.

was transparently a matter of party jealousy and animosity. Of the saintliness of that eminent servant of God there could be no reasonable question; the fame of his virtues and good works was universal, and the Church of France owed more to his lifelong self-devotion than it was possible to repay. But Vincent de Paul was strenuously opposed to Jansenism; and to this fact special allusion had been made, somewhat injudiciously, in the Pontifical decree. Nothing more was needed to wound the susceptibilities of many in the Parliament, and of the party among the clergy who shared their feelings. The curés and the avocats declaimed against the bull, opposed its registration, and threatened to appeal against it *comme d'abus*. The Parliament suppressed it on the pretext that it contained expressions inconsistent with the Gallican liberties and the maxims of the realm; but this *arrêt* was immediately annulled by order of the Council of State so far as related to the printing and publication of the bull, without any allusion to the principles upon which the Parliament had based its opposition.

Every ecclesiastical movement, at this unhappy period, was diverted from its real merits in order to serve as a fresh means of hostile aggression in the internecine war which distracted the Church. Archbishop Vintimille had introduced certain alterations in the Parisian Breviary, consisting chiefly of a new arrangement of the Psalms, which he appropriated, according to their respective subject-matter, to the different days of the week. The entire Psalter was thus to be repeated every week; and an approach was made towards equalizing the length of the various offices. In some instances, moreover, he substituted modern for the ancient hymns; he added considerably to the lessons from Holy Scripture; he carefully revised the extracts from the Fathers and from the Lives of Saints; and expunged several legends which seemed questionable on the score of historical accuracy.* The new Parisian Breviary was approved and adopted by fifty or more Gallican bishops; but the Jesuits and their partisans opposed it, and insisted on the exclusive authority of the Roman formularies. The differences which thus arose became associated with the long-standing roots of

---

* See his "Mandatum" prefixed to the Breviarium Parisiense, Pars Hicmalis. Lutet. Par. MDCCCXXXVI.

controversial bitterness; and an open feud broke out between Bossuet Bishop of Troyes, one of the most conspicuous of the Appellants, and his metropolitan, Languet Archbishop of Sens. Bossuet had published, like many of his colleagues, a new edition of the Missal for the use of his diocese; Languet complained of it as containing inadmissible innovations; and the suffragan defended himself in three mandements, asserting his right to regulate, within his own jurisdiction, minor details connected with the services of the Church.* Languet contended that the bishop had misused this prerogative; and the accusation had apparently some foundation, for Bossuet soon afterwards retracted several of the directions which had been excepted against in his Missal,—a step which gave sore umbrage to his party.

Archbishop Languet made himself on this occasion the instrument of the Jesuits, and of the animosity, both traditional and personal, which they cherished against the Bishop of Troyes for very sufficient reasons. A few years previously Bossuet had published several works from the manuscripts left

---

* The bishops of France possessed, from time immemorial, the right to revise the ritual used in their cathedrals, and to prescribe, within due limits, changes which they might deem necessary in the ceremonial of the Church. "Although the Catholic Church is one as respects dogma and morals, some diversity exists among particular churches as to the form of public prayers and the ceremonies of divine service. With regard to such matters, it is necessary to conform to the usages and prayers prescribed by the Breviaries and Missal of the diocese to which we belong. It is the practice of some regular communities to recite the Roman Breviary, as reformed by order of the Council of Trent, in whatever diocese their houses may be situated. There are others which have a breviary peculiar to their own Order. The bishops have sanctioned these various usages by the silence of several centuries, and could not at present compel such communities to follow the breviary of their dioceses. Whenever the bishops find in the office-books of their dioceses fabulous legends, or ceremonies which appear to favour superstition, it is their duty to cause them to be corrected, and to take care that nothing is inserted but what is edifying and useful for those who have to recite the offices. A great number of breviaries have been thus reformed since the middle of the last century. They are excellent models to follow for those who may be charged by the bishops with a similar undertaking. There was a time when it was believed in France that no change whatever could be made in the breviaries and missals without special permission from the Sovereign. They are now considered to be sufficiently authorized by the general privilege which is granted to the bishops under the great Seal, to print the Church formularies for the use of their dioceses. It is desirable that they should not introduce such changes except in concert with their cathedral Chapters." Héricourt, *Lois ecclésiastiques de France,* G. viii. 3, 4. This work has fallen under the common reproach of "Gallicanism;" it is, however, a collection of well-established authority. Louis de Héricourt was an advocate of the Parliament of Paris, and died in 1752.

by his illustrious uncle; the 'Élévations sur les Mystères,' the 'Meditations sur l'Évangile,' the 'Traité de l'amour de Dieu,' and the dissertation 'Sur la connaissance de Dieu et de soi-même.' Fichant, a writer in the Jesuit 'Journal de Trevoux,' had the hardihood to deny that these productions were really from the pen of the Bishop of Meaux; alleging that they abounded with sentiments which the great prelate was known to have repudiated as opposed to the essentials of religion. The Jesuits supported this insinuation; and Bossuet, in order to vindicate his honour, obtained an order from the Parliament summoning the Provincial and his colleagues to appear on a given day, that they might verify by personal examination the authenticity of the documents in question. They were forced to submit, and could not avoid acknowledging that the manuscripts produced were unquestionably in the handwriting of the late Bishop of Meaux, and that they had been faithfully reproduced in the volumes lately printed. The Bishop of Troyes published two Instructions Pastorales, each of the bulk of a thick volume, in which he exposed with pitiless severity the tactics of his calumniators, and repelled their aspersions upon his uncle's orthodoxy. They had pretended to detect, in these posthumous works, a tendency both towards Quietism and towards the Jansenistic errors on the doctrine of grace. Bossuet of Troyes showed no moderation in his triumph, and was an object of deadly enmity to the Jesuits for the rest of his days. A certain Abbé Pelletier attempted to answer his Instructions, but the *brochure* was an ignominious failure, and the Parliament condemned it to the flames.

The latter years of the younger Bossuet were embittered by continual opposition and contention. At length, in 1742, he resigned his see, and died shortly afterwards.

His distinguished fellow-appellant, Colbert Bishop of Montpellier, was removed from the scene somewhat earlier, in April, 1738. This prelate was a fertile and voluminous writer; in addition to his numerous publications in the controversy on the bull Unigenitus, he entered the lists against Le Courayer, the translator of Father Paul's 'History of the Council of Trent,' and against the Jesuit Joseph-Isaac Berruyer, author of the 'Histoire du peuple de Dieu, tirée des livres saints.' The professed object of this latter work was to render the study of Holy Scripture agreeable to persons living in the world; but in so doing Berruyer lost sight of the majesty and Divine authority of the inspired word, and transformed it into a mere secular narrative, fitted to captivate the imagination, like some tale of fiction or romance. The first part of the work was prohibited by the Congregation of the Index at Rome in May, 1734; and soon afterwards Bishop Colbert published a severe exposure of its errors in an Instruction Pastorale. He charged the Jesuit with deliberately corrupting Holy Scripture; with substituting the illusions of the human mind for the word of God; with putting profane language into the mouths of the sacred writers; with giving a false colouring to great crimes, and representing suicide as an act of heroism; with interpolating into the sacred text remarks and comments offensive to modesty. The eccentricities of Berruyer were condemned in the sequel by an assembly of French bishops, by the Sorbonne, and by the Parliament of Paris.

Jean Soanen, the suspended and exiled Bishop of Senez, was called to his rest in 1740; he died at the abbey of La Chaise Dieu, at the age of 95. Ever since his unrighteous condemnation by the Council of Embrun this prelate had been an object of extreme interest to the party of the Appellants; in their eyes he was a persecuted confessor, a martyr to the truth, an Athanasius or a Chrysostom; and numbers of them flocked to visit him in his retreat among the mountains of Auvergne. The bishop, however, alienated many of his admirers by defending, or allowing others to defend in his name, the fanatic excesses of the Convulsionists. De Bonnaire, an appellant doctor of the Sorbonne, had published, in 1736, a treatise in which those follies were denounced in terms of cutting severity. Soanen attacked this, and De Bonnaire rejoined with so much force of argument that the good bishop's reputation for wisdom was considerably damaged in the minds of the more calmly-judging of his party. But whatever estimate may be formed of his intellectual calibre and his controversial prejudices, the sanctity of his private life is indisputable; and it is scarcely surprising to find that the affectionate veneration of the Jansenists followed him after death, and that various miraculous events were attributed to his intercession.

Meanwhile the profligate Tencin, the prime mover of the

persecution which had driven the Bishop of Senez from his see to die in exile, was advanced to the highest honours and the most lucrative preferments in the Church. He was created a Cardinal in 1739, on the nomination of the prince who, proscribed in England under the name of the Pretender, was recognized at the court of Rome as King James III. In the following year he was made Archbishop of Lyons, and obtained soon afterwards, on the recommendation of Fleury, a place in the Council of State. These rewards flattered his self-love, and stimulated his ambition; and there is no doubt that he aspired to succeed Fleury in the supreme direction of affairs. A popular *jeu d'esprit*, which was first circulated at the time of the Council at Embrun, and which re-appeared at this moment, curiously illustrates the general estimate of his character and merits.

LES QUESTIONS DE L'ÉCHO DES MONTAGNES D'AMBRUN, AVEC LA RÉPONSE.

" Quel a été le motif du Concile assemblé dans cette ville metropolitaine ? "
"Haine."

"Es-tu bien informé de ce qui s'y est passé ? "
" Assez."

" Y a-t-on observé les loix prescrites par les canons ? "
" Non."

" Sur le dogme, les mœurs, la discipline, s'agissoit-il de quelque point ? "
" Point."

" Comment appeloit-on celui qui a été jugé dans le Concile présidé par Tencin ? "
" Saint."

" Qu'a-t-il soutenu pour engager les évêques à le traiter avec sévérité ? "
" Vérité."

" Que seront les évêques qui l'ont condamné ? "
" Damnés."

" Qu'obtiendra Tencin en récompense de ses indignités ? "
" Dignités."

" Parviendra-t-il au chapeau après un procédé aussi inouï ? "
" Oui."

" La simonie et l'agiotage ne lui nuiront-ils point ? "
" Point."

" Qu'était à ce prélat cette religieuse dévoilée qui . . . . et dont tout le royaume fut le censeur ? "
" Sœur." *

It is wonderful how, in the face of such unmistakable expressions of public hatred and contempt, Louis and his minister could have ventured to raise Tencin to posts of so much responsibility and influence. The Government at this period seems to have been systematically blind to the real significance

---

* See Soulavie, *Mémoires du Maréchal Duc de Richelieu*, tom. vii. p. 111.

of the prevailing temper of the nation. Some respect, however, for decency, some perception of what was due to the instincts of society, still survived; and Cardinal de Tencin never became Prime Minister. He was dismissed from office as a minister of State, and retired permanently to his diocese of Lyons, in 1751.

Cardinal Fleury had now outlived all capacity of actively directing the affairs of government; he secluded himself at his country house at Issy, and it was evident that his end approached. He breathed his last on the 29th of January, 1743, in the ninetieth year of his age. The description given by the Duke of Richelieu of the parting scene between Louis XV. and his minister, and of the advice tendered by the latter to his sovereign, is interesting, and may doubtless be relied on for substantial accuracy. He entreated him, it seems, never again to place a Cardinal at the head of the government. "They are dependent," remarked Fleury, "on a foreign power, and conceive that they are themselves a power, in respect of the commanding position which they hold in the Church. The affairs of France would suffer from this circumstance. My ecclesiastical rank often prevented me, during the troubles with the Parliament, from doing what I should have done had I been merely a layman. This is all that I have to reproach myself with. My administration has been pacific. . . . . The Church is at present tranquil. I have made some sacrifices in order to restore peace. The point of most urgent necessity is to attach the heads of parties to the interests of government, so as to detach them from the factions over which they rule. The Parliaments are the bodies which it is most difficult to control. They will either destroy the State or make essential changes in it, if they are suffered to gain the ascendant. I am aware of your Majesty's intentions on that head, and will not speak of it further. Religion, Sire, deserves your attention; if you will practise it personally, and protect it by your authority, you will not have to endure on your death-bed the anguish by which I am tortured at this moment. I trust in the mercy of God; but I dread a mistaken conscience, a blinded conscience." *

These last words throw a melancholy light upon the charac-

---

* Soulavie, *Mém. du Mar. Duc de Richelieu*, tom. vii. p. 95.

teristic weaknesses of Fleury. The chief faults of his ministry arose, not so much from the fact of his being an ecclesiastic, as from his being blind to the special duties imposed on him by his station, or lacking the energy and courage to respond to them. In the character of the king's preceptor, and enjoying as he did the confidence and affection of his pupil, he possessed immense advantages, of which it is to be feared that he made a negligent and unfaithful use. Had he employed them as he ought, it is scarcely conceivable that Louis could have plunged into those abject depths of moral degradation which disgraced his reign, and to which, in conjunction with other causes of popular alienation, we must ascribe the ultimate downfall of monarchical institutions in France.

After the death of Fleury, the department of ecclesiastical affairs was entrusted to Jean-François Boyer, formerly Bishop of Mirepoix. He had resigned that see on being appointed, in 1736, preceptor to the Dauphin, only legitimate son of Louis XV. Boyer was a man of very moderate capacity, but virtuous, conscientious, and disinterested. In his distribution of preferment, and in his general policy, he trod closely in the footsteps of his predecessor; and all dissentients from the bull Unigenitus were rigidly excluded from the dignities and emoluments of the Church. Boyer, however, to do him justice, seems to have been equally alive to the dangers with which both religion and society were menaced by the school of *philosophes* or freethinkers, whose ill-omened influence was at this period beginning to make itself felt throughout Western Europe. It was through his active interference, and urgent remonstrances with Louis XV., that Voltaire was defeated in his candidature for the chair at the Academy which was left vacant by Cardinal Fleury.* In his education of the Dauphin he showed an inadequate conception of the special difficulties of the task imposed on him, though it must be allowed that he acted rightly in point of essential principle. The hopes of the Church, and, indeed, of all intelligent men in France, were centred on the future of this young prince; for the gross scandals of the existing

---

* Voltaire was admitted an Academician, however, in 1746, having previously propitiated Boyer and the Jesuits by a vague declaration of his respect for religion.

régime were rapidly undermining the foundations of public order and hereditary authority. The preceptor, ably seconded by his colleague the Abbé de St. Cyr, laboured to imbue the mind of his pupil with profound reverence for religion, for the Catholic faith, and for all Catholic institutions; and the result was undeniably successful, for the Dauphin, surrounded as he was by an abandoned court, never yielded to its corruptions, and preserved intact both his belief in Christian truth and his blamelessness of morals. But the form of religion to which he attached himself was bigoted, sombre, superstitious; one which by no means qualified him for the duties of the position as a great public personage to which he was destined by his birth. He threw himself into the arms of the Jesuits, and learned to view everything in the light which their interests might dictate. By degrees he evinced a marked incapacity for exertion, whether political, military, or intellectual; and his second wife, a Saxon princess, described his ordinary habits not unaptly, by observing that he passed his time "like an owl."*

France was deprived, in the year 1742, of one of the last survivors of the race of her really great divines, by the death of Jean Baptiste Massillon, Bishop of Clermont. As a preacher, Massillon had achieved during the latter years of the reign of Louis XIV. a reputation second to none; and amid the orgies of the Regency he rendered inestimable service by fearlessly inculcating, both before the Court and in the chief pulpits of the capital, those great canons of mutual obligation between prince and people, the governor and the governed, upon which the safety and happiness of States depend. But his conscience would not suffer him to be a non-resident bishop; he quitted Paris in 1721, and devoted his energies for the rest of his life to the pastoral care of his diocese. Here he distinguished himself by fervent zeal and incessant labours; displaying at the same time a gentleness, considerateness, and moderation, which won for him the esteem even of those from whom he differed most widely in opinion. The appellants against the bull Unigenitus had little to complain of in the diocese of Clermont. The bishop himself, like the vast majority of his colleagues, adhered to the Constitution; he adopted the ordonnance of his predecessor enjoining the clergy

---

* Soulavie, *Mém. du Duc de Richelieu*, tom. viii. p. 130.

to conform to it; and he enforced compliance in cases where, in his judgment, it was necessary to resort to such acts of authority. But the spirit of his administration was eminently forbearing, conciliatory, paternal. He persuaded numbers of the non-acceptants to revoke their appeal, and in one way or another to satisfy the requirements of the law; and in the end he was able to congratulate himself that his diocese, which was once notoriously turbulent and divided, had become the most tranquil in France. All accounts agree as to the invariable charity and benevolence of Massillon's conduct towards Bishop Soanen, whose place of exile, La Chaise Dieu, was within the limits of his jurisdiction. Hearing that he was badly lodged in the abbey, he offered him one of his country houses, the Château de Beauregard; and in writing to him he observed a tone of profound respect for the venerable prisoner, though without dissembling the divergence of their sentiments on the distressing controversies of the day.* These truly evangelical virtues were not, apparently, regarded by Louis XV. and his minister as a sufficient recommendation for places of high trust and political power; and Massillon was suffered to live and die in the comparative obscurity of a remote province, while the honours of the State were lavished upon shallow mediocrities, totally incapable of grappling with the multiplied difficulties of the age.

Among the prelates whose names deserve honourable mention at this epoch was François Duc de Fitz-James, Bishop of Soissons, a son of the Marshal Duke of Berwick, and consequently a descendant, though illegitimately, of the royal house of Stuart. He is remarkable, not on account of any superior ability, but for the true Christian courage, firmness, and fidelity, which he exhibited under circumstances of no common difficulty. In August, 1744, Louis XV., who had joined his army for the purpose of repelling an Austrian invasion of Alsace, fell dangerously ill at Metz, and was soon reduced to the last extremity. The Duchess of Châteauroux, then the reigning mistress, supported by the Duke of Richelieu and other favourites, strove to exclude from the sick chamber all but their own partisans, and to keep the king in ignorance of his desperate condition. They were opposed by the Dukes of Bouillon and

---

* Massillon, Œuvres, tom. xiv. pp. 57 et seqq. (Paris, 1830.)

La Rochefoucauld, and the Comte de Clermont;* and the Bishop of Soissons, in his quality of premier aumonier, with a Jesuit named Pérusseau, the king's confessor, zealously co-operated with this latter party. The physicians at length abandoned hope, and an intimation of the fact was conveyed to Louis, in spite of all exertions to the contrary. Struck with terror, he expressed himself anxious to confess and receive the last Sacraments; and it was now that Fitz-James gave him to understand that this was impossible until he should have made some open reparation for his sins by banishing Madame de Châteauroux from his presence. The monarch, after much hesitation, submitted; and orders were issued that the duchess, with her sister Madame de Lauraguais, should retire forthwith to a distance of fifty leagues from Metz; a mandate which was punctually executed. The stern prelate exacted further, that Louis should make a declaration of his sorrow for the past in the presence of the royal family and his principal attendants; and the contemporary memoirs record the terms in which this humiliating avowal was expressed.† Finally, Fitz-James administered the Viaticum and extreme unction, which the king received with every external mark of penitence and devotion.

He recovered, as the reader is aware; and relapsed, after a brief space, into his dissolute habits. Madame de Châteauroux once more reigned supreme; and the first use which she made of her empire was to insist on the condign punishment of those who had plotted and effected her disgrace at Metz. The dukes of Chatillon, Bouillon, and La Rochefoucauld, were accordingly banished to their estates, and the Bishop of Soissons received orders to retire to his diocese. In 1748 he was stripped of his appointment as first chaplain to the king;‡ and a more serious privation was inflicted upon him in addition. He had been promised a Cardinal's hat whenever a presentation should fall to the turn of the exiled heir of the Stuarts; but when that opportunity occurred, he found himself passed over, in consequence, doubtless, of a plainly-notified veto from the court of Versailles.

---

* Younger brother of the Duke of Bourbon. He was Abbot Commendatory of St. Germain des Prés, but followed, nevertheless, the profession of arms.

† Soulavie, *Mém. du Duc de Richelieu*, tom. iii. p. 31.

‡ Barbier, *Journal*, tom. iii. p. 31.

Under such strokes of adverse fortune this bold rebuker of vice in high places remained immoveably faithful to his principles. As often as Louis visited the Château of Compiègne, which lies within the diocese of Soissons, he never failed to find in his cabinet a pastoral letter from the bishop, reflecting in no measured tone on his flagrant immoralities, and reminding him of the solemn protestations of repentance and vows of amendment which he had made when he believed himself at the point of death. These remonstrances his Majesty received without betraying indignation; but they had no practical effect whatever on his course of life.

The character of Bishop Fitz-James partook largely of the austere rigorism of the earlier Jansenists; and although he does not seem to have embraced their theological system as a whole, he gradually became identified with the Appellant party. The ablest among them constantly resorted to his house, and several publications which appeared in his name are known to have proceeded from their pen. He lived securely, however, in his retirement, without further molestation from the government, and died in peace at Soissons in 1765.

The death of Archbishop Vintimille occurred on the 13th of March, 1746. His immediate successor was De Bellefonds, Archbishop of Arles; but that prelate died suddenly within a few weeks after his translation. The public voice was now raised with some persistency in favour of the Abbé Harcourt, Dean of Notre Dame; Bishop Boyer, however, suspected him of secret leanings towards Jansenism, and declined to recognise his claims. He selected for the see of Paris one who was destined to acquire a wide and lasting, if not altogether an enviable celebrity, Christophe de Beaumont, Archbishop of Vienne.

De Beaumont belonged to a family of distinction in the Périgord, and was born at the Château de la Roque in 1703. He was unquestionably a man of sterling merit. He could not boast of shining talents, but he was gifted in a singular degree with the faculty of pleasing, the art of inspiring goodwill and confidence; he had an engaging mien and a gracious presence; his character was benevolent, and transparently sincere. While Bishop of Bayonne, he had made himself specially acceptable to the first Dauphiness, a young Spanish Infanta, who, on coming to France in 1744, suffered much from nervous apprehension as to the reception she might meet with in her new position. She never forgot the good offices of De Beaumont at this trying moment; and it was through her influence that he was preferred in 1745 to the Archbishopric of Vienne. "On being called to the see of Paris, his disposition," says a contemporary writer,* "seemed for some time pacific. He bore at first the character of a prelate secretly ambitious, but of a gentle, pliant temper, which had carried him from a third story in the Rue des Maçons to the archiepiscopal palace of the capital. It was expected that his rule would be mild and tranquil; but, after a courtier-like and peaceable behaviour at Bayonne and Vienne, he became all at once rude, harsh, proud, and inflexible in his dealings with the Court. He strove to persuade all France that his turbulence was active charity, and his ambition zeal for the unity of the faith. We have seen him set himself up as grand Inquisitor of France; and henceforward he arrogates to himself the cognisance of ecclesiastical affairs of every description. There are no intrigues to which he is not a party; no secret springs which he will not set in motion to annoy a man of worth who will not truckle to his caprices, or to protect a rogue and shelter him from the law, if he be known for one of his submissive proselytes." Richelieu, it must be remembered, was a partisan of the school of *soi-disant* philosophers, and a personal friend of Voltaire. He does justice, however, to the other side of the Archbishop's character. "While numbers of French bishops pampered their luxurious tastes at the expense of artists and skilled workmen, and died insolvent, Beaumont set them an example of good order, regularity, and decency of manners. He spent scarcely a third part of his revenue in keeping up the state of his office, in furniture and personal equipment; and all the rest he distributed among the poor. His charities were extended to the frontiers of France, and even to the Catholics of Ireland; but it sufficed to be poor and fanatical to enjoy a share of his bounty. The strictness of his morals is well known."

The character of Archbishop de Beaumont, though it embraced various admirable qualities, was not such as to fit him for the oversight of the diocese of Paris at a moment when the

---

* Soulavie, *Mém. du Duc de Richelieu*, tom. viii. p. 209.

Church was on its trial before a newly-constituted and jealous tribunal, which was every day making louder assertions of the plenitude of its jurisdiction—the tribunal of Public Opinion. He had been called to Paris because he was deemed a creditable interpreter and a promising administrator of the *old* system; but he soon found himself confronted by the apostles of a new dispensation; by propagators of strange novelties as to the soundness and authority of the institutions which had descended from antiquity; by a movement which dared to investigate, criticise, revise, reorganise, all the relationships between the governing aristocracy and the subject masses. He discovered that there were other difficulties to be dealt with besides that of silencing the Appellants and suppressing Jansenism. He discerned the symptoms of a deep-laid conspiracy against the entire status of the National Church, as it had flourished throughout the palmy days of the absolute monarchy; he foresaw that the hierarchy itself was to be attacked as a gigantic abuse, and its power denounced as an intolerable incubus on the natural rights and liberties of mankind. No sooner did he become sensible of the real danger with which the Church was threatened, than he cast himself into the struggle with all the vigour and decision of his unflinching nature; but the weapons which he employed were fatally injudicious and inadequate. The tactics of this noble-hearted prelate accelerated the catastrophe which he dreaded; but he was spared, at all events, the pain of witnessing the irretrievable ruin of his cause.

CHAPTER IX.

THREE royal edicts were published in 1749 and the following year, at the instance of Machault, comptroller-general of finance, which were looked upon as so many overt acts of hostile aggression on the Church. By the first, a tax of five per cent. was imposed upon all incomes, not excepting those of the ecclesiastical order; a clear infraction of the long-cherished immunities of the clergy from the ordinary burdens of French citizens. The second prohibited any further acquisitions of property by way of mortmain;—a stroke aimed directly at the system by which the possessions and wealth of the Church had been augmented so enormously from age to age. By the third, all holders of benefices were enjoined to furnish to the Government, within six months, a statement of the amount of their yearly revenues, with a view to "a more equitable distribution of the subsidies which the fidelity of the clergy bound them to supply."* Machault was a man of liberal views, and a convert to the new philosophy; especially to one of its fundamental principles, the necessity of a radical reform of the clergy. The treasury, by reason of the late war and the ruinous extravagance of Louis and his court, stood urgently in need of replenishment; and the minister, who knew that he should have the support of an intelligent and powerful party in attacking the overgrown wealth of the ecclesiastical Establishment, proposed this as a happy expedient towards liquidating the debts of the Crown.

The ordonnance of August, 1749, interdicted "all new foundations of Chapters, Colleges, Seminaries, religious communities, and hospitals, without express permission from the king, registered by the sovereign courts; suppressed all such establishments which had been formed since the year 1666 without the

---

* "Notre intention est que ces déclarations soient mises sous nos yeux, pour connoître par nous-même la véritable valeur des biens du clergé de France, et éclaircir les préventions désavantageuses auxquelles l'ignorance de cet objet a donné lieu." See Isambert, *Lois Françaises*, tom. xxii. p. 256.

authority of letters patent; and forbade all 'gens de mainmorte' to acquire property either in land, houses, or the public funds, without legal sanction from the government, which was henceforth to be obtained after a public enquiry into the usefulness of the proposed acquisition."* In this important enterprise it appears that Machault was fortunate enough to secure the concurrence of the veteran Chancellor D'Aguesseau;—a circumstance which goes far to prove that some restriction of the kind was wise and requisite. This was one of the last acts of the long public life of D'Aguesseau. That distinguished magistrate, perhaps the greatest master of constitutional jurisprudence that France has ever produced, resigned his office in 1750, and retired to his château of Fresnes, where he died in the year following, at the age of eighty-three.

The measure of immediate exigency was that which imposed the income-tax of the "vingtième." This was interpreted by the clergy, and justly, as a prelude to the forcible extinction of the fiscal immunities immemorially enjoyed by their order; and they accordingly resisted it with determined vigour. At the session of the General Assembly in August, 1750, the royal Commissioners were instructed to demand in his Majesty's name a subsidy of seven million livres and a half, payable by equal instalments in five years. The "vingtième" was not mentioned *eo nomine*, but the terms employed implied that the contribution was exacted by government as a right, whereas the clergy contended that all such payments on their part were purely voluntary and gratuitous. General indignation was expressed; a curt and almost insolent reply was drawn up, and presented to the king by Cardinal de la Rochefoucauld, to the effect that the Assembly would never concede as a compulsory tribute what had hitherto been given freely as a testimony of love and respect.† Thereupon the king abruptly dissolved the session, and ordered the bishops to retire to their dioceses. The intendants of the provinces were directed to levy forthwith the sum required upon the Church property throughout France. The Assembly, before

---

* See the Edict in Isambert, *Anciennes Lois Françaises,* tom. xxii. p. 226 et seq.

† "Notre conscience et notre honneur ne nous permettent pas de consentir à voir changer en tribut nécessaire, ce qui ne peut être que l'offrande de notre amour." *Collect. des Procès-verbaux des Assemb. du Clergé,* tom. viii. 1ʳᵉ partie p. 262.

separating, adopted a strong protest against the violation of its ancient privilege.

The zeal exhibited by the clergy in defence of their temporalities gave rise to much popular clamour and various satirical strictures. One pamphlet, entitled 'Remontrances du second ordre du clergé au sujet du vingtième,' was a parody of the address lately presented to the throne by the bishops. It drew an invidious contrast between the great dignitaries of the Church, "clothed in purple and fine linen, and fareing sumptuously every day," " purchasing the gift of God by vile adulation, accumulating riches under the pretext that luxury ought to be proportionate to rank, as if the patrimony of the poor were designed to foster the pride of aristocratic birth"—and the true pastors of the flock, " the second order in point of precedence, but first in respect of their labours, simple and frugal in their habits of life, devoting themselves to the service of the rustic poor, sharing with them the means of subsistence, guiding their minds, consoling them in trouble, watching over them from the cradle to the grave, and imbuing them with the only principles which could make them contented with their lowly station. These, Sire, are the true clergy of France, who now submit their humble representations to your Majesty against the haughty insubordination of their superiors, as shown in their attempt to excuse themselves from the impost of the "vingtième," in order that its whole weight may fall upon the rest of your Majesty's subjects." * Another sarcastic publication, printed anonymously, with the suggestive motto " Ne repugnate vestro bono," was indignantly denounced by the Assembly, and a circular letter was forwarded to the bishops, exposing its errors in detail. The author maintained in set terms the republican doctrine of the sovereignty of the people; stigmatized the clergy as the least useful portion of the community; and taught that Church

---

* This insinuation was but too well founded. By far the greater part of the grants voted by the clergy to the crown was supplied by the second order. " Les curés do tout le royaume, et tous les petits bénéficiers, sont accablés de décimes par la répartition qui se fait dans chaque diocèse, au lieu qu'ils ne payeroient, par l'imposition du vingtième, qu'à proportion de leur revenu effectif." Barbier, *Journal*, tom. iii. p. 102. It should be mentioned that during the ten years 1740—1750, no less a sum than sixty millions of francs had been drawn from the Church in " dons gratuits," independently of the " décimes ordinaires."

endowments, being the fruits of a mistaken and benighted piety, might be justly reclaimed by the State and appropriated to the public benefit. This *brochure* was generally believed to be written with the secret connivance, if not under the express direction, of the Minister Machault. Barbier describes it as a profoundly learned enquiry into the original institution of the French monarchy, the ancient status of the clergy, the steps which caused its aggrandizement, and the particulars of its gradual usurpations. The Council of State ordered it to be suppressed; but the only effect of this was to encourage the sale, and a second edition was published in consequence.

It may easily be conceived that these jealousies and divisions between the hierarchy and the working clergy seriously affected the general policy and interests of the Church. Archbishop de Beaumont and his colleagues became convinced that a tide of bitter animosity was setting in against their order, and it would seem that they ascribed it to a coalition between the "philosophes," the Jansenists, and the magistracy of the Parliaments; all of whom were well known to be agreed in the sentiment that a reform of the Church was indispensable, and that it ought to begin among those who enjoyed its highest dignities. Of the three disaffected parties, the Jansenists were the least numerous, the least influential, and the most easily assailed; and it was against them, accordingly, that De Beaumont directed his first measures of retaliation. He resorted, with grave unwisdom, to the system of demanding "billets de confession;" insisting upon their being produced in all cases of whatever rank where suspicion existed of complicity with proscribed heresy, or of opposition to the bull Unigenitus. The test was not a new one. It is said to have been originally devised as a safeguard against deception in the case of professing converts from Protestantism; and was subsequently enforced by Cardinal de Noailles, during his brief supremacy under the Regency, against the Jesuits and other Ultramontanes. The usage had since fallen into abeyance; but its revival at the expense of the Jansenists was, strictly speaking, no more than an application of the "lex talionis." An instance occurred in 1749 which caused considerable excitement. Charles Coffin, principal of the Collège de Beauvais, the friend and successor of the celebrated Rollin, and like him, a well-known Jansenist, was refused the last Sacraments by his

parish priest, Bouettin, Curé of St. Étienne du Mont. His nephew hastened to complain to the first president of the Parliament; the magistrate referred him to the Archbishop; and de Beaumont justified the refusal of the curé on the ground that there was no proof of orthodox confession. Meanwhile the sick man died without Absolution, Communion, or Extreme Unction; and some difficulty was made about interring him in consecrated ground. The younger Coffin, instigated by the anti-clerical party in the Parliament, pursued the affair in vindication of the respect due to his uncle's memory. Legal consultations were drawn up, maintaining that he had a right to redress; that the practice of requiring certificates of confession, from persons of established character, was contrary to the Paris ritual and to all ecclesiastical rule. These memorials were presented to the Parliament, and were about to be discussed, when the first president interfered, and the matter was postponed to a future day. The Court was now informed of the circumstances; and it was resolved to adopt the usual course of repelling all such attacks upon the spiritual jurisdiction by a peremptory exercise of absolute authority. The chief magistrates were summoned to Compiègne, where the king notified to them that the proposed subject of their deliberations was of such importance to the general welfare of the kingdom, that it could be dealt with only by the supreme power. He would take the measures which he judged most suitable to demonstrate both his respect for religion and his regard to the public tranquillity. He ordered the Parliament to suspend all action upon the affair in question, and to wait till he should make known his intentions, to which he expected immediate and implicit submission. An *arrêt* of the Council of State speedily appeared, suppressing the aforesaid consultations, which were pronounced to agitate dangerous questions, and to put forth claims tending to compromise the tranquillity of the State. The Parliament yielded for the time; and the result was that direct encouragement was given to the bishops to prosecute the scheme of inquisitorial oppression by which they hoped to root out the last vestiges of Jansenism.[*]
The "billets de confession" were soon exacted in almost every diocese of France; and refusals of the Sacraments, entailing

---

[*] Barbier, *Journal*, tom. pp. 83-93.

consequent exclusion from the rites of Christian sepulture, became matters of continual occurrence.

The curé of St. Étienne du Mont was an uncompromising ally of the Archbishop, and carried out his instructions with indomitable zeal and vigour. He was a canon-regular of St. Géneviève, and had formerly been a disciple of the Jansenists, who were predominant in that establishment. This made him all the more rancorous in his enmity against the party from whose camp he had deserted. In December, 1750, he excited fresh commotion by refusing the Sacraments to M. Coffin the younger, with whom he had already come into collision on the occasion of the death of his uncle. He strove to extort from him a recognition of the Constitution as an article of faith and a law of Church and State; and this being declined, he quitted him without administering the desired rites. Coffin was of the legal profession, a councillor of the Châtelet. The lieutenant-civil, attended by the whole official staff of that court, forthwith denounced this insult to their body in the Grand'-Chambre of the Parliament; and the magistrates, after due deliberation, summoned the curé personally to their bar. He refused at first, and officers were sent to compel him to appear. Being interrogated as to the motives of his conduct, he replied that his reasons were known to the Archbishop, his superior, and that whatever orders he might receive from him he was ready to obey immediately. He had nothing more satisfactory to offer in the way of defence; and the court decided on committing him to prison. He was taken into custody and conveyed to the Conciergerie; but was liberated the next day, and dismissed with a reprimand and a trifling fine. The "gens du roi" were directed to wait on the Archbishop and request an explanation. De Beaumont received them politely, and observed that certificates of confession were not usually required except in the case of persons unknown or without settled abode; but he avoided entering into further discussion, apparently from indisposition to recognise the right of the Parliament to question him.

Further embroilment soon ensued between the Archbishop and the Parliament, in consequence of the imperious policy of the former in the management of the Hôpital-Général of Paris. By his office he was one of the governors of that institution, but others were associated with him;—the first presidents of the

Parliamentary courts, the procureur-général, the lieutenant-général of police, and the prévôt des marchands. The Archbishop had conceived some suspicion of Jansenism against the sister-superior of the Hospital; he proposed to displace her in favour of a person for whose orthodoxy he could vouch, but who in other respects was by no means qualified for the post. On a division in the committee, the majority of voices was against the prelate; but he took upon himself to ignore that circumstance, and insisted that his proposition should be considered as carried, and executed forthwith. Sister Michel was accordingly dismissed, and the "dame Moysan" installed in her place. The Parliament was not likely to submit tamely to such treatment; they appointed two councillors to make a visit of inspection to the Hospital, and report to them on its condition. In consequence of the information thus obtained, they annulled the appointment of the new superior, and ordered a fresh election.[*]
Meanwhile De Beaumont had procured from the king a revised code of regulations for the government of the Hospital, the effect of which was to concentrate the supreme authority in his own hands. When this was presented to the Parliament for registration, they introduced alterations so numerous and important as altogether to counteract its object. An attempt was made to induce the committee of managers to accept the amendments; but this was overruled by the Archbishop upon the strength of an order which he produced from the Council of State. The first president Maupeou and other magistrates then retired abruptly, and the meeting broke up in confusion.

The king now summoned his Parliament to an audience at Compiègne; expressed his displeasure with their conduct, announced that they had no authority to alter the terms of edicts or declarations which they were required to enter on their register, and signified his will that the Hôpital-Général should be administered henceforth in exact accordance with the directions of the recent ordonnance. Subsequently his Majesty expunged with his own hands the records of their deliberations on this affair, and strictly forbade them to discuss it further, or to offer any remonstrances. The magistrates, provoked by this interference with the right of debate, which they regarded as

---

[*] *Nouvelles Ecclésiastiques*, 20 mars 1750, p. 45.

the most valuable of their functions, suspended their sittings, and refused to proceed with the ordinary course of justice. An accommodation was effected, however, before the close of the year.

"All this disturbance," says Barbier, "proceeds from the intrigues of the Jansenist party, and from the hatred which they bear to the Archbishop of Paris." * He might have added that the evil was greatly aggravated by the overbearing conduct of the prelate himself, as well as by the deep-rooted mistrust shown by the sovereign in his dealings with his Parliament, even in matters constitutionally belonging to their province.

The resistance of the clergy to the imposition of the "vingtième" was sustained with unflagging vigour, and with ultimate success. By a royal edict of January, 1752, the pecuniary demand made upon the Assembly of 1750 was withdrawn, and it was announced that new measures were in contemplation to regulate the contributions of the clerical order. This victory by no means added to the popularity of the Church with the rest of the nation.

The strife connected with the "billets de confession," which had abated for a while, burst forth with renewed bitterness in March, 1752. A priest named La Mère, an ex-member of the Oratory, attached to the household of the Duke of Orleans, fell ill, and demanded the last Sacraments from "frère Bouettin," the redoubtable Curé of St. Étienne du Mont. The curé suggested, as a preliminary condition, that he should declare his cordial acceptance of the bull Unigenitus. La Mère observing that he considered this unnecessary, Bouettin refused to officiate; La Mère preferred his complaint to the procureur-général, and the affair was reported to the Parliament. The magistrates proceeded as on former occasions. Having interrogated Bouettin, they passed an *arrêt* admonishing him not to repeat his offence, under penalty of the seizure of his temporalities and other exemplary punishment. They requested the Archbishop to take measures for preventing a recurrence of similar abuses in his diocese, and to cause the Sacraments to be administered to the Sieur La Mère within twenty-four hours. The king immediately cancelled this *arrêt*, and evoked the

---

* Barbier, *Journal*, tom. iii. p. 322.

affair to his personal cognizance. La Mère died without the Sacraments. The Parliament ordered Bouettin to be arrested; the king annulled the mandate. "Humble remonstrances" were thereupon made to his Majesty, who replied that, although he had no desire to withdraw such matters altogether from the cognizance of his Parliament, he had evoked the present case because the ordinary modes of procedure were not always sufficient to preserve public order.* Instead of bowing to the will of the sovereign, the magistrates adopted, on the 18th of April, 1752, a famous "réglement" prohibiting all ecclesiastics to take any step tending towards schism, and in particular, to refuse the Sacraments publicly, under pretext of default of a certificate of confession, or of specifying the name of the confessor, or of submission to the bull Unigenitus, which they denied to be obligatory as a "rule of faith."† Copies of this document were profusely distributed, together with an allegorical print representing the Parliament under the figure of Justice, surrounded by the pretentious motto, "Custos unitatis, schismatis ultrix." This engraving was suppressed by an order of the Council of State; "a somewhat petty proceeding," observes Barbier; "it ought to have been contemptuously ignored." ‡ Such measures only inflamed the already feverish agitation that prevailed.

The king now signified his intention to appoint a Commission, consisting jointly of prelates and lay magistrates, to consider the existing difficulties and propose expedients for the restoration of civil and religious concord.§ He named for this purpose Cardinals de la Rochefoucauld and Soubise, the Archbishop of Rouen and the Bishop of Laon, and MM. Joly de Fleury, Trudaine, Bidé de la Granville, and Castanier d'Auriac. The commissioners held repeated conferences, but without advantageous result. The irritation on all sides had by this time reached a point which defied repression; and scenes still more stormy were at hand. In December of the same year, the sacraments having been refused to an aged nun of the Convent of St. Agatha, Sister Perpetua, the Parliament once more

---

* *Nouvelles Ecclésiastiques*, ann. 1752, p. 84.
† Isambert, *Anc. Lois Françaises*, tom. xxii. p. 251.
‡ Barbier, *Journal*, tom. iii. p. 387.
§ *Nouvelles Ecclésiastiques*, ann. 1752, p. 123.

appealed to the Archbishop to put an end to such scandals. The prelate, in reply, exculpated the parochial clergy, took the whole responsibility upon himself, and declared that the administration of the Sacraments was a function of the ministry which he held from God alone. Provoked by his stubborn attitude, the magistrates expressed their wrath in a series of alarming *arrêts*. They decreed the seizure of the Archbishop's temporalities, which was executed accordingly, to the amount of 600,000 francs; they convoked the Court of Peers to sit in judgment upon him, and invited the king to preside on that occasion; they ordered the clergy of St. Médard to communicate Sister Perpetua and other sick persons making similar demands; and they refused to listen to the reading of royal *lettres de cachet* and orders of Council, by which their proceedings were censured and annulled. The bishops lost no time in protesting against the violence offered to De Beaumont. They proceeded in a body to Versailles, headed by Cardinals de la Rochefoucauld and Soubise, and insisted on making their complaint to the king in person; who testified some surprise at the intrusion of this unauthorised Gallican Synod. He soothed them by announcing, first, that he had evoked to himself, by an order of his Council, the affair of Sister Perpetua, and secondly, that he had already, previously to their arrival, countermanded the seizure of the revenues of the Archbishop of Paris. The clergy showed the liveliest sympathy with the prelate at this moment of trial. The treasury of the Assembly was placed at his disposal; the Chapter of Notre Dame guaranteed whatever liabilities he might contract; an unknown admirer offered him 200,000 francs in cash, without security of any kind; he was saluted with enthusiasm as the Athanasius of the Church of France. Meanwhile Sister Perpetua, who had somewhat suspiciously recovered her health, was removed by the king's orders from her cloister of St. Agatha to Port-Royal. This step gave great offence to the Jansenists, and was denounced in the Parliament as an attack on those slight remains of ancient liberty of which the French people had not yet been deprived.

During the early part of 1753 the Parliament was engaged in framing a catalogue of remonstrances to be presented to the king, relating not only to the matters lately contested, but to the general conduct of the Government with respect to the bull Unigenitus; including a very intelligible condemnation of the system of *lettres de cachet,* and other despotic abuses. An imposing list of twenty-two Articles was prepared; but the king, having been informed of their purport, declined to receive them, inasmuch as upon some of those points he had already explained himself, had given express commands with respect to others, while, as to the rest, he considered them likely to raise fresh obstacles to the maintenance of public tranquillity. On the receipt of this mortifying response, the Parliament decreed that "since it was found impossible, through the arts of ill-disposed persons, to put the throne in full possession of the truth, the courts had no other resource but to continue in permanent session, suspending all ordinary business, until it should please his Majesty to give a favourable hearing to their remonstrances." They were commanded, by *lettres de jussion,* to resume their functions; but declared that they could not obey without failing in their duty and betraying their oaths. Upon this the monarch, at the instigation, it is said, of Madame de Pompadour, exiled most of the councillors to various country towns, and imprisoned four of them in distant fortresses; these latter, it was understood, had proposed to designate the "ill-disposed persons" by name, and to specify the Chancellor Lamoignon, the Comte d'Argenson, and Boyer Bishop of Mirepoix. Much of the bitterness of this conflict was due to the rivalry which existed between the ministers D'Argenson and Machault; the former espousing the cause of the clergy, the latter secretly fomenting the insubordinate spirit of the Parliament. Louis inclined towards the counsels of D'Argenson; and, this being known, the Parliament at one time went so far as to discuss a proposal to arrest him, as well as the Chancellor.[*]

The Grand'Chambre was now transferred to Pontoise, and afterwards to Soissons. Civil affairs were totally neglected, and the magistrates were daily occupied in devising measures of vengeance against the inexorable Archbishop and his clergy. Dissensions of the same kind were raging, it must be remembered, in several of the provincial Parliaments, especially those of Rouen, Rennes, Aix, and Toulouse.

It was not long, however, before Louis and his advisers felt

---

[*] Barbier, *Journal,* tom. iii. p. 467.

it desirable to set on foot a negotiation with the malcontents; and this measure for a short time promised to issue in the happiest results. On the 1st of September, 1754, the Parliament, in virtue of an arrangement made with the first president Maupeou, was recalled to Paris; on which occasion a royal Declaration was issued, imposing silence impartially upon all classes of his Majesty's subjects as to the ecclesiastical disputes which had so long troubled the peace of the realm; and enjoining the Parliament to repress and punish any attempt to reopen such matters of dissension, or to contravene the intention of the present edict, from whatever quarter it might proceed. All previous prosecutions and penal measures were rescinded.* After some opposition the Declaration was registered in Parliament, with an additional clause to the effect that the law of silence was to be construed as prohibiting innovation in the public administration of the Sacraments. "By this registration," says Barbier, "the authorities of the Palais and the public, who have so long been sufferers (through the suspension of the course of justice), have substantially gained their cause."† By way of satisfaction to the clergy, Machault was transferred at the same time from the ministry of finance to that of the marine,—a step which was understood to imply the abandonment of his project for equalizing the distribution of the public burdens. Machault's successor as finance-minister was Moreau de Sechelles, a confidential friend of D'Argenson. Bouettin, curé of St. Étienne, who had been driven from his parish by an outburst of popular indignation, was now recompensed for his fiery zeal by promotion to an abbey. Cardinal de la Rochefoucauld undertook to mediate with his colleagues in the episcopate, and persuade them to yield the point of the "billets de confession," on the understanding that nothing more would be heard of the imposition of the "vingtième." The birth of the Duc de Berri, afterwards Louis XVI. (August 23, 1754), was hailed as a happy opportunity of banishing unpleasant recollections on all sides.

This, however, was but an empty semblance of pacification. The royal command was unscrupulously broken by the Jansenists,

---

* Isambert, *Anc. Lois Françaises*, tom. xxii. p. 260.
† Barbier, *Journal*, tom. iv. p. 39.

who "published several large volumes to prove the necessity of keeping silence;"* while, on the other hand, the Parliament was scarcely re-established at Paris before the refusal of Sacraments by the clergy commenced afresh. The Archbishop, being appealed to, declared that his sentiments were unchanged, and that he could only repeat the reply which he had made in 1752; the clergy had acted according to the dictates of their conscience, and in obedience to the express orders of their diocesan. This having been reported to the king, his Majesty sent the Duc de Richelieu to expostulate with the Archbishop. The latter pleaded that his conscience forbade him to agree to any compromise. "Your conscience, Monseigneur," the Duke retorted, "is a dark lantern, which enlightens no one but yourself."† Louis, provoked, signed a *lettre de cachet* exiling the prelate to his mansion at Conflans. The Bishop of Orleans, Montmorency-Laval, was punished in the same way; and the court having offered to translate him to the more manageable diocese of Besançon, he replied that he should be setting himself in opposition to the will of God if he were to seek repose in a peaceful diocese, while his duty called him to endure conflict and persecution at Orleans. The Parliament, on an "appel comme d'abus" against this prelate and his Chapter, inveighed eloquently against those who sought to enforce the Unigenitus as a rule of faith, and in the same breath insisted on the observance of the absolute silence prescribed by the recent declaration. The Archbishop of Aix, and the Bishops of Troyes, St. Pons, Montpellier, Vannes, and Nantes, experienced a like rigorous treatment from the local Parliaments. The magistracy throughout the kingdom were proudly conscious of the advantage they had gained in the late struggle with the Crown, and resolved to pursue it to its utmost lengths. In May, 1755, the Paris Parliament took upon itself to denounce certain theses argued at the Sorbonne, the subjects of which were declared to fall within the late prohibition. The court summoned the Syndic, reprimanded him, warned him to be more strict in examining theses for the future, and ordered the *arrêt* to be entered on the registers of the Faculty, and read publicly. An assembly of one hundred and

---

* Picot, *Mémoires*, tom. ii. p. 281.
† Soulavie, *Mém. du Duc de Richelieu*, tom. viii. p. 307.

fifty Doctors of theology refused to obey; upon which the Parliament commanded the attendance of all the superior officers and professors of the Sorbonne, and compelled them to register the *arrêt* on the spot without further demur. The Faculty was also forbidden to meet for deliberation until it should receive permission.

The General Assembly of the clergy held in the same year (June, 1755) testified with sufficient emphasis its dissatisfaction with these and other like enterprises of the judicial bodies. Their first step was to appeal to the king for the recall of Archbishop de Beaumont. They proceeded to remonstrate in strong terms against the growing spirit of encroachment shown by the secular courts in the domain of things spiritual. They besought the king to explain his Declaration of 1752 in conformity with that of 1730; to annul the Parliamentary *arrêts* against the Unigenitus; to restore to the bishops that freedom of action which was essential to their ministry, and to support the theological schools in the department of public instruction which belonged to them; to repress all attempts on the part of lay magistrates to exercise jurisdiction in the matter of the Sacraments, and to reverse all sentences passed against ecclesiastics by incompetent judges during the late troubles. But when the Assembly approached the delicate topic of the precise authority to be assigned to the Constitution, and the method of procedure to be followed in enforcing it, considerable difference of opinion was manifested. At the head of the more moderate section was Cardinal de la Rochefoucauld, Archbishop of Bourges and President of the Assembly; a prelate of high character and conciliatory temper, who had just been appointed to the administration of the *feuille des bénéfices* upon the death of Bishop Boyer. Those who adhered to him were in consequence styled "feuillans," since it was presumed that they were influenced by the prospect of professional advancement; while the advocates of a bold unyielding policy were called "théatins," from their sympathy with the impetuous Boyer, who belonged to the religious community so called.* The votes were pretty equally divided. The articles proposed by the "feuillans" were supported

---

* The Théatins were a society of regular priests, founded in 1524 by Giovanni Caraffa, afterwards Pope Paul IV., who was Bishop of Theate, or Chieti, in Apulia.

by seventeen bishops and twenty-two deputies of the second order; the dissentients numbered sixteen bishops and ten of the inferior rank. Under these circumstances it was agreed to transmit the articles to the Pope (Benedict XIV.), to request his advice, and to abide by his decision. This was done accordingly;* and the Assembly, after an unusually prolonged session, separated on the 4th of November, having previously addressed a circular letter to the bishops giving an account of their proceedings. The Abbé Chauvelin, one of the conseillers-clercs, a vehement partisan of the Appellants, denounced this document to the Parliament, but without result.

Archbishop de Beaumont, without waiting for the desired response from Rome, broke silence in a most indiscreet and extravagant mandement published *vivâ voce* from the pulpit of the parish church of Conflans in September, 1756. He enunciated, in a lofty magisterial tone, the principles of the Mediæval Church as to the absolute independence of the Spiritual Power, its paramount authority in expounding the faith, administering the Sacraments, and enforcing discipline; he exposed the fallacies by which the Parliamentary courts were accustomed to justify their intrusive action in matters clearly extraneous to their province; he repelled the imputation of fostering schism; he enlarged on the obligation of maintaining the Constitution as an organic law of Church and State. The prelate concluded by prohibiting all secular judges, under pain of excommunication incurred *ipso facto*, from taking proceedings in matters relating to the Sacraments, and the clergy from recognising any sentences pronounced by such usurped authority. He also forbade the faithful of his diocese to read publications tending to subvert the authority of the Church; and specified under that designation nine recent *arrêts* or extracts from the registers of Parliament.† The sovereign courts were at this moment in vacation; but the Châtelet instantly denounced the mandement as an illegal abuse of ecclesiastical power, and ordered it to be burnt by the public executioner, which was done forthwith.‡ Several

---

* The letter of the Assembly to Pope Benedict is given in the *Procès-verbaux des Assembl. du Clergé*, tom. viii. " Pièces Justif." No. v. p. 191.

† A full analysis of the Archbishop's mandement is given in the *Nouvelles Ecclésiastiques*, 10 novembre, 1756, pp. 186 *et seqq.*

‡ Barbier, *Journal*, tom. iv. p. 161.

bishops declared their cordial adhesion to the manifesto of their intrepid colleague.

Pope Benedict replied to the Gallican clergy by the brief or encyclical letter "Ex omnibus," dated October 16, 1756. This Pontiff (Prosper Lambertini) was among the most distinguished who have sat on the throne of St. Peter. To extensive learning and unaffected piety he united a singularly calm, luminous, discriminating judgment, a spirit of fairness and freedom from prejudice, and an enlightened zeal for the true interests of Catholicism. He had long deplored the intestine broils which distracted the Church in France, and had made various efforts to mitigate and repress the violence of parties. The object of his encyclic was to administer a rebuke to the bishops who were exasperating their flocks by acts of misguided and indefensible rigour, while at the same time he supported them in point of principle and essential doctrine. "Such is the authority of the Constitution Unigenitus," said Benedict, "that no faithful Christian can refuse to submit to it, or oppose it in any way whatever, but at the risk of his eternal salvation. Whence it follows that the Viaticum ought to be denied to the stubbornly refractory, according to the general rule which excludes notorious and impenitent offenders from the holy Eucharist." But he proceeds to point out that this designation is not to be too hastily applied; and that in cases where heresy is *not* notorious, but matter of suspicion, presumption, idle rumour, or private enmity, a wise indulgence may be exercised. He recommends, therefore, that the Sacraments, when demanded by sick persons, should be administered, but that warning should be given previously, that if received in a state of wilful disobedience to the laws and authority of the Church, they will not be profitable, but rather the means of heavier condemnation.*

This judicious project of reconciliation was not cordially accepted on either side. The Parliament suppressed the Papal

---

* The Duc de Choiseul, then ambassador at Rome, obtained at the same time from Pope Benedict a private letter to Archbishop de Beaumont, exhorting him to moderation and forbearance in the affair of the *billets de confession*. Choiseul dexterously managed this in the absence and without the consent of the Pope's minister, Cardinal Valenti. The latter, on being told of the step taken by his Holiness, exclaimed, "Alas! he has been writing heresy!"—Bezenval, *Mémoires*, p. 109 (Barrière's Collection).

brief as printed without permission. The king held a bed of justice on the 13th of December, and once more enjoined that the bull Unigenitus should be observed with profound respect and submission, though at the same time he declined to attribute to it the name, character, or effects of a rule of faith. All complaints relating to the refusal of the Sacraments were to be referred to the ecclesiastical judges; the civil courts were forbidden to order the Sacraments to be administered, though they were authorised to prosecute ecclesiastics who might withhold them from persons not notoriously refractory in their opposition to the Constitution. The law of silence was re-enacted, with an exemption in favour of the bishops, who might say what they pleased for the edification of the faithful, provided all were done in charity. The King announced on this occasion an important change in the organisation and functions of the Parliament. The cognizance of appeals was assigned exclusively to the Grand'-Chambre; the other courts could not assemble henceforth without the assent and order of the Grand'-Chambre; suspension of the course of justice was absolutely prohibited; two Chambers were entirely suppressed, including upwards of sixty judicial officers of various grades. The next day the great majority of the magistrates sent in their resignations, and the business of the courts was again brought to a standstill. No more than ten presidents and nineteen councillors retained their functions. General indignation followed these tyrannical proceedings of the Crown. Barbier concludes his Journal for the year 1756 by recording that "fanaticism reigned generally in Paris against the sovereign authority."*

The crime of the half-crazy assassin Damiens followed shortly afterwards (January 5, 1757), and was interpreted in contradictory senses, for which the amount of proof, or absence of proof, was about equal. Damiens had formerly been in service at one of the Jesuit colleges, and hence the blow was attributed by many to the instigation of that unscrupulous fraternity; on the other hand, he had been employed by more than one councillor of the Parliament, and this was used to colour the opposite insinuation that the stroke of vengeance came from the disaffected Jansenists. The criminal had undoubtedly been

---

* Barbier, *Journal*, tom. iv. p. 168.

in the habit of attending the Parliamentary debates, and had thus become accustomed to tirades against the injustice of the Sovereign, and his indifference to the demands of his subjects. He confessed, at one of his interrogatories, that if he had never set foot in the Palais de Justice, he should never have fallen into trouble; that hearing so much about the refusal of the Sacraments had turned his brain; that he did not intend to kill the King, but only to give him an admonition (*avertissement*) to pay more heed to the representations of the magistrates, and to punish the Archbishop, whose misconduct was the cause of all the mischief. He was evidently a weak-minded fanatic, without accomplices; and all attempts to fix the crime upon any particular school or party, political or religious, were fruitless.

The personal danger, however, to which Louis had been exposed, led to a temporary reaction of feeling in his favour. Much loyal attachment was displayed; the Parliament, notwithstanding the late irritating attack on their constitution and privileges, eagerly offered to resume their duties in order to root out the supposed conspiracy and restore public confidence. The King, upon his recovery, took advantage of the opportunity to propose conditions of peace. The Abbé de Bernis, a creature of Madame de Pompadour, who was now rising into power, was the principal negotiator. Under his adroit diplomacy the banished magistrates were recalled; and the King issued a decree interpretative of his Declaration of 1756, by which it was in fact withdrawn. The exiled prelates shared the benefit of this act of grace. On the 1st of October, 1757, Archbishop de Beaumont received the King's commands to return to Paris; the next day he had an audience of his Majesty at Versailles; on the 9th he officiated at Notre Dame. The Archbishop of Aix, and the Bishops of Orleans, Troyes, and Montpellier, were in like manner recalled to their dioceses. But early in the following year De Beaumont incurred afresh the displeasure of the Court. Some time previously he had been involved in a dispute with the nuns "Hospitalières" of the Faubourg S. Marceau, who had appealed to the Parliament, and elected a Superior in defiance of his orders. He punished them by laying an interdict upon their house; and as they refused to make the submission which he required, he declined to grant them absolution, though entreated to show mercy by the King himself.* He was now exiled a second time by *lettre de cachet*; and on this occasion his destination was a distant château belonging to his family, near Sarlat in the Périgord. There he remained for a year and ten months; the diocese being administered in his absence by four Vicars-general. In October, 1759, Louis once more relented in his favour, and he was reinstated in his post at Paris.

The Duke of Richelieu relates that at the time of the last-mentioned accommodation between the Parliament and the Court, great animosity was manifested by some of the most distinguished magistrates against the Order of Jesuits; and that they even made it a condition of their concurrence that that Society should be suppressed and extinguished. Those whose influence now predominated in the government—Madame de Pompadour, the Abbé de Bernis, the Comte de Stainville,† the President de Meynières, and others—became convinced that the Jesuits had been throughout the chief instigators of the late embroilments; and arrived in consequence at a tacit understanding that their existence as a corporate body was incompatible with the safety of the State. ‡

The General Assembly of 1755, in addition to its energetic remonstrances against the project of abolishing the financial immunities of the clergy, memorialized the Throne upon a subject of infinitely deeper importance, namely, the startling progress of the "new philosophy," as the doctrines of the freethinking school were designated. The topic had already been touched upon in the session of 1750, when De Montazet, Bishop of Autun, made a remarkable speech, in which he traced the origin of this insidious form of irreligion, exposed its fallacies, and uttered a note of solemn warning as to its tendencies and possible results. The same eloquent prelate, speaking in 1755 upon the dissensions between the Church and the civil authorities, said, "We cannot hide from ourselves that through the conflict between two powers which were designed to act in

---

* The interdict on the "Hospitalières" was removed in 1758 on appeal to the Archbishop of Lyons, in his character of "Primate of the Gauls." It is said that De Montazet, Bishop of Autun, was raised to the primacy on the distinct understanding that this was to be one of his first official acts.—Barbier, *Journal*, tom. iv. p. 262.

† Afterwards Duc de Choiseul and Prime Minister.

‡ Soulavie, *Mém. du Duc de Richelieu*, tom. viii. pp. 401, 402.

concert, and not to destroy each other, incredulity triumphs, error gains credit, and insubordination grows rampant; indifference is propagated, zeal loses heart, and even piety itself quails and stumbles. And is it not by such outbreaks that Heaven, in its wrath against the sins of a nation, prepares men sometimes for the infliction of that most terrible of its judgments, the total extinction of the Faith?"* The memorial drawn up by the Assembly† treats in detail of the systematic attacks which were now made on all sides against the time-honoured traditions both of religious faith and political subordination. "That thick smoke which ascends from the bottomless pit, and darkens the sun and the air,‡ seems to have spread itself, Sire, over the face of your kingdom. License, both of thought and writing, is carried to the utmost pitch of extravagance. A system of morals, of which the heathen world would have been ashamed, confounds the distinctions between vice and virtue. Self-styled philosophers, who glory in despising ordinary ideas and established rules of decency, do not hesitate to sully their pages with the most licentious images and expressions. Men speculate, with an amount of hardihood unparalleled under the French Monarchy, upon the origin of sovereign power, and the mode in which it should be exercised. That wholesome doctrine which sees in royalty the ineffaceable impress of the Divine Majesty, is altogether ignored. Vain and delusive attempts are rife to discover a primitive contract between the subjects who obey and the princes who command; and the use made of this chimerical engagement is to weaken the ties which ought to bind them together. Such is the inevitable course of the spirit of independence and revolt. It begins by casting off the yoke of that authority which reigns over the conscience; but as soon as this first step is taken, no other barriers remain which can arrest its progress. Men, disgusted with the notion of submission, and attracted by the flattering bait of liberty, accustom themselves to regard all power of government either as a deposit which they have the right to resume, or as an usurpation against which they may lawfully rebel. Proud imaginations are ex-

---

* *Procès-verbaux des Assemblées du Clergé*, tom. viii. 1ᵉʳ partie, p. 609.

† "Mémoire au Roi, concernant les libelles qui se répandent contre la religion."—*Procès-verbaux des Assembl. du Clergé de F.*, tom. viii. 1ᵉʳ partie, "Pièces Justificatives," No. vi.

‡ Revelation ix. 2.

alting themselves on every side against the knowledge of God. The mysteries which He has revealed, the laws which He has prescribed, His promises, His threatenings, all are contested, all become the prey of the rash and malignant criticism of our *esprits-forts*. They reject as incredible all dogmas which transcend their feeble reason. They contradict the best-attested facts and the most authentic records. They even extend this senseless spirit of pyrrhonism to truths cognisable by the light of reason. They deny the providence of God; they confound man with the brute; and in order to rid themselves of the stings of remorse, they pretend to confine their hopes and fears, and their whole being, to this transient and perishing life." The memorial proceeds to entreat his Majesty to take measures for repressing these fearful evils, by a strict application of the laws regulating the press, and by excluding from France publications of a suspicious character printed abroad.

The sceptical mania which had invaded the French mind during the last fifty years might well awaken sinister forebodings, not only among those who by their position as rulers of the Church were directly bound to uphold the Divine authority of Christianity, but among men of whatever class or calling who had any value for the one foundation of faith and morals, and for the immemorial institutions which were identified with their country's prosperity and glory. What was the real origin of this portentous phenomenon? Writers of the highest intelligence, of various shades of opinion both in religion and politics, pronounce it to have been the offspring of the Reformation; the natural fruit of the great moral insurrection which in the sixteenth century annihilated the supremacy of Rome. But this can hardly be accepted as a complete solution of the problem. Freedom of thought was, beyond all question, the characteristic watchword of the Renaissance; but there is reason to believe that the seeds of religious doubt were sown at a remoter date, and may be traced to the restlessness of speculation and dialectical combativeness which marked the reign of Scholasticism.

The elements of scepticism may be detected in the "Sic et non" of Abelard, and other productions of the Nominalist philosophy. Yet it cannot be denied that the tone of feeling and the course of events consequent upon the Reformation were such as fatally to impair the supremacy of the dogmatic principle. This resulted, not so much from any direct attempts to overthrow that principle, as from the collision, the antagonism, between opposite ideas or systems of authority. For the Reformers had their theory of authority, widely as it differed from that of preceding ages. Luther and Calvin, Knox and Bucer, Claude and Jurieu, were not less addicted to dogmatism than was the Sorbonne, the Inquisition, or the Pope. They proclaimed, indeed, the right of free examination and private judgment; but at the same time they set up standards of truth from which it was sin to depart; they promulgated laws, Confessions of faith, rules of discipline, which were enforced upon the conscience as of absolute obligation. They denounced intolerance, yet found it necessary, in their turn, to be intolerant of the errors from which they had separated, and to repress them with the utmost energy of moral, not to say of physical, force. Again, they appealed to Holy Scripture as the paramount criterion of truth; yet withal they assigned to the somewhat vaguely-defined quality of "faith" an interpretative supremacy over the written Word. On the one hand subjective faith was made the "verifying faculty" of the doctrines revealed in Scripture, while on the other, Scripture was maintained to be the sole test of the Divine origin of the truths which faith had embraced. On one side was the infallible self-certitude of personal assurance, on the other the equally infallible outward testimony of the Bible; and both were put forward conjointly in opposition to the traditional authority of the "Ecclesia docens."

All this tended towards religious chaos. Men repudiated their former teachers as blind and fallacious; but those who supplanted them failed to provide a consistent and harmonious system to replace what had been abandoned. To destroy had been comparatively easy; but to reconstruct, upon any principles of permanent cohesion and stability, was found an insurmountable difficulty. One innovation propagated another, and division multiplied indefinitely. The unchained intellect scorned all restraint on its passion for free investigation and universal criticism. Protestant Christendom was overrun by a motley host of discordant sects, each vaunting its distinctive Shibboleth, each hedged round by its individual exegesis of the Sacred Text, each self-complacently secure in the unerring intuition of its favourite apostle.

We know historically that the spectacle of these hopeless dissensions in the bosom of the Reformed communion perplexed and distressed beyond measure some of the ablest thinkers and writers of the seventeenth century. Two of them may be quoted by name, Isaac Casaubon and Hugh Grotius. In their case the scenes which they witnessed served only to inspire them with profound distrust of theological novelties, and to cause them to retrograde considerably in the direction of Rome. Others went further; they abandoned a society which seemed threatened with speedy disintegration, and sought a refuge from their anxieties in the arms of the ancient Church. But in regard to a *third* class of minds the effect produced was still more to be lamented, both for their own sakes and for the general interests of Christianity. Of these last Bayle may be cited as a fair example; a man of singularly acute critical powers, a subtle reasoner, and a giant in learning. Bayle, after manifold oscillations—after fluctuating uneasily first from Calvinism to Catholicism, then from Catholicism back to Calvinism—came to the conclusion that neither the one system nor the other met the requirements of the true philosopher. Nor did the theory propounded by Descartes bring him at all nearer to the wished-for goal of certitude. One resource failed after another; he saw that every creed, every system of metaphysics, every type of Christian communion, had its good points and advantages, but that somewhere or other they were all fallacious. He found himself wandering, in consequence, in a general haze of sceptical indifferentism.

Bayle was the real parent of French infidelity. He furnished the armoury of weapons by which his successors, pursuing at headlong speed the track which he had indicated, were enabled to carry dismay and havoc into the very heart of the Christian citadel.

While the memorable struggle between Rome and her rebellious children thus issued, in certain quarters, in the repudiation not only of Church authority but even of the principle of faith in supernatural truth, the National Establishment in France remained still in possession of its constitutional jurisdiction over the entire realm. Church and State were coextensive.

The laws of the Church were laws likewise of the State; and the latter, with much logical consistency, though with grievous want of wisdom, was in the habit of employing the secular arm to enforce obedience to the existing system. The shape in which religion presented itself to Voltaire and his confederates was that of a lordly arrogant hierarchy, exclusively recognised by the State, invested with vast temporal ascendancy, rolling in riches, and by no means remarkable for self-denying devotedness to the duties of the pastoral care. It was an odious compound, in their eyes, of superstition, despotism, and hypocrisy. But what they resented most of all was the attempt to compel conformity to the dominant creed by violence and judicial inflictions; the cruelties practised against the Huguenots—the prosecutions for heresy—the imprisonments and banishments, the fines and deprivations, so mercilessly accumulated on the opponents of the bull Unigenitus. Hence the earliest form of their hostility to Christianity was that of a battle with *intolerance;* a determined protest against the abuses of Church administration. They attacked religion through the inconsistencies, the vices, the misgovernment, of its ministers. "They uplifted their voice," says one of their apologists, "against all the crimes of fanaticism and tyranny; withstanding in religion, in political government, in morals, in legislation, whatever bore the character of oppression, of harshness, of barbarism. Their war-cry was reason, toleration, humanity." * Nor is it to be denied that by these energetic labours in the cause of civilization the school in question rendered important services to society. Could they have been content with applying themselves to the great task of administrative reformation—with vindicating the rights of conscience, and reprobating acts of persecution the chief effect of which was to exasperate men's minds and impel them to desperate extremes—they might have justly claimed a place, and a conspicuous place, among the benefactors of mankind. But they spoiled their cause by drawing false deductions from undeniable facts. Amid the passionate excitement which prevailed, they failed to distinguish between the practical abuses of the Church and its essential character as an institution. The paro-

---

* Condorcet, *Tableau historique du progrès de l'esprit humain,* ix⁰ époque.

chial clergy were intolerant, some of the bishops were immoral, bitter hatred reigned between conflicting sects, gross iniquities were perpetrated in the name and under the authority of religion; *therefore*, it was argued, Christianity is an imposture from beginning to end. The dogmatic teaching of the Church was impugned because it was believed to be the source, the root, the mainstay, of that corrupt system of political government which was daily becoming more and more insupportable to the nation; and henceforth the philosophers laboured, not only to inaugurate a new era with reference to personal liberty and equality of civil rights, but to subvert the fundamental basis of religious belief upon which the entire fabric of Christian society reposes.*

It does not appear that those who took up arms against revealed religion acted from the first upon any definitely concerted plan, although their purpose was one and the same. They were men of independent character, differing greatly as to mental idiosyncrasy, and as to their favourite types of theoretical opinion. Voltaire, their coryphæus, was a Deist; he acknowledged a First Cause, but had no belief in an objective Revelation, and held that man has no other law to guide him but that of nature and conscience. His object was to overturn Christianity as a theological system; to substitute a religion of sentiment, humanity, benevolence, for that of the Church Catholic, which rests on dogma and authority. Montesquieu, without denying the truth of Christianity, regarded it as a matter of indifference, both as to doctrine and practice. "The surest way to please God," he writes, "is to observe the rules of society and the duties of charity and humanity. As to ceremonies, they have no value in themselves; they are right only upon the presumption and to the extent that God has commanded them. But this is an extremely debateable question, on which it is easy to fall into error; for the difficulty is to choose the ceremonies of one religion out of some two thousand." † Con-

---

* "C'était bien moins comme doctrine religieuse que comme institution politique que le Christianisme avait allumé ces furieuses haines; non parcoque les prêtres prétendaient régler les choses de l'autre monde, mais parcequ'ils étaient propriétaires, seigneurs, décimateurs, administrateurs, dans celui-ci; non parceque l'église ne pouvait prendre place dans la société nouvelle qu'on allait fonder, mais parcequ'elle occupait alors la place la plus privilégiée et la plus forte dans cette vieille société qu'il s'agissait de réduire en poudre."—A. De Tocqueville, *L'ancien Régime et la Révolution*, liv. i. chap. ii. p. 23.

† Montesquieu, "Lettres Persanes," lett. xlvi. (*Œuvres*, tom. iv. p. 366).

dillac, again—who was an ecclesiastic, a relative of Cardinal de Tencin and of the Abbé de Mably—is considered as the chief exponent of the sensationalist or materialistic scheme; which became perhaps the most widely-accepted development of the philosophy of the eighteenth century. Condillac assembled round him a throng of enthusiastic disciples, of whom the most notable were the Marquis D'Argens, Baron Holbach, Helvetius, Lamettrie, and above all, D'Alembert and Diderot, the joint projectors of the 'Encyclopédie.' But a name commanding far more general interest than any yet mentioned is that of Jean Jacques Rousseau. Rousseau was neither a materialist, nor a profane scoffer, nor a supercilious sceptic. He professed respect for Christianity, and even for Catholicism; yet he did more to alienate the affections of his countrymen from the religion and the Church of their forefathers than any of the more pronounced freethinkers. His so-called "Spiritualism" was far more fascinating, though scarcely less anti-Christian, than blank infidelity or atheism. The articles of his creed were never clearly enunciated. It would seem that his leading idea was that of nominal adhesion to Christianity, interpreted with the most indulgent latitude, untrammelled by any precisely-defined dogmas, and regarded chiefly in a philanthropic point of view, as the system best calculated to promote the temporal well-being of mankind.*

To analyse the psychological peculiarities of these various seekers after truth, and the strange discoveries to which each was conducted in his chosen department of free thought, would be obviously beside the purpose of this work. But it is necessary to take some notice of the efforts made by the Church, with the co-operation of the executive government and the courts of justice, to check the torrent of their reckless speculations;—speculations which, as we now see too clearly, were directly preparing the way for the terrible cataclysm which was to close the century.

One of the earliest cases that occurred was the condemnation by the Sorbonne of a thesis by a Divinity student named De Prades,

---

* Rousseau states in one of his letters that his own views coincided with those set forth in the famous *Profession de foi du Vicaire Savoyard*, in the 'Emile' (Œuvres, tom. xviii. p. 80, edit. Paris, 1821). The creed of the imaginary Vicaire is (as might be expected) hazy, sentimental, and syncretistic.

who was known to be on confidential terms with the leaders of the new philosophy. This production was of considerable length, and marked by great ability. It was approved by the authorities at first; but afterwards, a report having spread that it was in great measure the composition of Diderot, it was re-examined more carefully, and meanwhile the author was suspended from proceeding to his degrees. One passage in particular was pronounced to deserve censure; it was to the effect that "the miraculous cures wrought by Jesus Christ, if regarded without reference to the prophecies, which gave them something of a Divine character, were but questionable miracles, since the cures performed by Æsculapius might present, in certain cases, the same phenomena." Other propositions were almost equally offensive; the abbé suggested that fire may perhaps constitute the essence of the human soul, and attacked the inequalities of social condition as contrary to sound reason. He was condemned by an immense majority of the Theological Faculty in January, 1752; and the sentence was confirmed by an order of the Parliament for his arrest. At the same moment Archbishop de Beaumont published a mandement against him in his usual vehement style, and interdicted him from his clerical functions. On this proceeding the avocat Barbier comments with much good sense and judgment. "The Archbishop," he says, "in censuring the propositions most injurious to religion, goes so far as to institute a comparison between the miracles of the god Æsculapius and those of Jesus Christ. Now assuredly Æsculapius never anticipated the honour of having his exploits analysed in the mandement of an Archbishop of Paris. The prelate complains of treatises, and even of volumes of great size, lately published; this is an allusion to the 'Dictionnaire encyclopédique.' He styles the Abbé de Prades a pupil of the materialistic philosophers; this is aimed against the sieur Diderot, &c. But whatever jealousy the Jesuits and others may betray in seeking to decry this Dictionary and stop its circulation, the Archbishop's mandement seems most unbecoming and ill-advised. In matters of such delicacy affecting religion it is not desirable to be so unreservedly outspoken. No doubt the thesis of the Abbé de Prades is rash and presumptuous; but it has been condemned by the Sorbonne, and its author likewise, and there the matter ought to rest. The circumstances were little known in Paris, except among certain classes. This 'Encyclopédie' is still a rare book, a dear book, full of abstract reasoning, not likely to be read except by intellectual scientific people, and their number is but small. What is the use of an Archbishop's mandement, which only excites curiosity among the faithful, and puts into their heads notions which may make them philosophical about religion, whereas the majority of such persons require nothing but their Catechism, having neither the time nor the ability to read anything else? This is imprudent. Meanwhile such is the animosity of the Jesuits (for it is they who have stirred up all this commotion *) that the mandement is eagerly cried about the streets; is sold cheap, so that even the petty shopkeepers buy it; and may thus be doing religion more harm than good." †

The Abbé de Prades, in order to escape imprisonment, fled from France, and sought an asylum at the court of Frederick II. at Berlin, where he was favourably received by that august patron of philosophical science, and was surrounded by the congenial society of Voltaire, D'Argens, Maupertuis, and others as deeply imbued with the liberal spirit of the age. But after a time he seems to have felt the incongruousness of his position, and returned to a more healthy frame of mind. In 1754 he published a formal retractation of his errors, and applied for absolution to Pope Benedict XIV. Subsequently he obtained preferment from the Bishop of Breslau, and died Archdeacon and Canon of Glogau in 1782.

The famous 'Encyclopédie' was all the more formidable as an attack upon the traditional system of belief and morals, inasmuch as it was the fruit of organised association, and concentrated all the energies of its authors upon one definite object. And although there can be no question that that object was revolutionary at once in the domain of religion, politics, and social order, it was not only pursued with extreme caution, but was veiled by an immense admixture of sound, enlightened, instructive teaching in various ramifications of human knowledge. By far the ablest contributor was D'Alembert; many of his compositions are efforts of a high order of genius, and his 'Discours préliminaire' is a

---

* Their hostility is said to have been occasioned by the refusal of the editors of the Encyclopédie to entrust them with the theological department of the work. D'Alembert, "Sur la destruction des Jésuites" (Œuvres, tom. v. p. 168).

† Barbier, Journal, tom. iii. p. 338.

masterpiece. He acknowledged without scruple that he was in the habit of practising reserve on points where candour might be indiscreet. Voltaire having objected to some of his articles, which he considered too favourable to religion, D'Alembert replied, " Doubtless we have some bad articles on theology and metaphysics; but with a theological censorship and an official privilege I defy you to make them better. There are other articles, less conspicuous, in which all errors are corrected. Time will demonstrate the distinction between what we have thought and what we have said." *

The government, however, was not blind to the real drift of the work. On the 7th of February, 1752, an order of the Council of State suppressed the first two volumes of the 'Encyclopédie' (all that had then appeared) designating them as "containing maxims subversive of the royal authority, fomenting the spirit of independence and revolt, and, under an obscure and equivocal phraseology, insinuating error, corrupt morality, irreligion, and infidelity." It was expected that the authors would be severely punished; Diderot, who had already been imprisoned at Vincennes for a satirical pamphlet against the Court, was threatened with a second visit to that fortress. But the conduct of the authorities in this matter was vacillating and capricious. Whenever the clergy, the Jesuits, and the Bishop of Mirepoix succeeded in making themselves heard, the Encyclopédistes were denounced as a band of desperate conspirators against the throne, the Altar, and the nation; but other influences prevailed in their turn; Louis XV. yielded to the all-powerful intercession of Madame de Pompadour, who rejoiced in every opportunity of mortifying the Jesuits; and the *philosophes* were again visited by the sunshine of royal favour. The third volume of the 'Encyclopédie' appeared in November, 1753, with a preface, in which the editors did not attempt to conceal their feelings of exultation.†

In January, 1759, on the publication of the seventh volume, the Parliament interfered; appointed a committee to examine the work, and ordered the four booksellers who had jointly taken

---

* D'Alembert to Voltaire, 21 juillet 1757 (*Œuvres de Voltaire*, tom. xli. p. 43 edit. Paris, 1818).
† *Œuvres de D'Alembert*, tom. i. p. 353 (Paris, 1805).

charge of it to suspend the sale until further instructions. Three doctors of theology, three advocates at the bar, and three professors of philosophy, were selected to conduct the scrutiny. But before their task was finished, an *arrêt* of the Council of State revoked the privilege which had been granted in 1746 for printing the work, suppressed the seven published volumes, and forbade the authors to continue it. "The writers of this Dictionary," it was stated, "had abused the indulgence shown them on a former occasion; and in the five additional volumes since circulated had given equal ground for scandal. Whatever advantage the public might derive from the work in connexion with the arts and sciences was infinitely outweighed by the evil which it had caused already, and might cause hereafter, with respect to morals and religion."* Pope Clement XIII., by a brief in September, 1759, approved this measure of the government; but so great was the influence which the Encyclopédistes and their friends had now acquired, that they succeeded in effecting a secret understanding with the Court, in virtue of which the late ordonnance became practically inoperative. The publication was resumed clandestinely, with the connivance of the authorities, who, since the work was no longer issued under the sanction of the censors of the press, conceived themselves free from further responsibility as to the result. The Chancellor Lamoignon defended this arrangement on the ground that it was required by the interests of commerce; since the foreign press would otherwise be needlessly benefited at the expense of France. It was impossible, he argued, to prevent the impression of such works; and, this being the case, it was better for the home trade that they should be printed within the realm than abroad.

---

* Barbier, *Journal*, tom. iv. p. 310. On this occasion D'Alembert complained bitterly to Lamoignon de Malesherbes, "directeur-général de la librairie," of the adverse criticisms which his work had provoked. The minister pointed out, in reply, that it was impossible to defend religion without noticing the published sentiments of those who attack it; and that it was no abuse of liberty to tax an author with irreligion, so long as the criticism is confined to works voluntarily submitted to the public. Within such limits, he was of opinion that a censor of the press could not interfere without the risk of making himself an accomplice in suppressing the truth. The philosophers, it thus appears, did not scruple to oppose the liberty of the press when the operation of that principle chanced to be inconvenient to themselves. See De Tocqueville's *Hist. philosoph. du règne de Louis XV.*, tom. ii. p. 88.

Some advantage, however, was secured. D'Alembert retired from the editorship, which devolved wholly upon Diderot. After this the work visibly deteriorated in genius and talent, at the same time that it became more avowedly and offensively irreligious. Voltaire complained loudly of these extravagances. Diderot himself was forced to confess that the later volumes were a heterogeneous jumble of things good and bad, true and false, crude and well-digested, vague, incoherent, and inconsistent. This huge compilation was at length completed in 1765; and in the same year it was condemned by the General Assembly of the clergy, in an elaborate document entitled 'Actes sur la Religion.'

The 'Émile' of Rousseau—the most popular, the most seductive, the most sophistical, of his works, in which he developes a system of education based solely on the laws of nature, and disallows the authority of any restraint except that which the young mind may voluntarily impose upon itself—appeared in 1762, and seriously alarmed the friends of religion. Lamoignon, who directed the censorship, was on terms of intimacy with the author, and sanctioned the publication for that reason; but the Sorbonne examined it minutely, and pointed out its errors in detail, classing them under various heads. Fifty-seven passages were specified for censure, relating to (1) God and the law of nature; (2) the necessity of Revelation; (3) the features of Revelation; (4) the means of acquiring the knowledge of Revelation; (5) miracles and prophecy; (6) revealed dogma; (7) intolerance, as imputed to the Catholic Church.

The Archbishop of Paris likewise attacked the 'Émile' in a vigorous *mandement*, but proved himself unable to contend on equal terms with the genius of Rousseau. The philosopher, in his reply, justified himself with all his characteristic ingenuity, mingled with professions of sincere respect for the prelate.*
An order of the Parliament was now signed for his arrest, and Rousseau evaded its execution by a precipitate flight to Switzerland.

"The Church," says Lord Macaulay, "made no defence except by acts of power. Censures were pronounced; books

---

* Rousseau, *Œuvres*, tom. x. pp. 1-118 (edit. Paris, 1821.)

were seized; but no Bossuet, no Pascal, came forth to encounter Voltaire. There appeared not a single defence of the Catholic doctrine which produced any considerable effect, or which is now even remembered."* This was indeed the case; but it is to be considered that the particular mode of aggression adopted by the philosophers was one that it was scarcely possible to repel. What could the Church do, systematically and effectually, against sarcasm and ridicule, against scurrility and buffoonery, against virulent malice and shameless misrepresentation? These are weapons scarcely to be met and overcome by sober argument, solid learning, and appeals to unimpassioned reason. Wit, *persiflage*, biting criticism, could not fail to carry the day against the denunciations and dry controversial dissertations of the Sorbonne, in the opinion of the great mass of a nation, and more especially of the French nation. And, again, the apologists for Christianity (there were many such, though their qualifications were not of the first order) wrote at this great disadvantage; they knew that religion was identified in France with an administrative system so corrupt that it was useless to defend it—that it was irrevocably condemned in the public mind. This consciousness discouraged them, and crippled their exertions. Such were the complicated difficulties of the crisis, that every position which might have proved a vantage-ground against the inroads of infidelity was practically unavailable. How was the Church to act with concentrated energy against those who assailed it from without, while its own children were tearing it in pieces by intestine feuds? While the Jesuits were moving heaven and earth to exterminate all opposition to the Bull Unigenitus—while Jansenists and Parliaments were caballing in concert against a tyrannical inquisition which tortured the consciences of the sick and dying, and inflicted penalties upon heretics, even after death, of which Rome herself would have been ashamed—what encouragement was there to undertake the humbler task of building up the external fortifications of religion? These scandalous dissensions had heaped such contempt on Christianity, that any attempt to rehabilitate it by argumentative demonstrations of its credibility was almost hope-

---

* Macaulay's 'Critical Essays,' vol. iii. p. 140 (8th edition, 1854).

less. The great facts of Revelation, the Divine constitution and authority of the Church Catholic, remained intrinsically clear and unassailable as ever; but they were obscured for the time by the glaring anomalies and contradictions which daily passed before men's eyes. Hence, while the enemy was pouring in like a flood, the efforts to stem the torrent were few, isolated, and defective in method and skill of organization.

It must not be supposed, however, that no steps were taken in this direction. The false philosophy of the day *was* confronted, and that strenuously and ably, by men whose names are well worthy to be had in remembrance. Among them must be cited Cardinal de Luynes, Archbishop Montazet of Lyons, Lefranc de Pompignan (Archbishop of Vienne), and Fitz-James (Bishop of Soissons). The veteran Duguet, too, at the close of a long, laborious, and troubled career, came to the rescue with his 'Traité des Principes de la Foi Chrétienne,' a work of sterling value. Nicolas Sylvestre Bergier, Canon of Notre Dame and confessor to the daughters of Louis XV., a writer of great fertility and of no mean controversial power, attacked the 'Émile' of Rousseau in his 'Déisme réfuté par lui-même,' Voltaire in his 'Apologie de la Religion,' Holbach in his 'Examen du Matérialisme,' and the anti-Christian school in general in his 'Dictionnaire Théologique.' But the most formidable antagonist of the prevailing unbelief was Antoine Guénée, a canon of Amiens, who published, in 1769, his 'Lettres de quelques Juifs Portugais, Allemands et Polonais, à M. de Voltaire.' Adopting a style of refined but trenchant raillery, Guénée turned the batteries of the philosopher of Ferney against himself. He pursues him through the entire course of his criticisms on the history of the Old Testament, and on the moral and ceremonial law of the Jewish nation, and convicts him, in language the most polished and deferential, of gross falsification of facts, of unpardonable ignorance, of numberless mistakes, and of damaging self-contradictions. He flatters him, at the same time, with the grateful incense of either real or affected adoration; and warmly applauds his benevolence, his labours in the cause of toleration, and his resistance to some of the vile abuses of the existing political system. This brochure greatly irritated Voltaire, who acknowledged that Guénée was an opponent of no ordinary calibre. "The Jewish secretary," he wrote to D'Alembert, "Guénée by name, is by no means deficient either in ability or learning; but he is as malicious as a monkey. He bites you to the bone while he pretends to be only licking your hand."* The 'Lettres de quelques Juifs' made a considerable sensation, have been several times reprinted, and still maintain their reputation.

But these and similar efforts availed not to repress or retard the irresistible march of events. The mind of the French people was by this time far gone towards a definitive rupture with antiquity, and was clamouring for change, novelty, reform, independence, upon any conditions and at all hazards. The light of Christianity was doomed for a season to wane in melancholy eclipse, and to give place to the pitiful shallowness, the wild extravagance, the deep moral corruption, the insupportable tyranny, of an Infidel Philosophy. The result to which things were tending was early foreseen by thoughtful observers. The Duc de Richelieu relates a conversation between himself and the naturalist Buffon, some passages of which are remarkable. The Duke, alluding to Buffon's work the 'Époques de la Nature,' said that *other* revolutions, besides those he had described as having agitated the physical system, seemed to be impending over the world. "Our ancient institutions are decaying day by day. This Sorbonne, which is tormenting you just now, and the priests, are not alarmed for nothing." "Consider," replied Buffon, "what is the strongest part, and what the weakest, of our constitutional system; look which is the most esteemed and which the most depreciated. You are young enough to live to see that the feebler and less valued institutions will gradually fall to pieces; after which the stronger will be better able to resist the attacks of time. The Episcopate and the Priesthood will be the first bodies sacrificed in France. They have no other support but public opinion, and this is no longer in their favour, nor will it permit a war of religion to be waged in case of resistance. I see the time coming," he continued, "when our prelates will have to content themselves with a stipend of twelve thousand livres a head, which indeed is paying dear enough for the services which they render to the State and Religion. But just as, after the reign of Chaos, the elements disengaged themselves and were arranged in harmonious order;

---

* Voltaire to D'Alembert, 8 décembre 1776 (*Œuvres*, tom. xli. p. 629).

as, in a burning fever, the body throws off from itself the secretions which interfere with its healthy action; even so the body politic, or rather those laws of nature which govern all bodies politic, will apply to its diseases the remedies proper for their cure; and those effectual remedies are repose and time."

Richelieu observes in a subsequent passage of his Memoirs, that the philosophers were wont to reproach the clergy with being actuated solely by the love of power, worldly honours, and worldly wealth. "When once the more intelligent part of the French people became persuaded of this truth, they showed an utter indifference to the interests of their pastors, and to all theological opinions. Religious ceremonial and religious books fell into discredit. The most trifling pamphlet directed against the offices and ministry of the Church was devoured with avidity. The Hierarchy was identified with the Throne; and when these two objects, venerated for so many ages by the nation, ceased to command respect, then, by slow stages, our Revolution began its course. A Jesuit named Longueval had placed on the title-page of his 'History of the Gallican Church' these singular words of Scripture, "Vestra fides nostra victoria est." One of the philosophers wrote underneath, "Votre bêtise est notre force." No sooner did this opinion of the philosopher become that of the people, than the old Gothic edifice of Sacerdotalism toppled down."*

---

* Soulavie, *Mémoires du Duc de Richelieu*, tom. vii. pp. 348, 362. The Duke's acquaintance with Scripture, as well as with Father Longueval's 'Gallican History,' was probably slight. The passage here quoted is not to be found in the Bible, though something resembling it occurs in the 1st Epistle of St. John, v. 4. It is not likely that the learned Jesuit historian committed the same inaccuracy; and certainly no such motto appears on the title-page of his work as we now possess it. The anecdote, nevertheless, forcibly illustrates the tone of sentiment propagated by the philosophers, with so much industry and success, with respect to "sacerdotalism."

CHAPTER X.

AMONG the signs of the times which presaged the disruption of the ancient Constitution, political and religious, in France, there was none more pregnant with meaning than the suppression of the Order of Jesuits. That event was in itself a revolution.

Historians differ in the explanations they suggest of a phenomenon of such magnitude, which, ten years before it occurred, might have seemed to ordinary observers as improbable as any within the whole range of human conjecture. By the admirers and advocates of the Society, its downfall is pronounced to have been part and parcel of a long-meditated and deep-laid conspiracy against the Catholic Church and the very existence of Christianity. "The Jesuits," says M. Crétineau-Joly, "were calumniated and sacrificed for no other reason than because they were the advanced-guard and reserved force of the Church. No design hostile to the Holy See, and consequently to religion, could succeed so long as the Jesuits were at hand to disconcert the schemes, and break through the mass of prejudice and hatred, which were constantly accumulating against them. The Jesuits were immoveable in their faith. They repulsed the slightest idea of opposition directed against the Spiritual Authority. They were attacked and condemned, because they refused to lend themselves to intrigues which threatened the security at once of the Holy See and of secular thrones."* Professor Ranke leans towards a similar view. "In every country," he says, "and at all the Courts, two parties were found; one making war on the Curia, on the accredited constitution and established doctrines of the time, while the other laboured to maintain things as they were, and to uphold the prerogatives of the Universal Church. The latter was more

---

* Crétineau-Joly, *Hist. de la Comp. de Jésus*, tom. v. p. 220. This is strongly corroborated by the Abbé Georgel, an ex-Jesuit, *Mémoires*, tom. i.

particularly represented by the Jesuits; that Order stood forth as the chief bulwark of Ultramontane principles, and it was against them that the storm was first directed."*

It has been contended on the other hand, by writers no less distinguished for intelligence and diligence of research, that the fall of the Jesuits is not to be ascribed to any deliberate plot or organized confederation; that although circumstances pointing towards such a result may have been long in preparation, the proximate cause which produced it was unpremeditated and almost fortuitous. This conclusion is maintained by Count Alexis de St. Priest, who attributes the expulsion of the Society from France almost wholly to the example set by the Marquis of Pombal in Portugal.† The ostensible ground upon which that minister acted was the desperate attempt upon the life of the king, Joseph I., in which it was alleged that the Jesuits were implicated; but it would seem that this was scarcely more than a plausible pretext. Three Jesuit fathers were denounced as accomplices in the crime; and one of them, Malagrida, forfeited his life by sentence of the Inquisition for this among other offences, at the stake.

There can be no doubt that the tragedy at Lisbon contributed greatly to ignite the inflammable materials which for many years past had been gathering round the doomed institution of Loyola. Barbier informs us, under date February 14th, 1759, that the printed judgment of the Portuguese tribunal made a wonderful sensation at Paris. "An immense number of copies have been sold, and the affair is the sole topic of conversation. Nothing less is talked of than the banishment of the Jesuits from the realm of France. Those who are most moderate in their sentiments think that it will be necessary to destroy the Society in this country by secularizing all the members who are priests, with a sufficient pension, so as to make them simply ecclesiastics unattached to any regular community; but this cannot be done without the consent of the Pope. The Jesuits show themselves as little as possible in Paris, for fear of being insulted by the animosity of the public."‡

But if the outbreak of hostility against the Order in France

---

* Von Ranke, 'History of the Popes,' vol. ii. p. 441 (Engl. trans., 1853).

† Cte A. de St. Priest, *Hist. de la Chute des Jésuites*, pp. 2, 3, 4 (Paris, 1846).

‡ Barbier, *Journal*, tom. iv. p. 306.

was to some extent accidental, and provoked by an act of doubtful justice on the part of a foreign Government, its original sources were of much older date and more complicated character. This history has been written to little purpose if the reader has not gathered from it that the policy of the Jesuits for upwards of a century past, pursued with undeviating consistency and unexampled success, must have roused the deadly jealousy of various sections of society, and that their position was, in consequence, one of extremely precarious tenure. The Parliaments had been their declared foes from the beginning. They had strenuously opposed the introduction of the Order into France; they had protested at every step against its growing ascendancy; they imputed to the intrigues of Jesuit confessors many a galling stroke of despotism which had violated their dearest privileges. To the same cause they referred, and not without reason, the whole train of mortifications and indignities to which they had been subjected in connection with the "billets de confession." That contest had indeed virtually terminated in their favour; but they had never forgiven the aggressors, and were eagerly on the watch for any opportunity of retribution. Again, if we cast a glance upon the long and bitter course of the Jansenist controversy, and picture to ourselves the feelings of a whole race of divines systematically excluded from the honours and prizes of their profession,—branded as heretics, persecuted by the bishops, proscribed by the State, driven from their homes and their country, reduced to the lowest depths of poverty, and even deprived of the last rites whereby the Church fortifies her children in their passage from time to eternity,—it is easy to conceive the odium in which the Jesuits were held by all opponents of the Constitution Unigenitus; that fatal measure being universally known to be their handiwork. The destruction of Port-Royal des Champs, had there been no other grievance, was a wound that could never be healed; a reminiscence that rankled in the depths of every Jansenist heart, and called unceasingly for vengeance.

The Society had made enemies, not less vindictive and far more powerful, in another quarter. They had mortally offended Madame de Pompadour; and her ill-will entailed that of the Duc de Choiseul, who owed his advancement to the reigning favourite, and had just succeeded to one of the highest posts in the service of the Crown.* The relations between the Marchioness and Louis XV. had of late ceased to be positively criminal; she professed herself anxious to repair the past, and to make her peace with the Church. For this purpose she appealed to one of the Jesuit fathers, De Sacy, and proposed to him, as an arrangement for the future, that she should continue to reside at Versailles in the quality of the king's confidential friend, renouncing for ever that connection which had been so notorious a cause of public scandal. According to her account (in a memorial sent through a private agent to the Pope†) the Jesuit seemed disposed to entertain this proposition; he prescribed certain changes in her habits, and a rule of life which she at once adopted and followed exactly. But the negotiation became known, and so much dissatisfaction was manifested, that the confessor found it necessary to give way. He intimated to the Marchioness that it was impossible for him to admit her to the Sacraments until she had retired altogether from her position at Court. After employing every resource of argument and persuasion to shake his resolution, she dismissed him; and it appears that subsequently she succeeded in effecting her object through the intervention of another adviser of more accommodating conscience. Father Pérusseau, the king's confessor, who was likewise consulted on this occasion, took the same line with his colleague De Sacy, and dissuaded his Majesty from approaching the Sacraments, though he expressed an earnest wish to do so. In this instance, at least, the Jesuits cannot be charged with countenancing lax morality. Had all the motives which led to the dissolution of the Order been of the same character, it would have fallen with signal honour to itself and to the great cause which it professed to represent.

The resentment of Madame de Pompadour, powerfully seconded by a statesman who had every inducement to further her views, and who sympathized with them individually, must then be added to all the other elements which were at work, secretly or openly, against the interests of the Society. It enjoyed, indeed, the confidence and support of the Dauphin,

---

* De Choiseul became Minister for foreign affairs, on the resignation of Cardinal de Bernis, in November, 1758.

† Printed by the Cte de St. Priest (*Chute des Jésuites*, pp. 33–41), from the MSS. of the Duc de Choiseul.

but this only served to aggravate the aversion of the Duc de Choiseul, who was personally at variance with the Heir Apparent, and strove in every way to counteract his influence. Nor was it less obnoxious to the philosophers;—a class who were rapidly becoming predominant in the world of letters, and who possessed the power, through the universal diffusion of their writings, of holding up their opponents to obloquy and ridicule throughout Europe. All religious Orders, all ecclesiastical corporations, were to the Encyclopédistes objects of impartial antipathy and contempt. In their eyes such institutions were hopelessly tainted with the poison of fanaticism. They were alike injurious to society and to the progress of civilization; equally dangerous to the peace of nations, the security of sovereigns, and the best interests of religion. The growing prejudice against the Jesuits was therefore with them a natural subject of congratulation. Every manifestation of such feeling they claimed as a triumph of their principles. They anticipated, as fruits of the abolition of the Order, the universal establishment of toleration, the extirpation of all the more disgraceful abuses in Church and State, and the advent of enlightened government based on the guarantees of a wise and beneficent constitution.

Such was the state of opinion which had grown up by degrees in France in opposition to the Jesuits, when an unlooked-for event occurred which suddenly brought the Order into a position of damaging discredit, and, by a singular combination of adverse influences, left it helplessly exposed to the malice of its enemies.

Father Antoine Lavalette, "procureur" of the Jesuit Missions in the Antilles, resided in that capacity at St. Pierre in the island of Martinique. He was a man of talent, energy, and enterprise; and, following an example by no means uncommon in the Society, he had been for many years engaged in mercantile transactions on an extensive scale, and with eminent success. It was an occupation expressly prohibited to missionaries; but the Jesuits were in the habit of evading the difficulty by means of an ingenious fiction. Lavalette was in correspondence with the principal commercial firms in France, and particularly with that of Lioncy Brothers and Gouffre, of Marseilles. He made frequent consignments of merchandise to their house, which were covered by bills of exchange, drawn in Martinique and accepted by them. For a time the traffic proceeded prosperously; but it so happened that upon the breaking out of the Seven Years' War, several ships belonging to Lavalette, richly freighted with West Indian produce, were captured by the English cruisers, and their cargoes confiscated.* The immediate loss fell upon Lioncy and Gouffre, to whom these vessels were consigned. They applied for reimbursement to Father De Sacy, "procureur-général des missions," Lavalette's superior at Paris. He assisted them to some extent, but had no means at his command of making good the entire deficiency, and referred to Rome for further instructions. At this moment the General of the Society died, and considerable delay occurred before a definite reply could be obtained from his successor. Meanwhile the Marseilles merchants were pressed by their own creditors; and, being unable to meet their engagements, were declared bankrupt. The new General of the Jesuits, Lorenzo Ricci, declined to be responsible for the liabilities of his subordinate; whereupon the creditors of Lioncy and Co. sued Fathers Lavalette and De Sacy in the Consular Court of Marseilles,† and obtained an *arrêt* condemning the former to satisfy their demands to the amount of 1,500,000 livres (60,000*l.*). It was altogether beyond his power to raise such a sum, and in consequence he became a defaulter, his debts being estimated at three millions of livres.

Under these circumstances the creditors determined to attack the Jesuit community as a corporate body, in discharge of the obligations of their accredited agent. The Marseilles tribunal pronounced in favour of the claimants on the 29th of May, 1760, and declared all the property possessed by the Order liable for the debt of Lavalette. At this stage of the proceedings the Jesuits ought obviously to have conjured the rising storm by effecting an amicable arrangement, at almost any price, with their opponents. But their good genius deserted them. Those who are about to be destroyed, says the adage, are first given over to infatuation. In the heyday of their prosperity they had obtained from Louis XIV. a special privilege authorizing them

---

* Barbier, *Journal*, tom. iv. p. 382.
† The magistrates called "juges-consuls," at Marseilles and other seaports, exercised the functions and jurisdiction which were transferred after the Revolution to the "tribunaux de commerce."

to appeal, for the final adjudication of any contested case affecting them, to the Grand Conseil, where it was pretty certain that their conduct would be indulgently viewed. Had they availed themselves of this resource on the present occasion, there is little doubt that some means would have been devised to extricate them from their perilous position. But they not only declined doing so, but committed the unaccountable and irreparable fault of carrying their cause before the Parliament of Paris; a step which placed them virtually at the mercy of their most determined enemies. They were misled into this ruinous error, it seems, by a consultation of some of the most experienced barristers of Paris, who maintained that the law was on their side; that there was no "solidarity" of interest between individual colleges and the Institute as a body, and that the establishment at Martinique was exclusively liable for all engagements contracted by its manager. They decided on adopting this line of defence; and when the case came on before the Parliament, their Counsel argued that, according to the constitutions of the Society, each college was perfectly independent with regard to its temporal property; that the Superior-General had no power to transfer or alienate endowments belonging to one, in order to benefit another; that it was his duty to see that such revenues were administered to the best advantage, but that he could not apply any part of them at his own pleasure to the general purposes or necessities of the Order. They contended, therefore, that the College of La Flèche, and the mission of Martinique depending on it, were solely answerable for the defalcations of Lavalette, and that the creditors had no legal claim against the Society in its corporate capacity. Thereupon the Parliament at once demanded that the constitutions thus referred to should be examined. The Jesuits were ordered to furnish a copy of them; they obeyed, and three councillors (Chauvelin, Terray, and Laverdy) were named to undertake the task.

The compulsory production of these mysterious records, which had never before been inspected by any but Jesuit eyes, was an event of crucial significance. It was the turning-point of the whole affair; and its consequences were disastrous. The Abbé de Chauvelin, who was not only a zealous partisan of the Jansenists, but also an ally of Voltaire and the Encyclopédistes, denounced the statutes on the 19th of April, 1761, as containing many things contrary to good order, to the discipline of the Church, and to the maxims of the realm. He dwelt specially upon the anomalous and dangerous constitution of the Society, governed as it was despotically by a Superior who was not a French subject, but a foreigner resident at Rome; one who claimed, moreover, to be exempt from ordinary ecclesiastical jurisdiction. His speech made a deep impression, and the court ordered the investigation to be prosecuted further. Meanwhile the appeal in the case of Lavalette's bankruptcy was disposed of on the 8th of May; when the *avocat-général* Lepeletier de St. Fargeau moved for judgment in a speech of brilliant eloquence, which was received by the audience with enthusiastic plaudits. The sentence followed. The court condemned the General of the Jesuits, and in his person the whole Society which he governed, to acquit the bills of exchange still outstanding, together with interest and damages, within the space of a year from the date of the *arrêt*. In default of payment the debt was made recoverable upon the common property of the Order, excepting only the endowments specially restricted to particular colleges. The delight of the public, who were present on the occasion in great numbers, "was excessive," says Barbier, "and even indecent. They escorted the first president down to the door, clapping their hands, and the result has been canvassed all day with the utmost satisfaction throughout Paris, which proves the great unpopularity into which this Society has fallen."*

Louis XV. did not love the Jesuits, but he feared them; and this latter feeling was diligently fostered by Madame de Pompadour, De Choiseul, and other enemies of the Order, who filled the king's mind with the terrors arising from the odious dogma of tyrannicide. They reminded him how often in times past Jesuit counsels had armed the hand of the assassin against the life of French sovereigns; and they confidently ascribed to the same source the recent crime of Damiens. Apprehension for his personal safety on one side, and on the other the earnest solicitations of the Queen, the Dauphin, and other members of his family, who warmly espoused the cause of the Order at this

* Barbier, *Journal*, tom. iv. p. 389.

crisis of its fortunes, at length roused Louis from his voluptuous apathy, and determined him to check the precipitate action of the Parliament. He commanded the magistrates to transmit to him the copy of the Society's statutes in their possession, that he might examine their contents in person. This was suspected to be a stratagem to obstruct the measures in progress. If the statutes were sent to Versailles, it was doubtful whether they would ever be returned. " But an angel," says Barbier, " or some charitable person, substituted an exactly similar copy, so as to put the Parliament in a position, after obeying the king's order, to pursue its own plan of operations, and thus to defeat the object of the *lettre de cachet.*" The friend in need, to whom the Parliament was indebted for this timely and successful act of intervention, is supposed to have been none other than the Abbé de Chauvelin.*

The king intimated that he would cause the statutes to be carefully scrutinized by his Council; and expressed his hope that in the meantime the Parliament would not come to any decisive resolution on the matter in hand. A royal *ordonnance* appeared soon afterwards,† enjoining the superiors of all Jesuit houses to exhibit to the Council of State their title-deeds and other documents relating to their property, as a preliminary to further arrangements contemplated by his Majesty with regard to the Order. The Parliament registered this declaration, though with sundry modifications; but on the same day they passed two *arrêts* which went far to neutralize the interposition of the Government, and proved that, in point of fact, they were already prepared to proceed to the last extremities against the Institute of Loyola. On the 6th of August, 1761, they condemned a quantity of publications by the Jesuits, dating from the year 1590 downwards, to be torn and burnt by the executioner; and the next day this was duly carried out in the court of the Palais de Justice. Further, the *arrêt* prohibited the king's subjects from entering the said Society; forbade the fathers to give instruction, private or public, in theology, philosophy, or humanity; and ordered their schools and colleges to be closed.‡ The accusation brought against their books was the same to

---

* Barbier, *Journal*, tom. iv. p. 395.
† Isambert, *Anc. Lois Françaises*, tom. xxii. p. 311.
‡ *Ibid.*, tom. xxii. p. 312.

which Jesuit divines, moralists, and historians, had been more or less exposed ever since the days of Jean Boucher, Martin Bécan, Mariana, and the Holy League;—namely, that of teaching "abominable and murderous doctrine," of justifying sedition, rebellion, and regicide. Sufficient evidence has come before us in the course of this history to show that the charge was not altogether groundless; but it is clear that it was resuscitated at this particular moment mainly *ad augendam invidiam;*—not because the wild theories of the sixteenth century were real causes of alarm, but because, in the already irritated state of public feeling against the Order, it was hoped that one vigorous onset might overthrow for ever an ascendancy which had been so grossly abused.

On the same day it was ordered that the *procureur-général* be heard on a motion of appeal, *comme d'abus*, against the bull "Regimini" (by which the Company had been instituted in 1540 by Pope Paul III.), as well as against other acts, decrees, and constitutions of the Holy See relating to the Jesuit body.

The Government replied to these bold measures by ordering the Parliament to suspend the execution of its *arrêts* for the space of a year. The Parliament affected to obey, but stipulated, in registering the letters-patent, that the delay should not extend beyond the 1st of April, 1762, and made other provisions which left them virtually at liberty to proceed as they might think proper.

The Jesuits, meanwhile, awoke to a full sense of the imminent danger which threatened them, and strained every nerve to disconcert their adversaries, whose aim, as they perceived, was nothing short of their destruction. But they relied too confidently on the protection of the Crown. In other days, any enterprise against an Order possessed of such formidable power in Church and State, and exercising such important functions near the person of the sovereign, would have been peremptorily repressed and punished; but the prestige of the monarchy was now seriously impaired, and it was no longer wise or safe for a King of France to undertake openly the defence of any institution which had incurred a deliberate sentence of condemnation from the mass of his people.

The philosophical school looked on in a spirit of serene complacency. "The Parliament," wrote D'Alembert to Voltaire, "is fighting *à outrance* with the Jesuits, and Paris is even more occupied with the contest than it is with the war in Germany. As for me, who have no liking either for Convulsionist fanatics or for the fanatics of Saint Ignatius, all that I desire is to see them destroy one another. At the same time I feel perfectly at ease as to the event, and am certain to find some one to laugh at, happen what may. I am tempted to say to the Parliament what Timon the misanthrope said to Alcibiades: 'You young scapegrace, how pleased I am to see you at the head of affairs! You will satisfy my spite upon these rascally Athenians!' The moment, perhaps, is close at hand when philosophy is to have its revenge upon the Jesuits; but who will avenge us upon the rest of the fanatics? Have we a right to flatter ourselves that the destruction of the Jesuit rabble will bring to pass the abolition of the Jansenist rabble, &c.?"*

It was suggested, very properly, by the committee of the Royal Council charged with the examination of the Jesuit Constitutions, that an affair of this nature ought not to be determined without previous reference to the Episcopate. The prelates were accordingly summoned, and were desired to give their opinion upon the following questions: I. "What is the utility of the Jesuits in France? what are the advantages and the disadvantages of the functions which they discharge? II. What has been the character of their teaching and conduct with respect to the doctrine of the security of sovereigns, the Gallican Articles of 1682, and in general with respect to Ultramontane principles? III. How have they acted as to the submission due to the chief pastors of the Church? have they attempted to infringe their rights and prerogatives? IV. What modifications may it be expedient to propose in France as to the extent of authority at present exercised by the General of the Jesuits?"

The prelates, fifty-one in number, met for the first time on the 30th of November, 1761, under the presidency of Cardinal de Luynes, Archbishop of Sens. They appointed a committee, who reported, after a month's deliberation, favourably to the Jesuits upon all the points of enquiry. The report was accepted

---

* D'Alembert to Voltaire, 8 Sept. 1761 (*Œuvres de Voltaire*, tom. xli. p. 139).

by the great majority of the assembly, most of whom, it must be remembered, owed their position in the Church to Jesuit influence (since the "feuille des bénéfices" had been almost constantly in the hands of the Order), and were pledged to the traditional tenets of the Jesuit school. There were, however, six dissentients, headed by Cardinal de Choiseul, who were of opinion that considerable changes should be made in the Society's constitution, chiefly bearing upon the subordination of its members to the ecclesiastical ordinaries. One prelate, and one only, voted for the total extinction of the Order— Fitz-James of Soissons.

Before making their report to the king, the bishops exacted from the Jesuits a formal attestation of conformity to the laws, maxims, and usages of the realm as to the temporal supremacy of the Crown, of adhesion to the doctrine of the Assembly of 1682, and of sincere submission to the authority of the Episcopate. Upon the strength of this document, which was signed by the Provincial, Superiors, and more than one hundred professed fathers,* they recommended the king to preserve the substantive existence of the Society, introducing at the same time, as reasonable concessions to public opinion, certain alterations in its statutes and practical administration. The government of the Order in France was to be delegated by the General to a vicar or deputy resident within the realm, who was to take an oath of submission to the laws before the Chancellor. The Gallican Articles were to be taught as necessary doctrine in their colleges; and all their establishments of whatever kind were to be open to the inspection of the Parliament. This project of compromise was forwarded to Rome for the consideration of the Pope and the General; and Louis gave them to understand, through his ambassador, that upon no other conditions would it be possible to stem the tide of opposition, and to maintain the Jesuits as a body corporate in France. It was now that the memorable reply was made, either by the General Ricci, or, according to other accounts, by Pope Clement XIII. himself—" Sint ut sunt, aut non sint ; " " Let them remain as they are, or let them exist no longer."

It must be observed that the proposed reform was, in reality,

---

* *Procès-verb. des Assembl. du Clergé*, tom. viii. part i. p. 349. Crétineau-Joly, *Hist. de la Comp. de Jésus*, tom. v. p. 260.

not a question of detail, but of organic principle; it was inconsistent with the normal idea upon which Loyola had based his institution, namely, that of unity and absolute centralisation of power. Even had it been accepted its success was problematical; but its rejection sealed the fate of the Order. Louis, notwithstanding the ungracious response from Rome, proposed his scheme of conciliation to the Parliament in March, 1762, and annulled at the same time all measures adverse to the Jesuits taken since the 1st of August preceding. The Parliament, secretly encouraged by the Duc de Choiseul, refused to register this edict; the king, after some hesitation, withdrew it; and no available resource remained to shield the Order against its impending destiny.

The Parliaments, both of Paris and the provinces, laid the axe to the root without further delay. By an *arrêt* of the 1st of April, 1762,* the Jesuits were expelled from their eighty-four colleges in the ressort of the Parliament of Paris, and the example was followed by the provincial tribunals of Rouen, Rennes, Metz, Bordeaux, and Aix. The Society was now assailed by a general chorus of invective and execration. Caradeuc de la Chalotais, Procureur-Général of Brittany, distinguished himself by his inflammatory appeals to the Parliament of Rennes. His two *comptes-rendus* against the Constitutions, followed by an elaborate *réquisitoire*, were performances of superior merit, and drew forth warm encomiums from Voltaire and others of the *philosophes*. Ripert de Montclar, who held the same office at Aix, and Dudon at Bordeaux, were equally vehement in their denunciations. Among the host of bitter attacks which poured from the press one deserves to be specially mentioned, entitled 'Extraits des assertions dangereuses et pernicieuses en tout genre, que les soi-disant Jésuites ont dans tout temps et persévéramment soutenues, enseignées et publiées.' The literature of Jesuitism had been ransacked to supply this heterogeneous mass of propositions, the drift of which was to convict the Order of systematically excusing, and even of directly suggesting and sanctioning, every species of enormity that figures on the calendar of human crime. It was replied that these pretended

---

* Isambert, *Anc. Lois Françaises*, tom. xxii. p. 312 *et seqq.*

citations were to a great extent garbled, perverted, and falsified; which fact is admitted, indeed, on all hands. "It cannot be denied," says D'Alembert, "that among a vast number of correct quotations some mistakes occurred; these have been frankly acknowledged; but even supposing they had been far more numerous, would they prevent the rest from being true? Moreover, if the complaint of the Jesuits and their defenders were as just as it seems to be the contrary, who will take the trouble to verify so many passages? Meanwhile, until the truth is ascertained (if such truths are worth the labour of investigation), this collection will have produced the result which was desired by the nation, namely, the annihilation of the Jesuits. The offences with which they are justly chargeable may be more or less numerous; but the Society will have ceased to exist; and this is the important point."*

All accounts concur to show that at this moment the case was no longer within the control of sound reason and calm judgment. It had passed into the region of blind impulse, of panic, of passion. The question was, not how much could be *proved* against the Jesuits, but how much could be successfully insinuated without proof; how much the multitude could be induced to swallow, whether true or false, for the purpose of justifying a foregone conclusion. Such, unhappily, has been in all ages the prevailing tone and practical course of important public movements in France, whatever may have been their original cause or their professed object.

The final blow was struck by the Parliament of Paris on the 6th of August, 1762, to which day the cause had been adjourned. The sentence then passed condemned the Society as "inadmissible, by its nature, in any civilized State, inasmuch as it was contrary to the law of nature, subversive of authority spiritual and temporal, and introduced, under the veil of religion, not an Order sincerely aspiring to evangelical perfection, but rather a political body, of which the essence consists in perpetual attempts to attain, first, absolute independence, and in the end, supreme authority. For this purpose the Society is monarchically constituted; so that the members which it collects in different countries are so many subjects lost to their lawful sovereigns, and bound to the service of a foreign monarch

---

* D'Alembert, "Sur la destruction des Jésuites" (*Œuvres*, tom. v. p. 95).

by an oath of absolute and unlimited subjection." The decree concludes by declaring the vows of the Jesuits illegal and void, forbidding them to observe the rules of the Order, to wear its dress, or to correspond with its members. They were to quit their houses within one week, and were to renounce, upon oath, all connection with the Society, upon pain of being disqualified for any ecclesiastical charge or public employment.*

The provincial Parliaments followed the lead of the capital, though in some few instances the decree of suppression was opposed, and carried only by a small majority; while at Besançon and Douai the decision was in favour of the Society. In Lorraine, too, under the peaceful government of Stanislas Leczinski, and in Alsace, where they were powerfully protected by Cardinal de Rohan, Bishop of Strasburg, the Jesuits were left unmolested.

Clement XIII. remonstrated against the harshness of the late proceedings in a brief addressed to the French Cardinals, in which he announced that he had already, in a secret consistory, annulled and abrogated an act so painfully offensive to the Catholic Church and to religion. The stout-hearted Christophe de Beaumont, again, was not wanting to himself in the emergency; in his Pastoral Instruction of October 28, 1763, he fulminated against the late proceeding of the secular courts as a gross usurpation of power in things beyond their province; he denied the truth and justice of the charges upon which the Jesuits had been condemned; he branded the collection of "extracts" as calumnious and spurious; he warned his flock that this was the first step in an aggression which aimed at demolishing the very foundations of religion.† Many of his colleagues—the Archbishops of Auch and Aix, the Bishops of Amiens, Vannes, Le Puy, Langres, Pamiers, Grenoble, and others—emulated the zeal of the "Gallican Athanasius," and published *mandements* of similar tenor. The magistrates were furious. They condemned to the flames De Beaumont's Instruction, and ordered him to be brought to trial before the Court of Peers. The king, dismayed by their violence, strove to compromise matters by exiling the Archbishop to La Trappe, forty leagues from Paris; but the Parliament refused to be

---

* Isambert, *Anc. Lois Françaises*, tom. xxii. pp. 328–378.
† Crétineau-Joly, *Hist. de la Comp. de Jésus*, tom. v. p. 280.

pacified; they reviled their diocesan in unmeasured language under colour of presenting a remonstrance to the king, and they vented their spite in still further severities against the Jesuits, who were now summoned to take the prescribed oath of abjuration of their Institute within one week, under pain of banishment from the realm for life. Out of the four thousand members of the Order domiciled in France, no more than twenty-five embraced the former alternative in preference to the latter. The edict of proscription was executed with unsparing rigour; even the confessors of the royal family were not exempted. The decree of expulsion, however, was not universal; it applied only to the ressorts of the Parliaments of Paris, Rouen, Toulouse, and Pau.

Vainly did the unfortunate fathers exclaim against a tyranny which destroyed their status as a religious Order, divested them of every shred of political ascendancy, and drove them forth to wander in disgrace, in many cases even as mendicants, in foreign lands. They met their fate on the whole with resignation, and in many quarters it excited compassion; but none could deny that they were the victims of a righteous retribution. In the days of their power had they not meted out to others the self-same measure of cruel oppression that now recoiled upon themselves? Had they not instigated persecution against fellow-countrymen and fellow-churchmen because they could not reconcile their consciences to all the extravagances of the bull Unigenitus? Were not *lettres de cachet*, ecclesiastical deprivation, confiscation, demolition, resorted to without scruple and without mercy by the agents of Ultramontane tyranny? If they were now sufferers in their turn, who could fail to see in that fact the working of a judicial Nemesis, adjusting the fluctuating balance of human destiny, and requiting the wrong-doer with the inevitable fruit of his misdeeds?

The suppression of the Jesuits—the most important act of the administration of the Duc de Choiseul—was consummated by a royal ordonnance of November, 1764, to which Louis did not give his consent without mistrust and regret. It decreed that the Society should cease to exist throughout his Majesty's dominions; but it permitted the ex-Jesuits to reside in France as private citizens, and to exercise their ecclesiastical functions under the jurisdiction of the diocesans. All former procedures to their disadvantage were by the same edict annulled; absolute silence was imposed as to the whole affair; and the Archbishop of Paris was once more recalled from exile. The Parliament registered this edict on the 1st of December; but exacted, as additional stipulations, that the fathers should reside in the dioceses in which they were born, that they should signify their presence in person every six months to the local magistrates, and that they should never come within ten leagues of Paris.*

Almost immediately afterwards, on the 7th of January, 1765, appeared the bull "Apostolicum," by which Clement XIII. condemned, with all the weight of supreme and infallible authority, the measure which had deprived the Holy See of its most valiant defenders.

"We protest," said the Pontiff, "against this grievous injury inflicted at once upon the Church and on the Holy See. We declare, on our personal authority and certain knowledge, that the Institute of the Company of Jesus exhibits in the highest degree the spirit of piety and sanctity; although men are to be met with who, traducing it by false representations, designate it as irreligious and impious, thereby outrageously insulting the Church of God, which they charge by those very terms with deception, in having solemnly declared an institution to be acceptable to Heaven which is essentially ungodly and worthless."

This bull was addressed to all Catholic bishops, who were directed to report to the Vatican as to the reception which it met with in the different kingdoms. Replies were received from only twenty-three prelates in all, of whom no more than two were French. It thus appeared that the Papal manifesto was considered indiscreet and inopportune. The Parliament of Paris suppressed it on the 11th of February; and those of Brittany, Normandy, and Provence ordered it to be publicly committed to the flames.

The only effect of the intervention of the Roman Curia was to excite further ebullitions of hostility against the prostrate Order. Charles III. of Spain, yielding, as it is alleged, to the exhortations of the Duc de Choiseul,† abolished it

---

* Isambert, tom. xxii. p. 424.
† Sismondi, *Hist. des Français*, tom. xx. p. 374. Crétineau-Joly, *Clément XIV et les Jésuites*, p. 171.

throughout his dominions by a sudden mandate of April 2, 1767. On the 9th of May following the Abbé de Chauvelin, in one of his most impetuous harangues, demanded of the Parliament of Paris that the Jesuits should not be more leniently treated in France than in Spain; the magistrates gladly assented to his arguments, and an *arrêt* was passed upon the spur of the moment, commanding all Jesuits who had not taken the oath to withdraw from the French territories within one week. The only exceptions allowed were those of great age or permanent infirmity. The court, knowing that resistance was useless, acquiesced, although the *arrêt* was directly at variance with the royal *ordonnance* of 1764; and the sentence of the magistrates was executed to the letter.

The Pope precipitated the final catastrophe by a further act of imprudence. The young Duke of Parma, a prince of the house of Bourbon,* had excluded the Jesuits from his duchy, and had published certain ecclesiastical regulations detrimental to the ancient pretensions of the Roman See. Clement XIII., reviving an antiquated title in virtue of which Parma was claimed as a dependent fief of the Papacy, was rash enough to launch a bull of excommunication against the Duke, and deprived him of his dominions as a rebellious vassal. All the Bourbon sovereigns promptly combined to resent this insult to their family. The Papal Bull was suppressed at Paris, at Madrid, at Lisbon, at Parma, at Naples. The Jesuits were expelled from Venice, from Modena, from Bavaria. The Pontiff was summoned to revoke his "monitorium;" and on his refusal French troops took possession of Avignon and the Comtat Venaissin, while the King of Naples seized Benevento and Pontecorvo. On the 16th of January, 1769, the ambassadors of Spain, France, and Naples presented a joint note to the Holy Father, demanding that the Order of Jesus should be secularised and abolished for ever. Clement, who had suffered severely from the manifold humiliations and reverses of his Pontificate, was overwhelmed by this last blow, from the effects of which he never rallied. He expired almost suddenly on the 2nd of February, 1769.†

---

* Ferdinand Duke of Parma, born 1751, was grandson, on his father's side, of Philip V. of Spain, and, on his mother's side, of Louis XV.

† St. Priest, *Chute des Jésuites*, p. 77.

The ensuing Conclave was memorable for a series of intrigues unusually complicated and protracted, of which a curious picture is given in the official correspondence between the Duc de Choiseul, the Marquis d'Aubeterre, French ambassador at Rome, and Cardinal de Bernis, who was confidentially instructed on the occasion by the cabinet of Versailles. The Italian Cardinals, most of whom were friendly to the Jesuits, made an effort to come to a decision without waiting for their French and Spanish colleagues, and very nearly succeeded in their project. The vigilance and skill of D'Aubeterre, however, kept the "Zelanti" in check until their opponents could muster in force; but even then it was found difficult to agree upon a plan of operations. The Spaniards proposed to make it a condition, before voting for any candidate, that he should sign a positive written engagement to dissolve the Jesuit Society. The French refused to sanction this scheme, which they pronounced corrupt and simoniacal. The Spaniards persisted, throwing the responsibility of any violation of the canons upon their sovereign, under whose express orders they were acting. But, since the main object of both parties was one and the same, namely the destruction of the Jesuits, it was arranged that the French, though they could not approve the expedient suggested, should not oppose it, and that they should support with all their influence the choice of their confederates. It was long before they could find a candidate suited to their purpose. The Conclave was agitated by divisions and conflicting manœuvres. Lorenzo Ganganelli, who was at length selected to represent the interests of "the Crowns," was a Franciscan monk, and for that reason as well as others was supposed to be adverse to the Jesuits; but he was also known to be of moderate views, was silent, discreet, reserved, and had carefully kept aloof from religious controversy. The Spanish Cardinals opened negotiations with him, and, according to the account of M. Crétineau-Joly,* obtained from him a note addressed to the King of Spain, stating that in his opinion the Sovereign Pontiff possessed the power and right to extinguish the Company of Jesus, without violating any canonical obligation; and expressing a hope that the future Pope would make every

---

* *Clément XIV et les Jésuites*, p. 260.

practicable endeavour to meet the wishes of the sovereigns. This was language sufficiently guarded to protect all parties from any imputation of simoniacal contract. But although no positive bargain was made, it seems clear that an understanding was arrived at. The Spaniards were satisfied, and consequently called upon De Bernis, who was kept in ignorance of the treaty until it was concluded, to co-operate in the election of Ganganelli. He complied, and two days later the cabal was astonished at the perfect success of its own enterprise. On the 17th of May, 1769, Ganganelli was declared Pope by the united suffrages of all the Cardinals in conclave, forty-six in number. De Bernis had obtained from him previously, in a private interview, an assurance that he would take immediate measures for settling all difficulties with the Duke of Parma; and although he spoke less explicitly upon the subject of the Jesuits, he made use of expressions which left the Cardinal in little or no doubt as to his intentions. On other points his promises were liberal; he even held out the prospect that Avignon might be ceded in perpetuity to France; and engaged to appoint certain individuals named by the French court to the highest posts under the Pontifical government.*

Cardinal De Bernis was now accredited as resident French envoy at the court of Rome, in succession to the Marquis d'Aubeterre. The new Pope, Clement XIV., professed to regard him with extreme gratitude as the instrument of his elevation, and treated him with unbounded confidence. De Bernis, flattered by this distinction, made such representations to his government, that for some time the Pope was not urged further upon the vexed question of the abolition of the Jesuits, which nevertheless weighed upon his conscience like a perpetual nightmare. But the evil day was only adjourned. The King of Spain lost patience, and in 1770 Clement was induced to write a letter to his Catholic Majesty, in the course of which he plainly admitted that "the Society deserved its ruin by reason of the restlessness of its spirit and the audacity of its proceedings." De Bernis observes, in a despatch of the same date, "The question is not whether the Pope would not be glad

---

* St. Priest, *Chute des Jésuites,* p. 104.

to avoid suppressing the Jesuits, but whether, after the formal promises which he has made in writing to the King of Spain, he can possibly help taking action against them. The letter which I have advised him to write to the Catholic king binds him so strictly, that unless some change of sentiment should occur at Madrid, the Pope is compelled against his will to terminate the affair. His Holiness is too intelligent not to see that if the King of Spain were to print the letter which he has addressed to him, he could not without dishonour refuse to keep his word by suppressing a Society the members of which he has already stigmatized as dangerous, turbulent, and seditious. It is commonly supposed that the Pope is very acute and clever; this opinion does not seem to me to be well founded. Had he been so sagacious, he would not have engaged in writing to destroy the Jesuits; he would not have portrayed them as ambitious, factious, and dangerous. According to that estimate of their character, it is easy to prove that he is obliged in conscience to suppress them. What then was his object in making this written engagement? To soothe the impatience of the courts, to procure for himself rest, to gain time by corresponding with the confessor of his Catholic Majesty, and in the end to suppress the Jesuits, if the sovereigns of the house of France persist in demanding it. This suppression, then, depends essentially upon the will of the three monarchs; and its execution will be accelerated or retarded according as they are urgent or languid in their instances." *

We cannot wonder that the Pope should have been reluctant to disband the Prætorian guard of the Vatican—to destroy a religious Order which for upwards of two centuries past had been labouring with such unexampled self-devotion to extend and consolidate the authority of the Apostolic See; but it is equally clear that it was impossible for him to withstand the combined and persistent pressure of the most powerful monarchs of Catholic Europe. He proceeded, nevertheless, with the utmost deliberation. He appointed a commission, investigated archives, collected evidence, entered into a fruitless negotiation with the court of Vienna, and consumed three years in preparing for a transaction which he felt to be inevitable. During this interval sinister rumours of all kinds were circulated to

---

* De Bernis to Duc de Choiseul, 29 April, 1770. Quoted by St. Priest, p. 120.

deter him from his purpose, and he became a prey to tormenting apprehensions of violence against his life. After some preliminary measures, the bull of suppression, "Dominus ac Redemptor noster," was at length promulgated on the 21st of July, 1773; the unfortunate Pontiff ejaculating as he signed it, "Questa suppressione mi darà la morte!"

The French government, having enforced upon Clement this last sacrifice to the necessities of his position, had no further pretence for retaining Avignon and its territory; and they were accordingly restored to the See. The Duc de Choiseul had purposed to improve the opportunity by exacting their cession in perpetuity to France; but that minister was dismissed from office in December, 1770. The success of his project, however, was not long delayed. It was one of the earliest acts of the Revolution to reunite Avignon and the Comtat Venaissin to the French territory.

Clement XIV. survived the suppression of the Jesuits somewhat more than a year. He had recovered to a remarkable extent his health and natural cheerfulness, notwithstanding which it appears that strange forebodings and predictions were current in Rome that his end was approaching. In the Holy Week of 1774, he suddenly experienced a violent attack of such a character that it was attributed both by himself and his attendants to the action of poison. He lingered for eight months, suffering at times agonizing pain of body and poignant anguish of mind; the powers of his constitution failed gradually, and at length sunk in total prostration; at intervals he was deprived of reason. More than once he started from a troubled sleep, exclaiming with sobs, "Misericordia, misericordia! compulsus feci! compulsus feci!" Death put a period to his sufferings on the 22nd of September, 1774.*

The real cause which proved fatal to Clement XIV. remains one of the secrets of history, and has become a sort of traditional touchstone of opinion between rival ecclesiastical schools. It is assumed that, if he died by violence, that violence must be laid at the door of the Jesuits; and accordingly the apologists of the Order with one voice negative all idea of poison, and explain the circumstances upon various natural considerations,

---

* St. Priest, *Chute des Jésuites*, p. 145.

Some rely with implicit faith on the *procès-verbal* of the post-mortem examination made by the surgeon Salicetti, which attributes the result to a constitutional infirmity aggravated by nervous excitement. Others believe that Clement was the victim of his own habitual terrors, suspicions, and despondency; others suggest that he ruined his system by the excessive use of antidotes. But there is no denying that there are facts which tell strongly in a different direction. Cardinal de Bernis, a witness on the spot, unprejudiced against the Jesuits, and possessing from his official position the best facilities for accurate and confidential information, remained profoundly convinced that the Pope met his death by criminal means. "The symptoms of the Pope's illness," he writes to the French minister of foreign affairs, "and, above all, the circumstances of his death, have given occasion to a prevalent opinion that it was not natural. The physicians who assisted at the opening of the body express themselves prudently, the surgeons with less circumspection. It is better to believe the report of the former than to attempt to clear up a mystery too distressing, which perhaps it is not desirable to penetrate." . . . "Those who are as well informed as I am, through authentic documents which the late Pope communicated to me, must pronounce the suppression of the Order most just and most necessary. The circumstances which preceded, attended, and followed the death of the Pontiff excite an equal measure of horror and compassion. I am now collecting together the true details of the illness and death of Clement XIV., who, Vicar as he was of Jesus Christ, prayed after His example for his most implacable enemies, and who, through extreme delicacy of conscience, barely allowed himself to breathe the cruel suspicions which had devoured him ever since Holy Week, when his illness began. I dare not conceal from the king truths, however melancholy, which will be perpetuated in history."* We learn from the testimony of the same diplomatist, that the successor of Clement, Pius VI., shared his persuasion on this painful topic. "I know better than any one," he writes in October, 1777, "the extent of the affection which Pius VI. bears to the Jesuits, but he treats them with caution even more than with love, because his mind and

---

* Despatches of Cardinal de Bernis, 28 août, 28 septembre, 26 octobre 1774. Quoted from the originals by St. Priest, *Chute des Jésuites*, pp. 152, 153.

his heart are governed rather by fear than by friendship. The Pope has his moments of openness, when he discovers his real sentiments; I shall never forget two or three impulsive avowals which have fallen from him, sufficiently intimating that he had full knowledge of the unhappy fate of his predecessor, and that he was not desirous of incurring the same risks."*

The Church of France acquiesced in the bull "Dominus ac Redemptor," but it was not officially published, since the Jesuit community had been already deprived of its legal existence by the edict of 1764. The Government contented itself with directing the prelates of the realm to give effect to the instructions of the Holy Father in their respective dioceses.

Archbishop de Beaumont, however, was not the man to submit to such a crushing blow to the Ultramontane system of Church administration without raising his voice in outspoken remonstrance. He wrote a letter to Clement XIV., dated April 24, 1774, explaining at length the reasons which made it impossible that he could ever accept or execute the mandate of suppression.† He contrasted this act with the Constitution "Apostolicum pascendi munus" given by Clement XIII. in 1765; and observed that the Church would stultify itself, and disprove its infallibility, if by one utterance it should decree the abolition of a Society which by another it had pronounced to be a model of sanctity and all Christian virtues.., "What manner of peace can that be," he exclaims, "which is said to be incompatible with the existence of the Jesuits? Doubtless it is that which Jesus Christ condemns as treacherous, false, delusive; that which, although bearing the name of peace, is not so in reality; peace, peace, and there is no peace;—that peace which is adopted by vice and libertinism, who acknowledge it as their mother; which never was allied with virtue, but, on the contrary, has always been the sworn enemy of piety. Against this kind of peace the Jesuits have constantly declared war in the four quarters of the world, and have waged it with determined vigour and

---

* Despatch of Oct. 28, 1777. St. Priest, p. 154. It should be mentioned that Father Theiner, the learned librarian of the Vatican, a writer by no means disposed to screen the Jesuits, rejects the imputation of foul play, and is sceptical as to some of the sensational incidents of Clement's last illness. A. Theiner, *Geschichte des Pontificats Clemenz XIV.*, vol. ii. p. 518.

† The Archbishop's language is somewhat unmeasured. He calls the Papal brief "un jugement isolé, particulier, pernicieux, peu honorable à la tiare, préjudiciable à la gloire de l'Église, nuisible à l'accroissement et au maintien de la Foi orthodoxe."

immense success. In order to exterminate it, they have sacrificed their talents, their labours, their zeal, and all the resources of their eloquence. Conspicuous proofs of this might be adduced from a long series of memorable actions, never interrupted from the day of the Society's birth down to that day, fatal to the Church, which has witnessed their extinction. These proofs are not of such a nature as to be unknown to your Holiness. If then, I repeat, it is *this* peace which could not co-exist with the Society, and if its re-establishment was indeed the motive of the destruction of the Jesuits, the event has covered them with glory. They have finished their course after the pattern of the Apostles and Martyrs; but good men weep for their fall, and deep and grievous is the stroke that has been aimed against religion and virtue."*

It was not long before the sovereign courts of Parliament, who had originally instigated the movement against the Jesuits, and had hailed its success with triumphant joy, were compelled to taste in their turn the bitter cup of humiliation. Circumstances arose which placed them in a position of such obnoxious antagonism to the Crown, that it became clear that either the one power or the other must succumb. The conflict had its origin in Brittany, where the Parliament, under the vigorous leadership of the Procureur-Général La Chalotais, braved the tyranny of the Duc d'Aiguillon, governor of that province. It was a reproduction, under a new form, of the great strife which had divided the French nation for fifty years. D'Aiguillon was the partisan and protector of the banished Jesuits, and represented all the traditions of absolutism in Church and State.† La Chalotais was a disciple of the new philosophy, and a patron of Jansenism; one who abhorred monkery and superstition, and cried up constitutional government and the liberties of the people. Being denounced to the king as a fomenter of sedition, La Chalotais was arrested, with four of his colleagues, and committed to the Bastille; they were afterwards sent into distant exile. The Parliament of Paris now made common cause with that of

---

* "Lettre de Monseigneur Christophe de Beaumont du Repaire, archevêque de Paris, en réponse au bref particulier adressé à lui par S. S. Clément XIV." Amsterdam, 1776.

† The Duc d'Aiguillon inherited his title and estates from the Duchesse d'Aiguillon, Marquise de Combalet, the favourite niece of Cardinal Richelieu. He was nephew of the Maréchal Duc de Richelieu, so conspicuous at the court of Louis XV.

Rennes, and presented a violent remonstrance to the throne against the treatment of the five magistrates. Louis retorted by holding a *lit de justice*, at which he made a speech of unusual indignation and severity. "I will not permit," said he, "the formation in my kingdom of a confederacy of resistance, which could not but destroy the peace of the monarchy. The magistracy is not a body or an order separated from the three constituted Orders of the realm; the magistrates are my officers, appointed to discharge in my name the truly royal duty of dispensing justice to my subjects. I know the importance of their functions; and it is a mere illusion to suppose that there exists any project to destroy the judicial bodies, or that the throne is hostile to them. Their true and sole enemies are those of their own members who maintain that all the Parliaments compose but one body, distributed in several classes; that this body is of the essence of the monarchy, and constitutes its basis; that it is the seat, the tribunal, the organ of the nation; that it is the protector and depository of liberty; that it is responsible in all departments for the public welfare, not only to the king, but also to the people; that it is the judge between the king and his subjects; that it co-operates with the sovereign in enacting laws, and that in some cases it may dispense with a law duly registered, and act as if it had no existence; and that if a collision of authorities should ensue, the Parliament is justified in abandoning its duties and tendering its resignation. By propagating such novelties," continued his Majesty, "the Parliament belies its own constitution and betrays its own interests. The supreme power resides solely in my person; my courts derive their existence and their authority from me alone; to me alone belongs the power of legislation, independently and undividedly; it is solely by my authority that the officers of my courts proceed, not to the enactment, but to the registration, publication, and execution of the law; and that they have permission to make representations to me as loyal and faithful counsellors." The king announced, in conclusion, that while the remonstrances of his courts would always meet with due consideration, his commands must be implicitly obeyed if, after deliberation, he should think proper to persist in them; and that, in case of obstinate opposition, he should be reduced to the sad necessity of employing all the power with which God had invested him in order to preserve his people from the fatal results of such unlawful pretensions.*

This despotic demonstration did not intimidate the Parliament. They proceeded to impeach the Duc d'Aiguillon of grave misdemeanours in his government, and demanded that he should be brought to trial in the court of Peers. The Duke himself concurred in appealing to the judgment of that tribunal; and the cause was heard accordingly before the king in person at Versailles in April, 1770. But after a time the proceedings were summarily arrested and annulled by royal edict; his Majesty declaring that he believed the Duke's conduct to be irreproachable. The Parliament, notwithstanding, pronounced that the charges against him subsisted in full force, and that his honour was thereby compromised; and suspended him from his functions as a peer until he should be acquitted in due course of justice.† Their *arrêt* was instantly cancelled by the Council of State. Remonstrances followed, a bed of justice was held, and Louis erased from the Parliamentary register all record of the recent trial. The magistrates protested vehemently against these multiplied acts of abusive authority, which were proofs, they said, of a deliberate design to change the form of government, and to substitute for the impartial procedure of the law the irregular impulses of arbitrary power. After much recrimination and additional provocation on both sides, the Parliament suspended its sittings and resigned in a body; proclaiming that "nothing now remained but that the magistracy and the laws they had sworn to administer should perish in a common overthrow." It was at this crisis that Choiseul, who throughout his ministry had firmly supported the Parliaments, and was suspected of having abetted these last acts of contumacy, was precipitated from power and exiled by *lettre de cachet*. His place was immediately filled by his enemies, the Chancellor Maupeou, the Abbé de Terray, and the Duc d'Aiguillon. One of the first measures of the new Cabinet (February, 1771,) was to abolish the ancient courts of judicature, and to replace them by six tribunals called *conseils supérieurs*, established in the cities of Arras, Blois, Châlons, Clermont-Ferrand, Lyons, and

---

* *Mercure historique*, mars 1766. Sismondi, *Hist. des Français*, tom. xx. p. 370.
† *Mémoires du* Baron de Bezenval, p. 195.

Poitiers. All the offices belonging to the mediæval Parliament were confiscated at a stroke, and a new judicial body was formed from the members of the Grand Conseil.* The provincial courts were dissolved and remodelled in like manner, together with many less important institutions of immemorial antiquity. The refractory and discontented were sent into exile, and all resistance was put down with a high hand.†

Considerable agitation was caused by these events, amounting, as they did, to another vast step in the rapid process of disintegration which was destroying the monarchy of France. Louis XV. was not blind to their significance; but he had now become indifferent to the future, and nothing was allowed to disturb his luxurious sloth and reckless nonchalance. "The machine will last as long as I shall," he was wont to remark; "as for my successor, he must shift as he can." It may be questioned whether his own life and example had not done as much towards undermining the foundations of the throne as either the machinations of popular demagogues or the sneers of infidel philosophers. But the scandals of this deplorable reign were drawing to a close. The king had latterly been impressed with a presentiment that his days were numbered; and attempts were made by Archbishop de Beaumont and others to arouse his conscience and inspire him with some concern for his soul's safety. The Abbé de Beauvais, preaching before the Court on Thursday in Holy Week, 1774, took for his text the denunciation of the prophet, "Yet forty days, and Nineveh shall be destroyed." The discourse contained allusions to his Majesty's private life so direct and startling, that it was generally expected that the abbé would be recompensed for his indiscretion by disgrace, or even with the Bastille.‡ The king, however, was so far from taking offence, that he appointed the fearless preacher

---

* Isambert, *Anc. Lois Françaises*, tom. xxii. p. 510.

† It was on this occasion that Lamoignon de Malesherbes, president of the "cour des aides," ventured to suggest to the king the convocation of the States-General, which had never been summoned since the memorable meeting of 1614.

‡ The following specimen of the sermon is preserved :—" Salomon, rassasié de voluptés, las d'avoir épuisé, pour réveiller ses sens flétris, tous les genres de plaisir qui entourent le trône, finit par en chercher uno espèce nouvelle dans les vils restes de la corruption publique." The Abbé de Beauvais was one of the most esteemed preachers of the day. He resigned the see of Senez in 1783, and died in 1790. His "Oraison funèbre" for Louis XV. was severely criticized by Voltaire.

to the vacant bishopric of Senez. Not long afterwards he was attacked by a complication of diseases, evidently destined to be mortal. He summoned his confessor the Abbé Moudon, and likewise conferred in private with the Grand-aumônier, Cardinal de la Roche-Aymon; and at the instance of these divines he consented to dismiss Madame du Barry from his presence. Before receiving the last Sacraments, Louis commanded the Cardinal to notify to those present that "his Majesty, although he was not accountable to any man, declared that he repented of the bad example he had given to his subjects, and that, if it should please God to prolong his days, he would employ them in studying their welfare."* He expired on the 10th of May, 1774, just within the forty days mysteriously foreshadowed by the Abbé de Beauvais; a period which he had repeatedly expressed his conviction that he should not survive.†

The inexperienced youth who succeeded to the throne under the name of Louis XVI. was amiable, virtuous, and full of excellent intentions; but his natural weakness, diffidence, and indecision were such as to nullify all that was good and noble in his character. One of his first acts was to re-establish the Parliaments, both of Paris and the provinces, according to their ancient constitution; a step recommended by the Comte de Maurepas, but adopted in opposition to the advice of the philosopher Turgot, whom the new sovereign had chosen as his minister of finance. The edict annulled all proceedings formerly taken by the magistrates in matters of religious controversy, and forbade them to enter on any such discussions for the future; but the effect of the measure, as on former occasions of the same kind, was only to make them more arrogant and impracticable than ever. Turgot was a man of true genius, and, had he been firmly and generously supported in his projects, might have succeeded in restoring something like order in the disorganized fabric of the State. But his connection with Voltaire and the 'Encyclopédie' made him an object of suspicion to the clergy, while his plans of economical reform excited the hostility of the aristocracy, the official classes, and of all who were interested in keeping up the old restrictive privileges of feudal society.

---

* *Mémoires de Bezenval*, p. 153.
† Soulavie, *Mém. du Mar. de Richelieu*, tom. ix. p. 465.

Turgot directed his most strenuous efforts against the unequal distribution of fiscal burdens; that inveterate abuse which was so deeply imbedded in the *ancien régime* that nothing could uproot it short of the whirlwind of a revolution. The Church, the nobles, the Parliaments, forgetting their mutual grievances and animosities, eagerly combined to crush a statesman who proclaimed, as a primary axiom of government, that subjects of all ranks and classes ought to contribute in just proportion to meet the common exigencies of the State. Turgot, abandoned by his sovereign, was driven from office in May, 1776. Voltaire heard the tidings with consternation. " What will become of us?" he cried; "miserable that we are, to have witnessed both the dawn and the extinction of the golden age! Now that Turgot is displaced, I see nothing but death before me; this thunderstroke has penetrated my brain and my heart."*

The National Church, meanwhile, continued to struggle against the flood of irreligion and infidelity which was inundating France, and lost no opportunity of warning the civil government of the extent of its progress; urging at the same time the employment of measures of repressive severity, which, if expedient at any time, were under existing circumstances manifestly powerless to arrest it. In their remonstrances to the throne in 1775, the Assembly of the Clergy inveighed with indignant eloquence against the general ferment which was rapidly loosening all the bonds of society. " Whence comes this restless spirit of examination in which all classes now indulge in respect to the conduct of the Government, its rights, and the limits of its authority? Whence arise these principles which are destructive of all established authority, disseminated in a multitude of writings, and repeated with unwearied eagerness in every country? All forms of disorder are connected together, and necessarily follow one another. The foundations of morals and of authority must needs crumble away concurrently with those of Religion." The Assembly prefaced with these remarks an " Avertissement aux fidèles sur les avantages de la religion et sur les effets pernicieux de l'incrédulité," which had been drawn up at their desire by De Pompignan, Archbishop of Vienne. The prelate enumerates, under seven heads, the advantages which faith secures, and of which men are deprived by unbelief.

---

* Voltaire to M. de la Harpe, 10 juin 1776 (*Œuvres*, tom. xxxviii. p. 469).

1. The repose of the mind in the knowledge of the truth. 2. The inward appreciation and love of virtue. 3. Restraint against vice and remorse for crime. 4. Consolation under suffering. 5. The forgiveness of sin. 6. The hope of immortality. 7. The preservation of order in civil society.* Under each of these articles he enlarges upon the beneficent results of Christianity as contrasted with the baneful fruits of the freethinking system. The Assembly of the same year put on record its renewed protest against the unbridled licence of the anti-Christian press; and condemned a numerous assortment of infidel publications, chiefly by Helvetius, Fréret, Holbach, and the Abbé Raynal. It also tendered the congratulations and thanks of the Church to the many writers who had distinguished themselves in the defence of revealed truth; among others to Guénée and Bergier (whose works have been already noticed), Gérard, Nonotte, and Berruel. The two latter were *ci-devant* Jesuits.

At their next meeting, in June 1780, the Clergy remonstrated, in a tone if possible still more energetic and emphatic, against the false liberalism and atheistical spirit of the age. The most learned and influential member of this Assembly was Dulau, Archbishop of Arles, who was placed at the head of the committee on "religion and jurisdiction," and presented to the House a very able report on the teeming productions of the infidel press. The prelate complained bitterly of the universal homage paid to "a famous writer (Voltaire) who was less remarkable for his genius and superiority of talent than for the implacable warfare which he had unhappily maintained for sixty years past against the Lord and his Christ; and who was nevertheless held up to public admiration, not only as the glory and model of literature, but as the benefactor of humanity and the restorer of social and patriotic virtue." He proceeded to denounce the subscription-lists recently opened for publishing various works inculcating a general contempt for authority in Church and State; and, passing on to consider what measures might be most advisable under the circumstances, questioned the wisdom of a recent *ordonnance*, which annexed the penalty of death to the offence of writing or diffusing works injurious to religion. "Called as we are," he said, "to a ministry of gentleness and charity, we find ourselves compelled to disguise the delin-

---

* *Procès-verb. des Assembl. du Cl. de France*, tom. viii. part ii. pp. 715 *et seqq.*

quencies of the most daring offenders, because we see the sword suspended over their heads. The same considerations may have restrained the activity of the most virtuous of our magistrates. A legislation less severe, and at the same time better executed, would be more effectual in suppressing the evil." The report goes on to advise greater vigilance and strictness in the public censorship; the punishment by fine or suspension of delinquent printers and booksellers; the abolition of "colportage" or book-hawking; frequent inspection of libraries and reading-rooms by the police; and an active supervision exercised upon the subject in all its bearings by the Episcopate. It was proposed, moreover, that the government should be requested not to sanction the publication of feeble apologies for religion, which were likely to do more harm than good.

The Report was adopted. It concludes with an eloquent expostulation against the apathy with which the prevalent assaults of infidelity had hitherto been treated by the authorities of the State: "Yet a few more years of silence, and the commotion will have become general, and will leave nothing to be seen around us but devastation and ruin."

Two other memorials were drawn up by the Archbishop of Arles in the name of this Assembly; the one on the encroachments of the Protestants, the other on the convocation of Provincial Councils. "Associations of all other kinds," he remarked, "are approved and patronized by government; why should the Clergy be denied the right to hold these venerable and canonical gatherings, so important to the welfare of their order? May not the Church justly look for at least an equal measure of protection with that accorded to the sciences, to literature, and even to Freemasonry?"

With respect to the Protestants, the memorial represented that they were constantly forming fresh enterprises with a view to recover that position of civil and religious independence which they had forfeited by the turbulence of former days. Of late years they had been admitted, contrary to law, to various public employments which naturally augmented their importance. Their worship was publicly celebrated, and they even insulted the worship and the faith of Catholics. The interference of the secular arm was invoked to repress their audacity; but at the same time the clergy strongly deprecated all punitive measures against the persons of their erring brethren, and acknowlodged that zealous teaching, persuasive example, fervent prayer, inexhaustible charity, are the proper and sole weapons of the Apostolate. "The ecclesiastical profession is perhaps of all others the most essentially opposed to all extremes of rigour."

Too confidently relying on the exclusive protection of an absolute monarchy, the Gallican prelates failed to perceive the necessity of large-hearted toleration and cordial recognition of the rights of conscience, even at a moment when the tempest was already lowering which was to sweep away not only their own immemorial privileges, but the throne of their sovereign, their national Christianity, and the whole assemblage of institutions which their country had inherited by the tradition of twelve centuries.

The Archbishop of Arles, in conclusion, deplored the false policy of the government in recently suppressing several religious communities. "In less than nine years nine different Congregations have disappeared from the face of the kingdom; the Servites, the Celestines, the Order of St. Brigitte, of St. Antoine, of the Saint-Esprit de Montpellier, &c. &c. And while reproach is heaped upon a saintly profession which has evangelical perfection for its glorious object, a wretched spirit of insubordination and revolt is ravaging our Church from within. The yoke of discipline weighs heavily on feeble minds. Zeal languishes, and resolution fails, under the flattering prospect of pensions and other worldly rewards, held out to the religious as temptations to abandon their profession. Who can wonder that families hesitate to entrust their children to houses whose existence is thus tottering and precarious? In a word, the axe is laid to the root of Monasticism as an institution, and will soon level with the ground that ancient tree, stricken as it is already with barrenness in many of its branches."

This Assembly expressed its disapproval of an edition of the collected works of Bossuet, which had been commenced some years previously by the Abbé Lequeux, and continued after his death by Dom Jean-Pierre Déforis, one of the Benedictines of Saint-Maur. Déforis was committed to Jansenist opinions, and laboured with all the fervour of unscrupulous party-spirit to impress a similar character on the writings of the immortal prelate; in order to which he loaded the text with a mass of notes, prefaces, and tedious explanatory dissertations, altogether foreign to the duties of an editor. The clergy were justly indignant at this attempt to give a false colouring to the utterances of the great Gallican oracle. They appointed a deputation to wait upon the keeper of the seals, and protest against the further progress of the publication; and in consequence orders were issued to Déforis to confine himself strictly to the reproduction of Bossuet's manuscripts, without note or comment. The Benedictine obeyed; but his labours were interrupted, as is well known, by the outbreak of the Revolution, and the work remained incomplete. The unfortunate Déforis perished on the scaffold during the "Terreur," in June, 1794.

Renewed efforts were made by the clergy, at an extraordinary meeting in 1782, to suppress the publication of irreligious books; and they adopted a special memorial to the throne against an edition of the complete works of Voltaire, which had been for some time in preparation under the auspices of Beaumarchais and Condorcet. This had already been complained of as an insult to religion by the Sorbonne, by Archbishop de Beaumont, and by De Pompignan, Archbishop of Vienne. The King, in his reply to the Assembly, promised satisfaction in general terms; and in pursuance of orders from the government, the editors of Voltaire established their press at Kehl, a town which, though not actually situate on French soil, was * separated from it only by the breadth of the river Rhine. The royal word was thus "kept to the ear," but it was nevertheless "broken to the hope." An order of Council appeared in conformity with the petition of the clergy, but no serious measures were taken to enforce it, and it was eluded without difficulty. The police paid Beaumarchais a domiciliary visit *pro formâ*, but it was known beforehand that nothing would be found to compromise him. All copies of the prohibited work had been previously removed to the Palais Royal, where they were safe under the custody of the Duke of Orleans, one of the most powerful patrons of the philosophers.

Among the mass of heterogeneous effusions which were thus first published to the world, a prominent place was occupied by the correspondence between Voltaire and D'Alembert; and the miserable fact was now demonstrated, which up to that time, though often asserted, had been pertinaciously denied, that these two friends not only disbelieved Christianity, but were

---

* I had written "is," but recent arrangements, to which I need not do more than allude, have necessitated the change of tense.

engaged in a deliberate conspiracy to overthrow it. During the later years of his life, this forms the theme of Voltaire's urgent and unwearied exhortations to his coadjutor. The phrases "écrasez l'infâme," "courir sus à l'infâme," and others of like tenor, recur continually in his letters, and leave no doubt as to the nature of the enterprise which was uppermost in his mind.

The "patriarch of Ferney" breathed his last at Paris on the 30th of May, 1778, at the age of eighty-four. Archbishop de Beaumont, when he first arrived in the capital, endeavoured to draw from him, by temperate and gentle solicitation, something in the shape of a disavowal of his errors. Voltaire, whose health was rapidly failing, at length consented to see a priest, and made a verbal profession tending towards reconciliation with the Church.* He rallied, however, for a time, and spoke jestingly of his recent act of weakness. On his deathbed he was visited by the curé of St. Sulpice, who questioned him as to some of the chief truths of Christianity; but the replies were ambiguous, and he died without receiving the last Sacraments. The "billets de confession," and the penalties inflicted in default of them, had for many years past fallen into disuse; notwithstanding which, the curé of St. Sulpice, in concert with the Archbishop, declined to sanction the interment of Voltaire's remains in holy ground. The Parliament showed no disposition, as of old, to coerce the ecclesiastical authorities; but the difficulty was cut short by the Abbé Mignot, nephew of the deceased philosopher, who hastily removed the corpse to his abbey of Scellières near Troyes, where it was buried with the accustomed rites. A missive from the Bishop of the diocese, prohibiting the funeral obsequies, arrived twenty-four hours after they had been performed.†

---

* It was expressed as follows: "Je soussigné déclare qu'étant attaqué depuis quatre jours d'un vomissement de sang, à l'âge de quatre-vingt-quatre ans, et n'ayant pu me traîner à l'église, M. le curé de Saint-Sulpice ayant bien voulu ajouter à ses bonnes œuvres celle de m'envoyer M. l'abbé Gauthier, prêtre, je me suis confessé à lui; et que si Dieu dispose de moi, je meurs dans la sainte religion catholique, où je suis né, espérant de la miséricorde Divine qu'elle daignera pardonner toutes mes fautes; et que si j'ai scandalisé l'Église, j'en demande pardon à Dieu et à elle.— Voltaire. Le 2 mars 1778, dans la maison de M. le marquis de Villette, en présence de M. l'abbé Mignot, mon neveu, et de M. le marquis de Villevielle, mon ami."—*Mémoires de Bachaumont* (edit. Barrière, 1846).

He acknowledged, however, that he did this only in order to secure a legal right to Christian sepulture. "Son refrain ordinaire est qu'il ne voulait pas que son corps fût jeté à la voirie." —*Ib.*

† Bachaumont, *Mémoires*. Droz, *Hist. du règne de Louis XVI*, liv. ii. p. 97. Lacretelle, *Hist. du XVIIIme siècle*, tom. v. p. 165.

The venerable Christophe de Beaumont departed this life, full of years, but in the possession of scarcely impaired mental energies, on the 12th of December, 1781. A vast multitude of the poor of Paris, who had been supported by his bounty, thronged the courtyard of the palace on the news of his death, bitterly lamenting the loss of their generous benefactor. The Archbishop was buried in Notre Dame, where his monument, like so many others, was brutally destroyed in one of the furious orgies of the Revolution. It was restored in 1811. He was succeeded in the see of Paris by Antoine Leclerc de Juigné, Bishop of Châlons, a prelate of eminent integrity and piety, but unfitted by natural temperament to cope with the tremendous difficulties of the time.

The attention of the clergy, at their ordinary meeting in the summer of 1785, was called to the judicial proceedings taken by the government against Cardinal De Rohan, Bishop of Strasburg, who was compromised in the mysterious intrigue known as that of the "collier de la Reine." The Cardinal, like many other prelates whose patrician lineage and powerful connections had been their passport to high rank in the Church, was a man of licentious morals, and was moreover egregiously vain and credulous. His weakness made him the dupe of a scheming adventuress called the Comtesse de Lamotte, who claimed descent from an illegitimate scion of the royal house of Valois. The particulars of the plot are familiar to all readers of French history, and need not be here recapitulated. Summoned suddenly to give an explanation to the king of the part which he had taken in the purchase of the famous necklace, the Cardinal avowed his indiscretion, and exposed the impudent fraud of which he was the victim. In the interests of all parties concerned, but pre-eminently in the interests of the throne, it would have been wise to avoid taking public cognisance of this discreditable affair. De Rohan, however, had the misfortune to be an object of violent personal dislike to Queen Marie Antoinette;[*] and it was at her demand, instigated by ill-advised counsellors, that Louis determined to submit the

---

[*] "Il avait, aux yeux de Marie Antoinette, l'irréparable tort d'avoir peint, de couleurs assez vraies, lorsqu'il était ambassadeur à Vienne, l'archi- duchesse, alors destinée au trône de France."—*Mémoires du Comte de Beugnot*, tom. i. p. 55.

case to legal examination. The Cardinal was arrested and sent to the Bastille; and, the option being offered him of taking his trial before a royal commission or before the ordinary courts, he preferred to trust himself to the justice of the Parliament. But he was speedily reminded that this was a step derogatory to his privileges as a prince of the Church. The Pope suspended him from the rights and honours of the Cardinalate for having recognised the competence of a civil tribunal, and threatened him with deposition if he persisted. He pleaded in his defence, that it was impossible for him to resist the positive commands of the king his master. Shortly afterwards the matter was taken up by the Assembly of the Clergy, who represented that the Cardinal, as a member of the Gallican episcopate, was entitled to the benefit of the Canon Law, which prescribes that bishops shall be judged by none but bishops. Upon this the prisoner retracted his appeal to the Parliament, and demanded to be tried by his ecclesiastical peers; and the Pope, informed of his change of sentiment, restored him to his place in the Sacred College. On the 7th of September, 1785, the Archbishop of Narbonne, president of the Assembly, moved that the affair of the accused prelate be referred to the Committee of "religion and jurisdiction;" and they made their report to the House in the sitting of the 13th of September. It established the right of a bishop to be judged by his colleagues, not only according to the provisions of ecclesiastical law, but on the authority of that acknowledged maxim of the civil constitution, which requires a French citizen to stand or fall by the verdict of his peers. The Assembly adopted a memorial to the king to that effect. It was presented by the president; but his Majesty's reply was evasive and unsatisfactory. He promised that the memorial should be taken into consideration; he assured the Clergy that they might depend upon his protection, and that he would carefully maintain the privileges which had been conceded to their Order by his royal predecessors. The cause, notwithstanding, was adjudicated by the Parliament. Nine months elapsed before it was decided. Court influence was brought to bear on one side to extort the condemnation of the prisoner, while on the other the many noble families to which he was related made every conceivable effort to secure his acquittal. Pending the proceedings, the Abbé Georgel, vicar-general to the Cardinal in his quality of Grand-aumônier,* had occasion to publish a Lenten *mandement*. He began by comparing himself to Timothy, whom St. Paul commissioned to supply his place in preaching the word of life to the disciples, while the Apostle was detained in bonds at Rome for his faithfulness to the Christian cause. Other ridiculous incidents occurred; and the popular feeling rose to a high pitch of excitement and irritation. The Parliament at length pronounced its *arrêt* on the 31st of May, 1786. The Cardinal, by a majority of five voices, was acquitted;† the Count and Countess Lamotte were declared guilty, and were sentenced, the husband to the galleys, the wife to detention for life at the Salpétrière. Such was the animosity at that moment against the court, especially against the Queen, that the result was hailed with enthusiasm by the people, and the Cardinal was conducted to his hotel amid shouts of triumph. Louis, most unwisely displaying his resentment, now deprived De Rohan of his office as Grand-aumônier, ordered him to send back the cordon of the Saint-Esprit, and banished him to his abbey of La Chaise Dieu in Auvergne. Two years later, on the intercession of the clergy, permission was granted him to reside at his palace of Saverne in the diocese of Strasburg.‡

The Church, the royal family, the monarchy, the aristocracy, lost prestige to a grievous extent by this unfortunate affair. The spectacle of an exalted dignitary, a member of the Roman Conclave, seized and ignominiously consigned to prison on a charge of swindling; the scandal of his intimacy with a person so notoriously unprincipled as Madame de Lamotte; the revelation of his almost incredible acts of folly in the fictitious negotiation with the Queen; the determination of the public to affix a sinister interpretation to the conduct of Marie Antoinette herself, in direct contradiction to the facts proved at the trial,—all these were circumstances of grave consequence in the critical state of France. And their effect was greatly

---

* The Grand-aumônier was *ex officio* ecclesiastical ordinary within the precincts of the court.

† "Purement et simplement déchargé de toute accusation."

‡ For a complete account of this strange passage of history, I may be allowed to refer the reader to the interesting work of M. Émile Campardon, *Marie-Antoinette et le procès du collier*, Paris, 1863.

enhanced in an ecclesiastical point of view by the too patent fact that the unedifying example of Cardinal de Rohan was by no means singular in the highest ranks of the clergy. The philosophism of the day was not without proselytes among the hierarchy; and the result was shewn not only in aberrations from the true standard of doctrinal belief, but in habitual worldliness of life and moral corruption. A thinly-veiled impiety had become fashionable in polite society; and aspiring Churchmen conformed without scruple to the dominant temper of the time. One of the most conspicuous of this class was the Abbé Talleyrand de Périgord, at this period one of the "agens-généraux" of the clergy, and soon afterwards Bishop of Autun; a man of no religious principle, who scarcely even pretended to believe the truths he was commissioned to teach, and who rudely broke through the trammels of his profession as soon as he caught sight of prospects which promised to gratify his thirst for worldly pre-eminence and power.

The last General Assembly of the Clergy of France was opened in May, 1788. The principal subjects of discussion were the resolutions which had been passed in the preceding year by the Assembly of the "Notables," convoked by the advice of the minister Calonne.* The Church had been represented on that occasion by fourteen prelates, three of whom, the Archbishops of Paris and Reims and the Bishop of Langres, sat as peers of the realm; among the rest were the Archbishops of Narbonne, Bordeaux, Arles, Toulouse, and Aix. The reforms proposed by Calonne were based on the great principle which had been asserted by Turgot and other statesmen, but hitherto ineffectually,—that of the extinction of fiscal privilege; the equal distribution of taxation among all orders of the nation. "What remains," he exclaimed in his opening speech, "to supply what is wanting, and procure all that is required to restore our financial prosperity? Abuses. Yes, gentlemen, it is in the abuses of our system that we possess a fund of wealth which the State is justly entitled to

---

* The Notables were a body whose counsels had been frequently resorted to in previous political emergencies. They were convoked at Tours by Louis XI.; twice in the reign of Francis I.; and by Charles IX. in 1560. The Constable De Luynes summoned them in 1619, and Cardinal Richelieu in 1628.

claim, and which may be the means of re-establishing order.* These abuses are founded on interests and antique prejudices, which have been spared by the lapse of ages; but what is the value of such considerations in comparison with that of the public welfare and the necessities of the State? It would be useless to attack small abuses; those which it is now proposed to annihilate are the most considerable, the most powerfully protected, those whose roots lie deepest, and whose branches are the most widely extended. Such are those which press upon the productive and labouring classes; abuses of pecuniary privilege, exceptions to the common law, the enormous disproportion of the contributions levied on different provinces and different subjects of the same sovereign, the manifold exemptions which enfranchise one part of the community only by aggravating the burdens borne by another. If such abuses, perpetually as they have incurred censure, have hitherto withstood public opinion and the repeated efforts of financiers to redress them, the reason is that it has been attempted to effect by partial operations what could not succeed but by a comprehensive and general measure."

The main feature of Calonne's programme was the imposition of a land-tax (*subvention territoriale*), to be assessed on the privileged orders equally with the rest of the nation. As the Clergy were by far the largest landed proprietors in the kingdom, this would have fallen with special severity upon their revenues; the prelates, in consequence, opposed the proposition, and succeeded eventually in defeating it, though several of them declared at the same time that they by no means wished to claim for their order immunity from ordinary taxation. The Archbishop of Narbonne, in the course of the discussion, protested with vehemence against a statement made by the minister, that the king had the right to impose taxes at his pleasure. Archbishop Dulau, of Arles, supporting his colleague, observed that it was doubtful whether any public body except the STATES-GENERAL was empowered to make additions to the national burdens. This appears to have been the first public mention of that great constitutional resource; of which no

---

* Calonne was affectedly careless in his phraseology. What he meant to say was, of course, that the sole hope for France lay in the *abolition* of these abuses.

government had availed itself since the beginning of the reign of Louis XIII., but which was soon to be invoked with clamorous eagerness by every mouth, as the sole remaining hope for the salvation of France. In the same sitting, M. de Castillon, Procureur-Général of the parliament of Aix, declared his conviction that no legal power existed which could enforce a land-tax in the proposed shape; neither Notables, nor Parliaments, nor provincial Estates, nor even the King himself; it belonged solely to the competence of the States-General.*

Without enlarging further on the debates in the Assembly of the Notables, it may be sufficient to remind the reader that Calonne, finding himself thwarted and undermined, retired from office in April, 1787, and that the control of the finances was then entrusted to Lomenie de Brienne, Archbishop of Toulouse. Brienne was one of the class commonly known as "prélats-administrateurs." In the government of his diocese he had shown considerable talent for business; but he was known rather as a political intriguer, a candidate for secular office and power, than as a model of piety and pastoral zeal. He was a man of advanced ideas, and an ally of the philosophers;† one, moreover, who stood high in favour with the Queen, to whom he was indebted for his appointment. Louis himself regarded him with aversion, on account of his latitudinarian views and irregular morals. Though his voice had been loudest in condemnation of the policy of his predecessor, the Archbishop had nothing original to propose on succeeding to his place; he advocated the same measures with slight modifications. Like Calonne, he laid great stress on the principle of impartial taxation; and this was accepted, theoretically, by the Assembly. But when he proceeded to recommend the land-tax, and define its amount, opposition arose in the same quarter as before, and the Notables declined to pledge themselves to any specific resolution on the subject. All parties began to feel embarrassed, irritated, wearied; and the minister soon judged it advisable to bring these fruitless deliberations to a close. The

---

* Droz, *Hist. du règne de Louis XVI*, liv. v. p. 174.

† De Brienne was an early friend of Turgot, and is said to have shared in the composition of his able work, *Le conciliateur, ou Lettres d'un ecclésias-* *tique à un magistrat*, published in 1754. In 1781 he was mentioned to the king as a possible successor to Archbishop de Beaumont. "No," said Louis; "it is still necessary that an Archbishop of Paris should believe in God."

Notables were dismissed on the 25th of May, having previously declared that "they referred it to the wisdom of the king to decide what imposts would be the least objectionable, in case it should be indispensable to demand fresh sacrifices from the nation."

Several edicts were now sent to the Parliament for registration. Three were accepted without difficulty; but the fourth, establishing a new stamp-duty, was resisted; and the magistrates demanded, as a previous condition, that they should be furnished with an account of the exact state of the national exchequer. This the government refused; and the royal edict was accordingly rejected. The Archbishop next presented the decree legalizing the tax on landed property. Under other circumstances this might have been expected to pass readily, as embodying the eminently popular doctrine of the equality of all ranks and classes before the law; but the Parliament was now possessed with a spirit of perverse obstructiveness. They clamoured vaguely for reform, yet when reforms were proposed in a definite shape, they forthwith denounced them as dangerous innovations. They negatived the king's demand, and announced in plain terms that "the nation, represented by the States-General, had alone the right to grant to his Majesty those subsidies which were manifestly necessary." Upon this a bed of justice was held, and the two edicts were registered under compulsion. The Parliament protested, as usual, the next day, and was thereupon exiled to Troyes. It was recalled, however, within a month, and the minister made an exhibition of his weakness by withdrawing the contested edicts.

Dissension recommenced immediately, and a decree authorizing a loan of 120 millions was registered by force in the king's presence. Another measure was proposed at the same moment, the object of which was to restore the Protestant separatists, to some extent, to the civil status of which they had been deprived under Louis XIV., by providing for the legal registration of their births, deaths, and marriages. Such a step had been long in contemplation, and had been repeatedly demanded by the Parliament; yet in the present state of embittered feeling it was not allowed to pass without being sharply questioned. A councillor named D'Eprémenil, a man of fearless courage, and highly distinguished as a popular leader, inveighed against the edict as a breach of the king's coronation oath, and an insult to the religion of his ancestors. Being reproved by several speakers for such language, he raised his hands towards the Crucifix at the further end of the hall, and exclaimed, in a burst of indignant enthusiasm, "What! would you crucify the Lord a second time?" D'Epréménil was a fanatic in religion, and had imbibed the delusions of the mystical sect called "Illuminés," or "Guerinets." His opposition, however, was not strongly supported. On a division, the edict in favour of the Protestants was passed by a majority of ninety-six against seventeen. It was but a niggardly instalment of relief; they were still to remain excluded from all judicial offices, and from all employments involving the right to give public instruction.*

Thus passed the eventful year 1787, which throughout its course portended more and more clearly the outbreak of the Revolutionary storm. Archbishop De Brienne, who had been accustomed to exercise great influence in successive Assemblies of the Clergy, summoned the extraordinary meeting of 1788 in the hope of obtaining the co-operation of his brethren in the important constitutional changes which he meditated, and also a liberal subsidy towards the necessities of the treasury. But he found them indisposed to meet his views. They remonstrated against the proposed "cour plénière," on the ground that such a tribunal would be suspected by the nation as dependent on the Crown, and might become a focus of dangerous intrigue in the event of a minority and a regency. They demanded, moreover, on the motion of the Archbishop of Arles, that the ancient immunities of their order in respect of taxation should be preserved, stickling with special earnestness for the "forms" of the ecclesiastical administration; that is, for the right of assembling in their own Chamber and regulating by their own votes the amount and proportion of their contributions. They deprecated, again, the late concessions to non-Catholics, and entreated the king to revoke that part of his edict. Finally, they expressed an anxious desire for the convocation of the States-General, thanked the king for his promise to resort to

---

* See the Edict "concernant ceux qui ne font pas profession de la religion catholique," in Isambert, *Anc. Lois Françaises*, tom. xxviii. pp. 472 *et seqq.*

their advice, and begged him to take that step without delay.

It is not easy to understand the policy of the Clergy in tendering this latter piece of advice to the Crown. That the Parliament should urge an appeal to the States-General is intelligible; for that body, no doubt, expected that the representatives of the nation would confirm and extend its privileges, and enact effectual guarantees against arbitrary interference by the sovereign. But it is strange that the *Clergy* should have imagined that, in the existing state of public feeling, the States-General were likely to legislate favourably to their pretensions and their interests. They could hardly have been ignorant that the overgrown wealth and vexatious privileges of the Church were hateful to the mass of the nation. They might have foreseen that the Tiers-état, when once permitted to deliberate upon the measures necessary to the safety of France, would vigorously attack abuses and anomalies which had long since been pronounced intolerable. Could they forget or ignore, again, the rampant hostility of the anti-Christian philosophy, and the cruel breaches it had made in the attachment of the people to the ancient Faith? Were they blind to the deplorable results of seventy years of bitter controversial agitation? To the still turbulent spirit of the Jansenists? to the subtle intrigues of the proscribed Jesuits? to the deep-rooted disaffection of the oppressed Protestants? All these quarters threatened danger to the National Church in its then position of exclusive authority; all these elements were ready to combine in the event of any serious attempt to legislate for the changed condition of society and the imperious demands of modern civilisation. The clergy, notwithstanding, fervently invoked the action of the States-General. Perhaps, as things then stood, it was too late to prevent that decisive intervention. But it might have been possible to guide its course and modify its character, had the privileged orders been wise enough to sacrifice in advance their odious exemptions, and to set an example of patriotic self-devotion while they were yet free agents, possessed of predominant influence on the movements of the State. They gained little credit by yielding afterwards, when it was manifest that they could no longer resist. It availed them nothing to abandon, in a moment of impassioned impulse, what they ought to have conceded long before as a matter of principle and duty.

The session of the Assembly terminated on the 4th of August. The remonstrances then presented by the Clergy are supposed to have mainly determined the policy of the government at this perilous crisis. On the 8th of August, 1788, a royal ordonnance postponed—in other words withdrew—the scheme of the "cour plénière," and fixed the meeting of the States-General at Versailles for the 1st of May, 1789.

Archbishop de Brienne now sank rapidly in credit. His financial difficulties were overwhelming; and at length he was compelled to announce that, for a specified time, the public creditor would be paid partly in cash, and partly by drafts or bills upon the treasury, which were to bear interest. This was looked upon as a confession of the imminence of national bankruptcy; and it was impossible, under such circumstances, that the minister should remain in office. He resigned on the 25th of August, to the general satisfaction of the nation. Honours were heaped upon him at the moment of his retirement; he had already exchanged the Archbishopric of Toulouse for that of Sens; he was now created a Cardinal by Pius VI., at the urgent request of Louis XVI. Several of his relatives received valuable appointments in the Church and at court; and in a word, De Brienne took his departure for Italy covered with marks of royal favour.* He was the last in the series of ecclesiastics who, with great diversities of intellectual capacity, but with an almost uniformly low average of moral and religious worth, enjoyed political ascendancy under the Feudal monarchy of France.

---

* This prelate held five great abbeys in addition to the archbishopric of Sens. His ecclesiastical income is said to have reached 680,000 francs (27,200*l.*).

CHAPTER XI.

The celebrated Necker, whom Louis recalled to the helm upon the fall of De Brienne,* re-assembled the Notables, and consulted them as to the composition and organization of the States-General;—questions which were now debated with intense vehemence throughout France. The Notables appealed to the precedent of 1614; when the deputies of the three orders had been nearly equal in number,† and had sat in three separate chambers, each possessing the right of a veto upon the proceedings of the other two. But it was not possible that such a glaring anachronism could be perpetrated under the present widely different circumstances of the nation. The Notables recommended liberal concessions with regard to the elective franchise; assigning, for instance, to every ordained priest, whether beneficed or unbeneficed, an equal right of suffrage for the ecclesiastical deputies. But they could not be persuaded to agree to the "double representation of the Tiers-état," although, strictly speaking, that principle was no innovation, having been already affirmed and acted upon in the case of the Provincial Assemblies created by Necker in his first administration. The question, like all others in revolutionary times, was destined to be practically settled, not by reference to tradition, but by the imperious exigencies of the hour. "The point to be considered," said Mirabeau, "is not what took place in former ages, but what ought to take place now."

Louis, urged by his Minister, overruled the judgment of the Notables, and decided that the number of deputies representing the Tiers-état should be equal to those of the other two orders united. This was announced by a royal ordonnance

---

* "Why did they not give me the fifteen months of the Archbishop?" exclaimed Necker; "*now it is too late.*" Madame de Staël, "Considérations sur la Rév. Française" (*Œuvres*, tom. xii. p. 164).

† The proportion of numbers on that occasion was as follows:—Clergy, 140; nobles, 130; commons, 192. But in those days the *number* of the deputies was a matter of little or no importance, since the voting was by orders and not numerically.

of December 27, 1788. Necker hesitated, however, to solve the further and more serious difficulty, whether the votes of the three orders were to be taken separately or in conjunction. In that problem lay the secret of the Revolution. The minister hoped to preserve his popularity by gratifying the commons in one point of their demand, while he withheld the other; but his own language at this juncture showed that he fully perceived the almost inevitable connection between the "double representation" and the numerical method of voting. "The importance attached to this question (that of the relative numbers of the deputies), is, perhaps, exaggerated on both sides; for since the ancient Constitution authorises the three orders to deliberate and vote separately, the number of deputies belonging to each order does not seem to be a question worthy of the degree of warmth which it excites. *It is, no doubt, to be desired that the orders should combine voluntarily for the examination of all affairs in which their interests are absolutely identical;* but since that resolution depends wholly on the wish of the orders, it can be looked for only from their regard for the welfare of the State." It suited Necker to speak thus guardedly; but his declared policy in making so large an addition to the numbers of the popular Chamber was universally understood to involve a further innovation which he did not dare to avow.

The States-General, when they met at Versailles on the 5th of May, 1789, consisted of 1158 members. The clerical Chamber numbered 290, including 47 prelates and 35 abbots and canons of cathedrals. The deputies of the Nobility were 270. The Tiers-état counted 598 voices, thus considerably outnumbering the collective strength of their colleagues. Their preponderance had been increased by the conduct of the nobles in Brittany and elsewhere, who had refused to proceed to any election of deputies.

The constituents of the Tiers-état, in their "cahiers" adopted in the various electoral districts, had already peremptorily demanded the grand concession which was to secure their supremacy in the work of legislation. They required that the votes should be taken individually, "so as to correct the inconvenience arising from the distinction of orders." They contemplated the possibility that the two privileged orders might refuse to accept this arrangement; and declared that, in that case, "the deputies of the Tiers-état, representing as they did twenty-four millions of Frenchmen, were both entitled and bound to act as a National Assembly, after offering to admit to their councils those of the Clergy and Nobles who might be willing to join them."* In pursuance of these instructions, the first movement of the Tiers-état was to invite their colleagues to meet them in the great hall (which had been assigned to them in consideration of their numbers), in order to proceed to the verification of their powers. The other Chambers had determined that this should be done separately; the clergy by 133 votes against 114, the nobles by 188 against 47.

The ecclesiastical order was much embarrassed by internal divisions. The great majority of its members were country curés, whose birth, social habits, and political ideas disposed them to sympathize with the Tiers-état; most of them were wretchedly poor, and they were not without grounds of discontent from the arrogant administration of their superiors. Many were Jansenists, smarting under the bitter memories of bygone wrongs and tyranny. On the other hand, the "haut clergé" were powerfully represented, and had every motive to identify themselves with the Crown and the aristocracy; these dreaded the assumptions of the popular order, which they hoped to repulse by ranging themselves resolutely on the side of privilege and prerogative. Both sections concurred, however, in proposing a joint committee of the three orders to arrange the point in dispute. The experiment was tried, but failed. An appeal was then made to the Clergy; they were adjured "in the name of the God of peace, and for the sake of the safety of France," to unite their deliberations with those of their brethren of the commons. This produced so marked an impression, that at one moment victory seemed certain; but the bishops contrived to prevent a division, and the debate was adjourned. The Court now interposed, and desired the Chambers to resume their conferences in the presence of the keeper of the seals and other royal commissioners, who were instructed to propound a compromise. The Clergy accepted the suggestion; the Nobles declined it; and on the 9th of June the negotiations were definitively broken off.†

---

* *Résumé Général des Cahiers*, tom. ii.
† Droz, *Hist. du règne de Louis XVI*. Bailly, *Mémoires d'un Témoin de la Révolution*, tom. i.

On the next day, June 10, the Tiers-état proceeded to a step which not only settled the point immediately at issue, but virtually predetermined the entire course of the Revolution. On the motion of the Abbé Sièyes, one of the members for the city of Paris, they sent a deputation to the clergy and nobles, to represent the necessity of no longer delaying to constitute the States for the despatch of business. They summoned them, for the last time, to repair to the Common Hall to verify their powers; they announced that the roll of the "bailliages" would be called over immediately; and that in every case of non-appearance the return would be declared null and void. On the 12th the examination of the "mandats" accordingly commenced. On the 13th, three curés of Poitou, Lecêve, Ballard, and Jallet, presented themselves in the chamber of the Commons, and tendered their credentials. They were received with joyful acclamations; it was looked upon as certain that the example would be speedily and largely followed. Six new adhesions were announced the day after; among them was that of Henri Grégoire, curé of Embermesnil, whose name, then scarcely known beyond his native province of Lorraine, was soon to become one of the household words of the revolutionized Church. Ten other clerical seceders joined the popular order on the 15th and 16th; and the impulse thus given was finally decisive in favour of the Tiers-état. It was on the 17th of June that Sièyes made the memorable speech in which he proposed that the deputies then present, representing the whole French nation in the proportion of ninety-six per cent., should proceed to discharge the duties for which they were elected, under the title of the NATIONAL ASSEMBLY. This motion, being put to the vote, was carried by a majority of 491 against 90. The first act of the self-constituted legislature was virtually one of sovereign authority, and formed a fitting prelude to its subsequent operations. The Assembly declared that it consented, in the name of the nation, to the collection of the existing taxes, although they had been illegally imposed. This arrangement was to remain in force up to the day of its separation; after which all taxes which had not been freely voted by the representatives of the people were to cease and determine throughout France.

The debates in the Clerical Chamber upon the question of verification of powers were protracted and tumultuous. The division was taken on the 19th of June; when the motion of the Archbishop of Paris, that the verification should be made separately, was affirmed by 138 votes, the contrary opinion being maintained by 127. Twelve deputies, however, declared themselves willing to adopt this latter course, with the addition of a proviso that the distinction of the three orders should be preserved in the verification. The minority entreated them to waive their exception, but, finding them resolute, they agreed to it by acclamation;—a move which transformed their minority into a majority of *one*. On the 22nd 149 ecclesiastics, headed by the Archbishops of Vienne and Bordeaux and the Bishops of Chartres, Coutances, and Rodez, figured in the procession of the National Assembly to the church of St. Louis.

The first outbreak of revolutionary violence occurred two days later, when Archbishop de Juigné was assailed by the populace on leaving the ecclesiastical Chamber; stones were thrown at his carriage, one of his chaplains was wounded by his side, and had not his coachman shown remarkable presence of mind, his life would have been in imminent jeopardy. He reached the Palace in safety, and a detachment of troops was sent to protect it; but the multitude was not to be intimidated; they became more and more furious, and it was found impossible to appease them until a promise had been extorted from the Archbishop that he would take his seat in the National Assembly. On the next day, accordingly, he yielded to this strange dictation, and was introduced to the Assembly by the Archbishop of Bordeaux. "Gentlemen," said De Juigné, "the love of peace brings me this day into the midst of your august assembly. Accept the sincere expression of my entire devotion to our country, to the service of the king, and to the welfare of the people. I should esteem myself too happy if I could contribute to these ends even at the expense of my life. May the step which I now take prove in some measure serviceable to the cause of conciliation and union, which must ever be the object of our desires!" Bailly, the president, replied by declaring that the Assembly congratulated itself on the presence of so eminent a prelate, that it had long and anxiously hoped for the benefit of his co-operation, and that the proof which he then gave of patriotism was the only crown that was wanting to his exemplary virtues.

Louis at length perceived that the tide had set in with a

force and volume which it was hopeless to resist. He yielded once more to the counsels of Necker, and laid his imperative commands upon the rapidly dwindling minority of the privileged orders to join their colleagues on the benches of the Assembly. Reluctantly and ungraciously they obeyed. Cardinal de la Rochefoucauld, President of the ecclesiastical chamber, distinctly notified, on taking his seat, that the Clergy reserved their constitutional right to deliberate and vote separately;— a right which they had neither the power nor the will to abandon during the present session of the States-General.

Extraordinary rejoicings followed the re-union of the three Orders. The king and the royal family were saluted with enthusiastic demonstrations of loyalty. Versailles was spontaneously illuminated. Hundreds of patriot voices proclaimed, with premature exultation, that the Revolution was accomplished, and accomplished without shedding a drop of blood.

It is no part of my design to undertake a detailed description of the momentous drama to which these scenes were introductory; but I am bound to place before the reader some account of those earliest enterprises of revolutionary legislation which bore so disastrously upon the status and fortunes of the National Church.

The object contemplated by the Constituent Assembly was to construct a new political system; to recast the whole framework of government, ecclesiastical and civil. As soon as it addressed itself to this gigantic task, the Church confronted it *in limine;* the most ancient, the most venerable, the most powerful, of all the institutions which belonged to the old *régime.* We have already reviewed, at some length, the causes by which that noble fabric had become to a great extent disorganized and dilapidated. We have seen the Church distracted for more than a century past by divisions of an altogether exceptional character; divisions more harassing than those of formal schism, inasmuch as both sides appealed with equal confidence to authority, tradition, and historical testimony, and both remained outwardly united within the pale of the same visible Communion. We have witnessed the outrageous abuses of ecclesiastical patronage through the concessions made to the Crown by the Concordat of Bologna;—the systematic prostitution of spiritual dignity to the claims of secular rank, political interest, worldly fashion, and other recommendations even more degrading. We have traced the rise and progress of a Philosophy "falsely so called," which, under colour of establishing the "rights of man," tended in reality to dissolve the essential bonds which hold society together, and to confound all sense of religious obligation in a hopeless maze of unbelief. We have noted that a desperate assault on the position of the Church, both as the authoritative Teacher of revealed truth and as an immensely wealthy corporation, was foreseen and predicted by sagacious observers as one of the first fruits of the turbulent spirit of the age. The aggregate of all these premonitory symptoms could not but entail a speedy catastrophe, when once the Revolution had acquired the great primary advantage which left it free to pursue its headlong career. The course of events which actually followed was unexpected and startling in its details; but the ultimate result was a foregone conclusion.

The population of France, whether in Paris or the provinces, was at this moment in a state of universal agitation and disorder. Brigandage and pillage prevailed to a fearful extent in many of the rural districts. The châteaux of the nobility were burnt by the peasants, and the proprietors subjected to gross indignities and cruelty. Crime of every kind was perpetrated with impunity; the law was powerless. The collection of the revenue, of rents, and seigneurial duties, was resolutely refused on all sides. An alarming report of these excesses was made to the Assembly on the 4th of August, and led to one of the most remarkable movements of the Revolution.

It was proposed, on the recommendation of a Committee, that the ancient laws of the realm should be maintained in force until they had been abrogated or modified by the Assembly; and that the taxes should continue to be levied until other less burdensome charges had been established. Upon this the Vicomte de Noailles suddenly rose, and, in an animated apostrophe to the clergy and nobles, exhorted them to make a general sacrifice of feudal rights and prescriptive privileges for the relief of their suffering fellow-countrymen. He demanded that the public burdens should be borne henceforth by all classes of Frenchmen in just proportion to their incomes; that pecuniary duties should be declared redeemable at a valuation to be hereafter fixed; and that *corvées* involving personal service should be abolished without compensation. The effect of his speech was electrical. These prodigious reforms were voted by acclamation; and, in a paroxysm of wild excitement, every vestige of Feudalism, with all its vexatious imposts, exemptions, and distinctions, was irrevocably swept away. The privileged orders vied with each other in devising schemes of self-spoliation; for several hours it was a scene of passionate competition for the honour of making the most costly and transcendent offering upon the national altar. Never was the characteristic impulsiveness of the French mind more strikingly illustrated.

Among the events of that memorable night, not the least important was the abandonment of the ecclesiastical tithes. This was included in the sweeping suppression of "droits de mainmorte." Hitherto payable in kind, the tithe was now to be commuted into a money-payment upon a principle to be determined by the Assembly; and its total redemption was to be provided for eventually. This was a serious change of system; but in its original shape it stopped short of confiscation. The agencies now in the ascendant, however, were not to be restrained within such moderate bounds. In the sitting of the 6th of August it was moved that the tithes, instead of being redeemed, should be extinguished without equivalent.* The maxim was now first enunciated, that Church property belongs to the nation; and the clergy were recommended to make a merit of necessity, and renounce of their own accord what the circumstances of the times no longer permitted them to retain. Redeemable rights, it was argued, imply an actual proprietorship; but the lands which pay the tithe were not granted to the clergy; tithe is a voluntary gift, which in process of time has become an impost; and it is always in the power of the nation to suppress it, on condition of making provision for the necessary expenses of the Church services and the relief of the poor. The Abbé Sièyes combated these assertions in a speech full of vigour and ability; contending that, although the estates liable to tithe had in the course of ages been repeatedly bought and sold, the tithe itself had never been included in the sale, and could not consequently be the property of any existing landowner. It was now proposed to abolish it, simply because the proprietors were unwilling to pay it any longer; but this would be, in fact, to make a present of upwards of seventy millions of francs to the land-

---

* The original decree provided that the tithes should continue to be payable in the usual manner as prescribed by law, until the tithcowners should have entered into actual possession of their "remplacement." Subsequently it was explained that this word was not to be taken to mean "un fournissement égal et équivalent," but only "un traitement honnête et convenable."

owner;—a measure of which he could not perceive the justice or expediency. His conclusion was that the tithe should be declared redeemable, that the produce should be capitalized, and the income applied, under the sanction of the law, to its original and only legitimate purposes.*

After three days of debate, a decision was arrived at independently of all considerations of reason and equity, by another outburst of tumultuous effervescence. A knot of curés, devoted to the popular party, handed to the President a paper bearing their signatures, by which they placed their tithes at the disposal of the nation, and urged their clerical brethren to follow their example. The invitation was warmly responded to. Ecclesiastics of all ranks hastened to append their names. No one seems to have reflected that the property which they were voting away was not their own, but held in trust on a life-interest, and that, consequently, they had no power or right to alienate it. " Let the Gospel be proclaimed," said Archbishop de Juigné; " let Divine service be celebrated with decency and dignity, let the churches be provided with virtuous and zealous pastors, let the poor be succoured in their need—such is the destination of our revenues, such is the object of our ministry and of our prayers. We place ourselves in the hands of the National Assembly, not doubting that it will secure to us the means of worthily discharging a mission so weighty and so sacred." " I declare," added Cardinal de la Rochefoucauld, " that the sentiments just uttered by the Archbishop of Paris are those of the whole clergy of France. We confide implicitly in the nation." Some objection having been made to the original document subscribed by the curés, as an invidious mode of proceeding under the circumstances, it was destroyed at once by its authors, and the tithes were thus abolished by an unanimous vote of the Assembly. Impelled by the same magnanimous spirit, the clergy likewise relinquished the plurality of benefices and the revenue arising from the " casuel " or surplice fees. The " annates," and other long-accustomed payments to the Court of Rome, were abrogated in like manner on the motion of the Abbé Grégoire.†

The consent of the Sovereign was asked, as a matter of form,

---

* Lacretelle, *Hist. de F. pendant le XVIIIme siècle*, tom. vii. p. 143.
† Bailly, *Mémoires*, tom. ii. p. 421. Ed. Berville et Barrière.

to this scheme of wholesale disendowment; whereupon Louis, while accepting it substantially, demurred to the wisdom of some few articles. But his observations were coolly disregarded. The Assembly requested him to promulgate their resolutions, and to give effect to them as law.*

The Abbé Sièyes now began to view his own work with misgiving, and bitterly remonstrated against a line of legislation which he had never contemplated. "You wish to be free," he cried, "and you know not how to be just!" Mirabeau's succinct announcement of the truth was little calculated to allay his apprehensions. "You have loosed the bull, M. l'Abbé, and you have no right to complain if he makes use of his horns!"

Madame de Staël, in her 'Considérations sur la Révolution Française,' explains with great perspicuity the ideas of the popular leaders at this crisis as to the temporal position and rights of the clergy. "The clergy in France," she says, "formed one of the four legislative powers; but as soon as it was judged necessary to make a change in this whimsical constitution, it was also necessary that the third part of all the property in the kingdom should no longer remain in the hands of the clergy; for it was in the quality of an order of the State that they possessed such an immense fortune, and administered it collectively. Since the property of the priests and of religious communities could not be made subject to those regulations of civil law by which the inheritance of parents passes in succession to their children, it would not have been wise to leave to the clergy an amount of wealth which might have enabled them to regain that political influence of which it was determined to deprive them. Justice required that the present holders should retain their life-interest; but what duty was owed to those who had not become priests, especially when the number of ecclesiastics was far larger than is needed to supply the spiritual wants of the people? Was it to be pleaded that nothing that exists ought ever to be altered? Was 'that which has been' necessarily established for all time to come?"

Again:—"Three-fourths of the possessions of the priests were bestowed upon them by the Crown, or by the ruling power of the day, not by way of personal favour, but in order to secure the due performance of Divine Service. Can it be questioned,

---

* Droz, *Hist. de Louis XVI*, liv. x. p. 348.

then, that the States-General, in conjunction with the King, had the right to make a change in the mode of providing for the maintenance of the clergy? But private founders and benefactors, it will be objected, bequeathed property to the ecclesiastical order; how can such endowments be with justice diverted from their destination? Yet man has no means of impressing a seal of eternity upon his resolutions. Is it possible to investigate, through the obscurity of ages, title-deeds which are no longer in existence, with a view to withstand the demands of living reason? The dissenting sects in England, it is true, provide spontaneously for the expenses of their worship; but the French were not disposed to submit to any sacrifice for the benefit of their priests. The prevailing unbelief arose precisely from the spectacle of the riches of the Church and the abuses thereby produced. It is with religion as with governments; if you attempt to maintain by force what is out of harmony with the feelings of the time, you debase the human heart instead of elevating it." *

Acting upon the principle thus broadly enunciated—that it is competent to the government and the nation to make alterations from time to time, at their discretion, in the public provision for the maintenance of religion and its ministers—the Assembly proceeded to legislate upon the whole subject of what had hitherto been accounted the sacred and inviolable possessions of the Church. A Committee had been appointed, on the motion of Talleyrand, Bishop of Autun, to devise measures for meeting the two ghastly calamities which stared France in the face, bankruptcy and famine; and the report was presented by that prelate on the 10th of October. After showing the utter insufficiency of all the ordinary resources at the command of the State, he pointed out that there existed an enormous fund which might justly be turned to account in such an emergency, namely, the property of the clergy. "The Clergy," argued Talleyrand, "are not proprietors of their possessions in the same sense with other proprietors. All that really belongs to them is that portion which is necessary to secure to them a moderate and becoming maintenance; of all the rest they are but administrators; it belongs to the fabrics of the churches and to the poor. If, then, the nation undertakes to provide for the sub-

---

* *Œuvres de Madame de Staël*, tom. xii. pp. 356 361.

sistence of the clergy;—if it relieves them from this administrative charge, and guarantees the repairs of churches, the expense of Divine Service, the relief of the poor, and other charitable obligations;—it is clear that the intention of founders is fulfilled, and that there is no violation of property. The surplus may rightly be appropriated to the extinction of the national deficit and the restoration of public credit." The Bishop went on to state that the territorial property of the Church was estimated at two milliards of livres, producing an income of seventy millions. The tithes amounted to eighty millions in addition. He proposed that for the future both lands and tithes should be at the disposal of the State; that out of the annual revenue thus acquired one hundred millions (four millions sterling) should be devoted to the maintenance of the clergy, none of whom were to receive less than 1200 livres, exclusively of residence and glebe; that all stipends should be paid quarterly in advance; and that the existing debts of the ecclesiastical Order should be defrayed by the State. It was believed that, after satisfying these claims, a sufficient balance would remain to reimburse the national creditor, and even to create a sinking-fund for future necessities.

The exposition of this scheme elicited loud applause. Considerable doubt was expressed, however, as to its feasibility; the sacrifice demanded seemed too vast to be submitted to without a formidable struggle, even though recommended by one of the most influential members of the episcopate. The question was debated long, vehemently, and with great ability; and various theories were broached as to the nature and tenure of Church property. Mirabeau was the principal speaker in support of Talleyrand's proposal, and was powerfully seconded by Barnave, Duport, and Treilhard. The most brilliant orator on behalf of the clergy was the Abbé Maury, afterwards Cardinal and Archbishop of Paris; but he showed a want of self-control and discretion, and indulged too often in angry invective which damaged his cause. One of the most sensible arguments was that of Malouet, who pointed out that even if it were true that Church property belonged to the nation, the Assembly had no right to alienate it from its traditional uses; the French people had not yet expressed its sentiments upon that question, and it was anything but certain that it would approve the course of radical innovation now proposed. He suggested the appointment of an

Ecclesiastical Commission, to enquire into the existing state of the bishoprics, chapters, parochial benefices, and conventual houses. After receiving its report, the Legislature would be better qualified to discuss a subject of such gravity, and to determine which establishments should be preserved and which it might be desirable to suppress.

But such moderate propositions were unheeded. A violent speech from Mirabeau brought the question to a definitive issue on the 2nd of November. He insisted strongly on the general principle that no designs of private benefactors can be allowed to come into competition with the public interest and the necessities of the State. The rights of the nation are prior to all such considerations; those who endowed the Church in days of yore had no power to fetter the action or compel the acquiescence of all future generations. "The nation is the sole and absolute owner of all ecclesiastical property." He moved, therefore, that the possessions of the clergy be declared at the disposal of the nation; charged, however, with the duty of providing for the expenses of public worship, the support of the priesthood, and the relief of the poor, under the superintendence of the provincial authorities. A second clause provided that the minimum stipend of incumbents should be 1200 livres, exclusively of house and garden. On a division the motion was carried by a majority of 568 against 346.*

These resolutions, which at a stroke reduced the clergy of the National Church from the position of an independent order of the State to that of a body of stipendiaries at the mercy of the popular will, were carried into immediate execution. On the 20th of December the Assembly ordered that a sale of ecclesiastical property should take place forthwith, to the amount of 400 millions of livres; and on the 5th of February, 1790, the beneficed clergy were enjoined to declare the nature and value of their preferments before the local municipal officers. Much difficulty was experienced, however, in the further prosecution of the scheme. Estates were offered for sale, but a sufficient number of purchasers was not forthcoming. In this dilemma it was arranged that a large portion of the property should be sold to the municipal corporations, who paid for it by promissory notes or debentures. These "billets municipaux" were after-

---

* Lacretelle, *Hist. de F. pendant le XVIII*^{me} *siècle*, tom. viii. p. 12.

wards put into circulation on the credit of the government, and were exchangeable, at the pleasure of the bearer, for their value either in land or in coin. Such was the origin of the famous system of "assignats," which, during the subsequent course of the Revolution, proved so fruitful a source of public distress and calamity.*

But the National Assembly, though it had no scruple in secularising the inordinate wealth which had been so grossly misused by the later generations of the hierarchy, was not prepared to risk a complete rupture with the Catholic Church. In the midst of the general wreck of the civil institutions of Feudalism, the Revolutionists were far from meditating the destruction of its religious organization. Proclaiming, as they did, universal toleration, unbounded liberty of conscience, the equality of all forms of religious worship in the eye of the law, they desired at the same time that the new Constitution which they were about to publish should have the sanction of Christianity, in that shape which was so immemorially and unalterably endeared to the heart of the French people. Disendowment they practised with a high hand and without remorse; but, with singular inconsistency, they shrank from disestablishment; they could not reconcile themselves to a positive sentence of divorce between Church and State. Hence, concurrently with their labours in remodelling the political institutions of the country, they digested a plan for bringing the ecclesiastical administration into harmony and union with the civil;—a scheme which was destined to prove signally abortive.

The "Constitution civile du Clergé" was framed by the so-called "Ecclesiastical Committee," and was submitted to the Assembly on the 6th of February, 1790. Its provisions amounted, without doubt, to a very serious invasion of the external economy of the Church as it had existed for some ten centuries in France. Its principal feature was that by which the ecclesiastical circumscriptions were to be assimilated to the new division of the kingdom into eighty-three departments, each department constituting a diocese. All existing sees beyond that number were suppressed. By the 5th Article, French citizens were forbidden to recognise, in any case and under whatsoever pretext, the authority of an ordinary or metropolitan whose see is within

---

* Rabaut de Saint-Étienne, *Précis de la Révolution Française.*

the territories of a foreign power, as well as that of its delegates residing in France or elsewhere; without prejudice, however, to "the unity of the Faith, and the communion which is to be maintained with the visible head of the Church universal." Bishops and parochial clergy were henceforth to be elected by the people; the only qualification for the electoral suffrage being that of having attended Mass immediately before proceeding to the election. The newly-elected bishop was to be confirmed by the Metropolitan, who might examine him, if he thought proper, as to his doctrine and life. Bishops were expressly forbidden to apply for institution to the Pope. They were simply to notify to him their appointment, in attestation of the unity of faith and of the communion which they were bound to preserve with the visible head of the Church universal.* Every bishop, before consecration, was to take an oath in the presence of the municipal officers, the clergy, and the people, to watch diligently over the flock committed to him, to be faithful to the nation, the law, and the king, and to maintain to the best of his power the Constitution decreed by the National Assembly and accepted by the sovereign. The same oath was imposed upon all curés before their institution by the bishop; and both bishoprics and cures were to be considered vacant until the incumbents-designate had taken the prescribed test.

The emoluments to be enjoyed by the clergy of the new Establishment were on a miserably parsimonious scale. The revenue allotted to the Bishop of Paris (the title of Archbishop being abolished) was 50,000 livres (2000*l.*). That of other bishops ranged from 12,000 to 20,000 livres, according to the size of their cathedral cities. Parish priests in the capital were to receive 6000 livres; in large country towns, 4000 livres; in smaller places, from 3000 down to 1200, in proportion to the population. Residence was enforced upon all ecclesiastics without distinction; even bishops were not authorised to be absent from their dioceses for more than fifteen days consecutively, except in case of absolute necessity, and with the consent of the civil authorities of the department.

---

* Art. XIX. "Le nouvel évêque ne pourra s'adresser au Pape pour en obtenir aucune confirmation; mais il lui écrira comme au chef visible de l'Église universelle, en témoignage de l'unité de foi et de la communion qu'il doit entretenir avec lui."

This scheme was subjected to a long series of searching debates in the Assembly. The spirit in which many of its regulations were conceived was clearly that of a return to the primitive principles of Church government, anterior to the usurpations both of the Papacy and of despotic royalty.* The chief author of the project was a *ci-devant* advocate of the Parliament of Paris, named Camus, a strict Jansenist in religious opinion, and well-known for his extensive acquaintance with the Canon Law, which had procured for him the appointment of counsel to the Clergy of France. His influence had been predominant in the deliberations of the "Comité ecclésiastique."

It was plain, from the first moment, that the proposed Constitution would not meet with unanimous acceptance from the clergy. The discussion upon it was opened by the Archbishop of Aix, who contended that the Assembly had no authority to legislate on the discipline of the Church, and that such matters could not be lawfully determined but by the bishops assembled in a National Council. He was answered by Treilhard, who argued that spiritual authority ought to be confined to articles of faith and morals, and that the external mechanism of religion in its public aspect has in all ages been more or less subject to the control of the temporal power. Camus pointed out that the territorial limits of dioceses are not of Divine institution; that they were adopted originally in conformity with the civil circumscriptions established by the Roman government; and that, since the State had thought fit to sanction a fresh division, it was the duty of the Church to regulate its own arrangements on that model. With regard to the appointment of bishops and pastors, he contended that the right of election resided, according to the primitive legislation of the Church, with the people; and that the transfer of that prerogative to the Crown and the Pope was a mere modern usurpation. Appeals to Rome, he said, must be suppressed, and ecclesiastical causes determined by judges acting on the spot. A question having been asked as to the interpretation of the Article repudiating the jurisdiction of foreign prelates, the Abbé Grégoire replied that "it was the intention of the Assembly to reduce the authority of the Pope

---

* The original right of Metropolitans to consecrate and confirm their suffragans was one of the points repeatedly insisted on in the critical conjunctures of Gallican Church history. See Vol. I. p. 348; Vol. II. pp. 74, 76.

to its legitimate dimensions; but that it was equally resolved, at the same time, to take every precaution against the calamity of schism."

After a discussion which was kept up with great energy for several weeks, the new Constitution of the Clergy was adopted by the Assembly on the 12th of July, 1790. Louis XVI. long hesitated to accept it. He had received a brief from the Pope, earnestly warning him against it as a sacrilegious attempt to overturn and degrade the whole structure of the Catholic Church. Negotiations followed with his Holiness, which occupied a considerable time, and of which the particulars were never divulged. The king at length signified his assent on the 24th of August.

A manifesto of the utmost importance, drawn up by Boisgelin Archbishop of Aix, and entitled "Exposition des principes sur la Constitution civile du Clergé," appeared on the 30th of October, bearing the signatures of thirty prelates belonging to the Assembly. It was an elaborate protest against the late legislation upon matters which, although they might be called external and temporal, were in point of fact inseparably connected with the spiritual functions and jurisdiction of the Church. Special exception was taken to the Article which transferred the canonical institution of bishops from the Pope to the Metropolitan, and that which enjoined newly-elected prelates simply to notify their appointment to his Holiness, instead of seeking at his hands the jurisdiction or mission essential to their ministry. This document was adopted by the great majority of the clerical members of the Assembly; it was circulated throughout France, and was signed by nearly the whole of the Episcopate, together with a large number of cathedral chapters and parish priests.[*] Nevertheless the legislature, uninfluenced by such expressions of opinion, proceeded to decree, on the 27th of November, that all ecclesiastics who, within one week from that date, had not taken the oath of adhesion to the Constitution civile du clergé should be deemed to have resigned their offices, and that their successors should be named without delay. If, notwithstanding, they should continue to exercise their ministry, they were to be declared rebellious to the law, deprived of their emoluments,

---

[*] Picot, *Mém. pour servir à l'hist. ecclesiastique pendant le XVIIIme siècle*, tom. iii. pp. 155-158.

stripped of the rights of citizens, and punishable by the tribunals, according to the circumstances of each case. The royal sanction was extorted, rather than granted, to this most impolitic act of rigour.*

The Assembly committed a grave error in judgment in attempting to force the new system upon the consciences of the clergy by the coercion of an oath. This false step became the source of fierce and calamitous dissension.

> "Hoc fonte derivata clades
> In patriam populumque fluxit."

For the third time in its history, the Church of France was now rent asunder by an internecine schism. On one side the Constitutional oath was accepted, on the other it was repudiated as incompatible with the first principles of ecclesiastical obligation. Henceforth the clergy were of two opposite designations;—jurors and non-jurors, conformists and nonconformists, "prêtres assermentés" and "prêtres insermentés." The issue between them was in reality none other than that which has always formed the point of departure between the rival systems of Gallicanism and Ultramontanism. If the Pope be not only the first bishop of Christendom, the visible ministerial head of the Church, the common Father of the faithful, but also the source and root of spiritual Authority, the sole and indispensable channel of mission to the diocesan Episcopate, then it was a matter of plain duty to refuse to acknowledge the lately-promulgated Constitution; for there can be no doubt that it ignored, and was intended to ignore, these latter pretensions on the part of the Roman Pontiff, and to revive the ancient discipline, as distinguished from the innovations of the Forged Decretals and the usurpations legalized by the Concordat of the sixteenth century. On the other hand, it was incontestably desirable to preserve a public recognition of Christianity by the French Government and people, provided this could be done without any sacrifice of essential principle; and many minor defects in the Constitution might well be excused in consideration of that vast advantage. Considering how much might fairly be pleaded on both sides of the dilemma, the good faith of those who felt at liberty to take the oath ought no more to have been impeached or

---

* Lacretelle, tom. viii. pp. 28-34.

questioned than the conscientious objections which governed the recusants. But to denounce pains and penalties, disabilities, deprivations, public infamy, against those who might demur to what were in their eyes unlawful changes decreed without competent authority, was, to say the least, a policy which betrayed a strange amount of short-sightedness and ignorance of human nature on the part of its authors. It contradicted the elementary principles upon which the Assembly had hitherto claimed the support of the nation; especially that of impartial toleration as laid down in the "Declaration of the Rights of Man."* It procured for the dissentients that sympathy which never fails to attach to those who suffer for their religious convictions— who are persecuted for conscience' sake.

The Abbé Grégoire was the first to swear allegiance to the Constitution. He took occasion to declare his persuasion that that step was consistent with profound attachment to the laws and institutions of Catholicism. After mature and serious examination, he and those who acted with him were unable to perceive in the new organization anything at all derogatory to the sacred truths which they were bound to believe and teach. "It would be to defame, to calumniate the Assembly, to impute to it a design to lay presumptuous hands upon the censer. In the face of France and of the universe the National Legislature had made a solemn profession of respect for the Catholic, Apostolic, Roman religion. Never had it harboured a thought of depriving the faithful of any of the means of salvation; never had it designed to make any aggression upon doctrine, upon the hierarchy, or upon the spiritual authority of the head of the Church. It fully acknowledged that such concerns are beyond its province."

About sixty curés, members of the Assembly, enlisted after the example of Grégoire under the banners of the Revolutionary Establishment. Of the bishops who were deputies, two only accepted the oath; Talleyrand, Bishop of Autun, and Gobel, Bishop of Lydda *in partibus* and suffragan of Basle. Three prelates not belonging to the Assembly gave in their adhesion afterwards, namely, Lomenie de Brienne, Archbishop of Sens; Jarente, Bishop of Orleans; and De Savines, Bishop of Viviers. With these five exceptions, the Gallican Episcopate remained calmly resolved to risk all temporal loss and suffering rather

---

* See the *Déclaration des droits de l'homme et du citoyen*, Articles x. xi.

than betray what they conscientiously believed to be the cause of the Church and of truth, by acknowledging the intervention of a secular power within the domain of spiritual jurisdiction. Their sees were forthwith declared vacant, and the severities of the law were executed to the full extent. It is not wonderful that, under these circumstances, the clergy who rejected the Constitution should have commanded the respect, confidence, and affection of the vast majority of Catholics in France.

On the 25th of January, 1791, the first constitutional bishops, Expilly and Marolles, were consecrated in the church of the Oratoire at Paris by the Bishop of Autun, assisted by Gobel of Lydda, and Miroudot, another bishop *in partibus*. This was manifestly an irregular proceeding, even according to the new code of jurisprudence; for neither Talleyrand nor his assistants could pretend to metropolitan rank, and were therefore not empowered to confirm or institute bishops; so that although a true succession was secured by their ministry, it remained a debateable question whether the new prelates possessed a valid mission. The elections to eighty vacant sees were now proceeded with throughout the country. Gobel was chosen Bishop of Paris, in the room of Archbishop de Juigné, who had quitted France with the first batch of aristocratic emigrants on the outbreak of the Revolution. Grégoire was elected in two dioceses, and made his option for that of Loir-et-Cher, fixing his residence at Blois. The new body of rulers thus intruded on the Church were for the most part men of small capacity and no weight of character. Many were promoted as a direct reward for the votes by which they had contributed in the Assembly to subvert the ancient constitution of France in Church and State; while the success of others was due to the general reputation they enjoyed for unqualified zeal in the cause of Revolution.*

The Court of Rome lost no time in announcing publicly the view taken of the "Constitution civile du clergé" by the supreme authority of the Church. In a brief, dated March 10, 1791,

---

* Several of the new prelates, however, were men of undoubted ability and merit; among such may be named Lamourette, Metropolitan of Lyons; Le Coz, Bishop of Ille-et-Vilaine; and Moyse, of the Jura. Bishop Grégoire, too, though widely mistaken in many of his opinions, possessed a high character for integrity, piety, and pastoral zeal. He courageously denounced the apostasy of Gobel, and the appalling acts of impiety connected with the "culte de la Raison."

and addressed to the bishops of the National Assembly, Pope Pius expressed at some length his disapproval of its principal articles; combating particularly the idea that matters of discipline are comparatively unimportant, and may be altered at pleasure without detriment to purity of doctrine and the integrity of Church communion. He severely reprobated the new arrangement for the election of bishops, the control which was to be exercised over them by the departmental and municipal officers, the suppression of monastic Orders, and the reckless alienation of ecclesiastical property. A month later his Holiness published a second brief, directed to the episcopate, clergy, and faithful laity of France, by which he peremptorily commanded all ecclesiastics, secular and regular, of whatever rank or order, who had submitted to the new Constitution, to signify their retractation within forty days, under pain of suspension, and of being declared irregular if they should continue to exercise their functions. By the same act he pronounced the recent consecrations null and void, and suspended from all episcopal functions the two prelates, Talleyrand and Gobel, who had taken the chief part in consummating the schism.*

The existing breach among the Gallican clergy was thus widened and intensified. The "insermentés" were compelled to look upon their conforming brethren as sacrilegious pretenders, destitute of valid ministerial authority; while the partisans of the Constitution, finding themselves repudiated by the Pope, perceived that they had little or no chance of acquiring the confidence of the people unless the antagonist priesthood could be decisively dislodged from their position and driven out of the field.

Open strife was the inevitable result of such a state of feeling in the then condition of France. Agitation and violence broke out, almost immediately, in various districts;—in the Pas-de-Calais, in Normandy and Brittany, in Poitou, in Languedoc. Day after day reports were made to the Legislature of fierce brawls, not unfrequently ending in bloodshed, between the rival religionists; sometimes the aggressors were agents of the "prêtres réfractaires," sometimes the supporters of the State clergy insulted and persecuted the nonconformists. Disorder, confusion, anarchy, reigned on all sides. Contradictory propositions were put forward as to the best means of meeting these new perils. One deputy

---

* Picot, *Mémoires*, tom. iii. p. 173.

moved that priests who had refused the civic oath should be confined (*internés*) to the chief towns of the departments, under the surveillance of the authorities. Another insisted that the law should be put in force impartially against all priests, whether constitutional or non-juring, who were found disturbing the public peace. On one side it was demanded that religious liberty should be secured by paying the ministers of all persuasions indiscriminately; on the other it was urged, with a view to the same object, that all public provision for religious purposes should be suppressed, and the citizens left to remunerate on the voluntary principle those whose ministrations they preferred. The notorious Fauchet, constitutional Bishop of Calvados, after declaiming vehemently against intolerance, persecution, and fanaticism, concluded by requiring that the non-jurors should be deprived of all salary from the national treasury, inasmuch as the State recognised no form of Catholicism except its own.* "Why should we pay these troops of *ci-devant* canons, abbés, monks, and beneficed clergy, who have abjured the conditions of their ministry, and are remarkable only for their intriguing spirit and their intense hatred of the Revolution? Of what use are they? They only play into the hands of the 'émigrés,' they send money out of the kingdom, they foment sedition at home and abroad. They would be content to see blood flow in torrents, provided only they could recover their lost privileges."

The Girondist Gensonné proposed to separate the ministrations of religion from everything connected with civil government; to confine the clergy to their strictly spiritual functions, and take from them the duty of registering secular acts—births, deaths, and marriages—together with the management of schools, hospitals, &c. After which there would be no necessity to exact the oath to the "Constitution civile," and the main cause of the prevailing commotion would be at once removed.

The result of these discordant reasonings was a decree passed by the Legislative Assembly on the 29th of November, 1791, to the following effect:—that refractory priests should no longer receive payment or support of any kind from the public funds;

---

* The Non-jurors, though they had no share of the provision made for the clergy by the new constitution, still enjoyed a scanty pittance from the funds produced by the sale of the ancient patrimony of the Church.

that they should be reputed "suspects" of disaffection, rebellion, and traitorous designs against their country, and as such placed under surveillance; that the authorities might remove them from any localities in which disturbances occurred; that they might be imprisoned for any period not exceeding two years; that none but "prêtres assermentés" should be allowed to officiate in churches maintained by the State; and that a list of those who refused the oath should be drawn up and laid before the Assembly. But this measure was loudly exclaimed against in various quarters; and the king, after a month's deliberation, interposed the veto assigned to him by the Constitution, in virtue of which it fell to the ground.

The "insermentés" interpreted this as an encouragement to persevere in their factious conduct; and the ferment of religious agitation, especially in the rural districts, rose higher than ever. "What with fanaticism on one side and persecution on the other," cried Cahier-Gerville, minister of the interior, "it seems as if toleration were banished from the realm." The only remedy, he added, was a complete separation between Church and State. France ought to renounce the idea of a national religion, and leave it to the consciences of individuals to support whatever creed and form of worship they thought proper.

But the outbreak of the war with Germany, which was attributed, not without reason, to the persevering intrigues of the emigrants, and the intimate connection of this latter party with the clergy opposed to the Constitution, threw the Assembly into a state of excitement and indignation which made it impossible that the religious difficulties of the moment should receive a wise and maturely-considered solution. In the midst of the alarms of impending foreign invasion, a fresh debate commenced on the 13th of May upon the penal enactments to be applied to the Non-jurors. The question had been referred to a committee of twelve members; and in pursuance of the recommendations of its report, the House at length resolved that, having regard to public order and security, it was necessary to banish the refractory priests from France.* Upon the joint demand of any twenty inhabitants of the same canton,

---

* " La déportation des ecclésiastiques insermentés aura lieu comme mesure de sûreté publique et de police générale."

the magistrates of the department were authorized to pass a decree of transportation (*déportation*) against an accused ecclesiastic; and in case of resistance, the punishment was to be carried into effect by armed force. Those priests who might return to France after once quitting it were made liable to imprisonment for ten years. This was undisguised persecution; yet it cannot be denied that the conduct of the "insermentés" had in too many instances given cause for exasperation; and, indeed, matters had by this time reached such a pass, that the only choice lay between enforcing the authority of the new Constitution by the terrors of the law, and allowing it to be practically repealed and abolished. But the religious conscience of Louis XVI. revolted against deliberate outrage to the Church. For the second time he notified his veto, in spite of the vehement remonstrances of Roland, minister of the interior, who warned him that if this decree were rejected, disturbances of an alarming character would infallibly follow; that the priests would be exposed to the fury of popular vengeance, and that the cause both of religion and of the monarchy would be finally sacrificed. The king refused to be convinced, and expressed his feelings by dismissing Roland and two of his colleagues from office. This last chivalrous effort to oppose a barrier to the resistless march of revolution precipitated the fate of the unfortunate Louis. The "veto" was one of the pretexts too successfully employed by the Commune of Paris and its bloodthirsty satellites for the purpose of instigating the insurrection of the 20th of June; which led in its turn to the decisive catastrophe of the 10th of August.*

The Revolutionary organization of the Church, in spite of all the good intentions of its authors, was foredoomed to failure by reason of the heterogeneous nature of its component elements. It had its origin in Liberalism as to politics; in Jansenism as to doctrine; in Gallicanism as to matters of discipline. It was a crude attempt to engraft modern ideas upon old institutions; to reconcile the principles of mediæval,

---

* See a luminous narrative of these latter transactions in the work of M. Mortimer-Ternaux, *Histoire de la Terreur, d'après les documents authentiques*, tom. i. pp. 301-339. It is well known that the law of "déportation" was rigorously carried into execution during the Reign of Terror. The number of ecclesiastics who were thus driven from France has been calculated at twenty-eight thousand. De Prat, *Les Quatre Concordats*, tom. ii. p. 34.

and even of primitive Christianity with the rationalistic philosophy and the self-willed lawless spirit of regenerated France. The enterprise was Utopian; yet it will hardly be denied, save by those who are incurably steeped in Ultramontane prejudice, that as a tentative scheme it deserved sincere respect. After surviving the combined shock of Terrorism and Atheism, after witnessing the massacres of September, the abolition of Christianity, and the conversion of Notre Dame into the "Temple of Reason," the Constitutional clergy, upon the fall of Robespierre, re-opened the churches for Catholic worship, and laboured, not without success, to revive some sense of religion among a scoffing and brutalized people.* They made it their object to show that the vaunted "principles of 1789" were not incompatible with Christianity; and that, rightly understood, they had been professed and practically exemplified by the Church Catholic in every age. They claimed for "liberty, equality, and fraternity" a distinct and legitimate place in the economy of the Gospel. They exhibited the Church as insisting on the spiritual brotherhood of all members of the one baptized family throughout the world; they appealed to the historical facts which prove that the Church has been constantly the benefactor and champion of the enslaved and oppressed; and that all the most important movements towards securing the franchises and elevating the condition of the people have been due to her benign influence. Their exertions could not be imputed to motives of self-interest, for one of the first acts of the Convention, after the Reign of Terror, was to proclaim freedom for all forms of worship (*liberté des cultes*), and to announce that no religious denomination would henceforth be supported by grants from the public funds.†

But the task undertaken by the Constitutionals was hopeless in the anarchical condition of the nation. A strong reaction had set in against the tyranny, the barbarities, the hideous profanations, of the earlier stages of the Revolution; and that rebound of feeling was not favourable, but directly the reverse, to the ecclesiastical system inaugurated in 1790. The "insermentés" were, at

---

* No less than eight of the Constitutional bishops suffered by the guillotine during the Reign of Terror. Among them was the eloquent Lamourette of Lyons, who is said to have formally retracted, in the near prospect of death, his oath to the Constitution, and to have expressed penitence for the part he had taken in the "schism." The wretched renegade Gobel perished by the guillotine on the 14th April, 1794.

† Decree of September 20, 1794.

this moment, proscribed and persecuted by the Government, and destitute of popular prestige; yet, before the century closed, their star was once more perceptibly in the ascendant. In proportion as men's minds revolted from the monstrous crimes and excesses which had heaped disgrace upon the name of the Republic, they were drawn towards the old familiar forms and institutions which that terrible convulsion had overthrown; and the Constitutional Church found itself gradually compelled to succumb before this vigorous reflux of religious thought.

An attempt was made in 1797 to arrive at an amicable understanding, and extinguish the schism. A Council assembled at Paris, under the presidency of Claude Le Coz, Metropolitan of Ille-et-Vilaine, addressed a letter to the Pope, imploring him to aid them in the sacred work of healing the divisions of the Church; protesting their deep veneration for his office, and canonical submission to his authority; and justifying their past conduct on the ground of the necessities of the case, and the acknowledged services which they had thereby been enabled to render to the cause of religion.* The bishops likewise opened communications with their nonconforming brethren, in the hope of persuading them to unite in devising the means of a solid and lasting pacification; and even went so far as to propose that, in places where at present there were two bishops, one consecrated previously to 1790 and the other since that date, the senior should be recognized as rightful diocesan, the junior being designated as his successor, should he survive him. But their overtures were altogether fruitless. Pius VI. vouchsafed them no reply, and the non-juring clergy acknowledged the proposals of the Council in terms which betrayed a total want of cordial sympathy.

The revolt of La Vendée, in which the undisciplined peasantry of a single district of no great extent withstood, and sometimes routed, the best armies of the Republic, conveyed a lesson which no intelligent reader of contemporary history could misunderstand or ignore. It proved that there were localities in which the old Constitution in Church and State under which so many successive generations had grown up was still, notwithstanding all its faults and abuses, unspeakably dear to the popular mind; and that to attempt any permanent settlement of the religious

---

* Vid. *Annales de la Religion*, tom. vi. p. 73.

difficulty without paying due regard to these profound convictions, would be wildly imprudent and unstatesmanlike.

Napoleon Bonaparte, on assuming the reins of government in 1799, at once perceived that the ecclesiastical programme of his predecessors was wholly inadequate as a provision for the religious wants of the nation; and that no proposal had a chance of leading to a satisfactory final arrangement unless based upon the ancient relations between the Gallican Church and the Apostolic See. It is not to be supposed, indeed, that the First Consul examined this grave problem with the exactness of a theologian, nor even that he troubled himself to review and master all the historical evidence upon which its true solution depends; but, as a measure of political wisdom and expediency, and for the selfish object of consolidating his own power, he resolved to lose no time in effecting a definitive reconciliation with the Sovereign Pontiff. The result was the Concordat signed at Paris on the 15th of July, 1801, between the government of the French Republic, represented by Joseph Bonaparte, and Cardinal Consalvi, as plenipotentiary of Pope Pius VII.

The leading principle upon which this treaty was concluded was one of unprecedented novelty. It was nothing less than the compulsory resignation of their sees by the entire episcopate of France, whether appointed under the *ancien régime* or under the Constitution civile. This was to be extorted from them, as a matter of canonical obedience, a sacrifice to the pressing necessities of the Church, by the Pope; and a new circumscription of dioceses was thereupon to be created, the number being reduced to sixty, including ten archbishoprics.* To these sees the First Consul was to nominate, selecting the objects of his choice from the ranks of the Constitutionals as well as from the ancient hierarchy; and the Pope, according to the provisions of the former Concordat, was to give the canonical institution. The bishops were to nominate to the parochial cures; but their choice was to be previously approved by the government. The Catholic religion was declared to be

---

* Among other rude changes, the Concordat of 1801 suppressed the archbishopric of Reims, with one or two exceptions the most ancient, and in point of historical associations the most venerable and glorious, of the Gallican sees.

that of the great majority of Frenchmen; its worship was to be free, public, and protected by the State; the government undertaking to provide a fitting remuneration for its ministers. The clergy were to take an oath of allegiance to the existing Constitution; and a prayer for the Republic and the Consuls was to be inserted in the Church Service. Lastly, the Pope accepted, as a *fait accompli*, the confiscation of the property of the Church, and covenanted that the actual possessors should not be disturbed in their acquisitions.

The brief "Tam multa,"* by which Pius VII. demanded of the bishops of the *ancien régime* the immediate resignation of their sees, was by no means unanimously obeyed. The survivors of the original Episcopate were eighty-one in number; forty-five of these submitted to the mandate; the remaining thirty-six demurred on various grounds. Ten days only were allowed them for signifying definitively the course they intended to pursue; at the end of that time the Pope and the First Consul proceeded to legislate for the future organization of the Gallican Church, disregarding remonstrances, protests, and petitions for delay which reached them from different quarters, particularly from the bishops who had taken refuge in England. These latter, of whom there were fourteen, remained obstinate in their non-compliance. Another brief, "Post multos labores," was addressed to the Constitutionals, exhorting them to return without delay to Catholic unity, to declare in writing their submission to the Roman Pontiff and their acquiescence in his decisions concerning the affairs of the Church in France, and to retire forthwith from the dioceses of which they had taken possession without institution by the Apostolic See. Some few complied with the demand; but the majority treated the Pope's summons with studied disrespect. It was useless, however, to resist the will of the government; and accordingly the Constitutional bishops resigned their preferments into the hands of the First Consul.

On the 29th of November, 1801, the Sovereign Pontiff, by the bull "Qui Christi Domini," promulgated the new division

---

* See *Annales de la Religion*, tom. xiv. p. 97. The work thus entitled consists of a series of 18 octavo volumes, extending from 1795 to 1803. It is of great interest, affording a complete insight into the principles and purposes of the ecclesiastical reformers of the time. It was edited chiefly by Bishop Grégoire.

of French dioceses; announced the acts of resignation or deprivation by which the existing sees were rendered vacant; created in their place the new episcopate of ten archbishops and fifty bishops according to the arrangement just mentioned; and empowered Cardinal Caprara, whom he accredited as legate *à latere,* to confer on the prelates-designate the Apostolical institution. The Concordat was presented to the Corps Législatif on the 5th of April, 1802, by M. Portalis, minister of public worship, who, in a speech evincing considerable research and learning, descanted on the vast importance of a National Church, and the necessity of applying a remedy to the grave disorders originating in the schism among the clergy.* He also combated the apprehensions which might be felt of a renewal of extravagant pretensions on the part of the Papacy; reminding his hearers of the jealous limitations by which such enterprises had always been repressed in France; and pointing out that under the system about to be inaugurated it would be the interest of the clergy to support the paramount authority of the civil power, since their own rights and liberties would thus be most effectually guaranteed against undue pressure from the side of Rome.

Portalis, however, avoided all mention of the "Articles organiques," or series of regulations which had been appended to the Concordat by the French Government without the knowledge or consent of the Pope. Their general drift was to reduce the Church into direct and servile dependence on the secular administration. No missive or official document from the court of Rome was to enter France without the previous approbation of the government. No legate or emissary of any kind was to exercise ecclesiastical functions, or discharge any public mission, without a similar sanction. The government was to examine the decrees of foreign Councils, not only Provincial but even General, and to satisfy itself that they were not injurious to the peace and well-being of the State, before they could be lawfully published in France. The ancient usage of appeals *comme d'abus* was re-established, and their cognisance assigned to the Council of State. Restrictions were imposed upon the bishops even as to the right

---

* *Annales de la Religion,* tom. xiv. pp. 496–553.

and conditions of conferring Holy Orders. The clergy were forbidden to celebrate marriages except between persons who produced a certificate that the civil contract of marriage had been executed previously before the lay magistrate. The Pope protested, in an allocution in full Consistory, against these supplementary enactments; declaring that he had demanded of Bonaparte their suppression or modification, but without success.

The nomination of the new Episcopate followed immediately; that prerogative being exercised by the adventurous soldier to whom France, in recompense of his brilliant services in the field, and of his zealous exertions in behalf of order and settled government at home, had thought proper for the time being to confide her destinies. It was a primary object with the First Consul to put an end to the existing schism among the clergy; and this he resolved to effect by means of a fusion between the contending parties, allotting to each a fair share in the honours of the hierarchy now to be created. The Papal legate strongly objected to the appointment of any of the Constitutional bishops; but Bonaparte steadily adhered to his plan, and carried it into execution. Most of the prelates were selected from the ranks of the Non-jurors; but twelve belonged to those who had taken the Revolutionary test. The latter class included Le Coz, who was named Archbishop of Besançon, and Primat, who became Archbishop of Toulouse. Bishop Grégoire, the ablest and most influential man of his party, who had been personally consulted by Bonaparte as to the policy to be pursued at this critical moment, found himself, nevertheless, omitted from the list. The legate Caprara attempted to extort from them a formal retractation of their oath to the Constitution civile; but the First Consul intimated that he did not consider this expedient; and after a brief but sharp struggle, the Cardinal gave way, and contented himself with a simple acceptance of the Concordat and declaration of submission to the Holy See. A grand ceremonial at Notre Dame, on Easter Day, April 18, 1802,—attended by the three Consuls, the diplomatic body, the Cardinal-legate, the new Archbishops and Bishops, and a numerous *cortége* of civil and military authorities,—announced with becoming solemnity the restoration of a National Church Establishment in France.

Such were the circumstances under which the Priesthood and the Empire, the sovereign powers of Church and State, once more adjusted their differences, and concluded a definitive treaty of alliance, as soon as the desolating fury of the Revolution had so far subsided as to render such a movement possible. The reader will naturally be led to compare the general character and tendency of the settlement of 1801 with those of the compact between Leo X. and Francis I., known as the Concordat of Bologna; and will not fail to observe the close correspondence which reigned between them.

As in the sixteenth century, so at the opening of the nineteenth, the high contracting parties pursued their own views of interest, and reaped great mutual advantages; but the Church for which they professed to negotiate was at both epochs weakened and damaged rather than benefited by their agreement. The second Concordat had little to recommend it except as a temporary expedient for putting an end to intestine discord. The schism was healed; but the price exacted for that boon was immense. Instead of profiting by the liberal theories and reforming spirit of the Revolution, France soon relapsed, in a religious point of view, into a condition of servitude more oppressive and abject than ever. No sooner was the "Constitution civile" abolished, than Ultramontanism reappeared; the reaction in its favour being all the more fervent and passionate, inasmuch as all the abominations and impieties of Republican fanaticism were imputed, with manifest injustice, to the opposite system. It was now that a writer of distinguished powers, enthusiastically devoted to the cause of the Roman Curia and of Pontifical supremacy, Count Joseph De Maistre, made himself the interpreter of the changed feelings which were gradually taking possession of the Catholic mind of France. His earliest work, 'Considérations sur la France,' was published in 1796. He inveighed sarcastically against Gallicanism, taunting it with the infelicitous efforts lately made in its name to effect a reformation in the Church; but he apparently forgot that the multiplied scandals and corruptions which had rendered reformation a matter of imperative necessity were, in great measure, the direct fruit of Ultramontanism. The public seems to have been affected by a like obliviousness; so that the theories advanced by De Maistre were eagerly embraced, and his writings exercised a prodigious amount of influence both in forming and in giving utterance to the religious sentiment of France during this reactionary period. He was followed at the distance of a few years by one who was not his inferior in genius, and who, at the outset of his eccentric career, was a no less zealous advocate both of monarchy and of the autocracy of Rome;—the impulsive, energetic, eloquent Abbé Lamennais. The Vicomte de Bonald was another successful labourer in the same field. Their principles became predominant among the bishops and clergy of the restored Gallican Church; the more so, in proportion as they discovered that the new Concordat had imposed on them a heavier and more grievous yoke, in the way of secular encroachments and restrictions, than had been attempted by the most despotic of former governments. Even Louis XIV., imperious as he was, had never ventured to place any such galling checks upon the independent action of the episcopate; he had never dictated in the ordinary details of diocesan administration. Bonaparte's government was liberal in profession, but intensely tyrannical in practice. He constantly appealed to the "Gallican liberties" and the Four Articles of 1682; he reaffirmed those principles as integral parts of the national legislation, and ordered them to be taught and subscribed in the Seminaries throughout France.* Yet never was the Church more helplessly enslaved by the State than while the supreme power remained in his hands.

It is mortifying to have to record this inglorious termination of the many struggles and sacrifices of the Gallican Church in defence of the true constitutional principles both of civil and ecclesiastical government. The net product, as it would seem, of that long traditional warfare was to leave the Church in a state of degrading thraldom to a double absolutism; on one side a secular, on the other a spiritual dictatorship had invaded and effaced its liberties. No doubt it was a circumstance seriously detrimental to the Gallican cause that it had allied itself, at a moment of unprecedented national peril, with the apostles of Republicanism and Revolution. It cannot be denied that the "Constitution civile du clergé" contributed largely

---

* See the "Articles Organiques," No. XXIV.

to stimulate the passions and to aggravate and prolong the animosities of that troublous time; but it is of the utmost consequence to observe that the ultimate result cannot with justice be laid to the charge of Gallicanism, properly so called; rather it was the fruit of influences radically opposed to it. A brief retrospective glance at the principal acts of ecclesiastical legislation in France, for the purpose of establishing the truth of this assertion, may serve to bring the present work not inappropriately to a conclusion.

Complete mutual independence between the Spiritualty and the Temporalty—true, sound, and philosophical though it be as a matter of theory—has probably never been realized in practice since Christianity became the dominant religion of Europe. Traces of the interference of secular authority in regulating the concerns of the Church appear in some of the earliest pages of French, or rather Frankish, history. Merovingian princes usurped, under various pretexts, the right of nominating to bishoprics; the Carlovingians invested the heads of the Church with civil offices, and domineered over them by virtue of this confusion between their spiritual jurisdiction and their duties as functionaries of the State. The Feudal aristocracy tyrannized over the ecclesiastical order in their turn; habitually violating the right of free election, and converting the richer preferments into hereditary appanages in their families. In *principle*, however, these early ages distinctly recognized the autonomy of the Church; the authority of ecclesiastical legislation; the administrative power of ecclesiastical Courts and Judges. In proof of this we need only turn to the Pragmatic Sanction of St. Louis, so constantly cited as the Magna Charta of Gallican liberty. The Church, according to the terms of that famous ordonnance, is to be administered in conformity with "the common law, the canons of Councils, and the statutes of the ancient Fathers." Prelates, patrons, and ordinaries are to exercise their lawful rights, and to enjoy the jurisdiction which belongs to each. Appointments in Cathedrals and other Churches are to be made by free election; and all ancient immunities, privileges, and prerogatives granted to the Church are approved and confirmed. Not a hint is here to be found of the comparatively modern practice of applying to Rome for the confirmation and institution of bishops; but on the contrary, the exorbitant pecuniary imposts levied by the Papacy are severely censured, and forbidden for the future except in case of urgent and absolute necessity. The Pragmatic Sanction of Bourges, in 1438, was a second movement in the same direction. It solemnly protested against the crying abuses of Mediævalism. It denounced the "réservations," "dévolutions," "expectatives," by means of which the richest benefices of France were often conferred upon unknown foreigners, who never resided among their flocks, and could not speak their language; and this to the exclusion of the native clergy, who were thereby discouraged, and "abandoned the study both of Divine and human science, since they saw no reasonable prospect of advancement in their profession." It prescribed canonical election, and confirmation by the Metropolitans. It abolished the "annates." It regulated the system of appeals to Rome, and enjoined that all ecclesiastical causes should pass through the various gradations of local jurisdiction.

In an evil hour for the Gallican Church, Louis XI. was persuaded, by the counsels of an ambitious and unprincipled prelate, to abrogate the Pragmatic Sanction. Pope Pius II., adroitly practising upon the despotic character of that monarch, assured him that the liberties of the Church are but so many fetters upon the power of the Crown; and the misguided Prince, to whom liberty in every shape was odious, announced that he found it necessary to revoke the great legislative act of his father, which had "erected a temple of licence in his kingdom." Thereupon the canonical elections were suppressed; and a tacit assent was given to all the usurped prerogatives of the Roman Curia. The Pope, transported with vindictive joy, caused a copy of the hateful Pragmatic to be dragged through the mire in the streets of Rome.

I have described elsewhere the series of intrigues which followed under Louis XII., and the conjuncture of circumstances which brought about the memorable negotiation between Leo X. and Francis I., resulting eventually in the Concordat of Bologna.

This celebrated treaty amounted to a complete revolution in the administration of the Church. It substituted absolutism for constitutional government. It was a private bargain between the King and the Pope, by which each conferred upon the other a boon of no common magnitude, while the rights and interests of a *third* party, namely the National Church of France, were superciliously ignored and sacrificed. The Crown assumed the arbitrary nomination to bishoprics and other consistorial benefices, to the final extinction of the primitive rule of free election; the Pope acquired the right of confirmation or institution, to the exclusion of the Metropolitans and their Comprovincials, to whom that duty was assigned by the invariable legislation of antiquity. The obstinate and long-protracted opposition offered by the great constituted bodies ecclesiastical and civil is the best proof of the extreme gravity of the change, and of the clear-sighted intelligence which discerned its danger to the true interests of the nation. The Parliament of Paris protested that on this occasion its action was not free, but compulsory; that if any publication of the Concordat took place, it was not by the vote of the magistracy, nor with their consent, but simply by the express and reiterated command of the Sovereign; that they could never approve the ratification of the Concordat, but would use their utmost efforts to secure the execution of the canons of Councils and of the Pragmatic Sanction. We have seen how similar protests were multiplied in the course of the 16th and 17th centuries, in the "cahiers" of the States-General and in the "remontrances" of the Assemblies of the Clergy. Whenever the Church had an opportunity of declaring its sentiments as a body, the restoration of free election was invariably one of its first demands. From the days of St. Louis down to the eve of the Revolution the national convictions upon these vital points underwent no change. Among the "cahiers" drawn up at the election of deputies to the States-General of 1789, the greater number, not only of those presented by the clergy, but likewise by the Tiers-état, contained petitions for the abolition of the Concordat, the revival of the primitive rules of ecclesiastical election, and the discontinuance of all pecuniary tribute to the Court of Rome.

The Concordat, then, was totally irreconcileable with the principles of Gallicanism. It struck a fatal blow at the independence of the Church; it imposed upon it the concurrent yoke of two masters, the Crown and the Sovereign Pontiff; and it provided no sufficient guarantees against the abuse of the powers acquired on either side. Stipulations were inserted, indeed, with respect to the distribution of preferment, in favour of graduates of the Universities, but a special exception was made, at the same time, on behalf of candidates of royal or aristocratic birth—" consanguineis regis ac personis sublimibus " —who were to be eligible for the highest dignities without producing any academical evidence of their capacity. The natural effect of this clause was to create in France, during the halcyon days of the old Constitution, an episcopate belonging almost exclusively to noble families; the gay parasites of the Court, and the "grands seigneurs de province," obtained as it were a vested interest in those tempting prizes for the benefit of their younger sons. Hence arose the mischievous distinction between the "haut clergé" and the inferior pastors who did the real work of the Church; a severance of classes to which must be ascribed in great measure the helpless weakness of the ecclesiastical order at the epoch of the Revolution. Bossuet was one of the few members of the Gallican episcopate who could not claim the prefix of the aristocratic particle to his name; and even in the case of Bossuet, it is understood that the absence of patrician blood operated as an insuperable bar to his elevation to the metropolitical throne of Paris.

That the system introduced by the Concordat did not prevent Bossuet and others of his stamp from rising to the honours of the episcopate is a circumstance to be regarded with thankfulness; but it concludes nothing as to the intrinsic merit of the principle of that arrangement. Under whatever plan of Church administration, men of their vast moral and intellectual superiority could not have been overlooked; had the elections been in the hands of the Chapters, they would assuredly have been nominated; indeed, under such circumstances, it is probable that the number of wise appointments would have been greater, and the influence of the Gallican school of theology would have been widely augmented. But what was the actual course of events? The race of prelates of the type of Fénelon and Bossuet, ever memorable as it is, was short-lived. While Louis XIV. reigned, his characteristic elevation of mind would not brook anything like flagrant abuse in matters affecting the public ministry of the Church; but how different was the *régime* inaugurated by his successors! What defence can be offered for a government which inflicted on the Church a Dubois, a

Tencin, a Lafiteau, a Jarente, a De Rohan? What can be said for Cardinal Fleury's determined and exclusive patronage of men pledged to enforce the disastrous Bull Unigenitus? Can we wonder that under such blighting influences the standard of ecclesiastical virtue and attainment rapidly declined, and that, when at length the sanctuary was assaulted by an anti-Christian philosophy, no adequate resources were forthcoming wherewith to meet the shock, and the educated mind of France deserted to the camp of the invaders?

But if it was a gross violation of the liberty of the Church to abandon to the Crown the nomination to its highest dignities, much more abnormal was the innovation which placed the right of institution at the sole discretion of the Pope. Nothing is more certain, from the testimony of antiquity and the teaching of the greatest masters of theology, than the fact that bishops were originally elected, confirmed, and consecrated, without any direct intervention of the authority of the Papal See. The evidence adduced by De Marca, Thomassin, and Bossuet establishes this point conclusively.* Nor is this a mere question of external discipline; it involves the crucial issues between the two antagonist schools which divide Catholic Christendom as to the nature and extent of the authority of the Pope over the Church. It is the same question, in a slightly varying shape, which was so violently agitated at the Council of Trent, and which that Assembly in the end deliberately forbore to determine.† Institution signifies the conveyance of ecclesiastical jurisdiction; to acknowledge, therefore, that this is obtainable from the Pope alone is to acknowledge that there is no mission, no lawful vocation to the cure of souls, except from him; from which it would follow that he is in reality the sole and universal Bishop; the absolute monarch of the Church. It is unquestionably competent to the Church, duly assembled in Œcumenical Council, to pronounce such a momentous decision, and to arrange its rules of discipline accordingly. But in the case of the Concordat the entire negotiation was conducted between

---

* De Marca, *De Concord.*, lib. vi. cap. ii. iii. Thomassin, *Vet. et Nov. Eccles. Discip.* p. ii., lib. ii. cap. xxx. Bossuet, *Defens. Declarat.* p. iii. lib. viii. cap. xi. Thomassin may also be consulted with advantage as to the use and meaning of the Pallium. p. i. lib. ii. capp. liii. liv.

† See *supra*, Vol. I. pp. 153–158.

Leo X. and the minister plenipotentiary of the King of France. When the terms had been settled, they were submitted *pro formâ* to the fifth Lateran Council, a small body of Italian prelates wholly subservient to the will of the Pope; but to the Gallican Church the result was announced as a *fait accompli*, without even the form of consultation. Thenceforward France stood committed, by a compulsory agency *ab extra*, without cooperation or consent of her own, to the essential principle of Ultramontanism.

In what manner the provisions of the Concordat were employed by the Papal Court for the purpose of extorting submission, in moments of critical difficulty, both from the Crown and from the Church, has been already circumstantially recorded in our pages. The Pope was empowered to refuse the bulls of institution at his absolute pleasure; he was not restricted by any condition as to the duration of such refusal; there was nothing to hinder him from prolonging the vacancy of Sees indefinitely; he might keep whole provinces destitute of canonically commissioned pastors, and thus *starve* the Church into a capitulation. The entire organism of ecclesiastical government was by such legislation placed at the mercy of the individual Pontiff.

Instances of the refusal of the bulls of institution were, however, very rare for many years after the passing of the Concordat. The most remarkable was the case of De Marca, who, having been named by Louis XIII. in 1642 to the see of Conserans, was denied these indispensable documents until he had retracted certain statements in his work 'De Concordiâ Sacerdotii et Imperii.' Six years elapsed before he was qualified to enter on the duties of the episcopate.

The immense advantage thrown into the hands of the Pope by the Concordat was alarmingly manifested on the occasion of the Four Articles of the Assembly of 1682. During eleven years in succession Rome refused to institute the prelates nominated by Louis XIV.; in thirty-five dioceses the normal government of the Church was virtually suppressed. Such was the embarrassment and disorder thus created in Church and State, that surrender was inevitable. The bishops-designate humbly renounced and revoked the part which they had taken in the proceedings of the late Assembly; the king, the haughty arbitrary Louis XIV., withdrew his edict, so that the doctrine of the Four Articles was reduced to little more than a protest on paper, instead of being universally enforced and inculcated by authority, as was at first intended. These measures, however, did not imply any repudiation of the *principles* affirmed in the famous "Declaration of the Clergy;" principles which were not then formulated for the first time, but represented the traditional belief of the French Church, and the legislation of the great Councils of the fifteenth century. Louis yielded to the Pope so far as to refrain from insisting that the Four Articles should be taught officially in the Universities and other centres of national education; but at the same time he refused to permit the avowal of Gallican doctrine to be made a ground of disability, or visited with penal inflictions. Such is the import of a well-known letter which he addressed to Pope Clement XI. in 1713, on the occasion of the nomination of the Abbé de St. Aignan to the see of Beauvais. "It would not be just," observed Louis, "that I should hinder my subjects from expressing and defending their sentiments upon matters which lie freely open to discussion on both sides, like many other theological questions, without impugning in the slightest degree any articles of faith." He reminded Clement that he was bound by the Concordat to grant institution to the nominees of the Crown, unless they were chargeable with heresy; "and his Holiness is too enlightened," he continued, "to undertake to declare those maxims heretical, which have been followed for so many ages by the Church of France." The Pope could not gainsay the force of this remonstrance. He offered no rejoinder, but despatched the bulls to the Abbé de St. Aignan, without attempting to exact from him any disavowal of the proceedings of the Assembly of 1682.*

Experience showed, then, in the typical contest between Louis XIV. and Innocent XI., that the Concordat had furnished the Vatican with a weapon so formidable that in extreme cir-

---

* D'Aguesseau, "Mém. sur les affaires de l'Égl. de F." (*Œuvres*, tom. xiii. p. 424). Bausset, *Histoire de Bossuet*, tom. ii. pp. 214–216. The theology of Rome, however, has made giant strides since the days of Louis XIV., Clement XI., D'Aguesseau, and Bossuet. In an article on "Liberalism religious and ecclesiastical," in the 'Dublin Review' for January, 1872, we read as follows:— "Since July, 1870, it has been infallibly certain, that Gallicanism directly contradicts revealed truth."

cumstances it could hardly fail of success, if employed with sufficient firmness and pertinacity. The consciousness that Rome had in its possession this sharp instrument of coercion, applicable at once to the civil government and to the national clergy, greatly favoured the current towards Ultramontanism which set in with the reign of Louis XV. The bishops renounced their independence, and hugged the chains of foreign servitude, accepting more and more blindly the counsels and control of the Jesuits. Of this fact the history of the Constitution Unigenitus is a perpetual illustration. That unfortunate measure, which was simply a device of Le Tellier and his brethren for crushing out the remains of the rival school which challenged their supremacy, strained the principle of submission to the Pope as the infallible exponent of revealed truth to an extent from which the Church has never since recovered. The infatuated rigour with which it was forced upon rebellious consciences led to a concatenation of events which hopelessly deranged the framework of society, and frustrated every effort made to reconstruct it. It was this spectacle that aroused the deep disgust and indignation of Voltaire and his fellow-philosophers, and impelled them to declare open war against religion. It was the intolerable pressure of Ultramontane centralisation that drove the Jansenists into their last desperate excesses. It was this that gave birth to the fanatical mummeries of the Convulsionists of St. Médard. It was this that provoked the stubborn antagonism between the Parliaments and the clergy in the affair of the refusal of the last Sacraments to the sick and dying. And inasmuch as the Crown espoused the quarrel of the hierarchy, encouragement was thus given to the incipient spirit of disaffection to the Monarchy. The sovereign power, already tottering under the ravages of internal decay, was paralysed by a series of weak concessions and ignoble defeats; the machinery of the State became irremediably disordered; and the struggle ended in the total collapse of authority and the disintegration of the social system.

When the Revolution had scattered to the winds every fragment of the mediæval Constitution, an indefinite field was thrown open to the inventive genius of reform and reconstruction. And now supervened that singular episode in the history of French Christianity, the "Constitution civile du Clergé." This, as we have seen, was a well-intentioned, but anomalous and ill-digested, attempt to restore some of the distinctive principles of primitive Church organization;—especially the free election of the clergy by the suffrages of the faithful, and the institution of bishops by the Metropolitans. But while proclaiming these organic innovations on the existing system, the Church reformers of the National Assembly fully acknowledged the authority of the Pope, and professed inviolable fidelity to the Roman See. It was not to be expected that such a position could prove practically tenable. The Concordat, though radically vicious in principle, had never been repealed, and was therefore, in the eyes of the Pope, the legitimate order of the Church; it was certain that Rome would never voluntarily relinquish an arrangement which, both in theory and practice, was so propitious to her claims. The Pope anathematized the Constitution civile; and from that moment it had not the faintest prospect of success. No arguments were strong enough to persuade the mass of French Catholics that orthodox doctrine and the ordained means of salvation were to be found in a community which had been pronounced schismatical by the Apostolic See. It was useless to appeal to antiquity—to quote the legislation of Constance and Basle—to invoke the Gallican liberties and the Articles of 1682. There was no denying that matters had been ruled differently in modern times, with the general acquiescence of the Catholic world; and to contravene that prescriptive polity was to be self-convicted of disloyalty and revolt against the Church. The Constitutional priesthood thus became a discredited sect; and though its services were acknowledged and rewarded in the measures of conciliation adopted in 1801, it was impossible that its views and influence should be predominant under the reactionary *régime* which commenced from that date. The counter-revolution inevitably took the shape of advanced Ultramontanism. In proportion as the men of 1789 had attempted to correct and curtail the exaggerations of Papal prerogative, the prevalent impulse now gravitated towards a revived theocracy upon the model of the middle ages. No incense was too costly, no homage too lowly, no submission too unqualified, to be offered in sacrifice at the shrine of St. Peter.

In 1813, during the captivity of Pius VII. at Fontainebleau,

Napoleon made an effort to restore the balance, by exacting certain concessions from his prisoner which would have circumscribed the power of the Papacy with respect to the institution of bishops.* But his Holiness resolutely refused to subscribe to any such modification of the terms of the Concordat. The negotiation failed; and the fall of Napoleon in the following year finally defeated the project. Since that time the theory of the Pope's sole and absolute monarchy has been, with occasional though scarcely audible murmurs of dissent, the creed of the ecclesiastical body, and of the religious mind, in France.

The end, however, is not yet. Even after all that has passed within the memory of the present generation, the oppressive dogmatism of the Roman Curia has not succeeded in blotting out that venerable tradition which is for ever enshrined in the faithful records of Catholic Antiquity. Gallican theology, however painfully depressed by recent decisions, and banished from the schools where it once reigned in peerless lustre and unquestioned authority, is not extinct. It is reduced for a time, through the pressure of adverse circumstances, to the level of an antiquated theory, interred in the dusty half-forgotten folios of the seventeenth century, and incapable of exercising practical power over the convictions, the policy, or the fortunes, of the existing Church. Yet this despised tradition, which is not that of one age or one nation, but coextensive with the universal and undivided Church of Christ, is in reality indestructible. "Fluctuat, nec mergitur." † It is tossed upon the troubled waters, but it sinks not. The Church cannot, if it

---

* It was on this occasion that the Abbé Lamennais published his treatise *La tradition de l'Église sur l'institution des évêques*. The following sentences from the Preface will give an idea of the author's course of argument:— "Les clés, dans l'Écriture, sont l'image et le symbole de la souveraineté. C'est donc toute sa puissance que Jésus-Christ remet à Pierre, sans exception ni limites. Il l'établit en sa place pour lier et délier; il le substitue, si on peut le dire, à tous ses droits; et Celui qui disait de lui-même, Tout pouvoir m'a été donné au ciel et sur la terre, confie au prince des Apôtres ce pouvoir infini, qui doit être jusqu'à la fin des temps la force et le salut de l'Église. Or, toute juridiction est une participation des clés qui n'ont été données qu'à Pierre seul; il est donc l'unique source de la juridiction. De la plénitude de sa puissance émane toute autorité spirituelle, comme nous l'apprenons des Pères, des Papes et des Conciles."

† This is the ancient motto belonging to the armorial bearings of the city of Paris; the device on the shield being a ship breasting the waves. It will not perhaps be considered out of place on the title-page of this work.

would, sever itself from its past history. Catholic truth will assuredly avenge itself, sooner or later, by recurring to the original sources from which it derives its life and strength ; to the normal rule which imposes on the Christian conscience those verities, and those alone, which have been held " always, everywhere, and by all." We are told, indeed, that the doctrine of the autocracy and infallibility of the Roman Pontiff *does* form an integral part of the original Deposit of faith, and has been believed, at least implicitly, by the Church in every age ;—the explicit definition of it having been providentially reserved for the times of special difficulty and perplexity in which we live. But, as the great Bossuet observes, " if the fact was so abundantly clear—if the doctrine was so positively revealed, as they pretend—what has so long prevented its being affirmed in categorical terms as an article of the Catholic Faith ? Or in what sense could this authority of the Pope have benefited the Church, so long as it remained doubtful, its certainty not having been hitherto universally proclaimed ?—this authority I say, of the Pope pronouncing *ex cathedrâ*, in which our opponents place the sum and substance of the faith ? Is it possible that the Church should have been destined to wait till our own days, till nearly the close of the seventeenth century, for the boon of absolute security and peace ? If not, we must teach religious minds to look for complete tranquillity in nothing short of the consent of the Catholic Church. . . . . . It was not this doubtful infallibility (of the Pope) tha Christ bestowed; had such been His gift, He would have revealed it from the very beginning to His Church, lest, if left uncertain or imperfectly made known, or unconfirmed by manifest tradition, it might become unprofitable." *

Unhappily it is all but hopeless that any reconsideration or revision should take place of that latest action of the dominant power at Rome, by which the opinion of one particular section of the Church, seldom distinctly formulated before the sixteenth century, and always strenuously disputed, has been transformed into an universally obligatory article of faith. Yet in the interests of the reunion of Christendom—that glorious consummation towards which the hearts of Catholics in all quarters of the

---

* Bossuet, *Gallia orthodoxa*, sect. xcvii.

globe are turned with an ever-increasing intensity of ardour—it would seem that some such reaction towards the unchangeable standards of Ancient Orthodoxy is an indispensable condition of success. It is clearly beyond the power of Ultramontanism to bring about a cordial understanding between the East and the West. The Council of the Vatican will never win the sympathies or heal the intestine divisions of Anglicanism. A policy dictated by Jesuitical intrigue is ill calculated to dispel the prejudices of the Protestant sects. Even minds sincerely disposed to bow to the legitimate authority of the Church and of a Council really Œcumenical revolt instinctively against demands which would place them in desperate antagonism to the mighty stream of historical truth. If a definitive reconciliation is ever to be effected between faith and reason; if Christianity is to resume its rightful empire over the world of intellect and science; if the Church is to gather together and reorganize within her fold the now disjointed and contending fragments of our common humanity,—that work must be accomplished by reasserting the primitive Rule of Faith and the primitive laws of ecclesiastical government. Already some auspicious signs of such a reformation are discernible in the horizon. It may be premature and presumptuous to speculate upon their exact import; "the vision is yet for an appointed time." Meanwhile, those who are willing to " wait for it " will re-echo in their suspense the ejaculation of the holy Bernard, " Quis mihi dabit, antequàm moriar, videre Ecclesiam Dei sicut in diebus antiquis?" *

---

* St. Bern., *Epist.* ccxxxviii. "Ad dominum Papam Eugenium." (Migne, *Patrolog.* tom. clxxxii. p. 480.)

LIST OF THE ARCHIEPISCOPAL AND EPISCOPAL SEES OF FRANCE BEFORE THE REVOLUTION OF 1789.

PROVINCE OF ARLES.

			Revenue. Livres.		
Archbishopric.	Arles.	Arelate.	33,000		
Suffragan Sees.	Marseilles.	Massilia.	30,000		
	St. Paul trois Châteaux.	Tricastinum.	10,000	Suppressed	1801.
	Toulon.	Tolonium.	15,000	,,	1801.
	Orange.	Arausio.	10,000	,,	1801.

PROVINCE OF AVIGNON.

Archbishopric.	Avignon.	Avenio.	48,000		
Suffragan Sees.	Carpentras.	Carpentoracte.	10,000	Suppressed	1801.
	Vaison.	Vasio.	10,000	,,	1801.
	Cavaillon.	Cavallio.	16,000	,,	1801.

PROVINCE OF AIX (en Provence).

Archbishopric.	Aix.	Aquæ (Sextiæ).	37,000		
Suffragan Sees.	Apt.	Apta.	9,000	Suppressed	1801.
	Riez.	Reii.	15,000	,,	1801.
	Fréjus.	Forum Julii.	28,000		
	Gap.	Vapincum.	16,000		
	Sisteron.	Sistaricum.	15,000	Suppressed	1801.

PROVINCE OF EMBRUN.

Archbishopric.	Embrun.	Ebrodunum.	30,000		
Suffragan Sees.	Digne.	Dinia.	10,000		
	Glandève.	Glandeva.	10,000	Suppressed	1801.
	Grasse.	Grassa.	22,000	,,	1801.
	Vence.	Vincium.	7,000	,,	1801.
	Senez.	Sanitium.	10,000	,,	1801.

PROVINCE OF VIENNE.

Archbishopric.	Vienne en Dauphiné.	Vienna.	22,000	Suppressed	1801.
Suffragan Sees.	Die.	Dea.	15,000	,,	1801.
	Genève, ou Annecy (Savoie).	Genova.			
	Grenoble.	Gratianopolis.	28,000		
	Maurienne (Savoie).	Mauria.			
	Valence.	Valentia.	16,000		
	Viviers.	Vimarium.	30,000		

PROVINCE OF BESANÇON.

Archbishopric.	Besançon.	Vesontio.	36,000	
Suffragan See.	Bellay.	Bellicium.	10,000	

LIST OF THE ARCHIEPISCOPAL AND EPISCOPAL SEES—*continued*.

PROVINCE OF NARBONNE.

			Revenue. Livres.	
Archbishopric.	Narbonne.	Narbo (Martius).	160,000	
Suffragan Sees.	Agde.	Agatha.	70,000	
	Alais.	Alesia.	16,000	
	Alet.	Alecta.	30,000	
	Béziers.	Biterræ.	30,000	Suppressed 1801.
	Carcassonne.	Carcaso.	35,000	
	Lodève.	Luteva.	26,000	,, 1801.
	Montpellier.	Mons Pessulus.	45,000	
	Nismes.	Nemausus.	26,000	
	Perpignan (or Elne)	Perpinio, vel Elne.	18,000	
	St. Pons?			
	Uzès.	Uscia.	25,000	Suppressed 1801.

PROVINCE OF AUCH.

Archbishopric.	Auch.	Ausca.	26,000	
Suffragan Sees.	Dax.	Aquæ (Tarbellicæ).	14,000	Suppressed 1801.
	Lectoure.	Lactora.	28,000	,, 1801.
	Comminges.	Convena.	60,000	,, 1801.
	Aire.	Adura.	26,000	,, 1801.
				Re-estab. 1817.
	Bazas.	Vasate.	18,000	
	Tarbes.	Tarba.	30,000	
	Oleron.	Elorona.	13,000	Suppressed 1801.
	Lescar.	Lascura.	27,000	,, 1801.
	Bayonne.	Baionna.	26,000	

PROVINCE OF BOURGES.

Archbishopric.	Bourges.	Biturigum.	40,000	
Suffragan Sees.	Clermont.	Claro-Mons.	15,000	
	Limoges.	Lemovia.	20,000	
	Le Puy.	Podium.	25,000	
	Saint-Flour.	Floriopolis.	12,000	
	Tulle.	Tutela.	12,000	

PROVINCE OF ALBY.

Archbishopric.	Alby.	Albiga.	120,000	
Suffragan Sees.	Cahors.	Cadurcum.	60,000	
	Castres.	Castra.		Suppressed 1801.
	Mende.	Mimata.	60,000	,, 1801.
	Rodez.	Ruthena.	50,000	
	Vabres.	Vabræ.	23,000	Suppressed 1801.

PROVINCE OF BORDEAUX.

Archbishopric.	Bordeaux.	Burdigala.	55,000	
Suffragan Sees.	Agen.	Aginum.	50,000	
	Condom.	Condomus.	70,000	Suppressed 1801.
	Angoulême.	Engolisma.	20,000	
	Saintes.	Santones.	21,000	Suppressed 1801.
	Poitiers.	Pictavium.	30,000	
	La Rochelle, before Maillezais.	Rupella prius Malleacensem.	50,000	
	Luçon.	Lucionia.	24,000	Suppressed 1801. Re-estab. 1820.
	Périgueux.	Petrocorium.	24,000	
	Sarlat.	Sarlatum.	20,000	,, 1801.

THE GALLICAN CHURCH.

List of the Archiepiscopal and Episcopal Sees—*continued*.

PROVINCE OF LYONS.

			Revenue. Livres.	
Archbishopric.	Lyons.	Lugdunum.	50,000	
Suffragan Sees.	Autun.	Augustodunum.	22,000	
	Châlons-sur-Saône.	Cabillonum.	14,000	
	Dijon.	Divio.	25,000	
	Langres.	Ligones.	50,000	
	Mâcon.	Matisco.	21,000	
	Saint-Claude.	S. Claudius.	27,000	Erected 1742.

PROVINCE OF PARIS.

Archbishopric.	Paris.	Lutetia.	200,000
Suffragan Sees.	Blois.	Blesæ.	24,000
	Chartres.	Carnutum.	30,000
	Meaux.	Meldæ.	25,000
	Orléans.	Aurelianum.	50,000

PROVINCE OF REIMS.

Archbishopric.	Reims.	Remi.	70,000	Suppressed 1801. Re-estab. 1817.
Suffragan Sees.	Soissons.	Suessiones.	23,000	
	Laon.	Laudunum.	30,000	Suppressed 1801.
	Beauvais.	Bellovacum.	55,000	
	Noyon.	Noviodunum.	37,000	Suppressed 1801.
	Châlons-sur-Marne	Catalaunum.	27,000	
	Senlis.	Silvanectum.	18,000	Suppressed 1801.
	Amiens.	Ambianum.	30,000	
	Boulogne.	Bononia.	20,000	Suppressed 1801.

PROVINCE OF SENS.

Archbishopric.	Sens.	Senones.	70,000
Suffragan Sees.	Auxerre.	Autissiodorum.	50,000
	Nevers.	Nivernæ.	20,000
	Troyes.	Trecæ.	20,000

PROVINCE OF ROUEN.

Archbishopric.	Rouen.	Rothomagus.	100,000	
Suffragan Sees.	Avranches.	Abrinca.	22,000	United to Coutances 1801.
	Bayeux.	Bajocasses.	90,000	
	Coutances.	Constantia.	35,000	
	Évreux.	Ebroïca.	28,000	
	Lisieux.	Lexovium.	50,000	Suppressed 1801.
	Séez.	Sagium.	16,000	

PROVINCE OF TOULOUSE.

Archbishopric.	Toulouse.	Tolosa.	110,000	
Suffragan Sees.	Lavaur.	Varum.	50,000	Suppressed 1801.
	Lombèz.	Lombarium.	35,000	,, 1801.
	Mirepoix.	Mirapicum.	30,000	,, 1801.
	Montauban.	Mons Albanus.	35,000	
	Pamiers.	Pamiæ.	25,000	Suppressed 1801. Re-estab. 1817.
	Rieux.	Rivi.	26,000	Suppressed 1801.
	Saint-Papoul.	S. Papuli.	22,000	,, 1801.

VOL. II. 2 F

LIST OF THE ARCHIEPISCOPAL AND EPISCOPAL SEES—*continued*.

PROVINCE OF TOURS.

			Revenue. Livres.	
Archbishopric.	Tours.	Turones.	48,000	
Suffragan Sees.	Angers.	Andegavi.	25,000	
	Dol.	Dola.	22,000	
	Le Mans.	Cenomanum.	40,000	
	Nantes.	Nannetes.	30,000	
	Quimper-Corentin.	Corisopitum.	21,000	
	Rennes.	Redones.	16,000	
	Saint-Brieuc.	Briocum.	20,000	
	Saint-Pol de Léon.	Leonia.	12,000	Suppressed 1801.
	Tréguier.	Trecorium.	20,000	,, 1801.
	Vannes.	Venetiæ.	24,000	
	Saint-Malo.	Maclovium.	35,000	Suppressed 1801.

Suffragan Sees to the Archbishopric of Trèves.	Metz.	Metæ.	120,000	
	Toul.	Tullum.	30,000	
	Verdun.	Virodunum.	74,000	
Suffragan to Mayence.	Strasbourg.	Argentoratum.	400,000	

The See of Versailles was created 1801.
The See of Saint-Dié was created 1777.

NOTE TO CHAPTER VI., VOL. II.

Pp. 233–240.

To this period belongs the remarkable correspondence which passed between Dr. Wake, Archbishop of Canterbury, and certain Doctors of the Sorbonne, with the avowed object of promoting a reunion between the National Churches of England and France. The original documents relating to this affair are preserved in the Library of Christchurch, Oxford; and access to them has been allowed me by the kind liberality of the college authorities.

A detailed account of the circumstances, with extracts from the letters, may be seen in the Appendix by Dr. Maclaine to the fourth volume of Mosheim's 'Ecclesiastical History;' in an anonymous 'Examination of Dr. Maclaine's Defence of Archbishop Wake, addressed to a respectable Layman' (London, 1769); in a publication by the Anglo-Continental Society, 'D'un projet d'Union entre les églises Gallicane et Anglicane' (Oxford, 1864); and in the 'Eirenicon' of the Rev. Dr. Pusey, 1865, p. 210 *et seqq.*

Both parties in this negotiation (if it can be termed such) incurred severe censure for their conduct; and in consequence it has become a question somewhat sharply contested, whether the first overtures proceeded from the Anglican or from the Gallican side. Had the project been as reprehensible as it was in truth eminently meritorious, greater anxiety could not have been manifested, on behalf both of the English Primate and of the Parisian divines, to repudiate the charge of having taken the initiative. The evidence is conflicting and ambiguous; and the point, after all, is of secondary importance. The truth may be, not improbably, that a conjuncture of circumstances existed at the time on both sides of the Channel, which, to minds of a certain theological cast, seemed suggestive of the desirableness and feasibility of an approximation; that a favourable opportunity occurred, or was procured, of expressing these reciprocal sentiments in influential quarters; and that the path thus opened was pursued with more or less of zeal, skill, and judgment, until at length it could not be concealed that there was no reasonable prospect of success.

Dr. Wake had been in former days attached as chaplain to the British Embassy at Paris; and had acquired among the French literati the reputation of a man of learning and a powerful critical writer. He entered the lists with no less an opponent than Bossuet, and published more than one volume of strictures on the famous 'Exposition de la Foi Catholique.' In 1705 he became Bishop of Lincoln, and in 1716 was elevated to the throne of Canterbury. All the leading doctors of the Sorbonne were well acquainted, without a doubt, with his character and abilities.

The Rev. W. Beauvoir, of a French family who emigrated to England at the revocation of the Edict of Nantes, was at this time Chaplain to the Earl of Stair, British Ambassador at Paris. He was known to Archbishop Wake, and corresponded with him occasionally on literary matters. In December, 1717, this gentleman became the means of opening communications between the Archbishop and the famous Dr. Louis Ellies-Dupin; with whose talents, vast acquirements, and voluminous contributions to ecclesiastical learning, the Primate was doubtless already familiar. The moment was that of the outbreak of organized opposition to the bull Unigenitus. The four bishops had recently published their act of appeal to the future General Council. Cardinal de Noailles was universally known to sympathize with them, though he had not yet openly taken the same defiant attitude; the movement was spreading rapidly, and the Appellants, excited and over-sanguine, imagined that the whole nation was about to rise in arms against the extravagant mandate of the Roman Curia. At this crisis Dupin and three other doctors of the Sorbonne expressed to Dr. Wake, through Mr. Beauvoir, their desire for an union of the Gallican Church with the Anglican, as the most likely means of effecting the reconciliation of "all the Western Churches." The Archbishop responded in general terms of interest and goodwill; and an interchange of letters then ensued, in the course of which Dr. Wake declared his belief that there were but few things either in the doctrine or the discipline of the Church of England which Dupin and his friends would wish to see altered. He also exhorted his correspondents to take advantage of the growing resistance to the late Constitution to establish and extend the ancient liberties of the Gallican Church; and he breathed the hope that "a second Reformation" might eventually be inaugurated, in virtue of which not only the best of the Protestants, but likewise a large section of the Roman Catholic Communion, might be visibly united with the English Church.

Dupin upon this applied himself to the task of drawing up a methodical plan of reunion between the two Churches; and the result was his 'Commonitorium,' which was forwarded to Archbishop Wake in August, 1718. For an analysis of this *brochure* (the original of which seems unfortunately to be lost), I must refer the reader to the works above mentioned. It is an ingenious attempt to interpret the Thirty-nine Articles of the Church of England in a sense not repugnant to the doctrinal standards of the Church of Rome.

Gallican divines, it must be remembered, though they rejected the Ultramontane theory of Church government, the supremacy and infallibility of the Pope, &c., yet considered themselves strictly bound, in matters of scientific theological doctrine, by the Tridentine definitions, which they held to express the authoritative tradition of the Church Catholic. The whole teaching of the Sorbonne proceeded systematically on that basis; no other could possibly have been accepted by any important part of the "Ecclesia docens" of France. Any project of reunion with the Reformed Church of England involved, consequently, much more than the question of the precise ecclesiastical position and jurisdiction of the Roman Pontiff. Even if the Appellants from the "Unigenitus" could have been brought to acquiesce in the views of Archbishop Wake on that subject, and to reduce the Papal supremacy to a mere priority of rank in the Episcopal College, there were other rocks ahead still more dangerous to any hopes of a return to unity of faith. Wake, indeed, seems to have thought that if the Gallicans could be induced boldly to cast off the usurped yoke of the Pope, they would proceed in course of time to a reformation in points of essential doctrine; and he urged them, accordingly, as preliminary to any future arrangement, to seize the present opportunity of breaking with Rome, and proclaiming their independence as a National Church.

It is clear, however, that he had no sanguine anticipation of any such measure; nor, though he continued to write to Dupin in an encouraging and friendly tone, was he satisfied with the 'Commonitorium.' The following is an extract from his letter to Mr. Beauvoir of the 30th of August, 1718. (Wake MSS. Ch. Ch. Library, tom. xxix.) "I cannot well tell what to say to Dr. Du Pin. If he thinks we are to take their directions what to retain and what to give up, he is utterly mistaken. I am a friend to peace, but more to truth; and they may depend upon it I shall always account our Church to stand upon an equal foot with theirs; and that we are no more to receive laws from them, than we desire to impose any upon them. In short, the Church of England is free, is orthodox. She has a plenary authority within herself; she has no need to recur to other Churches to direct her what to believe, or what to do; nor will we otherwise than in a brotherly way, and with a full equality of right and power, ever consent to have any treaty with that of France. If, consistently with our own establishment, we can agree upon a closer union with one another, well; if not, we are as much, and upon as good grounds, a free independent Church as they are.... You see, Sir, what my sense of this matter is; and may think, perhaps, that I have a little altered my mind since this affair was first set on foot. As to my desire of peace and union with all other Christian Churches, I am still the same. But with the Doctor's *Commonitorium* I shall never comply; the matter must be put into another method, and whatever they think, they must alter some of their doctrines, and practices too, or an union with them can never be effected. Of this, as soon as I have a little more leisure, I shall write my mind as inoffensively as I can to you, but yet freely too. If anything is to come of this matter, it will be the shortest method I can take of accomplishing it, to put them in the right way. If nothing (as I believe nothing will be done in it), 'tis good to leave you under a plain knowledge of what we think of ourselves and our Church; and to let you see that we neither need nor seek the union proposed, but for their sake as well as our own, or rather, neither for theirs nor ours, but in order to the promotion of a Catholic Communion (as far as is possible) among all the churches of Christ."

Mr. Beauvoir, in his reply, says, "Your Grace hath perfectly convinced me, that there is little hope at this time of an union. The State doth not seem in a condition to do it, if it was designed; and the Doctors and Divines here are as yet too full of prejudices. But a friendly correspondence may in time open insensibly their eyes; and, perhaps, afterwards incline the Court to shake off the yoke of Rome. These thoughts I keep to myself, and, according to your Grace's wise commands, I conceal from them."

Upon the appearance of the bull "Pastoralis officii," Mr. Beauvoir wrote to the Archbishop as follows:—"The Pope's late brief to separate from those that have not received his constitution Unigenitus hath obliged Cardinal de Noailles to own publicly his appeal. Cardinal de Rohan hath sent a mandate to his diocese excommunicating all those that should appeal from the Constitution; and so have Cardinal de Bissi and the Bishop of Évreux into theirs. So that we are like to see a formal schism in France, which may induce the Appellants to seek the protection of the Church of England. I am assured that Cardinal de Noailles seems *now* earnest for an union. But that, time is to discover. But I most humbly presume, that the only way for them to come to an union is sincerely to reform their Church. For *then* the union is of course made, without the formality of perhaps impracticable treaties."

The correspondence proceeded; and Dupin and his colleague Dr. Piers de Girardin warmly expressed their admiration of the Archbishop's letters, and their entire satisfaction with his account of the succession of the English bishops, upon which latter subject they had been "in an error." "Your Grace's letter to Dr. Dupin," writes Beauvoir, under date Nov. 8, 1718, "hath been communicated to the Cardinal de Noailles, who hath a copy of it. The Procureur-Général (M. Joly de Fleury) is also to have one when he comes to town, and he is expected this day. 'Tis blaz'd about, that there is a correspondence carry'd on still to unite the Gallican with our Church; and that this correspondence is carry'd on with your Grace. I find that the Anti-constitutionists industriously spread this rumour for their advantage here." Again, Dec. 9, 1718, "They labour under great difficulties, which yet with God's blessing may easily be overcome. It is as clear as the day, that unless they honestly and without prevarication assert broadly the authority of their

Church, they'll labour still under as great inconvenience as formerly, and that the Court of Rome will be at last too hard for them, and contrive heavyer chains to load them with, when a fit occasion offers."

The negotiation having now become a matter of public notoriety, the French government felt it necessary to interfere; the more so, inasmuch as Dubois, the Regent's principal adviser, was ambitious of the Roman purple, and eager to recommend himself to the Curia by some signal service. Mr. Beauvoir informs the Archbishop, on the 14th of February, 1719, that Cardinals de Rohan and Bissy had complained, in a memorial to the Regent, that Cardinal de Noailles was seeking to induce the Sorbonne to join with the Church of England and withdraw from the Church of Rome; and that Dr. Dupin was employed by him to negotiate the treaty of union. De Noailles, being questioned thereupon, declined to enter into particulars, and gave only a general answer, which was not satisfactory. The Abbé Dubois was then desired to examine Dupin. He treated him civilly, but required him to surrender all Archbishop Wake's letters, together with copies of his own. "I was at the Palais Royal at the moment when his papers were brought in," says Lafiteau (Hist. de la Constit. Unigen. tom. ii. p. 87). "It was advanced in them that, without impairing the integrity of Catholic teaching, it would be possible to abolish auricular confession, to make no mention of Transubstantiation in the Eucharist, to suppress religious vows, to permit the marriage of priests, to do away with fasting and abstinence in Lent, to dispense with the Pope, and have no further intercourse with him, nor respect for his decisions." Lafiteau's testimony, however, may be suspected of some exaggeration.

"Abbot Dubois," writes Mr. Beauvoir on the 13th of April, "having secured the letters, &c., says not one word about them. So then his design is to keep them from public view. But then the business of a union is suspended. Dr. Dupin and Dr. P. (Piers de Girardin) appear very easy about the matter. The first visibly decays; and the other hath much abated of his courage. Both the Doctors continue in their just value and veneration for you, my Lord."

Before Dr. Wake's reply to this latter communication reached Paris, Dupin had been removed from the scene by death. He expired on the 6th of June, 1719, in the sixty-third year of his age. This event was fatal to any hopes which might have arisen out of the preceding correspondence. Dr. Piers de Girardin, unsupported by the genius of his colleague, showed no eagerness to resume the scheme. Cardinal de Noailles, intimidated and overpowered, signified his adhesion to the terms of reconciliation with the Pope negotiated by the crafty Dubois; and the "accommodement" of 1720 was the result. The success thus achieved by the Constitutionists became the foundation of the decided superiority which they were enabled to maintain, without any important check, from that date down to the Revolution.

The accusation brought against Archbishop Wake by the notorious Archdeacon Blackburne, author of 'The Confessional,' —that of having sanctioned concessions amounting to organic changes both of discipline and doctrine in order to promote the union of the Church of England with a branch of the "Popish" communion—appears to be by no means borne out by facts. It is true that he was willing to acknowledge the primacy of the Roman Pontiff, in the sense of an external privilege or mark of honour originally bestowed on him as bishop of the Imperial city. And it is also true that he was anxious to remove from the Service-books whatever might be a hindrance to intercommunion in religious offices; "that so, whenever any one comes from us to them, or from them to us, we may all join together in prayers and the holy sacraments." He considered that the only thing in our Liturgy which Roman Catholics would disallow is the "rubric relating to the Eucharist;"—that commonly known as the "Black Rubric." It may be inferred, therefore, that the Archbishop was favourable to some alteration in that statement, or even to its entire excision. But in all other respects he was a staunch assertor of the orthodoxy of the Anglican formularies; and insisted that any doctrinal reforms necessary to reunion must come from the side of Rome.

INDEX.

A.

ACARIE, Madame, i. 241, 245.
Adrian II., i. 37.
Advocates of Paris, ii. 265, 272, 274, 275; ten of them exiled, ii. 276.
Agde, Council of, A.D. 506, i. 27.
Agen, Bishop of, Cardinal de Noailles, remarkable letter to, ii. 210.
Alexander V., i. 88.
Alexandre, Noël, ii. 171.
Amboise, conspiracy of, i. 134.
Amelot, ii. 225.
Amour, Louis de St., i. 403, 413.
Amyot, Jacques, i. 125.
Annat, F., i. 457.
Annates, an oppressive impost, i. 81; abolition of, i. 96.
Ansegisus, Archbishop of Sens, i. 38.
Appeal of the four Bishops to the Gallican Episcopate, i. 469.
Appeals to Rome began first to prevail, A.D. 404, i. 5–8.
Appel comme d'Abus, institution of, i. 74–77.
Aquaviva, General of the Jesuits, i. 179, 256, 259.
Arles and Vienne, dispute between Bishops of, i. 6, 8.
——, First Council of, A.D. 314, i. 5.
Arnauld, Agnes, Abbess of St. Cyr, Coadjutrix of Port-Royal, i. 342.
——, Antoine, i. 197, 374; defends Jansenius, i. 389; his treatise on frequent Communion, i. 392; the Jesuits intrigue against him, i. 395; triumphant acquittal of, 399; on the Five propositions, i. 403; condemned by the Sorbonne, i. 425; deprived of his degrees, i. 427; emerges from his retirement on the "Peace of Clement IX.," i. 472; withdraws into voluntary exile, ii. 20; on the Gallican Articles, ii. 53; on the Revocation of the Edict of Nantes, ii. 67; reply to Malebranche on Mediation, ii. 83; malice of the Jesuits, ii. 85; death of, at Brussels, ii. 87.
——, Marie Angélique, consecrated Abbess of Port Royal, i. 340; becomes Head of the Maison du Saint Sacrement, i. 345; her death, i. 453.

Arnoux, F., i. 290.
Arnulf, Archbishop of Reims, i. 40, 43.
Articles, the Gallican, ii. 50.
Assembly, general, of the Clergy, i. 49; Bossuet's sermon before, ii. 36; Declaration concerning ecclesiastical power, ii. 49; prorogued, ii. 55; measures against the Huguenots, ii. 65; Augustiniana Ecclesiæ, &c., ii. 162; Vineam Domini, ii. 177; reign of terror, ii. 250; demands permission to hold Provincial Councils, ii. 259; disapproves of the Legend of Hildebrand, ii. 277; Unigenitus, ii. 320; submits the articles to Pope Benedict, ii. 321; on the "new philosophy," ii. 325; struggles against irreligion, ii. 371; efforts to suppress the publication of irreligious books, ii. 375; last general, ii. 380.
Assembly of bishops of province of Paris, ii. 154.
Attrition and Contrition, i. 370.
Auger, Edmond, confessor to Henry III., i. 179.
Augustine, St., i. 377; on grace and free-will, i. 378–380.
Aurelius, Petrus, i. 365, 367, 369.
Auvergne, First Council of, A.D. 535, i. 17.
Auxerre, Bishop of, ii. 277.
Avignon, Popes at, i. 79.
Avosmediano, Bishop of Cadiz, i. 153.

B.

BAIUS, i. 382, *note*, 386.
Barbier, Avocat, ii. 266, 333.
Barclay, John, i. 264, *note*.
——, William, i. 261, 264, *note*.
Basle, Council of, i. 95.
Bausset, Cardinal de, ii. 165.
Bayle, the real parent of French infidelity, ii. 329.
Beaumont, Christophe de, Archbishop of Vienne, afterwards of Paris, ii. 304, 310, 313; exiled to Conflans, ii. 319; recalled to Paris, ii. 324; and the Jesuits, ii. 356; letter to Clement XIV., ii. 365; death of, ii. 377.

Beauvais, Abbé de, preaches before the Court, ii. 369; appointed Bishop of Senez, ii. 370.
Bécheran, Abbé de, ii. 284.
Beda, Noël, i. 117.
Bellai, Eustache du, i. 150.
Bellarmine, Cardinal, i. 261, 263.
Bénard, Laurent, i. 334; founder of the Congregation of St. Maur, i. 334.
Benedict XIII., Pope, ii. 253; reply to Cardinal Noailles' congratulatory letter, ii. 254; address to the Dominicans, ii. 254; on the Unigenitus, ii. 256; is compelled to endorse the Unigenitus, ii. 258.
———, XIV., Pope, ii. 321; reply to the Clergy, ii. 322.
———, St., order of, revived, i. 333.
Bernard, Claude, founder of the Seminary of the Thirty-Three, i. 332.
———, St., on the "two swords," i. 55.
Beruis, Cardinal de, ii. 324, 361; on the death of Clement XIV., ii. 364.
Berruyer, Joseph Isaac, ii. 296.
Bertin, Claude, i. 267.
Bérulle, Cardinal Pierre de, i. 249, 292; founder of the Oratory of Jesus, i. 250; and Richelieu, i. 314.
Besons, Archbishop of Bordeaux, ii. 231.
Beza, Theodore, i. 127; at the Colloquy of Poissy, i. 141.
Bishops, meeting of the, to discuss the "droit de Régale," ii. 32.
Bissy, de, Bishop of Meaux, ii. 206; made Cardinal, ii. 227.
Blackwell, Archpriest, i. 260.
Boisgelin, Archbishop of Aix, ii. 403.
Bologna, Concordat of, A.D. 1516, i. 105-112.
Boniface VIII., Pope, i. 58; his quarrel with Philip the Fair, i. 59; despatches five separate bulls to France, i. 62; excommunicates Philip, i. 69; retires to Agnani, i. 70; taken prisoner, death, i. 70.
Bossuet, Jacques Bénigne, account of Retreat at St. Lazare, i. 325; appointed Archdeacon of Sarrebourg, ii. 13; consecrated Bishop of Condom, ii. 14; Bishop of Meaux, ii. 36; his sermon before the General Assembly, ii. 38–43; dispute with Choiseul about the Pope's infallibility, ii. 48; prepares the Declaration of the Clergy concerning ecclesiastical power, ii. 49; 'Defensio Cleri Gallicani,' ii. 57; advises the distribution of French translation of the New Testament, ii. 62; on the Revocation of the Edict of Nantes, ii. 67; opinion of Malebranche on Mediation, ii. 81; Madame Guyon submits her writings to him, ii. 110; his pastoral letter, ii. 120; head of a commission to report on Madame Guyon's works, ii. 113; estrangement of Fénelon, ii. 126; death, ii. 175.
Bossuet, Bishop of Troyes, ii. 295.
Boucher, Curé, King of the League, i. 191; sermons at St. Merry, i. 201.
Boüettin refuses the Sacraments to M. Coffin and others, ii. 312, 314, 318.
Bouillon, Cardinal de, ii. 142.
———, Duke of, i. 295.
Bourbon, Duke of, ii. 253.
Bourdoise, Adrian, ii. 5.
Bourgeois, Doctor of the Sorbonne, i. 398.
Bourges, National Council of, A.D. 1438, i. 97; Pragmatic Sanction of, i. 98; revoked by Louis XI., i. 100; re-established by the Parliamentary Courts, i. 101; finally abrogated, i. 107.
Boursier, Laurent François, ii. 266, note.
Boyer, Jean François, ii. 300.
Bretonvilliers, M. le Ragois de, ii. 4.
Brienne, Loménie de, Archbishop of Toulouse, ii. 382; resigns the control of the Finances, ii. 386.
Brunechilde, Queen, i. 28.
Buffon, ii. 310.
Bulls :—Ausculta, fili, i. 67; Unam Sanctam, i. 67; Pastor æternus, i. 107; In eminenti, i. 386; Cùm occasione, i. 412; Ad Sacrum, i. 446; Regiminis Apostolici, i. 465; Vineam Domini, ii. 177; Unigenitus, ii. 217, 323; Pastoralis Officii, ii. 239; Ex omnibus, ii. 322; Apostolicum, ii. 358; Dominus ac Redemptor, ii. 363; Qui Christi Domini, ii. 414.
Burgundy, Duke of, ii. 204, 207.

C.

St. Cæsarius, i. 9.
Caisse des Conversions, ii. 63.
Calonne, ii. 380; speech before the Assembly of the Notables, ii. 380.
Cambrai, Council of, A.D. 1566, i. 169.
Camus, his influence in the Comité ecclésiastique, ii. 402.
Carmelite nuns in France, establishment of, i. 240.
Casaubon, Isaac, i. 222; goes to England, i. 223.
Caulet, François de, Bishop of Pamiers, ii. 26; death of, ii. 29.
Celidonius, i. 7.

Cerle, F., ii. 29.
Chalmette, Abbé, ii. 225.
Chamier, i. 233.
Champflour, Bishop of La Rochelle, ii. 200.
Chantal, Madame de, i. 247; foundress of the Congregation of the Visitation, i. 249.
Chardonnet, St. Nicolas de, ii. 5.
Charlemagne, his capitularies, i. 18, *note*; convokes five great Councils of Arles, Mayence, Reims, Tours, and Châlons, i. 30.
Charles the Bald, Emperor, i. 38.
—— VII. sends ambassadors to Pope Eugenius, i. 95; assembles a great national council at Bourges, A.D. 1438, i. 97.
—— IX., i. 135, 163.
Châtel, Jean, i. 227.
Chauvelin, Abbé de, ii. 348.
Chinese ceremonies, ii. 166.
Choiseul, Duc de, ii. 344, 357, 363.
——, Gilbert de, Bishop of Comminges, afterwards of Tournay, i. 457; conference with F. Ferrier, i. 458; dispute with Bossuet, ii. 48.
Church and State, relations between, i. 263.
Church, the Gallican, its acme of prosperity, ii. 160.
Clemangis, Nicolas de, i. 83.
Clement V., i. 78.
—— VII., i. 80, 121.
—— VIII. i. 201; grants absolution to Henry IV., i. 203.
—— IX., i. 467; letter of the four bishops to, i. 471; peace of, i. 473; death of, i. 476.
—— XI., ii. 168; addresses the bull Vineam Domini to the Assembly of Clergy, ii. 177; condemns the New Testament of Quesnel, ii. 183; appoints a special congregation to examine the New Testament, ii. 209; issues the bull Unigenitus, ii. 212; indecision of, ii. 223; confession to Amelot, ii. 226; addresses a conciliatory brief to Noailles, ii. 237; death, ii. 246.
—— XIII., publishes his bull, Apostolicum, ii. 358; excommunicates the Duke of Parma, ii. 359.
—— XIV., ii. 360; signs the bull suppressing the Order of the Jesuits, ii. 363; remorse and death, ii. 363.
Clergy, General Assembly of the, i. 49. *See* Assembly, general, of the Clergy.
——, Gallican, on royal marriages, i. 359.

Clermont, Collége de, i. 146.
——, Council of, A.D. 1095, i. 21.
Coffin, Charles, ii. 310.
Cointe, Charles le, i. 254.
Colbert, Bishop of Montpellier, ii. 296.
——, statesman, ii. 37, 46.
Coligny, Admiral de, i. 129, 135.
Comité ecclésiastique, ii. 400.
Concordat of Bologna, A.D. 1516, i. 105–112.
—— of Worms, i. 22.
—— of Paris, ii. 413.
Condillac, ii. 331.
Conseil de Conscience, or ecclesiastical commission, ii. 247.
Constance, Council of, or 16th Œcumenical, A.D. 1414, i. 88; decrees of, i. 91; not œcumenical, i. 92, *note*.
Constitutionnaires, les, ii. 259, 270.
Contrition and Attrition, i. 370.
Convulsionnaires, the, ii. 284, 286, 287.
Cornet, Nicolas, Syndic of the Faculty of Theology at Paris, i. 401; his five propositions, i. 402.
Cotton, F. Pierre, i. 233, 259, 265, 290, 310.
Councils:—Agde, i. 27; Arles, i. 5; Auvergne, i. 17; Basle, i. 95; Bourges, i. 97; Cambrai, i. 169; Clermont, i. 21; Constance, i. 88; Douzi, i. 37; Early, on episcopal elections, i. 17; Embrun, ii. 263; Epaone, i. 27; Florence, i. 3, *note*; Lateran, i. 104; Mouson, i. 43; Orleans, i. 27; Pavia, i. 94; Pisa, i. 87; Pontyon, i. 38; Reims, i. 18; Sardica, i. 6, *note*, 7, 33; Sens, i. 118; Sorbonne, i. 116; Trent, i. 122; Troyes, i. 18; under the Carlovingians, i. 29; Vienne, i. 18.
Courts, ecclesiastical, i. 71.
Cugnères, Pierre de, i. 72.
Cyran, St., Abbot of, i. 345, 359, 364, 367; arrested, i. 371; imprisoned at Vincennes five years, i. 373; released, i. 376, death, i. 376.

D.

D'Achery, Dom Jean Luc, i. 338.
D'Aguesseau, ii. 78, 93, 153, 169, 183; his famous réquisitoire before the Parliament, ii. 156; tenders his resignation, ii. 244; death, ii. 308.
D'Aiguillon, Duc, ii. 366.
D'Ailly, Pierre, Chancellor of the University of Paris, i. 82, 87.
D'Alembert, ii. 334.
Damiens, the assassin, ii. 323.
D'Andelot, François, i. 129.

Danès, Pierre, i. 123, 190.
Daniel, F., i. 442.
D'Argenson, Marquis, ii. 190, 191.
Daubenton, F., ii. 126.
D'Aubeterre, Marquis, ii. 360.
Decretals, forged, i. 35, 41, *note*.
Déforis, Dom Jean-Pierre, ii. 374.
Del Monte, Cardinal-Legate, i. 123.
D'Espinac, Pierre, Archbishop of Lyons, i. 184.
D'Épresménil, ii. 383.
D'Étampes, Leonor, Bishop of Chartres, i. 304.
Diables de Loudun, i. 353.
Diderot, ii. 335.
Dom Didier de la Cour re-establishes the Rule of St. Benedict, i. 333.
Dominis, Antonio de, Archbishop of Spalatro, i. 287–289.
Dorsanne, Abbé, ii. 231.
Douai, fourberie de, ii. 86.
Doucin, Louis, ii. 232.
Douzi, Council of, A.D. 871, i. 37.
Dragonnades, ii. 64.
Droit de Régale, established in the time of Philippe le Bel, i. 77, ii. 23.
Dubois, Abbé, ii. 242; ordained priest, ii. 243; consecrated Archbishop of Cambrai, ii. 243; made Cardinal, ii. 246; death of, ii. 252.
Dubourg, Anne, i. 132; tried for heresy and condemned to death, i. 133.
Dufaur, Louis, i. 133.
Duguet, Jacques Joseph, i. 254.
Dulau, Archbishop of Arles, ii. 372; his two memorials on the encroachments of the Protestants, and the Convocation of Provincial Councils, ii. 373, 374.
Dumoulin, Charles, i. 168.
Duplessis-Mornay, i. 218; conference with Du Perron, i. 219.
Duprat, Antoine, Archbishop of Sens and Chancellor of France, i. 105.
Dupuy, the brothers, i. 350.

E.

ECCLESIASTICAL buildings, restoration of, i. 215.
Ecclesiastical power, declaration of the Clergy concerning, ii. 49.
——— property, sale of, ii. 399.
Edict of Nantes, i. 205.
Edicts, three, imposing taxes, ii. 307; protests of the Clergy against, ii. 309.
Elections, episcopal, early councils on, i. 17.
Elisiens, the, or Vuillantistes, ii. 286.

Embrun, Council of, A.D. 1727, ii. 263; suspends Soanen, Bishop of Senez, ii. 265.
'Émile,' the, of Rousseau, ii. 337.
'Encyclopédie,' the, ii. 332; suppressed by Government, ii. 335; reaches its seventh volume, ii. 335.
Erasmus, i. 117; denounced by Noël Béda, i. 117.
Erigona, John Scotus, ii. 98.
Eudes, Jean, ii. 6.
Eudistes, congregation of, ii. 6.
Eugenius IV., i. 94; deposed by Council of Basle, i. 97.

F.

FABRONI, Cardinal, ii. 181.
Faculty, theological, of Paris, ii. 235.
Fénelon, François de Salignac de Lamothe, ii. 70; mission to the Protestants, ii. 71; refutation of Malebranche, ii. 83; acquaintance with Madame Guyon, ii. 104; opinion of Madame Guyon, ii. 107; nominated to the Archbishopric of Cambrai, ii. 115; Articles of Issy, ii. 115; consecrated Archbishop, ii. 119; estrangement from Bossuet, ii. 126; appeals to Rome for judgment on his book, ii. 135; exiled from Paris, ii. 138; publishes his celebrated Apology, ii. 146; submission to the Pope's decision, ii. 151; confidential relations with Le Tellier, ii. 195; on the Unigenitus, ii. 217; death of, ii. 228.
Fenouillet, Pierre, Bishop of Montpellier, i. 360; mission to Rome i. 361.
Ferri, Paul, ii. 14.
Ferrier, du, at the Council of Trent, i. 161.
———, F., i. 457; conference with the Bishop of Comminges, i. 458.
Feudalism, effect of, on the Church, i. 19.
Figuristes, the, ii. 286.
Filesac, i. 367.
Filles de la Charité, i. 328.
Fitz-James, François Duc de, Bishop of Soissons, ii. 302.
Flèche, Père Timothée de la, ii. 222. *note*.
Fleury, André Hercules de, ii. 253; supports the Constitutionnaires, ii. 259; advanced to the rank of Cardinal, ii. 260; and the Parliament, ii. 291; death of, ii. 299.
———, Claude, author of the 'Histoire Ecclésiastique,' ii. 232; death of, ii. 250.

Florence, Council of, i. 3, *note*.
Flotte, Pierre, i. 61, 65.
Fontaine, Jacques de la Roche, editor of the 'Nouvelles Ecclésiastiques,' ii. 288.
Force, Marquis de la, i. 296, 297.
Formulary, the, condemning the Five Propositions. i. 445; enforced at Port Royal, i. 453; enforced by royal edict, i. 461.
Fourberie de Douai, ii. 86.
Franchises, the affair of, ii. 73.
Francis I., i. 105; Erasmus appeals for protection to, i. 117; hostility of Charles V., i. 122.
——— II., i. 133; death of, i. 135.
Fresne, Canaye de, i. 222, 234.
Fronde, war of the, i. 400.

G.

GALLICANISM, general character of, i. 1; early relations with Rome, i. 4, 5; in its true sense, i. 14; ancient and modern, i. 15.
Ganganelli, Lorenzo, ii. 360; *see* Pope Clement XIV.
Gap, Protestant synod at, i. 228.
Garlande, Mathilde de, foundress of the Port-Royal des Champs, i. 339.
Génebrard, Gilbert, Archbishop of Aix, i. 190; member of the Council of Ten, i. 191.
Geoffrey, Abbot of Vendôme, i. 54.
Gerberon, F., ii. 89.
Gerbert, on Papal administration, i. 41; elected Archbishop of Reims, i. 42; *see* Pope Sylvester.
Gerson, Jean, i. 88; on general councils, i. 89.
Givri, Anne Escars de, i. 226.
Godet-Desmarais, Bishop of Chartres ii. 109; death of, ii. 195.
Gondi, Henri de, i. 226.
———, Jean François de, i. 226.
———, Jean François Paul, i. 226.
———, Pierre de, i. 225.
Gonzalez, Thyrsis, ii. 165.
Grandier, Urbain, i. 353; accused of sorcery and condemned, i. 355.
Gravamina against the bishops, i. 72.
Gregory VII., i. 45.
Guises, assassination of the, i. 185.
Guyon, Madame, ii. 102.

H.

HABERT, Isaac, Dr. of the Sorbonne, i. 389.

Hallier, François, i. 367.
Harlai, Achille de, i. 186, 230.
———, François de, Archbishop of Rouen, afterwards of Paris, i. 476, ii. 38, 47; death of, ii., 89.
Hauranne, Jean du Verger de, i. 345, 385. *See* St. Cyran.
Henry II., i. 123; protest of, at Trent, i. 125; persecution of the Huguenots by, i. 130; proceeds in person to Parliament, i. 132; death of, i. 133.
——— III., i. 172; object of the Catholic League to imprison him, i. 175; helplessness and imbecility of, i. 181; summons the doctors of the Sorbonne to his presence, i. 183; causes the assassination of the Guises, i. 185; forms an alliance with Henry of Navarre and the Huguenots, i. 188.
——— of Navarre, excommunicated by Pope Sixtus, i. 180; public abjuration of Calvinism, i. 200; absolution by Pope Clement VIII., i. 203; difficulty with the Huguenots, i. 204; Edict of Nantes, i. 205; revival of the catholic religion, i. 209; concludes peace with Spain, i. 210; corruptions of the Church, i. 213; lays the first stone of the new cathedral of Sainte Croix at Orleans, i. 215; conference at Fontainebleau, i. 219; recall of the Jesuits, i. 227; reply to the Parliament, i. 230; assassinated by François Ravaillac, i. 257.
Heresy, trials and arrests for, i. 133.
Hersent, Charles, or Optatus Gallus, i. 351.
Hesychasts, or Quietists of Mount Athos, ii. 97.
Hilary, Bishop of Arles, i. 7.
Hildebrand, i. 45. *See* Gregory VII.
———, St., Legend of, ii. 276, 277
Hincmar, Archbishop of Reims, i. 19, 32, 38.
———, Bishop of Laon, deposition of, i. 37.
Holstein, i. 10, *note.*
Honorius, Pope, i. 10, *note.*
Hotman, François, author of 'Franco-Gallia,' i. 187.
l'Hôpital, Michel de, head of the Tiers-parti, i. 135; created Chancellor of France, i. 136.
Hugh, Abbot of St. Victor, i. 55.
Huguenots, or French Reformers, i. 128; persecuted by Henry II., i. 130; insurrection of, i. 294; repulse Louis before Montauban, i, 297; defeated at Ile de Rhé, i. 297; submission of, i. 299; revolt again, i. 301; edict of grace, i. 313.

Hugnes, Abbé Gaspard de, ii. 264.
———, Bishop of Die, i. 45.

I.

INFALLIBILITY, Papal, theory of, i. 449.
Innocent I., Pope, i. 5.
——— III., Pope, on papal jurisdiction, i. 57.
——— X., Pope, appeal of Bishops to, i. 405; discussion of the Five Propositions, i. 407; condemns them, i. 412.
——— XI., Pope, ii. 27; his briefs to Lous XIV., ii. 28, 30; reply to the General Assembly, ii. 44; affair of the Franchises, ii. 73; death of, ii. 75.
——— XII., Pope, ii. 76; letter of the Bishops-designate to, ii. 77; appealed to by Fénelon, ii. 135; decides against Fénelon's 'Maximes des Saints,' ii. 149.
——— XIII., Pope, address of the seven bishops to, on the bull Unigenitus, ii. 248; death of, ii. 253.
Inquisition, attempt to establish, in France, i. 132.
Investitures, war of, i. 20.
Irenæus, i. 4.
Ivo of Chartres, i. 45; remonstrance to Paschal II., i. 46.

J.

JANSENISM, ii. 168.
Jansenistic controversy, commencement of the, i. 377.
Jansenists, i. 387, 399, 407, 417, 420, 437; provoke a renewal of hostilities, ii. 161.
Jansenius, Bishop of Ypres, i. 345, 371, 385; his 'Augustinus,' I. 387, 417.
Jean d'Angély, St., i. 296.
Jesuits, the, first obtained footing in France, i. 146; banished from France, i. 197; re-established, i. 228; ascendency of, i. 265; re-open the Collégo of Clermont, i. 290; and the Parliament of Paris, i. 309; and the Bishop of Chalcedon, i. 365; their intrigues against Antoine Arnauld, i. 395; conduct in China, ii. 166; animosity against the, ii. 312; Madame de Pompadour and, ii. 345; condemned by Parliament, ii. 349; expelled from their colleges, ii. 354; destruction of their order, ii. 355; suppression of, ii. 357; abolished in Spain by Charles III., ii. 359.

John Lateran, St., Council of, A.D. 1725, ii. 258.
——— XV., Pope, i. 42.
——— XXIII., Pope, i. 88, 91.
Joigny, Count de, i. 319.
Joyeuse, Cardinal de, i. 224, 255.
Juigné, Antoine Leclerc de, Bishop of Châlons, afterwards Archbishop of Paris, ii. 377, 391.
Julius II., Pope, i. 101; excommunicates Louis XII., i. 103.
Jurisdiction, patriarchal, of the Pope, i. 9.
———, provincial and national, i. 24-27.
———, spiritual, development of, i. 72.

L.

LA CHAISE, F., ii. 26, 194.
Lacombe, F., ii. 102, 145.
La Flèche, Jesuit establishment of, i. 235.
Lafosse, miraculously restored to health, ii. 281.
Lainez, general of the Jesuits, i. 144, 146.
Languet, Jean Joseph, Bishop of Soissons, ii. 288, note, 295.
Lansac, St. Gelais de, i. 185.
La Parisière, Bishop of Nismes, ii. 279.
La Rochelle, general assembly of the Huguenots convoked at, i. 294.
Lateran Council, fourth, A.D. 1215, i. 22; fifth, A.D. 1513, i. 104; eleventh session of, A.D. 1516, i. 107.
Laubardemont, i. 354, 372.
Launoi, Jean de, i. 10, 426.
Lavalette, F. Antoine, ii. 346.
Law, the adventurer, ii. 262.
Lazare, St., priory of, i. 323; "Tuesday Conferences" at, i. 324; general retreats at, i. 326.
League, the Catholic, or Holy Union, i. 172; discovery of its secret aims, i. 174; distrust of Henry III., i. 176; pillars of, i. 178; secret treaty with the King of Spain, i. 179; seek the sanction of the Holy See, i. 179; Pope Sixtus V. persuaded to issue a bull against Henry of Navarre and Prince of Condé, i. 180; dominant power in France, i. 184; rebellion in Paris, i. 187; contradictory principles of, i. 187; principal leader of, Claude de Saintes, Bishop of Évreux, i. 189; Council of Ten, terrorism, i. 191, 192; decline of terrorism, i. 193; the Satyre Menippée, i. 195; formal sub-

mission to the Bourbon Government, i. 197.
Ledieu, Abbé, ii. 57, 90.
Lefranc, Anne, miraculous recovery of, ii. 283.
Legates, Papal, i. 44; restrictions on, i. 47.
Legations, system of, i. 44.
Legras, Madame, i. 328; institution of the Filles de la Charité, i. 328.
Lemaître, Antoine, i. 374.
Le Mans, Bishop of, i. 212.
Le Moine, Cardinal, i. 67.
Leo the Great, i. 7; his decision between Arles and Vienne, i. 9.
Leo X., Pope, i. 104; abrogates the Pragmatic Sanction, i. 107.
Lescure, de, Bishop of Luçon, denounces the New Testament of F. Quesnel, ii. 200.
Lesdiguières, Marshal, i. 292; abjuration of Calvinism, i. 298; death, i. 299.
Lestonnac, Jeanne de, Marquise de Monferrant, i. 245; foundress of the earliest institution in France for female education, i. 246.
Le Tellier. *See* Tellier, Le.
Liancour, Duc de, i. 421.
Liber Diurnus, i. 10, *note.*
Liberty, ecclesiastical, i, 11, 12.
———, perversion of Gallican, i. 13.
Ligny, de, plot against, ii. 87.
Linières, F. de, ii. 251.
List of the Archiepiscopal and Episcopal Sees before the revolution of 1789, ii. 431.
Loi fondamentale, the, i. 282.
Longueville, Duchess of, i, 467, 473; death of, ii. 22.
Lorraine, Armagnac de, Bishop of Bayeux, ii. 261.
———, Cardinal of, i. 129; instigates the persecution of the Huguenots, i. 130; revives the Inquisition, i. 131; at the Colloquy of Poissy, i. 142; at the Council of Trent, i. 151; preserves throughout the position of mediator, i. 155; proceeds to Rome, i. 159; interview with Pius IV., i. 159; returns to Trent, i. 164; termination of the Council, i. 166; death of, i. 173.
Loudun, Protestant assembly at, i. 205.
Louis, St., his famous ordinance, the Pragmatic Sanction, i. 23.
——— XI., i. 100; revokes the Pragmatic Sanction, i. 100.
——— XII. re-establishes the Pragmatic Sanction, i. 101; excommunicated by Pope Julius, i. 103; reconciled to Leo X., i. 104; death of, i. 105.
Louis XIII., i. 276; re-establishes the Catholic religion in Béarn, i. 291; proceeds to Pau, i. 293; takes possession of Saumur, i. 296; is repulsed at Montauban, i. 297; submission of the Huguenots, i. 299; death of, i. 376.
——— XIV., religious policy of, i. 451; determines to proceed against the four Bishops, i. 466; declaration of, on the Droit de Régale, ii. 25; signs the Revocation of the Edict of Nantes, ii. 66; letter to Pope Innocent, ii. 148; appeals to the Pope, ii. 176; demands a bull condemning the errors contained in Nouveau Testament of Quesnel, ii. 209; orders an assembly of the Bishops to report upon the Unigenitus, ii. 216; death of, ii. 228.
——— XV., his sloth and indifference, ii. 369; dismisses Madame du Barry, ii. 370; death of, ii. 370.
——— XVI., ii. 370, 410.
Louytre, i. 243.
Luçon, Bishop of, his speech at the prorogation of the States-General, i. 284. *See* Richelieu.
Luther, his works condemned by the Paris divines, i. 116.
Luynes, de, i. 290.
Luzançi, Henri Arnauld de, i. 374.

M.

Mabillon, Jean, i. 338; ii. 160.
Machault, Comptroller-General of Finance, ii. 307.
Mailly, Archbishop de, ii. 236.
Maintenon, Madame de, ii. 104, 109; and Cardinal Noailles, ii. 184.
Maistre, Count Joseph de, ii. 417.
Malebranche, Nicolas, ii. 79.
Mallet, ii. 19.
Marca, Pierre de, i. 294, 352.
Mariana, the Jesuit, i. 259.
Martelière, Pierre de la, i. 270; his speech against the Jesuits, i. 270.
Martin V., Pope, i. 92.
Mascaron, Jules, Bishop of Agen, i. 255.
Massalians, or Euchites, ii. 97.
Massillon, Jean Baptiste, Bishop of Clermont, i. 255; death of, ii. 301.
Matthieu, Claude, the "Courier of the League," i. 179.
Maubuisson, Convent of, i. 341.
Maur, St., congregation of, i. 335.
Mayenne, Duke of, i. 187, 191, 192, 194.

Mazarin, Cardinal, i, 364, 395, 400, 415, 419, 450.
Médard, St., tomb of François Pâris at, ii. 282; miracles at, ii, 283.
Medici, Mary de', i. 276, 291.
Medicis, Catherine of, i. 135; letter to the Pope, i. 139; attends the Colloquy of Poissy, i. 140–145.
Medina, Bartolomeo, ii. 164.
Mercuriales, i. 132, note.
Mirabeau, ii. 398.
Miracle of the Sainte Épine, i. 435 439.
Molé, Matthieu, de, i. 309, note, 403.
Molina, Luis, i. 383.
Molinists, the, i. 401, 423.
Molinos, Michel de, ii. 100.
Mont, Sainte Marie du, i. 221.
Montanus, heresy of, i. 4.
Montauban, defeat of Louis XIII. before, i. 297.
Montazet, de, Bishop of Autun, ii. 325.
Montgéron, Carré de, ii, 285.
Montholon, i. 271.
Monton, last editor of the 'Nouvelles Ecclésiastiques,' ii. 283.
Montpellier, siege of, i. 299.
Montpensier, Duchess of, i. 183.
Mouson, Council at, A.D. 996, i. 43.
Mysticism, or Quietism, ii. 96, 106.
Mystics, the, or Theosophists, ii. 99.

N.

NANTES, Edict of, i. 205; revocation of, ii. 66, 69, 72.
Napoleon Bonaparte, ii. 413; the Concordat of 1801, ii. 413.
National Church Establishment, restoration of, ii. 416.
Necker, ii. 387.
Négrepélisse, town of, i. 298.
Nicholas I., Pope, i. 32–36.
Nicolas V., Pope, i. 100.
Nicole Pierre, ii. 15.
Noailles, Louis Antoine de, Bishop of Châlons, afterwards Archbishop of Paris, ii. 89, 113, 163, 176, 188, 192; his remorse about Port-Royal, ii. 193; signs the declaration, ii. 193; his principles attacked, ii. 202; appeals to Madame de Maintenon, ii. 203; Le Tellier's plot against him discovered, ii. 204; opinion of Le Tellier, ii. 205; deprives the Jesuits of their licence, ii. 206; remarkable letter to the Bishop of Agen, ii. 210; and the nine protesting bishops, letter of, to Louis XIV., ii. 218; forbidden to appear at Court, ii. 220; restoration of, ii. 230;

"feuille des bénéfices" bestowed on, ii. 232; the Pope addresses a conciliatory letter to, ii. 237; publishes his appeal to the General Council, ii. 240; resigns his seat in the Council of Conscience, ii. 240; draws up a statement about the Unigenitus for Benedict XIII., ii. 256; failing faculties of, ii. 267; accepts the Unigenitus, ii. 268; death of, ii. 269.
Noailles, Vicomte de, ii. 393.
Nogaret, Guillaume de. i. 70; treatment of Boniface VIII., i. 70.
Notables, Assembly of the, ii. 330; re-assembled, ii. 387.
Notre Dame, congrégation des filles de, i. 245.
Nouet, F., i. 395.
'Nouvelles Ecclésiastiques,' a Jansenist journal, ii. 288.
Noyers, M. des, ii. 9.

O.

OLIER, Jean Jacques, i. 331; founder of the Seminary of St. Sulpice, i. 331.
Omer Talon, i. 308.
Optatus Gallus, i. 351.
Oratory of Jesus, founded by Cardinal de Bérulle, A.D. 1610, i. 250.
Orleans, First Council of, A.D. 511, i. 27.
———, Fifth Council of, A.D. 549, i. 17.
———, Ordonnance of, i. 136.
———, Duke of, his marriage impugned, i. 357.
———, Philip, Duke of, Regent, ii. 230.
d'Ossat, Arnaud, Cardinal, i. 224.

P.

PALMA-CAYET, i. 173, 199, 218.
Papal power, development of, i. 31.
Pâris, François de, ii. 281.
Parliament of Paris registers the Pragmatic Sanction, i. 100; opposes the Concordat, i. 107; yields to the king, i. 109; contests the decrees of the Council of Trent, i. 167; expels the Jesuits, i. 227; resists their return, i. 230; disputes with the clergy, i. 305, 307; and the Jesuits, i. 309; denounces the sentence of the Inquisition, ii. 239; signs the Declaration, ii. 245; appealed to by Soanen, ii. 264; attacks the judgment of the Council of Embrun, ii. 265; collision between, and the ecclesiastical authorities, ii. 273; disputes between,

and Archbishop Beaumont, ii. 312; rebuked by the king, ii. 313; transferred to Soissons, ii. 317; recalled to Paris, ii. 318; summoned to Compiègne, ii. 289; its principal members banished or imprisoned, ii. 290. suppresses the bull for the canonization of St. Vincent de Paul, ii. 293; condemns the Jesuits, ii. 349; expels them from their colleges, ii. 354; destruction of the Order of the Jesuits, ii. 355; re-established by Louis XVI., ii. 370.
Pascal, i. 420; his provincial letters, i. 428, 434, 441; his death, i. 444.
Paschal II., Pope, i. 46.
Patroclus, Bishop of Arles, i. 6.
Paul III., Pope, convokes the Council of Trent, A.D. 1544, i, 122.
Paul, St. Vincent de, on Seminaries, &c., ii. 1. *See* St. Vincent de Paul.
Pavia, Council of, A.D. 1423, i. 94.
Pavillon, Nicolas, Bishop of Alet, i. 417, 454, 465; ii. 28.
Pélisson-Fontanier, Paul, ii. 63.
Péréfixe, Hardouin Beaumont de, i. 454; Archbishop of Paris, i. 461; ejects the abbess and nuns of Port Royal of Paris, i. 463.
Périer, Marguerite, i. 435.
Perron, Jacques Davy du, i. 203, 216, 217; conference at Fontainebleau, i. 219; reply of to De Mornay, i. 220; made Cardinal, i. 221; at the meeting of the States-General, i. 279.
Petitpied, ii. 287.
Philip the Fair, i. 58; his quarrel with Pope Boniface, i. 59; arrests the Pope's Nuncio, i. 61; convokes the Estates, i. 63; impeaches the Pope, i. 69; causes him to be arrested, i. 70.
Pibrac at the Council of Trent, i. 148.
Piccolomini, Æneas Sylvius, i. 95, *note*. *See* Pius II.
Pirot, F., i. 440.
Pisa, Council of, A.D. 1409, i. 87; deposes Benedict XIII. and Gregory XII., i. 88, 102.
———, Pseudo-Council of, i. 103; transferred to Milan, i. 103; suspends Pope Julius II., i. 103.
Pithou, Pierre, author of 'Treatise on the Liberties of the Gallican Church,' i. 195.
Pius II., i. 95, *note*, 100.
——— IV., i. 147; interview with Cardinal of Lorraine, i. 159; summons the Queen of Navarre, i. 163.
——— VI., ii. 304; disapproves of the Constitution civile du clergé, ii. 407.

Poissy, Colloquy of, i. 40, 48, 145.
Polignac, Abbé de, ii. 181, 224.
Pombal, Marquis of, ii. 343.
Pompadour, Madame de, and the Jesuits, ii. 344.
Pompignan, Archbishop of Vienne, ii. 371.
Poncet, Maurice, i. 181.
Pons, St., Bishop of, ii. 174.
Pontyon, Council at, A.D. 876, i. 38.
Port-Royal des Champs, i. 339, 463; ii. 185; its downfall, ii. 189; dispersion of the nuns, ii. 190; levelled with the ground, ii. 191.
——— de Paris, i. 343, 420; the Sainte Épine, i. 436.
——— Royalists, ii. 21; persecution of, i. 453, 463, 464.
Portail, Antoine, i. 320.
Portalis, M., ii. 415; presents the second Concordat to the Corps Législatif, ii. 415.
Prades, Abbé de, thesis by, condemned by the Sorbonne, ii. 332; flies to Berlin, ii. 334; publishes a formal recantation, ii. 334.
Pragmatic Sanction, A.D. 1268, i. 23.
Prelates invested with temporal peerages, i. 19.
Probabilism, doctrine of, ii. 164.
Propositions, the Five, i. 402-411; bull upon the, i. 412.
Protestant places of Worship, i. 127.
Protestantism, French, rise and progress of, i. 113.
Protestants, French, numerical strength in the 16th century, i. 127; party leaders, i. 129; efforts to convert the, ii. 61; the Avertissement pastoral, ii. 61; mission to the, ii. 71; emigration, ii. 72.
Pucelle, Abbé, ii. 220, 231, 272.
Puisieux, Marquis de, i. 300.

Q.

Quesnel, Pasquier, his 'Réflexions Morales,' ii. 92.
Quietism, ii. 166.
Quietists, the, ii. 100, 102.

R.

Rancé, de, Abbot de la Trappe, ii. 37, 88, 144.
Ravaillac, François, i. 257.
Reims, Council at, i. 22, 43.
Reine, Sainte, hospital of, ii. 10.
Retrospective view of ecclesiastical legislation in France, ii. 419.

Retz, de, i. 400, 415, 449, 454.
Rhotad, Bishop of Soissons, i. 32.
Richelieu, Armand Jean Duplessis (afterwards Cardinal), i. 277; first public speech, i. 284; made Prime Minister, i. 301; policy of, i. 303; undertakes the siege of La Rochelle, i. 312; solicits the appointment of Legate, i. 347; forbids the Papal Nuncio Scoti to appear at Court, i. 349; instigates the outcry for a Gallican Synod, i. 349; and De Marca, i. 352; impugns the marriage of the Duke of Orleans, i. 357; unjust taxation of the clergy, i. 362; imprisons St. Cyran, i. 371; death of, i. 375.
Richer, Edmond, Syndic of the Faculty of Theology at Paris, i. 265; his veto at the Chapter-General of the Dominicans, i. 267; his treatise 'De Ecclesiasticâ et Politicâ Potestate,' i. 268; is superseded, i. 273.
Rochefoucauld, Cardinal de la, i. 287.
Rochelle, La, siege of, i. 313.
Rohan, Cardinal de, Bishop of Strasbourg, ii. 377, 379.
———, Duke of, i. 296, 301.
Roland, Minister of the Interior, ii. 410.
Rollin, Charles, ii. 212.
Rose, Guillaume, Bishop, i. 182, 193, 197.
Rousseau, Jean Jacques, ii. 332; his 'Émile,' ii. 337.

S.

SACRAMENTS, refusal of the last, to dying people, ii. 292, 293.
Saint-Simon, Duke de, ii. 197.
Saintes, Claude de, i. 189.
Saisset, Bernard de, Bishop of Pamiers, i. 61.
Sales, François de, i. 224, 236; his mission in the Chablais, i. 237; made coadjutor of Geneva, i. 238; preaches a course of Lent sermons in Paris, i. 239; consecrated Bishop of Geneva, i. 240.
Santarelli, Antoine, i. 307; his book condemned to be burnt, i. 308; censure of, i. 310.
Sardica, Council of, A.D., 347, i. 6, note, 7, 33.
Saron, Abbé Bochart de, ii. 205.
Satyre Ménippée, i. 195.
Scepticism, rise of, ii. 327.
Schelstrate, Emmanuel, Librarian of the Vatican, i. 91, note.
Schism of the West, i. 78.
Schoolmen, the, i. 380.

Seminaries, ecclesiastical, ii. 1-7.
Seminary of the Thirty-three, i. 332.
——— of St. Nicolas de Chardonnet, ii. 5.
Senault, Jean François, i. 255.
Sens, Provincial Council of, A.D. 1527, i. 118.
Servin, Advocate-General, i. 270, 275; his sudden death, i. 308.
Sièyes, Abbé, ii. 390, 396.
Sixtus V., Pope, i. 180; his bull against Henry of Navarre, i. 181.
Smith, Richard, Bishop of Chalcedon, i. 365.
Soanen, Jean, Bishop of Senez, ii. 261; appeals "comme d'abus" to the Parliament of Paris, ii. 264; exiled to La Chaise Dieu in Auvergne, ii. 265; death of, ii. 297.
Solminiac, Alain de, Bishop of Cahors, ii. 3.
Sorbonne, Faculty of the, i. 116; condemns the opinions of Luther, i. 116; censures the 'Colloquies' of Erasmus, i. 117; releases the people from their oath of obedience to Henry III., i. 186; orders the king's name to be erased from the formularies of the Church, i. 187; outcry against the Jesuits, i. 258, 270; refuses to register the bull prohibiting the 'Augustinus,' i. 388; reception of Pope Innocent's bull on the Five Propositions, i. 415; deprivation of Arnauld, i. 427; division about the Constitution Unigenitus, ii. 220; pronounces the decree false, cancelled, ii. 233; ratifies the decree, ii. 271; censures Rousseau's 'Émile,' ii. 337.
Soubise, Duke of, i. 296, 297, 301.
Sourdis, François d'Escoubleau de, i. 225.
———, Henri de, i. 225, 312.
Staël, Madame de, on the French Revolution, ii. 396.
States-General, i. 184; at Suresnes, i. 194; meeting of, A.D. 1614, i. 276; refuse to receive the decrees of the Council of Trent, i. 277; summary of proceedings, i. 283; speech of the Bishop of Luçon, i. 284-286; Archbishop Dulau refers to the, ii. 381; meet at Versailles, ii. 388.
Suarez, the Spanish Jesuit, i. 274.
Sully, i. 200, 221, 229.
Sulpice, St., Seminary of, i. 331; ii. 4.
Supremacy, judicial, of the Church, i. 53.
Suresnes, Conference at, i. 194.
Syagrius, Bishop of Autun, i. 28, note.
Sylvester, Pope, i. 42.
Symmachus, i. 9.

Synods, of Paris, i. 17; diocesan and provincial, i. 25; national, i. 26.
——, ancient and modern, compared, i. 50, 51.

T.

TABARAUD, i. 253.
Talleyrand, Bishop of Autun, ii. 397; his scheme for appropriating the property of the clergy, ii. 397.
Talon, Advocate-General, ii. 35; on the Franchises, ii. 74.
Tarisse, Dom Jean Grégoire, Superior-General of the congregation of St. Maur, i. 336.
Tellier, le, Chancellor, ii. 67.
——, Michel, Confessor to Louis XIV., ii. 189; character of, ii. 194; plots against de Noailles, ii. 204; exiled to La Flèche, ii. 232.
Ten, Council of, i. 191.
Tencin, Pierre Guerin de, Archbishop of Embrun, ii. 262; convokes by Royal Edict the Council of Embrun, ii. 263; created Cardinal, ii. 298; jeu d'esprit on, ii. 298.
Testament, Nouveau, de Mons, ii. 19.
Thomassin, Louis, i. 254.
Thomists, the, i. 380.
Tiers-parti, the, i. 135.
Tithes, abolition of, ii. 395.
Tournelle, the, Court of Justice, i. 132, note.
Tournon, Cardinal de, i. 140.
Tours, Council of, A.D. 1510, i. 101.
Tremoille, Cardinal de la, ii. 196, 209.
——, Duke of, i. 295, 312.
Trent, Council of, A.D. 1544, i. 122; removed to Bologna, i. 123; re-assembled at, i. 124; protest of Henry II. at, i. 125; suspension of, i. 126; seventeenth session, A.D. 1562, i. 147; French prelates under Cardinal Lorraine at, i. 151, 153;. Articles of Reformation, i. 157; French ambassadors retire to Venice, i. 162; termination of the Council, i. 165.
Tridentine Decrees, i. 165, 168.
Tronson, Louis, ii. 4.
Trophimus, i. 6.

Troyes, Council at, A.D. 1107, i. 22.
Turgot, ii. 370.

U.

ULTRAMONTANISM, i. 15; ii. 417.
Unam Sanctam bull, the, i. 67.
Union, Council-General of the, i. 187.
University of Paris, i. 82; appeal of, against the Jesuits, i. 270.
Urban VI., Pope, i. 80.
—— VIII., Pope, i. 348, 352, 365; letter of the Bishops to, i. 397.

V.

VAILLANT, ii. 286.
Vaillantistes, the, ii. 286.
Vanne, St., i. 333.
Vasquez, Gabriel, ii. 165.
Verna, Council of, i. 29.
Vervins, Peace of, i. 210.
Victor II., Pope, i. 45.
Vienno, Council at, A.D. 1112, i. 22.
Vieuville, Marquis de la, i. 300.
Vincent de Paul, St., i. 317; originator of the "Sœurs de la Charité," i. 319; founder of the "Congregation of the Priests of the Mission, i. 320; establishment at St. Lazare, i. 324; Retreats at St. Lazare, i. 327; originates the "Compagnie des Dames de Charité," i. 329; his death, ii. 11.
Vintimille, Gaspard de, Archbishop of Paris, ii. 271, 275, 288, 294; death of, ii. 304.
Vio, Cardinal di, or Cajetan, i. 103, note.
Visitandines, order of the, i. 247.
Voltaire and his confederates, ii. 330, 332, 371; death of, ii. 376.

W.

WAR with Germany, ii. 409.
—— of investitures, i. 20.
Worms, Concordat of, i. 22.

Z.

ZOSIMUS, Pope, i. 6.

THE END.

www.ingramcontent.com/pod-product-compliance
Lightning Source LLC
Chambersburg PA
CBHW022112300426
44117CB00007B/680